CONSERVATISM

CONSERVATISM

The Fight for a Tradition

EDMUND FAWCETT

Princeton University Press
Princeton and Oxford

Published by Princeton University Press
41 William Street, Princeton, New Jersey 08540
6 Oxford Street, Woodstock, Oxfordshire OX20 1TR

press.princeton.edu

All Rights Reserved
ISBN 9780691174105
ISBN (e-book) 9780691207773

LCCN: 2020020532

British Library Cataloging-in-Publication Data is available

Editorial: Ben Tate, Sarah Caro, and Josh Drake
Production Editorial: Debbie Tegarden
Text Design: Lorraine Doneker
Jacket/Cover Design: Pam Schnitter
Production: Erin Suydam
Publicity: James Schneider
Copyeditor: Gail K. Schmitt

Jacket images: ROW 1: Edmund Burke, Konrad Adenauer, William McKinley,
Ronald Reagan, Donald Trump, Charles de Gaulle; ROW 2: Margaret Thatcher,
Carl Schmitt, Boris Johnson, William F. Buckley, Robert Gascoyne-Cecil, 3rd Marquess
of Salisbury, Marine Le Pen; ROW 3: Otto von Bismarck, Benjamin Disraeli,
Joseph de Maistre

This book has been composed in Arno Pro with Industria Solid Display

Printed on acid-free paper. ∞

Printed in the United States of America

10 9 8 7 6 5 4 3 2 1

To Natalia

CONTENTS

PREFACE

To survive, let alone flourish, liberal democracy needs the right's support. It needs, that is, conservatives who accept liberal and democratic ground rules. Yet conservatism began life as an enemy of liberalism and never fully abandoned its reservations about democracy. Conservatism endured in modern politics by cooperating with liberalism and soon learned how to prevail in democracy. Liberal democracy of the kind that thrived in Western Europe and the United States after 1945 grew from that historic compromise by the right. When, as now, the right hesitates or denies its support, liberal democracy's health is at risk.

With the left in retreat, both intellectually and in party terms, the right commands politics at present. But which right is that? Is it the broadly liberal conservatism that underpinned liberal democracy's post-1945 successes or an illiberal hard right claiming to speak for "the people"?

By saying what liberal democracy is and why for all its flaws and vulnerabilities it matters, *Liberalism: The Life of an Idea* (2nd ed., 2018) aimed to show what we risk losing. *Conservatism: The Fight for a Tradition* is the other half of the story. It describes the right's present contest with itself in the light of the past.

Conservatives from the start have quarreled with each other as well as with liberalism and democracy. Should they compromise with their historical opponents, or resist? Should the fight be primarily in party politics over power and government, or in intellectual and cultural life? Those questions for conservatives have never gone away. A chaos of voices has often made it hard to say what, if anything, conservatives stand for. At the same time, the very fierceness and endurance of the contest suggests that all sides have believed that there existed something tangible worth fighting for.

Conservatism's history is told here in four periods, given artificially sharp dates for clarity: frontal resistance to liberal modernity (1830–1880); adaptation, compromise, and catastrophe (1880–1945); political command and intellectual recovery (1945–1980); and the contest for supremacy between liberal conservatism and the hard right (1980 to the present).

In each of the four periods, a party-political narrative ("Parties and Politicians") is followed by a characterization of conservative thought at the time ("Ideas and Thinkers"). The first recounts the "endless adventure of governing men"—more lately, governing women—as parties of the right form, split, and re-form in a running conservative renegotiation with liberalism and democracy. The second describes the public appeals, defenses, and philosophical vindications by writers, journalists, speechwriters, and thinkers working in the conservative tradition. As their words multiplied, a conservative outlook emerged, loose and tangled to be sure, but recognizable and, roughly speaking, continuous. Its particular content changed over time, but its broad character stayed the same.

Conservatives throughout were guided by a wise angel and by a worldly angel. In the perplexing rush of modern change, they have spoken to a universal human desire for familiarity and stability—for tomorrow to be like today. As defenders of order and property, however, conservatives overcame their hesitations and soon spoke up for capitalism and its demands—the great servant of material progress that restlessly turns society, lives, and outlooks upside down.

Conservatives, that is, have forever faced two ways. They promise stability and upheaval, continuity and disruption. By temperament, they swing from confidence in their record and pride in their creed to fear that success will be snatched away and that their beliefs are widely ignored. Puzzling as it sounds, conservatives have largely created and learned to dominate a liberal modern world in which they cannot feel at home.

The focus is on four countries: France, Britain, Germany, and the United States. That choice may look like chauvinism. The excuse is that liberal democracy is a framework of politics with distinctive values on which those four countries, despite obvious differences or provincialism, all converged in the twentieth century, especially after 1945. There is nothing eternal about liberal democracy. Many shrewd and well-informed people worry that its day is already done. Whether they are right or wrong, few will quarrel that these large countries represent liberal democracy's historic, albeit nonexclusive, core.

Readers already confused by the labels and categories here—notably the interchangeable use of "conservatism" and "the right"—are urged to glance at appendix A, "Conservative Keywords," where the book's main terms are pinned down and ground-floor distinctions made. The chapter 2, "Character, Outlook, and Labelling of Conservatism," addresses such general matters more fully. A second appendix, "Philosophical Sources of Conservative Thought," recalls thinkers from Plato onward, on whom conservatives (among others) have drawn. A third appendix, "Conservatives: A Gazetteer," gives micro-lives of more than two hundred conservative politicians and thinkers. This extended historical essay has neither footnotes nor scholarly bibliography. In "Works Consulted," readers can find works from which the essay grew and which they may want to look into themselves.

As a left-wing liberal, I do not claim that this history is neutral. I trust it is objective. I have tried to avoid two standbys of political writing, celebration and caricature. If that has worked, readers on the right will recognize themselves and their tradition. Readers on the left will get a view of their opponent's position, which they are prone, like rash chess players, to ignore. *Conservatism: The Fight for a Tradition* is written in comradely spirit with a question for the left: if we're so smart, how come we're not in charge?

Conservatism's epic is told here in recognition, puzzlement, and alarm: *recognition* of the right's party-political and intellectual strengths; *puzzlement* at neglect of those strengths, by a left that knows too little of how the right thinks and by a right that exaggerates its own intellectual and cultural disadvantages; *alarm* at the rise of the hard right, which faces mainstream conservatives with a clear choice: find allies to their left with whom to rebuild and hold a shaken center or join the rightward rush from the liberal-democratic status quo.

ACKNOWLEDGMENTS

For this extended historical essay on the political right, I have plundered widely from the works of many writers and scholars. I am in their debt and thank them all. In person, I thank wholeheartedly Charles Hope and Chaim Tannenbaum, who read drafts, caught errors, and made valuable suggestions. Thanks also to sound guidance from two anonymous academic reviewers for Princeton University Press. Martin Ruehl, together with two other earlier reviewers for PUP as well as David Wiggins, helped me clarify and improve the original outline. In London, Kwazi Kwarteng, Oliver Letwin, Roger Scruton, and Jonathan Wolff made time to talk to me about conservatism. So too in Berlin did Frank Bösch, Dieter Gosewinkel, Norman Gutschow, and Paul Nolte. At PUP, my editors Ben Tate and Sarah Caro encouraged and helped throughout, and Debbie Tegarden and Gail Schmitt saw the book skillfully through production. Pam Schnitter designed a striking cover. Maksimiljan Fras helped factcheck. Conny Günther, a peerless bureau manager, interpreter, and guide arranged my Berlin interviews. Over the years, I had many fruitful, enjoyable talks about conservatism with Adrian Wooldridge as well as with Oliver Black and Tony Thomas, good friends, both of whom died in 2019. In talks or letters, Karl-Heinz Bohrer, Elliot Y. Neaman, and Fred Studemann gave valuable guidance on the German right. Edward Chancellor and Antonia Phillips, Donald and Diana Franklin, and Tom and Rosemund Graham generously put me up with fine, quiet places to work. As ever, greatest thanks go to my wife, Natalia, to whom this book is dedicated. She gave unstinting support while editing, with her sister, a book of her own. With written work, as with most things, she knows what, and what not, to conserve.

PART I

Conservatism's Forerunners

1

Critics of Revolution

i. The Hard Authority of Punishment and the Soft Authority of Custom: Maistre and Burke

Conservatism, like liberalism, has no Decalogue, no College for the Propagation of the Faith, no founding Declaration of Independence, and no doctrinal compendium to match the Marx-Engels Standard Edition. Into that gap, at the end of the nineteenth century, when conservatives were hunting for an intellectual tradition, the writings of Edmund Burke (1729–97) on the French Revolution were rediscovered as a rich and ever-giving second best. Burke's themes—the authority of tradition, the folly of political intellectuals who ignored tradition, and the organic but vulnerable character of society—were singled out as dialectical weaponry.

Burke's writings gave conservatism in retrospect, particularly conservatism in Britain and the United States, a tone of balance, openness to facts, and all-round moderation that stood out in contrast to the blind zeal of conservatism in France and Germany. The works of Joseph de Maistre (1753–1821), a Savoyard lawyer and exile from the French Revolution, were commonly cited to illustrate the extreme, unbridled character of the continental right. Burke bequeathed to Anglo-American conservatism a tone of enlightened good sense and worldly-wise competence. Maistre became the Counter-Enlightenment forerunner of right-wing authoritarians and fascists. This contrast sees too much of the early twentieth century in the late eighteenth. It relies on selective editing and neglects telling elements that the thinkers shared. Maistre was never going to sit well in conservatism's front parlor but belongs in the household as much as Burke.

Maistre and Burke each had unusual rhetorical power and a rare gift of phrase. Maistre argued in black and white with Manichean ferocity. He drove contrasts to extremes and stretched good points past breaking. "Every government is despotic: the only choice is to obey or rebel." "The only institutions that last are religious." "Liberty was always the gift of kings." As if to seize back the guillotine from unworthy hands, he wrote of the scaffold's sacredness and the hangman's piety. Burke's writings, which often began as speeches, were less angry and more to the English taste. His targets—religious enthusiasm, political intellectualism, legal codification—were welcome to ears at ease in their world and suspicious of meddling questioners. Burke's irony was parliamentary and teasing; Maistre's, wounded and, like Jonathan Swift's, savage. Maistre was a lawyer. Burke studied law. Neither argued as philosophers, although Burke had so argued when younger in his attack on the thought that there were presocial people, and when establishing the *sublime* among the categories of aesthetics. On political topics, Burke's favorite argumentative pace was presto, and he could be vicious as well as lyrical. The Boston council was "vermin"; the commoners of 1789 were like "a gang of Maroon slaves suddenly broke loose from the house of bondage."

Both he and Maistre were social outsiders. Burke was a Dublin-born commoner of Anglo-Irish parentage. Maistre was a member of the provincial administrative nobility from Savoy, the French-speaking part of a northern Italian kingdom that had bounced back and forth between France, Spain, Austria, and fragile independence since the sixteenth century. As workaday officials or servants to political masters, both wrote of politics from the inside.

Both thinkers suffered a long decline and slow recovery in their reputations. William Gladstone read Burke through (as he did most things), and Burke had a following among bookish American Whigs, notably Rufus Choate (1799–1859), who ranked him with Homer, Cicero, and John Milton as required reading to "liberalize" the study of politics and law. Walter Bagehot, by contrast, ranked Burke as an early influence on conservatism lower than Pitt the Younger. T. E. Kebbel's *A History of Toryism* (1886), one of the tradition's first scholarly surveys, mentioned Burke only in passing.

In the liberal ascendancy of the 1830s, criticisms of the French Revolution of the kind Burke and Maistre had made were widely felt to have missed their historical mark. Blackening "constitutional" 1789 with the "popular-despotic" 1793–94 and treating the Revolution as a single criminal folly were unconvincing, given how widely the gains of 1789 were accepted and how even the Restoration had not reversed the French middle classes' economic gains. As for the Terror, Maistre and Burke had grasped the self-defeating character of revolutionary excess, which made sustained opposition look redundant. The Revolution, to Maistre, was "a monstrous interlude" in an otherwise reasonable and virtuous national history, albeit an interlude with a purpose. As "divine chastisement," the Revolution had purged and rescued France. Recast in terms of his God-governed history, Maistre was echoing Burke's insight into the self-curing character of revolutionary delusion. For the Jacobins, the Revolution itself, Burke wrote, was "just punishment for their success." The liberal middle classes of the 1830s and 1840s did not need reminding that Terror was bad, the wrong way to govern, and, above all, self-destructive.

Neither Burke nor Maistre believed that people in general were capable of self-government, though for different reasons. Maistre took a bleak view of unregenerate humanity. It could never be relied on to keep the rules and it needed harsh discipline and submissive faith together with the threat of swift punishment. Burke was sunnier in his philosophical anthropology. Unlike Maistre, he made no sweeping factual claim that, given a chance, people were free riders (who recognized rules but counted on others to keep them) or wantons (who recognized no rules). The trouble with trusting people to govern themselves lay for Burke not in their inability to keep rules but in their incapacity to make rules. For nobody, strictly, made rules. To think so was the intellectualist mistake of declaration writers and legal codifiers. Rules emerged from custom, and the customs that endured were those that suited a society and its people.

Whether the rules of society came from a divine source, as Maistre insisted, or from custom, as Burke held, their origins were closed to intelligent enquiry. Divine providence was for Maistre inscrutable. The roots of custom were for Burke obscure. Neither could be argued with and made to yield up a standpoint of criticism for the rules they had generated. Without "ancient opinions and rules of life," Burke wrote, "we have no compass to govern us" and no longer know "to what port to steer." Try as they might, intellectualists in politics could not escape that difficulty. So each claimed.

Neither God's providence nor custom, however, could be relied on alone for social order. Both Maistre and Burke thought a common faith guided and sustained by an established church was also needed. Each recognized the usefulness of religion as a social expedient. Burke made the point soothingly: "The consecration of the state by a state religious establishment is necessary also to operate with a wholesome awe upon free citizens." In a letter in 1815, Maistre declared much the same about faith's utility in terms cynical enough to shock a secularist: "If I were an atheist and a sovereign, . . . I would declare the Pope infallible . . . for the establishment and the safety in my states."

After the Revolution and the Napoleonic Wars, the first conservatives asked themselves whether the turmoil, suffering, and criminal excess had been due to liberty or to its perversion. Burke mildly and Maistre savagely had blamed modern liberty, that is, liberty understood in the wrong way. It was plain to Burke that, once freed from custom and good sense, people were capable of the worst follies and crimes. Maistre thought the same once people were freed from God and his earthly ministers. The foe for Burke was unrestricted, goalless dissent; for Maistre, satanically proud disobedience. For both, mistaken liberty led morally to bewilderment, politically to revolution, breakdown, and counterrevolution. Whether for Burke in this world or for Maistre in a next world, disruptive modern liberty made human life not better, but worse.

Maistre's and Burke's ideas ran side by side into the tradition of conservative thought that was later labelled anti-rationalist. They did not merge. Burke proscribed political reasoning that judged customary arrangements by insecure external standards. He trusted to common morality and social habit that doing without critical reason of the unwanted kind could yet be reasonable. Maistre proscribed reasoning in politics as such, celebrating instead faith and obedience. The less reasonable anti-reason could be, particularly the more offensive to Enlightened opinion, the more Maistre relished the shock.

In this regard, Burke was more open. In politics, he allowed for faction, argument, and disagreement. He spoke loudly against disrupters who sought to leap out of the frame of common assumptions that made argument possible. That aspect in Burke pointed to eventual accommodation slso with liberal diversity. Burke insisted on the need for shared customs and a common faith within a unified society, without which, argument risked slipping into intellectual warfare.

Maistre, by contrast, wanted from politics authority and obedience. His anti-rationalist legacy passed to authoritarian, illiberal conservatism. The legacy runs to Charles Maurras, Georges Sorel, Carl Schmitt, and latter-day right-wing populists. The authority each appealed to varied: for Maistre, the Pope; for Maurras, a French monarch; for Sorel, the disaffected working class; for Schmitt, a temporary dictator; for present-day right-wing populists, "the people," understood as excluding those with views populists dislike as well as elites whom populists of like background seek to replace.

What each of these thinkers wanted from authority was an argument-ender that would cut off debate and silence disagreement. They wanted something that, in the liberal view, would shut down politics itself, because politics to liberals meant unending dispute in a diverse society. The liberal side of Burkeanism could eventually come to terms with that picture of politics as argument. To the Maistrian side, the liberal picture was wrong in whole and part. No reconciliation was possible. Maistre has appealed to the rejectionist element in conservatism and to its authoritarian fringe, as well as to cultural anti-moderns like Charles Baudelaire, Friedrich Nietzsche, and their descendants, who relished his mocking disdain.

Unlike Burke, who saw them from the safety of Westminster, revolution and war made Maistre an exile. In 1792, French troops occupied Savoy, part of a dynastic kingdom that included Piedmont and Sardinia. As judge and senator, Maistre feared himself a marked man and fled. Years of wandering began in Switzerland and Italy. After Napoleon

Bonaparte's victories, when Austria ceded its Italian territories to France, the Savoy court decamped to Sardinia. Maistre followed, picturing the rest of his life as that of "an oyster stuck to a rock." In 1802, he was sent to Russia as an envoy. His job was to plead for money and status on behalf of a crown without a kingdom. The Russians had more pressing worries but approved a small subsidy. Many small countries or minor powers were tinder that reignited war after moments of exhaustion in the long European conflict (1792–1815)—Sweden, Canada, Portugal, and the Romanian lands. Sardinia was too small to bother with. Once they grasped how little their island kingdom counted, Maistre's employers in Cagliari cut his pay and told him to shorten his dispatches. Often Maistre ate his servant's soup. In such conditions, Maistre wrote his best-remembered works.

At evening by the Neva River, in the *Petersburg Dialogues* (published posthumously in 1821), a worldly senator, a Catholic nobleman, and a count argue out the problem of evil: how to reconcile belief in an omnicompetent, well-meaning God with the fact of human suffering. Maistre's younger brother, Xavier, an army officer and author of a satire on the Grand Tour, *Journey around My Room* (1794), may have written the descriptive prelude, on the charm of Russian summer nights, which lulls readers for the sustained dialectical skirmish to follow. With more wit and oratory than close argument, the count, speaking for Maistre, puts forth the old Christian answer that human suffering, even undeserved suffering, had its place in an inscrutable divine plan. For God's justice, though perfect, was slow. In human eyes, the innocent suffer and malefactors go free. It may not look it, but on God's plan every ill was compensated for and every crime punished, so long as time was allowed. As a rationale for a moral economics of retributive and compensatory justice, such argument was never going to win adepts in the early nineteenth century, when philosophers were commonly looking for a naturalistic, post-theological grounding to morality. The *Dialogues* contain also Maistre's sallies against Francis Bacon's mechanistic world picture and John Locke's empiricist account of the mind, English thinkers he wished had thought more like Burke.

Of more political moment were Maistre's critique of the Revolution and his constitutional thinking found in the earlier works, *Considerations on France* (1796–97) and *The Generative Principle of Constitutions and Other Human Institutions* (1814). The Revolutionary Terror was God's punishment for Enlightenment denial of faith. Once purged in blood, France merited salvation and was duly rescued by the European allies from Napoleonic captivity. The Enlightenment took a callow view of humanity's preoccupations and capacities that ignored its irrationality and violence, as well as its need for sacrifice, obedience, and submission. There were no presocial humans, but neither was humankind one society. There was no "man in general," only particular men belonging to one of many national types.

Maistre took his predecessors' lessons and drove them to the limit. With David Hume he agreed that feeling, not reason, underlay political obligation, yet what Maistre meant was not worldly prudence and sensible habit, as with Hume, but human self-abnegation and the solidarity of collective guilt. Burke noted that some obligations were not chosen. Maistre insisted that none of our deeper obligations were chosen. Endurance in a human institution was evidence of divine—that is, ungraspable—origin and whatever the human mind could not grasp should not be touched. A state did not win credit by support from an established church; rather, the state itself should make itself sacrosanct. Nations did not have constitutions, let alone write them. Habits, manners, and norms constituted a nation. The most authoritative law was unwritten law. There was no humankind, only the French, Spanish, English, and Russians. Politically, Maistre, following Burke, claimed to reject ideal constructions but insisted that theocracy was the best form of government. Social order was unachievable without an undivided, sovereign power submitted to unquestionably in a latter-day equivalent of religious awe. Institutions could not survive if they were subject to impious doubt: "If you wish to conserve all, consecrate all." Obedience to authority, whether from faith or fear, must be blind and unquestioning, at the risk, otherwise, of anarchy. Maistre's shadeless picture of politics and society was too stark ever to serve as conservatism's official portrait. His overblackened picture of unregenerate, undependable humankind was still a conservative one. It stood out against the liberal picture, which allowed for human improvability and progress. That liberals could and often did oversweeten their picture in no way erased the contrast.

Readers who come to Burke's works for the first time are struck by their rhetorical power, fertility of metaphor, and subtlety of argumentative suggestion. They are also struck that many or most of the contemporary traditions that Burke was defending as essential to the well-being of society—a dominant landed interest, limited suffrage, an authoritative national church—are long gone. Indeed, they were going or had gone by the late nineteenth and early twentieth centuries, by which time conservatives, particularly those in Britain, began to rediscover a forgotten Burke and adopt him as their intellectual godfather. Scared by the Paris Commune (1871) and prodded by Taine's counter-revolutionary history of modern France, conservatives revived Burke's *Reflections on the Revolution in France* (1790) as the nearest thing to a founding text. Grand as it is, the work raises a second puzzle, which is, how, for all its literary brilliance, an occasional and in ways polemical work should have earned its high place in conservative thought.

Burke's topical attack on the French Revolution took aim at intellectuals in politics and at the holders of public debt. Burke's "political men of letters" had come to the fore as shapers of public opinion for a growing and demanding readership. The state's creditors had sought profits in lending against the security of nationalized church lands. Intellectuals, tied to no particular class or interest, were prone to indeterminate ideals and callow impracticality. Self-seeking creditors, often foreigners, were anonymous and without stake in France's institutions. Both intellectuals and financiers were given to experiment and innovation, with unpredictable but, as Burke also insisted, reliably grim results. The intellectuals were unflightworthy "aeronauts," both foolhardy and out of touch. Their carping undermined the twin guardians of social "manners" and public faith on which a decent commercial society depended: an open, economically productive aristocracy and a tutelary church. Right or not on those requirements for a decent commercial society, Burke recognized the indecent kind, well aware of what the colonial rapine by come-and-go fortune hunters had done to Indian society.

The political men of letters in Burke's picture had griped and exaggerated, without presenting a viable alternative. They had delegitimized one institution after another by sapping public faith in social artifice and ignoring the need for a "veil" of unreflecting custom to cloak destructive natural passions. The financiers in their turn had abetted a perilous financial scheme that brought France a ruinous inflation and wrecked public confidence in the state's fiscal responsibility. France's innovators, in sum, had together destroyed the moral authority and monetary trust on which social order depended.

Drawing on a classical sequence of constitutional decline familiar since the Greeks, Burke foresaw growing instability and a descent into anarchy that would be met by popular disorder, growing violence, and, eventually, military rule. Burke's awesome vision, fixed and clear when he began to write late in 1789, struck readers across Europe as prophetic. His reputation as the seer of war, Terror, and Napoleon lent him continent-wide credit in the 1790s but obscured his wider life and writings.

Burke was an outsider who advanced by superabundant talent and good connections in service to the Marquess of Rockingham, a Whig grandee and leader of the anti-ministerial faction in parliament. The Rockingham Whigs wanted to preserve oligarchic government in the interests of landowners and commerce. They were hostile to crown attempts under reforming ministers to limit their power. When Burke spoke of defending tradition, he had that conflict in mind.

A confessional Gemini by family background, Burke had been born in Dublin to a Protestant father and Roman Catholic mother. After Trinity College, the city's Anglican and only university, he studied law in London and made his literary and philosophical name before he was thirty with works that nourished his responses to the Revolution. The ironically entitled *Vindication of Natural Society* (1756) satirized the idea that there had ever been presocial people or that people could be coherently imagined as outside or detached from some particular society. Burke's essay *Of the Sublime and Beautiful* (1757) invoked a familiar distinction between the social passion of love and the self-preserving passion of fear in order to enrich the conceptual resources of aesthetics. To love of beauty, Burke added an engaging astonishment at the sublime, that is, at scenes or objects that strike us as overscaled, obscure, or overpowering. In astonishment, an image arises for us of threatened pain at a safe distance, and we sense "tranquillity shadowed with horror." Burke impressed most who met him with his eloquence and argumentative fertility. He became the editor for the *Annual Register*, a yearly review of politics and intellectual life, which he oversaw for many years. In 1765 he obtained a seat in parliament, where he sat till 1794.

Burke was a thinker-advocate, each task locked to the other. As the agent for the New York assembly, he spoke up for its protests against British taxation and in 1775 called for reconciliation in speeches on the American colonies. In ways, Burke was a modernizer and reformer. He wanted a lessening of disabilities for Irish Catholics and a reduction in tariffs so as to collect more revenue from taxes, as well as a cutting of the royal payroll and cleaning up military patronage. In 1783, he and his then ally Charles James Fox wanted the government to wrest the administration of India from the irresponsible, rapacious East India Company. After their bill failed, Burke began a nine-year campaign to impeach the company's governor for malfeasance.

In other ways, Burke was behind his times. He feared the democratization of government and opinion. He rejected John Wilkes's radical proposal for more direct representation by binding members of parliament with written instructions. Burke was leery of banking, which he saw as a spur to "innovation" and a corrupting paymaster for its political friends. Of mobile capital, he wrote: "Being of recent acquisition, it falls in more naturally with any novelties. . . . The kind of wealth which will be resorted to by all who wish for change." That the wealthy should be taxed to reduce poverty Burke thought absurd. Cut the throats of all the rich, Burke wrote, and share what they eat in a year, and it still would not serve. He came to see the slave trade as abhorrent and thought it must end in time. Meanwhile it should be humanized by a code of treatment, not abolished. Among Burke's ideas for improving slaves' lives, drafted in 1780 and sent to a correspondent in 1792, were clothes for them on slave ships, schooling for slave children, Sundays off, and lashes limited to thirteen at a time. Burke was for religious liberty but spoke against extending it to Unitarian dissenters, who denied the orthodox doctrine of the Trinity.

The scholar's Burke has been freed in recent decades from his reputational jail as the French Revolution's scold. For most conservatives, he remains the author of the *Reflections*. Without them, people would say what Burke said of Bolingbroke, the Tory butt of his *Vindication*, "Who reads *him* today?" France made and shaped the conservative Burke in reverse. On a visit to Paris in 1773, he marveled at the eighteen-year-old dauphiness but found the godless levity of his intellectual hosts offensive. In May and June 1789, Burke greeted the French upheavals as a "wonderful spectacle." By late summer, when the king's party was in retreat, he turned hostile, provoked partly by the enthusiasm of British radicals. It took his rhetorical skill to balance the jarring claims that Britain should mortally fear a revolution to which, in its stolidity, it was immune.

The authentic, scholar's Burke says too much to be politically useful. "The only specimen of Burke is all that he wrote," Hazlitt quipped in 1807. The first task in creating a useable Burke was accordingly to cherry pick. Burke's copiousness was here an asset, and noticed early. No politician of whatever party, Thomas Moore wrote in 1825, finds himself in "any situation for which he could not select some golden sentence from Burke" to strengthen his argument or "adorn it by fancy."

A second task was to purge the Burkean critique of exaggeration. Maistre's exaggerations were naked and cried out to be scoffed at. Burke's were more suggestive and insinuating: the Terror was as good as fated in 1789, radicals are all revolutionaries, social criticism of any kind is either folly or betrayal, and reform reliably overruns and defeats itself. Although Burke hinted more than stated, exaggeration of that kind became a heady part of what the American political scholar Albert O. Hirschman aptly called "the rhetoric of reaction."

A third task was to rescue Burkeanism from the defense of the undefendable: not simply from the vain defense of what Britain's right-wing Whigs were seeking to preserve from the 1770s through the 1790s, but from the vain defense of any passing and unstable status quo. The task was to find in Burke's writing answers to the question that recurs for conservatives in capitalist modernity: in an ever-shifting society, where there is never dependable ground underfoot, what can and must be rescued?

Rather than as a guide to the kinds of policy to follow or the types of institution to protect, Burkeanism was accordingly recast so as to offer higher-order, reusable advice in changing circumstances. The advice focused on the prudent management of unavoidable change in order to limit its social disruptiveness. Less was said about the hard part of identifying which values had to be defended. Burkeanism of this second-order kind is rightly thought of as a historically relative Utilitarianism, cast in negative terms: minimize disruption according to what the standards of the day find disruptive.

The distinctive maxims of that higher-order Burkeanism turned on tradition, ignorance, and the vital but vulnerable character of human sociability. By "tradition" was meant norms or institutions handed down from past generations that people at present had a duty to uphold and pass on in good shape. However opaque their origin, the endurance of traditions was first-pass evidence of their legitimacy: "That which might be wrong in the beginning is consecrated by time and becomes lawful." If a tradition was in question, the burden of proof was on its questioner, not the other way around.

Humans' knowledge of themselves and, second, their society was imperfect. Not only were they complex by nature, society itself was growing complex. Prudence called on them not to pretend to know more about either than they did know. It enjoined against making a habit of faultfinding in society and then hunting for cures to overdrawn ills that sped change and often made things worse. Faultfinding suffered typical flaws: it relied on "abstract" claims and it invoked maxims that worked in some places but not in others.

The word "abstract" is both a multipurpose philosophical term of art and a rhetorical term of abuse. Borrowing in his early philosophical writing from Locke, Burke had distinguished three sorts of abstract idea: natural kinds (*trees, sheep, humans*), properties (*colors, shapes*), and "mixed" ideas such as *virtue, vice, honor, law,* which matched nothing in the natural world but which brought to mind past experiences of virtuous or vicious actions, or previous encounters with, say, soldiers and magistrates. The circularity of reasoning—how might the past action be recognized as, for example, an instance of virtue?—was not convincingly answered by Burke.

In his political writing, "abstraction" became more loosely a term of criticism for the kinds of reasoning that Burke objected to in politics. One was to propose innovative arrangements that had to be talked of in "abstract" terms. Like "virtue," for example, terms for innovative arrangements were innocently abstract in corresponding to nothing in nature. Unlike "virtue," such terms were also culpably abstract. Because they were new, they evoked no past experiences. When an innovation of the suspect kind was spoken of, nothing graspable came to mind. Innovative talk was for Burke a kind of nonsense.

Exporting maxims from where they worked to where they did not work was the second kind of reasoning Burke proscribed. Morals and norms that served all humanity were at their most general, but their specific forms varied locally. They had all grown over time, surviving only because they suited where they grew. Uprooting them in hope they would flourish elsewhere was folly; institutions fitted their nations and were not readily copied. Efforts to speed or reverse social change were equally futile. Revolution and reaction were mirror faults.

Burke's prime exhibit of abstraction was the Declaration of the Rights of Man and of the Citizen (1789). In the declaration, the mistake of France's intellectual men of letters was not that there were no rights— there were rights wherever there was law, and there was law wherever there was society. Those particular rights; however, had all grown up locally in civil society, as tended by an emergent law of the land. There were no uprootable, transportable rights; that is, there were no universal rights. Rights were common to a society, not to humankind.

Reform, in sum, must step away from past practice. Innovation ignored that precept and hence was bound to fail. To the fictive young French correspondent to whom Burke imagined himself writing in *Reflections* he said that France's unwritten constitution had indeed fallen into disrepair but that it had not been necessary to tear down the building and find a new site. Instead, "you might have repaired those walls, you might have built on those old foundations."

The melancholy modern record of obstinate resistance to wholesale, imposed reform followed by brutal counterresistance might seem to speak in Burke's favor, yet his case against innovative reform relies on an unsupported, backward-looking assumption. A modern society's judgment of whether reform is with or against the grain is seldom clear or conclusive. It is not that modern society, morally speaking, is cross-grained. Even in modernity, there can be a shared core of political morality. The trouble is that in liberal modernity how shared morality is to be applied and adjudged in given cases will always be open to argument. One group's perilous innovation will be another's prudent repair. Simply declaring a harmony of proper morality and custom's lessons does not make that argument go away.

Together the bad habit of abstraction and foolish trust in innovation amounted for Burke to what has here been called intellectualism in politics. It was a fair and useful target for conservatives, who nevertheless soon had to explain how a liberal weakness for intellectualism differed from their own growing reliance on intellectuals, beginning with men like Burke. Despite a professed indifference to ideas, conservatives in time found their own political men of letters. Samuel Taylor Coleridge, as will soon be seen, was an early conservative who called for a "clerisy" of brains that, instead of dreaming up possible futures, would identify and promote the upkeep of national traditions.

Burkeanism's third leading theme was that human sociability was universal and everywhere fragile. In whatever society people found themselves, they grew by nurture and education into a "second nature." Burke wrote of that acquired nature as a "cloak" or "veil" of habits, attitudes, and norms. Superficial but vital, they varied from place to place. Whatever local form they took, they were needed for sociability. They might seem old and worn. They might not meet the taste of social critics. But trying to see through them or tear them away was still dangerous. Changing the material of his metaphor, Burke preferred "the rust of superstition" to bumptious critical "impiety."

Once he was canonized for conservatism, the urge to box and re-box Burke never died. Philosophically, he was packaged as a Lockean contractualist, a Humean moral skeptic, a historically minded relativist, a natural-law theorist, or a rule Utilitarian ("In all moral machinery," Burke wrote, "the results are the best"), perhaps both those last two together, the first in morality, the second in politics. Burke himself advanced no philosophical defense in depth of what he was about politically.

Was Burke conservative or a liberal? Of the historical Burke, the question is anachronistic. There were none of either in Burke's day. Still, the question is not pointless, and for Burkeanism the answer is "both," for the Burke distilled into Burkeanism attracted liberals as well as conservatives. Burke said much that right-wing liberals could agree with. Liberty required order, which required property. Tampering with trade was generally a mistake. Many of our duties were unchosen duties, and people had not only rights to liberty but also due expectations for social order.

Burke, more generally, thought healthy politics should reflect society. Society was diverse and in conflict. Politics, accordingly, required faction and argument, as liberals also believed. Sovereign power, further, was necessary but capturable. Institutions for its exercise had to be arranged so that, in Burke's words, no group or interest should "act as if it were the entire master." Avoiding an "entire master" animated the pre-conservative James Madison in his thoughts on the United States Constitution. It underlay how the liberal François Guizot thought of sovereignty's exercise as lying beyond the reach of any one interest or faction and as controllable in the end only by morality and law. *That* Burke opened paths of liberal-conservative compromise.

Conservatives, however, had fellow feeling for the less liberal, anti-cosmopolitan Burke. In international terms, he was a conservative nationalist, an early exponent of geopolitics treated as a conflict of ideologies (England, Burke wrote in 1796, "is in war against a principle") or as a down-to-earth defender of British power concerned with efficient taxes, lively commerce, and a stable empire. The national conservative Burke stressed a common faith and shared allegiances as a framework to contain vigorous faction. He celebrated British customs and attitudes as tested by time and somehow uniquely worthy. That is the Burke who echoed in the patriotic oratory of British conservatism from Benjamin Disraeli to Stanley Baldwin and beyond. It is the Burke who warmed the spirit of an American author shivering in a Scottish winter, Russell Kirk. In *The Conservative Mind* (1953), Kirk not only reminded American readers of Burke's existence but also elevated him into a presiding intellectual deity of that mid-twentieth-century invention, the Anglosphere.

Burke's concern for continuity in the morality of politics was profound and compelling. He handed down to conservatism the puzzle of how to hold to established values amid remorseless modernity. The puzzle was not strictly partisan, but conservatives, especially Burkean conservatives, made it their own. The values Burke had in mind were shared public and private duties, pieties, allegiances, and loyalties, without which, it was feared, social order in modern conditions could never stabilize. The character of the list was plain enough. Giving it actual content in their own times has occupied conservatives of Burkean mold ever since.

ii. The Call of Faith and Beauty: Chateaubriand and Other Romantics

None of Burke's rhetorical flights was better known than his cry of dismay on behalf of the queen when a Parisian crowd burst into the royal palace at Versailles: "I thought ten thousand swords must have leapt from their scabbards to avenge even a look that threatened her with insult. But the age of chivalry is gone." That of "sophisters, economists and calculators" had succeeded. The "sentiments which beautify and soften private society" were vanishing. The decent veils of expedient belief on which social order depended, the "drapery of life" from the "wardrobe of the moral imagination," were, Burke feared, being ripped away.

Burke's fear echoed the alarm at social change sounded by moral satirists from Juvenal to Swift. Manners were changing, it was true, but whether manners themselves were being abandoned, as Burke seemed to suggest, was less certain. A new fashion is not nakedness. Burke's difficulty was why one should prefer old to new manners once all manners, in the broad sense of social norms, were seen as useful pretenses. If new manners brought stability, then on Burke's own requirements, it would seem they served as well as old manners.

Burke's metaphor of social beliefs as clothes, later worked up by Thomas Carlyle in *Sartor Resartus* (1836) and before long absorbed into the sociological vernacular, had good and bad sides. The good side was that a social norm's authority depended in part on the breadth of its credit. Norms of courtesy, reasonableness, mutual respect, and cooperation are like that. They weaken or break down when widely ignored (which is not to say they must first be widely agreed on to come into force). The bad side of the metaphor is that it threatens to turn acceptance of social norms into expedient dissembling. The metaphor blurs the fact that whereas we cannot see through clothes, we can see through beliefs. Clothes do their work for decency, although we all know what we look like naked. If, on the contrary, social norms are taken for a useful pretense that veils our primitive and asocial nature, it will be perilous to count on them to do their work for social order once the pretense is seen through and constantly remarked on. Keeping up social pretenses is harder than getting dressed in the morning. Philosophers from ancient Greece through the Christian Middle Ages had questioned the force and sources of social norms. Only in the Enlightenment with the spread of reading was the practice of asking why democratized and made part of public argument. Once it had been, as Burke acknowledged, it was difficult to stop the seed of doubt from growing and spreading. Burke's awkward metaphor pointed to an enduring difficulty for conservatives in their contest with liberal modernity. It runs through to the present day: how can we sustain a belief that we are convinced society needs when we ourselves offer not grounds or evidence for the belief but only a conviction that the common holding of the belief is useful for social order?

Another Enlightenment Romantic and critic of the French Revolution, François-René de Chateaubriand, captured the difficulty well.

Lingering aside in distaste, he described the Restoration *sacre* of the last Bourbon, Charles X, by the archbishop of Reims (1825) at the cathedral where French kings had been crowned since the Middle Ages. The jostling attendance included royalist emigrés as well as veterans of the Revolution and Napoleon who had switched coats in time. Who, Chateaubriand asked, could be taken in by such a spectacle? It was "not a *sacre*," he wrote, "but the representation of one."

A younger son from an old Breton noble family, Chateaubriand was by turns naval cadet, apprentice courtier, American voyager, wounded volunteer in the army of the anti-Jacobin emigrés, London exile, bestselling novelist, Catholic revivalist, Napoleonic envoy turned critic of the emperor, constitutional pamphleteer, founder-editor of *Le Conservateur*, Restoration foreign minister, knight errant for the Bourbon Ultras, liberal critic of those same Ultras, defender of the press, and internal exile from the bourgeois monarchy of Louis Philippe. From that wholly modern muddle of adventure, dissidence, and incompletion, Chateaubriand fashioned an eighteen-hundred-page autobiography that gave shape to the tributaries, diversions, and repetitions that made up his life, the *Mémoires d'outre-tombe* (1849–50), which ranks with Augustine's and Jean-Jacques Rousseau's *Confessions* among masterpieces in the unconservative genre of self-invention.

Little of that, though fascinating, would have won Chateaubriand a place in the story of conservatism had he not he passed down to it a repertoire of disavowal for the "empty world" of liberal modernity and a counterpart trust in the "full heart" of faith and loyalty. Chateaubriand was a Romantic among conservatism's anti-rationalist forerunners. He was less philosophical than Burke and, though cross about many things, not as angry as Maistre. As a child of the eighteenth century, he sought to answer disenchantment with reenchantment. Passionate attachments, he urged, counted more in life and politics than prudential reasoning or partisan obedience, a claim he pressed in *Le Génie du Christianisme* (1802), the book that first made his name. Friends saw in him personally a sturdy egotism. Unflatteringly for them, he himself wrote that his strongest emotion was boredom. Many questioned his sincerity, yet Chateaubriand preached his Romantic gospel of resistance to the emerging world of liberal modernity with a sense of conviction that won converts and imitators.

Politically, he called himself "Republican by nature, monarchist by reason, Bourbonist from honor." Though too skeptical for legitimism, he shared with the Ultras their disgust at watching regicides and Bonapartists land on their feet in the post-1815 Bourbon court. Waiting in an anteroom to see Louis XVIII, as Chateaubriand described the scene in his memoirs, he watched lame Talleyrand, Napoleon's diplomat, shuffle out of an audience with the king helped by Napoleon's police chief, Fouché, and murmured to himself, "Vice supported on the arm of crime." Arbitrary force repelled him, especially by power against defenseless victims. Among the strongest passages in the *Mémoires* is his dry but outraged account of the Duc d'Enghien's execution, with Napoleon's connivance, after a kangaroo trial (1804).

In Chateaubriand's capacity to question almost everything but his own judgment, an ungenerous later French conservative, Maurras, saw a pagan libertarian. Admirers have seen in Chateaubriand's suspicion of power a liberal streak found in the rebel Albert Camus or in the self-described Tory anarchist George Orwell.

Chateaubriand believed in a constitutional monarchy, in representative government constrained by fixed, nondemocratic institutions that were designed to ensure security of property and protect subjects from arbitrary power. He believed also in personal liberties and freedom of the press. He blamed the Revolution on royal dithering and interference, and he supported the Bourbons not from out-of-the-drawer legitimist theory but for the practical and somewhat cross-cutting reason that the dynasty had, broadly speaking, provided good rulers. After 1815 he believed in a "possible Restoration," not in the self-defeating reaction of the Ultras. It was folly, Chateaubriand thought, to bring back old congregations, compensate property losses, restore primogeniture, muzzle the press, and make sacrilege a capital offense. To Louis de Bonald, the author of that last bill (1825), he cried in the chamber, "You reject the norms of our day to return to times we cannot even recognize."

For all that, Chateaubriand could sound like a proto-liberal, which in a limited way he might have been, except for his distance from middle-class life and values.

Chateaubriand shared that suspicion of bourgeois society and what he took for its politics of mutual interest in an article in *Le Conservateur*. It contrasted a "morality of interest" with a "morality of duty." Society could not be governed by violence, only by *séduction*, that is, persuasion. The persuasive force of mutual interest, it might be said, could be stronger than that of duty; for duty rested on "fiction," whereas interest was actual. No, Chateaubriand answered. Interest was fickle and unstable, never by evening what it was in the morning, resting on no more than chance and ever fluid. There existed by contrast an unbreakable chain of duty running from families into society that tied fathers and children, kings and their subjects, into mutual obligations.

Like William Wordsworth in Britain and Adam Müller in Germany, Chateaubriand disliked the commercial society he saw eating away at an earlier, supposedly more natural way of life. The natural life was imagined socially in terms of older habits and institutions, and psycho-geographically in terms of the countryside, especially wild countryside. Were that all, Chateaubriand's writing might have gone the way of Étienne Sénancour's *Obermann* and other writers of the day swept up in the Romantic idea of pure nature and tainted society. In addition, he had a hard, knowing eye for worldly affairs and an ambition, however misplaced, to fight at the top of the political game. Some saw in his obsession with Napoleon an unhinged wish to supplant Napoleon. Chateaubriand's Romantic side, which he poured into his novels, imagined America as a Rousseauesque open field, cherished and tended by wise original peoples. His worldly side reminded him how it was. On arrival in Delaware, he was helped on to the dock by a young black woman, to whom he gave a handkerchief, noting to himself how incongruous it was to be greeted in the land of liberty by a slave.

Le Génie du Christianisme caught a moment of religious conciliation. It was published soon after Napoleon's Concordat with the Vatican in 1801 reestablished Roman Catholicism as the primary religion of France and permitted the return of emigré priests. *Le Génie* aimed to reawaken religious feeling by stressing the aesthetic aspects of Christianity and helped make it acceptable, even fashionable, in intellectual drawing rooms. It contributed to the Catholic revival after 1815, when peace returned, military careers closed, and a religious calling looked again to be a fair alternative among the upper classes.

As a Counter-Enlightenment manifesto for the beauties of the Christian faith, *Le Génie* tied together Romantic longing, contempt for bourgeois worldliness, and Catholic lessons in piety and humility. By rejecting false gods, Christianity had ended our intellectual infancy but compensated us for the loss of childish wonder. By chasing divinities from the woods and returning nature to its solitude, Christianity had given us an object of solace, contemplation, and religious awakening. Worldly busyness and its reductive understanding of life had limits. We needed ritual. Whether classical or Christian, ritual appealed to us in its poetry. Nothing was lovely, winning, or beautiful without an element of mystery. Religion deepened art by pointing us toward ideals that could be intuited, not justified. Last, self-assertive mockery was corrosive and deadening. Among the enemies of Christian piety from the start had been sectarians, sophists, and the frivolous who "destroy everything with laughter." Christianity, into the bargain, had served sound government and blessed the forgiveness of enemies in the cause of national reconciliation.

The topics that moved Chateaubriand and that were widely anthologized from the six-part *Génie* were ruins, oceans, feast days, church bells, and love of nation. That last element, which was foreign to Catholic universalism but not to Gallicanism, belonged indispensably to Chateaubriand's politics of feeling and allegiance. A common religion was one way in which a shared allegiance might heal a divided nation. The nation itself was another. Tapping patriotic feeling to unite a country against its internal foes became a theme for the nineteenth-century right, for use first against liberalism and later against international socialism. Nor for Chateaubriand was the pursuit of French pride mere literary exhortation. As foreign minister he promoted, against British reservations, an invasion of Spain to crush its liberals (1823) and pressed for an alliance with Russia to break up the Ottoman Empire, for a

French foothold in Latin America, and for a "just expansion" of France's frontier along the Rhine. Napoleon III eventually tried all of it, with disastrous results for France and Europe. Charles de Gaulle, an admirer of Chateaubriand's prose, also heard his cry: "I wanted the French to want glory." De Gaulle, however, understood France's limits. By his time, national glory was not on offer. The representation of glory had to serve in its place.

Appended to *Génie* were the wildly popular Romantic novellas, *René* and *Atala*, which were written or published earlier. Their antihero, René, is an unhappy young man without a home in society who, unlike Goethe's Werther, rather than kill himself seeks purpose from life in the American woods. These short works counted heavily toward the success of a long book that Chateaubriand made longer by adding doctrine and theology, as if to appease serious Christian thinkers who expected better defenses of faith's claims to truth than his "I wept, so I believed." Chateaubriand's religion of sentiment had limits, but it lit up a problem facing later conservatives looking to Christianity to provide a civic religion that liberal modernity, they believed, was too thin and too divisive on its own to allow for. Félicité de Lamennais, a cofounder of *Le Conservateur*, was one of several nineteenth-century conservative religious thinkers—Wilhelm von Ketteler, John Henry Newman, Charles Hodge, and Orestes Brownson—who, as will be seen, also hoped to reconcile faith and modernity.

Maistre, Burke, and Chateaubriand each handed down to conservatism an intellectual target for use by the right against the left. The target could be thought of as a triangle that might be hit on any one of its sides: an apostasy or denial; a wrong way of thinking; and a suspect kind of thinker. First, revolutionaries denied divine providence (Maistre), custom and tradition (Burke), or enchantment (Chateaubriand). Second, they thought about politics in the wrong way, whether by corrosive "raison individuelle" (Maistre), delusory "pure metaphysical abstraction" (Burke), or the deadening "l'esprit positif" (Chateaubriand). Just what those highly general charges were and whether they were one charge or many were left to conservatives to wrestle later in the twentieth century, when efforts were made to give the idea *rationalism in politics* more philosophical shape and weight. In contrast, the third side of the triangle, the suspect intellectual, gave a clear, palpable target. Revolutionary thinkers, on this last charge, were "men of letters" without recognized status or interests of their own save the practice of moral and political criticism itself. Their aim was not, as they proclaimed, to make a new, better, or reformed society but rather to maintain unending argument about a new, better, or reformed society. For only unending argument gave political men of letters a rationale. The political intellectual, on that unflattering picture, was a half-trained doctor who was quick to spot ailments, real or imagined, but with no grasp of health and no ability to cure.

iii. Order in Nations and Among Nations: Gentz and Other Germans

The right might abjure intellectualism in politics, but it needed brains of its own who could take on the intellectuals of the left. An outstanding early model was Friedrich von Gentz (1764–1832), who spent a career of drafting and arguing in the service of established order, both within and among the nations of Europe. For intellectual combat of that kind, he was well equipped. As a young man, he went to Königsberg with a recommendation from Moses Mendelssohn to study under Immanuel Kant, heard him lecture, corrected the proofs of Kant's *Critique of Judgment*, and was returned to his father, in the philosopher's words, "in good health and well-schooled." Besides translating the first French critics of the Revolution, in 1793 Gentz put into German Burke's *Reflections*, teasing out Burke's thought in long footnotes that tidied up the argument in rationalist spirit.

Revolution for Gentz was not an assault by reason but an assault on reason. The revolutionary error to his mind was not reasoning about politics in strange ways that were wrong even when done well, but reasoning in familiar ways, only doing it badly. Revolution was not as for Burke an attack on custom by reason but an attack by poor reasoning on good. For Gentz, the primary question of politics was how power was best used for the maintenance of peace and stability, both within and among nations. If that was an "abstract" principle, so be it. If broad maxims drawn from some combination of prudence, reasoning, and experience were "abstract," so be it. Gentz was not interested in fighting battles against the Enlightenment, nor after his early sallies was he much involved in philosophy.

Gentz's thought looked back and ahead. It looked back to the six-teenth- and seventeenth-century modern tradition of *raison d'état* (the idea, present in the writings of Niccolò Machiavelli and Thomas Hobbes, that obligations on states and their trustees were specific to politics and not neatly exportable from the sphere of personal moral-ity). It looked forward to what later became known as realpolitik, or realism (the idea that geopolitics, the first element of statecraft, involved an amoral contest among sovereign nations unregulated by suprana-tional norms or ideals save rudimentary counsels of prudence). For Gentz, reasoning well about politics meant thinking out what *raison d'état* required in the turbulent status quo of revolutionary and Napole-onic Europe. For later conservative realists, his question generalized. In whatever turbulent status quo they found themselves, they too had to ask, "What here and now does *raison d'état* require?"

Established as a lawyer and state official in Berlin, Gentz ran the jour-nals *New German Monthly* (1795) and the *Historical Journal* (1799). His grasp of foreign affairs and finance won him a reputation. When his hostility to Napoleon left him politically homeless in peace-seeking Prussia, he left for Vienna (1802), where he worked as a writer-adviser for hire to the Austrians and British. French occupation (1805) made him an exile again, but he was back in Vienna by 1810 as an aide to the Austrian chancellor, Metternich. Pleas for a court post went unheard, and he operated as a commoner with only Metternich's protection. As drafter and frequently creative notetaker, he was at the five post-Napoleonic congresses. Although no democrat, he thought the idea of restoring France's Bourbons after 1830 by force absurd, and lost the chancellor's favor.

A rake and gambler ever in debt, Gentz was frowned on by the pious. In his sixties, he fell in love with an eighteen-year-old dancer, the daughter of Joseph Haydn's copyist, who without claiming to be faithful made him happy in old age. Romantic conservatives took Gentz for an eighteenth-century leftover, democrats and socialists for a reactionary, and Prussian nationalists for a faithless cosmopolitan. He was little read and soon forgotten. He reads today more like a familiar, realist conservative than his backward-looking contemporaries. As a political intellectual serving the chancelleries of Europe, Gentz's first concern was less with speculating about how power should be exercised than vindicating how it was exercised. He was an early model of a familiar present-day figure, the clever policy intellectual with top degrees circulating between right-wing think tanks, conservative magazines, and political leaders' private offices.

In thinking about revolution, Gentz was an enthusiast for 1789. He followed Kant in taking the National Assembly for legitimate and not, as Burke claimed, a usurpation of royal authority; however, Gentz soon turned against the Revolution. The revolutionaries' mistake was not in having universal, innovative ideals, it was in leaving them general, unanchored, and out of practical reach. Gentz did not mock the Declaration of the Rights of Man in the satirical manner of Justus Möser (1720–94), the north-Saxon critic of market society and Enlightenment princely reform. Nor did Gentz fault the declaration, as Burke had done, for misunderstanding the character of rights. Gentz instead subjected the declaration to an article-by-article critique (1793) for errors of drafting and logic in the manner of a philosophically attuned lawyer. The declaration to his mind was not so much misconceived as ill-done.

Gentz wrote not as a philosopher but as a publicist and political adviser. He understood the role of political intellectuals as laying out simple principles and defending the policies of their political masters in depth. Gentz's essay "On the Balance of Power" (1806) spelled out the guidelines for European peace that served the post-Napoleonic settlements. Within states, locally chosen arrangements, republican or monarchical, should prevail unless they upset continental order. In the German lands—Prussia, Austria, and the other territories of the defunct Holy Roman Empire—politics should promote faith (which fostered obedience) and hold democracy at bay.

A defender of free opinion as an editor in Berlin, Gentz supported its suppression in the press and universities in the climate of reaction after 1815. Public opinion, he wrote, should be formed, not followed. Afraid of Prussian domination, Gentz opposed confederal institutions that might serve to unite Germany as well as Friedrich List's common market. As for nascent socialism, it was to be stifled at birth. Over dinner at the Congress of Aix (1818), Gentz suavely told the cooperativist Robert Owen: "We do not want the mass to become wealthy and independent of us. How could we govern them if they were?"

Gentz's tone and style were at their clearest in *On the State of Europe before and after the French Revolution* (1801), his reply to the case against Britain by Alexandre d'Hauterive, Napoleon's diplomatic aide. Monarchy had not brought eighteenth-century Europe to darkness and poverty, Gentz argued; rather, reforming monarchs across the continent had raised standards of living. War had broken out in 1792 not because of British belligerence, but because the Westphalian system had broken down under the weight of Prussian growth, Russian pressure, and the general growth of trade. British commercial interests had not prejudiced France; the Navigation Acts hindered Britain more than they did its competitors. Britain had not exploited superior naval power; it had fought at sea through the eighteenth century on equal terms. France and Britain were both colonial powers, neither with a clear advantage. Nor did Britain monopolize industry; its products sold widely in Europe because they were better. They were better because Britain had freed itself from false economic doctrines. Gentz was on retainer from the British and writing what he judged served his masters' cause. What strikes the present-day reader is a tone familiar from "realist" conservatism: the coolly factual style; the confident dismissal of radical claims, especially claims about the dismal past; and a presumptive framework of competitive national goals.

Gentz had tried at first to engage in the dispute among German philosophers about the nature and desirability of the French Revolution but soon withdrew, aware that his talents lay elsewhere. The leading philosophers in Germany—Immanuel Kant, Friedrich Schiller, J. G. Fichte, and G.W.F. Hegel—were, to begin with, favorable on the whole about the Revolution. They saw in it, each in their way, hope for social progress and a more reasonable politics. Kant thought that although there was no right to rebellion in general, the French Revolution might prove beneficial if people's enthusiasm turned to civic engagement and support for a constitution. As if to welcome to its cause the author of the anti-tyrannical play *The Robbers*, the French republic made Schiller an honorary citizen (1792). Schiller greeted 1789 as a step for freedom but wondered if people were ready for it, writing to a friend in 1793, "You have to constitute citizens before you can give them a constitution." The Terror shocked even progressive German opinion. The change was evident in Hegel's work, when he looked back in the 1800s. Fichte, who blamed the Terror on the belligerence of France's neighbors, had at first to fight off claims by German reactionaries that he was a Jacobin. But Fichte himself then turned against the Revolution when France (1806–7) turned against Prussia.

Less well-known thinkers who influenced later German conservatives were against revolution from the outset. August Rehberg (1757–1836) was a German Burkean and scholar from Hanover who took the Revolution to be antihistorical. He mistrusted broad, universal principles and faulted the French Revolution for flying against what was locally achievable at that moment in history. A defender of Germany's small states and an opponent of centralism, Rehberg was not against change or reform itself but only change in the wrong hands. With that in mind, he called on Germany's privileged classes to reform themselves. He disapproved of Kant's rationalistic enthusiasm, as he saw it, for 1789. Rehberg took Kant's support for the Revolution as a failure to gauge the gap between universal maxims and their practical achievability. For the political romanticism of his friend Adam Müller (1779–1829), Gentz had little patience. However sharp was Müller's critique of new ways to think of state and society, Gentz took his approach as backward looking. Müller's hopes for preserving Germany's legally privileged classes, its old "estates," and restoring an imagined premodern unity struck Gentz as out of touch. Revolution had to be fought, Gentz insisted, not with nostalgia but with modernity's own weapons.

Hegel is a telling bookend to German reactions to the French Revolution. Like Kant, the liberal Hegel believed that satisfactory arrangements in politics must be reasonable. They must, that is, be intelligible and acceptable to those who must live under them. Those conditions of acceptability and intelligibility need not, however, be the same for everyone at all times. Reason, on Hegel's view, ought not to try to apply itself in isolation from the society in which people found themselves. France's revolutionaries pressed too fast with principles that were too detached from actual circumstances. The Revolution took a wrong turn, left history's "rational" march for freedom, and slipped into violent unreason. The Terror, on that understanding, was a contingent horror, as little part of an intelligible human history, Hegel wrote, as "chopping the head off a cabbage." Instead, in Hegel's superhistory the motor force of history—humanity's urge for freedom—passed in Napoleon's hands from France to Germany, where the old, "irrational" patchwork of the German empire was discarded and political freedom found new expression in Prussian constitutionalism.

After his death, Hegel's heritage divided like the French assembly into right and left. Right Hegelians were on the whole religion-minded conservatives who found in his works a vindication of prevailing arrangements, understood as the achievement of world history's march toward freedom in Prussian constitutionalism. The left Hegelians took from Hegel a tool for the criticism of prevailing arrangements, understood as only the latest stage in an unfinished struggle for recognition by the weak against the strong. In its Marxist variant, left Hegelianism turned world history into a tradition of revolution.

Hegel himself paid little attention to the recent revolution in America. In the early 1820s, the oversight made sense. In his *Philosophy of History* (1822), Hegel took the new country as too fluid and open in its likely futures to say anything world-historical about it. Such philosophical caution had been no constraint on Gentz, the policy intellectual, when thinking of contemporary upheaval and war experienced by peoples across the Atlantic world. Two decades earlier, he had written a spirited essay contrasting the French and American Revolutions, which was published in his *Historical Journal*. Its characteristic brio caught the eye of the American envoy in Berlin, the young John Quincy Adams, later president and a leading conservative Whig. Adams translated the essay and had it published soon after in the United States (1800). He was glad to welcome an article from "one of the most distinguished political writers in Germany." For Adams, it rescued the American Revolution "from the disgraceful imputation of having proceeded from the same principles as that of France."

iv. Revolution to Prevent Revolution: Madison and Other Americans

The left charged supporters of 1776 who opposed 1789 with inconsistency. The charge was commonplace across the Atlantic world and needed answering by the right. In Europe, it was heard against Burke. In the United States, it was popular among Jeffersonian anti-Federalists. Gentz's answer to the charge was scholastic and lawyerly. As he described them, the American Revolution was defensive; the French, offensive. The Americans were defending established rights that had been injured or abridged by the British. Their aims were fixed and limited. Revolution prompted little resistance from within the colonies; widespread support for independence created a nation. The French Revolution stood in contrast on each point. The revolutionaries usurped power and trampled on rights. They had no aim but set off "in a thousand various directions, continually crossing each other." Far from creating a unified nation, they provoked a mass of resistance and plunged the country into civil war. The good American and the bad French Revolutions became part of conservatism's intellectual armory.

In fact, there was not just one American response to the French Revolution but varied, shifting responses. The Americans in Paris—Thomas Jefferson and Gouverneur Morris—offer a telling contrast. Jefferson was the American envoy in Paris (1785–89), sent there the year before to join Benjamin Franklin and John Adams in negotiating commercial and diplomatic treaties with the major powers. When it came, France's revolution excited him. He believed in "the good sense of man" and his "capacity for self-government." If reason could exert its force, Jefferson was confident he was seeing the "first chapter of European liberty" (August 1789). He did not feel tied to past, believing with Thomas Paine that "the earth belongs in usufruct to the living."

Jefferson took events in France and America as expressions of popular resistance. Two years earlier, rioting by armed country debtors in Massachusetts who stormed a tax house had scared the wealthy and powerful of the new land, but not Jefferson. "I like a little rebellion now and then. It is like a storm in the atmosphere," he wrote in a letter brushing off the affair (February 1787). Jefferson looked on government as dangerous to people's liberty. Rulers needed warning from time to time that people "preserve the spirit of resistance," he wrote of popular unrest in general later that same year. The answer was not violence but conciliation. "Let them take arms. The remedy is to set them right as to facts, pardon & pacify them. What signify a few lives lost in a century or two? The tree of liberty must be refreshed from time to time with the blood of patriots & tyrants. It is its natural manure" (November 1787).

In May 1789, Jefferson, now envoy for the United States, eagerly attended the Estates General. To James Madison back home he wrote of what he took for a French sense of common enterprise: "Our proceedings have been viewed as a model for them on every occasion." The American constitution was treated "like . . . the bible, open to explanation but not to question." With the Marquis de Lafayette, Jefferson began to sketch out a declaration of rights for France.

Jefferson's successor as American envoy when he returned to America in autumn 1789 was a constitutional monarchist, the wealthy New Yorker Gouverneur Morris (1752–1816). A frequent speaker at the Constitutional Convention (1787), he had chaired the Committee on Style, which wrote the final draft and added the phrase with its fateful pronoun which opens the Preamble, "We, the people of the United States." A strong federalist, he was antislavery but exclusive in his understanding of democracy. Morris believed, like the conservative Whigs to come, that substantial property was a requirement for political participation. Morris was an exemplar of what Jefferson later called the "Anglo-Monarchio-Aristocratic" Federalists—the bankers for commerce and traders in public debt, "timid men who prefer the calm of despotism to the tempestuous sea of liberty."

He and Jefferson saw revolution differently. After a meeting with him in May 1789, Morris wrote to a friend that Jefferson had "too sanguine expectations of a downright republican form of Government." Putting Burke's point in fewer words, Morris saw the difficulty so: "The literary people here, observing the abuses of their monarchical form, imagine that everything must go the better in proportion as it recedes from the present establishments, and in their closets they make men exactly suited to their systems. But unluckily they are such men as exist nowhere else, and least of all in France."

Jefferson's "sanguine expectations" of downright republicanism reflected the American spirit better than did Morris. Republican mistrust of monarchs and top-down authority persisted in the United States late into the nineteenth century. Uprisings in France, which had helped America in its fight for independence, were welcomed: outside the conservative Whig press, which shook its head at any sign of bottom-up democracy, France's July Days (1830) were welcomed in America. So was the declaration of the Second Republic (1848) and the collapse of the Bonapartist Second Empire. American disapprovers were in the minority. They included Southern Democrats, alarmed by the abolition of slavery in France's colonies (1848) and by the fall of their European backer in the Civil War, Napoleon III (1870). Among the Americans who cheered in 1830 was an aged Madison, who greeted the end of the last French Bourbons with delight.

Madison serves as an instructive middle case between Jefferson's and Morris's understanding of revolution. Morris wanted strong authority to defend property and order, and Jefferson, despite talk of resistance and liberty, did not disagree. He had no wish to sow disorder or despoil property. Like Madison, he owned slaves and had little quarrel with electoral property franchises. Within those undemocratic confines, however, lay differences that were to reemerge in the conservative contest with liberalism. Jefferson, in republican spirit, trusted to the resources of citizens and society to ensure peace and prosperity. He was wary of an overbearing central power. Madison shared Jefferson's belief in the need for popular control of government, but he thought peace and prosperity elusive without overall central power and uniform national laws.

"In framing a government which is to be administered by men over men," Madison wrote (*Federalist 51*), "the great difficulty lies in this: you must first enable the government to control the governed; and in the next place oblige it to control itself. A dependence on the people is, no doubt, the primary control on the government; but experience has taught mankind the necessity of auxiliary precautions." Such for Madison were the building blocks of a sound constitution. In a letter to Jefferson (October 1787), who was not a delegate, Madison reported his understanding of those auxiliary precautions as they were put together at the Constitutional Convention in Philadelphia. Madison's triple aim was to establish unique national authority, recognize popular sovereignty, and prevent majoritarian tyrannies.

As Madison reported, it was rapidly agreed in Philadelphia to preserve the union. The radical departure was a federal government that "instead of operating on the States should operate without their intervention on the individuals composing them." Sovereign power, that is, was to work directly on citizens, not through states or intermediaries. Federal law would oblige and protect people one by one. Bar that principle, there was no political nation. The federal government must be "energetic" and "stable" enough to do its work, but it must answerable to the people. Terms of office should be limited, and the exercise of power should be in many, not one or a few, hands.

Popular control could not be exercised directly. The judgment of the people had to be filtered and articulated. Madison accepted that in modern states of any size and complexity direct participation, which, in *Federalist 51*, he called "democracy," was neither practical nor desirable. Representation was one of the ways in which popular sovereignty could be contained. Given representation, people did not decide or make laws themselves. They sent delegates to do it for them. Pure, or direct, democracy was in that way avoided. A second way to contain popular sovereignty was articulation. Some kinds of representation did too little to filter or articulate the popular will. A single legislature that controlled the executive and the judiciary, for example, would do too little. Such an arrangement, soon favored by Jacobinism and the democratic traditions of the socialist left, relied on a false equation of the popular will with the will of the majority. Representative institutions needed to be articulated and complexified to balance the authoritative force of popular will against its commonly inarticulate content.

The American Constitution, as Madison described it to Jefferson, brimmed with articulation. Its powers were divided—into executive, legislative, and judicial. Each had some control over the others, but none had final say in appointments to all. The legislature was divided into the Senate and House, a division that soothed the anxieties of small states that they would be overwhelmed by big ones and the concerns of the rich minority that they would be despoiled by the less rich majority.

The tyranny of majorities was Madison's anxiety. It was vital "to guard one part of society against the injustice of the other part" (*Federalist 51*). Popular government entailed majority decision. There had, all the same, to be ways to prevent majorities from oppressing minorities. A Bill of Rights, added afterward, was one way, but not soon enough for Madison's fellow Virginian, George Mason, to vote against the Constitution before storming home. Madison himself came around to accepting the Bill of Rights. His still stronger hope for containing majorities lay less in constitutional safeguards than in the fact of social diversity. Society was divided and would remain divided. Factions were inevitable and troublesome but equally a source of benefit. A tyrannous majority was indeed the worst despotism to fear, but in a large, diverse republic such tyranny was unlikely.

The new framework was criticized on all sides. French reformers such as Jacques Turgot and the Marquis de Condorcet were disappointed by the creation of a senate and strong president. They believed that representative government required a strong assembly. The Founders, they felt, had missed their chance by mimicking oligarchic British tradition and accepting "Gothic" muddle rather than an intelligible structure transparent in its aims and working.

The Constitution was born in compromise and survived a civil war when compromise broke down only by radically changing itself. It had relied on the Great Compromise between the small and big states and on a second, "rotten" compromise between the free North and the slave-holding South. In return for empowering the federal government over trade and commerce, the future of slavery was left aside, although slaves were counted as three-fifths of a person for purposes of apportioning representation.

Legally, the "rotten" compromise between North and South was abandoned with the abolition of slavery and the passage of the Fourteenth Amendment, a constitutional passkey for establishing personal and corporate rights in federal and, increasingly, in state law. The passkey became a liberal tool, used first by right-wing liberals to enfranchise business from the claims of labor and later by left-wing liberals to free citizens from the moral interferences of law on their private conduct.

Madison's "harmonious system of mutual frustration," as the historian Richard Hofstadter called it, survived in continuity through many changes. The constitutional debates of 1787–88 fed into the contests of political modernity, giving it new terms and new metaphors. The Constitution itself became a stake in the American version of the contest between liberalism and conservatism. Appointments to its legal guardian, the Supreme Court, were fought over in partisan terms by the White House and Senate. The justices decried the labels, which they said caricatured their work. For the bulk of legal disputes that reached them, the point was fair, but for the rarer but headline cases of deep political division and high constitutional controversy—slavery, business and labor, personal morals, institutional powers—the complaint missed the mark, as a historic record of reliable partisanship along liberal-left and conservative-right lines suggested.

v. What the Critics Left to Conservatism

The critics of the French Revolution handed down to early conservatives a rich store of arguments, metaphors, and rhetorical appeals for use against their first opponents, the liberals of the mid-nineteenth century. Revolution had a wrong picture of society as conflicted and competitive, when society was in fact organic and harmonious.

Revolution had destroyed stability and order, misled by false ideas about the practicability or desirability of change. Society's members did not, in disruptive insolence, question and dictate to society. Rather, society guided and showed them their duties. People were not all "naturally"—that is, presocially—good until society, especially modern competitive society, made them bad, as Rousseau, the spirit of Revolution, had preached. They were not all reliably capable of wise choice and self-government, as the Revolution's book-read but foolish lawyers trusted. People in the main were weak, imperfect, and in need of firm guidance. They could not step away from society and judge it from the outside as philosophical critics of society pretended, for they themselves drew standards of judgment from their own place in society's framework of ranks and stations. Even were they so able, society was too subtle and complex to be assessed by overarching principles, which were inevitably loose and ill-fitting. Society properly understood was the embodiment of tradition, itself a store of knowledge and the foundation of self-understanding.

Such was the legacy of conservatism's forerunners. Denial of social harmony, limits of political reason, and human moral imperfection fostered a ruinous belief in progress: overconfidence in the steady betterment of society and either sentimental faith in people's intrinsic goodness or a naive trust in their improvability. History, like providence, was inscrutable. Society was opaque. People were imperfect and inept at self-direction. On that anti-revolutionary arsenal crafted in the 1790s—anti-individualist, anti-egalitarian, and politically skeptical—conservatism was to draw richly when in the mid-nineteenth century its arguments with liberalism were openly engaged.

PART II

What Conservatism Is

2

Character, Outlook, and Labelling of Conservatism

i. Conservatism as a Political Practice

Before the story goes on, some ground needs to be cleared. What is conservatism? What is this a story of? There are no knockdown facts here. The questions find many answers as well as self-defeating claims that they are too difficult to have any answer. The terms in play are tricky, but "what is conservatism?" is not about labels or meanings. The question bears on conservatism's character and its kind, which have to be understood historically.

If you ask what kind of thing conservatism is, you will hear that it is a party-political family, counsel of government, philosophy of society, mouthpiece of the haves, voice of all classes, unexalted picture of humankind, or universal human preference for the steady and familiar against the changeable and strange. Each answer catches some aspect of conservatism. All are partial. Conservatism as understood here is a tradition or practice of politics. As with any practice, that involves three things. Conservatism has a history, it has participants in the practice—politicians, thinkers, backers, voters—and it has an outlook to guide them. Neither who conservatives are nor what they think can be put into a phrase or formula. Its practice is complex, but that is poor reason to stop before the story starts.

Conservatives were not were heard of before the early nineteenth century. Like liberals, their first opponents, conservatives faced new social conditions previously unimagined. Although their social and intellectual roots were old and deep, the scale and pace of change was disorienting. After creeping along for centuries, populations and economies had suddenly exploded in growth. Technical innovation was altering settled forms of life. Movement from country to town freed people from old authorities and customary ties. People who read and argued about politics were no longer counted in the thousands but hundreds of thousands, soon millions. Money was spent to make things that created yet more money. Capitalist modernity, in short, was turning economic methods, social patterns, and people's outlooks upside down. It enriched and impoverished, empowered and disempowered, shuffled social ranks, created high expectations, and reframed ethical norms. In this exciting, destabilizing new condition of society, politics had to rethink itself. Liberalism and conservatism were born.

Liberals, to schematize, embraced capitalist modernity. Conservatives responded by opposing the liberal embrace. The first liberals welcomed capitalism and critical thought, the twin turbines of modern change. Liberals favored freer markets, moveable labor, and the self-generative force of money. They embraced religious indifference and social and cultural diversity, as well as the constructive power of disagreement. The first conservatives defended closed markets and stable patterns of life while fearing the solvent powers of finance. They stressed social unity, shared faith, and common loyalties. Liberals saw themselves as opening up society, releasing energies, and letting people go. Conservatives saw liberals as breaking up society, spreading disorder, and leaving people bewildered. Liberalism offered experiment and endeavor. Conservatism promised certainty and security. Without having to claim that liberals caused capitalist modernity, conservatives blamed liberals for embracing capitalist modernity. It quickly became for conservatives a liberal modernity.

Conservatives linked liberals with blind encouragement of change, just as liberals linked conservatives with blind resistance to change. By the 1830s, when two Baden liberals began publishing their massive study of contemporary politics, the *Staatslexikon*, liberals were described in it as the "party of movement," conservatives as the "party of resistance or standstill." Conservatives, by implication, were obstructionists. Conservatives turned the imputation around: liberals were destructionists; they stood for disorder and insecurity, whereas conservatives stood for order and stability. Both in fact were looking for social order but did not think of it in the same way.

Were politics chess, liberals had white; they moved first. Conservatives had black; they countered liberalism's opening moves. In time, the initiative changed hands. Conservatives, who began as antimoderns, came to master modernity, for the right was in telling ways the stronger contestant. It spoke for the powers of wealth and property—first, land against industry and finance, then for all three, and soon for small property as well as large. Conservatism, in addition, would rely well into the twentieth century on the organs of state and on society's many corps—law, religion, armed forces, universities—which tended to a stand-pat conservatism in the everyday, prepolitical sense of wanting tomorrow to be like today and not forever changing the furniture. Conservatives overcame fears of political democracy and by the early twentieth century were regrouping—in ascending order of coherence, in Germany, France, the United States, and Britain—as formidable electoral powers.

Those triple advantages—the backing of wealth, institutional support, and electoral reach—helped the right prevail at the liberal democratic game. Puzzling as it sounds, conservatism's ultimate reward for compromising with liberal democracy was domination of liberal democracy. Though cast by the left as politicians of the past, the right became the leading force of modern times, as its party-political record in office confirms. After 1914 in the France's Third Republic (1870–1940), Republicans (right-wing liberals) traded office (often in coalition) with Radicals (left-wing liberals), keeping socialists and communists at bay. A similar pattern followed in the Fourth Republic (1944–58). In over sixty years of the French Fifth Republic, the president was on the right in more than thirty-nine, on the left in twenty (and those presidents— François Mitterrand and François Hollande, were of the palest, most center-minded left), with a centrist, Emmanuel Macron, making up the remainder. In Britain, the twentieth century was a "Conservative century" in terms of office. From 1895 to 2020, the Tories governed alone or were the majority party in coalition governments for 81 of

126 years. The right's dominance in the United States was harder to spot. In thirty-one presidential elections (1896–2016), Republicans won seventeen, Democrats fourteen. Republicans controlled the Senate for only fifty-four years, against the Democrats' sixty-eight, and only fifty-two against seventy in the House. On another measure of dominance, Republicans held the White House and both houses of Congress for forty-four years, against forty for the Democrats. That seeming balance masked the fact that a solid white South returned conservative, segregationist Democrats until the 1970s. If control of the national agenda is the test, reform Democrats framed the political argument only for a time after 1913 and then again from the 1930s to the 1960s.

The German right in the twentieth century might seem with little question to fall outside that pattern. Until 1918, conservatives split over reforming or resisting reform to the Wilhelmine Reich. They split again from 1918 to 1933 over support or subversion of modern Germany's first attempt at liberal democracy, the Weimar Republic. Despite brave acts of resistance, the right collapsed and collaborated with Nazism, persuading itself that the bigger fight was against Bolshevism. After the calamity that Germany brought on itself and the world, a liberal-democratic German right was born in the wreckage, led by Christian Democrats. Since the founding of the Federal Republic (1949), the German chancellor was a Christian Democrat in fifty-one of seventy-two years. Was there a single German right? An unbroken, continuous right—no. Nevertheless, when a post-1945 German right re-formed itself, it had German, not imported or imposed, sources to draw on.

The more elections conservatives won and the more they governed, the larger their responsibilities grew. Having opened by opposing liberal modernity, mainstream conservatives came to own it. In representing more and more of modern society, they found themselves more and more on both sides of the conflicts that racked modern society— business's need for innovation against people's longing for stability; the demands of global competition against the nation's common good; the useful fragmentation of knowledge and multiplication of viewpoints against the need for the shared loyalties and common assumptions that make public argument possible. Taken together, those tensions could be labelled "efficiency against community." In standing for both, the right was soon arguing as much with itself as with rivals to the left.

From the late nineteenth century on, party-political success combined with a high degree of inner-party disruption. A recalcitrant hard right, which refused compromise with liberals or with democracy, was louder at times, softer at others, but always there. It harried the mainstream right in Republican France and Wilhelmine Germany during the 1880s and 1890s. Over Ireland, trade, and empire, it divided Britain's Tories during the 1910s and 1920s). An anti-liberal, segregationist right controlled the US South politically from the 1880s through the 1960s, misshaping modern American conservatism. In Germany, the failures of war and economic depression prompted a right-wing search for alternatives to liberalism and parliamentary democracy during the 1920s and 1930s, with calamitous results. At present, a postindustrial hollowing out in society, a financial crash, failed wars, and geostrategic fears have shaken voters' faith in the conservative claim to prudence and superior understanding. With increasing pace during the 2010s, a broadly liberal-minded center-right found itself on the defensive against a confident, disruptive hard right.

Recalcitrant conservatives—those, that is, who refuse compromise with one or more aspects of liberalism—have come in many varieties. Some have focused on structures and institutions: latter-day monarchists, anti-parliamentarians, corporatists, right-wing populists; some on the nation and its prerogatives: colonialist diehards, go-it-alone unilateralists; some on the character of the national people: anti-immigrants, anti-Semites, Klansmen, Southern resisters to civil rights, white-nation extremists, latter-day dark-web "incels." They tend to vanish to the fringes in democratic liberalism's better times (before 1914; again after 1945). In worse times, 1918–45 and with rapid tempo, now, the recalcitrant right moves in to disrupt and divide a conservative mainstream committed to compromise.

Although liberal democracy is a child of the left, its growth and health have relied on support from the right. As the historian Brian Girvin expressed it in *The Right in the Twentieth Century* (1994), "A democratic right is a necessary condition of democracy." A data-minded political scientist, Daniel Ziblatt, put the point with empirical sophistication in *Conservative Parties and the Birth of Democracy* (2017), adding a further condition: to give support, the right must be strong and united. When, as now, the right is divided, the haves sleep less easily that government is in safe hands. "A robust conservative political party," Ziblatt wrote, "may actually be a precondition for democracy." Girvin and Ziblatt were echoing Joseph Chamberlain, then a radical Liberal, when he was appealing to business to support social reform in 1885. "What ransom," he asked, "will property pay for the security which it enjoys?" When property paid the ransom—higher taxes, social welfare, worker protections, business regulation—conservatism sustained democratic liberalism. When the ransom for property looked too high, conservatives hesitated and drew back. Liberal democracy has done best when the competing demands of property and democracy were in balance.

For all the right's historical success in party politics, its thinkers and intellectuals have tended to shine more for individual brilliance than for gradual consolidation of undisputed principles. Throughout conservatism's history, party politics has drawn on and shaped conservative ideas. That interplay is one reason for the familiar difficulty of summarizing what conservatives think. There are others. Whereas the liberal outlook has a canon of characteristic thinkers—Wilhelm von Humboldt, John Stuart Mill, Aléxis de Tocqueville, Leonard Hobhouse, Karl Popper, John Rawls—conservatives lack a canon. To confuse matters, two thinkers cited by some as mapping points for late-twentieth-century conservatism—Friedrich Hayek and Michael Oakeshott—also belong in the liberal canon, on its right-hand edge. The muddle, it should be noted in passing, is only apparent: Hayekians follow their master and deny he was conservative; many, though not all, followers of Oakeshott deny he was liberal; but those labels are not authoritative. Liberal conservatism became orthodox after 1945, and each thinker gave primary voice to one aspect of that orthodoxy: Hayek to efficiency, Oakeshott to community.

A further difficulty is that, intellectually speaking, the right never entirely shook off the oppositional spirit of its birth. In looking into the conservative mind, it often seems in consequence to be a brilliant repertoire of counterblows against liberals and suspicion of democrats but without large aims or principles of its own. In answering the implied charge that something positive is missing in the conservative outlook, two paths of reply are open.

The pragmatic path, often linked to "realism," is to treat strong performance in office as its own legitimation. Though no longer society's natural rulers, conservatives, on that view, have proven to be its most reliable rulers. To justify themselves and show others what they were about, conservatives accordingly did not require large aims or ideals; to think that they did was to misunderstand the tasks of politics. All that was needed was a driver's manual of prudent maxims about governing well: go cautiously, don't try many things at once, don't expect much of people or politics, don't upset the haves, and—to adapt an image from the philosopher Anthony Quinton, a lucid British conservative—keep the bus on its "narrow, winding road."

The rules-of-prudence approach has a British flavor and was less common in France, Germany, and the United States, where conservative thinkers on the whole were bolder. They searched for large, positive ideas that they believed conservatives needed: in political economy (market against society); in religion's part in secular society; in the rights of anti-liberal minorities; in the character of nations and peoples. As if inspired by the title of a small, overlooked but prescient book from an American conservative, *Ideas Have Consequences* (1948), that search for a conservative outlook was fostered in the second half of the twentieth century by a well-financed Gramscian campaign of intellectual renewal in think tanks, institutes, the media, and universities, first in the United States and Britain, then also in France and Germany. The search sharpened the right's tools in public argument, even when it did not find a counterliberal orthodoxy or end disputes on the right.

In the absence of a settled party-political orthodoxy, a broad, quite different path for conservative thought lay open not in party politics but outside it, in aesthetic and ethical criticism of liberal modernity. As thinkers and writers, they were often the right's most distinctive voices. They reminded liberal-democratic society of its costs, neglects, and failures: disavowal of authority, social fragmentation, human damage, empty promise of progress, license for willfulness, and sentimental attachment to human equality. The critics might be literary, philosophical, or religious. They included poets and writers (Leopardi, Wordsworth, Coleridge, Hawthorne), critics (Ruskin, Sainte-Beuve), satirists (Mencken), early Greens (Cobbett, Riehl), and lawyers, philosophers, and historians (Stephen, Bradley, Carlyle, Gierke), as well as religious thinkers (Lamennais, Newman, Ketteler, Hodge, and Brownson). Such critics wrote with the zest of battle in faith that the harms of modernity might yet be held off. As cultural democracy strengthened and cultural authorities declined in the twentieth century, that confidence weakened. Conservative critics grew angry or elegiac. They included writers who championed escape into unthinking action (Drieu, the early Jünger) or retreat to religion or aesthetics in a spirit of noncooperation and withdrawal (Eliot, Scruton, and strands of American Catholic thought).

ii. The Conservative Outlook

The early labels "party of movement" and "party of order" were catchy but misleading. Both liberals and conservatives were looking for order and stability, but they did not think of them alike. Liberals pictured modern order as achievable in a fluid society of self-possessed, mobile, and well-provided-for people. Authority under law in such an order would flow outward from the mutual accommodations of reasonable, live-and-let-live citizens. Authority, though established and effective, would be conditional and open to question.

Conservatives kept to an older picture. Social order for them depended on stable institutions and social hierarchy with settled ranks and familiar duties. Authority on that picture flowed downward through fixed, recognized channels. Conservatives had venerable ideas to draw on. To Plato, authorities should be obeyed because they were wise and in touch with higher truth. To Hobbes, the intellectual godfather of the "realist" right for whom security was the highest social value, authorities were needed as sovereign arbiters to stop people's inborn competitiveness from running out of control. For Hume and Burke, authority was what people had grown used to obeying and whose origins (in conquest or usurpation) were now thankfully forgotten. Authority, on each account, was absolute in this sense: it was to be obeyed and not forever asked for credentials by tiresome questioners. To be settled—to become "established," to use a favored term—social order required unreflective acceptance, loyalty, and faith, not doubt, critique, and "maybe."

That vertical understanding of authority could be thought of in older ways as religious or military, or in newer pluralistic terms. Conservatives could picture an orderly society as a community of believers under a superior, divine authority; as a military hierarchy of command flowing down from higher to lower units; or as a manifold whole of corporations and associations each with a downward authority, from whole to part, of their own. On that last, newer picture, authority was more than rulers and lawmakers; it included orderly society itself, with its settled customs, norms, and conventions.

Conservatives understood that society was rarely, if ever, perfectly ordered. They recognized the immemorial scourges of famine, war, disease, rebellion, and bad government (wicked princes, greedy oligarchs, angry mobs). They grasped, too, that a settled society was not fixed or frozen but open to gradual change. What they had not expected and what in capitalist modernity the first conservatives faced was something altogether more daunting: a new kind of social order that, as it seemed, continually sowed disorder and insecurity by itself. The perpetual disturbance of capitalist modernity promised a tearing down of established ranks, an overturning of settled patterns of life, and widening disregard for ethical and cultural authority—not once, but again and again.

If conservatives were to persuade others to share their picture of "established" order, the picture would have to be adapted and modernized to retain credit in changing times. Conservatives would have to turn its early lessons from critics of the French Revolution—society's unity, reason's limits, and human imperfection—into a contemporary, counterliberal outlook. First, they had to accept that a conservative outlook was needed. For those who had been used to ruling but no longer ruled, the lesson was painful and difficult to accept.

iii. Conservative and Liberal Outlooks Contrasted

A German historian of conservative thought, Rudolf Vierhaus, nicely summed up the attitude to political ideas of the old ruling classes. For them, he wrote, "social order and political power belonged to the sphere of 'is,' not to that of 'would' and 'should.'" On turning to "woulds" and "shoulds," early conservatives heard and read liberals, then disagreed with them. Each made themselves clearest in opposition to the other. The first conservatives were anti-liberals; the first liberals, anti-conservatives.

To four questions facing any coherent political outlook, conservatives and liberals answered differently. Is society cohesive or conflicted? Are there moral limits to the exercise of power? Does human life improve? Is everyone equal in society or are there superiors and inferiors?

Liberals, to put it in summary terms, took society to be competitive and conflicted. They distrusted power and questioned customary authority. They believed in human progress and social equality, with its requirement of civic respect for all. They had high expectations of political action. Conservatives took society to be harmonious. They respected power and accepted customary authority. They did not believe in progress or in equality. Respect in their eyes was due not to everyone regardless but to merit and excellence.

Gentz's friend, the German Romantic Adam Müller, was an early objector to treating society as competitive and conflicted. Although his attachment to princely rule and estate privileges was nostalgic, his nose for liberal faults was sharp. The flaw in the liberal picture, he judged, was to place people outside society and then try to put them back. People could not, without cost to themselves and to what they were leaving, abandon their society or deny its hold on them. There were never new societies, as if a new society could be winched into history by pulling timeless ideals to earth; there were only ongoing societies with pasts and futures, whose bounds, if they existed, nobody knew. Society, lastly, was not a tool to be used at will for selected purposes, however beneficial or worthwhile, but instead was something of general value on its own terms that could not have a number put to it by how well or badly

society executed particular tasks. Those mistakes about people and society could be called—to use present-day terms—costless exit, time-
lessness, and instrumental use. Conservatism's opening charge that
liberals misunderstood the moral power of the social bond continued
to enjoy a late-twentieth-century return in conservative ethical criticism, as well exemplified by the thinkers such as Alasdair MacIntyre and
Roger Scruton. A parallel charge, that liberalism exaggerated people's
desire for autonomy and underplayed their need for authoritative
norms, came in post-1945 Germany by Arnold Gehlen and by American
neoconservatives.

Both conservatives and liberals agreed that authoritative power was
needed for social order, but they disagreed on how power was to be
legitimized and made authoritative. To conservatives, power once "established," that is, settled and accepted, was just and hence authoritative, although legitimate holders of authority could act unjustly. To
liberals, for power to be just it had to be more than obeyed from habit
or put up with. It had to be shown to be just. The difference revealed
itself, among other ways, in the liberal attachment and conservative hostility to written constitutions. Power for liberals was ever open to "Why
must I obey?" "Why should I pay?" and "Why must I conform?" To
conservatives, that was backward. Power, in their eyes, became acceptable and established by assuring order. It followed that law, property,
and custom, the pillars of social order, were to be respected, not carped
at, criticized, and deflected from performing their order-supporting
tasks. To a conservative Ultra like Bonald, the leading brain of France's
post-Napoleonic restoration, the idea of public argument was itself
anathema. With characteristic morgue, Bonald said, "One should only
ever assemble people in church or in the army, because there they don't
argue; they listen and obey."

A favorite object of conservative mockery, especially from writers and
poets, was trust in the achievability of human progress, the third element
in the liberal outlook. Musing about the lava-crusted slopes of Etna in
his great poem *The Broom* (1836), Giacomo Leopardi taunted: "Etched
on these slopes is the magnificent, progressive fate of humankind." In his
fable, "Earth's Holocaust" (1844), Nathaniel Hawthorne teased liberals

for their callow preoccupation with novelty. For Charles Baudelaire, progress was "a doctrine of laziness" that childishly pictured history as a cozy train taking everyone to a happier and better destination.

What liberals counted as a better life was questioned. "Commerce has enriched thousands," Coleridge acknowledged. It had been, he wrote, "the cause of the spread of knowledge and science," but he asked, had it "added one particle of moral improvement?" The French historian Hippolyte Taine openly lamented the "causes of modern unhappiness, which puts a leaden sky over our heads." In a celebrated passage from *L'Ancien régime* (1875), he contrasted the bourgeois rat race with the ease and liberty of aristocratic life: "No demanding, early jobs in those days; no furious competition; no ill-defined careers and unbounded vistas. Ranks were clear, ambitions were limited and there was less envy. People were not continually discontent, bitter and preoccupied as they are today. Privilege and favors mattered less when there were no rights. We long to get ahead. They longed to amuse themselves."

Material progress was contrasted unfavorably with the supposed moral emptiness of liberal modernity. Thoughts of the kind continued through the nineteenth century and beyond. Although not directly political, they became ammunition to fire back against liberals when liberals invoked morality in their own political causes. Arthur Schopenhauer's and Søren Kierkegaard's philosophical pessimism was deployable in high-level critiques of liberal progress. Nietzscheanism was on hand to upset liberals with the suggestion that their humanitarian impulses to protect the weak were rooted in envy and resentment. Thinkers in the twentieth century continued to shake their heads at liberal modernity's philosophico-moral failings, whether for its superficiality and inauthenticity (Martin Heidegger, who thought us "too late for the gods, too early for Being") or for its pseudo-critical recklessness (Theodor Adorno, for whom "the fully enlightened earth radiates disaster").

Openly political charges against liberal progress focused on its undue costs and unintended consequences. Even if desirable, broad human progress would not be achievable, conservatives argued. In a pointed study of the right's critique of liberal progress, *The Rhetoric of Reaction* (1991), the American thinker Albert O. Hirschman suggested that the charges could all be brought under one or other of the heads of futility (hoped-for change is not improvement), perversity (recommended cures make the ailment worse), or jeopardy (repair causes other harms). In those terms, cultural critics of liberal progress from Coleridge to Heidegger and Adorno made the charge of futility (modern change is not for the better). Late twentieth-century national-minded critics of economic globalism made the charge of perversity (foreigners' gains did not outweigh heavy local costs). Twenty-first-century critics of liberal-modern planetary neglect—who, it must be stressed, cross the left-right divide— make the charge of jeopardy (economic growth stifles the globe).

Where in the fourth element of their outlook—demanding that state and society treat everyone with equal respect—liberals saw public virtue and fellow feeling, conservatives saw fond hope and sentimentality. Respect, in conservative eyes, was due to merit and rank. Respecting everyone whoever they were and whatever little they did for society or achieved for themselves in worldly terms was not respect but a hypocritical kind of mockery. Respect shown to anyone at all and without measure became worthless. People were not equal in energy, talent, achievement, or character. Some excelled in what they did, some in what they were. Beyond equal treatment at law, nobody deserved society's respect as such.

The conservative denial of equality could take antique and modern forms. A vision of hierarchic society lingered late into the nineteenth century, notably in official Roman Catholic thinking. In an encyclical (1878), Pope Leo XIII, an advocate of Christian corporatism, pronounced that God had ordained "various orders in civil society, differing in dignity, rights, and power, whereby the State, like the Church, should be one body, consisting of many members, some nobler than others."

The modern form of conservative inegalitarianism was subtler. It had been heard at the beginning of the century from the Hanoverian sceptic Rehberg. In *Über den deutschen Adel* (On the German aristocracy, 1803), he wrote: "You can strip nobles of their names, titles, and crests, but nobility itself is indestructible." He wanted to distinguish rank from what is expected from rank by way of good performance. Some nobles ruled well (he had Britain and Hanover in mind), others ruled badly (pre-1789 France). As for aristocracy, so for every class. Some members of a class performed well, others did poorly. Membership itself was no guide. Rehberg was expressing conservative meritocracy before its time.

Conservatives had a further argument against equality. Liberal promises of respect for everyone led in practice to diffuse action and inattention to particular needs. Liberals preached but failed to deliver equal respect. Indeed, they encouraged or shut their eyes to new tyrannies of strong over weak, rich over poor, owners over workers. Rather than promising equal respect, it was better, in conservative eyes, to ensure effective concern, gauged to people's varying needs and merits.

Liberal deceit was worse still when the promise of equal respect was made to all, democratically. The promise threatened then to become empty, if not destructive. People, to the conservative mind, were not equally given to self-mastery, let alone to governing others. They were not, economically speaking, due equal rewards for unequal efforts. They were not, ethically and culturally, all equally sound in judging what mattered in life and what aesthetic standards to uphold. But out of tactical prudence, mainstream conservatives, especially after 1945, came to compromise with the egalitarian language of democratic liberalism. They tempered and quieted their belief in inequality. They learned not to bellow like the young Salisbury had done in 1862 about "the insane passion for equality" but to speak like Dwight Eisenhower in his first inaugural, in January 1953: "Any man who seeks to deny equality among all his brothers betrays the spirit of the free and invites the mockery of the tyrant"—equality for sisters came later. The conservative adoption of a democratic, egalitarian language never wholly hid the right's original conviction that humans were not equal and that trying to make them equal was imprudent and unachievable. Tension between democratic discourse and conservative conviction runs through the right to this day.

iv. Bonding Spaces for Conservatives with Liberals

When socialist or reformist demands for economic democracy— roughly, a more equal stake in prosperity for all—grew loud later in the nineteenth century, conservatives and liberals saw points of accord.

Differences of outlook were softened. Liberals, on closer look, did not distrust power as such; they were wary of its arbitrary exercise. As believers in progress, liberals were not aiming to replace one society *by* another society but to remove ills *in* society. They, too, grasped, that duties came with rights. In return, conservatives acknowledged that established power need not be unlimited, immune to question, and able to do as it pleased. They accepted that a settled, unified society might well need topical repair. Conservatives did not deny rights as such. How could they? Security in property depended on them. What conservatives objected to was inflating and devaluing rights by declaratory overextension.

Politically, those bonding spaces allowed for durable alliances, as the party-political narrative will soon show. Intellectually, they made it harder for conservatives to say what made their outlook special or why they came to accept economic liberties but never felt wholly at home with cultural liberties.

A blurring of conservative and liberal outlooks was noticed early on. Moderate conservatives, the German political observer Friedrich Bülau wrote in 1847, were not for no change, and moderate liberals did not call for total change. During the radical upheaval of 1848, the right-wing German liberal David Hansemann told a friend, "What was liberal yesterday is conservative today and former conservatives happily link up with former liberals." In "Intellectual Conservatism" (1856), Walter Bagehot reversed the direction of fit but made the same linkage, writing, "To a great extent every liberal is now a Conservative." These early observers had spotted something new and valuable for conservatives to hold onto, a frame of modern politics that can be called a liberal status quo.

The blurring was clearest in the United States, where the Whigs, who became Republicans, combined liberal and conservative elements from the beginning. Crudely, Whigs were economically liberal as procapitalists, semiliberal on slavery, and conservative in their fear of electoral and cultural democracy. The liberal-conservative cross type was evident also in Europe. A German example was Wilhelm von Kardorff, a landowner-businessman who led the pro-Bismarck Free Conservatives and founded the German industrial federation, and Gustav Stresemann, the leader of the right-wing liberals in the Weimar Republic. Typical of liberal conservatism in post-1945 France was the pro-market Antoine Pinay, who called himself "Mr. Consumer." He led the Independents, which later fed into the center-right party of Valéry Giscard d'Estaing. In the United States, until the 1970s, the liberal conservative was easy to spot in the pro-market, culturally open-minded "Rockefeller Republican." A British archetype was the "Wet" Tory Prime Minister Harold Macmillan (1957–63).

v. The Adaptability of Conservative Ideas

An unavoidable question arises at this point. How far are conservative ideas put forward in historically different circumstances two hundred years ago the same ideas conservatives put forward nowadays? If they are not the same, it seems wrong to talk about a conservative outlook common to then and now. And if there is no common outlook, the very idea that there is one tradition or practice here looks mistaken. Coherence here seems to fight with continuity.

Scholars have sought to solve the continuity-coherence problem in various ways. For Karl Mannheim in 1927, conservatism was a principled defense of landed interests and their institutions against destabilizing modern change, but his timebound conservatism risked stalling in the nineteenth century. Samuel Huntington, in contrast, argued in 1957 that conservatism was "situational." Its "essence" was defense of the prevailing order, whatever and whenever. Over time, his conservatives had and did not need to have anything common to think or say. In 1996, Michael Freeden sought to link continuity and change by allowing each their measure. Conservatives then and now have shared a common outlook, on his account, while adapting its particular content to shifting circumstances.

Conservatives have proved adept at restating their outlook, in the way Freeden suggested, to fit the times. The outlook's character, that is, has remained as the content changed. For example, *social unity* among the first conservatives was thought of in "organic" terms as a hierarchy of ranks and estates. Believing them or not, Disraeli was still talking in such terms at midcentury. The organic metaphor, however, was giving way to the visible facts of class conflict and democracy. Social unity was rethought in terms of people and nation. The people were imagined as a cultural or racial whole, acting together as a nation with an agreed past and common destiny—often imperial—to spread Englishness, Frenchness, or Americanness to the world. After 1945, talk of a unitary "people" was proscribed as totalitarian or racialist, and exclusionary nationalism was treated as dangerous and discredited, but in time, the lessons were forgotten. With the rise of a hard right in the twenty-first century, unitary talk of "the people" returned. Competitive nationalism was taken for good sense. With *social unity*, what did the idea's work throughout those changes was what a united society had little patience for: diversity, divisiveness, and troublemaking.

The *authorities* that conservatives first defended were particular and personal: local squires and judges, clergymen, and teachers, but authority has grown impersonal: the state's legal authority (to have the final say); the market's economic authority (to deny those who cannot pay); society's normative authority (to police ethical and cultural standards).

The idea of *property* was, to begin with, tied for conservatives to particular places and types of owner, above all the landed classes. Defending property blended easily with defending country against towns, farming against industry, gentry against merchants. Later in the nineteenth century, as William Mallock's and William Sumner's writings will illustrate, defending property blended for conservatives with backing bosses against workers and markets against the state. Property is still among the first things conservatives defend, but it has grown diffuse. Owners are no longer a distinctive social kind. Property used to be the visible face of society, fenced in and to be walked past in admiration, envy, or longing. It is now also promissory or virtual. The thought is at least as old as Karl Marx, but capitalism's champion Joseph Schumpeter was alive to the change, writing in 1942 that "by substituting a mere parcel of shares for the walls of and machines in a factory" capitalism "takes the life out of the idea of property." Finance was not the only kind of property to acquire an impersonal, virtual character. Property has now come to include a diverse, essential portfolio known as "human capital": skills, education, privileged access, and social connections. Through those changes, the idea *property* has kept its role in conservative thought as a stabilizer of society providing people—to use Hegel's term—with "personality," a capacity for effective action in civic life they would otherwise lack.

In weight and reach, the *state* of the 1830s bears little likeness to the state of the twenty-first century. The peacetime state in rich nations then spent well less than 10 percent of its national income, not, as now, 40–60 percent. Taxes were similarly low, and few owed them. Talk of the state then and now is in a way like calling the mail coach and the World-Wide Web "communications." By contrast, conservative concerns about the state's reach and weight are alike. Economic pressures that make the state grow or shrink—war or peace; prosperity or penury—are alike. Then as now states cycled between economic openness to each other and back. Ethically and culturally, conservatives then as now were having arguments of the same character about how far the state should support churches or police speech and personal morals.

The *wisdom of custom and tradition* was gradually detached from endangered or superannuated institutions. It was decoupled also from older beliefs and philosophies. After 1945, the wisdom of custom and tradition was neatly transmuted to fit the times. Custom in politics was rethought as prudence and firmness, undistracted by ideology. Custom in economics was replaced by the supposed self-correcting character of markets. The work done by the idea *custom* remained. It was to debar critical or overblown ideas from politics and state meddling from economics.

vi. "Conservatism," "the Right," and Other Label Troubles

The conservative story involves moderates and radicals, centrists and extremists, the economically minded and the ethically minded, excluders and includers, dividers and uniters. Conservatives have been pigeonholed as "reactionary," "status-quo," "revolutionary," "ultra," "neo," and "paleo." They have been marshaled according to their primary focus as political, cultural, religious, environmental, and moral conservatives. In the apt phrase of the philosopher Simon Evnine, conservatism is an "endemically contested entity."

"The enemy of conservatism," Samuel Huntington wrote, "is not liberalism, but radicalism." Conservatives, it is true, have often complained of radicals on the right. Metternich cried in exasperation that all legitimists could legitimize was revolution. At the beginning of France's Third Republic, Adolphe Thiers rebuked a royalist opponent: "It was necessary to pacify but for fifty years you have angered and no government could become established—you have all served the left more than the conservatives." The error is to think of radicals as political types or of radicalism as a set of ideas. The terms "radical" and "moderate" are not substantive but adverbial. Radicalism and moderation bear on pace, posture, and style, not content. The difference turns on how aims are held and acted on: rigidly or flexibly, zealously or temperately, in attacking thrusts or defensively dug in, bent on annihilating opposition or allowing for compromise, unable to live without conquest or able to survive defeat and failure.

Conservatives can be radical or moderate. It depends on the state of the contest, on the stakes in the contest, and on which party is attacking, which defending. "Conservative" appeals to custom, unity, and even political modesty can take temperate forms: stress on duty to society; "one-nation" conservatism and deprecation of class division; policy gradualism. They can take also intemperate forms: stigmatization of the Other; denial of social diversity and hounding of internal enemies; exclusionary nationalism; tarring of moderate opponents as radicalized and extreme.

When pressed, elements of the right are commonly willing to play as radicals against the majority opinion, the rule of law, or established custom: French anti-republicans from 1870 to 1880); Britain's Tory "ditchers" (over reforming the Lords, in 1910), or the Conservative leader Bonar Law encouraging armed rebellion in the north against Home Rule for Ireland in July 1912—"I can imagine no length of resistance to which Ulster will go, which I shall not be ready to support"; German conservatives who backed armed opposition in the early Weimar Republic; Southern conservatives in the United States who resisted court-ordered desegregation of schools in the 1950s and 1960s; British anti-European Conservatives, who after 2016 who ignored opinion in a divided country, flouted constitutional norms, and, replaying an appeal of the radicalized right familiar since the late nineteenth century in Europe and the United States, set an elected parliament they did not control against a being of their own populist imagination, "the people of Britain."

The coiners of "liberal" as a label in party politics were the Spanish constitutionalists in the 1810s. The label "conservative" came soon after in France. Chateaubriand's journal, *Le Conservateur* (1818), is cited as an early partisan use, although the term was heard earlier for the broad attitude of political caution. Soon after, a German lawyer, Ludwig Harscher, favorably contrasted "conservative liberalism" with "disruptive liberalism" (1823), giving early verbal baptism to a rich later history of intellectual merger and cross-party alliance. British Tories in the 1820s were still in a distancing manner using French neologisms. Viscount Castlereagh spoke of "our English *libéraux*," the Duke of Wellington of "the *parti conservateur* of this country." The new labels were soon Englished. By 1830, the Tory *Quarterly Review* could announce that Tories were called "with more propriety" the "conservative party."

In the United States, "conservatism" and "the right" are used interchangeably for the entire family of oppositions to liberalism. In republican France, it is often claimed that a genuine conservatism never existed. In 2017, the historian of ideas François Huguenin called conservatism France's "great absentee." The same has often been claimed of liberalism in France. Either practice can be tied so tightly to a favored exemplar as to be unexportable (Britain's Conservative Party, for example) or sketched so generally as to be actualized nowhere. In France, the term *la droite* embraces streams elsewhere called conservative. In Germany *die Rechte* is used the same way. If words alone guide, conservatism has not existed in Germany for a century. Since 1918, *Konservatismus* has suggested failed reaction, stuffy pretention, or over-the-line radicalism, associations that smart young conservatives of the German hard right are working to overcome.

Among the parties of the right in the four countries considered, only Britain's long-lived Conservatives have adopted and kept the name. The German right dropped "conservative" as stuffy and baggage-laden after 1918. France's mainstream right has since the 1900s employed a mini-dictionary of permutational acronyms—UR, ARD, AD, RPF, RPR, CNI, UNR, UDR, UDF, UPR, UMP—none of which contain the word "conservative." In the United States, Democratic opponents of Reconstruction in the Southern states briefly called themselves conservatives, but since the 1900s, Republicans in the United States have been seen as the conservative party, and the Democrats as liberals or progressives.

A sense of order can be brought to this seeming muddle if the left-right distinction as basic to liberal-modern politics is recalled. Unless we treat politics as a zero-sum game in which the whole field is to be won and held by one side, recognition of an enduring left-right divide across the field reflects, in rough terms, an acceptance of politics as unending argument amid diversity. It reflects acceptance, in short, of a core element in liberal democracy: the acknowledgement of unsettleable social conflict, fought over politically by the right and the left. The British thinker Steven Lukes put it well in 2003: As a "natural-seeming but historically contingent spatial metaphor," the left-right division is "pervasive, adaptable, general and exceptionally versatile," embodying as it does "the principle of endemic and legitimate conflict between alternatives of equal standing."

Trailing the left-right metaphor of politics in an open field is a call to reject preeminence or dominance. The left never wholly dropped its myth of speaking for humankind. The right never wholly dropped its self-image as the wise head on an unthinking social body. The distinction is often said to be redundant or worn out, but it endures. Thinkers of right and left find it easiest to recognize themselves as anti-thinkers of the other. Without a contestant, argument and—for a liberal, at any rate—politics itself dies.

vii. Dilemmas for Conservatives

Reflecting on the difficulties of being a conservative, in 1962 Clinton Rossiter called conservatism the "thankless persuasion." The German thinker Niklas Luhmann had something like that in mind, when he wrote—to reverse the order of his crack—that progressives normally end in frustration, whereas conservatives are frustrated to start with. Conservatives began as natural-born rulers who had lost authority, but they rewon it by compromising with the liberals and democrats they had started out opposing. They found themselves in command of a modern world they could not love in their hearts.

The frustration here is not temperamental but political. Conservatives can be grumpy or cheerful in their frustration. It depends on who and when. When the historical dice go against them, grumpy conservatives will say, "I told you so." Cheerful conservatives—in the bonhomous spirit of Hume—will laugh off frustration as what is to be expected from "the politics of imperfection." Treating conservatism as a moral temperament seems, in addition, to be oversensitive to the times. An American political scientist, Herbert McClosky, polled conservatives in 1958 and found them typically "alienated," "submissive," and "somewhat spiritless." A social psychologist, Jonathan Haidt, did the same and in *The Righteous Mind* (2012) found the typical conservative to be in better balance with life's demands than the typical liberal. If so, we might reasonably wonder why conservatives at present can sound so angry. Perhaps the point is that conservatism is a category in politics, not social psychology.

Political conservatism is frustrating because its dilemmas never go away. In appealing to social unity and common faith, are conservatives sincere or cynical? Is their preferred mode of action the valiant stand or the regrettable compromise? Have they principles by which to decide what to keep amid capitalism's creative destruction, or is theirs an improvisational pursuit of what works *here and now*, wherever and whenever that is?

Unity and order in society depend together on a common faith, so many conservatives have thought. Such a faith need not be religious, but it does have to be serious and strong enough to bind people in un-reflecting loyalties. If so, a question arises for conservatives. Should people hold such a faith because it is true or because their believing it is useful for social order? If institutions on which social peace and order depend are to be believed in with due piety and protected from the glare of enlightened criticism, their contingent origins and sometimes self-serving purposes must be veiled with an aura of mystique. Society, that is, needs protecting from that staple of moral satire: unmasking selfish interests behind publicly proclaimed virtues. Unmasking society and civilization itself as practiced by the "hermeneutics of suspicion" (Marx, Nietzsche, and Freud) posed for conservatives (and not only conserva-tives) a graver threat. It could be answered by challenging the unmask-ers on the facts, or by agreeing that society and civilization were indeed masks, but necessary masks.

The thought that a wearable orthodoxy, no matter what, was needed for social peace was latent in Richard Hooker's misgivings about Puritan zeal and Catholic doctrinalism that underlay his vindi-cation of the Elizabethan religious settlement. It was explicit in Hobbes's and Spinoza's work. In *De Cive* (1651), Hobbes wrote of the sovereign's duty to keep a firm grip on the universities lest they turn out seditious thinkers who, if clever, would cloud "sound doctrine" on which civil peace depended, or, if stupid, would stir up the igno-rant from the common pulpit. Spinoza, who mistrusted clerics and churches, argued in the *Tractatus Theologico-Politicus* (1670) that al-though a person's beliefs were private and could not be controlled from outside, worship in public was a social matter. "If we want to obey God rightly," he wrote in chapter 19, "the external practice of religion must be accommodated to the peace of the republic." The state, that is, should supervise a common faith for the sake of social order. Hooker, Hobbes, and Spinoza were each in their way respond-ing to the troubling, seemingly irreversible fact of confessional diver-sity. They were confirming in argument what the Peace of Augsburg (1555) and the Treaties of Westphalia (1648) had politically en-trenched: acceptance of religious differences as a historical fact and the end of medieval universalism.

The conservative defense of religion as social bulwark could be sincere. The leader of the Wilhelmine German Conservative Party, Otto von Helldorff, was not playacting when in 1878 in Reichstag debate on Otto von Bismarck's antisocialist laws he endorsed the view that "only a religious view of occupation and work . . . can overcome Social Democracy." Power's use of religion could also be theatrical. Recall Chateaubriand, repelled by the coronation of Charles X and asking himself who could be fooled by such a spectacle. The American scholar Jerry Z. Muller neatly summed up the dilemma in 1997: "The family that prays together may stay together. But members of a family that pray together in order to stay together may eventually find themselves neither praying nor staying."

The list of arrangements conservatives defend or have defended is long. It includes not only the "previous regime" that lingered into the nineteenth century of princely rule, established churches, noble privileges, limited suffrage, and confessional disabilities: conservatives have also stood for plebiscitary authoritarianism, constitutional monarchy, written and unwritten constitutions, centralized and federal states, religious intolerance, and religious liberty. Many institutions that conservatives have sought to keep have buckled, lost authority, or died. Did that make conservatism vain, a heroic failure, a tragicomic posture? Were conservatives like the "gallant cavaliers" in Byron's *Don Juan*, who "fought in vain / For those who knew not to resign or reign"?

Tough-minded, "realist" conservatives have a ready answer. Customs serve social order until they cease to serve. As long as they serve, customs must be upheld. It is foolish to mock or undermine them. Once they weaken under the pressure of historical change, there is no call on conservatives to keep them alive. Customs, along with norms, institutions, authorities, and standards, are not of value in themselves. They are valuable only insofar as they are useful at keeping social peace and sustaining prosperity. Asking a conservative "realist" for a transhistorical standard by which to judge what to keep or let go is vain. Theirs is a historical consequentialism that judges custom by an outcome: is the custom useful in its time?

Conservatives must still apply that test. They must judge when to stop preserving the unpreservable. Their *triage* of custom—let be, let die, or repair—presumably has to rely on more than hunches. Without clear principles, it is not obvious how reasonable judgments are made. Conservatives have often overrated the life chances of institutions they favored, blaming their collapse not on inner flaws but on mischievous interference. Burke judged that the French monarchy and French society were in reparable shape in 1789 if only the lawyers and intellectuals of the Third Estate had not turned the Estates General into a futile row about ideal constitutions. American mid-nineteenth-century conservatives, with Calhoun in the lead, thought that the slave society of the Southern states was sustainable if only the Northern abolitionists had not agitated and interfered. German conservatives in the 1920s, unreconciled to the Weimar Republic, claimed that the Prussian monarchy was savable but for its betrayal by hostile Bolsheviks and timid Social Democrats. A "realist" conservative could reply that the test of conservative judgment lay in the historical record: despite failures of the kind noted, adaptive conservatives, it might be held, had got it more right than wrong when judging when to defend shaken institutions or values and when to bow to unavoidable change. That historical claim, even allowing it were true, would not show the principles, if any, that underlay what, on this defense at any rate, come to look like an astonishing series of canny guesses.

viii. Fighting for a Tradition

Conservatism's story can be told, in the phrase of a British Tory from the 1920s, as "the endless adventure of governing men" (and, lately, women who govern). It involves also sustained, many-sided politico-philosophical argument. Without argument, the story is pointless, as if the adventurers have no idea what they are adventuring for. Without the adventure, arguments and ideas spin on their own without historic content. In four periods given sharp dates for clarity, parallel stories are here told of conservative parties and politicians, together with ideas and thinkers.

Amid destabilizing change, the first conservatives sought order in the prevailing institutions (crown, church, and aristocracy), prevailing legal patterns (ownership and inheritance), or prevailing social forms (deference, faith, and loyalty). Liberal modernity was generous in keeping its dialectical opponent occupied with giants to slay and enemies to oppose: first liberal capitalism, solvent of the previous political order (mid-nineteenth century); then the demands of economic democracy, either in its weaker reformist or stronger socialist forms (late nineteenth and early twentieth century); and, finally, ethical and cultural democracy, an anything-goes normlessness, as conservatives saw it, for which they blamed liberal indulgence and bad philosophy (late twentieth and early twenty-first century). In each period, conservatives have had to reframe and rethink their original commitments, which were inherited from the critics of revolution: social unity, authority of custom, disbelief in progress and equality, limits of political action.

Running through the conservative story is a contrast between political success and intellectual uncertainty. The mainstream right considers itself to have governed and overseen liberal democracy more sensibly than has the left. It claims to have managed better the competing demands of modern society—for innovation and stability, for business efficiency and social equity, for global range and local well-being. If asked what they stand for, conservatives of compromise will point to their long record as the dominant government of liberal democracy and to liberal democracy, for all its flaws, as the least bad of political systems. For the doubters of the right, who question that picture, the mainstream, liberal right is complacent and out of touch. In party politics, for the hard right, the modern liberal status quo is not something to be proud of but something to be overturned. Outside party politics, among the right's ethical and cultural critics, that same status quo is a wrong and ugly way to live.

In the modern flux, what of value should conservatives keep and pass down? Have conservatives an intellectual orthodoxy of their own or simply a set of anti-liberal criticisms and grievances? Is conservatism a substantive tradition with distinctive values or a stylistic tradition of prudent management? Those questions recur throughout the conservative story. Running through it, also, is an argument over how far to compromise with liberal modernity. That contest gives the story of conservatism vitality and shape. It makes it the fight for tradition in two senses. Conservatives fight to identify and protect traditions that liberal modernity undermines, and they fight among themselves for ownership of their own conservative tradition.

PART III

Conservatism's First Phase (1830–80)

Resisting Liberalism

The Year 1830

Peoples, trade, and travel were growing fast. France had 33 million people; Britain, 24 million; and the United States, 13 million, of whom 2 million were slaves. Crowded London was home to 1.5 million souls, and Paris to 800,000. Berlin had 250,000; and New York, 200,000. Most French people lived and worked in the country. Already in Britain, a quarter worked in cities, many in factories. Life expectancy at birth was around forty years. Children who survived to ten could expect to live into their fifties.

Manchester and Liverpool were joined by rail. The sewing machine and the lawnmower were patented. The German publisher Baedeker planned his first tourists' guides. Schinkel's neoclassical Altes Museum opened in Berlin.

Books published included Lyell's *Principles of Geology*, Stendhal's *The Red and the Black*, and Joseph Smith's *Book of Mormon*. Berlioz's *Symphonie Fantastique* premiered in Paris.

William Hazlitt and Benjamin Constant died. Camille Pissarro, Emily Dickinson, Robert Gascoyne-Cecil (Lord Salisbury), and Louise Michel, anarchist deportee from the Paris Commune, were born.

In Paris, the Restoration monarchy was overthrown. A divided Tory party in Britain lost power to the Reform Whigs. Across the German lands, conservative courts stifled calls for liberty and popular participation. Jacksonian Democrats and the proto-Republican Whigs divided American politics. Conflicts grew between a free-labor, industrializing North and an agrarian, slave-holding South.

President Jackson signed the Indian Removal Act for "transfer" beyond the Mississippi. French troops began a bloody occupation of Algeria.

3

Parties and Politicians

A RIGHT WITHOUT AUTHORITY

The first liberals took themselves for constructors. They saw their task as replacing a rigid, ill-adapted framework of government that had been shattered by social change. They took themselves as society's new authorities, stepping in to ensure political order within a flexible new framework after the previous authorities had lost their grip and been discredited.

To conservatives, liberalism's flattering self-image rested on a mistake. Liberals, in their eyes, were disruptors, little better than revolutionaries. Conservatives were the natural party of government. Liberals, by contrast, were inexperienced usurpers. Unrealizable dreams and a mistaken picture of society in conflict with itself together with inevitable blunders would quickly discredit them. The right's authority had not been lost, only obscured by mischievous liberal politicking. Conservatism's first task was to dispel the error and reestablish its authority.

That dream of reestablishment misread the balance of social forces and failed to grasp the character of the new political game. Landed elites, local *notables*, gentry, squires, and *Honoratioren* and old hierarchies and institutions survived, it is true, with many old powers intact. They and their conservative helpers—judges, officials, military officers, priests, and professors—would survive, indeed, for much of the nineteenth century. In Britain, 325 of the 652 MPs in the House of Commons in 1880 were younger peers, baronets, or gentry. As late as 1912 in Germany, two in five of the parliamentary members of the German Conservative Party were titled aristocrats. Liberal modernity, however, had brought a telling change that undercut the appearance of continuity.

The uncontested authority of such elites was gone. If power was to be held and kept, power was to be disputed, shared, and exchanged. If the right was to reclaim authority—that is, accepted, established, legitimate power—the right would have to argue for it. Liberals who had successfully undermined the legitimacy of the previous regime were not all envious, upstart scribblers, as Burke caricatured the French of 1789. Liberals were in a sense only messengers. They spoke for a demanding new kind of citizen who was happy to question authority and on whose consent political order now largely rested. Such a citizen, spied with a sharper eye by Benjamin Constant soon after Burke, belonged to the middle classes, on whom social order and economic prosperity would depend. Conservatives would have to persuade and win such people.

As modern party politics emerged in the early nineteenth century, conservatives faced, accordingly, a strategic choice. They could try to recoup undisputed authority, either as restorationists looking to the past (French pre-1830 Ultras, German pre-1848 absolutists) or as authoritarians attempting to control the present (Napoleon III, Bismarck). Or they could abandon dreams of absolute control, accept parity with liberals, and strive to win the new game on liberalism's terms. The second was the majority choice of the British right and, except for the South, the American right. To do that, conservatives would have to accept a politics of contested authority and endless argument. They would have to fight for control within a framework of government that liberals favored.

That liberal framework included parliamentary sovereignty, wider franchise, and civic equality. It gave body to the core liberal ideals of limited power and equal respect. Those ideals in turn took content from the institutional frame they called for. Since liberals, in addition, believed that society could improve, they favored a state with the reach and authority to foster social progress and unblock what stood in its way, that is, they favored large unified nation-states, undivided markets, and consolidated central powers. As it emerged in the early nineteenth century, that liberal framework faced conservatives with a choice. Some conservatives worked to prevail within it, others to replace the framework with nonliberal alternatives. The powers of parliament, the rights of citizens, and the reach of the state became the stuff of argument among conservatives themselves.

The form, intensity, and timing of choice varied. In France after 1789, the old social authorities and old political structures had gone. New authorities and structures needed to be established. The task of finding a durable new framework took till the 1880s, in part because the French right mostly hindered that search. Only with the acquiescence of the moderate right did liberal democracy begin to consolidate itself in France's Third Republic. In Britain, new social authorities emerged after 1830 as old institutional structures were kept but democratically adapted. Here, too, the right fought a long, strategic retreat, ending in compromise and preparation for twentieth century recovery. In Germany the old powers survived but struggled for democratic authority in improvised, hybrid structures created in the 1860s and 1870s. They broke down early in the next century under the strain of democratic pressure and war. In a divided United States, creating new structures and new authorities was fought about into the 1870s and beyond, to be settled only in the mid-twentieth century. In each country, how well liberal modernity fared depended heavily on how the right chose between compromise or resistance.

i. Improvisations of the French Right

On the right in France, compromise proved the winning choice. By the end of the nineteenth century, democratic liberalism had stabilized. Getting there had been a winding, unsettled course. Other paths for the right—reaction, autocracy—were tempting alternatives. At moments of republican or democratic upheaval from the left—1848 and 1871— fear of revolution united the right, otherwise at odds with itself over which alternatives were least bad. Constrained absolutism in the Bourbon Restoration (1815–30) defeated itself. Liberal monarchy under Orleanist *notables* from 1830 to 1848 promoted modern markets in a central state but ignored pressures for democracy until the explosion of 1848. Bonapartism (1848–70) succeeded for a time in combining economic liberalism, plebiscitary autocracy, and reempowerment of the church only to yield to liberal reform and defeat itself by provoking war with a stronger Germany. Latter-day monarchism ended farcically in the first decade of Third Republic (1870s) with three claimants—a legitimist, an Orleanist, and a Bonapartist—squabbling, as Thiers put it, over an empty chair.

In France, the idea that the left-right contest required a final victor proved tenacious. On the right, supporters of reaction, liberal monarchy, and autocracy all took the French state as a prize to be captured and used for the service, respectively, of the old order, propertied wealth, or that imagined being, the people, thought of as the sensible and propertied middle classes. So, on the other side, did republicans, democrats, and socialists, who sought to win the state for the people, thought of classlessly as equal citizens or in class terms as the working masses. The left might claim to speak for all but only grudgingly wanted to hear from the right. It was happiest when imagining that the right and the interests it spoke for were a small, recessive minority that could somehow be banished from politics altogether.

Only in 1870, with the arrival of the Third Republic—after the successive failures of the Restorationists, July Monarchists, republican 1848ers, and Bonapartists to find a framework of modern order amid capitalist change—was the liberal idea of conflict without final victors accepted on the right. Even then, it was not accepted by all the right. Politically, an anti-republican fringe rankled and obstructed. Intellectually, liberal democracy's sources were held to be tainted. The first part of Taine's history of the French Revolution, published soon after the Paris Commune, described how 1789 had come about not only from a "long suicide" of France's elites but also from the tradition-sapping ideas of the Enlightenment: Voltaire's irreligion, Rousseau's nature-worshipping contempt for society, and undue trust in reason to create and sustain novel institutions.

The errors and failure of post-Napoleonic reaction were a generous gift to French progress. The sixteen years of the Restoration (1815–30) in effect killed off French monarchism, leaving it a phantom, undead after 1830 but without hope of life. Under Louis XVIII and the constitutional *Charte*, a timid semi-representative brake on absolutism, the

Restoration stabilized and openings were made to reform. When Louis died (1824), his stubborn brother took the throne as Charles X, ruling with support of the Ultras. When in July 1830 Charles closed the newly elected chamber of deputies, imposed censorship, and excluded middle-class voters, protests spread across Paris, as bankers, journalists, supporters of the Orleanist royal branch and ordinary people in Paris made clear they had had enough. After three "glorious days" of protest, barricades, and occupied public buildings, Charles abdicated early in August. He fled to England, granted entry under an assumed name by the prime minister Wellington.

Conservatives took heart, nevertheless, from the disappointments of liberal monarchy that followed from 1830 to 1848 and the failure of France's Second Republic in 1848–51. In class terms, the fall of the Bourbons marked the triumph of an ascendant bourgeoisie. Politically, control passed to the liberal monarchists, the Orleanists. Louis-Philippe, son of the regicide Duc D'Orléans, took the title King of the French and was known as a "citizen king." Marx was close to the truth in calling the July Monarchy a joint-stock company. Creditors' financial interests were served, although government offices and authority remained in the hands of *notables*. Of more than sixty ministers, most came from high professions or the peerage. Companies were given greater freedom in law. Railways spread: the state kept taxes low, borrowed heavily, and paid for the track, while private companies ran the trains. The governing outlook of the July Monarchy was economically liberal in its friendliness to capitalist progress but hostile to electoral democracy. It was exemplified in the right-wing, anti-democratic liberalism of François Guizot. His watchwords were peace, compromise, and a politics of the "happy medium." Guizot's top-down liberalism of economic freedom for business combined with a narrow franchise and tight political control was not, however, stable.

The July Monarchy's end came in turn, in February 1848, after the financial crash and years of poor harvests of the mid-1840s. Calls for reform went unheard by a government grown deaf to events. Campaigns for change spilled into the Paris streets. At a soirée, Guizot's confidante, Mme. Lieven, a reputed Russian spy, was talking anxiously to the chief of police. They asked Guizot about the rioting. "Oh," he told them, "You needn't worry about *that*." In days, the king had sacked him, and he was on a coach bound for exile in England, disguised as a German footman. In a mêlée outside the Foreign Ministry, nervous troops fired into a crowd of demonstrators, killing many. Barricades went up across Paris. The king abdicated in favor of a nine-year-old grandson, a tacit admission that state authority had vanished. In the vacuum, France's Second Republic was declared.

France's first modern party of the right was formed in May, when monarchist deputies met at the Rue de Poitiers to form a conservative defense. The prospect of change that they did not control frightened France's *notables* and middle classes. It mattered little whether change came from a popular legislature or from the Paris streets; both were alarming. Middle-class fears lessened when the April elections returned an antiradical majority but came back when economic demands from the poor and workless grew. The slogan of the Rue de Poitiers was "Order, property, religion." The party of order included legitimists and Orleanists, absolutists and constitutionalists, liberals and anti-liberals. None were democrats. None trusted the republic.

In the party of order, Guizot and Thiers stood out. Each exemplified a distinctive conservative compromise with liberal modernity. The paternalistic, anti-democratic Guizot, who returned from England only in 1850, was spoken for at the Rue de Poitiers by his followers. Their rigid top-down liberalism was ill able to meet popular pressures. By contrast, the long-lived, ever-adaptable Thiers played leading roles in the July Monarchy, Second Republic, Second Empire, and Third Republic. His career matched the several stages of conservative reconciliation with liberal democracy: against Ultras and reaction as the "party of movement" (1820s), support for constitutional monarchy (1830–48), antiradical flirtation with autocracy (1848), and rejection of monarchism and final embrace of liberal democracy as first president of the Third Republic (1871–73).

Bonapartism appeared to offer the offer the French right an alternative. Lately returned from England, Louis Napoleon relied on a third framework, plebiscitary autocracy. It combined the short-term gains and long-term flaws of monarchist reaction and Jacobin democracy. For three years, Louis Napoleon governed as the republic's president, supervising conservative measures to put the Catholic Church back into education (the Falloux laws, 1850–51), muzzle the socialist press, and provide welfare aid to steal the left's thunder. None of the measures allayed underlying complaints or quieted dissent. Radical gains in elections to the National Assembly re-alarmed the right. In December 1851, Louis Napoleon and his interior minister launched Operation Rubicon, a coup against the republic which they led. Police arrested opponents, including Thiers, who had earlier supported Napoleon. A rigged plebiscite approved the coup. Following a sequence of his uncle's, Napoleon was made president for ten years and then emperor (November 1852).

Louis Napoleon later joked that the Second Empire could not be pigeonholed. The empress was a legitimist; his cousin Jérôme, a republican; he himself a socialist; and his ally, Charles de Morny, an Orleanist. "The only Bonapartist is Persigny"—the interior minister—"and he's mad." The Second Empire was in fact an experiment in top-down modernization with freer markets and a strong state but limited politics. Its claim to authority rested on what is nowadays called performance legitimacy, that is, delivering social order and rising prosperity while denying civil and political liberties.

The regime, however, rarely looked stable or lasting. The agents of state control, France's prefects, included authoritarian reformers, liberal reformers, old reactionaries, and moderate democrats, but the options were not open for choice because public argument had been largely shut down. Orleanist notables—Charles de Rémusat, Victor de Broglie, Tocqueville—were cast aside to write memoirs and histories. Their right-wing liberalism lived on in silence. It was secular, ungreedy for national glory, and keen on small budgets. In the 1860s, the empire became more liberal, both economically and politically: free-trade agreements with Britain and Prussia, further company laws, political concessions, and relaxations on the press. As often with autocracies, the Second Empire's end came as it liberalized and as it paid the price for provocative adventures abroad. Napoleon III's armies were defeated in an ill-chosen war with Prussia (July–September 1870), the emperor himself was captured and sent, by way of Germany, to exile in England.

A republic, France's third, was declared in a capital surrounded by the enemy. When, to seal victory and end the war, the Germans besieged Paris, the French sued for terms. War-weary voters chose a right-wing government under the unsquashable Thiers, who accepted a stringent peace. Paris, however, was out of step. Radicals had swept its parliamentary seats. They were revulsed by France's capitulation, angry at government help for state creditors as the city starved, and stirred by hopes for civil rights and social reform. After regular troops fraternized with a radicalized Paris militia in March 1871, Thiers withdrew the army to Versailles. Shut in by a hostile army, abandoned by its own defenders, and robbed of state authority, Paris elected a self-governing commune of some ninety members, further radicalized when twenty delegates from rich *arrondissements* refused to sit.

As Marx admitted, the Commune was neither socialist nor proletarian. Its members were mostly self-employed artisans or minor professionals. Anarchist and Utopian talk rang in political clubs. The Commune's practical goals were less ambitious: more self-government for Paris and help for craftsmen and small businesses. The Commune lasted seventy-two days, scant time to meet goals of any kind but time enough for Thiers to regroup and send General MacMahon to crush, with great brutality, a spontaneous insurgency his government had done much to bring about. The facts of the Commune soon mattered less than its myths. For the left, 1871 was another hope-giving might-have-been, to add to those of 1793 and 1848. For the right, it showed the limits of democracy and the perils of the mob.

The Third Republic survived its turbulent birth and uncertain early years under a recalcitrant right that hoped to stem the democratic tide. After 1871, however, the choices for the French right rapidly narrowed: accept democratic liberalism as the political framework or face irrelevance. Thiers had put down the Commune and averted German occupation, but at a heavy cost: the loss of Alsace and part of Lorraine, the latter exacted by Bismarck in exchange for reducing France's large indemnity. Anti-republicans were not assuaged. Monarchist dreams re-vived. Thanks to a crushing electoral victory (1871), the right controlled parliament and, to begin with, anti-republicans controlled the right. Parliament repaid Thiers by replacing him (1873) as president with Mac-Mahon, the butcher of the Commune. The anti-republicans, however, overplayed their hand as Bourbon, Orleanist, and Bonapartist claimants vainly competed for a throne the nation no longer wanted. Reconciled conservatives hesitated, allowing parliament to pass constitutional laws in 1875 that consolidated a republican and parliamentary regime, with universal male suffrage, a strong parliament, and a weak, seven-year president.

The unreconciled right had one last try at thwarting the republic from inside institutions it detested but did not comprehend. When MacMahon misjudged his authority and sacked a reforming prime min-ister in 1877, the French right expected to sweep the ensuing elections, unaware that conservative opinion had moved on. Moderate conserva-tives had resigned themselves to the republic, as had moderate republi-cans to working with them. Both saw a common foe in rising socialism. Pro-republican parties won the election by almost two seats to one. The recalcitrant right was pummeled. Its practical options lay outside parlia-ment, in the street, which despite noise and tumult proved a blind alley.

ii. The British Right's Divided Heart:
Peel or Disraeli

Because British conservatives avoided the dead ends and calamities of the nineteenth-century right in France and Germany, it is tempting to treat conservatism in Britain as a historic exception, perhaps a type all its own. The apparent continuity and good sense of British politics was, in counterpart, admired, envied, and misunderstood by conservative thinkers on the continent from Rehberg and Stahl in Germany to Guizot, Rémusat, and Thiers in France. Britain had had its civil war and "revolution" in the seventeenth century, the thought ran, but by the late eighteenth century, it was entering capitalist modernity with a stable framework of familiar institutions and two-party competition. Left-right parity had, it seemed, become built in with mutual recognition of leading factions. Because Britain had no written constitution, there was nothing to write, rewrite, or tear up; hence there were no points of breakage to disturb an alluring institutional picture of continuity and seminatural origins. Obvious ruptures and innovations—the removal of a suspected Catholic king, the imposition of Dutch then German kings, the revolt of British America, the creation of a modern trade in slaves, the commercial predation of India, the nineteenth-century introduction of an administrative empire, the national fault lines within a nominally United Kingdom—were either ignored or ingeniously defended as quite other than what they seemed. Far from breaks or novelties, such changes were variously explained as a return to old practices, as regrettable but temporary expedients, as the extrusion of foreign elements, a recovery of customary rights, or as the natural extension of the British nation.

Hume, a Tory with Whig sentiments, ironized on the collusive nature of the party contest in Britain, asking himself how hard it was to tell Tories and Whigs apart. The names themselves were hostile terms of mockery adopted by their targets. In Irish, *toraigh* was a word for "bog-trotter" or "bandit." It was first used politically in the late seventeenth century by court Protestants against the Stuart crown. The "whiggamors" were Scottish Protestant protesters (1640s) against the English church. Shortened to "whig," the label was used by James's camp against his anti-Catholic enemies.

For much of the eighteenth century, competition for office and preferment was less between Whigs and Tories than among Whigs. They disputed influence with the crown until the Hanoverian succession of George I, in 1714, after which die-hard Tory support for a Stuart restoration discredited the party at court, though not in parliament's country seats. The ministries were largely led by Whig cliques until the 1760s, when war debt and colonial unrest strained executive capacities, pushing George III, who acceded in 1760, to seek more power for the crown and free government from faction. George was backed by Pittite Whigs and opposed by the Rockingham Whigs, whose parliamentary spokesman was Burke. It seemed as if Bolingbroke's court-versus-country quarrel had returned, setting central against local powers, Whitehall against "the people." In fact, radicalism and revolution were making a new division, out of which Britain's modern, post-oligarchic parties eventually formed. In 1794, the Rockingham Whigs, now under Portland, split over the French Revolution. Fox, a former ally of Burke but an enthusiast for 1789, favored peace with revolutionary France. Portland backed Pitt the Younger in rallying Europe for a counterrevolutionary war. The Pitt-Portland Whigs became Tories. The Foxites, as anti-Tories, kept the Whig label for themselves. The party labels remained in use until the early mid-nineteenth-century. The Tories formally renamed themselves Conservatives in 1834; the Whigs, Liberals, in 1859.

In settling on or resisting a liberal-modern frame of politics, nineteenth-century Toryism had key moments of political choice (suffrage extension, 1832 and 1867); economic choice (free trade or protection, 1846), and ethico-cultural choice (Catholic emancipation, 1829). The figures facing those choices who led the party in this period were Peel, Derby, Disraeli, and Salisbury. Peel, a right-wing liberal, split the party over Catholic emancipation and abolition of the protective Corn Laws. Through decades of opposition, from the 1840s to the 1870s, Derby and Disraeli skillfully shepherded conservatism toward accommodation with liberal democracy. Lord Salisbury was a Tory Ultra in youth who in age after 1880 became a Conservative pragmatist. (He will be returned to in part IV.) Derby and Disraeli left Salisbury the groundwork of a successful modern mass party on the right.

The first leader of the modern conservative party, Robert Peel (1788–1850) was twice prime minister (1834–35; 1841–46) and, in Salisbury's jibe, twice betrayer of his party. As a spokesman for limited, effective government, Peel represented one half of British conservatism's divided soul. The brainy, devout son of a newly rich calico maker, Peel was a reforming home secretary from 1822 to 1827 in Liverpool's administration and again under Wellington, from 1828 to 1830, when he made criminal law less savage and won removal of civic disabilities for Catholics (1829). The bill opened crown offices and parliament to lay Catholics (not clergy), forbade Catholic priests from wearing religious garb in public, and made membership of the Jesuits or other

Catholic orders an offense (although the ban was not strictly enforced). Peel's reluctant support for the Catholic cause came not from liberal belief in religious freedom, being himself a narrow-minded Protestant. Rather, he shared the fear of his prime minister, Wellington, that religious concession was the only path in Ireland between home rule and military occupation.

Catholic emancipation opened a breach between Tory compromisers under Peel, and Tory Ultras, led by diehards in the Lords. Peel initially opposed, but after enactment accepted, the Reform Act (1832). The reform abolished fictive, grandee-owned "rotten boroughs," created new constituencies in northern cities, and gave votes to owners or leasers of property worth ten pounds or more, bringing in small tenant farmers and country shopkeepers, as well as some tenants in towns. It also legally defined voters as male. Reform raised the electorate from a figure of around 500,000, estimated in the absence of a national register, to some 750,000, roughly 7 percent of the adult population. When the Lords blocked an early version of the bill, protests erupted in towns and cities hoping to get representation for the first time. In Bristol, rioters disrupted the city for three days.

Peel's hopes for British conservatism were to rally economic liberals in defense of the established order, thus thwarting Tory Ultras but holding off radical reform. The name "conservative" was in currency. With help from editor of the *Times*, Thomas Barnes (1785–1841), Peel drafted the Tamworth Manifesto (1834), which laid out the elastic twin themes he hoped his party would follow: resistance to unneeded social change where possible and accommodation when necessary. The manifesto took the Reform Act (1832) as "a final and irrevocable settlement of a great constitutional question" (that is, there were to be no further reforms); promised, without commitments, a "review" of civil and church institutions; accepted reform in the form of the "correction of proved abuses" and "redress of real grievances"; but drew a line against heedless change and "a perpetual vortex of agitation." On the Whigs' electoral defeat in 1841, Peel became prime minister. He introduced an income tax and, fatefully, Corn Law repeal, over which the Conservatives split. The anti-Peelite majority rallied to Derby, whereas Peel kept support only of a Conservative minority, the Peelites, who joined the Whigs—later Liberals—after Peel's death in 1850.

Disraeli mocked Peel's career as "one long appropriation clause." He is remembered admiringly as creator of liberal conservatism and unadmiringly as a faith-justified, free-market dogmatist. Peel's efficiency-minded economic liberalism represented one half of conservatism. It was part of a single heart, the other being a unifying appeal to society and nation. Conservative appeals to nation were not only emotive but also economic. Liberal free trade continued to vie with Tory mercantilism inside the Conservative party into the twentieth century.

An ex-Whig, Edward Stanley, Lord Derby (1799–1869), was prime minister three times in the 1850s and 1860s and Tory leader from 1846 to 1868, in the party's wilderness years, when he steered it between the right-wing liberalism of Peel and the *jusqu'auboutisme* of the Tory Ultras. As colonial secretary for the Whigs, Derby drew up the bill for abolition of slavery in the colonies in 1833, which released slaves from servitude in steps over seven years and compensated plantation owners for loss of "property" with the equivalent of £20–30 billion in today's money. As Irish secretary, he gave modest state support for nondenominational schooling. An opponent of the Irish Catholic reformer Daniel O'Connell, he left the Whigs over the weakening of Anglican supremacy in Ireland in 1834 and moved with his small following to join Conservative MPs under Peel. Only narrowly did Derby's Knowsley Creed lose to Peel's Tamworth Manifesto as the new party's founding document. Derby then broke with Peel and led the opposition to the repeal of the Corn Laws. After 1849, he was seconded in the Commons by his protégé Disraeli, who after Derby's death largely dropped him from the Conservative epic. An early sign of conservative-liberal rapprochement on the right was Derby's support for the liberal Palmerston in the early 1860s. He disapproved of Palmerston's foreign adventures but shared his hostility to radicals.

Derby, along with Disraeli, had responsibility for the party's open concession to electoral democracy. It was "a leap in the dark," Derby believed, but "unavoidable." Unlike the Conservatives of 1832, Derby had grounds for thinking that conservatism could prosper at the democratic game. His and Disraeli's Second Reform Act (1867) almost doubled the national electorate (grown from natural increase) to 2.2 million (16 percent of the population) by adjusting the property qualification to put the vote in reach of rural smallholders, tenants, artisans, and town laborers.

A landowning Lancashire grandee with a large estate at Knowsley, then on the edge of Liverpool, Derby was sensitive to the complaint that over the previous century English magnates had displaced smallholders and called for a land registry that he hoped would show the opposite. (The upshot was unclear.) In a similar spirit of concerned paternalism, Derby saw to the relief of local weavers hurt by the cotton famine during the American Civil War. An educated nob who translated Homer, he was at ease with horse trainers and stalkers, not with the press or the middle classes, who did not get his detached, world-weary tone. His last words when asked how he felt, were, it is said, "Bored to the utmost power of extinction." Derby's sense of the public was confined to parliament and his conservatism was pragmatic, more a style of maneuver than a body of ideas. A Victorian essayist wrote soon after his death that Derby added "nothing new to the political thought of the age," which presumed an unduly narrow conception of political thought. Derby was a conservative pragmatist aiming to channel or stifle radical reform by political concession and social alleviation. Progress's boons came with harms, he believed. An alert conservative should watch out for unexpected ones. Railways, for example, destroyed working-class housing. From the unstoppable "machine" of change, good might come with "a skilful hand," but if change was "recklessly accelerated," then "overwhelming wreck" was inevitable. Derby's conservatism rested on an intuitive grasp of what twentieth-century sociopolitical studies called latent functions and unintended consequences. The liberal riposte that unintended consequences could be good as well as bad did not stop unintended consequences from joining the right's repertoire of arguments against government intervention and social reform.

As a statesman, political novelist, party leader, and prime minister (1868; 1874–80), Benjamin Disraeli (1804–81) epitomized the British right's chary accommodation to liberal modernity. A Romantic "Young

England" Tory, he began as an opponent of suffrage extension and a defender of established institutions—landed property, English church, crown, old universities, and the Lords—which embodied in his mind not vested interests but conservative ideals of loyalty, deference, and faith. He ended as a pragmatic manager-tactician largely reconciled to mass democracy, social reform, and the upper classes' loss of cultural privileges.

Disraeli gave his political ideas fictional and nonfictional form. In his popular fiction of ideas, Disraeli ranged over the expediency of Peel (*Coningsby, or The New Generation*, 1844), class conflict in the "Hungry '40s" (*Sybil, or The Two Nations*, 1845), Britain's emergent empire (*Tancred*, 1847), and confessional politics (*Lothair*, 1870). An early essay, *Vindication of the English Constitution* (1835), was a galloping tract, not a careful argument. It opened by attacking what Disraeli took for the house philosophy of reform, Utilitarianism: it understood happiness as narrow self-interest; it assumed that anyone granted power would act as tyrant or robber; then, in a logical leap, it argued for democratic government by all. Utilitarians, as "new schoolmen," thought abstractly, neglected local circumstances, and failed to grasp that sound institutions could not be measured by calculating "utilities" but instead reflected national character and history.

In Burkean fashion, Disraeli called the state "a complicated creation of refined art," dismissed natural rights, and treated law as arisen historically by convention. Britain's sturdy institutions stood out in contrast to the gimcrack constructions France had suffered under since 1789. The French experimenters of 1830 soon found themselves "at the head of a people without a constitution, and not possessing any elements to form one." Amid Europe's "general commotion," to which England also succumbed, only stolid, autocratic but well-governed Prussia remained calm.

Disraeli's attack on mistaken ideas tracked the criticisms made by Burke. His party-political complaint echoed Coleridge's historical romance of political and social harmony disturbed by greed and disaffection. As Disraeli redrew the picture, two great camps were at odds. The Whigs represented an oligarchy. The Tories stood for the nation. On one side, were Whig magnates, bankers, and urban dissenters. On the other, crown, church, and common people, that is, the "gentlemen" of England's counties and boroughs. Upstart commercial elites had power without responsibility. Unlike paternal squires, who took care of their tenants and laborers, the new owners treated their workers as factors of production to be bought and sold for what the market would bear. Limited government would ask better of industry, not demand better by law. In the 1830s, moral suasion was already an empty hope. Once in office, Disraeli invoked law to protect workers and clean up cities. Disraeli's social-minded conservatism was a small step toward the welfare state.

Two years before his second ministry, Disraeli laid out the triple core of his broader outlook—British institutions, empire, and "the elevation of the condition of the people"—in his Crystal Palace Speech (June 1872). How far Disraeli's attachment to crown, church, and the Lords was sincere, rather than instrumental, is disputed. As with Burke, Disraeli's appeal to faith and sentiment in defense of established institutions had a trace of cynicism, which was never fully dispelled. Was religious faith good because it was true or because it was useful? His was an exemplary case of the conservative dilemma noted earlier. Disraeli's Crystal Palace defense of empire was rhetorical and sentimental. He held that the liberal attempt to "disintegrate" the empire by showing that there was never "a jewel in the crown" as costly as India—by treating empire, that is, as an unpaying commercial proposition—had failed because liberals ignored "the sympathy of the colonies for the mother country." Whatever the reasons, Disraeli was sincere about his third concern, and as prime minister, he did undertake reforms to better working conditions and city living.

Historians disagree on how far Disraeli earned his contrasting labels of social reformer, People's Democrat, and One-Nation Tory. Charming, raffish, self-promotional, and often in debt, he was seen by his great rival, the Liberal Gladstone, as "all display . . . without genuineness." Perhaps Disraeli did deflect hearers from conservatism's dilemmas with his golden tongue. In loyalty to party, feel for maneuver, and nose for office, Disraeli nevertheless epitomized a distinctive element on the

British right: an instinct for self-preservation underlying the remarkable continuity of a single dominant party. Like Baldwin after him, Disraeli had a pitch-perfect ear for the sentiments of the conservative electoral core, middle England: cool to pretention, to oligarchic privilege, and to intellectualism when met in person or from opponents but fervent when appealed to on behalf of ungraspables such as nation, crown, and empire.

Peel, Derby, and Disraeli together created a modern party that allied the interests of business, finance, and land with the defense of Britain's familiar institutions, crown, Anglican church, and Lords. As they blended with right-wing liberals, their former rivals, Britain's conservatives reflected the social elites that their party, in the first instance, served. Both were absorptive and adaptable, preferring to smother rather than crush their foes. That character lived with British conservatism into democratic times. The party spoke for empire and for union with Ireland, causes that in England had wide popular appeal. Early attachments, in addition, evolved and found new objects. In 1830, British conservatism stood for church against chapel, farms against manufactures, and country against city. By 1880, the ethical shape of those attachments—orthodoxy against dissent, tradition against novelty, virtue against vice—was still recognizable but flexibly and more pragmatically held. In urban-industrial conditions of modern capitalism, the Conservatives were becoming an adaptable right-wing party of wide democratic appeal. As society changed, success would depend on how well they adjusted the balance of those attachments and how open an ear they kept to popular opinion.

iii. German Conservatives without Caricature

The guiding spirit of German conservatism was the Junker, an ignorant country squire from East Prussia who duped peasants at country fairs with cheap tricks that he hoped might one day fool the nation. So the poet Heinrich Heine wrote in a preface to his political dispatches from France in 1832. Prussian censors cut the passage about the Junkers, along with much else, although it saw light in a French edition the following year. Heine's mockery of France's indolent "citizen-king" Louis-Philippe and the biddable politicians of the July Monarchy were mild beside his unforgiving picture of Germany in thrall to a backward, landowning class.

Heine's caricature died hard. It was once close to a historical commonplace that Prussian Junkers had delayed and then helped destroy liberal democracy in Germany. Their hold on the state, army, and church in Prussia late into the nineteenth century and beyond had enabled national unification by war, modernization from above, and avoidance of civic freedoms and electoral democracy that emerged in "normal" neighbors such as France and Britain. Compared with theirs, German conservatism was one-dimensional, tied to landed interests, ill-organized, and ill-adapted to democratic conditions.

There was an incoherence in the caricature, however, as there was with the fatalistic picture of liberal democracy's poor chances in Germany, which drew on that caricature. If the Junkers as a class were uniformly thick, unrepresentative, and backward, how did they command a rich and varied new practice of politics—conservatism—let alone a vast and complex modern nation? Prussia in the mid-nineteenth century was more than a land of stunted squires and mute peasants. It included the rapidly industrializing Rhineland as well as civil servants, schools, and universities that won the admiration of the world.

Some Prussian conservatives were backwoodsmen. Others were right-wing professors or civil servants. Elard von Oldenburg-Januschau, for example, was a blunt Junker diehard, who never finished high school, loved his time in an Uhlan cavalry regiment, and is remembered for telling fellow deputies in the Reichstag: "The Kaiser should be always be on stand-by to send a lieutenant and ten men to close this house." Bismarck's thorn in the Prussian parliament, Hans von Kleist-Retzow (described below) came from Prussia's high administrative class. He went on to university and several degrees, having started at Schulpforta, the high-pressure school near Leipzig that taught Nietzsche and Bethmann-Hollweg.

Far from the fixed outlook of a unified Prussian nobility, German conservatism was, like conservatism in France and Britain, rich in conflicts and cross-tensions. German conservatives included ultras and reconcilers, defenders of the *Ständestaat* (old prerogatives and localism) against the *Beamtenstaat* (modern administration and centralism); the competing claims of banks, factories, and farms; large regional variations; and the confessional divide between Protestants and Catholics, which broke up the first attempts to create a modern conservative party in Germany amid the clamor for liberalization and representation in the 1830s. Conservatives disagreed on how far to accept or co-opt the liberal and democratic opposition on the field of modern politics.

The German right divided also on the social question, which came to the fore in the hard times of the 1840s as poverty entered political argument. (The word *Pauperismus* had first appeared in the Brockhaus dictionary in 1840.) By 1848, 30 percent of Cologne's people were estimated to live in poverty. Conservatives agreed that poverty, especially urban poverty, was a problem, but they disagreed on what caused the problem and how it should be met. Some blamed poverty on liberal industrialists, others on the workers' idleness and poor morals. Some wanted modest state aid, others, in effect, a welfare state. There was not one uniform conservative answer to the social question.

In an unstable Confederation (1815–48; 1850–66), it complicated their disagreements that German conservatives had to decide also what their modern field of politics was to be: a continuing loose confederation under Austrian leadership (the *großdeutsch* solution) or a unified German nation-state guided by Prussia (the *kleindeutsch* answer). Conservatives from the smaller German states, anti-Prussians, and anti-liberals tended to support Austria. Conservatives willing to compromise with liberals and liberals who disliked Austrian autocracy more than the Prussian kind supported Prussia.

Another source of division on the German right was Bismarck. On his emergence with powers of decision in the 1860s, when Prussia's nascent parliament hesitated and weakened, conservatives had further to decide if they were pro- or anti-Bismarck. As Bismarck changed in his attitude to conservatives, so did their attitude to him. He began as a pious right-wing Ultra only to emerge, in office, as pragmatist without obvious scruple. A dwindling band of Ultras, through their newspaper the *Kreuzzeitung*, held out against him. Most conservatives rallied to him, and the anti-Bismarck torch passed from the old right to Catholic conservatives, democratic liberals, and socialists.

Germany's first conservatives were politically spoiled. They had never fully lost authority; they kept access to the instruments of state. Only intermittently were they democratically tested. In party terms, conservatism had begun as informal networks of local notables after the settlement of 1815. Defenders of the old order were determined to protect princely power from liberalism and democracy. Old privileges were abolished, late-feudal practices ended, and nods made to constitutional government. With exceptions such as Baden, a compromised, uncertain absolutism prevailed. Prussians were promised a constitution in 1815; it took till 1848 to arrive, was imposed from above, and was at once truncated and further revised half a dozen times in the 1850s. Franz Joseph withdrew a hastily drafted Austrian constitution in 1851. Old elites monopolized positions in princely courts, the churches, armed forces, and officialdom. Their authority, however, was no longer unquestioned.

If the French Revolution awakened German political thought, the Revolution of 1848 pushed German conservatives into public argument. They began to broach ideals, arguments, and policies. They drafted statements of aims and manifestos. Already, in response to France's July Monarchy, a weekly paper, the *Berliner Politisches Wochenblatt* (1831), had been launched but efforts to start a party of the right failed when Catholics and Protestants went their separate ways in 1837. Matters were more urgent a decade later. "Think what you like about political clubs," the newly founded *Kreuzzeitung* announced in June 1848, "it's here we have to fight the enemy at its own game or get hammered." A group of four hundred rich and mainly noble conservatives founded that summer in Berlin the Union for the Defense of Property and Promotion of the Welfare of All Classes, known more simply as the Junkerparlament. Its aims were to fend off interference in property, promote general welfare, and foster class unity. On organizing itself as a party in the Prussian parliament in 1861, it described its aims as unity from above, maintaining a strong Prussia with a strong army, ensuring social and moral discipline, as well as keeping control of banks.

German conservatives were beginning to play by the rules of liberal modernity. They had to argue for policies and interests, not simply issue directives. Playing by the rules allowed, as elsewhere, for electoral manipulation, suborning the press, and, generally, gaming the system. To picture Wilhelmine conservatives as top-down string-pullers, however, is as distorting as the Junker caricature. Conservatism was also bottom-up. Popular movements and local demands across Germany put pressure on party politicians in Berlin. Engagement in public argument gave rise to divisions. Appealing to the people was, for many, unconservatively *völkisch*, that is, populist or popular in a bad sense. For others, appealing to the people was the only path to survival. Such a conservatism would be, by contrast, *volkstümlich*, that is, popular in a good sense. The implied contrast in understandings of democracy came to matter later. Conservatives who accepted the modern game first had to organize themselves. It cost Germany because they were not good at the task. The Wilhelmine Reich's right remained lukewarm about democracy, locally scattered, and disorganized.

For nearly twenty years after German unification (1871), the three main right-wing parties together won close to half the votes for the Reichstag, now chosen by universal male suffrage. They were the Deutsche Konservative Partei (DKP, German Conservative Party); the Frei Konservative Partei (FKP, Free Conservatives); and the National Liberals (NL).

The DKP and the FKP grew out of the pro-ministerial faction in the Prussian assembly that had fought the liberals in the early 1860s over the budgetary powers of parliament. Both came out of the old right in the Junkerparlament (1848), which was determined to resist the liberal and democratic tide but could not agree on how. The Free Conservatives descended from the moderates of the 1850s and 1860s, who wanted to use new means to conservative ends; the DKP arose from the old anti-modern diehards. The diehards agreed to mix in party politics, but on terms that proved ever harder to defend: limited suffrage, subordinate parliaments, and maintenance of old privileges, including tax freedoms and a hereditary say in politics. As those redoubts weakened, by the late 1860s they faced more pressing questions: unification by war and a new Reich constitution, which included universal male suffrage. Since Bismarck, an avowed conservative, pressed for both, the choice for the right became, in effect, for Bismarck or against him.

The business and bankers' party, the FKP, backed Bismarck. It was his first building block for conservative coalitions in the Reichstag. It was strongest in Rhenish Prussia, where industrialization was rapidly taking hold. The party became less useful to the chancellor after it split over free trade and its electoral appeal began to slip. Unlike the DKP, which was still guided by old attachments and suspicions of liberalism, the Free Conservatives were concerned for efficient administration, national strength, and above all, resistance to socialism. They were, like their pro-Bismarck allies, the National Liberals, right-wing modernizers from above, wary of electoral democracy but resigned to using it as best they could. Both parties supported Bismarck in his attempt to bend two independent forces in German public life to the will of the state, the Catholic Church, and the socialist movement, although within each party there was a liberal-minded minority that objected to those campaigns.

The old German conservatives in the DKP came out of the die-hard bloc in the pre-Reich Prussian and North German parliaments. Faced by war with Austria and German unification, it also split into pro-Bismarck and anti-Bismarck wings. The first wing had the upper hand in the Reichstag, under the DKP leader, Otto von Helldorff-Bedra, a Bismarck loyalist. The other wing controlled the Prussian parliament.

On unification, these old conservatives together accepted universal suffrage for the Reichstag but sought a Reich upper house as a blocking device against unwanted reform. Although the diehards failed, in compensation they had the parliament of Prussia, which on unification accounted for two-thirds of the German population. Unlike the Reichstag, the Prussian parliament had wide taxing powers. Controlled until 1918 by the DKP, it made life miserable for reforming chancellors and kept most taxation out of democracy's reach.

When founded formally as a national party, in 1876, the DKP announced its aims in loose terms as support for the Reich constitution, rejection of wide suffrage for states and localities, civic freedoms, and restraint on the powers of central government. The DKP wanted religion to keep a place in politics, because religion alone, in the party's view, could answer people's "growing bewilderment" and halt the "dissolution of social bonds" caused by the triple menace of undue liberty, finance capital, and socialism. Conflicts among the parties of the right enabled the Catholic Center (founded 1870) to act as a hinge party. When the Reich and the Vatican were reconciled after 1878, as Germany's anti-Catholic *Kulturkampf* lost impetus, the Center allied itself with the DKP, only to break again later.

Such conflicts and cross-alliances give the lie to a misleading picture of Wilhelmine conservatism as a solid bloc of Junker-led reaction. Far from delaying liberal democracy in Germany from a position of unity and strength, a divided right helped obstruct or misdirect it out of weakness. Powers, interests, and elites who felt threatened by liberal reform, economic democracy, and the decline of cultural authority lacked a self-confident right-wing party that they could rely on to temper modern change.

Those dramas had actors who exemplified distinctive right-wing types. Their contrasting roles and temperaments underline the variety of the mid-century German right: the Ultra, the social-conservative, the thwarted modernizer, the party balance holder between moderates and diehards.

Typical Ultras were the Gerlach brothers, Leo and Ludwig. They formed the core of the camarilla that guided the rudderless King Friedrich Wilhelm IV. Their patriotic outlook was shaped by wars with France (both were veterans), their religious conviction by the Pietist awakening, with its call to personal faith and community action. The early social-Christian conservative tradition was represented by Hermann Wagener, an ex-churchman and publicist who campaigned as the conscience of resistance to the modern society that capitalism was creating.

Conservatives willing to bend to the times included thwarted modernizers such as Joseph von Radowitz. A Catholic, he began on the reactionary right with the *Berliner Politische Wochenblatt* but became a liberal-minded constitutionalist keen to appease working-class demands. Like the Gerlachs, Radowitz was close to the king but, unlike them, learned from events. In the 1830s, he had argued for church and crown against reform. By the straitened 1840s, Radowitz wrote in *State and Church* (1846) that the government should act to reduce poverty. Conservatives were foolish, he believed, to shut out liberals when the threat was working-class radicalism. Radowitz's ministerial rival was Otto von Manteuffel, a clever civil servant schooled at Schulpforta who was interior minister from 1848 to 1850, then premier and foreign minister from 1850 to 1858. In the period of stunted constitutionalism after 1848, Manteuffel held the balance in Prussia's government between the moderates and ultras.

Although such figures, whose lives can be read more about in appendix C, illustrate the variety of early German conservatism, they were in their different ways all engaged in a similar holding operation. Their predemocratic manner of politics became irrelevant with the rise of Bismarck, German unification, and the creation of a national parliament, the Reichstag, elected on universal male suffrage. The Bismarck system replaced an older conservatism of court politics and limited representation with a democratic-authoritarian hybrid. It relied on a complex interplay among the crown, bureaucracy, and parliament, all under Bismarck's guidance, although less under his control than authoritarian legend made it seem.

A party conservative who rallied to Bismarck was Otto von Helldorff-Bedra (1833–1908). He led the German Conservative Party from its founding (1876). Helldorff marshaled Prussian conservatives behind Bismarck, holding off the last of the Ultra diehards on the one hand and the social conservatives led by Wagener on the other. A Prussian obstructionist who turned against Bismarck was Hans von Kleist-Retzow (1814–92). Like Britain's Salisbury when young, Kleist was at first a brilliant defender of ideas that were past their prime. He then fell in with Bismarck (whose niece he married) only to revert after 1870 to the Christian-patriarchal right.

A common problem for the first German conservatives was this. Although they still held the reins of power, they were no longer fully in charge. They lacked popular acceptance, which they sensed they needed but were afraid to grasp. They were taxed, in short, by democratic legitimation. What price should they pay for living in calmness with a more liberal and democratic modernity? The coinage of payment was old conservative attachments—to crown, princely power, noble privilege, social unity and hierarchy. Giving up many or most was, for conservatives who were willing to compromise, a price worth paying, so long as property, the basis of social order, was protected.

Diehards of the old right, unhappy with so high a price, clung to crumbling institutions. A newer, younger right, more popular and attuned to the time, detached conservative loyalties from old interests and refocused them in new ways. Social unity was no longer pictured as hierarchy but as shared nationhood and Germanness, though thought of in exclusionary ways. Other conservatives hung on in pragmatic hope of somehow avoiding choice. Bismarck's success and failures as the Prussian first minister and later Reich chancellor (1862–90) depended on managing those countercurrents, both avoiding calamity and storing up trouble for the future, as the section "The Ambivalence of German Conservatives," in chapter 5, will suggest.

Rueful, unreconciled German conservatives fell back into resignation and withdrawal before popular forces they could neither accept nor resist. Theodor Fontane caught that attitude of conservative refusal to engage in modern politics in his last novel, *Der Stechlin* (1898). Set in the early 1890s in the Brandenburg lake country, north of Berlin, the story centers on an old Prussian squire, Dubslav. He is a latter-day Junker of the kind Heine mocked and whose world had passed. He is reluctantly persuaded to stand for parliament in his district as a conservative. On election night, the Social Democrat is declared the runaway winner. The liberals are disappointed. Dubslav is relieved. Unimpressed by democratic politics, he cannot take electioneering seriously. He goes to eat with his agents, happy in the thought that "Winning is good, but dinner is better."

iv. United States: Whigs and Jacksonians; Republicans and Democrats

In January 1831, the American statesman and former president John Quincy Adams worried in his diary about the likely impact of Europe's liberal upheavals on his own country. They would, he judged, "strengthen the principle of democracy" and "proportionably diminish the securities of property." Reducing taxes would lead to "sponging" the national debt (that is, losses for bondholders) and a "shattering" of confidence in credit. Political reform and "religious infidelity," especially in France, would destroy authorities "obnoxious to democracy"—bishops and hereditary peers—neither of which could withstand the "consuming blaze of public opinion." In his anxiety, Adams was unsure what to conclude. On the one hand, he thought "the doctrine of European democracy" would "find no favor here." On the other, he wondered if American institutions could withstand popular conflict over slavery. The looming abolition of British slavery threatened to pass "like a pestilence" from the West Indies to the United States. There it would be resisted alike by Southerners and by Northerners keen to keep the South in the Union. Even so, Adams worried that democratic pressure for abolition promised the United States "bitter fruits."

Adams (1767–1848) is a good counterinstance to the claim that the United States lacked a conservative tradition. He was a right-wing Whig, and although both terms need explaining in the local context, Adams exemplified a distinctively American conservatism, both in his commitment to national unity and social order as well as in his iron presumption of a quasi-natural duty to govern. Adams was US president (1825–29), like his father before him, secretary of state (1817–25), US senator (1803–8), and representative for Massachusetts (1831–48), as well as American envoy in the Netherlands, Prussia, Russia, and Britain. Framer of the Monroe Doctrine, Adams stabilized his country's foreign position after renewed war with Britain and Spain's retreat from Latin America.

As that high-performing record suggests, politics for Adams was primarily statecraft. A believer in his nation's destiny, he detested the spirit of party but was nevertheless a great hater and capable infighter. Humorless, quick to anger, and self-disciplined, for fifty years he kept an impersonal, political diary. A stern Calvinist, he treated the American Transcendentalists' milder gospel of worldly redemption by way of spiritual self-improvement as an irresponsible deception. Emerson he dismissed as "a crackbrained young man." In Adams's bleak view, only

God's unpredictable grace could tame and guide a depraved human nature.

Less doctrinally, Adams understood the ineliminable role of chance in human life and what he called the "lottery ticket of a new-born infant." His own distinguished but star-crossed family was an extreme instance. Two brothers and a son died early of alcoholism. Another son died young after a wastrel life. Yet the Adams grand lineage included, besides its two presidents, Adams's third son, who became a leader of the Free Soil Republicans, and a grandson—later to appear—the writer Henry Adams, historian of the United States, satirist of Washington corruption, and rueful critic of modern progress.

In party-political terms, Adams became an anti-Federalist opponent of overbearing central government, then an anti-Jacksonian Whig after 1824, wary of popular democracy. American Whigs emerged in the 1820s and 1830s as opponents of Jacksonian Democrats, forming the second of three commonly identified nineteenth-century party systems: Federalists and Democrat-Republicans (1792–1824), Whigs and Democrats (1824–56), Republicans and Democrats from the Civil War to the Gilded Age (1856–92).

Whigs were liberal in their belief in material and moral progress, conservative in their trust of elites and distrust of democracy. They were not dogmatically free market but looked to taxation and government for public "improvements"—first of all, roads and canals—that a flourishing national market needed. Looking back, Adams wrote in July 1834 of his hopes to have made "the national domain the inexhaustible fund for progressive and unceasing internal improvement." At the same time, Whigs treated the executive branch with suspicion as a trough of corruption, linking them to a later tradition of good-government Republicanism. As to moral progress, they were sternly top-down about improving people, who needed guidance from their betters. Without radical improvement in the character of the citizenry, Whigs feared that democracy was bound to founder. They looked therefore to churches, newspapers, schools, and universities to tame an unruly, masculine culture. They thought of themselves as the improving heirs of English traditions—common law, aristocratic responsibility, orderly politics—that had weakened or grown tired in the old country.

The contest between democratic Jacksonians and conservative Whigs was accordingly often presented as a class politics of haves versus have-nots, privileged elites versus the American people. The conflict was in fact more between sectional elites, the South and West on the one hand, the North on the other. It was less about overturning the social order than about the proper direction of the nation. Was the first task of politics to improve or expand the United States?

Whigs wanted to improve America and Americans before they spread across the West. The great Whig newspaperman Horace Greeley wrote that "opposed to the instinct of boundless acquisition stands that of internal improvement." A nation, he intoned, could not "simultaneously devote its energies to the absorption of others' territories and improvement of its own." By contrast, the Jacksonian *Democratic Review* cried, not longer after, "Yes, more, more, more! . . . Till our national destiny is fulfilled and the whole boundless continent is ours."

Whigs appealed to those doing or hoping to do well in the modern market economy. It won upwardly mobile white Protestants, city clerks, and those in skilled occupations, as well as farmers near to transportation tying them into city markets. Whig elites included bankers, wealthy business owners, and other insiders in the growing cities of the East. The Whigs' Democratic opponents in the North rallied artisans whose skills were being discarded with the spread of industry, Catholics who resented Whig interference with their saloons and schools, and up-country farmers who disliked city slickers and bankers.

"Whig" was not just a party-political label but also the name of a climate of opinion, as Daniel Walker Howe characterized it in a classic study, *The Political Culture of the American Whigs* (1979). To Whig reformers the rest of America was not the Wild West but the Wild Everywhere, a bride-short, male-dominated free-for-all scarred by dueling, drinking, whoring, and rioting. In the 1830s only one American in fifteen lived in a town of more than eight thousand. Compared to Paris or London, the biggest US cities—New York, Boston, and Philadelphia—were provincial towns without metropolitan culture. Like early nineteenth-century Germany, the United States had no single urban focus. Unlike Germany it had no princely courts with distinctive cultural traditions, and only a handful of university towns.

In such a society, reforming American manners required new cultural institutions, as the Whig lawyer and educationalist Rufus Choate (1799–1859) argued in two celebrated lectures, "Mental Culture" (1844) and "The Conservative Force of the American Bar" (1845). Key for Choate was the law school and the "profession of the Bar," for they fostered in the popular mind opinions "indispensable to conservation." In Europe, social and political institutions still needed reforming, but not in the United States, for "with us the age of this mode and this degree of reform is over; its work is done." To Choate, a patriotic American was a conservative who upheld the traditions of law in a perfected constitutional frame. In Burkean mode, Choate explained the value of such traditions, for there was "a deep presumption in favor of that which has endured so long." (Before his late nineteenth-century rediscovery in Britain, Burke had an American vogue, with seven editions in the 1830s. In letters and lectures Choate included Burke in a permutational mini-pantheon of worthies, classical or English-speaking, that Americans were wise to admire: "Cicero, Homer, Burke, Milton"; "Burke, Plato, Hamilton"; "Milton, Bacon, Burke, Johnson.")

Early Democrats, by contrast, had the unconservative spirits of Thomas Jefferson and Andrew Jackson to guide them, the one libertarian, the other popular. In the Jeffersonian vision as finely evoked in Walter Russell Mead's "The Jacksonian Tradition" (1999), citizens were all equally free and, if not fine as they were, in no need of improvement from interfering outsiders. Nor were they under obligation to interfere in efforts to improve society, which could flourish in liberty and equality if left to itself. For Jacksonians, Americans had ample resources for self-guidance. There were, it was true, good people and bad. The good, however, could punish or exclude the bad as they chose without interference from moral busybodies. Jacksonians in their way were as strict as Whigs, but their strictness was exclusionary and bottom-up, whereas Whig strictness was elite-driven, inclusive, and top-down. Neither were permissive in the late-modern "I'm okay, you're okay" sense. Each fed twentieth-century moral conservatism in the United States both in its low and high variants—right-wing evangelism and neoconservative ethical preaching.

The Enlightenment spoke to Jeffersonians. Blithe to actual inequalities, they imagined everyone, on Russell Mead's telling, to be self-interested but reasonable beings capable of republican life together in a bucolic harmony of farms and small towns. Evangelism preached to Jacksonians. Fighters by circumstance, they divided the world into friend and enemy, whether Indians in their path or older elites in their way. They were quick to treat the Christian Awakening in postmillennial spirit. As a counter-Enlightenment restoration of religious confidence, the Awakening echoed Wesleyanism and Pietism, which had swept Protestant Europe but took a distinctive form on the American frontier. For postmillennials, Christ's Second Coming was nigh, when the good (friends) would be saved and the wicked (enemies) damned.

For Whigs, the message of the Christian Awakening was different. They took it in the premillennial spirit as a gospel of social progress and reform. The end was not nigh and Christ was not due. An imperfect world—with its friends and foes, its motley of people good and bad—was not about to be simplified and resolved in a choice-relieving final judgment. Awakened Christians of millennial cast had the harder task of improving the world in order to make it worthy of Christ's eventual Second Coming.

As moral and cultural improvers in a violent, male-heavy society, Whigs were prominent in campaigns for temperance, women's rights, and abolition of slavery. Only reluctantly and prudentially were they electoral democrats who accepted votes for free men as well as freeholders. John Adams, for example, had resisted the change in Massachusetts in 1820. Though he failed, the Whigs put up losing fights against universal suffrage in other states with wealthy elites, such as New York and in the plantation South. A vehicle of intellectual Whiggery, the *American Whig Review* (1845–52), sermonized against democracy in Burkean tones before eventually changing its mind. Western expansion did much to weaken conservative resistance. In a frontier society, it was not practical to sustain top-down politics. Like adaptive conservatives in Europe, Whigs saw that they had to validate claims to guide the country by braving the political marketplace. As in Europe also, American Whigs found they could win elections as successfully as Jacksonians. When the Whig champion William Henry Harrison won the presidency in 1840, a Jacksonian ruefully remarked, "We have taught them how to beat us."

A well-known version of the claim that the United States lacked a conservative tradition was Louis Hartz's *The Liberal Tradition in America* (1955). The nation was liberal at birth, Hartz argued, for it had neither an *ancien régime* nor feudal traditions, hence there was nothing for liberals to attack or conservatives to defend. Without roots in a liberal-conservative contest, American politics was pragmatic, ideological, and consensual, leaving no room either for socialism, its other missing tradition.

Hartz's story of a liberal American founding was child of a consensual post-1945 interlude, much as Charles Beard's classic account in *An Economic Interpretation of the Constitution of the United States* (1913) of the document's origins in class conflict between the rich and poor, creditors and debtors, was child of the Progressive Era. Similarly, pluralist histories of the early republic reflect present-day preoccupations with diversity, conflicts over "identity," and world-sensitive refusal to believe in American exceptionalism. Were Hartz writing today, he would perhaps have expanded his confining idea of conservatism as resistance to modernity by a dying class. Resisting modernity lies indeed at the conservative core. The task, however, is neither class specific nor rooted in time. Allowing for Hartz's contestable social picture of a post-feudal, post-traditional United States, the new nation was soil for conservatism in its counter-democratic mode. The dilemma for America Whigs was like that facing European conservatives: how far should they compromise with liberal—and democratic—modernity, as popular demands grew. Whigs were liberal in their confidence in progress but undemocratic in not trusting people to make progress by themselves. They were conservative in their insistence that competent elites should supervise the economy and elevate the mind without popular interference.

It was confusing that Jacksonians and Whigs both spoke for liberty since they did not think of liberty alike, as Walker Howe explained. For Jacksonians, the Revolution had freed America not just from Westminster and England but from the whole European past, and in a sense from history. For Whigs the Revolution was also a triumph for liberty but understood differently—as a culmination and recovery of English liberties. For the Whig Daniel Webster, "American liberty" had "an ancestry, a pedigree, a history. Our ancestors brought to this continent all that was valuable in their judgment in the political institutions of England." In English tradition, American Whigs found what conservatives look for amid the churn of modernity: things of value to cherish and hand on.

The New Englander Daniel Webster (1782–1852) and the Kentuckian Henry Clay (1777–1852) were the two leading anti-Jacksonians besides Adams. Webster was a Whig lawyer from Massachusetts. From 1823 to 1850 with short intervals, he was a US representative and later a senator from that state. A conservative nationalist, Webster thought and spoke of the nation as a unity. When he talked of "the laboring classes," he meant bankers as well as mechanics and farmers, yet he also opposed a wider franchise in Massachusetts (1820). Economically liberal, he argued before the Supreme Court to uphold private contracts and for federal powers to prevent states from interfering with commerce. He opposed alike Clay's high federal tariffs and Calhoun's state campaign to nullify them (1830s). Annexing Texas, Webster feared, would destroy the North-South balance, and he disapproved of the Mexican War (1840s). Like Clay, and later Stephen Douglas, but unlike Abraham Lincoln, he wanted Western expansion of slavery left to "popular sovereignty," that is, to voters in new territories.

Henry Clay also was a conservative nationalist and promoter of the "American System" (protective tariffs, federal public works, a national bank). The new nation, Clay believed, must be prosperous, independent, and united. Born in Virginia, young Clay moved to Kentucky, where he inherited a slave plantation. Clay was Speaker of the House and a US senator and a representative from Kentucky (1806–52, with intervals). A believer in gradual emancipation and the return of freemen to Africa, Clay, like his party, could not resolve the slavery question. A border politician, "Harry of the West" was a "great conciliator" to admirers, a principleless deal maker to foes. Like Adams, his family fortunes were desolate. Of his eleven children, all six daughters died early and three sons were mad or alcoholic. His favorite son died in the Mexican War for Western expansion, which he opposed.

Clay and Webster were formidable in the Congress, as much for speechmaking as for winning votes. The Whigs had poor luck, by contrast, with the White House. It was a sorry record. Having won the presidency, the Whig Harrison died of a cold within weeks of a chilly inauguration. His replacement was the nonparty vice president, John Tyler. In 1848, the Whigs opportunistically passed over Clay and nominated the victor of the Mexican-American War, General Zachary Taylor. He was popular in North, where he was believed to be against the westward expansion of slavery and also in the South as a military hero (where he obtained 55 of his decisive 163 electoral votes). When Taylor died of cholera (1850), his weak successor, Millard Fillmore, was popular mainly with the anti-Catholic, anti-immigrant Know-Nothings and powerless in the mounting North-South conflict. Fillmore signed the bills that traded free California for tightening the Fugitive Slave laws (1850). His successor, Franklin Pierce, signed the Kansas-Nebraska Act (1854), which by leaving Western voters to decide for or against slavery in effect revoked the Missouri Compromise (1820), which had accepted slavery in a future Southwest but left the Northwest free.

The Whigs had become factionalized and were widely believed to lack a compass of principle. The North-South problem was for them not the wrongness of slavery as such but slavery's threat to the survival of the nation. Webster might proclaim "Liberty *and* union, now and forever, one and inseparable!" Whig insistence on the unity of the nation foundered on the facts of disunity, not least on conflicting understandings of liberty: as liberty from slavery and liberty to hold slaves.

American party-political camps were recast by the Civil War, which Adams had feared and which Clay and Webster vainly tried to prevent. The war left the forces of conservatism in awkward alliance across a regional and party-label divide: South and North, Democrats and

Republicans, a new party, that had been founded in 1854 to promote the free-soil cause. The Republicans were in turn divided, most immediately about how to deal with a defeated South. Lincoln, assassinated as the war ended, had laid out the lines for a postwar South (1863): rapid re-establishment of civilian government and reintegration into the Union. Republican Radicals wanted reparations and negotiated readmission to the Union.

Reconstruction began along Lincoln's lines in Arkansas and Louisiana, only to be subverted by Southern resistance (black codes, which tied emancipated slaves to indentures and limited their movement; anti-black violence). Congress then passed and, over President Andrew Johnson's veto, repassed the Reconstruction Acts (1867–68). They imposed military rule and conditioned readmission to the Union on writing new state constitutions and on ratification of the Fourteenth amendment, which guaranteed civic and legal equality to all Americans. Amid continued white Southern resistance, widespread corruption, and Northern weariness, compounded by antiblack prejudice, in a third phase (1870–77), reconstruction was gradually abandoned. Texas, Virginia, Mississippi, and Georgia completed the South's reentry to the Union in 1870. Political corruption, the crash of 1873, and lack of support for Reconstruction combined for an electoral disaster that cost the Republicans ninety-three House seats in the Congressional election of 1874. Reconstruction was acknowledged as dead after the presidential election of 1876. The Democrats won, but the electoral votes of three states were successfully challenged in court and switched in return for a promise to withdraw the last federal troops, giving the presidency to the Republican, Rutherford Hayes.

With the end of Reconstruction, conservatism in the United States was reshaped along sectional and class lines across a North-South divide. In a flourishing, fast-growing urban-industrial economy, Northern Republicans spoke for business interests, which resisted unions and kept control of the factory floor. In a backward rural South, impoverished white elites under a Democratic Party flag divided poor blacks against poor whites, enjoyed unbreakable majorities in state legislatures, and resisted democratic liberalism until the 1960s, when a South grown richer gave in to a combination of federal pressure and pragmatic calculation. Cultural conservatives in the South—for example, the Southern Agrarians (to be noted later)—defended the region's "higher" values against the crude "materialism" of the North. Theirs was an example of the "withdrawal" strategy taken by critics of liberal modernity on the right who chose to resist in books rather than politics.

As the first American conservatives, anti-Jacksonian Whigs inherited a new means of controlling social conflict in a large, diverse republic: constitutional law. Since they shared that inheritance with their Jacksonian rivals, the law itself was opened to politics. Questions of how the mechanism was to be understood and elaborated became themselves partisan. American conservative tradition allowed for the partisan character of constitutional argument and for the changeability of law in a fluid modern society. Chapter 4 will introduce a prominent example of the constitutional defense of slaveholding interests by a formidable conservative brain, John Calhoun.

Despite evident large differences in the growth of early conservatism in the four countries in focus here, there were common challenges that the right faced in restoring its authority in a liberal-modern world. In the 1830s, the right's primary choice was either to resist or to compromise with liberal modernity. By the 1880s, it faced the further question of how far to accept democratic modernity. Compromise with liberalism was one thing, compromise with democracy another. Liberalism promised the boons of protection from power and equal respect for all, whoever they were. It said little about who was to enjoy such boons. It fell silent about how far "all" stretched. Democracy, by contrast, insisted on liberalism's boons for everyone. Democratic liberalism, that is, demanded that protection from power—the power of state, wealth, or social pressures—be available to everyone, whoever they were. The "everyone" here included not only majorities—the less educated, the less well-off—it also included minorities, be they rich or poor, upon whom majorities might prey. When democracy is narrowed to a simple, unchecked principle of majority rule, it ceases to be truly democratic and becomes demotic. It can then be exclusive and illiberal, tyrannizing over "the few" in the name of "all" with false appeal to the will of the people. That is illiberal democracy, often called populism, a scourge, as will be seen, with which the latter-day right in the twentieth and twenty-first centuries often plays.

When liberals first asked the established powers to explain themselves, public argument went on within voice range in modest halls among handfuls of literate men informed by small-run reviews and newssheets. Early liberal calls to insulate property from the interference of the state came when owners were a small minority among property-less masses with few or no economic powers of their own. When liberals originally rebuffed the tutelage of cultural authorities, they imagined that ethical and intellectual freedoms would be exercised by propertied, educated men. Democracy blew that confining picture apart. The exigent new kind of person that power had to answer to in democracy, whether the power of state, wealth, or society, was potentially every citizen.

By the late nineteenth century, equality in politics, though hedged and filtered, was largely conceded. Economic equality, however, alarmed liberals and conservatives alike. Its demands reshaped the political field. New coalitions formed on both the right and left. Conservatives moving centrally toward liberalism met liberals moving rightward from economic democracy. Liberals moving leftward toward economic democracy met socialists moving centrally toward liberalism. Neither coalition was stable. Left-liberals and socialists fought forever over the degree of economic democracy. Right-liberals and liberal conservatives came together to defend property and prosperity against economic equality in anything but palliative quantities. Unlike right-wing liberals, however, conservatives, even the market-minded kind, never felt at home in cultural democracy. The party-political story of conservatism's next period, 1880–1945, turns on how well or badly the right managed those powerful crosscurrents.

4

Ideas and Thinkers

TURNING REASON AGAINST LIBERALISM

Thrown into public argument, the right needed to find justifications for a conservative politics that would grip the minds of critical and demanding modern people. Much as the right needed ways to restore lost political authority, so intellectually the right had to find a compelling outlook without recourse to old defenses. It needed arguments to win over people to whom the promises of liberalism and democracy appealed.

That second task was in a way harder. Politically, the right inherited old habits and long experience of government, which it turned to advantage when in office. Intellectually, the right found itself having to do what the once-established powers it spoke for—crown, church, landed elites—had rarely expected to have to do, that is, justify themselves to a large, literate public whose compliance and consent could not be taken for granted. A frontal approach by appeal to unquestioned authority was no longer enough. Conservative thinkers and writers attuned to the times sought arguments in politics, religion, and philosophy, which they hoped would win contemporary ears.

Two exemplary mid-nineteenth-century right-wing thinkers, John Calhoun and Friedrich Stahl, mixed modern learning with legal reasoning on behalf of predemocratic, semiliberal regimes. Both were lawyers, and though conservative, both made concessions to a new intellectual climate. Calhoun used constitutional and historical arguments to defend the slave-owning American South as a safer path toward eventual social progress than liberal modernity offered. With a mix of philosophical, legal, and theistic scholarship, Stahl spoke in rapidly modernizing Prussia for limited monarchy, clerical authority, and indirect representation by social class. Both were trying, by constitutional means, to immunize weakened powers—the South's plantocracy; the sociopolitical hierarchy of old Prussia—against the twin dangers of centralizing modern government and growing popular discredit. Neither succeeded in his immediate aim: Calhoun to defend the indefensible, Stahl to keep alive the unsustainable. Each thinker, nevertheless, left claims of principle that later conservatives were able to draw on long after the institutions they were defending had gone: Calhoun's for why counter-majoritarian forces are needed in democracies; Stahl's that the conservative goal of social order was achievable in a variety of institutional forms—more representative, more authoritarian—given the unquestioned final authority of law.

Of the once authoritative traditions threatened by modernity and defended by conservatives, none looked more vulnerable than religion. Its authority in public argument had already weakened. Science had undermined religion's traditional metaphysical premises. Confessional division had reduced its public authority and limited its usefulness for social cohesion. But in its own sphere, whether shared ritual or private belief, religion remained strong. Faith, not nonbelief, was still the rule. In such a climate, it was barely thinkable for conservatives to do otherwise than defend faith against its detractors and stand up for religious authorities, divided as they might now be. Conservatives in person were not commonly obliged to choose between cynicism and sincerity. Most presumed that social order depended on the presence of widespread religious faith. Most themselves believed.

That still left it unclear how wide the sphere of religion was and where religion was to settle in public life. Should it continue to seek a public role? Or should it retreat to a private conviction, needed to make good members of society, yes, but effectively silent in public argument? Further, should religion engage in party politics? If it did, it risked losing its distinctive, unsecular role. But how, when standing aloof, could religion shield itself from secular pressures? For religious conservatives, the problem of secular modernity had the shape of the question facing political conservatives with liberal modernity: compromise or resist, adapt or withdraw?

Félicité de Lamennais in France and Wilhelm von Ketteler in Germany gave a pragmatic answer. They found a contemporary role for Christian faith in its social mission. Across the bridge of Leonine papal teaching after 1878, they opened paths to Christian Democracy in post-1945 Europe. John Henry Newman, an Anglican disbeliever in democracy, came to see in the Roman church a ready source of countermodern authority. In the United States, the Constitution separated church and state by proscribing an established church and ensuring free worship, but it did not keep faith out of politics or politics out of faith. Among a religious people with diverse confessions, how could it? American confessions themselves divided into right and left wings, as illustrated by the scholar Charles Hodge, an anti-modernist force among Presbyterians, and Orestes Brownson, a liberal Catholic often at odds with his conservative church. Concerned by liberalism's appeal and by the growing authority of science, the writer-poet Coleridge called for resistance from a kind of lay clergy—he named it a "clerisy"—that would sustain the ethical and spiritual values of a traditional culture and promote conservative ideas. He was arguing, in effect, that conservatism needed its own intellectuals.

When liberal thinkers had shown more of a target in their own writings, conservatives later in the century took aim at liberalism philosophically. Outstanding examples were the judge and writer James Fitzjames Stephen who wrote against Mill on civil liberties and social equality; the legal historian Otto von Gierke, who lent historical weight to the conservative claim that a healthy society needed voluntary institutions that were neither creatures of a centralizing sovereign state nor products of mutable private interests; and the philosopher F. H. Bradley, who argued against ethical "individualism" (in one of that slippery term's many understandings), which a political liberalism was commonly assumed to need among its philosophical defenses. Stephen was the most openly political of them, Bradley the least, with Gierke, an early liberal who ended as a nationally minded conservative in between. Thin as the linkages were between scholarship and partisanship, work of their kind began a long twentieth-century shift in the balance of public argument, which eventually put liberals into the defensive position of having to justify themselves to conservatives rather than, as at the start, the other way around.

i. Constitutions for Unacceptable Ends: Calhoun

John Calhoun (1782–1850) is remembered with justice as an apologist for the slave-owning interests, although the word "apologist" sounds as if he were cynical or short of arguments when he was neither. Not only did he think himself right with blind sincerity, but he exercised his great ill-used talent, argument, with relentless skill from his entry into Congress (1811) to shortly before his death, when his last speech on the South's behalf was read for him as he listened on the Senate floor, too ill to speak.

Listeners to Calhoun's speeches were often more awestruck than persuaded. A German visitor heard in them a "Mephistophelean scorn" for the "absurdity" of his opponent's views. Harriet Martineau thought Calhoun made of "cast-iron" and mentally "possessed." Everyone was struck by his alarming, fiery eyes. He was often outmaneuvered by colleagues with feebler mental powers but a better grasp of the human make. Mill judged Calhoun superior as a "speculative political thinker" to anyone in the United States since Madison or Hamilton. Such praise for a Southern slaveholder was startling from the author of *On Liberty*, one of the few prominent figures in British politics to take the Union's side in the Civil War. Mill nevertheless had heard in Calhoun the same demoralizing question for majoritarian democracy that troubled him: how by a simple head count may the views and concerns of the minority be justly "blotted out"?

Calhoun's unbending defense of the South gave coherence to what otherwise looked like a course without plot. His father was a prosperous slaveowner in the backcountry Carolinas, where settlers fought for living space with those already settled. A grandmother and uncle had died in an Indian raid. As soon as he could, the clever, earnest boy, who read political classics for choice, escaped the confines of the frontier for Yale and public life. He was hard to match in his grasp of politics but was poor in his feel for fellow politicians, whom he tended to view with suspicion or contempt.

Calhoun was a Whig, a Democrat, and neither, a rivalrous vice president to both John Quincy Adams and Andrew Jackson, and by turns a defender, enemy, and compromiser on tariffs. He lead the Southern Warhawks calling for war with Britain over its interference with American ships and stirring up of Indians on the frontier (1812)—"The honor of a nation is its life!"—only to change his mind as talk of secession spread in the North and the conflict seemed to imperil the Union. Calhoun later opposed war with Mexico over Texas, a popular cause with Democrats, out of the similar fear that victory would sharpen conflict between the sections over slavery's future in the West. Twice he failed to win the presidency (1824; 1844). Jackson bested him (1832) politically over South Carolina's try at nullifying federal tariffs, personally by dropping him as a running mate, and socially by publicly mortifying Calhoun's prudish wife. His higher ambitions were done for, and over the next eighteen years, bar a brief return to government, Calhoun spoke in the Senate as a voice of the South.

In speaking for the South, Calhoun to his own mind was also speaking for the Union. They belonged together. Each had to live and prosper with the other. One might be smaller and weaker, but it was still in justice owed equal say and equal concern. The North could no more ask the South to northernize than the South could insist that the North southernize. To do either was to deny parity, their equality as partners. That said, the South had lessons for an exploitative, money-grubbing North, being better attuned to the social virtues and life's higher aims. So Calhoun vigorously argued in speeches and in the works published after his death, *Disquisition on Government* (1851) and *Discourse on the Constitution* (1851).

The first book faced how to protect a large and stable minority interest in an electoral democracy. Calhoun's answer was, in effect, legislative co-decision and local executive blocking powers. The second book sought to show that the US Constitution, properly read, demanded that answer. Although his interpreters have heard a variety of influences,

Calhoun, like the Founders, was arguing with people schooled in law, not philosophy. After brisk preliminaries—people were social and self-ish; without government, no society; without constitution, no government—Calhoun got to the nub: what constitutions were for. They were, in his view, blocking devices against undue power. Constitutions protected the governed from government, which tended to tyrannize unless checked. When properly made, constitutions also protected minorities against majorities.

By "minority" Calhoun did not mean, in its late twentieth-century sense, a once disregarded group—say, blacks, women, or Hispanics. He meant an enduring regional or social "interest" large enough to bear weight in the nation but too small not be out-votable. Nor by "interests" did Calhoun mean economic classes, sectors, or pressure groups. His interests had political and cultural unity. They had history. They were, in effect, mini-nations. More than that, Calhoun did not spell out. Though he argued in broad terms, one minority interest was ever present: the American South, with its plantations and slaves. The majority "interest" was the North, which was rapidly outgrowing, outproducing, and out-arming the South.

For Calhoun, interests together made up a national community. The "sense of the community" could be taken either directly by "right of suffrage unaided" (that is, roughly speaking, one person, one vote) or filtered "through a proper organism" (that is, some means of voting by interests rather than by people one by one). When "an interest or portion" of the community might be "unequally or injuriously affected," its "concurrent" judgment was needed in making law. If an offending law was passed, an outvoted interest could veto its execution.

Despite a forest of terminology and a lack of specifics, Calhoun in the *Disquisition* drove all he said to one clear, simple point: "It is this negative power, the power of preventing or arresting the action of the government, be it called by what term it may—veto, interposition, nullification, check, or balance of power, which, in fact, forms the constitution."

The idea of qualified, "concurrent" or "super" majorities was not new. Rousseau had urged in the *Social Contract* (1762) that "the more grave and important the questions discussed, the nearer should the opinion that is to prevail approach unanimity." Madison had worried in the *Federalist Papers* about poor majorities despoiling rich minorities. He had calmed his fears with the thought that in a large, diverse republic there were too many competing interests for any one to dominate the others. Besides, the Constitution itself was rich in counter-democratic mechanisms to filter simple majorities of the kind Calhoun was after. Calhoun was not mollified. The Constitution had to be interpreted and adjudged. Its injunctions had to be enforced. Over the courts and the executive, political majorities were likely to prevail.

Calhoun left hard questions open. What was to count as a large, enduring interest? How widely available (among topics; among wielders) might veto powers be made before government paralysis set in? Who within a minority interest was to wield its veto? What, in justice, is a minority veto worth if captured by a bullying sub-majority or by a self-appointed mini-tyrant? Such questions taxed liberals and conservatives in nineteenth-century Europe who were struggling with the conflicting pressures of modern nationhood in democratic times. Efficiency pressed for large nations, big markets, and central government. Equity called for attention to local customs and concerns. Few solutions worked fully, and many did not last. Calhoun's challenge to majoritarianism returned in the liberal-democratic late twentieth century with mounting calls for regionalism, multiculturalism, and separatism.

Calhoun realized that no institutional mechanism could by itself turn the trick. Among modern peoples, in the end, sections and communities would live in peace together within a single nation only if they chose to. In a pre-Rawlsian touch, casting forward to the thought that in an ideal commonwealth just institutions and just citizens would reinforce each other, Calhoun wrote that the existence of a mutual veto among the sections would presume a mutual recognition that made using the veto unnecessary. Bar acceptance of each other, there was no fail-safe constitutional answer, only separation or war.

The *Discourse* sought to find those lessons from the *Disquisition* in the American Constitution. The Founders on Calhoun's telling had recognized the danger of federal power treading on the reserved powers of the states and so had allowed for the idea of a "concurrent" majority—that is, major steps to be taken only with minority approval. Only so could the twin threats of "consolidation" (overpowerful central government) and "disunion" (federal breakup) be avoided.

Calhoun left the *Discourse* unfinished. In earlier, less doctrinal speeches, he had amply laid out arguments for the American causes that occupied him in his last two decades: resistance to tariffs and defense of slavery. The arguments were more pragmatic than principled and showed his strength as an advocate. Rather than demolish a single target, he scattered fire wide, leaving the opposition everywhere wounded.

Tariffs for protecting industry were unfair, Calhoun argued, for they raised prices. In the North, wages could be increased to compensate, but that was not possible in the slave South, which had no wages. Second, the South's economy relied on exporting cotton, for Americans bought at most a seventh of yearly production. When protective tariffs shrank exports, who would buy the shortfall? Third, protection benefited those who least needed it: the rich and their agents "who crowd Congress with petitions for bounties"; the "active, vigilant and well-trained corps" of officials and regulators who lived from government; and the banks, which financed industry.

Calhoun took a similarly pragmatic approach with slavery. Without a principled defense, his outlook came apart, because all else he said relied on the presumption, spoken or not, that slavery was just. Take it away and Calhoun's arguments, even the valid ones, became unsound. A brief middle section of the *Disquisition* did touch on inequality and, obliquely, on slavery. In a final moral sense people were equal, Calhoun allowed. In talent and energy, they started out unequal. Moral and material progress relied on that inequality, for it spurred people to better themselves. Liberty was not a right but came only with effort leading to social progress. Effort, however, must be personal, not governmental. A progressive society was like an army on the march. Were government to force the back to the front, forward movement would stop and "arrest the march of progress." How unfree men and women, forbidden in many places to read or write, could better themselves by personal effort, he did not say.

As a public orator, Calhoun was blunter. Slavery, far from "sinful and odious," was "a positive good," he declared in a notorious speech of 1837 that stands as a small lexicon of plausible-looking excuses for the unacceptable. Slavery created bonds of sympathy between master and slave. It was slowly civilizing a barbarous people. It united Southern whites across boundaries of class. It served a farm economy that fitted with Northern industry. In a Burkean note suggesting that custom brought legitimacy, Calhoun also said of slavery, "Be it good or bad, it has grown up in our society and institutions." Webster, who respected Calhoun as an adversary, would have none of that. In his speech of 1850, directed at the dying Calhoun, Webster reminded the Senate that Southerners had changed their minds to suit the times. Earlier, they had agreed that slavery was evil, at best a temporary and costly aberration that economically would soon die. Then slavery became profitable, first because of the cotton gin, then with the opening of the West. For its defenders, slavery was no longer an evil but a boon, though a boon, as Lincoln later said, that no man wanted for himself.

Calhoun had an unexalted view of politics and bleakness of tone heard in later conservatives such as Bismarck (without the sardonic humor) and Salisbury. He weighed up the balance of forces in politics with an open eye, an attitude sometimes taken as peculiarly conservative and dubbed, with a multitasking word, "realist." No "wealthy and civilized society," Calhoun said, had ever existed in which "one portion of the community did not in fact live on the labour of another." Peering ahead to Southern defeat in its historical contest with liberal modernity, he glumly predicted in 1828, "After we are exhausted, the contest will be between the capitalists and the operatives." In fear of being thought pious, Marxists have favored the unexalted tone. Noting the likeness, the American historian Richard Hofstadter nicely called Calhoun the "Marx of the Master Class." Despite claiming to believe that the slave South, not the capitalist North, stood for civilization's advance, Calhoun had little Whig hopefulness about human progress or Jacksonian sense of democratic equality. His sweeping historical claim about true progress was little more than a debating point. Perhaps Northern capitalism was corroding civic values, but it did not follow that a slave South was the better choice.

Although Calhoun shared with Mill the liberal's suspicion of majoritarian power, his conservatism stands out clearly in four ways. He did not believe in liberal equality—in civic respect, that is—for all; he feared the destructive pressure of a reforming, central state on traditional rights and local customs; he understood how the political right must now fight for opinion, noting how abolitionism, the fiend that haunted him, had "taken possession of the pulpit, of the schools, and to a considerable extent of the press, those great instruments by which the mind of the rising generation will be formed." As for democracy, Calhoun was a procedural, not a substantive, democrat. He accepted the electoral procedures of democracy but fought to limit their operation by constitutional devices to protect a privileged minority. As a disbeliever in liberal equality, Calhoun had no time for the substantive idea that liberalism's benefits must be extended democratically, that is, to everyone. After his death, conservative resistance to the liberal state was pushed to the point of war. For the unreconciled American right, the American Civil War followed the French Revolution as conservatism's second founding.

ii. Reason for the Right Replaces Nostalgia: Stahl

Heckled by defiant young Hegelians at his inaugural lecture in Berlin, in 1840, the new professor, Friedrich Julius Stahl, rebuked them: "Gentlemen, I am here to teach, and you are here to listen." The Prussian authorities had appointed him to counter what they feared were harmful, rationalistic beliefs among the nation's ever-disruptive students. Stahl, as best he could, obliged by putting forward a conservatism he believed might be argued for with sound reasoning. He accepted a constitutional monarchy while insisting on the equal sovereignty of the Christian faith and the Prussian nation, whose demands on people did not arise from choice or consent. "Authority, not majority" was Stahl's anti-democratic watchword.

In that spirit, the first volume of Stahl's *Philosophy of Law* (1830) took issue with the legal theories of modern thinkers whom officials might not deeply understand—seventeenth-century natural-rights writers, Kant, Hegel—but whose ideas and repute they blamed for stirring critical disaffection among the young. Stahl's second volume (1833) lent weight to anti-liberals and anti-democrats alike with its comprehensive picture of law as arising not from human custom or social decision but within a universal, God-given moral order. It was notably harsh about the ambiguities and dangers of Left Hegelianism.

Nowadays little heard of and scarcely read, Stahl (1802–61) was a leading figure in his day. Lord Acton told Gladstone's daughter that Stahl had more talent and influence in Germany than Disraeli had in Britain. Stahl was the son of a Jewish merchant from Munich. Although Prussia granted Jews civil rights in 1812—several decades before laggard Britain—Stahl converted to Protestantism, as did Disraeli, on coming of age.

Stahl was learned, dry, and, like Calhoun, eager to beat his opponent on every point. He dressed in gray or black, the shade for lawyers, professors, and churchmen, being himself all three. Late in life he was a high governing official in Prussia's Evangelical state church. Stahl, it seemed, exemplified membership in a "clerisy" of the kind (soon to be described) that the Germanophile Coleridge longed for in Britain: a clergy-like body of teachers and intellectuals who would keep alive the normative traditions of a nation's culture and faith. The snag was that neither the society nor institutions for such a unifying "clerisy" existed. Stahl's Germany was a diverse land of many regions and confessions with a tangle of thirty-nine discordant religious authorities, not the orderly, top-down structure of law and loyalty he speculated about and sought to validate in his lectures. The Evangelical Church itself was a recent union of Lutherans and Calvinists imposed in 1817 by a newly devout Prussian monarchy, disputed by Saxon Lutherans (who went to jail or immigrated to the United States), and soon abandoned in an unofficial schism.

Stahl was thrust into party politics by the Revolution of 1848. He fell in with Prussia's anti-liberals and wrote a manifesto of conservatism for their new newspaper, the *Kreuzzeitung*. Its main points were to combat revolution but avoid reaction, respect law, spurn arbitrariness whether princely or popular yet keep the crown supreme, allow freedom of labor and inheritance, defend the legal equality of Christian people, and maintain both German unity and the independence of German states. Stahl lent his legal expertise to drafting Prussia's overdue constitution and entered the Prussian Senate. There Stahl stayed till his death, pressing the conservative cause.

Although the Revolution of 1848 failed, it lived on in the minds of its makers and unmakers. Loosely connected protests, risings, and constitution-drafting by liberals and democrats across Europe were soon rebuffed, by force or otherwise. The turbulent episode, as Marx saw, was not 1789 come again. But it reconfirmed the division of the political field into left and right. It sharpened each side's awareness of its own weaknesses. The left struggled to see why it had lost. The right sensed the strength of the left, which it feared would win next time. Unlike in France and Britain, however, the right was in power. Stahl grasped that to stay there, the right would need to prevail in argument. His manifesto in the *Kreuzzeitung*, "The Conservative Banner" (July 1848), laid out a strategy for the right: not to turn back time but to take control of the present. Conservatives, he urged them, should not blame the crown for accepting a constitution but praise it for adapting to the times.

Stahl was talking to two sorts of listeners. One was the conservative Ultra, shaken by 1848 and unable to tell a constitution from a guillotine or a religious modernist from an atheist. The other was liberal opinion, by which Stahl understood the property-owning middle classes. They had fomented 1848 and then pulled back in alarm at radicalism and democracy. Looking right, Stahl hoped to pull the Ultras toward the liberals. Looking left, he hoped to pull the middle classes to the conservative side. Stahl expressed both the reconciled and unreconciled sides of the conservative soul. He saw that conservatives had to live in liberal modernity but hoped to limit the terms of cohabitation.

The iniquity that organized Stahl's thoughts was revolution—in politics, philosophy, or religion. Revolution, he explained, was not a rebellion or uprising. Protest against evident wrongs or removal of bad rulers brought undisputed benefits. Examples he cited were Magna Carta, the Glorious Revolution (1688), and even 1789 in France. Who in France, Stahl asked, wanted to bring back arbitrary arrest, unfair middle-class taxes, subjugation of peasants, and exclusion of Protestants? Those were wrongs, since properly corrected. They were, however, revolution's smaller part. For revolution, truly seen, was not an episode or event but an attitude of mind.

Revolution, for Stahl, was human willfulness, ethical license, disregard for authority, and the embrace of a world without norms. It was, in sum, the primary source of liberal modernity's social and moral ills. By generalizing, Stahl's work served as a staging post between earlier writers against the French Revolution and the anti-liberal vernacular of conservative thought in the later nineteenth and twentieth centuries. By detaching revolution from conservatism's originating historical episode, Stahl was able to "revolutionize" the liberal point of view. He turned a pragmatic, piecemeal liberal search for social order into a normless campaign of ethical destruction.

Similar thoughts had lurked in the first writers against the French Revolution, passionately in Burke, incisively in Gentz. For both writers, events were too many and too close. Political liberals, let alone liberal philosophers, were not yet in view. Stahl brought the anti-liberal lesson into the open and made it clear. The inspiration for his malign 1789 was, it is true, more Maistre's than Burke's. Whereas Burke's scribblers were foolish to deny custom, Maistre's were wicked to deny God. Revolution, in Stahl's understanding, came from Luciferan pride. Hellfire, by contrast, was not the Lutheran style. Stahl's *psychomachia* was cooler, less angry, and more usable than Maistre's. His answer to the apostasy of revolution was not the hangman but the rule of law.

Without the rule of law, there was no social order. Private law was needed to referee disputes among people. Public law was needed to control the state. It was notably rich in Germany. (When the English jurist John Austin first had to lecture on public law he found too few English sources and turned to German authorities.) Stahl took public law as a surer way to contain state authority than constitutions and parliaments. To suggest its strength, he contrasted the patrimonial state favored by Haller and which still existed in Russia, where a ruler's say was a matter of private law and the state belonged, in effect, to the crown, with the new Prussian state, where law constrained citizens and state agencies alike. Sovereign power, vested in the crown, was absolute and indivisible, it was true, but its exercise was nevertheless tempered by the advice of society's propertied and professional elites and by public law. In deference to the times, Stahl allowed that the advice might be channeled through a parliament with limited powers. A constrained monarchy of the kind was, in Stahl's phrase, "institutional" or, more familiarly, "constitutional."

Liberals and democrats each misunderstood constitutions, Stahl insisted. The Halves (Germany's liberals of 1848) looked needlessly to parliamentary constitutions to restrain power, when they had already in their hands the ready means of public law. The Wholes (Germany's democrats of 1848 calling for wider representation) were for Stahl revolutionaries in disguise. Imagining people to be equal—in interests, capacities, and rights—democrats claimed to speak for a single, uniform humanity. By neglecting actual differences, they roused dissatisfaction, sowed discord, and encouraged unbelief with a zeal found only in fanatical religions.

Stahl gave constitutional body to those thoughts by helping draft and defend (and later trim) the Prussian Constitution of 1850. The crown kept the power of final decision, guided and to a degree constrained by upper and lower houses. The lower house was elected on a triple franchise: a third each of its seats was picked by electoral assemblies chosen by three tax classes: roughly the rich, middle-income, and low-income—in other words, the few, the some, and the many. Whereas the Reichstag after 1871 was chosen by universal male suffrage, which gave the Catholic Center, liberals, and Social Democrats, divided as they were, a majority voice there by the end of the century, the Prussian lower house remained solidly in conservative hands until its abolition in 1918. More an improvisation than a system, the Wilhelmine mix of crown and parliament, Prussian and Reich, fiat and law, inheritance and invention owed much to Stahl's attempted reconciliation of opposites.

Stahl's improvisation was an adaptation of Germany's old "estates" in new constitutional guise. As with all he wrote, it spoke to the past and present, right and left. Representation was, strictly, a misnomer. The exercise of sovereignty could not be shared (liberal error). It did not derive from the people (democratic error). Parliaments, all the same, were to guide and caution the crown. The landed nobility had been the natural voice of parliament. It stood between crown and people, and its role was to defend the people, not, or not merely, to fight its corner. The heights of society were to perform that same task of selfless mediation. How the tax classes reliably matched the old "estates" and why the dutifulness of the nobility should be counted on, Stahl left unclear. He leaned instead on the point that noble status and privilege had been abolished in law, but the tasks of nobility remained. In a cryptic phrase that left the claims of democracy unanswered, Stahl claimed to be recommending *Stände* (estates or social ranks) "of responsibility, not privilege."

To fill the hole Stahl believed he had found in modern philosophies of law, he turned to his Protestant understanding of the Christian outlook. Social order rested on law and morality. Together they drew authority in the end from a personal God, who presided over "a moral kingdom." The Christian state, with its ethic of free agency and responsibility, was its highest form. A sympathetic, post-theological understanding could hear Stahl as insisting that moral order was not a social, human, or philosophical artefact. It could not, that is, be thought of as coming from collective decision, actual or presumed, or from *tu quoque* reasoning in a spirit of reciprocity. Nor could it be undermined by skeptical reasoning, whose probing presumed a moral order it sought to deny.

Stahl's theological clothes made for a loose fit in politics. His Christian injunctions were both clement and lax, as well as punitive and strict. He was against serfdom and slavery (though loth to condemn it in the American South). He welcomed more humane punishments. He was for many civic freedoms, including the right to choose a religion (at least in private) and to change country. In contrast, he disapproved of lawful divorce, favored capital punishment, took blasphemy for a criminal offense, and thought suicides should be refused "honorable" burial.

Liberals as well as Left Hegelians like Bauer and Feuerbach found Stahl unprincipled and circular in argument: he used authority to justify authority, they held, and left obscure how practical judgments flowed from higher premises. Their doubts had force but missed Stahl's less reasoned attachments to a certain idea of Prussia and to the high value Christians put on the human person, without which his political morality made little sense.

The Prussian social character, to Stahl, was orderly, effective, law-governed, and dutiful. Remove a sense of duty among Prussia's elites, and Stahl's constitutional structures fell apart. Whether apt or not, pride in Prussian efficacy and duty was a patriotic commonplace, contrasted with French frivolity and British shopkeeper-mindedness.

Stahl's second less reasoned attachment was to Christian respect for the human person, whatever their worldly standing. Among philosophers he admired for their reconciliationism were Friedrich Schelling (who had encouraged him in his philosophy of law) and Hegel, both of whom tended to argue that any one thing was an aspect of everything else. Stahl pulled back from them because a personal God seemed to have vanished from their thinking and, without a personal God, Stahl could find no way to rationalize his other deep conviction: the untouchability of the human person. As no other faith, Protestant Christianity, Stahl believed, had treasured and freed the human person to live with others in a society of laws.

Stahl saw his conservatism strategically and as a matter of principle. He took industrial capitalism as unstoppable but hoped capitalist modernity might yet be stopped from becoming liberal, let alone democratic, modernity. Pragmatically, Stahl saw his task, as many conservatives see theirs, of sustaining if he could what was valuable in the old order. To adapt Calhoun's metaphor, society was on the march. A conservative's task was to persuade the van not to race off, the rear not to sit and sulk. Stahl sought to persuade old elites to trade *ständisch* privilege for primacy in the representative arrangements of government. He sought to win the middle classes to conservatism from fear of socialism and democracy. Philosophically, he trusted that a rationally defended faith could support both a conservative politics and a strict ethics, though the practical guidance given by his theology was limited. The ethics he favored seemed to be more those of his milieu and time rather than an ethic that the theology by itself called for and that could be reapplied when the time and the milieu changed.

iii. How Conservatives Should Defend Religion: Lamennais, Ketteler, Newman, Brownson, and Hodge

Stahl was not alone in his hostility to liberal thought. To religious conservatives generally the adversary was clear. Liberalism "pulverizes humanity" and turns society into a "rational-liberal calculating machine" (Bishop Ketteler). Once liberal ideas take hold, "nobody should expect progress in society, happiness or even liberty" (Abbé Lamennais). It was scant consolation that liberalism was "too cold a principle to appeal to the multitude" (Cardinal Newman). People needed a creed. The "mad attempt to separate the progress of society from religion . . . has rendered modern liberalism everywhere destructive and everywhere a failure" (Orestes Brownson). The foe, liberalism, was in view. So much was agreed.

The problem was this. If, as it seemed, liberalism was winning in society, what was its Christian opponent to do? Confront or concede? Resist or adapt? If religious thinkers confronted and resisted, how were they to argue? Like conservatives generally, religious thinkers faced a puzzle of intellectual strategy. If they argued against liberal modernity in religious terms, they risked not being heard. If they argued in nonreligious terms, had they not given in before the contest began?

In secular modern societies, religious reasons tend to be discounted in public argument. It is not that believers' claims and causes are silenced, rather, arguments made by believers for their claims—political, social, or moral—need from prudence to be cast in nonreligious terms if they are to win wide assent. In France in the 1960s, to look forward, when parties of the right resisted bills to legalize abortion, their arguments were secular: France needed more babies; even competent abortions were dangerous; loose living was encouraged by reducing its costs. An argument of principle was added, but it was still a secular argument: abortion was an unjust taking of life. So in the United States, for example, abortion continues to be publicly opposed by religious believers not on the grounds that it is divinely forbidden but because they hold it to be unjust killing. Secular moderns will not credit arguments from divinity. They can agree that unjust killing is wrong. Religious believers and secular moderns can then argue—*is* abortion unjust killing?—rather than talk past each other.

If, in addition, there are many competing confessions, each with their own beliefs and doctrines, there is a second purpose to excluding religious reasons from public debate. It serves believers and nonbelievers alike: keeping the argumentative peace and allowing for collective decision-making in diverse, conflicted societies.

Those pressures for keeping religious and political reasoning apart could be called the fact of public secularization (to the extent that it is a fact) and the policy of privatizing religious reason (excluding it, that is, from public debate). Those pressures are so familiar nowadays as to be almost unnoticeable. That was not so in the mid-nineteenth century, when they were fresh as a cold spring wind and keenly felt. Together they shaped how religious conservatives strove to preserve what they feared liberal modernity was in danger of losing.

The lives and thoughts of five conservative Christians serve here to illustrate approaches to that choice of resistance or adaptation. It faced the Christian confessions equally. Lamennais, Ketteler, and Brownson were Roman Catholics, Newman was a high-church Protestant who became a Roman Catholic. Hodge was a strict Presbyterian. Each saw large failings in contemporary public life that they believed a Christian approach could and should address.

They dismissed appeals by liberals and democrats to human equality, which sounded empty when set against the social facts. Egalitarianism to their minds exaggerated people's capacities, set unreachable goals, and distracted from practical needs. They denounced liberalism's heartless exploitation of the working poor as well as the encouragement it gave to godless help for them under the name of socialism. They complained also of modern society's moral decay: loose living, not listening to authorities, breaking rules, and listening to clever thinkers who denied there were rules or claimed we made our own. Ethical fears of the kind grew intense with rapider urbanization after the 1830s. City living was linked in worriers' minds with uppity apprentices, mixed marriages, and general laxity of folk torn from the rural hold of parson and squire. Such ethical dislike of cities was linked in Europe with Romantic celebration of the countryside. American Whigs were geographically more evenhanded in their worries. They fretted both about unmonitored conduct on the male-heavy Western frontier and about slovenly living in crowded city slums.

One anxiety for Christian intellectuals wrapped together the rest: fear for the Christian faith itself. Social order, morality, and faith made a chain in their minds. If faith went, so did confidence in morality, and if that went, social order was imperiled. Natural science, scholarly criticism of religion's written sources, and critical philosophy were together sapping Christian confidence not just in the facts of their faith but in the reasonableness of religious belief as such. Lamennais and Newman felt sharply, and tried to deflect, modernity's relentless demand for reasons. Newman wrote that "rationalism," by which he meant not just denying but overthinking religion, was "the great evil of the day." If faith was shown to be unreasonable, would not the reasonableness of morality be next?

The answer Lamennais gave to finding Christianity's new place was, nevertheless, more practical than doctrinal. So it was with Ketteler. Christianity was to show its worth in liberal modernity not by testifying to higher truth but by doing good. Ketteler summed up that pragmatic creed: "Religion and morality by themselves cannot cure the plight of the workers." He and Lamennais spoke for a Catholicism of social action that put help for the needy before engagement in church polemics or party politics. Theirs was a social version of the attempt, later stressed by Durkheim, to find religion a home in modernity by treating it as a shared way of life, not a theology or counter-scientific story of the world.

Ketteler was the more strategic. An engaged Catholicism, he believed, could both hold off socialism and protect Germany's Catholics.

Lamennais, who began as a right-wing Ultra, became a radical democrat whose draft constitution in 1848 was dismissed by fellow republicans as too extreme. Ketteler was an insider, clear in aim but careful to keep in with his secular opposite number in Hesse, a reactionary prime minister, as well as with the Vatican. He came, in time, to accept the idea of a Catholic party in Germany. Lamennais was an outsider, who swung from right to left, fell out with the Pope, and ended with no political home of his own. He nevertheless opened a space in France for a left-wing Catholicism that never lost its hostility to free-market liberals.

Félicité de Lamennais (1782–1854) was the self-taught son of a rich Breton, recently ennobled. At five, when his mother died, he was packed off to his uncle's estate, where he made himself erudite by reading all he could find in the large library. Early experience turned him against politics. Brittany suffered notable cruelties in the Revolution, when his family hid priests from anticlerical Jacobins. Napoleon's truce with the Church in 1801, which gave the French state broad control over the Catholic clergy in return for paying their bills, confirmed young Lamennais's dislike of politics. A modern state that paid for a national religion on prudential grounds was bound, he judged, to end up strangling genuine faith. Lamennais dreamed instead of a theocratic European federation guided by the papacy. In the Restoration monarchy, he wrote for Chateaubriand's *Conservateur* and, like him, was repelled by the corruption and incompetence of the Bourbons. Lamennais set his task instead to prying a beneficent, universal faith from the defense of national despots.

In 1830, Lamennais helped found a radical newspaper, *L'Avenir*. It was printed in Belgium, which had a tolerant new constitution, and promptly condemned by the Vatican. He was censured by the Pope again for supporting the uprising of Poles against their Russian occupiers, when the papacy found it more urgent to defend Orthodox despotism against patriotic Catholics (1830–31). By the Hungry '40s, Lamennais's open embrace of popular, social-minded Catholicism put him at war with the church hierarchy. Now close to socialism, Lamennais considered market liberalism, if not tempered by social responsibility and anchored in a common faith, as a war of all against all. He favored personal liberties but doubted how achievable they were in unfettered economic markets. As a newspaper publisher, Lamennais remarked how much money you needed to enjoy free speech.

The religious work Lamennais was most remembered for, his early essay *On Indifference* (1817), might seem to cut across that social radicalism. It addressed the place of faith in modern society. It attacked common evasions, as he saw them, that moderns used to avoid religious conviction: the skeptical claim that religious faith was improbable but useful for social order and needed only by the mass of people; the anti-universalist claim that, as all faiths were equally doubtful, the wise course was to adopt the faith of your society; and the Protestant anti-clerical claim that, since Biblical revelation needed interpreters (and its claims as historical record had been exploded by biblical criticism), appeal to Scripture was no ground for challenging clerical authority.

The link between the earlier and later Lamennais was hostility to liberal "individualism," a loose idea that was fast becoming a liberal target for conservatives to fire at. Lamennais in *On Indifference* took to task Luther, alone with his God, and Descartes, alone with his Demon, for overprizing private judgment and neglecting that language and reasoning were necessarily social. Some habits of thought, he wrote, were local, others "natural," or common, to humanity. Those formed a *sens commun*, which Hume called "habit" and Lamennais, echoing Burke, called "prejudice." In religion, such habits of mind inclined people, without reason or argument, to religious faith. In politics, the opinion of the people inclined to the proper answer. Skeptical critics and tiresome minority opinions got in the way. For the anti-liberal Lamennais, the gap between papal authority and popular authority was not, in the end, very large.

As bishop of Mainz from 1850 to his death, Wilhelm von Ketteler (1811–77) was a leading German spokesman of top-down social Catholicism. For the sake of social peace between capital and labor, Ketteler thought working-class economic, but not political, demands should be met. He opposed Bismarck's anti-Catholic *Kulturkampf* and favored Catholic-Protestant reconciliation.

Ketteler saw his clerical task as shielding the German church, in a majority Protestant nation, from the pressures of a reforming state, particularly in church government and education; his diplomatic task, with like-minded Catholic bishops, as reining in the Vatican's intrusions into national politics; and his political task as heading off socialist demands for collective ownership and democratic control of the economy by appealing across confessional lines to the working classes in favor of cooperatives and trade unions.

Ketteler's family was from old Westphalian aristocracy. He had been schooled by Jesuits, studied at four universities, and lost the tip of his nose in a student duel. A lawyer and civil servant before becoming a Catholic priest, Ketteler quit as a government official in protest over the arrest of the archbishop of Cologne (1838), an early shot in the conflict between Protestant and Catholic authority that was to burst out in Bismarck's anti-Catholic *Kulturkampf* (1870s). As a delegate to the abortive Frankfurt parliament hoping for a pan-German constitution (1848–49), he sided with the moderate liberals. When the Rhineland's industrialization quickened in the 1850s, Ketteler preached and wrote against the neglect of its harsh social effects. In *The Labour Question and Christianity* (1864), he blamed liberals for a ruinous picture of society that took people for "atoms of stuff" to be ground to powder and "blown over the earth." Influenced by the socialist Ferdinand Lassalle, he thought workers should be able to unionize and, if need be, strike. Ketteler's social message had little to say about the labor conditions on farms in East Prussia that were later to horrify Max Weber. He was for personal liberties but followed his church's patriarchal view of men and women without demur. He shared the casual anti-Semitism of his class and creed, which he veiled in generalized disapproval of banking.

Ketteler was among the German bishops who feared that by digging itself in against the modern world the Roman papacy was marginalizing Catholicism and asking for retaliation from secular powers. At the First Vatican Council (1868), Ketteler argued against the declaration of papal infallibility in grave doctrinal matters (1868), afraid of the reaction it would cause in Germany, yet he took care not to affront the Pope or tread on the Vatican's authority. Without retreating over doctrine, a more flexible pope, Leo XIII (1878), listened to the social message, saying of Ketteler, "I learned from him." The encyclical *Rerum novarum* (1891), appealed for tempered labor-capital relations and the right to unionize (though employer-worker associations were preferable). It opposed socialism and strikes.

On German unification, when Catholics were outnumbered in the new Reich by Protestants two to one, Ketteler came round to thinking that Germany needed a Catholic party. He had earlier hesitated, thinking the church's role was social and clerical, not political. A confessional party, he feared, would stir up anti-Catholicism. As the *Kulturkampf* burst on his church anyway, that argument fell away. Ketteler spoke up for the new Catholic Center Party in *Catholics in the German Empire* (1873). It combined a neo-Thomist view of natural law with Hegel's picture of a socially articulated state. The Catholic party's aims, Ketteler wrote, should be to resist the ethical and intellectual errors of the day, fend off an overpowerful state, protect personal freedoms, and safeguard the natural rights of intermediate institutions such as the church, schools, and family.

Ketteler was conservative in his hostility to political liberalism and in his suspicion of mass democracy. Political liberalism, on his understanding, exalted the state by making it the sole source of law and denying any higher authority—notably Christian morality—above the state: "If the state is God, then the entire development of the Christian religion is senseless." (That seemed to rest a political point on a philosophical exaggeration; a political liberal could accept the higher authority of morality over law and allow that a positive law, while still being law, might well be unjust.) Ketteler sensed, nevertheless, an intellectual cousinage between Christianity and liberalism. Freedom and duty were not separable, nor was freedom at war with authority. Authority showed the reflective, free person what they had good reason to do. There was little in either of those claims for liberals to disagree with, although they might think Ketteler had left more to be said when he wrote: "No institution is more liberal than the Catholic Church."

Finding a democratic, bottom-up frame for social Catholicism preoccupied the Center Party. It struggled with German regionalism. Bavarian Catholics did not join the party till 1894 then split away again in 1920. The Center voted for the enabling law in 1933, which opened the path to a Nazi dictatorship. Conservative Christians in Germany found a liberal-democratic political home only after 1945 in a new center-right party that allied Catholics and Protestants.

Unlike Lamennais and Ketteler, John Henry Cardinal Newman (1801–90) was little engaged in the world around him. An Oxford-educated banker's son, he looked on Christianity more as a spiritual guide than a social presence. Newman, like Friedrich Schleiermacher and Søren Kierkegaard, treated faith as the make-or-break element of a person's life, not a friendly helping hand or psychic adjunct that might be supplied in other ways.

Newman saw the Christian task as maintaining "religion in an anarchical world." Democracy he thought "dreadful," Whigs to his mind were "vermin," and liberalism was fated to remain a minority creed of interfering busybodies. Not all conservatives felt Newman's alarm at the condition of society, but most shared his scorn for liberals together with his conviction that society needed a religious faith, although they might not have put the point with Napoleon's bluntness: "Society cannot exist without unequal possessions and inequality of possessions cannot subsist without religion." Conservatives as a rule would still agree that a sound, shared religion was essential for social order. The problem was, which religion? Christianity had many confessions. Each confession had various traditions, self-understandings, and philosophical defenses. For a worldly, practical-minded conservative, the confessional choice was secondary; any familiar creed that was widely accepted and undisruptive would do. For Newman, as for many believers, to answer the question of what faith to follow in terms of social utility was frivolous. The matter of choice—if it was a choice—Newman found acute. His life became a search for a religious home, which proceeded as a series of encounters, rejections, and further searches. His life was equally a search for the religious intellectual's role in a rapidly secularizing culture.

Newman searched by exclusion. He grew up in a period when science and philosophy were advancing side by side with a reawakened enthusiasm for religion. Unfamiliar forms of common worship and Christian belonging showed themselves on both sides of the Atlantic. Some came from Pietism, Quakerism, Methodism, and other post-clerical offspring of the seventeenth and eighteenth centuries. Others were new. The common element in these evangelical awakenings was emphasis on religious feeling and personal conviction rather than on doctrine and scripture. From secular liberals, religious awakening tended to provoke pity or disregard. To conventional believers, evangelicals were little better than anarchists. In 1807 Sydney Smith called them "one general conspiracy against common sense and rational orthodox Christianity." Smith took the religious awakening of his time for a Second Coming of sixteenth-century Puritanism, which Hooker had seen, along with Roman Catholicism, as an enemy of the Elizabethan religious settlement.

Among philosophers, Schleiermacher was the revival's philosopher of encouragement and calm, Kierkegaard of struggle and anxiety. Newman had an ear for both registers. In his discontent with orthodox Anglicanism, Newman was first attracted to evangelical Christianity of an intellectualized kind but came to look on it as a step toward renewed doubt and overpersonal judgment. Biblical criticism, on the other hand, had shaken Protestant attachment to scripture and, besides, no book could "make a stand against the wild, living intellect of man." Instead, Newman turned to a kind of creedal archaeology, seeking to recover Christianity's spiritual core by studying its earliest teachings. He argued for such an approach in *Tracts for the Times* (1833–41), which drew a large following in Oxford, where he was an Anglican priest.

That approach, too, soon disappointed Newman. To fortify faith amid modern doubt, what was needed, he decided, was not a pure, ancient source, untroubled by later doctrine and interpretation, but an unchallenged present-day authority. In 1845, he became a Roman Catholic—later describing the steps of his personal conversion in *Apologia pro vita sua* (1864)—when stung by the charge that, like Napoleon, he was calling cynically for unreflective faith because it was useful.

Newman gave a more philosophical defense of "fideism" in *The Grammar of Assent* (1870). Fideism, loosely, was the view that it was reasonable for a person to accept a claim of great moment in their lives when the weight of evidence on either side was evenly balanced or unclear. In greater argumentative detail, Newman's essay echoed Lamennais's attack on indifferentism.

Politically, Newman moved from die-hard Toryism to social-minded, Catholic paternalism. Humanity, in his view, was corrupt and society imperfect; not even a society of good Christians would be just. Society could nevertheless be stable and healthy provided it shared a religion. A common faith would bind society, enabling authority to govern by consent. Of four ways to govern, which he described in an essay, "Who's to Blame?" (1855)—"subordination" (authoritarianism), "participation" (mass democracy), "delegation" (a bureaucratic variant of the first), and "co-ordination"—Newman preferred the last. In the spirit of European corporatism, Newman pictured a social union that would reconcile the classes, offering protections and liberties under a single, overarching belief.

The Catholic Church he encountered in Rome disappointed him. A sympathetic philosopher, Anthony Kenny, wrote that Newman spent the first half of his life trying to persuade the Church of England to be more like the Church of Rome, and the second half wishing that Roman Catholics were more like Anglicans. Newman had hoped to find in Rome a faith that was more believed in, more authoritative. He found one that was more born into, more taken for granted, and, despite its claims to authority, less obeyed.

Orestes Brownson (1803–76) faced an American version of Newman's difficulties with a universal church that was not the leading church of his homeland. As a Catholic exponent of faith-based Americanism, Brownson offered a defense against Protestant prejudice. He was also a defender of working people, and a conservative who understood freedom for government and citizen alike as obedience to just laws. He began as Lamennais ended, a passionate defender of the working classes, but he abandoned progressive politics and like Newman turned to accept the Roman church. Brownson became a Catholic a year before Newman (1844) and like him wrote an autobiography of his spiritual journey.

Born on a Vermont farm, Brownson was given up to Calvinist neighbors for adoption as a six-year-old when his mother died. The gloom of his adoptive home repelled him, and as a young man he fell under the spell of Channing and the Unitarians. Self-taught, Brownson read voraciously, threw himself into intellectual life, and founded the *Boston Quarterly Review*. He took the Whigs as hypocritical elitists and the middle classes for whom they spoke as enemies of working people. The new power was industrial capital, and although Southern slavery was abhorrent, it was less cruel on its sufferers than Northern free labor, as he wrote in "The Laboring Classes" (July 1840). Soon after, Brownson abandoned all confidence in progressive politics. Any attempt at sweeping reform of society was hubristic, a vain human attempt to "be as gods." Order and acceptance, not carping and disruption, were required in society. Protestantism had too many sects. Only Catholicism offered the coherence needed. The verve that he had shown against capitalist Whigs Brownson deployed against Protestants, Transcendentalists, individualists, nihilists, and all other "ists" flawed by the primal stain of liberalism.

Brownson took himself in that anti-liberal regard for a conservative, which in a large sense he was, although his political opinions were moderate and his instincts conciliatory. Anti-Catholic feeling had burst out in the United States as the number of Catholics rose from the 1820s to the 1840s, swollen by Irish and Rhineland immigrants. A vein of prejudice among the Protestant majority remained strong. In *The American Republic* (1865), Brownson hoped to show suspicious Americans that good citizens could be Catholics. At the same time, he hoped to persuade a defensive, tradition-bound church that Catholics could be good Americans. Brownson spoke up for religious freedom, against religious prejudice on all sides, and for the separation of church and state. The Vatican repaid him and his follower Isaac Hecker, editor of the *Catholic World*, by denouncing "Americanism" as an error in a letter to American bishops (1899).

Although he sided with religious liberals in his church, Brownson in *The American Republic* (1865) criticized political liberalism for misrepresenting freedom and society. Freedom, for government and citizen alike, was obedience to just laws. Society was not a compact but "an organism, and individuals live in its life as well as it in theirs." Brownson was conservative in seeking to temper democratic liberalism by beneficent moral guidance. A Catholic exponent of faith-based Americanism offered as defense against Protestant prejudice, he spoke for a paternalist social Christianity, then emerging also in Europe.

Charles Hodge (1797–1878) was a Presbyterian theologian at Princeton Theological Seminary who upheld scripture as the word of God and defended a strict, pessimistic Calvinism that inspired twentieth-century Fundamentalists and conservative Evangelicals. Although learned in German biblical criticism and philosophy, Hodge invoked neither Kantian rationalism, Hegelian metaphysics, nor Schleiermacher's religion of feeling. He defended his strict theology by appealing to intuition and common sense, for which, in ways that might have surprised them, he cited thinkers of the Scottish Enlightenment. Firmly and courteously, he led the Old School of Presbyterians in their disputes with their New School coreligionists in controversies of the day. Darwinism, in Hodge's view, equated to atheism. He opposed religious revivalism and hung back from condemning slavery. Revivalism, whether in the radical, popular vision of the abolitionist Charles Finney (1792–1875) or the moderate, upper-crust gospel of William Ellery Channing (1780–42), was for Hodge a worldly, that is, ungodly, campaign of moral uplift and self-improvement.

Cast in theological terms, revivalism stressed the Christian believer's capacity to end spiritual anxiety and redeem their life by a free embrace of faith. Hodge's bleaker Calvinism denied people's control over the time and means of their salvation. In secular terms, Hodge turned his back on the American gospel of self-reliance, with its hopeful promise of self-improvement. He accepted both Lutheran "individualism" (lone believers answer directly to God) and "corporate solidarity" (because of Adam, we are all sinners; because of Christ, we may all be saved). A holder of slaves, Hodge took the institution as being biblically justified, but he decried Southern mistreatment of slaves and found the laws that denied them schooling abhorrent. All the same, Hodge, a strong nationalist, backed the Union in the Civil War. The faithless kind of nation that the United States must not become was typified for him by France, where, as Hodge pronounced (1852), "the intelligent part of the population have no religion and the religious part no intelligence." Hodge wanted a conservative religious orthodoxy, but one with the intellectual weaponry to defend itself. Over his long career at Princeton Seminary, Hodge taught, it was calculated, more than three thousand students.

If a feel for Hodge's mental climate is difficult to grasp for postreligious minds with no patience for biblical disputation, the fictional imagination can fill the gap. A contemporary writer who powerfully evoked the American Calvinist mind was Nathaniel Hawthorne. His novels and allegorical tales offered a reimagination of the Puritan element in American thought, with its assurance of human depravity and scorn for ameliorative hope. Hawthorne was an anti-Whig by experience and conviction. In Boston, he was pushed out of his government career as a Democrat, and he believed neither in liberal progress nor the abolitionist cause. A sense of sin and folly pervaded his work. Every new society, a Hawthorne character intoned, soon found itself needing a prison and a graveyard. His popular allegory "The Earth's Holocaust" (1844) mocked evangelical hopes for this-worldly reform of imperfect humankind. *The Blithedale Romance* (1852) satirized the Fourierist commune at Brook Farm, which he helped pay for and where he briefly lived. *The Scarlet Letter* (1850) posed, without resolving, Puritanism's abiding conflict between personal conscience and social shame. In their different modes, Hodge and Hawthorne were conservative counterinstances to the callow picture of the early American national spirit as liberal, democratic, and optimistic.

Those several conservative thinkers showed contrasting ways of finding a modern place for religious faith in public argument. Three spoke to religion in politics. Lamennais chose the personal pursuit of Christian social ideals in defiance of clerical authority. Ketteler chose the clerical pursuit of similar ideals from a framework of church authority, which he also sought to defend against the state. Brownson argued that a modern democracy needed the guidance of a universal morality.

The other two spoke to a contest of right and left within religion. Against religious liberals and modernists, Newman sought to show the reasonableness of accepting an unreasoned faith together with the authority of a hierarchic church. Against similar opposition among liberal-minded coreligionists, Hodge asserted the authority of scripture, as strictly understood by authoritative interpreters. Neither won an opening for papal or biblical reasons in public argument. Both aimed to create secure cognitive spaces for thoughtful believers in a skeptical, science-minded culture.

All five were conservative in a broad sense. Negatively, they thought political liberalism was inadequate as public morality and liberals were too complacent about the ills of modern society. Positively, they sought to isolate and hold on to what mattered in human life amid the churn of capitalist progress, an endeavor commonly cast as rescuing (high) spiritual values from (low) material preoccupations. In doctrinal terms, that meant protecting faith from science and, if possible, supernaturalism from naturalism, or at any rate from versions of naturalism that left little or no room for religion. These thinkers wanted the intellectual and religious worlds to reinforce each other in the cause of morality and social order. Newman wanted "the intellectual layman to be religious and the devout ecclesiastic to be intellectual." Hodge believed that "liberty can exist only on the foundation of intelligence and religion."

iv. Conservatism's Need for Intellectuals: Coleridge's Clerisy

Neither Newman nor Hodge were directly engaged in politics, and neither spoke nationally. Newman embraced a universal church. Hodge spoke for the conservative side of one of the many large American confessions. It fell to the poet Coleridge to call in national politics for the creation and nurture of a figure that barely existed in their lives but which has achieved recognition and authority in ours: the conservative intellectual.

The work in which Samuel Taylor Coleridge (1772–1834) focused his many political thoughts was *On the Constitution of Church and State* (1830). Its occasion was the Catholic emancipation act (April 1829). Coleridge was against granting Catholics in Britain civil rights, partly on the old grounds that Catholics owed allegiance to a foreign power (the Vatican) and partly on the odd grounds that its priests were celibate. Despite the topical context, both of the book's main points were of general interest for conservative thought. One was familiar among Romantic writers distressed by the social and human costs of early industrial capitalism, which was more advanced in Britain than elsewhere. The other was an original proposal of Coleridge's own.

Coleridge was among the poets and writers who took their cultural distance from liberal modernity by turning to the past and to the right. They included other radicals turned conservative: Wordsworth, the ex-enthusiast for the French Revolution with whom Coleridge had published their manifesto-anthology, *Lyrical Ballads* (1798), and Southey, now a contributor to the Tory *Quarterly Review* and poet laureate, with whom Coleridge had once hoped to start a Utopian commune in Pennsylvania. They also included William Cobbett, a people's Tory, who loved the country and the crown but hated upstart trade, as well as the courtiers, moneymen, and "borough-mongers" (bought politicians) who fed off "the Wen" (London). Among them, too, was the historian Thomas Carlyle. He published his attack on a spiritless, mechanical age, *Signs of the Times*, in the same year as Coleridge's *Constitution* and became liberal society's conservative scourge.

What these writers shared was a roster of dismay at the cultural failings of liberal capitalism: an atomistic, one-dimensional philosophy handed down from Locke and Newton, a pitiful idea of happiness as material prosperity and a popular culture that was emerging not, as hoped for, in a natural-grown rural idyll or in deference to excellence and great men, but as something urban, coarse, and manipulable. Anxieties of this kind, it will be seen, enjoyed a long life in the conservative tradition. They had counterparts, particularly in Germany, of the more philosophic or academic kind—Müller, Rehberg, as noted—but they were strongest in Britain, where the urban-industrial upheavals of liberal modernity came earliest. The worries ran through Coleridge's copious writing and table talk, which he put into political shape in *Constitution*.

Coleridge saw a "wretchedness of division" in British society and regretted the lost harmony of life, which was imagined to have prevailed before modern times. A responsible say in government required property, it was true, but in industrial capitalism, Coleridge feared an "overbalance of commercial spirit." Its boisterous energies required restraint by the landed interest, that is, oversight of the Commons by the Lords. Coleridge dressed up those social and institutional thoughts in an Anglicized vocabulary of contrast-collapsing German idealism that he had picked up in Göttingen.

To grasp a thing's nature, you had to understand its "Idea," its aim or end. The aim of a state or nation—Coleridge did not carefully distinguish them—was to become constitutional, that is, established, settled, accepted. A constitution was not a contract among people of the day; rather, like a living organism grown over time, a constitution balanced a nation's competing inner forces. Those forces were permanence (which strove to remain) and progression (which pushed forward). Permanence, in Britain, could be found in landed property and farming, progression in commerce. The "barons" spoke for the first in the Lords. They assured political stability. The "franklins and burgesses," or in postmedieval terms, commoners or middle classes, spoke for progression in the Commons. They ensured prosperity and personal freedoms. As in Hegel's system, the crown represented the higher unity of the state, which reconciled the interests. Hiding in the verbosity was an accurate but unoriginal thumbnail sketch of Britain's oligarchic institutions.

Coleridge's second point in *Constitution* was more telling. A conservative modern society, Coleridge went on, required more than barons and franklins to hold it together: it needed a common civic creed that could be articulated and propagated by conservative intellectuals. Creed and intellectuals would together form a "clerisy or national church." Its purpose would be to curb the dangers of liberal society—undue freedom and ethical diversity—as well as the cultural coarsening of mass democracy.

Coleridge's neologism, "clerisy," was suggestive. Its intellectuals would, he hoped, have the tutorial authority of the old clergy without (necessarily) their priestly status or religious doctrines. They would be neither clerical nor lay but—more reconciliation of opposites—in between. Some would be "fountain-heads of the humanities," tending and enlarging knowledge. Others would be teachers, spread throughout the nation to leave no part without "a resident guide, guardian and instructor." The teacher (a Burkean touch), would "bind the present with the past" and so "connect the present with the future." The nation was to pay for this "permanent class or order" out of the "nationality," money set aside for public purposes; that is, in plain language, out of taxes. The creed would be broad and varied but coherent enough to serve as a unifying force, like a religious faith, but without divisive, doctrinal content.

More a conservative of reconciliation than resistance, Coleridge recognized the inevitability of social change. He allowed that society might progress but wanted broad education and high cultural standards to push progress in a chosen direction, but not toward civilized "polish" (which served to mask the bad behavior of dissolute eighteenth-century nobs) nor toward efficiency and comfort (the higher hopes of the middle classes). Coleridge spoke, as he saw it, for a more humane and more moral culture, without which society would be "neither permanent nor progressive."

Hazlitt wrote of Coleridge that there was no subject on which he did not touch and none on which he rested. His *Constitution* raised other topics, including education. Was the clerisy to be educational or political? It should be both, Coleridge thought. Preserving a humane education in technical and instrumental times preoccupied Newman, who struggled without success to instill values of the kind in the curriculum as the rector of a new Catholic university in Dublin. It concerned Matthew Arnold in *Culture and Anarchy* (1869), as it continued to preoccupy the right's cultural critics of liberal modernity deep into the twentieth century, with brave latecomers to the cause in our own times. Throughout, the critics had to ask themselves, "Who or what are we fighting for?" The question will recur when more recent cultural critics of the right are discussed later, notably T. S. Eliot, the American neoconservatives, and Scruton. The true and obvious answer to the question was that they were fighting to keep and propagate high cultural values. For that, however, they had to struggle in society for speaking time and cultural attention.

Coleridge did his best to hide the point in a cloud of words, but he had seen clearly that conservatives were in a contest of ideas and that, in a modern society, the contest would need institutions and money. Anticipating the idea of "soft power," Coleridge threw in an argument that he hoped might appeal to taxpayers. A clerisy would "secure for the nation, if not a superiority over the neighbouring states, yet an equality at least, in that character of general civilization, which equally with, or rather more than, fleets, armies, and revenue, forms the ground of its defensive and offensive power."

Mill grasped Coleridge's point. With Jeremy Bentham, he took Coleridge for one of "the two seminal minds of the age." Each, Mill wrote in 1840, was "a great questioner of things established," only each was asking a different question. Bentham asked of traditional opinion. "Is it true?" Coleridge asked. "What is the meaning of it?" Received opinion to Bentham was a sign of the selfish interests of aristocracy, priests, or lawyers. To Coleridge, it was a sign of "struggle to express in words something that had reality for them" and that, by implication, should be preserved. Politics aside, Mill saw Coleridge as a fellow spirit in his own attempt to humanize Benthamism. The phrase in *On Liberty* with which Mill hoped to open up Bentham's narrow idea of human happiness as enjoyment of pleasure and avoidance of pain—"the permanent interests of man as a progressive being"—owed much to Coleridge.

How conservative was Coleridge? He began as a Unitarian radical, an enthusiast for the French Revolution, a would-be Utopian, and a campaigner against Britain's slave trade, as well as an opponent of Britain's taste for foreign wars. He ended a defender of Britain's religious and political institutions as they appeared in the 1820s, just as they were about to change for good. He was abstract, speculative, and impractical. He lacked skepticism about political knowledge, but that was perhaps because he knew so little of politics and politicians. A letter of his in 1807 to Lord Liverpool urging the Tory prime minister to lead a campaign against empiricism and other philosophical errors met understandable bafflement. Like Burke, Coleridge had undemocratic liberal leanings toward personal liberties—for men, that is, of certain standing. Less liberally, he wanted a national creed and common morality. Rather than representation one by one, he favored, like German conservatives of the time, representation by interests or by "estates," which he did not greatly distinguish. Both Coleridge's Burkean view of the constitution as an "organic" growth and his German idealist view of it as the visible form of the state's "Idea," or purposes, was conservative (because anti-progressive) in what it silently denied: the existence of a state machine that might serve liberal or Utilitarian goals.

v. Against Liberal Individualism: Stephen, Gierke, and Bradley

If conservatives took liberalism as their partisan foe, they treated individualism as their political opponents' great error of principle. But what error was that? A disengagement from society and withdrawal to private networks? Alexis de Tocqueville thought he had spotted something of the kind in American society, describing individualism in 1840 as "a mature and calm feeling, which disposes each member of the community to sever himself from the mass of his fellow-creatures, and to draw apart with his family and friends." An unpatriotic disengagement from duties to the nation? The conservative Whig Henry Clay implied as much when asking the Senate in July 1850: "What is an individual man? An atom, almost invisible without a magnifying glass.... Shall a being so small, so petty, so fleeting, so evanescent, oppose itself to the onward march of a great nation, to subsists for ages and ages to come?" Or was individualism an egoistic withdrawal from community and civility themselves? So Frédéric Le Play, the French social thinker suggested in 1864: "Wherever individualism comes to dominate social relations, people rapidly descend to barbarism."

The term "individualism" had no settled use. As an innocuous moral shorthand, it picked out four profound and well-attested convictions with long pedigrees in the common tradition. First of all, morally speaking, people mattered as people, not as men or women, Jews, Christians, or Muslims, blacks or whites, rich or poor. Nobody went naked in society. Everyone had to wear something. Their particular social clothes, however, were morally irrelevant. Second, everyone mattered equally. If social clothing was morally irrelevant, nobody could properly be excluded from society's concern, denied its protections, or exempted from its demands. Third, everyone had a sphere of privacy that was no one else's business and on which neither state nor society might intrude. And fourth, everyone had in them seeds of capability and personal growth, which could not be left untended without moral loss.

Calling those moral claims "individualist" was in one way harmless, although "humanist" was a less contentious, more informative label. Those moral convictions concerned the proper treatment of human beings, whoever they were. Their point was universality (what was due to anyone), not singleness, separation, or isolation (how any one person differed from another or from some larger whole). Unlike the label "individualist," the label "humanist" carried no suggestion of setting one person against others. Without denying people's proud, "don't touch me" sense of distinctiveness, those four moral convictions bore on what each person had in common. They aimed to shield people from morally irrelevant hierarchies, categorizations, discriminations, and neglect. The convictions, furthermore, were "humanist" in concerning the human person rather than non-people such as transcendental entities, other animal species, or the planet. They were singular and not, or not directly, about the respect due to collections of people such as nations, tribes, or social classes. The label "individualist," with its tangle of misleading, prejudicial associations stuck nevertheless and was freely used by conservatives in various contexts to berate liberals.

Thrown into politics, those four moral claims—dignity, equality, privacy, and self-development—were grafted to disputed theories about how people belonged in society—indeed, how any one person belonged in larger groupings or endeavors. As a doctrine of method, thought up as the study of society and economics was seriously underway, individualist theory gave people, one by one, a constitutive or explanatory primacy. It pictured the human person, complete with his or her aims and capacities, as abstract in the sense of detachable, uprootable, and transportable—indeed, to some extent as anonymous and interchangeable. Such was the picture of people handed down to political liberalism by Benthamite Utilitarianism. It was not the only philosophical picture that liberalism could call on. Nevertheless, by the mid-nineteenth century that "individualist" picture was commonly taken to be one that liberals embraced and that their outlook needed. Lecturing at Harvard (1898), the British constitutionalist A. V. Dicey made the dependence, in effect, an equivalence: "Benthamite individualism . . . in accordance with popular phraseology, may often be conveniently called liberalism."

Conservative critics had acquired a target in what, with some caricature, could be treated as liberalism's house philosophy: a loose mix of empiricist methodology, associationist psychology, and Utilitarian ethics. The philosophy started with particulars in the hope of moving toward larger wholes—explanations in science, communities in history, normative unities in morals. Science accumulated singular facts. History recorded the singular acts of men and women, not larger movements or forces. Ethics attended to the satisfactions of people singly, not in groups. It drew force from people's needs and choices, counted one by one. To conservative critics, that picture of human life and society was false. Not because it was all false, but because it started in the wrong place. It gave the questioner—any questioner of social customs and norms—a kind of argumentative primacy, allowing them to ask of society and demand an answer to the question, "What are these norms and customs to *me*?"

Although three representative thinkers—Stephen, Gierke, and Bradley—were all in some sense anti-individualist, their preoccupations were different. Stephen sought to defend the authority of social convention. Against Mill, he insisted on the primacy of conformity over individuality. Stephen was less concerned with the constitution of society or the sources of value. Gierke aimed to counter a picture of law and the state that took them to speak directly to citizens singly, without the intermediaries of civil society. Law and the state, for Gierke, had grown up out of "estates,, "corporations," and other collective bodies. Those mid-level collectivities had their own rights and opinions that could not be parsed into the rights and opinions of their several members. Bradley, a pure philosopher, was concerned by the content and character of morality's claims on us. Morality's content, for Bradley, was social. Detached from society, people lost anchorage for their duties. Morality, on the other hand, had a character found everywhere. Among morality's marks was a binding authority on people one by one. Was Bradley anti-individualist or individualist? Despite a misleading reputation as a philosopher of communitarianism, he was both and neither. Stephen was the most openly political, Bradley the least, with Gierke, an early liberal who ended as a German conservative, in between.

In family terms, James Fitzjames Stephen (1829–94) was a conservative sport in a liberal milieu. The family spirit on both sides was evangelical Victorian reform. His maternal grandfather was vicar of Clapham and Unitarian anchor of the antislavery movement. His father, a colonial civil servant, had helped draft the abolition of slavery in the British Empire, in 1833. As stars in the Bloomsbury firmament, his nieces Vanessa Bell and Virginia Woolf were living reproof to Stephen's antique understanding of gender.

Politically, Stephen exemplified the growing alliance between conservatives and right-wing liberals, both alarmed by the pressures of democracy. Though no friend of economic democracy (a topic of chapter 6), Stephen was most exercised by ethical and cultural democracy. The location of political wisdom had shifted in conservative minds. For Burke, people—meaning society's elites—were not as wise as custom or tradition. For Stephen, people—that is, the masses—were not as wise as the elites.

In argument, he was bullish. At university, where Stephen was nicknamed "the Gruffian," he charmed friends and teachers but barely scraped a degree and went to the bar, where he also failed to shine. Elevated in time to a judgeship, he served in India from 1869 to 1872. Like Mill, he believed that liberal standards served Indian people better than prevailing customs and, in that spirit, established caste-blind rules of evidence. On the bench again in Britain, contentious judgments in notable murder trials and declining health led to Stephen's removal. After striking his head on the handle of a water pump, he became mentally unstable and was declared legally insane.

Stephen's main earnings were from journalism, chiefly his writings for the conservative weekly founded by Salisbury's brother-in-law, the *Saturday Review*. Known for its derisive tone and scorn for liberal humbug as the *Saturday Reviler*, the publication was a perfect outlet for Stephen, who claimed to sense the popular pulse better than did improving liberals. Aping Bentham's disregard for high taste, he boasted that *Robinson Crusoe* was his favorite book. Stephen might be remembered only as a Victorian eccentric but for his outstanding talent as a right-wing controversialist. Like the critics of the French Revolution, Stephen fed the conservative cause with simple but effective weapons in public argument. Neither topical nor philosophical, they were general enough to be reusable but not so elevated as to leave partisan politics altogether. They were also apt for the times in that they skirted earlier agonies of faith and science. Stephen appealed to a secular conservatism happy to treat faith as socially useful but not intellectually necessary.

For Nietzsche, customary morality was an unreasoned protection thrown up by the weak against the strong. For Stephen, it was an unreasoned tool for the strong to control the weak. On that instrumental view, the task of morality was prohibition backed by threat. "You ought not to do x," Stephen claimed, should be taken to mean that if you did x, "God will damn you, man will hang you if he can catch you and hate you if he cannot, and you . . . will hate yourself." The content of morality came from society; that is, what was prohibited came from social convention, which might or might not be encoded in a religious creed. Law's task, as the promoter of society's good—order and stability— was to uphold conventional morality, not try to improve it or ask if it was true. Conscience and a sense of duty were useful for social order, but neither were enough on their own. The main task fell to law— above all, criminal law. It was to be rationalized and modernized but not weakened.

Stephen feared that a "second orthodoxy" of liberal pieties was softening educated opinion and distracting it from its proper task of social control. His most concentrated attack came in *Liberty, Equality, Fraternity* (1873), which he wrote on the ship home from India. Its immediate target was Mill's *On Liberty*. Like Mill, Stephen was a Utilitarian. Good and bad were to be gauged socially, by benefit or harm to "the greatest number." From a shared starting point, Stephen reached opposite conclusions. Although both feared democratic society, Mill hoped for social order and moral progress through education, whereas Stephen did not believe in social progress and looked to moral order from criminal law.

The order on which society depended required moral restraint. There would, however, always be "an enormous mass of bad and indifferent people," whose "depth of moral failings" could be checked only by compulsion. Because people were not much improvable, liberal faith in progress rested on delusion. Because people were not equal, hopes for democratic sovereignty were blind: "Wise and good men ought to rule over foolish and bad." Because people were not fraternal but partial, "the religion of humanity" was a fraud. Stephen dismissed or restricted each of Mill's watchwords in turn. There was "a vast number of matters in respect of which men ought not to be free." People were "fundamentally unequal" and they were "not brothers at all."

In courtroom fashion, Stephen bored away at weaknesses in Mill's proscription of coercive interference with personal liberty, which Mill himself recognized and had sought to patch. Society had no say over personal conduct, Mill insisted, unless it harmed others. To that "harm principle," Stephen made familiar objections. The distinction between harm to self and others was unstable. Besides, Mill gave no usable gauge for the wrong of coercion or the worth of liberty. Mill's arguments for free speech either failed or clashed with his utilitarian principles. Nor was Stephen persuaded by Mill's "eulogies to individuality." Variety was not in itself useful. To the extent that it had value, individuality required not liberty but discipline and inhibition. Replaying a fear of Tocqueville's about the leveling effects of democracy, Stephen wrote that, given "social macadamisation," liberty for all sapped individuality.

Equality was required, but only in the legal sense of treating like cases alike and applying the law person-blind. In any other sense, people were and would remain unequal. Women were weak and should be kept under the "captainship" of men. An adequate social order could endure only if people kept to four rules: commit no crime, inflict no wrong, do your duty, and keep what you can for you and yours. Such an order did not require equality in any large sense. There was no harm to inequality in itself. Elites were often kinder to the poor than were egalitarians. An equal say for each in politics often led, in practice, to despotism: the result of cutting up political power "into little bits is simply that the man who can sweep them into one heap will govern the rest."

Fraternity was a false hope resting on neglect of the facts. There would always be enmity between classes. People would never agree about the content of happiness. In the human makeup, altruism was undersupplied. Social order depended not on mutual respect, still less on a sense of brotherhood, but on fear of punishment, either in hell or in this life.

Here in blunt terms was a modern moral conservative catechism. To dismiss Stephen's views as those of an unsubtle, combative judge is to see them from too narrow an angle. Stephen is better seen as a bridge between Maistre and present-day "moral conservatives." Maistre, they, and Stephen all laid weight on society's sanction—clear standards, exemplary punishment, the infliction of shame as vital for social health and social order. Moral conservatives are less extreme and more hopeful about improvement from education in sustaining social order. They have in reserve, if opinion swings their way and constitutional protections allow, the instrument that Stephen foregrounded, criminal law.

The work of Otto von Gierke (1841–1921) is a reminder that whereas the first defenders of the modern state were efficiency-minded, nation-building liberals, its first opponents were community-minded conservatives with local or sectional loyalties. Gierke's scholarly career as a historian of German law may be taken as an attempt to vindicate that second view. In distinguishing the two sides, one divisive issue was how the authority of the state and its laws worked. Did laws operate directly on citizens, one by one? Or did law work through intermediary bodies? To schematize, liberals tended to want a unified national market with uniform laws under a single, sovereign authority. Conservatives on the whole had for various reasons resisted such a power. They had hoped to defend the rights and opinions of collectivities and other midway authorities that existed in between state and citizens. Those might be customary social "estates," with their powers and privileges, or they might be old regions that had kept a degree of autonomy.

A higher-order disagreement framed in "individualist" versus "collectivist" terms was about the constitution of society. Was society a derivative assemblage of independent people, taking its moral powers from them (the individualist view)? Or was it a self-standing community of socially dependent people with moral powers of its own (the collectivist view)? The individualist team claimed Locke, Hugo Grotius, and Kant as intellectual guides, whereas the collectivists sought forebears in medieval traditions and Hegel. Gierke, in those terms, was a collectivist.

Collectivists faced in turn a telling further question. Was society one community or composed itself of subcommunities? That is, was society unicellular or multicellular? Gierke thought society was multicellular. Together with the modern state and its laws, a national society had emerged out of many independent and long-standing communities. His answer blended liberal and conservative concerns. It was conservative in insisting on respect for the rights and opinions of intermediary bodies between the citizen and the modern state. Gierke's understanding drew notably on the German experience of scattered and overlapping sovereignties. The modern state to his mind did not link sovereignty and people with nothing between. That picture, popular in the liberal canon, was conceptually and historically wrong. The modern state had emerged gradually as lower instances and local powers merged or blurred. Gierke was liberal in insisting on the plural, diverse character of society's many groupings.

In party-political terms, Gierke began as a liberal. By unification, he had become a fervent German nationalist. He described an epiphany on Unter den Linden in Berlin (July 1870), when he felt an overpowering sense of oneness with a patriotic crowd that had gathered in anticipation of the war about to start with France. In his later writing, Germanness and the exceptional character of its law and history came more to the fore. In a passionate address after Germany's defeat in a second

war (1919), Gierke spoke of "the German idea of the state." Shortly before his death, he joined the new German National People's Party
(DNVP). That "Germanizing" of his thought was not inevitable. His
British champion and translator, Frederick Maitland, heard Gierke's
larger message—take seriously the life and being of intermediary bodies—
as transportable and not rooted in German soil.

The character of corporations turned on how they came to be and
whether they had rights of their own, independently of their members.
A view inherited from Roman law was that corporations were legal
fictions—an idea crafted by Italian papal lawyers in the fourteenth
century during the long quarrel with the German empire. As legal fictions, corporations came into being only when recognized by the law.
Gierke took the opposite view. Corporations grew up on their own. The
Romanist conception, he argued, confused legal recognition with independent life. With that in mind, Gierke rejected a leading implication
of the legal-fiction view: that if they were fictions, corporations had no
actual personality, aims, or rights of their own. They were treated as if
they had only for legal purposes. No, Gierke held, corporations were
entities on their own, with personality, aims, and rights. As to the character of law, the Roman tradition made it the will of the sovereign. That
was the top-down view, which was favored by German liberals. Gierke
took a bottom-up view. Law had grown from custom. The difference, in
what at the time struck nonparticipants as a chiefly scholastic matter,
became evident in disputes over harmonization and codification of German law after 1870. The National Liberals wanted a uniform law that
would defend property and suit a vigorous capitalist economy, whereas
Gierke and other conservatives opposed early drafts of the code, which,
they believed, failed to protect customary rights.

In his *History of the Law of Fellowship* (1868–1913), known in English
as *The German Law of Associations*, Gierke provided a massive survey of
the life and character of many German "collective" bodies since the early
Middle Ages. His running presumption was that such bodies had personality and moral value of their own, independent of their members.
From the great mass of material, several thematic elements stood out.
One was variety. Gierke described guilds, towns, leagues, and estates.

Another was change. Guilds, as Gierke described them, became corrupt over time, as membership and offices became hereditary and tradeable. Towns, at first more equal in their government, became hierarchical as urban "aristocracies" and class-consciousness emerged. Gierke also told a sweeping historical story, in the Hegelian or Marxist manner, from before Charlemagne to the nineteenth century. The running theme was competition between *Genossenschaft* (fellowship) and *Herrschaft* (lordship). Fellowship was strong before 800, weak under feudalism, strong in the Peasant's Revolt (1525), weak under absolutism (1525–1806), and strong again in the nineteenth century, when Gierke was thinking of trade unions (the left) and agrarian leagues (the right).

On Gierke's account, democratic representation did not emerge from representation by estates. It was modern. In a Burkean echo, Gierke wrote of the representative speaking not for his constituents but "for the whole people." Elsewhere, in language easily twisted into populism, he spoke of representative government expressing "the spirit of the people." More innocently, Gierke could be heard as talking simply about public opinion.

The lessons of Gierke's work for conservatism were mixed. He was against an overmighty modern state. His "multicellular" society was alive with intermediary bodies of many kinds: associations, guilds, corporations, unions. In both regards, he might be thought to be taking civil society's side against what critics of liberal modernity have often viewed as twin enemies: the all-suffocating state and the isolated, asocial liberal citizen. But Gierke said more than that. For him, the authority of nation and people rose above that of state, society, and individual. That conservative, anti-individualistic outlook pointed two ways. It could be pressed either toward liberal pluralism and diversity, or toward an illiberal holism.

In Britain, F. H. Bradley (1846–1924) was a leading thinker of late nineteenth-century British idealism, a metaphysical tradition that owed more to Kant, Hegel, and other German thinkers than to British forebears. Its animating core was suspicion of philosophy's common binary choices and a determination to reconcile its familiar oppositions: parts and whole, mind and world, self and community. Holistic idealism of the kind never found a settled home in Britain, and the reputation of Bradley's ethical and social thought suffered as a consequence.

Contrary to appearances, Bradley's aim in his work *Ethical Studies* (1876) was to rescue our commonsense beliefs about morality from competing philosophical exaggerations. We recognized that we were responsible for our actions. We thought it was we who initiated action, not outside forces. We believed we made free choices without imagining we had magical powers. We sought pleasure, but not for pleasure's sake, and did our duty, but not for duty's sake. Society showed us our duties. If we thought back to how, as children, we were inducted into morality, it was hard to see conscience and duty otherwise. Such were our intuitive convictions, which by selecting and tidying much philosophy falsified. A better psychological grasp of ethics was needed, Bradley thought. But ethical thinking in Britain and America was about to circle away from psychology, as it was in logic.

Yet Bradley's own intimation about how such a psychology of morals might work sounded far from commonsensical. Satisfaction, on Bradley's account, was not a relation (like, for example, possession) between persons and what they desired, say an apple. Satisfaction, rather, was the closing of a gap between distinct thoughts: a person's wish and its "ideal object" (the thought-of apple). Wanting and getting an apple was a trivial case of "self-realisation," the aim in all we did. That compacted term did duty for the simplest satisfaction, in which *my* aim is realized. It did duty also for the grand, overarching aim of becoming one's ideal "self," the kind of person one would or should ideally be.

Bradley's ethical writing won him a reputation as a philosopher of conservatism. He was, for liberal critics, a "defeatist" who saw society with "Hegelian complacency" and took a "shopkeeper" view of politics. That caricature rests on a selective misreading of one passionately "communitarian" chapter in *Ethical Studies*. Its title alone gave it wing, "My Station and Its Duties." A hierarchical, tradition-minded conservative looking for ammunition against liberal carpers and improvers could find it in the chapter aplenty. "The 'individual' man, the man into whose essence his community with others does not enter, who does not include relation in his very being is, we say, a fiction." The "individualist" mistake of treating human communities as " 'collections' held together by force, illusion or contract" was not only philosophically inept but discredited by science (Bradley meant Darwinism), which had shown us as evolved from social animals. As for our higher aims in life, we should keep our place, it seemed, as there was "nothing better than my station and its duties." Aiming to better ourselves, or by implication society, was presumptuous, for all was well in the garden: "To wish to be better than the world is to be already on the threshold of immorality."

Bradley, an ailing, eccentric man, is said to have shot at stray cats from his college window. That was not his manner in philosophy. He cycled between extreme positions, exposing the failings of each, pressing on in hope of resolution. "My Station and Its Duties" ended by announcing that its communitarian, socially rooted picture of morality was in fact a failure. One reason was that the opposition between the "good" self that aligns "is" and "ought" by being as society requires and the "bad" self that pursues its own ends cannot be suppressed or blotted out. For another, any person may step outside the conventional frame and come to see that society is in "rotten condition." Bradley was acknowledging that the "individualist" who was ready to let the team down and the social critic who demanded better of society might, in circumstances, be right after all.

In the next chapter, "Ideal Morality," Bradley further disappointed anyone still hoping for a denouement. Like morality itself, we were a "self-contradiction." Meaning by "really" what is more commonly meant by "ideally," he wrote: "We never are what we feel we really are; we really are what we know we are not; and if we became what we are, we should scarcely be ourselves." That was not, gnomically expressed, the banality that we were imperfect and left much of what we wished to do or be undone. For Bradley, incompletion was the fate of all our thought. Every judgment was partial and provisional. In metaphysics, science, or morals, we aimed for completeness, which was needed as a limiting case but, as such, was unattainable. For ethics, Bradley put the point with another aphorism: "Morality aims at the cessation of that which makes it possible." That "contradictoriness" of morality, at once overdemanding and inescapable, was not to be lamented but understood. It arose from the "structure" of wanting and choosing, which was part of our human make. Perhaps, but if morality was overdemanding, it breached the appealing principle that "ought" implied "can." Morality, in that case, would be unreasonable.

Bradley briefly considered, but rejected, the thought that our wish to "realize" our ideal selves, and so achieve morality's largest demands, might be met in religious experience. That is, he gave no final defense of morality's reasonableness. As a nonbeliever, he was content to offer an entirely secular story of morality's hold on us, only to suggest that his story was incomplete.

That engagement with morality was needed for social order was a principle that belonged for most conservatives to their catechism. Such engagement, it seemed, required confidence that morality's demands were achievable, but because the demands were hard and not fully meetable, further reassurance was needed. Christian faith offered such reassurance. Christians believed in a divine redeemer, who would close the gap between the imperfect "is" and the overdemanding "ought." Christian faith promised redemption. It had promised, that is, that the "ideal self" was achievable after all. Denial of faith removed that reassurance. Hence the urgency of Christian conservatives to show the reasonableness of faith, for on faith, the reasonableness of morality turned.

A communitarian conservative troubled by the fluidity of liberal society might find attractive a line of thought that Bradley himself did not pursue. Society could be "rotten" in various ways. Bradley had dwelt on how persons could fail themselves and society by self-isolation or refusal of duty, but there was a counterpart risk in society. It could fail people by not providing stations and stability from which binding duties and a sense of themselves arose. Such a thought was to run like an arrow in the twentieth-century critique of hyperfluid modern liberal society. (It will return, for example, in the discussion of MacIntyre in part V.)

There was nothing strictly political in Bradley's view of our social embeddedness. People, after all, could be embedded in a liberal progressive society as much as in one that was traditionalist and conservative.

Nor did social rootedness mean that everyone reached the same moral or political conclusions. Observation and judgment, using the commonsense morality of his or her liberal society, could enable a moral conservative to take issue with liberalism's laxity or anomie. Wilberforce could stand up against slavery to the same extent as Shaftesbury against child labor.

To judge from his few topical writings, Bradley's nonphilosophical views were fierce and illiberal. He had no more patience than Stephen with the "the religion of humanity," which—like conservatives to this day—he took for do-good sentimentality. On punishment, Bradley wrote, "The rights of the individual are . . . today not worth serious criticism," and "Over its members the right of the moral organism is absolute." On war and peace, he wrote: "A nation must aim at the peace of mankind and at peace in the end but, as things are, this principle will in some cases justify violence, and even extermination. . . . The meek will not inherit the earth." Like others of his day, from right to left, he was worried by the "degeneracy" of the lower orders and outraged by "the right of the individual to spawn without restriction his diseased offspring." His view of gender, on show in *Aphorisms* (1930), which was published according to his wishes after his death, was primitive. None of that, however, should muddle the point that Bradley was a conservative and a philosopher rather than a philosopher of conservatism. As philosophers must, he raised, without answering, the question of the reasonableness of morality's hold on us. He did not say, as some conservatives would have him do, that morals were socially rooted. Rather, he tried to reconcile how morality's demands could be both local and universal, communal and personal. Morality was one example of Bradley's broader campaign to overcome familiar oppositions in philosophy that, he believed, were rejected by common sense. It was a noble aim but promised little success in public argument, where loose, ill-understood ideas such as *individual* and *community* were set against each other like prize fighters.

As those three thinkers have shown, conservative thinkers, when facing what became known as liberal individualism, could pull in different directions. One was toward the "collectivist" pole, in which the community or social organism became itself a sort of superindividual, endowed with aims and purposes for which its members were passive followers. That picture was useful to conservative populists, nationalists, and others of the exclusionary right claiming to speak for the people. The other pull was toward a liberal-minded recognition of personal worth and moral independence, particularly in the Protestant tradition of religious "individualism," which placed no intermediaries between the believer and God or between the agent and his or her conscience.

There were also down-to-earth, economic ways to understand the public contest between individualism and collectivism. They turned on economic interests and the conflict between labor and capital. Henry Sidgwick in *The Elements of Politics* (1891) offered this account of the economic contrast: "What one sane adult is legally compelled to render to others should be merely the negative service of non-interference, except so far as he has voluntarily undertaken to render positive services; provided that we include in the notion of non-interference the obligation of remedying or compensating for mischief intentionally or carelessly caused by his acts—or preventing mischief that would otherwise result from some previous act. This principle for determining the nature and limits of governmental interference is currently known as 'Individualism.' ... The requirement that one sane adult, apart from contract or claim to reparation, shall contribute positively by money or services to the support of others I shall call 'socialistic.'" In the defense of economic liberties against the "socialistic" principle, conservatives joined right-wing liberals, as the critics of economic democracy—Mallock, Sumner, and Schumpeter—will show in chapter 6.

PART IV

Conservatism's Second Phase
(1880—1945)
Adaptation and Compromise

The Year 1880

Cologne Cathedral was finished after more than six hundred years. The Palermo catacombs were closed. A four-day stand-off between Benedictine priests and police southwest of Avignon highlighted the expulsion of fifty-six hundred members of French unauthorized religious orders from their abbeys and monasteries.

The American magazine *Science* went on sale. Electric street lighting was installed in Indiana. Frozen mutton from Australia arrived in England. The cash register was perfected and soon patented, the first pay telephones installed, and Venn diagrams devised for picturing sets. The University of London gave degrees to women. Winter fog blanketed London. British troops defended the empire in South Africa and Afghanistan. France annexed Tahiti.

European and American economies enjoyed a long expansion, broken by busts and crashes. After the short-lived bust of 1873, new growth ended in 1884, followed by quick recovery. Low prices that hurt farmers continued through the decade. Wealth and property spread unevenly. In Prussia, 60 percent of the population owned land but more than half the land was in the hands of fifteen thousand big owners.

Henry James published the first installments of *Portrait of a Lady*, and Henry Adams published *Democracy*. Gustave Flaubert and George Eliot died. Apollinaire, H. L. Mencken, Sean O'Casey and Oswald Spengler were born.

The thin look for women of the 1870s gave way to full skirts, tight waists, and large bustles. In a class convergence, men's suits began to replace frock coats among the middle classes, and smocks gave way to jackets among artisans and laborers.

5

Parties and Politicians
AUTHORITY RECOVERED AND SQUANDERED

"The Republic will be conservative or it will not survive," Adolphe Thiers proclaimed in November 1872. Liberal champion of 1830, on-and-off ally of Louis Napoleon, and nemesis of the Paris Commune, the long-lived, ever-adaptable Thiers was the Third Republic's president. He was warning all sides that liberal democracy would not endure without a liberal-minded, moderate right.

Thiers did not speak of liberal democracy, but that was what he meant. In French terms, "republicanism" picked out the same political space as "liberal democracy" came to name in English. In a quarrelsome nation that had struggled since 1789 to find a frame for modern politics, republicanism—by which he meant liberalism of a democratic kind, extended to all—was for Thiers, the frame that "divided the least." Republicanism could lean left or right. It could be more or less inclusive in its promises. But it had to work at the liberal center and not be pulled toward the collectivisms of either side. Thiers's warning to France's conservatives was to ally with right-wing liberals or risk irrelevance. The warning to the left was to lower its political and economic ambitions and not treat conservatism and property as historic relics that could somehow be swept from the field.

Thiers's warning applied not just in France. The party-political story of the right (1880–1945) turned largely on how far conservatives heeded Thiers's warning: how well or badly right-wing liberalism met the tasks of the time and how well conservatives held together their competing forces of compromisers and rejectionists. In compressed, capsule terms, the story can be put this way. Where it prevailed—in France, Britain, and, up to a point, the United States—the conservatism of compromise enabled liberal democracy to survive the fears and hesitations of the post-1880 right, as well as its own self-inflicted calamities of imperial overreach, war, and economic slump. By giving ground to liberalism and democracy, compromise enabled conservatism itself to survive as a party-political force. Where rejection prevailed on the right, conservatism degenerated into extreme forms, either populist or authoritarian. At worst, conservatives abandoned the liberal-modern field of politics altogether and fell in with fascism or Nazism.

To unpack that capsule and restate the terms being used here, liberalism and democracy each made several demands. Liberals sought to restrain the coercive power of the state and the cultural power of society. Liberals of the left wanted also to limit wealth's power, whereas liberals of the right wanted to leave wealth alone. Democrats wanted those liberal restraints on power for everyone. Since liberal democracy came in more than one combination, compromising with it allowed conservatives degrees of engagement. It gave them bonding points with liberals of the right and points of opposition with liberals of the left.

Conservatives who compromised ceased to resist electoral democracy (a vote for all), but together with right-wing liberals, they resisted economic democracy (an economic share for all), whether under the banner of left-liberal reformism or, more radically, socialism. Eager to preserve ethical and religious authorities and loath to end moral policing, conservatives also tended to resist cultural democracy. Conservative compromise, that is, was partial, gradual, grudging, and reversible. Yet in 1880–1945, compromise from the right did come, and where it came, a democratic liberalism was eventually embedded in the West after 1945 with a center-left and center-right in open, constrained competition.

Electorally, compromise proved a strategic winner for the right, but at a cost to its distinctiveness and sense of itself. Winning elections and holding office made conservatives owners of the liberal present. In party terms, it left them open to a recalcitrant right that rejected compromise with liberal modernity, either in the cause of a dying past or in pursuit of post-liberal visions. Intellectually, adaptation left conservatives unsure of what made their outlook special or what they stood for.

An unreconciled right that rejected liberal modernity lived on into the twentieth century. It delayed the full achievement of liberal democracy in the United States until the 1960s, threatened it in France's Third Republic, and destroyed its promise in post-1918 Germany. Conflict between the liberal and the anti-liberal right was harder to track in Britain. It went on within a single, disciplined national party. At frequent risk of capsize, Britain's Tories maneuvered the crosscurrents of the right, though with less success after 1980.

In this second period (1880–1945), mainstream conservatives who stayed in party politics and competed for office became, in economic matters, market-minded liberals, or what Clinton Rossiter called, in an economic sense, "laissez-faire conservatives." They spoke of old attachments but fought for broadened interests, invoked the symbols of their tradition while adopting liberal economic agendas, and resisted the stronger demands of economic democracy.

When made democratically, the liberal promise of protection from the power of wealth was for everyone. Economic democracy, in aspiration, would leave nobody powerless in markets that refused custom to the penniless or at work, where the boss's word was final. As adopted in practice in the mid-twentieth century, economic democracy came to offer social welfare, union rights, product standards, consumer protections, and regulation of markets.

Economic democracy, it needs stressing, came in liberal and nonliberal forms. In liberal forms, it extended the promise of protection from power to all. Though this was easy to miss, the promise was double. It offered people protection from the power of wealth, and wealth protection from the power of state and society. In liberal form, economic democracy acknowledged both requirements. In nonliberal forms, economic democracy withheld that acknowledgment. It gave state and society an unanswerable trump against wealth and markets, leaving them politically unprotected. Between the liberal nondemocracy of unchecked markets on the one hand and the illiberal democracy of collectivized economies on the other lay an ocean on which liberals and conservatives, left or right, could navigate and argue.

Turning a lack of ideas to advantage, conservatives began to appeal to voters less because what they offered was different from what liberals offered than because conservatives delivered it better. Conservatives began to reframe their ideals to suit democratic sensibilities. For example, as their embodiment of social unity, class hierarchy made way for one people in one nation, an appeal that could be pressed in nativist, populist, and totalitarian directions. Conservatives still insisted that property and authority were required for social order, but they thought and talked of both in new ways.

Property had changed shape. As the party of the haves, conservatives had not only landed property to defend but also industry, commerce, and banking, together with their rapidly growing tail of lawyers, accountants, salesmen, and clerks in urban offices and shops. The conservatives' primary opponents were no longer liberal grandees competing for dominance in the tight circle of semi-democratic politics. Often in the arms of right-wing liberals, laissez-faire conservatives by the end of the nineteenth century faced industrial trade unions, economic planners, and state interventionists, together with their own smaller but confidently articulate tail of government officials and intellectuals.

In 1880–1945, conservatives in government allied or merged with existing liberal parties of the right keen to resist organized labor and to temper administrative interference in markets. In a historic compromise, they stopped fighting to replace the institutional framework of liberal democracy or resist its economic engine, market capitalism. Instead, they turned to managing the competing demands of what had evolved as a mixed tradition of right-wing liberal and old conservative elements: the demands, that is, for a limited state and an authoritative state; for innovative free markets and stable communities; for self-reliance and social cohesion. Open and fierce today, those conflicts within conservatism have roots in the late nineteenth and early twentieth centuries.

How far conservatives should allow laissez-faire to prevail also in ethical and cultural matters continued to divide the right. Old authorities were weakening or vanishing. Previously independent instances of decision or control—monarchical, aristocratic, or clerical—were in this period absorbed or contained by an overarching modern state. To begin with, the modern state upheld old controls on ethical standards and cultural life. It did so directly through the law and courts or indirectly by backstopping the authority of cultural arbiters such as churches, schools, universities, the press, and publishing. In time, the state gave in to campaigning liberal pressure for reform and to changes in public attitudes. Slowly from the late nineteenth century—and in a rush after 1945—one bulwark after another fell to cultural democracy, in which nobody's life choices about what aesthetically to cherish or ethically how to think or carry on could be gainsaid by the state or by society's ethical and educational arbiters. In that emerging new climate, conservative defenders of the old order had a painful choice. They could fight bravely but in vain to defend the undefendable. Or they could live in vexation with liberal modernity, criticizing it from the side for having, to their eyes, abandoned standards of any kind. After 1980, as conservatives succeeded in rolling back economic democracy, anxiety grew on the right about cultural democracy and ethical anomie.

i. The Moderate Right in France's Third Republic

By 1880, the responsible right in France had abandoned hope of holding off liberal democracy. Social and professional elites lived on in the Third Republic, but France's previous *notables* no longer formed a governing class. In January 1879, after the Republicans capped an earlier victory in the National Assembly by winning control of the Senate, President MacMahon bowed to the new forces and resigned. The republic, having survived a turbulent first decade, steadied and embedded itself. Royalist heirs were banned from the presidency. Exams replaced patronage as the ladder of ascent in the civil service. Press restrictions were lifted. Mayors (save that of Paris) became elective. Sunday work was legalized. Hospitals and cemeteries were secularized. Religious teaching ended in state schools and the French state stopped paying for Catholic clergy. Internationally, revenge against Germany ceded priority to colonial expansion. Much, however, did not change. Life terms for senators were abolished but the Senate itself remained. Little was done to reduce the overrepresentation of rural interests. Working-class demands were neglected.

Electoral wins in the 1880s and 1890s consolidated the pro-republican right and pushed the unreconciled, anti-republican right into the street. Over the course of nine pre-1914 elections, from 1876 to 1910, the anti-republican majority in the National Assembly—monarchists of both stripes and Bonapartists—shrank away to a minority presence with a third of the seats and then to a ghostly remnant. In parliament, the left-right contest came to be fought by a liberal left, known as Radicals under various party names, and a liberal right, known as Republicans.

Two obstacles to understanding French conservatism in the Third Republic can here be quickly dealt with. First, party contests in France were masked balls. French conservatives in parliament called themselves liberals, moderates, progressives, even left republicans, and the names of parliamentary groups often failed to match those when electioneering. During the old right's dying campaigns in the 1880s, its remnants came together in a *union conservatrice*, but the Boulanger fiasco put paid to the label *conservateur*, which vanished from electoral politics. Nobody mistook dropping the word for the disappearance of conservatism or the right itself.

Second, conservative success depended throughout on shifting alliances. Unlike in Britain or, allowing for the large exception of South, the United States, the French right did not develop a single, united party. In part, it did not need to. Conservatives could rely on great strength in regional pockets—the Catholic west, parts of the northeast, and the southern edges of the Massif Central. Conservative deputies, in addition, tended to become unbudgeable, both because two-round elections by constituency (1875) favored the local incumbents of whatever party and because conservative voters deferred by habit to authority. Parliamentary politicians of the right did not need an interfering national party to succeed.

At first, members of the majority right in the National Assembly were known as Opportunists (the term originating as mockery with Radicals for the leader of the republican right, Léon Gambetta). Opportunists and Radicals disagreed about institutions (for or against an upper house in parliament), about church and state (moderate or radical anticlericalism), and about their respective affinities (for the old right; for the new socialists). Unity broke down in the 1890s, when the Republicans split into their own left and right wings. The Republican right, in turn, split into the more lay, urban Alliance Démocratique (1901) and the more clerical, rural Fédération Républicaine (1903).

Those families of pro-republican, parliamentary conservatism flanked to their left by the Radicals in their own changeable groupings provided a ministerial carousel of twenty-seven prime ministers from 1880 to 1914. It looked rickety to a quick eye but turned on a steady underlying center. Parliament found bargains that satisfied the bourgeois elites and France's diverse smaller interests: family businesses and small farms and provincial professionals and shopkeepers. Missing from that social contract was a growing industrial working class as well as women of all classes, who did not get the vote until 1944. Although run by male-heavy elites, the republic with its festivals and symbols, enjoyed popular appeal. To link the republic with the good Revolution of 1789, the Quatorze Juillet (Fall of the Bastille) was made a holiday. In her bonnet of an emancipated slave, Marianne, the secular daughter of a once-protective mother church, was chosen as the republic's emblem. Unlike Britain's John Bull, who personified a national character type, or Uncle Sam, who stood for the federal power, Marianne personified an idealized frame of common life.

That conservative-tinged "republican synthesis" survived scandals of bribery, honors-selling, and kickbacks. It weathered economic slowdown during 1882–96, profited from a subsequent long period of rapid economic growth from 1896 to 1914, disregarded France's few critics of liberal empire, and saw off three late nineteenth-century campaigns from hostile conservative "antis": anti-German revanchists, nationalist anti-Semites, and Catholic anti-republicans.

A leading advocate of *revanche* was Paul Déroulède (1846–1914), a soldier poet, prisoner from the Franco-Prussian War, and hard-right skirmisher. Déroulède made his name with *Chants du soldat* (1872), a short book of ballads that lamented fallen comrades, called for national revenge, and linked love of the French countryside with mourning for its war dead: "They're there in that dark wood. . . . There in our France." The Ligue des Patriotes, which Déroulède started in 1882 as a nationalist pressure group on parliament, grew into an anti-republican street force. Déroulède became an ever rowdier and soon-derided figure. He took an ineffective lead in the Boulanger Affair (1889), when a weak and unreliable republican general was miscast by rich anti-republicans in the role of latter-day Bonaparte as the nation's strongman-savior.

In a country where Catholic tradition remained strong, prejudice against Jews, as with hostility toward Protestants, was endemic. To put anti-Semitism into democratic politics nevertheless took work. The hardest of the Third Republic's toilers was Edouard Drumont (1844–1917), author of *La France juive* (1886) and editor of the anti-Semitic *La libre parole* (founded in 1892). Drumont's skill was to make prejudice sound acceptable by distinguishing reasonable-seeming from evidently unreasonable varieties. Drumont identified Christian-traditional forms of anti-Semitism (Jews as Christ killers), anthropological forms (based on "scientific" racism), and politico-economic discontents (Jews as controllers of finance capitalism). The suggested implication was spurious but tempting to the unwary: whereas the first form was a myth and the second probably a myth, the third was rooted in fact.

Drumont's mischief paid off in the Dreyfus Affair, in which a French army captain, a Jew from Alsace, was falsely condemned as a German spy, cashiered from the army, and sent to prison on Devil's Island (1894). National campaigns for and against Dreyfus divided national opinion. For a time, "Dreyfusard" and "anti-Dreyfusard" became interchangeable with "left" and "right." Easily forgotten from the affair is that the right lost. Dreyfus was exonerated, reinstated in the army, and compensated by the French state. Anti-republican officers were sacked or retired early, and civilian control over the armed forces was asserted, though at a cost. The government's unapologetic use of spies and denunciations to purge the army shocked even Dreyfusards.

In its early decades, the Third Republic's drive for cultural authority, particularly in education, met strong resistance from the Catholic Church. Top-down secularization had to compete with clerical obstruction and mobilization of middle-class Catholics. Renewed popular devotion was to be seen in the many pilgrimages and celebrations of Marian apparitions. Membership in religious orders grew. Catholic schools kept pace with, and on some measures outgrew, state schools. Priests in their sermons warned parishioners that voting for Republicans was a mortal sin. Official church hostility, however, was abruptly reversed in a *ralliement* (1892), when Catholics were urged by the papacy to support the republic. Softening the Vatican's hostility was the larger cause of a global faith. The Roman papacy had come to see a harmony of interests with republican France. The republic favored rapid colonial expansion, and the most active Catholic missionaries were French.

The French conflict of clericals and anticlericals lived on, with neither side winning complete or final victories. Both Ferry's educational reforms (1880s) and the separation of church and state (1901; 1905) involved compromises. Ferry reasserted lay control over state schools while allowing privately financed religious *écoles libres*. Combes's later reforms removed church privileges and rearranged how the French state subsidized the nation's majority faith. It did not, as the most thoroughgoing anticlericals had hoped, remove Catholicism's ethico-cultural presence.

Economic recovery in the 1890s lessened grievances and dampened conflicts. A mood of well-being spread, later remembered as the Belle Epoque, for which sparkling Paris was the cultural center. Anti-German revanchism died down, and some wounds from the defeat of 1870 were already closing. France had quickly paid off the hated indemnity to Germany, which was financed by state debt paying a tempting 5 percent (when interest was 3.5 percent). In occupied Lorraine, French iron ore and German coal were soon serving both countries in making steel. Bismarck, uninterested in colonies, got on well with France's Republicans, who as liberal colonialists were keener to extend and consolidate France's foreign empire than to recover Alsace-Lorraine. Beyond the hard right, anti-Semitism retreated to private, if common, prejudice. A telling sign was the popular press. In the 1900s, the circulation of the anti-Semitic *Petit Journal* declined, overtaken by the *Petit Parisien*, which after initial hesitation and once it was clear they were winning, came round to supporting the Dreyfusards. Hostile passions on the recalcitrant right smoldered all the same. They were kept alive notably by Action Française, founded by Charles Maurras (1898), and flared again in the extremist leagues of the 1920s and 1930s.

Yet more pressing were economic and social questions. France's economy faltered in the 1880s but in the mid-'90s grew rapidly until 1914. A question that divided the French right, as elsewhere, was trade protection. The free-trade lobby—exporters—yielded to the farming interest, led by Jules Méline (1838–1925), a conservative protectionist. A lawyer from Vosges, Méline entered parliament (1872) and, as barriers went up elsewhere, led France's lobby against free trade. He pushed through the Méline Tariff (1892), which raised the levy on farm imports from 3 percent to 21 percent. From 1903, he was a leader of the Fédération Républicaine, the pro-clerical party of the moderate right that appealed to farming and small commercial interests with a mix of antistatism (opposition to income tax), mutualism (Méline promoted the Crédit Agricole in 1894), and support for Catholic schools.

Labor protections remained slight, although concessionary reforms were made for industrial workers. Unions were regularized in law (1901), but strikes were brutally put down by Radicals (with Georges Clemenceau in the lead) as well as by Republicans. As state revenues relied heavily on regressive tariffs and sales taxes, the conservative-led Senate was able to quash a liberal proposal for an income tax (1895). When Joseph Caillaux's income tax bill passed the National Assembly in 1914, it took two years even in revenue-hungry wartime for a reluctant Senate to concede.

When peace came in 1918, France's all-party Union Sacrée broke up and voters returned a solidly conservative National Assembly, organized as the Bloc National. The moderate French right acquired a kind of inertial weight as the solution that fewest could dislodge. No stable majority existed in parliament for the social reforms the country needed. Their natural advocates, the parties of the left, were split. The Radicals had come to look paternalist, overpreoccupied with parliamentary maneuver, and out of touch. Socialists vied for domination of the left with Communists, nervously but obediently following the changeable line from Moscow. Narrow wins for the radicals-and-socialist Cartel des Gauches (1924; 1932) and a big victory for the radical-socialist-communist Popular Front (1936) led to cabinets of the left that nevertheless soon broke down in disputes over taxation, public spending, and social protections.

The leader who best personified the Third Republic's conservative centrism was Raymond Poincaré (1860–1934). A Lorrainer, he had seen German occupation as a boy. Although his hostility softened in the 1900s, it revived with the war, when Poincaré became an unremitting anti-German hawk. He pressed for a hard peace in 1919 and sent French troops to the Ruhr when German reparations were late in 1923. A bourgeois and a lawyer, Poincaré spoke for the middle-class values of work, thrift, and honesty. Party corruption was rife in the Third Republic, but in forty years of public life no hint of scandal touched Poincaré, known for being "white as ermine." Although he and Clemenceau were at one in their anti-Germanism, Poincaré took his great rival to be unprincipled, much as Clemenceau took Poincaré for a prig. Poincaré outshone his rivals in acumen and dedication to work but lacked a popular feel. He led the country in wartime as president from 1913 to 1920 but, in France at least, Georges Clemenceau (*Père victoire*), together with the military leaders Foch and Pétain took larger credit for the victory, while Poincaré won foreign odium for insisting on a Carthaginian peace. Stiff and upright, he preferred the role of statesman to that of party stalwart, although his most regular allegiance was to the Alliance Républicaine Démocratique. As prime minister, once before the war and twice after, Poincaré held office both when the left and when the right controlled parliament. As the bankers' hard-money man, in 1926 he rescued a fast-diving franc, an operation so successful as to flood the Bank of France with gold, helping later to worsen Europe's financial instabilities.

Poincaré's conservative vision of politics rested on tangible outcomes more than on causes or ideals. The vision included the familiar conservative elements of social order, anchored economically in sound money, and social unity, rooted in national strength. In party terms, Poincaré thought that government was best conducted at the center by moderate conservatives, helped, if need be, by a responsible left. Poincaré's post-1945 heir was Antoine Pinay, leader of the party that itself descended from Poincaré's ARD, the Centre National des Indépendants. Middle-class, lay, economically liberal, and right-wing, Pinay's party blended in turn with the Giscardian Independents of the 1970s, who added the element of cultural liberalism.

French foreign policy was hampered in the 1920s and 1930s by conflicts that froze both the left and the right. The urgent tasks were managing war debt, responding to a world slump, and containing a revived Germany. The post-1918 left was in the main pacifistic. On the right, the desire to keep Germany down jostled fears that a weak Germany would mean the triumph of Bolshevism. In addition, fascism's rise in Italy and Germany encouraged the dream among a vocal minority of the French right that a homegrown variety might solve the nation's social and foreign problems together at a stroke.

Despite failing to meet France's economic and foreign tests, conservative centrism survived into the 1930s, as ministries passed on unsolved difficulties from one to the next. They were hampered on the right by outright opposition in the street from the extra-parliamentary Ligues and by growing complaints within the *classe politique* itself among politicians and intellectuals convinced of the nation's backwardness and need for *redressement* (recovery).

In the street, anti-republican ghosts from the 1880s and 1890s returned. Veterans' grievances were channeled in François de La Rocque's Croix de Feu, which changed from a diffuse, popular movement of support with three million followers into a smaller right-wing strike force. Returning to its earlier anti-liberal hostilities, the Catholic Church let it be understood in its parish sermons and newspapers that communism was a worse peril than fascism. In their detestation of the liberal-conservative compromise, the extremes of politics blurred. Jacques Doriot, the Communist mayor of Saint-Denis, in Paris's "red belt," turned anticommunist and founded the far-right Parti Populaire Français (1936). Dissident causes of the kind got money from businessmen, for example from the *fascisant* perfume manufacturer, François Coty, as well as indulgence from a minority of the Fédération Républicaine.

The anger and theatrical vehemence of such groups shook but failed to break the Third Republic. Anti-parliamentary rioting in Paris (February 1934) was withstood and soon largely forgotten. The state's authority was reaffirmed by the Popular Front prime minister Léon Blum, who banned political leagues (1936). A less theatrical but larger threat to republican stability was middle-class resistance to the Popular Front's social reforms. It was partly assuaged by the Daladier government, which curbed or suspended the Front's improvements to hours and wages (1938). To soothe anti-immigrant fears, Édouard Daladier also opened concentration camps for Republican refugees from the Spanish Civil War and other undocumented newcomers. By decade's end, the Third Republic had survived the disruptions of France's hard right, but at a heavy price in concessions to illiberal or undemocratic demands.

Preoccupation with national decline is a conservative staple that takes ethico-cultural as well as political forms, as later chapters will explore. Politically, in the 1920s- and 1930s, the preoccupation focused on France's supposed "structural" backwardness and need for comprehensive modernization. The marks of backwardness in such a view were many. France was too dependent on farming, too sluggish economically, too lax in its upkeep of bridges and roads, too stick-in-the-mud socially, too partisan, and too poorly served by an out-of-date administration. Whether or not such a view was apt—and much suggests it was luridly overdrawn—it had prominent followers, particularly after the political dramas of 1934–36.

One principal advocate of technocratic modernization was André Tardieu (1876–1945). He was a conservative politician and journalist who entered parliament in 1914 and held all the top ministerial posts, including the premiership (three times, 1929–1932). His watchwords were strong defense, social modernization, and an effective state. Tardieu took no interest in religious politics and was untroubled by the putative erosion of France's *ordre morale*. A modernized nation, in his view, would be more rational, specialized, industrial, urban, and democratic (among other things, he wanted votes for women). He saw an obstacle in the "cloud of dust" thrown up by party bickering, which contrasted unfavorably with what he saw as the broad business-like agreement between the main parties in the United States, which he admired. Reform required a supportive frame of vigilant peace (hence his defense of the Versailles Treaty) and exclusion or deflection of the left ("Le socialisme," he would say, "voilà l'ennemi").

Tardieu's actual public-works plans in the 1920s were modest and, as premier during the economic crisis, his pre-Keynesian policies were confused and timid. He is remembered as an early representative of the technocratic spirit that later marked France's center-right in the Fifth Republic after 1959. More immediately, Tardieu's growing doubts about the viability of mass democracy—expressed in his unfinished work, *Completing the Revolution*—together with his stress on French backwardness gave nourishment to a blame-shifting view that became popular on the right after the fall of France in 1940. Military defeat, it was held, came not from political hesitation, military miscalculation, and bad luck but from national decadence. Where the right could not agree with itself was on what caused France's perilous vulnerability: failure to modernize, as Tardieu believed, or blind abandonment to modernity, as cultural conservatives held.

The Third Republic survived disaffection from the right and left, hostility from the Catholic Church, German military occupation of the entire northeast, and loss of 10 percent of its military-age men (1914–18), as well as an economic slump from which, deep as it was, France was recovering by the end of the 1930s. The republic succumbed only after military defeat (1940), and then "succumbed" is a half-truth, as if the Third Republic had suffered a natural disaster or given in to a disease. In July 1940, both houses of parliament—meeting at an Auvergne spa town in unoccupied France—voted overwhelmingly to replace the republic with the authoritarian Vichy regime. Only socialists and left-radicals opposed the change, although other radicals and a few conservatives in the Fédération Républicaine abstained. (Communist deputies, loyal to a Soviet Union at peace with France's German invader, were ineligible.) After liberation, the Third Republic's self-suppression was stricken from France's constitutional record. The law of July 1940 was declared void, the Vichy regime was erased as an un-French interlude, and, after twenty-eight months of provisional postwar government, France's Fourth Republic succeeded the Third, as if without break.

Without France's defeat, there would have been no Vichy interlude. But without the anti-liberal and anti-democratic traditions of the pre-war French right, the Vichy regime would not have known what shape to take. Under Pétain, jostling factions of the unreconciled right—authoritarian, *ordre morale*, clericalist, corporatist, fascist—saw their chance and fought for influence. Vichy's watchwords were "Travail, famille, patrie," a wishful alternative to the republican trio of "Liberté, egalité, fraternité." In practice, the Vichy government oscillated between the conflicting aims of national renewal, "shielding" the French people, and preserving order. It mattered little that Vichy's factions disagreed on whether national renewal should be moral or technocratic. The regime lacked the means for either. Shielding the French people—from German occupation and exactions—was claimed by some to have been in part achieved but was dismissed by others as a poor excuse for hard-right agendas that Republican France had rejected for seventy years. In time, Vichy's aims narrowed to keeping order, which meant more policing, more violence against its own people, and more concessions to the German occupiers, including co-operation in the deportation of French Jews.

The figure who represented those conflicts was Pierre Laval (1883–1945), a migrant like Doriot from left to right, twice premier in the Third Republic, and twice vice premier under Pétain in Vichy (1940; 1942–44). Son of an innkeeper from the Auvergne, Laval rose from labor lawyer and socialist to anti-parliamentary authoritarian, grown rich with the help of business friends. Undoctrinal, he saw his job in Vichy not as chasing moral recovery but as Franco-German rapprochement. Despite his self-belief that he was a shrewd judge of power, Laval failed to grasp the disparity in strength of occupier and occupied. His preoccupation with "the deal" blinded him to the nonrational, untreatable character of Hitlerian Germany. After a controversial trial in 1945, Laval was executed. For the party-political families of the French right that had voted to end the Third Republic, 1944–45 was a zero point from which the only direction was up.

ii. British Conservatives Adapt

In Britain, conservatism's accommodation to liberal capitalism and electoral democracy was personified in the long career of Robert Gascoyne-Cecil (1830–1903), better known as Lord Salisbury. From being an anti-liberal scourge as a young journalist and MP at midcentury, after 1880 Salisbury became the consolidator of a successful mass party that governed Britain in the spirit of right-wing liberalism for much of the next one hundred and forty years. Aloof and erudite, Salisbury was the founding architect of a modernized Tory party that successfully triangulated its liberal-democratic foes—economic, institutional, and social. Under Salisbury, Toryism learned to speak for business and finance, as well as for the landed interest. It continued to revere while gradually abandoning old institutional attachments (crown, Lords, established church) in favor of vaguer but equally passionate loyalties to empire and nation. It made itself popular enough among middle-class and other voters, especially in England, to become the strongest party in the twentieth century and after. On Disraeli's death (1881), Salisbury led the party from the Lords. He was prime minister three times (1885–86; 1886–92; 1895–1902) and had four turns as foreign secretary (1878–80; 1885–86; 1887–92; 1895–1900).

Young Salisbury, who needed the money, poured out articles for conservative magazines such as the *Quarterly Review* and the *Saturday Review*. He took aim at liberal-democratic pieties with a scorn that never left him, though in public he later softened his acerbic tone. Liberalism, Salisbury held, was like an "untenable religion," rooted as it was in sentimental views of humanity and a misunderstanding of Christianity: "The common sense of Christendom has always prescribed for national policy principles diametrically opposed to those that are laid down in the Sermon on the Mount." As for democracy, Salisbury thought that all communities threw up "natural leaders" to which people unthinkingly deferred unless misled by egalitarians. Unlimited democracy would promote careerists and professionals, not better or more consensual government. Worse, it would encourage spoliation of the rich by the poor, who were no less vicious than the rich, only more numerous.

Seeing himself as a "pathologist of states," Salisbury, like Calhoun, was near-Marxian in his view of politics as governed by the pursuit of material interests. To custom and tradition as such he was no more attached than were Utilitarians. Institutions were to be judged by results, not by familiarity or endurance, which he thought poor gauges of their usefulness. The test of any arrangement for young Salisbury was: did it contribute to stability, security, and prosperity, above all for landed society, high and low, without which social order was impossible?

Salisbury's belief in the primacy of the rural interest ceded in time to the recognition that the haves included large holders of property in general, that is, bankers and industrialists, not only landowners. His unexalted picture of politics remained unchanged in essentials, although acquiescence with liberal capitalism darkened its tone. In "Disintegration" (1883), Salisbury lamented the destabilizing effect of economic cycles on modern society. In good times, prosperity spread, together with material inequalities, which people begrudged more than aristocratic rank and privilege. In bad times, growing material need was exploited by the "radical agitator," who turned popular resentment against the institutions of society. Salisbury glumly looked forward to a "long conflict between possession and non-possession, which was the fatal disease of communities in ancient times."

The task of conservatism, Salisbury thought, was to keep order without cramping freedom, which in Millian vein, he took for liberty to "do what he likes as long as he does not injure his neighbour." Keeping order involved suppressing the "boiling lava of human passion" and stifling the delusory hopes of progress, which ignored the brittleness of civilisation's "crust."

As party leader and prime minister, Salisbury bent that picture of conservatism to circumstance without betraying it or blurring its distinctiveness. When his father died (1868), he inherited an income worth £50 million in today's money together with the title Marquess of Salisbury. He resigned from Derby's government in protest against suffrage extension (1867). The 1870s occupied him with ministerial responsibilities in India and eastern Europe. On his return from diplomatic affairs, Salisbury's elevated early grumbling about democracy was little guide

to his skillful maneuvers in practice. Conservatives surprised themselves by winning the first election after the franchise reform (1884),
which extended the vote to poorer classes in the countryside. Salisbury
continued to moan in private about the delusions of progress, but in
public he played the patrician democrat with success.

Ireland gave Salisbury his opening. Home Rule blew apart the Liberals and won Salisbury an ally in the ex-Liberal Joseph Chamberlain. His
Unionists supported Salisbury and allied with the Conservatives from
1895, before merging in 1912. Like Bassermann's National Liberals in
Germany, Chamberlain was a new force on the right: for big business,
empire, and tariffs and above all, to keep socialism at bay. With Chamberlain, Salisbury created winning majorities or coalitions in three elections (1886; 1895; 1900).

Although implacable on Ireland and empire, Salisbury made concessions to liberal reformism under pressure from Chamberlain. His government introduced worker's compensation (1897). Far from obstructing the suffrage of 1884, it deepened electoral democracy by making
county councils elective and so breaking the last hold of country landowners on city government. As tellingly for the future of British conservatism, the party under Salisbury modernized itself into a disciplined
national organization able to prevail in the democratic game. The Prim-
rose League, founded in 1883 to promote popular conservatism, claimed
a membership of 1.5 million by the early 1900s. Local "wire-pullers" were
replaced by professional party agents. Election manifestos were introduced, and a shadow cabinet was created to prepare for office in opposition. The Conservative Central Office (opened originally in 1870) was
strengthened and run at first under the parliamentary chief whip. The
contrast with party fluidity on the French right and regional unevenness
of support for German conservatives was striking. The reach and coherence of a single large right-wing party after 1918 made it easier for British
conservatism to absorb or deflect the hard right in the 1920s and 1930s.

Like Garibaldi, Salisbury was shy in company but good with crowds.
He sneered that the *Daily Mail* (1896) was "written by office boys for
office boys" but grasped the need to use the press and took to briefing
journalists. Remembered by grateful Conservatives for the next century

and beyond, Salisbury's career was a master class on how to play a weak hand with a diffuse creed on behalf of a declining, overstretched power.

Although for Salisbury interest drove politics, he grasped that politics also had to be thought and talked of in symbols. Artfully, he blended nation, empire, and crown as objects of common loyalty. In a speech for Queen Victoria's Diamond Jubilee, in June 1897, Salisbury praised the nation's "great experiment" of "trying to sustain such an empire entirely upon the basis of mutual goodwill." As a new conservative attachment, empire had great popular appeal, unlike the church and Lords. J. R. Seeley's pro-imperial *Expansion of England* (1883) sold eighty thousand copies in three years and was selling over ten thousand twenty years later. Until it soured in unexpected losses, the Boer War was popular in England, helping the Tories win the Khaki Election in 1900.

Salisbury's twenty-one years in power were a holding operation, which on his melancholy view of conservatism counted as an achievement. He left his successors doubts as to what the party stood for, which tactical gambits and patriotic appeals could not conceal. Soon after Salisbury handed on the premiership and party leadership to his nephew Arthur Balfour in 1902, the Tories were crushed by a revived and social-minded Liberal Party, which had converted from laissez-faire to social reform. In the 1906 election, the Tories crashed to 157 seats, 100 of which were held by either Chamberlain Unionists or supporters of his protectionist policies. Conservatives were torn. For the protectionists, tariffs promised to solve three problems at once: they would help British industry, which was losing ground to foreign competition; they would pay, as in France, for social reforms to deflect the left without directly taxing the rich; and as its very name suggested, a policy of protection would assuage generalized anxieties about Britain's loss of preeminence, its relative economic decline, and its military weaknesses, as exposed in the South African conflict, which did not turn out as jubilant early crowds had expected. To free traders such as Arthur Balfour and Winston Churchill, who bolted to the Liberals, protection was a sure way to lose elections. Free trade, with its promise of cheap food, had become for many voters as much a part of Britain's unwritten constitution as the National Health Service was to become after 1945.

British conservatism was facing its version of the right's dilemma already seen in France: whether to compromise with liberals wary about democratic forces pushing liberalism leftward or bend rightward to appease Conservative Ultras over Ireland, the Lords, and trade unions. Was the party to bow to the democratic will as expressed through parliament? Or should it risk an extra-parliamentary denouement? The party was split between hedgers and diehards, compromisers and recalcitrants. Civil war loomed over Ireland, fanned by Conservative diehards, who were given comfort by Tory leaders.

Toryism (1913), a small book by the historian of conservatism Keith Feiling, put the dilemmas and anxieties of the early twentieth century right in Britain into a wry dialogue among four typical Conservatives. Together they spanned the party's inner spectrum: a "cynic of noble birth" and "real Tory" (the ghost of Salisbury); "a man of means and leisure" who was a Tory "on principle" (that is, a rich man who was a Conservative from personal interest); an ex-Liberal MP (a political careerist, a Tory by convenience); and a radical, imperialist Tory Democrat (a campaigning Chamberlainite with grand ideals). All four worried that the "ship is top-heavy": large empire, small country; big taxes, small class to pay them; big imports, fragile currency; uncertain world, small army. Without clear result, they worried, too, that the Conservative Party was its losing purpose and distinctiveness. The book's playful tone did not hide the fear that, as after 1846, the party was divided, unsure of itself, and without guiding ideas. In 2020, put four similarly distinct British Tories together and replace "empire" with "Brexit," and the worries about the state of the nation and party would not be much different.

World war saved the Conservatives from despondency. It froze party competition (in 1916, the Tories joined the Liberals in government under David Lloyd George), postponed Ireland, and gave the Conservatives time to rethink and regroup. They had not won back the agenda by 1918 but were on top in parliament, a position they kept for all but three of the next twenty-seven years. In the first postwar election (1918), Bonar Law's Tories won 382 seats, and the divided Liberals lost over 100, beginning a slide toward the margins. From 1908, MPs were paid, opening the Commons to representation for an ascendant Labour Party. The trade unions had doubled their membership from four million (1914) to more than eight million. In that same postwar election, Labour won 57 seats. Five years later, it won 197, overtaking the Liberals and making it the second-largest party.

In right-left terms, parliamentary socialism, in the shape of a reformist Labour Party, was replacing the Liberals as the Tories' foe to the left. Business-minded Conservatives of a new type—"hard-faced men who have done well out of the war," in Lloyd George's sneering phrase—sat on former Liberal benches. The leader of the Tories' recovery was the son of a manufacturer from the Midlands, Stanley Baldwin. Despite its inner conflicts, the party he inherited from Salisbury and Bonar Law was, compared to its rivals, a formidable national machine.

With lightness and skill, Baldwin (1867–1947) fashioned conservatism as the natural, inevitable politics of middle England, centered on national unity, common values, and classlessness. Dismissed by the unwary as a bluff know-nothing, Baldwin grasped the importance of words. His cousin, Rudyard Kipling, called him the true poet of the family. In speeches and essays, which were anthologized in *On England* (1926), Baldwin fashioned a vision of the English people and what mattered to them that long served his party. Baldwin blended patriotism with conservatism, and love of England with hostility to socialism and intellectualism.

He was three times prime minister (May 1923–January 1924; November 1924–June 1929; June 1935–May 1937) and had three election wins. After the Carlton Club meeting in 1922, when Conservatives voted to abandon their coalition with the hated Lloyd George, Baldwin emerged as the strong man of the party and became leader in May 1923. Baldwin saw off the brief General Strike (1926), weathered the Depression, held off the Mosleyites, and managed the abdication of Edward VIII, which disturbed a nation that still favored the crown. Against that record, Baldwin lost two of three elections as prime minister, gave way to his party's high-tariff wing, cosseted the south while ignoring the north, and failed—like others—on Hitler. He was among the few Conservatives to leave when he chose (1937), rather than from illness or being ousted by a party quick to abandon weak leaders.

Baldwin took his adversaries to be reasonable and open to compromise. He accepted left-right parity and treated Labour as a legitimate rival, while hunting for working-class voters. He avoided stigmatizing opponents. He brushed off calls (from Churchill among others) to meet the General Strike with force, presented it as a test for the nation, not a matter of class, and let it peter out. At first, he resisted calls from the right of his party to clamp down on unions but he later gave in, accepting the Trades Disputes Act (1927), which banned sympathy strikes and restricted compulsory party donations from union dues—a big source of money for the Labour Party.

Baldwin had public tact. He let opponents throw the first blow; he kept his strong religious convictions to himself; and he was quiet about his piano playing, love of painting, and wide reading, aware that English voters as a rule disliked cultural showing off and suspected intellectuals of bogusness. "Intelligentsia," he once wrote, "is a very ugly word for a very ugly thing." Baldwin's picture of an island people at ease with itself and somehow insulated from the world was a beguiling fiction with a long afterlife.

Despite a do-nothing reputation, Conservatives took steps in the 1920s and 1930s toward social reform: the Widows, Orphans and Old-Age Pensions (1925); slum clearance and housing; shifting of property taxes, known as rates, from industry and farms and filling the revenue gap left for local authorities with central-government grants; and industrial "rationalizations" in coal, textiles, and electricity. Under Baldwin, the government chartered the noncommercial British Broadcasting Corporation (1927), and reduced the voting age for women to twenty-one (Equal Franchise Act, 1928), secure in the belief that women voted more right than left. In 1935, when women made up more than half the electorate, the Tories won 386 seats.

Thanks to a single, inclusive party with a strong national organization, British conservatism left little space in the 1920s and 1930s for a disruptive right-wing fringe, as in France, or a destructive extreme, as in Germany. There was widespread early admiration in the Conservative Party for Hitler's strong leadership and suppression of the German left and for Germany's economic revival, but little for Britain's marginal, homegrown fascism. The other parties in Britain were in decline or divided. The Tories shared power in national governments from 1931 to 1935, but no other party won a parliamentary majority in the 1930s.

Baldwin encouraged practical efforts to overcome Toryism's sense of intellectual inferiority. The problem had been met earlier by denial. The conservative writer Arthur Boutwood rationalized the party's lack of ideas by insisting in the *National Review* (1913) that it had no need of "a philosophy of politics" or "a distinctive ideal" since conservatism was a practical attitude. He was repeating what Hugh Cecil had argued in *Conservatism* (1912): conservatism was less a body of aims and ideals than a second-order attitude to governing. Cecil's book was a reply, requested by the publisher, to Leonard Hobhouse's *Liberalism* (1911). Unlike liberalism, with its hopes and ideals, conservatism for Cecil was rooted in a natural "disposition" to be wary of big or rapid changes, in "distrust of the unknown," and, in a mysterious phrase, in a "preference of that to which we are accustomed, because custom had actually assimilated our nature to it." That "natural" attitude had taken historical form in conservative responses to the French Revolution. From such premises Cecil inferred, in the words of the philosopher Anthony Quinton, "more or less ingenious defences of limited taxation, the maintenance of the British Empire and other, fairly contingent elements, of the platform of the Edwardian Conservative party."

Not all conservatives shared Boutwood's and Cecil's complacent disregard for ideas. In *A Defence of Conservatism* (1927), Antony Ludovici lamented the Tory silence in the face of intellectual ferment on the left. In the 1920s, Conservatives faced intellectual opposition from the left, with the Left Book Club, the Fabian Society, and the Workingmen's Educational Association. Pressed by Lloyd George, liberal intellectuals turned out color-coded policy documents—Yellow Books, Orange Books, and so on. Open-eyed Conservatives responded. Harold Macmillan published (with others) *Industry and the State* (1927) and *The Middle Way* (1938). With money from the Bonar Law Memorial Trust, Ashridge College was opened in 1929 to train a conservative cadre. That year, the Conservative Research Department was also started. The concern was to know more about how society was, less about how it had been or should be. The spirit was that of technocrats like Tardieu in France. In conservative discourse, talk of custom and tradition was giving way to present-day problems and how to solve them. Expertise was replacing natural authority as the right's entitlement to rule.

Initial sympathy for Hitlerism on the British right was encouraged by fear of German communism. Should Hitler weaken and German communism revive, Europe's right, perhaps Britain's also, looked imperiled. But as Germany's strengths and demands grew, fear of Hitlerism rose, leaving British Conservatives unsure what to think. The Labour Party, like the left in France, was pacifistic. British officials and diplomats were both for and against appeasement. It depended on where and how. Tactical concessions should be made for the greater aim of resisting German pressure. That much was common ground. But which concessions? Among the key players there was a blocking majority on all options: concessions in the empire or in eastern Europe; alliance or not with France; building up the navy or the air force. The Treasury said there was no money for either. Nor was Germany the only threat. Britain had Japan to fear (for Britain's Asian colonies), as well as Italy (for freedom of the Mediterranean). An isolated Britain, the military chiefs warned, could not fight a three-front war. Neither Baldwin nor Neville Chamberlain, who succeeded him as prime minister in 1937, resolved the puzzle.

Baldwin's postwar reputation as sleepwalker in a lost decade, encouraged by Churchill and his friends in the Beaverbrook press, was unearned. Historical reevaluation in the 1970s and 1980s painted Britain's 1930s as less bad than professionally and popularly imagined. Baldwin, in turn, was given credit for social and economic achievements and for modernizing the party. The new judgment, though more balanced, risked distortion of its own. An avowedly one-nation party governed a two-part nation that was divided into a sheltered, prosperous southeast and Midlands (where engineering and cars did well, raising labor productivity), and an impoverished north, for which Baldwin's conservatism had little to say. National pride and imperial ambition misled Churchill into setting the pound (and interest rates) too high in 1925, and falling-price depression was met by continued austerity, which failed to reduce the level of public debt in the economy. Although the number of workers was higher in 1939 than in 1929, unemployment jumped in the mid-1920s and stayed high until the Second World War.

Even after correcting that under-judgment, Baldwin was never going to outshine in the historical imagination the party colleague who had harried him from the right of the party for two decades, Winston Churchill. Once prime minister, Churchill took charge of a party that had considered him a self-serving maverick and became an inspirational wartime leader. Like Disraeli or Margaret Thatcher, Churchill (1874–1965) seemed to resolve in one capacious personality the party's inner conflicts. First Conservative, then Liberal, then Conservative again, Churchill held high offices of state from 1908 on and was twice prime minister (1940–45; 1951–55). Blunder and failure dogged him in office, as did alcohol, depression, and debts, yet with luck and determination he was never conclusively bested or driven from the field. Impetuous and undeflectable, Churchill faced blame and derision by the decade: military calamity (Gallipoli, 1915), mismanaging the currency (sterling's return to gold at too high a rate, 1925), imperial nostalgia, admiration for fascism, and ambiguity on appeasement (1930s), military calamity again (Norway, 1940), and indifference to home affairs (1940–45). Had the party's first choice, Lord Halifax, agreed to become prime minister in May 1940, Churchill would be remembered as a divisive, quixotic figure. Once in charge as wartime leader, he communicated an indomitable will to resist, first by ruthless harrying of the cabinet and generals, then to the nation by radio and Commons speeches. Like de Gaulle, whom he never got on with, Churchill had the creative power of words to form simple pictures and lay out clear paths in the minds of millions, making first Hitlerism then communism unarguable, implacable foes in a war that somehow combined protection of the hearth with the survival of civilization. His *Second World War* (1948–53) was criticized as victor's history and his *History of the English-Speaking Peoples* (1956–58) faulted for creating in its very title a post-imperial fiction, yet they stamped common memory and were hugely popular, winning him the Nobel Prize in Literature (1953).

Indifferent to party and impatient with doctrine, Churchill claimed always to have been a liberal. He was, it is true, a right-wing liberal of a laissez-faire kind. He believed neither in telling people how to behave nor in much helping them with their lives. Unlike Victorian moral scolds or Edwardian social reformers, neither vice nor poverty much concerned him. Churchill had, on the other hand, an un-Cobdenite relish for war and a paternalist belief that his natural position was to lead, being born to wealth (his American mother's side) and aristocratic British title (his father's).

Churchill grasped the theatrical element in mass democracy. His speeches and histories crafted a credible national epic. He himself played a character part: showman and rascal; self-indulgent lover of champagne and cigars; unapologetic go-getter often in debt and greedy for money; and above all, undentable fighter, seizing success from failure and vice versa, as in a serial story. Not that Churchill was a mere actor. The part he played was an exaggeration of himself. Among voters mistrustful of their supposed betters, Churchill's lack of pretense lent him credit. For an out-of-touch conservative, Churchill, like de Gaulle, had a feel for popular sentiment.

Britain escaped the worst of the 1930s but was less an exception than it looked. It became a liberal democracy more smoothly than in France and without self-inflicted disaster as in Germany. Still, it took Britain time. Undemocratically liberal for much of the nineteenth century, it began early in the twentieth to grow liberal in more democratic ways. Votes for all, a say at work for labor, and social protections were introduced and became part of the constitutional furniture. Conservatism hindered and helped. It obstructed and delayed, but it stole liberal— and later socialist—clothes. The main weight of British conservatism followed the strategic line of Derby and Salisbury: sound obdurate but concede rather than battle in vain. The Conservatives' course from 1880 to 1945 confirmed to that extent what the historian E.H.H. Green called its "incremental absorption and ascendancy of liberalism." Tory diehards remained but turned their radicalism outward, toward defense of an undefendable empire, to the Protestant cause in Ireland, and later to anti-Europeanism.

iii. The Ambivalence of German Conservatives

Because of the catastrophe that Germany later visited on itself and the world, it is difficult not to tell the party-political story of Wilhelmine and Weimar conservatism as a sequence of fatal steps on the road to 1933. On such an account, Germany was first unified from above in war and then browbeaten by Bismarck, a conservative authoritarian in the service of East Prussian reaction. Once he was gone, a military caste egged on by shipbuilders and arms makers harried conservative elites, who were afraid of socialism and national "encirclement," into a disastrous Europe-wide war. On Germany's defeat, a discredited right found its sole purpose in subverting the new republic and enabling Hitler's rise.

Elements of that caricature are true, but its depiction of a single path to disaster, which clears away complexity and luck, is false. German conservatism from 1880 to 1945 was not simple or uniform. It was not the mouthpiece of one interest. It was neither a passive tool of the Junkers before 1918 nor fascism in the germ afterward. Wilhelmine conservatism had support outside East Prussia and appealed to the middle classes and small farmers, as well as to the upper classes. Weimar conservatism included supporters as well as enemies of the republic. Nor was what the right faced peculiarly German. In confronting liberal modernity, the German right faced the familiar choices of adaptation or resistance, which the right faced in France, Britain, and the United States.

Conservatism had peculiarities wherever it was. Each was special in its way, but German conservatism was not uniquely special. It shared with France's right the handicap of having ill-organized, competing factions rather than a single, strong national party as in Britain. Arguments among German conservatives over policy—tariffs or free trade; for or against empire; indirect taxes or progressive taxes on wealth and income—were common also on the right in France, Britain, and the United States. Confessional frictions—Catholic versus Protestant, Lutheran versus Calvinist—affected German conservatism but were present to a degree also on the British and American right. A "backward" East and "modern" West gave German conservatism a regional shape, but so did the sectional conflict of North and South in the United States.

That said, distinctively German factors complicated conservative choices about hastening or delaying liberal democracy. One was the confusion of authorities in the Wilhelmine Reich. The other was the newness of parliamentary government after 1918. During the 1870s and 1880s, the confusion of authorities was disguised by the domineering figure of Bismarck and the relative weakness of parliament. After a young Kaiser eager for his own say contrived Bismarck's resignation (1890), the confusion became open when parliament was strengthened. In the Weimar Republic, parliamentary authority was recognized in theory; it needed, but never fully received, support from a liberal and democratic right.

After Bismarck's fall, the Bismarck myth grew up that nothing worked without him. "He's never linked with failure and nothing counts but him," his loyal aide and publicist Lothar Bucher reflected. Well before Max Weber's judgment that Bismarck had left the nation without a political education, the left-liberal Theodor Barth wrote in 1888, "He is a kind of master who leaves no school. He has followers but no successors."

The Bismarck myth was at best half true. Wilhelmine parties, politics, and institutions worked without Bismarck and despite themselves. The truth in the myth lay in the undue space Bismarck occupied on the right. His dominating presence helped spare the fractious German right from organizing itself better as a party force in democratic politics.

Among conservatives of the nineteenth century, Otto von Bismarck (1815–98), the Iron Chancellor, belonged to a special type. He was a pragmatic authoritarian who despised liberals and democrats but would work with either so long as his word was final. He was the prime minister and foreign minister of Prussia from 1862 to 1890, bar a ten-month interlude in 1873, chancellor of the North German Federation from 1867 to 1871, and imperial chancellor from 1871 to 1890. His domination of German politics for nearly thirty years relied on personal closeness to the crown (his authoritarian side) and command of the public stage, both in parliament and in the popular imagination (the liberal and democratic elements). A North Saxony–born Junker, he had the attitudes of his class: suspicion of business and the middle classes, disdain for the masses, and—like Salisbury—a bleak view of life's possibilities, sustained by a Pietist faith. His overbearing personality drew much from a huge frame, sardonic wit, and devouring appetite for work, despite sleeplessness and hypochondria. As richly evoked with Bucher's help in *Thoughts and Recollections* (1898), sound politics for Bismarck meant playing off parties and institutions against each other. Skillful diplomacy (as epitomized in his Kissingen Memorandum, 1877) involved playing off competing foreign powers.

More by force than by persuasion, Bismarck pursued German unification from above in three wars (against Denmark, Austria, and France). Once he became imperial chancellor, he sidelined the parliamentary liberals and turned the state's powers first on the Catholic Church (whose preaching questioned the Reich's authority in 1872–78), then on the Socialists (whose call for electoral representation alarmed business and finance in 1878–90). To balance the latter attack, social-reform schemes for sickness insurance, industrial accident coverage, and state-run old-age insurance were introduced from 1883 to 1889. Antisocialist laws were extended four times, but the Reichstag turned down a fifth request, by which time Bismarck's moment was over. Internationally, Bismarck joined the turn from liberal free trade in 1878 but spurned the liberal race for colonies to focus instead on ensuring German dominance in Europe.

Bismarck improvised a complex constitution for the Reich that called for his directorial talents. It combined universal male suffrage with a weak parliament that lacked proper taxing powers; a chancellor with ministers whom the emperor chose and dismissed; and no bill of rights, independent courts, or immunities for deputies outside parliament. The Reich flanked the old institutions of Prussia, which were headed by a king (in person, also emperor) and controlled by an obstructionist, undemocratically elected right.

To work at all, such a contrivance required, it would seem, a strong hand. After his death, hundreds of totemic Bismarck towers and statues of Bismarck in armor rose across Germany. Few monuments were erected to the Reichstag or its party politicians. Veneration in stone can, however, be misleading. Bismarck was not all Wilhelmine conservatism, which was as much a tale of weakness as an epic of strength.

After unification, the Wilhelmine right largely accepted that it must fight on democratic terms. It accepted, that is, that it needed popular support and that, with energetic new rivals to the left, passive acquiescence from people no longer counted as support. Yet from the 1880s onward, the right's electoral weakness began to tell. After a high point in 1887, when together they won 47 percent of the national vote, the three parties of the right—the German Conservatives (DKP), the Free Conservatives (FKP), and the National Liberals (NL)—steadily lost ground in the Reichstag. By 1912, the DKP, FKP, and NL had shrunk in total to 26 percent of the vote. While support for the right's old parties dwindled away, support for the Social Democrats and Catholic Center grew until they comprised more than half the Reichstag in votes and seats. The Center party, which had liberal and conservative wings, leaned sometimes left, sometimes right.

Their decline at the polls reflected the failure of conservative parties to break out of the countryside into Germany's rapidly growing cities. In 1912, the right won 55 percent of the vote in localities of less than two thousand people, but only 25 percent in cities of one hundred thousand or more. The right had support outside East Prussia, but it was generally outvoted in conservative districts by the Catholic Center. With a steady pace after 1890, when the ban on the Social Democratic Party (SPD) officialdom and electioneering ended, the electoral maps of the German Reich after 1890 came to resemble a three-color flag: black for the Catholic Rhineland and Bavaria, where the Center was strong; red in industrial Saxony (SPD); and blue in East Prussia (conservative).

A deeper difficulty was uncertainty as to what conservatives stood for. Their original adversary, liberalism, had changed. As some liberals turned left and some right, liberalism no longer offered a clear target against which conservatism could define itself. Neither liberals nor conservatives had a single, dominant party. Bismarck's turn to free trade split the National Liberals (1880). A breakaway formed the small but vocal left-liberals. The remaining majority backed Bismarck and worked together with the two "name" conservative parties. All three faced internal disputes over aims and policy as well as the threat from outside of capture by one or other of the special-interest right-wing leagues militating for yet higher tariffs, more colonies, a bigger navy, and fewer immigrants, especially Jewish immigrants.

Those pressures buffeted Wilhelm von Kardorff, who led the Free Conservatives from 1880 to 1906. As a spokesman for business, Kardorff founded industry's national lobby in 1876. His party relied on middle-class urban voters, much like the National Liberals, which in outlook and interest it resembled. As did urban Tories and right-wing Liberals in Britain, the Free Conservatives wanted efficient local government freed from landowning interests, which Kardorff successfully pro-moted. To serve big business, he supported protective tariffs but failed to win support for bimetallism and cheap money. He also failed to sat-isfy his party's third constituency, small farmers in the West. They wanted higher tariffs on farm imports, which city voters opposed as a food tax. Kardorff's difficulty was not uniquely German. To their country-city conflicts, the French and British right, as just seen, had few ready answers either. Kardorff's star fell as his party's vote dwindled to vanishing—3.5 percent (1903).

The task of Helldorff as head of the German Conservatives (1876–92), was no less awkward. Few of the fractious troops under his nominal control wanted to march in the same direction. They included latter-day Christian Romantics, social-welfare conservatives, and anti-Bismarck obstructionists in the Prussian parliament. Despite the difficulties, Hell-dorff gave Bismarck staunch backing in the Reichstag through the 1880s. Loyally, it supported the failed fifth attempt at renewal of Bismarck's antisocialist laws in 1890. The mood had changed, however, and the right had split. Left liberals were joined in opposing it by the Catholic Center and by National Liberals who thought it wiser to tame than out-law socialism.

Helldorff was brought down in 1892, when his party lurched further right. Its fear was to be outflanked by popular anti-Semitism. Helldorff's nemesis was Adolf Stoecker, a Lutheran preacher and demagogue. He had founded his own Christian Social Party in 1878, which combined hostility to bankers, Jews, and liberals with appeals to Christian piety in aid of the poor. Stoecker had a following at court, where he preached, and a rapport with big-city crowds, who took Helldorff's DKP to be stuffy and old hat. Together with the historian Treitschke, Stoecker called for a halt to Jewish immigration from the east. (Treitschke's right-wing nationalism will be a topic on its own in chapter 6.) Stoecker's appeal scared the DKP into making anti-Semitism official policy in its Tivoli Programme (1892). The shift gained the party little, won it no seats, and proved a handicap when public anti-Semitism died down, as in France. Disappointed by rabble-rousing, the DKP refocused on defending tariffs and resisting the taxation of wealth. Stoecker's star fell, but he had written the script for a demotic conservatism of a new kind that stigmatized enemies within.

German conservatism in the Weimar Republic shows the strength of absence. The republic's birth, brief life, and death are too well known to require summary, but the role of the German right in each of those phases belongs in the party-political story of conservatism.

On the collapse of the Wilhelmine Reich at the end of the 1914–18 war, the three parties of the parliamentary right dissolved and reformed as two new groupings. A majority of the old National Liberals formed the German People's Party (DVP in its German initials), led by Gustav Stresemann. Hostile at first, it came to support the republic. The former German Conservatives and Free Conservatives together created a single right-wing party, the German National People's Party (DNVP). Besides uniting the two Wilhelmine parties, it drew in the remnants of Stoecker's Christian Social Union and the National Liberals' ultraright fringe, as well as followers of two popular lobbies, one new, one old: the Stahl-helm, which rallied postwar veterans and the pro-farmers Land League. For its organization, the new party relied on the weak national networks of the old German Conservatives. Though calling itself "national," the DNVP was strongly Protestant and concentrated in East Prussia. It hovered between frank hostility and grudging acquiescence toward the new republic.

The new party's name—the German National People's Party—was telling. Upon its founding (November 1918), it rejected the label "conservative." The name, so objectors argued, was tarnished by association with the discredited Wilhemine elites, whom voters hated for the war. Traditional conservatives grumbled in turn about calling it a "people's" party. In their view, it was groveling to the crowd. Quarreling over the name reflected the new party's two-facedness. It was elite and popular, moderate and radical, ready to work with the republic and willing to wreck the republic.

In its perilous first years, as chances arose to wreck the republic, the right seized them but failed. In the constituent National Assembly, both conservative parties, the DNVP and DVP, voted in vain against the Versailles peace and the Weimar constitution in 1919. Leading members of the DNVP supported the failed Kapp Putsch (1920). Neither party, however, had a serious alternative to accepting labor-business peace, as embodied in the Stinnes-Legien Pact (1918). After the crises of 1923—attempted coups by left and right, foreign occupation, hyperinflation—the republic stabilized. The economy improved, social peace returned, Franco-German relations eased, and parliamentary government worked.

In this second period, 1924–28, DNVP moderates, led by Kuno von Westarp, moved the party toward cooperating with the republic. In a free vote, half the party voted for the Dawes Plan, which eased hated war reparations with an American loan. Westarp had earlier backed the failed Kapp Putsch but had come to see the futility of open resistance. Anti-republican radicalism was losing appeal. As the republic stabilized, the promise of cabinet portfolios worked its appeal on Westarp's party. After 1924, the DNVP took posts in several ministries. Conservatism grew less radical in a larger way. As society steadied itself, the political cost to the right of resistance and disruption grew. In the everyday, non-partisan sense of preferring order to chaos and stability to uncertainty, the forces for conservatism in business, courts, churches, universities, and even Germany's shrunken army came to see the republic as a lesser evil than the dreamed-of ultraright alternatives. Briefly, as the republic held on and began to stabilize in the mid-1920s, the path of the radical right looked blocked. As a new normal appeared to settle in, a resistant core on the right abandoned party politics for the intellectual fringes. It will be met again as the "conservative revolution" in chapter 6.

Respite for Germany's new liberal democracy was brief, however, as was Westarp's hold on the DNVP. It was unclear what it stood for. If the party blended with right-wing liberals, it lost distinctiveness. If it refused, it blurred into the anti-Weimar "conservative revolution." They excited readers of small reviews but had little grip in party politics. Bar its theatrical proposal to restore a constitutional monarch, Westarp's party was no longer openly anti-Weimar.

As the party for business, Stresemann's DVP had more weight. Outside East Prussia, in the parts of Germany where the economic weather was made, the DNVP came to look upon many on the right as irrelevant. Electoral disaster struck in 1928. The party's share of the vote fell in half and it lost thirty seats. Its right wing, under Alfred Hugenberg, deposed Westarp, who, with a handful of allies, formed a powerless and soon forgotten breakaway, the Conservative People's Party. Westarp subsequently retired to write a multivolume history of the German right. Hugenberg moved to the front of the stage to a leading part in Weimar's calamitous third period (1929–33).

If one man combined the interests and preoccupations of the unreconciled right in the Weimar Republic, it was Alfred Hugenberg (1865–1951). His business empire included arms making, newspapers, and film. Making money blended well with his political aims: making Germany strong and preventing it from becoming socialist. German strength, in his view, meant national power and unalloyed Germanness. Help for small businesses and hard-pressed farmers was needed to prevent socialism. As a believer in mutual aid and mutual banks, Hugenberg was wary of corporatist pacts between big capital and big labor.

His interests in business and politics became hard to tell apart. He became financial manager of the arms maker Krupp, which raised its dividend under his guidance by 75 percent in five years. At the outbreak of hostilities in 1914, he set out annexationist war aims. In 1920 he was among the hard-right National Liberals who joined the postwar DNVP (via brief passage through the wartime Fatherland Party, which had been formed to oppose a negotiated peace). Hugenberg's media interests included press services, advertising agencies, parliamentary reporting offices, regional newspapers, newsreels, and the film studio, UfA.

Hugenberg, for all his reach and business power, was oddly bad at party politics. Unlike the bulk of the party that he took over and tried to run, he was neither a monarchist nor anti-Semitic, although he did not interfere when newspapers of his railed against Jews. His referendum against the Young Plan (1929), a second try at relieving the weight of reparations, failed. On the rebound, Hugenberg fostered the Harzburg Front (1931), a short-lived alliance between the DNVP, the Nazis, and the Stahlhelm. Its chief result was to give the Nazis an entry into previously conservative middle-class districts. As unemployment rose to more than 17 percent in 1932, the Nazis had a trump card. They were party-political outsiders, an untried alternative that had not yet failed. Unlike the pro-Weimar parties and the conservative right, the Nazis were not to blame. Communists could claim the same, but Nazis were less frightening to the middle classes. Hugenberg, like other German conservatives, saw all that too late. When they moved to stop Hitler, they were no longer able to do so. To control him, as they hoped, they needed the liberal and democratic means they had done too little support.

The Weimar Republic was Germany's breakthrough into liberal democracy. But liberal democracy requires a parity of left and right, under which each recognizes the other's legitimacy and opportunity to alternate in office. The German right after 1918 was not organized or committed enough to meet either condition. Historians argue whether the strength of an active and hostile right undermined the Weimar Republic, or whether, on the contrary, the right hung back in fear that it was too weak to prevail at the democratic game. Either way, conservatism in Germany showed the power of absence. Weimar's collapse owed much to the weakness of a liberal-democratic conservatism.

iv. The American Nonexception

The Gilded Age in the United States—the period roughly from the end of Reconstruction to beginning of the new century—had two faces. Epic nation building and massive economic expansion was one; social neglect, city squalor, and a persistent North-South division the other. Which face you focused on depended on where you stood. Wealth and its defenders saw manifest, quasi-natural success. Poverty and its opponents saw corrigible social failure. Those contrasting views divided stand-pat conservatives on the right from eager reformers on the left. Since Republicans largely monopolized office, the contrast ran as much among Republicans as between them and Democrats.

In the half-century after the Civil War, the United States remade itself in an astounding burst of economic growth that was concentrated in the industrial North and Midwest. A small Atlantic economy that drew modest capital from farming, trade, and slavery transformed itself into a modern dynamo spinning reinvestable wealth out of technical innovation and industry. A great continent open to capture together with the stimulus of war aided the takeoff, but those advantages, inert on their own, had to be seized. By the 1880s, the US had overtaken Britain as the world's leading steel producer. In 1913, it had built over two hundred thousand kilometers of railroads, twice as much as Western Europe. Early in the new century, the US overtook Britain, which till then, bar Australia, had the highest GDP per head. American prowess was visible in the overall annual average growth rates for the economy from 1870 to 1913: Britain, the laggard, at 1.3 percent; France, 1.4 percent; Germany, 1.8 percent; and the US, 2.2 percent. That astounding transformation gave the party of the haves much to be proud of.

In the great entrepreneurs and financiers of the period—Andrew Carnegie (steel), John D. Rockefeller (oil), Cornelius Vanderbilt (railroads), J. P. Morgan (finance)—American conservatism found itself modern-day heroes who did not need exhuming from the past or sketchily hoped for from the future. As models of ambition and agents of progress, these giant figures spoke for laissez-faire conservatism with an authority that no party politician or political thinker could match. Better than a party manifesto, they embodied in person a conservative "gospel of wealth," as preached eloquently by Andrew Carnegie (1835–1919) in his essay "Wealth" (1889) and in the hugely popular *Autobiography* (1920). According to Carnegie's gospel, social progress was treated as a force of nature, best left alone to spread its net benefits unaided. Society advanced, Carnegie wrote in his essay, according to a "law of competition," which was often "hard for the individual" but "best for the race," because competition, untroubled by well-meant interference, insured "the survival of the fittest in every department."

Ethically, progress alone told right from wrong. "Humanity is an organism," Carnegie reflected in his *Autobiography*, published just after his death, "inherently rejecting all that is deleterious, that is, wrong, and absorbing after trial what is beneficial, that is right." Such a grandiose but factual-sounding way of talking Carnegie had picked up from Herbert Spencer and the Social Darwinists. In the wrong hands, it could be made to sound as if justifying dog-eat-dog competition and not looking after the weak. For Carnegie, the "organic" metaphor worked differently. Believing that "a man who dies rich dies disgraced," Carnegie acknowledged the social-minded emotions of shame and gratitude. He gave millions for public libraries and other purposes as well as founding institutions to study and promote world peace.

In party terms, Republicanism divided. A majority of officeholders, known originally as "Stalwarts," were glad to let business and their cozy ties to business alone. A minority of reformers sought to clean up politics and business, above all by stopping them from eating off each others' plates. These Republicans were variously known as "Half-Breeds," "Mugwumps," and, later, "Progressives."

The laissez-faire majority thought business was best left to itself to create wealth, the law best directed to that end, and elected officeholders safest when bought off rather than when crusading. A New York Republican fixer supreme, Roscoe Conkling, summed up the Stalwarts' unexalted view of a politicians' duties: "Parties are not built up by deportment or by ladies' magazines or by gush."

The reforming Republican minority started out by pressing for cleaner politics and cleaner cities. They were not yet for government interference with business or for state protection of factory workers and small farmers. That changed in the 1890s, after a long farm depression and the 1893 Crash, when Republican Progressives called for a new course. Led by Theodore Roosevelt, they split the party into right and left, conservatives and anti-conservatives, allowing Progressive Democrats to win the White House under Woodrow Wilson (1912).

Democrats, too, had a right and a left. Bourbon Democrats, North and South, formed a laissez-faire right. Almost Cobdenite in their economic liberalism, they were against high tariffs, loose money, and imperial expansion, which the United States was pursuing in the Americas and Pacific. Twice they took the White House from Republicans with victories in 1884 and 1892 for Grover Cleveland, who had broken the corrupt city machine in Buffalo, New York. The Bourbon Democrat aim was for business to rely on markets rather than on government, and for government to keep out of politics. Bourbon laissez-faire was different in the South. There it meant leaving in place the impoverished planter elites and not disturbing the subordination of black to white. With the abolition of slavery, that subordination had to be re-embedded in discriminatory laws that Democrat state legislatures supplied until the 1960s.

On the Democratic left, Bourbon Democracy was overtaken at the close of the Gilded Age after 1896 by the rise of the Populist Democrats (under William Jennings Bryan) and Progressive Democrats (under Woodrow Wilson). Those were respectively working-class and middle-class campaigners for an expansive idea of the state's duties to society. As in Europe, that new democratic vision of an active, dutiful state was to color the partisan contest in the United States in the twentieth century. It gave American conservatives in both parties a well-outlined Other against which to define themselves. Neither Populist nor Progressive Democrats included interference with the South among an expansive state's duties, and both were sensitive to pervasive antiblack prejudice in the North.

During the sixty-four years from 1869 to 1933, Republicans held the White House for forty-eight, the Senate for fifty-six, and the House for thirty-two. They owed that success to several factors. One was electioneering. Throughout that time, they spoke for business but, like business, they adapted as society changed. To begin with, Republicans won the votes of rural, small-town America across the North with a variety of national appeals. Helping at election time to begin with was the Grand Army of the Republic, a veterans group that "waved the bloody shirt" by painting Democrats as the "party of rebellion." As memory of the Civil War faded, Republicans appealed to nativist fears of American dilution by painting Democrats as the party of immigrants—Catholics from Ireland, Italy, and Poland, Jews from eastern Europe—spreading foreignness in unhealthy cities. However, as in Europe, appeals to national pride and prejudice were not always vote winners. They were too easily trumped by lunch-pail concerns about pay and prices to be an all-weather campaign resource. Modern techniques, above all fundraising, were also needed. Typical of the new, election-minded Republicanism was Mark Hanna (1837–1904). Like Salisbury's Conservative agents in Britain, Hanna created a tool kit for twentieth-century American electioneering.

Hanna was a Cleveland-raised businessman and Republican political manager who ran William McKinley's successful campaign for president in 1896. Hanna exacted more than $100 million in today's money from Standard Oil, the Morgan bank, and other interests; kept the uncharismatic McKinley on his front porch in Ohio; and sent Republican speakers across the nation talking up sound money, high tariffs, and restored prosperity. McKinley's opponent, William Jennings Bryan, who was running jointly for the Democratic and the Populist Parties, appealed to factory workers, small farmers, and the urban poor, talking up cheap money to cure the depression. He came close to his Republican opponent in the popular vote but scared enough middle-class voters outside the South and the Plains and Mountain West to lose heavily in the Electoral College. Twice more Bryan lost, in 1900 and 1908, his vote share dropping each time as Republicans began to eat into the working-class vote. Facing organized labor, their first choice, as in Europe, was conciliation, though quick with coercion in reserve. As governor of Ohio, McKinley, for example, had stood up for labor unions. He preferred to embrace them than fight a class war. His emollient slogan was "Good for business, *so* good for labor." Republicans did not forget working-class loyalties and prejudices. They asked for votes from "working Americans." By stressing the first word, they could quietly reprove shirkers. By stressing the second, they silently excluded Catholics, immigrants, and blacks.

Control of institutions, above all Congress and the law, was a second factor in the conservative success. As Woodrow Wilson wrote in *Congressional Government* (1885), the presidency was weak, Congress strong. It may be recalled that the ur-liberal-conservative Madison had helped design the Constitution with the fear of intrusive government in mind. For conservatives who wished to obstruct an overactive executive, the techniques of delay and misdirection for use by Congress abounded. A fine example of conservative obstructionism was Joseph Cannon (1836–1926), a long-serving congressman from Illinois. As all-controlling Speaker of the House from 1903 to 1911, Cannon saw his task as thwarting the ill-judged experiments proposed by Theodore Roosevelt and his Progressive Republicans. Pugnacious "Uncle Joe" Cannon allotted committee places to ensure that reforms bills did not sneak past his Old Guard. The Republican William Howard Taft, Roosevelt's successor in the White House, had looked forward to using Cannon in the conservative cause. Democrats, however, allied themselves with Progressive Republicans to break Cannon's grip on power and, with it, the House's conservative veto on change. The shift enabled the reforms of Wilson's first administration (1913–17), which included passage of an income tax and direct election to the Senate, both previously blocked by an obstructionist Congress.

Senatorial blocking power in the new century fell to conservative coalitions of Republicans and Southern Democrats. Right-wing Democrats won elections in the South, thanks to laws that in practice prevented blacks from voting. Without Republican opposition or Democratic rebels to contend with, Southern congressmen and senators were reelected as if for life, accumulating seniority and chairmanships. With the help of conservative Republicans in the North, the South made the Senate a blocking chamber whose power was broken only in the 1960s. It voted with Northern Democrats for big government in the New Deal after 1933, when federal works helped a needy region and federal price support helped farmers, especially big farmers. After 1945, the South became richer and more industrial. Southern Democrats voted with Northern Republicans against big government and big unions but supported high defense spending, which helped the South. The hold of Southern Democrats in the Senate delayed the vote for women and civil rights for blacks and thwarted compulsory health insurance and the humanization of punishment. For many, though not all, American conservatives, congressional obstruction was a worthy stand against mischievous or inept social engineering. Against Wilsonianism (1910s), the New Deal (1930s), and the Great Society (1960s), obstructionists in Congress could invoke the triple conservative argument against liberal reform: it was too costly for the benefits it brought, it was often futile and ineffective, or it was perverse in its unintended consequences.

A final factor in conservatives' success was the law. In the nation-building period between the Civil War and the New Deal, American law served the large purposes of protecting the freedom of businesses to expand the economy and spread prosperity, creating a national market by removing internal barriers, aligning state laws, and easing the progress of transport, notably railways, and insulating the states of the South from federal intrusions that might threaten their legal subordination of black Southerners.

The Supreme Court limited efforts by unions to organize; struck down state regulations setting standards for minimum wages, maximum hours, and child-labor conditions; rejected a federal income tax as unconstitutional; and recognized corporations as legal persons with the full rights of ordinary citizens, which extended them the due-process protections of the Fourteenth Amendment. The Supreme Court and other American courts gutted postwar Civil Rights laws and upheld the notorious "separate but equal" doctrine underpinning Southern segregation.

A leading conservative jurist of the day was the Californian and Union loyalist, Stephen J. Field (1816–99). On the Supreme Court from 1863, Field joined like-minded justices in upholding federal law in the defense of economic liberalism. Their doctrinal wedge was "substantive" due process, as opposed to the procedural kind. The Fifth and Fourteenth Amendments to the Constitution protected US citizens from infringement of rights, save by "due process of law." Field took those rights to include property rights so invested or entrenched as to be invulnerable to interference by social legislation from the states.

The "conservative force of the American bar" that Choate had looked forward to forty years earlier was coming into view. Eager to raise standards, harmonize the states' qualifications, and rebuff charges of malfeasance, the American Bar Association was founded (1878). Law schools grew in number, from 28 with sixteen hundred students (1870) to 100 with thirteen thousand by the end of the century. The top law schools served, like Oxford or Cambridge in Britain or the *grandes écoles* in France, to train a national elite that staffed government, served politics, and directly or indirectly gave public argument in the United States its distinctive, legalist shape.

In the 1920s, much as an elegiac tone became popular in American conservative thinking, a reassuring, nostalgic element entered Republican speeches. The tone was like that of Baldwin's "one-nation" hymns to Englishness. It spoke to original conservative concerns for social unity and shared loyalties, sought to quiet anxiety about rapid, bewildering change, and tried to say who Americans were and what the United States stood for. Conservatism needed eloquence, for society, the economy, and the nation were not as conservatives wished. Society was diverse and divided. Government was small but growing fast. And like it or not, the United States was engaged in the world. How far it should go to accept or try to alter that disturbing state of affairs vexed the American right. The question touched three areas of concern: social coherence, the government's role, and the use of national power. Doing nothing meant accepting the unacceptable. Resisting meant turning conservatives into radicals or revolutionaries. The dilemma preoccupied and divided the American right through the nineteenth century and beyond.

A nation that had seen itself as predominantly white and Protestant and scattered in small towns had greatly changed. Industry was familiar enough, but the new century had brought profound further changes. As in Germany, a country that had been agricultural for most of living memory had raced through industrialism and was making its fastest productivity gains in shops and offices. The transition to a service-based economy was rapidly under way. The market was spreading itself into ever larger areas of human life. Buying and selling of human skills, a point half-spotted by Marx, was visible not only in fields and factories but everywhere. Pride in better conditions of life and the growing profusion of convenient, affordable goods reawakened the old conservative disquiet about the value of material progress. Recall Coleridge's doubt about "moral improvement" and Taine's worries about "modern unhappiness." In like spirit, American conservative thinkers worried about the ethical consequences of this-wordly success. Religious conservatism gained ground in the churches, Protestant and Catholic alike.

The image of an older, more sheltered American world lingered accordingly in right-wing writing and speeches. The Republican tone of the 1920s was set by Warren G. Harding and Calvin Coolidge in their inaugural addresses. The speeches were drafted by Judson Welliver (1870–1943), Harding's and Coolidge's "literary clerk" in the White House. A Midwestern reporter who later lobbied for the American Petroleum Institute, Welliver exemplified the growing professionalization of political work

Harding's themes in 1921 were American providentialism and unilateralism. The nation, for Harding, was chosen and exceptional. "Surely," he told listeners, "there must have been God's intent in the making of this new-world Republic. . . . We have seen civil, human, and religious liberty verified and glorified." The United States was to other nations a model, not a guardian or protector. It was sovereign and unbindable: "It can enter into no political commitments, nor assume any economic obligations which will subject our decisions to any other than our own authority."

Coolidge's inaugural in 1925 took as its themes national pride, the true value of property, and the virtue of thrift. Calls for fairer economic shares he deflected with an equivocation about property: "We need not concern ourselves much about the rights of property if we will faithfully observe the rights of persons. Under our institutions their rights are supreme. It is not property but the right to hold property, both great and small, which our Constitution guarantees." As for thrift, it applied to government as much as to households: "The very stability of our society rests upon production and conservation. For individuals or for governments to waste and squander their resources is to deny these rights and disregard these obligations. The result of economic dissipation to a nation is always moral decay."

Coolidge was talking in ways that were about to be cast aside. A crippling slump soon savaged American prosperity. Not the market but government and war came to the rescue. Democrats won the presidency and the Congress (1932). They held the one for twenty years, the other, bar two brief intervals, for nearly fifty. To critics on the left, government-led reform by Democrats—successively, the New Deal, Fair Deal, New Frontier, and Great Society—were too timid in correcting social ills and economic inequities. To critics on the right, using the state for social ends was a socialistic target at which conservatives, despite their other disagreements, could agree to aim fire.

Although electorally in the wilderness, in the 1930s the Republicans began a long, intellectual fight back. With money from the du Pont Brothers, the American Liberty League was founded in 1934 to promote free enterprise and resist government interference. The writings of Friedrich Hayek and Ludwig Mises, largely ignored as economists in Europe but welcomed as publicists for business in the United States, won a small but growing following on the American right. As cited by Kim Phillips-Fein in *Invisible Hands* (2009), Jasper Crane, Hayek's American promoter, nicely recast Coleridge's founding lesson on the need for conservative intellectuals in latter-day terms: "What the high-brows upstairs talk about today has such a decisive influence on the public's opinion of tomorrow." With the libertarian Leonard Read and others, Crane established the Foundation for Economic Freedom (1946), a forerunner of the free-market think tanks that became part of the politico-government landscape from the 1970s onward.

In the American context, it might look as if Thier's warning to the right with which this chapter began—accept liberal democracy or face irrelevance—was not needed in the United States. For was not American politics liberal at birth and democratic soon after? As we are seeing, that is at best a half-truth. American conservatism was strong from the beginning. It was liberal in some ways, not in others. American conservatives, to schematize, were economically laissez-faire but dubious about the liberal faith in open-ended progress. They did not believe in equality, doubted people's capacity for self-government, and opposed direct, unfiltered democracy. In religious terms, American conservatism tended to an Augustinian, not a Pelagian, view of humankind as flawed and, in this world, unredeemable. Resistance to the ethical and cultural free-for-all of liberal capitalism found early support in the Protestant and Catholic churches.

American conservatism was odd but not uniquely odd. It shared inner conflicts and tensions with its European counterparts. All faced an onrush of modernizing change under capitalism, liberalism, and democracy. Each had to decide how far to compromise with their early liberal foes. They all had to weigh up, economically, how much compromise the interests of the haves, their first responsibility, would bear. They all had to gauge, politically, how much compromise with liberals their party distinctiveness would bear.

Answers did not fall from the sky. Conservatives might mouth but they no longer believed Burke's claims about the political right not needing large ideas. Starting with the defense of property and capitalism, a great intellectual battle was engaged against the liberal and nonliberal left.

6

Ideas and Thinkers

DISTRUST OF DEMOCRACY AND OF PUBLIC REASON

Conservatism's historic compromise with liberalism was never neat, complete, or final. By the end of the nineteenth century, liberalism itself was changing in response to the demands—electoral, economic, and cultural—of democracy. Progressive liberals were moving left to appease economic discontents with welfare and regulatory reforms. Market-minded liberals were moving rightward to resist those palliative efforts. Coming toward them from the right they met conservatives who had turned from preserving the "world of yesterday" to forestalling a socialist future. The conservative liberalism spotted by a farsighted German lawyer at the start of the century was by its end in full view.

The first question was whether conservative thought had more to offer than just maxims of prudence and monitory advice. Had it more to say than that conservatives ran liberal democracies better than liberals and democrats? If conservative thought had more to say, could that extra be articulated in a distinctive body of aims and ideals? And if it had, were those ideas more than negative and reactive, more, that is, than a critical handbook for use against liberalism's and democracy's own attempts to justify themselves? From the late nineteenth century onward, conservative thinkers tended to divide into those content to expose the flaws of their opponents and those who continued to seek a conservative philosophy of its own.

Conservative thinkers from 1880 to 1945 gathered powerful ammunition against democratic liberalism. They rejected the economic claims of socialism and the effectiveness of palliative liberal reform; they questioned the reasonableness of people en masse together with the limits of public reason; they lamented the ethical aimlessness and satisfaction with mediocrity encouraged by democratic culture. The right's critics bored away at a core weakness of liberal democracy: either liberalism promised the wrong things, or, if it promised the right things, those things could not be extended to all. Not everyone was equally capable or deserving. The harshest conservative critics drew the disruptive—indeed, revolutionary—lesson that, in modern conditions, democratic liberalism's characteristic form—elective, multiparty parliamentary government—was bound to fail.

Alarmed by democracy's threats to economic efficiency, Mallock, Sumner, and Schumpeter sought to rebuff socialist hopes for popular control of the economy. Mallock and Sumner stressed the futility of well-meant social reform. All of them insisted on society's need for competent elites.

Others focused on the social and cultural aspects of liberal modernity. Le Bon, Treitschke, and Sorel concentrated on people's unreasonableness and the volatility of mass society, which the overthinking, unduly trusting liberals did not grasp and had no answer for. In like vein, the writers Maxime Du Camp, Henry Adams, and H. L. Mencken scorned popular taste and common opinion, retouching for the modern right an ancient picture of common people as stunted, herdlike, and easily led.

Faced by what they took for a debased, spiritless culture, conservative writers such as Eliot urged a withdrawal to excellence. Writers alienated from liberal-democratic society preached renewal of national values (Moeller) or escape into action (Jünger). Loathing of the liberal-modern world underlay the funeral orations for parliamentary democracy given by Maurras and Schmitt.

As representatives of late nineteenth-century to early twentieth-century conservative thought, those several thinkers shared common preoccupations. Their writing was largely critical. They were clearer in what they were against than what they were for. They criticized democratic liberals for their belief in equality and trust in people's reasonableness. And underlying their social and cultural criticisms was a bass-note insistence on something that in their eyes social order depended upon and that liberals stubbornly refused to recognize: people's desire to believe, to follow, and to belong.

i. Defending Capitalism: Mallock, Sumner, and Schumpeter

William Mallock (1849–1923) was an English novelist of ideas, a prolific political writer, and a spokesman for conservative causes who disbelieved in the upward progress of humankind. Convinced that left-wing liberals and socialists were out-arguing conservatives, Mallock set out to shake the British right from mental torpor. Faced by what he took for the right's mental sloth, the antisocialist roared in frustration (1882): "All that bears any semblance of organised thought or system has belonged to the attacking party"—he meant the left—which was met from his own side by nothing but "an obsolete dogmatism that cannot even explain itself."

On their founding in 1884, the British Fabians, who called for a mild, parliamentary socialism, quickly attracted a following of well-known intellectuals, including Beatrice and Sidney Webb, Bernard Shaw, H. G. Wells, and Emmeline Pankhurst. Earlier, Henry Hyndman, a wealthy conservative turned Marxist, had started the Social Democratic Federation (1881). Henry George's *Progress and Poverty* (1879), which argued that workers and capitalists should keep what each duly earned but that unearned rent from land belonged to all, helped inspire the tax proposals in the Radical Programme (1885) of a Liberal party ginger group supported by Joseph Chamberlain.

To Mallock, the claims of economic democracy, whether packaged as socialism, social democracy, Marxism, or Georgism, relied on wishful thinking. Calls for state direction of production, for public provision of social welfare, or for workers' say in industry might be buttressed by tables and statistics, but they rested on a double error: the underestimation of productive complexity in modern economies and an overestimation of people's capacity for self-organization. As Mallock argued in his many antisocialist books from *Social Equality* (1882) onward, material betterment and sustainable prosperity depended on wise guidance by a talented elite. His elite was not a hereditary class or social caste but a pool of entrepreneurial talent. The particular skills and excellences might vary, but the general requirements of entrepreneurship remained constant: innovativeness, organizational know-how, and a talent for giving orders. By their nature, such productive virtues were in short supply. It was foolish to expect that they could be spread to the masses by education or reembodied in shop-floor democracy. "The only means by which the total product of a given population can be increased," Mallock wrote, "is not any new toil on the part of the labouring many but an intellectual direction of the many by the supercapable few."

Mallock was not a Malthusian pessimist. He was confident that economic prosperity might grow and spread. It could not come, however, from improving the productive skills of the majority. Their role was as shoppers to increase demand. Material progress would come, as Mallock wrote in *Aristocracy and Evolution* (1898), only from "the talents and activity of an exceptionally gifted minority." As wealth spread, in addition, everyone's material conditions might improve, but the outcomes would never be equal. Poverty might be reduced, even eliminated, but inequality would not disappear.

Mallock extended his frank inegalitarianism to political democracy. His skeptical view of democratic legitimacy echoed the elaborately argued doubts of the elite theorists Pareto, Mosca, and Michels. Politics in his eyes was not a reflection of popular opinion but instead a contest for power among small groups. He thought conservatives should resist rather than acquiesce in further widening the franchise. The 1884 Reform Bill had extended the vote, in effect, to most working-class men in cities. In all, around 60 percent of British men in Mallock's time had a vote, and he feared the knock-on effects on economic democracy: heavier taxes on wealth to pay for welfare schemes to help industrial workers and the poor; overprotection for trade-union authority in the workplace.

By the 1900s, the Conservative Central Office was using Mallock's *Labour and the Popular Welfare* (1893) as campaign material for speakers. The book, which drew on Alfred Marshall's *Principles of Economics* (1890), offered rebuttals of popular socialist claims: that "all wealth was due to labour," that profit was exploitative, and that wealth was sufficient to give force to redistributive taxation (he faulted Georgism for overestimating the revenues from land rent in Britain by a factor of seventy-five). Like Schumpeter later, Mallock stressed entrepreneurship as a fourth factor in production after labor, land, and capital. He called it "industrial ability," although in his pretechnical hands it remained unquantified and, to an extent, mysterious. Mallock did not set himself against all economic and social reform. Unions could improve labor-management relations and encourage wage stability, but they could not permanently raise the level of wages. Spending on certain public services was useful and necessary, and if such spending was "socialistic," then Mallock accepted that he, too, was socialist.

Though chiefly reliant on the pen, Mallock was involved with the antisocialist Liberty and Property Defence League, founded (1882) by peers, railway magnates, and big industrial owners. Mallock toyed with running for parliament but drew back. He dabbled briefly in business but was put off by the mundane give-and-take of board meetings. Cooperation was probably not Mallock's thing. "No enterprise undertaken by a number of persons," he grumpily recorded in his *Memoirs* (1920), "can possibly succeed unless it has some man of exceptional strength at the head."

Social Darwinian narratives were stock-in-trade in Mallock's day. In *Aristocracy and Evolution* (1898), he presented evolution as in small part "an orderly sequence of the unintended" directed in larger part by the "intentional activities of the few." Determined to find a providential authority, Mallock would not accept the random force of nature. His account of evolution was an improvised amalgam. It yoked animal evolution as applied to society with Christian providentialism, in which the part of God was replaced by the "supercapable" few.

Mallock was a better polemicist than thinker. A clergyman's son from Devon, he was mediocre student at Oxford but a skillful writer who lived from his frequent articles and more than thirty books. He made his name with *The New Republic* (1877), a novel of ideas mocking liberal and secular intellectualism set in an English country house whose guests are obliged by their host to talk at dinner about "the Aim of Life." Heavier than Love Peacock and without Waugh's bitchiness, Mallock's satire made labored fun of some of the day's leading brains including Arnold, Huxley, Jowett, and Ruskin.

Mallock had a weakness for false either-ors. In economics and politics, he leaned hard on the supposedly exclusive alternatives of individualism and collectivism. By recognizing the existence of personal excellence and superior talent, he seemed to suggest that one had to deny authority or moral worth to human collectivities of any kind. His essay on faith and morals, "Is Life Worth Living?" (1879), argued as if by abandoning belief in the supernatural people had left themselves with no defense against nihilist rejection of morality itself.

By temperament a knocker and balloon pricker, Mallock yearned nevertheless for religious faith, troubled as he was by the modern loss of spirituality. In that same essay, he noted as "peculiarities" of the modern age the shaping impact of Christianity on Western society; the insignificance to which science was now reducing Christianity; and the strained "self-consciousness of the modern person," whom Mallock saw as overpreoccupied with themselves and unduly self-critical. By losing belief in the supernatural, Mallock held, people had robbed art of "all its strange interest" and created a world in which "the moral landscape" was "ruined." Although he never joined the Roman Catholic Church, Mallock admired, like Newman, its claims to magisterial authority. The Catholic Church, he wrote, was "the growing, moral sense of mankind organised and developed under a supernatural tutelage."

Rather than engage with secularists in hunting out nonreligious grounds for morality, Mallock mocked the very attempt, which he called "positivism." It was a "superstition" that replaced a providential creator with an idealized humanity as the world's moral guidance. Because humanity was weak-willed, diverse, and undersupplied with generosity or altruism, positivism found itself obliged to take people for better than they were. The secular morality of positivism accordingly puffed up an artificial "enthusiasm of humanity" that when faced by the melancholy human facts collapsed into the disappointments of "self-reproach, life-weariness and indifference." Another false either-or was on exhibit here. The enthusiasms of religious faith were equally subject to disappointment. The lack of cogency in Mallock's critiques mattered less than the verve with which they were expressed. Attacks of his kind on liberal do-goodism and liberal secularism lived on to serve the twentieth-century conservative canon.

Like Mallock, the American social thinker William Graham Sumner (1840–1910) was convinced that to answer socialists and liberal-democratic reformers, conservatives had to raise their intellectual game. Unlike Mallock, Sumner was happy to trade the supernatural authority of God for the this-worldly authority of nature in the hope that the latter would give morals and politics solid ground.

Sumner had grown up with religion and become a pastor only for religious beliefs to slip off him. He recorded that he did not abandon his religious faith; he simply left it in a drawer, as he put it, and on opening the drawer later found nothing there. His passage from preaching to teaching seemed as easy. Without formally dropping clerical office, Sumner became a professor at Yale University (1872), where he taught the study of society for the next thirty-seven years. Yale was evolving from a finishing school for young men plus clerical-training college into a modern university with graduate studies along German lines dedicated to bankable knowledge in science and the humanities. Sumner was part of that evolution. Studying society was to him an empirical matter, little different in character from the natural sciences.

Sumner in his many books and articles put forward a laissez-faire conservatism that pictured human life as driven by the "spur of competition," treated unfettered markets as the surest guarantee of rising prosperity, and took the state to owe people "nothing but peace, order and guarantees of rights." He was not a Utopian anarchist or dogmatic believer in spontaneous, self-correcting order. The ceaseless competition he had in mind was not a Hobbesian war of all against all. Society needed institutions and common norms; children had to be inducted into moral life and educated.

There, however, the common ground with Sumner's liberal-democratic and socialist opponents ended. Sumner did not believe there were blanket moral standards for humanity across the world. Societies had the norms and arrangements—he called them "folkways"—that suited them. Folkways changed slowly and imperceptibly, driven by forces of adaptation and selection over which people had little or no control. Social criticism was empty and well-meant interference, futile. Nor, on Sumner's unsunny picture, were people equal. The inexorable demands of competition sorted people into the "fit" and "more capable," who had "personal and social value," and the "not fit," who were less capable and had less value. Equality was a "flagrant falsehood" and all great achievements came from the elites of humankind. "Only the elite of any society, in any age, think," he wrote in *Folkways* (1906).

From those confident premises, which magically transmuted moral facts into "natural" facts, practical recommendations were drawn. Since people's "folkways" varied across the world, imperial attempts to impose foreign ways were bound to fail. Sumner objected to his country's liberal-imperialist annexations in Spanish America. Because people were not greatly improvable, government and cultural authority were best left to the few with brains and judgment. Democratic-representative government gave too little assurance that the "fit" would rule. Sumner, who had a brief exposure to it in New Haven, thought that, in local government, property owners should get an extra say and that "idlers" should have none. A postwar visit to Louisiana as part of a delegation to investigate voting fraud (1876) persuaded Sumner that denying free blacks a vote was a legitimate, if temporary, expedient.

Though no democrat with a small *d*, Sumner was a thoroughgoing economic liberal. Poverty was not caused by exploitation, he insisted, and would not be cured by impoverishing capitalists. Instead, poverty was to be cured by raising productivity and for that, as Mallock and Schumpeter believed, wise capitalists, not interfering do-gooders, were needed.

Sumner's defense of elites was not the defense of a class. Going one further than Rehberg, who thought some aristocrats unfit to rule, Sumner took the line earlier taken by the British liberal Lord Acton that every class was unfit to rule. All interests sought to capture government. The rich tended to rent-seeking, and tariffs were there to pamper uncompetitive industries. Sumner's belief in the primacy of free markets was robustly stated but not always easy to live up to. When the Progressives took aim at the business and banking trusts in the name of competition, Sumner, a conservative anti-Progressive, sided with the trusts.

True to his confidence that moral facts were to be found in "natural" facts, Sumner told an impressive, all-encompassing tale of social evolution from which those various general claims and practical recommendations supposedly flowed. A less sympathetic way to organize his political thinking is to reverse the logical order of argument. Almost all Sumner said about politics flowed from a pair of laissez-faire, moral assumptions with which he started: the undeserving poor were nature's inevitable losers whom it was wasteful to spend resources to help; all large-scale efforts to change a society's habits and moral attitudes by abrupt, "arbitrary" reform were fruitless and wrong to pursue.

Although commonly called a Social Darwinist, Sumner formed his chief views before reading Darwin's work. He used Spencer's phrase "survival of the fittest," but his social evolutionism was distinctively his own. He did not liken human society to the animal kingdom or try to reduce social facts to biological facts. He was wary of treating instincts as inherited characteristics born by physical traits transmitted to present-day people from distant animal forbears. Social change on Sumner's picture, was, it is true, governed by "natural selection," but selection for Sumner worked on competing beliefs, practices, and institutions rather than on biological variation. Institutions that "fit" their conditions survived. They alone were "good" or "right," and endurance proved their worth.

The mechanics of social competition and selection were vague. Sumner distinguished "struggle for existence" (humans versus nature) and "competition for life" (humans versus each other) but found it hard to keep the contests apart. To Sumner's doubters, the entire evolutionary apparatus was stage decor for independent laissez-faire views. When arguing for the natural resistance of norms in *Folkways*, Sumner turned from Darwinism to ordinary history with a parade of Renaissance humanists, New England Puritans, Austria's Josephine Reformers, and *Sozialpolitiker* in Wilhelmine Germany, who all failed, on Sumner's account, to graft foreign ways onto their own societies or to accelerate a supposedly natural rate of imperceptible cultural change. Suspicion that Sumner's conservative opinions floated loose from his social evolutionism was strengthened by the presence in contemporary argument of progressives and feminists who used an evolutionary apparatus to defend views distant from Sumner's.

Sumner is perhaps best remembered for his "forgotten man" argument against interference with society's "natural" working, originally published in *What Social Classes Owe Each Other* (1883). State-mandated aid for the needy, for example, fell on taxpayers generally but unevenly. The "forgotten man" here was the hard-pressed person A who paid taxes to help poor B with reform programs chosen by a distant, interfering C. Or the "forgotten man" might be the would-be worker shut out of a job by a trade union that restricted membership to keep up wages. In this interference Sumner included moral policing—temperance campaigns, for example—which he called the "the gospel of gush." "Almost all legislative effort to prevent vice is really protective of vice," he held. Such laws, Sumner argued, interfered with "nature's remedies" against vice, that is, "decline and dissolution." Consider a drunk in the gutter, Sumner suggested. It was pointless to pay the police or others to help him, for the drunk in the gutter was "just where he ought to be, according to the fitness and tendency of things." Rather than pay to rescue him, it was better to let "nature" do its work to "get him out of the way."

Although arrestingly stated, jostling here were separate claims that a social reformer could answer. Taxes could equally be seen as paying for the benefits of the social order enjoyed by all. The costs of unions had to be netted against their benefits, which other conservatives, Mallock, for one, had acknowledged. The drunk might be useless to society but calling him nature's refuse simply dodged the actual question of why he should be denied fellow feeling.

Sumner's demotion of compassion from social virtue to social vice led a historian of sociology, J. H. Abraham, to call his work an "extreme and inhuman approach to society." Sumner perhaps was overgeneralizing hard lessons in self-reliance learned young. His mother's death when he was eight left him in care of a loveless stepmother. An affectionate but often absent father, a mechanic from Lancashire, roamed the western frontier, then not far beyond Ohio, in search of fortune died broke. Sumner's remarkable ascent through theology and classics to higher studies in Germany and at Oxford, thence a professorship at Yale, had little obvious explanation for him but talent and hard work. If he could do it, why not others? The lack of fellow feeling behind the question spoke for a liberal harshness that not all American conservatives were happy to embrace.

If Sumner's celebration of lonesomeness make his laissez-faire conservatism an outlier, he belongs in other ways squarely in the conservative tradition. Although markets on his view were to be left free to work their changes undisturbed, authoritative elites, enduring customs, and stable institutions were also needed for social order. His was an attractive, influential sell in a free-for-all society where material conditions were rapidly, if unevenly, improving but where society's elites were alarmed by democratic pressures from below.

Sumner's positive ideas of how conservatives could reconcile tradition and change were vaguer and weaker than his negative certitude about the limits of good intentions. His scorn for reforming "sentimentalists" in politics who failed to grasp the so-called law of unintended consequences became part of the right's twentieth-century rhetorical arsenal for use against progressive liberal proposals for social reform. But as the philosopher C. D. Broad pointed out in another connection not long after Sumner's death, rational skepticism about reform cuts two ways. It is indeed likely that not all the effects of a proposed change are always foreseen; however, the "law of unintended consequences" claims more. It alleges that those unforeseen consequences are likelier to be bad than good, which there is no adequate reason to believe.

A less extreme, more worldly, and better-grounded thinker was Joseph Schumpeter (1883–1950), an Austrian-born economist and conservative defender of capitalism. Setting aside historical nostalgia and moral critique, Schumpeter put political economy at conservatism's heart. Liberal capitalism, he argued in *Capitalism, Socialism and Democracy* (1942), was the best of the bad ways to organize a stable society, the good ways being unachievable. His conservative compromise with liberal modernity was subtle, Hegelo-Marxist in its reconciliation of opposites, and rich in "Yes, if" and "Yes, but." Capitalism was creative but destructive. Innovation continually destroyed familiar goods, firms, and jobs, replacing them with unfamiliar ones. Capitalism needed such innovation together with entrepreneurs who put them into the market but, grown large and complex, capitalism yearned for bureaucratic rationalization. Without popular acceptance, capitalism was unsustainable, yet democratic interference threatened its efficiency. Could capitalism survive democracy? Schumpeter did not think so but at once added a "Yes, if": capitalism could survive with an open, authoritative upper class, an efficient, uncorrupt bureaucracy, broad social consensus, and institutional breakwaters against majority pressures, especially in economic and financial management.

Schumpeter's year of birth (1883) was notable for economics: John Maynard Keynes also arrived and Karl Marx died. Unlike Marx, Schumpeter did not take capitalism's self-devouring character for fatal. Unlike Keynes, he did not think state action could tame its cycles. The turbulence of capitalism was, as it were, a fact of modern life. "Creative destruction," he wrote, "is the essential fact about capitalism. It is what capitalism consists in and what every capitalist concern has got to live in." Economic life for Schumpeter was not a search for equilibrium but, as he wrote, a "process of change." For a conservative, especially a liberal, laissez-faire conservative, that was a hard doctrine to articulate and defend. Schumpeter, an ironist, was aware of the conflicts.

Schumpeter had a lifelong contempt for anti-capitalist intellectuals who wrote dismissively about business and finance with no experience of either, yet he regretted the old elites' loss of cultural authority and habits of control that capitalism had undermined. His own background was mixed. In class-conscious Austria, Schumpeter was both commercial and upper-class.

Reflecting on capitalism and imperialism at the end of the 1914–18 war, Schumpeter denied the Leninist linkage of capitalism and world conflict. In an echo of eighteenth-century thinkers who had looked to commerce to soften manners and retire combat as a form of life, Schumpeter wrote in "Sociology of Imperialisms" (1918) of the civilizing, pacifying effects of liberal-democratic institutions. A quarter of a century later in the middle of a yet more terrible world war, Schumpeter, in a spirit of doubt reinforced by events, wrote of democracy's and capitalism's weaknesses.

In the 1920s and 1930s, much of Europe—Italy, Spain, Portugal, Poland, Greece, Lithuania, and Yugoslavia—had fallen under fascist or authoritarian dictatorships. Germany and Austria had succumbed to Nazism. In the United States, where Schumpeter was now teaching, the economy had recovered from a deep slump thanks in part to the American preparation for war. Intellectually, the defenders of market capitalism were on the defensive. Socialist planning, public ownership, and Keynesian intervention were canvassed on the left as necessary rescues for a failing socioeconomic system. The Polish economist Oskar Lange and others were offering answers to Mises's antisocialist claim that prices needed markets and that since resources could not be efficiently allocated without prices, a marketless, planned economy was bound to fail.

In that climate of self-doubt, Schumpeter described in *Capitalism, Socialism and Democracy* the many ways in which capitalism was undermining itself. It encouraged social vices that sapped its health and discouraged the social virtues of thrift, delayed gratification, and discipline needed for its survival. In the disorder it caused, capitalism stimulated exaggerated concern for the victims of the turmoil, as epitomized in Gladstonian liberalism and bequeathed to Keynesian reform. "Radicals may insist that the masses are crying for salvation from intolerable sufferings," Schumpeter wrote, but "there never was so much personal freedom of mind and body for all . . . never so much active sympathy . . . [and] readiness to accept burdens as there is in modern capitalistic society."

Instead of a well-defended fortress, Schumpeter saw capitalism's "crumbling walls." He worried that he was witnessing a decline of the adventurous, innovative spirit of early capitalism. Entrepreneurship, he feared, was giving way to corporate managerialism and government regulation. Limited companies with tradeable shares had broken the vital link between ownership and innovation.

A subtler trouble was the sweeping away of "feudal" holdovers—the sustaining practices and authoritative habits of old precapitalist elites— that Schumpeter feared had no replacement in fluid market capitalism. Like Weber, he worried that a rationalistic, unheroic bourgeoisie, incapable of national seriousness, was "ill equipped to face the problems, both domestic and international, that have normally to be faced by a country of any importance." In a metaphor that mixed a New Deal dam with a Gothic cathedral, Schumpeter wrote: "In breaking down the precapitalist framework of society, capitalism . . . broke not only barriers that impeded its progress but also flying buttresses that prevented its collapse."

As in other providential stories of capitalism's future course, it was not clear what was causing what, as Albert O. Hirschman pointed out in a bravura essay, "Rival Interpretations of Market Society" (1982). If indeed capitalism softened manners and made competition less warlike, was that good or bad? Schumpeter first thought it good, by making nations less eager to fight each other. Later he worried that "softening" both disarmed the bourgeoisie for its historic task of throwing off the "shackles" of the old order and robbed it of the self-denial needed to be effectively capitalistic. Like another observer at mid-century, the liberal Louis Hartz, Schumpeter wondered if a capitalist society given over entirely to the authority of the market would not work better if some of the old shackles providing cultural and moral guidance were somehow retained. As Hirschman suggested, there were part truths in each of those grand claims. They lived on in thinking about the "cultural contradictions" of capitalism, which took wing among German and American neoconservatives in the 1950s and 1960s.

Among capitalism's travails, Schumpeter's greatest concern was about anti-capitalist intellectuals. Amid "growing hostility," Schumpeter wrote, there emerged the social critic whose corrosive damage threatened to make "the bourgeois fortress . . . politically defenseless." The intellectual required a talent for words but had no responsibility for the conduct of affairs. Their disaffection made them unemployable.

Liberal bourgeois commitment to freedom of speech made them un-controllable. Only authoritarians kept intellectuals in their place. No lesson of Schumpeter's was more taken to heart by post-1945 conservatives than his plea to the right to gird for the battle of ideas in defense of capitalism.

Like the elite theorists, earlier mentioned, Schumpeter believed in popular sovereignty only in a most limited or figurative way. He saw electoral democracy as a contest among small groups for office: "Democracy is the rule of politicians." Old bottom-up justifications of democratic government—that it served the common good or expressed the popular will—did not work. The common good was either a theoretical figment or a genuine quantity but impossible to gauge. People singly or en masse were not reasonable enough to have a settled, discernible will. Schumpeter proposed instead a top-down theory of competition for leadership. Electoral democracy, Schumpeter wrote, was an "arrangement for arriving at political decisions in which individuals acquire the power to decide by means of a competitive struggle for the people's vote." Among the benefits of accepting but confining democracy in that way, Schumpeter listed the creation of an undisputed space for decisive leadership, the blunting of class struggle, regular opportunities to remove unwanted governments, and the dropping of populist appeals against minorities in the name of the people's will.

So that that democratic "rule of politicians" should not injure capitalism, Schumpeter set several conditions. There should be politicians of caliber. The range of political decisions should be limited, especially in economic and monetary matters. Democratic "self-control" should prevail: that is, people must accept duly imposed laws even if they disapproved of them, and everyone should be encouraged to tolerate diverse opinions. Taken together, those conditions were stringent enough to ask if Schumpeter was not, in effect, saying that, no, capitalism could not survive, or that it could live on, but neutered by a well-meaning, socialist reformism.

As if to stress that melancholy vision, Schumpeter made clear who—or rather, who was not—in charge. "Mankind is not free to choose," he wrote. "Things economic and social move by their own momentum and the ensuing situations compel individuals and groups to behave in certain ways whatever they may wish to do—not indeed by destroying their freedom of choice but . . . by narrowing the list of possibilities from which to choose. If this is the quintessence of Marxism, then we all of us have got to be Marxists."

Schumpeter, recall, was an ironist. His drift was not always what it appeared. He was too conservative to trust to hope and too aware of the failures and catastrophes of his century for hymns to progress. Surrounded by optimists about socialism, he playacted the pessimist about capitalism. If that reading of Schumpeter's thought is correct, he was more hopeful for capitalism than he seemed. The half century after his death in 1950 proved him right. His irony had another side, however. How confident was he that conservatism could survive capitalism?

Schumpeter revered the analytical economics of Walras and though not strongly mathematical himself championed the econometrics of which Walras was an originator. Yet modeling an economy as an equilibrium-seeking system struck Schumpeter as incomplete. It robbed economies of historic shape. Schumpeter was not alone in seeing that economics must be dynamic, not just static. By his day, business-cycle and growth theories abounded. Schumpeter, however, went further, or perhaps turned sideways. The historic shape he found in capitalism was, in a nontechnical sense, chaotic. Technical innovations and the entrepreneurship that brought them to market were ceaselessly turning upside down the socioeconomic patterns of how people worked and lived.

To conservatives, who were concerned either with people's chosen aims or with their duties, that was an alarming vision. A founding thought for conservatives in their objections to liberalism was that people's aims and duties made sense only in a settled frame of society that changed at most slowly. If, as it seemed inevitable in capitalism, the frame was continually and unpredictably shifting, talk of aims and duties lost its grip. The basis for a common ethics and culture began to disappear. Would such a capitalism permit society to conserve habits, practices, and allegiances that made human life more than a market free-for-all in which everything was tradable but rarely at yesterday's price?

Schumpeter the ironist gave no clear answer, but his drift was another "yes, if." Liberal conservatism could survive capitalism if there were open, absorbant upper classes, a proficient, independent bureaucracy, and a degree of agreement among people about the ethical and cultural values in their common life. Liberal conservatism could survive, in a word, if the market did not devour society.

Schumpeter handed down to late twentieth-century conservatism economic counsels of prudence and a social riddle. He restated old conservative cautions about quiet politics and competent government in terms of sound economic management. It was urgent, he stressed, to insulate economic and especially monetary management from democratic pressures, to beware of policies and reforms that discouraged entrepreneurship, and to counter disruptive intellectuals of the left with vigorous defenses of capitalism. Save in the most general terms, he left hanging the social riddle that taxed later conservative thinkers, especially in Germany and the United States, of how excellence, authority, and ethical values could yet be preserved in the productive churn of creative destruction.

When facing how to reconcile the competing demands of economic liberalism with conservative concern for the ethical fabric of society, thinkers of the mainstream right after Schumpeter in the second half of the twentieth century had a choice of avenues. Either they resolved the conflict by force and subordinated society to the economy in the hope that efficiency, given time, would take care of ethics. Or they continued to search, Diogenes-like, for social values that had to be saved as familiar norms and respect for ethical authorities seemed to vanish at bewildering pace.

ii. Six Ways to Imagine the People: Treitschke, Le Bon, Du Camp, Adams, Mencken, and Sorel

By 1880, nation building and democracy had created a new being, the nation-state. Yet what was a nation-state? The *Oxford English Dictionary*'s entry for "nation-state" reads: "An independent political state formed from a people who share a common national identity, histori-cally, culturally, or ethnically. More generally, any independent political state. A nation-state may be distinguished from states which comprise two or more historically distinct peoples, or which comprise only part of a historical people." With loud understatement, the entry adds: "However, such distinctions are frequently problematic." No less than liberals, conservatives struggled to get their understanding of those volatile ideas—*people, nation,* and *state*—into order.

Since classical times, "the people" had meant different things. As a political term, it might mean a *citizenry* of a city, commonwealth, or state, that is, men with civic duties, common rights, and a role in public argument as opposed to everyone else without. As a head-counting term, it could mean simply a *populace,* a body of people in a recognized territory, whatever their age or status, including perhaps foreigners. Next, as a class term, "the people" could mean the *common people,* the great mass of society without wealth, status, or voice but who, when angry or hungry, might form a demanding mob.

Finally, and most knottily, "the people" might mean a *national people* or *nation,* a natural-seeming but recent, contested idea that took ele-ments from the other three. The people of a nation—the French, the English, and so on—were distinct from those of another (foreigners). They were neither noble, rich, nor common but from any class. They were subject to the same laws and government, which, if wise, listened to what the people had to say. In conditions of broad social ignorance, who composed the nation—who the national people were and what, if anything, they were like—was left first to the work of the imagination.

When putting those jostling ideas together, nineteenth-century lib-erals and conservatives, to sharpen a contrast, started at opposite ends. Of anything unfamiliar or disputed it is natural to ask, where did it come from and what it is made of? So too of the nation. How did na-tions form? How did people become a nation? In answering those questions, liberals began with the citizens of a state and drew out of them a nation. If the liberals were democrats, they included common people in the citizenry. For liberals, the nation was, accordingly, a de-rivative, political idea. Conservatives, by contrast, began with the nation and built from it a citizenry. As a distinct body of people, the nation was imagined ancestrally or culturally; that is, its people could be treated as sharing origins or as sharing beliefs, attachments, and historical memories. Without one or the other, a people could not make a citizenry. The nation, for conservatives, became accordingly a foundational, social idea.

Although starting at opposite ends, the competing sides found meeting points. Liberals might stress that to form a nation, people in practice needed "like-mindedness" of some kind. Mill, for example, eloquently pressed the point in *On Representative Government* (1861). Conservatives in turn might stretch the shared beliefs required for people to form a citizenry to include explicit commitments to a given political way of life.

Until the nineteenth century, such puzzle-questions of people, nation, and state chiefly exercised lawyers or clerics advising monarchs and grandees. In the democratic age, they burst into politics in two forms, one horizontal, the other vertical. Separated but like-minded people wanted to unite (Germany, for example). Unlike-minded people wished to separate (American southerners; peoples of the Austro-Hungarian and Ottoman Empires; Ireland as a disputed part of the United Kingdom combined both problems). The vertical question touching people, nation, and state was the character of popular sovereignty. How wide and tight was democratic control to be? Popular sovereignty had meant one thing when exercised by small, quarrelsome but familiar in-groups. It meant another when exercised by a formidable, little-known popular mass.

Conservatives knew a lot about people. Landowners knew tenants. Bosses knew workers. Politicians knew voters. Priests knew parishioners and teachers knew students. Their knowledge, however, was more intimate than social, more personal than anonymous. The right's knowledge of people, that is, tended to be thick and narrow rather than thin and broad. That gave it an edge of a kind over the left, whose knowledge of people en masse, for whom it professed to speak, overleaned on books and theories. The right, however, also had to think of the people en masse if it was to thrive in democracy. Were the people hostile or friendly? Fickle or reliable? Disruptors of society or the bedrock on which it stood? The right needed answers. Yet where was it to turn? Social theory abounded but social statistics, opinion sampling, and knowledge of society generally were in their infancy. From the 1840s, as earlier noted, social observers—Friedrich Bülau, Eugène Buret, Friedrich Engels, and Louis-René Villermé—had studied factory work and urban poverty. In the 1850s, the French engineer and proto-sociologist Frédéric Le Play had studied family structures and patterns of property transfer. The German historical economist Gustav Schmoller had opened Europe first socioeconomic think tank, the Verein für Sozialpolitik (1872). Yet little solid was known yet of the people en masse, whom conservatives now reluctantly took for their new masters. As the counting, classifying, and typifying of society got slowly under way, the right turned also to its imagination. It filled the gaps in what it knew about people with pictures. To begin with, they were anxious and dark.

In imagining the people, conservative thinkers and writers in the late nineteenth and early twentieth centuries typically organized their pictures around one or other of six themes: the primacy of the people's *national* character, as stressed by patriotic historians such as Heinrich von Treitschke; the *nonrationality* of crowds, as pressed by Gustave Le Bon; a debased variant of that thought, their *bestiality*, as recounted in Maxime Du Camp's superheated account of the Paris Commune; their everyday *venality*, as regretted by Henry Adams in his ambivalent satire on electoral democracy; their *stupidity*, as ridiculed by H. L. Mencken in his lampoons against liberal opinion and middle-class culture; and their redemptive *hostility* as invoked against liberalism and parliamentary democracy by Georges Sorel, a hard-to-classify radical who shared a conservative loathing for the hypocritical liberal talk of progress and who saw the people as mute but effective saviors.

The *nation* was a unifying idea that served late nineteenth-century conservatives as a way to lower tension between their hopeful vision of a people at peace with itself and the manifest divisions of society. Internally, the idea *nation* could be used in temperate, inclusive ways as a focus of common loyalty, like the old monarchy. Or it could be used intemperately, in exclusive, often racialist, ways to divide those who belonged and those who did not belong in the true nation. Externally, the nation was thought of as one state in a competitive world of others, either pacifically, as a model and improver for the world, or belligerently, as an armed righter of national wrongs. In each of those ways, the nation served as a unifying idea: by symbolizing the people (a common whole), purifying the people (excluding the unwanted), and, in pride or vengeance, animating the people (to action in the wider world). Disraelian Conservatives and American Republicans appealed to the inclusive nation as a symbolic unity. During the 1880s and 1890s, segments of the French and German right adopted exclusionary, purifying ideas of their nations. Liberal imperialists in Britain and France and Bismarckian *Realpolitiker* in Germany invoked national-mindedness for military-diplomatic ends.

An outstanding example of a nationalist historian who combined realpolitik and exclusion was Heinrich von Treitschke (1834–96). Looked down on by fellow scholars, he was a writer of great power and popularity. His multivolume history of Germany in the eighteenth and nineteenth centuries graced the shelves of the educated middle classes and lent public support to Germany's strategic demands for equal status among the world's powers. The historian Theodor Mommsen, who doubted his scholarship and rebuked him for his anti-Semitism, called Treitschke's pen the nation's sharpest sword. Treitschke had intellectual and political platforms as a university professor, longtime editor of the political monthly *Preussische Jahrbücher*, and member of the Reichstag. He sat as a National Liberal, although his liberalism was thin. A Dresden-born Saxon, he became a Prussian superpatriot. An early free trader, he turned protectionist. Originally a Bismarck skeptic, he became a Bismarck worshipper. Treitschke's exaltation of the Hohenzollern dynasty and his anti-Semitism caught a moment on the German right in the 1880s and 1890s. Conservatism was torn between cautious liberal reform and national self-assertion coupled with popular activism. Treitschke's conservatism was the second kind.

Treitschke wrote a national history that gathered the complexities and divisions of the German lands onto a single path leading to the Wilhelmine Reich under a Prussian monarch. German diversity—Rhineland

and East Prussia, Catholic and Protestant, farms and industry—was blended into the higher unity of the Prussian state. His history found German national feeling before the Napoleonic age, attacking the post-Napoleonic German Federation, Austrians, and southern Germans for together obstructing German unity. It attacked French liberals, natural-law rationalists, and Jewish cosmopolitans and took shots at the poet Heine. Treitschke also attacked socialism for "alienating its comrades from the state and the fatherland" in the name of "envy and greed" (1874). He treated palliative liberal reforms of the kind proposed by Schmoller as sentimental refusals to acknowledge natural inferiority and weakness. Yet he accepted universal suffrage and was hostile to the three-class Prussian franchise.

Writing to a friend (1879), Treitschke complained of political correctness *avant la lettre,* moaning that the harshest things could be said against the national failings of the Germans or French but not against the Jews. In a notorious pamphlet written in 1880, he lent his authority as a historian to growing anti-Semitism. "Year after year out of the inexhaustible Polish cradle there streams over our eastern border a host of hustling, pants-peddling youths, whose children and children's children will someday command Germany's stock exchanges and newspapers." Mommsen blamed Treitschke for fomenting anti-Jewish protests by Leipzig students. The dispute between them turned on competing understandings of assimilation. Mommsen thought Jews should integrate themselves politically into the Reich. Treitschke confused civic assimilation of that kind with Jewish abandonment of their faith. Dividing them was a liberal-inclusive and a conservative-exclusive idea of nationality. For the liberal Mommsen, to be a good German you had to be a good citizen. For the conservative Treitschke, to be a good German you had to be a particular kind of person.

Treitschke turned Karl Rochau's 1853 coinage *Realpolitik* from a warning by liberals to themselves to heed actual circumstances into a right-wing call for the uninhibited use of national power. "The state," for Treitschke, was not "a good little boy, to be brushed and washed and sent to school." The state, as in Hegel's thinking, was the most comprehensive frame of "ethical life," the common, norm-governed life of people together in society. The frame rose from families, through law, commerce, and bureaucracy to the highest organs of state power. Hegel had divided them into crown, executive, and legislature, but Treitschke did not believe in the separation of powers.

Of German unification, he wrote that the army was the stronger national bond, not the Reichstag, where people learned to "hate and abuse each other." Treitschke wrote as if following a schema that contrasted weakness (peace, society, middle classes, and liberal social policy) with strength (war, state, army, and Junker conservatism). In his hierarchy of control, Prussia oversaw Germany; Germany, Europe (especially hypocritical England); and the German empire, the inferior people of the colonies.

Who were the German people? For Treitschke, they were above all patriots, sharing devotion to the national idea. In that devotion, not in ancestry or biology, lay their Germanness. That devotion was shared by all true Germans, but although present in the nobility and the lower classes, it was strongest in the social core: the educated middle classes. "Without overprizing itself, a people does not arrive at knowledge of itself at all. . . . The Germans are always in danger of losing their nationality because they have too little of this solid pride." Fellow-feeling, a sense of shared past, and national pride were not far from how Mill and many other nineteenth-century liberals saw the nation. A difference between that and Treitschke's conservative view lay in this. For a liberal, attachment to nation was one political virtue among others. It was not a trump. For Treitschke, it was as if national feeling were all.

In the light of Germany's early twentieth-century history, it is tempting but wrong to treat exclusionary nationalism as typical of all Germans or unique to Germany. Such nationalism in Germany, though powerful, was neither pervasive nor stable. German jingoism of the 1890s and the rally to arms of 1914 contrasts with detente of the 1910s and the military disillusion, peace efforts, and mutinies of 1917–18. The Wilhelmine Reich lacked national symbols. There was no official German anthem until 1922. The red-white-black flag of 1871, called for not from patriotic feeling but by shipping companies who needed a national ensign, was chosen to satisfy both Prussia (white and black) and Germany's great trading cities (red and white). The imperial title was never settled. The German states kept their own symbols and institutions. The Reich constitution, as noted, was widely thought of as an international treaty, not the baptismal certificate of a new nation.

Unifying national myths were popularized in the second half of the nineteenth century also in the United States, Britain, and France. George Bancroft's epic history (1854–78) treated the founding of the United States and its subsequent course as a purposeful crusade by selfless Americans for the freedom of the civilized world. John Fiske's popular histories mixed Darwinist speculation with providential Americanism. Theodore Roosevelt's best-selling history, *The Winning of the West* (1889–96), recounted how, in settling the frontier, good, that is cooperative, "savages" were relocated and bad, that is resistant ones, were swept aside. In Britain, the "bible of imperialism," J. R. Seeley's *The Expansion of England* (1883), wrote of a de-territorialized Englishness spreading peacefully across the world, although not, Seeley thought, in India. It sold eighty thousand copies in three years and was still selling more than ten thousand a year in 1911. Thomas Carlyle's biographer and Oxford history professor, James Froude, wrote an anti-Catholic history of Ireland and jingoist celebrations of the British Empire. Edward Freeman's *History of the Norman Conquest* (1867–79) contrasted early Britain's Saxon liberties with Norman oppression from France. Although in party terms a Gladstonian Liberal, Freeman was a notorious bigot, free in his contempt for blacks, Jews, and the Irish. Across the Channel, the French archaeologist and historian Numa Fustel de Coulanges expunged the German tribes from his scholarly studies of early France. The great educationalist and "national teacher" of the Third Republic, Ernest Lavisse, supervised historical textbooks for schools that celebrated the French epic. His primer for the youngest children told them: "You must love France because nature has made it beautiful and because history has made it grand."

National feeling was nowhere spontaneous. The national imagination needed prompting and fostering everywhere by writers and intellectuals. That said, nations were not imaginary. To prompt and foster them, there had to be common beliefs and attachments to start with. What mattered among conservatives was whether nations were imagined in inclusive or exclusive ways.

Common tradition had treated people in crowds as awesome, foolish, terrifying, savage, and bestial. When calm, people in crowds acted thoughtlessly, in herdlike imitation of each other. When roused, they behaved like violent drunks, capricious women, or lunatics. Thus had common tradition pictured people en masse. The contribution of Gustave Le Bon (1841–1931) was to place immemorial fear of the mob on a factual-sounding pedestal. An omnicurious French doctor, social thinker, and scientific popularizer, Le Bon won a name among politicians and thinkers who, while doubting his methods, welcomed his conclusion that people en masse were not to be trusted.

Part of Le Bon's success was to reframe ancient prejudice. Crowds were not mindless, Le Bon insisted, rather, they had a mind of a special kind. In *La Psychologie des foules* (*The Crowd: A Study of the Popular Mind*, 1895), Le Bon wrote of a collective mind driven by hidden instincts that silenced even the crowd's most reasonable members. "Isolated," he wrote, "a man may be a cultivated individual; in a crowd, he is a barbarian." The aphorism was typical of him. As a well-known Paris *saloniste*, Le Bon was an early example of a now familiar type, the gifted social-science popularizer who reduced complexities and uncertainties to palatable nuggets. When the French writer and hostess Marthe Bibesco was asked why political luminaries put up with Le Bon, she replied that he gave them formulas and that politicians lived by formulas, the way cooks lived by recipes.

For readers alarmed by mass democracy, *The Crowd* had good news and bad. Societies were never remade by radical intervention. They changed slowly in a gradual evolution of ideas and routines. Comforting as that might sound, it had to be accepted that predemocratic frameworks had gone. The threat of the masses lay less in their weight of votes than in the daunting content of their demands. Worse, the masses were irrational. Still, they were governable if understood as crowds.

A crowd, Le Bon explained, was not a chance agglomeration. It was organized and purposeful, albeit unconsciously and not reasonably. Crowds formed without their members realizing. Each member felt "invincible power" bestowed by numbers, yet all were "suggestible" and the crowd acquired its own purpose by "contagion." In a crowd, everyone became "a barbarian, that is, a creature acting by instinct." Instead of reasoning, crowds thought in pictures and analogies. They did not act intelligently, although they might have a "mood," fixed by circumstances. The mood could be joyful and peaceful or hate-filled and aggressive. Crowds, accordingly, were capable of acting criminally (riots) or heroically (battle).

In mass society, the old controls on people were ineffective. Neither religion nor customary institutions could master the crowd; however, leaders inevitably emerged from crowds and served as their guides. They might be tyrannical or statesmanlike, evil or good. They were always despotic and drew their authority not from intelligence or superior ability but from understanding the crowd and typifying its members. The successful leaders of crowds never explained or sought to justify what they said but simply pronounced and then repeated themselves.

Le Bon divided crowds into heterogeneous (with mixed membership) or homogeneous (the same sort of members). The first kind could be "anonymous" (street crowds) or "non-anonymous" (juries or parliaments, both prone to groupthink). Homogeneous crowds included sects and castes (for example, priests, judges, military officers, or factory workers), as well as social classes (the peasantry, the middle-classes). When crowd-thinking seized a social caste, it tended to crystallize and last. The caste then listened only to itself and sought to capture authority in order to control the masses.

Since proneness to thinking like a crowd did not distinguish social elites and "civilized" peoples from the lower classes or "primitive" peoples, Le Bon fell back on common prejudice for his hostile views of women (who were naturally inferior to men); of free universal education, an aim of Ferry's 1880s reforms (few people were improvable by schooling); and of blacks ("One can award a negro a bachelor of arts degree, a doctorate," Le Bon opined, "one cannot make him civilized.")

Universal suffrage, in Le Bon's opinion, was regrettable but unavoidable. Government was ever less able to direct opinion. Nevertheless, for "civilised peoples," parliamentary assemblies were still the best form of government, Le Bon allowed, adding ironically, "at any rate for thinkers, writers, artists and learned men." Crowds were intolerant, dictatorial, and conservative, with an "absolute fetish for tradition, an unconscious horror of any novelty that might change the condition of their lives." They were governable by a dominating, powerful leader.

Despite evident inconsistencies and overlaps in Le Bon's sketch for a fact-based study of mass behavior, his vivid picture of people en masse as a crowd pressed by forces that it did not fully comprehend stamped the imagination of all those, left or right, who questioned whether liberal parliamentarism could meet the Third Republic's tests: economic downturn in 1893, fiscal weakness, corruption scandals, and spreading strikes.

Le Bon denied partisan intent, but *The Crowd*, which quickly ran through many editions, nourished conservative doubts about democratic liberalism in obvious ways. By stigmatizing collective action as crowd action and crowd action as irrational, it seemed to vindicate the right's fears of working-class organization and demands (trade union rights together with electoral pressure for social reform and state controls in the economy). By suggesting that all action by social groups was prone to crowd-like irrationality, Le Bon's work fortified conservative doubts about the influence, even the existence, of the reasonable, independent-minded citizen on which political liberalism leaned.

Without calling him the first to do so, in 1921 Sigmund Freud paid Le Bon the compliment of having recognized the role of "unconscious mental life." In Schumpeter's opinion, Le Bon, "dealt a serious blow to the picture of man's nature which underlies the classical doctrine of democracy and democratic folklore about revolutions." For all his exaggerations, Schumpeter wrote, Le Bon "made us face gruesome facts" of "primitive impulses, infantilisms and criminal propensities" that "everybody knew but nobody wished to see."

Le Bon was more borrower and bricoleur than systematic thinker. From the social Darwinism of the Spencerians he took the idea of a biocultural hierarchy dividing humanity into higher and lower civilizations. From Alfred Fouillée (1838–1912), Le Bon took the thought that our understanding of morals and society, far from being silently shaped by material forces of which we were unaware, was to the contrary shaped by guiding ideas, which Fouillée had called "*idées forces.*" Le Bon's work came after Gabriel Tarde's (1890) on the force of imitation in social life and Scipio Sighele's (1891) on criminal crowds, prompting priority disputes. Writing of the kind stamped conservative thinking about liberal-democratic society into the next century, typified by *The Revolt of the Masses* (1930), from the right-wing Spanish thinker, José Ortega y Gasset. It ran on into the dismal view of democratic ethics and culture that preoccupied American and German neoconservatives after 1945.

The study of people en masse became more sophisticated, more empirical, and more professionalized. Yet despite aspirations to science, such studies were never successfully depoliticized. Distinct twentieth-century traditions of people en masse emerged, one prominent in social psychology, the other in free-market economics. The first was friendly to conservative fears about democracy. It sought to confirm Le Bon's claims about the folly of crowds and their submissiveness to despotic leaders. The collapse of liberal democracies in the 1920s and 1930s, together with the rise of fascism, Nazism, and Soviet Communism, encouraged the midcentury study of irrationality in politics, disruptive mass movements, and the supposed "authoritarian" (that is, submissive) personality. An enquiry into the roots of fanaticism by the American social psychologist Eric Hoffer, *The True Believer: Thoughts on the Nature of Mass Movements* (1951) became a best seller and was said to be the book Eisenhower most liked to give to visitors.

The second, economic, tradition stressed, by contrast, the wisdom of crowds. Drawing on rational choice theory and claims about the superior information-gathering capacities of free markets, this more hopeful tradition looked without anxiety on decision-making by people en masse. Collective decision-making was mined with diverting traps and paradoxes, but none so grave as to ruin confidence in the wise crowd. As long as the crowd in question was diverse, independent-minded, and, above all, not guided, bullied, or bossed about, collective decision-making grew better the bigger the crowd was.

To schematize, the foolish crowd preoccupied anxious conservatives from the late nineteenth to the mid-twentieth century. After 1945, conservatives-turned-market-liberals welcomed the wise crowd without entirely forgetting the foolish and authority-craving one. Conservatism became stretched between anxiety and hope. Defense of property, trust in markets, and suspicion of government pushed conservatives to see sagacity in the blind, unguided judgments of the numerous, disconnected, wise crowd. Pulling them the other way was their original fear of the equally numerous but fused and foolish crowd. Conservatives never fully shook the suspicion that the wise crowd of economic theory, far from being a source of spontaneous order, was in fact an amoral free-for-all in disguise.

Le Bon's simple but graspable picture of the people as crowd lived on in conservative fears of mass democracy, regret at cultural leveling, and rejection of political liberalism's picture of the self-reliant, reasonable citizen. It was given lurid color by literary writers who wrote in contemporary terms about the fickleness and dangers of the mob. A notable French example was Maxime Du Camp (1822–94). A minor writer and adventurous early photographer, Du Camp was best known for literary friendships with Gustave Flaubert and Baudelaire, who dedicated to him "Le Voyage," the caustic hymn to disenchantment from *Fleurs du mal*. Du Camp might well be forgotten but for a vehement, four-volume account of the 1871 Commune, *Convulsions de Paris* (1878–80). It added the Commune to 1793 and 1848 in the conservative canon of horror at the Paris mob. A masterpiece of vituperation and scorn, Du Camp's work was set in a deceptively factual frame of Communal documents and official reports. As a national guardsman in 1848, Du Camp had fought insurgents, been wounded, and retained a loathing for republicans that gave his book literary force. *Convulsions* presented a polemical, fantastical picture of the city's common people as weak-willed, malady-prone simpletons led astray by a few hundred half-educated villains.

In demonizing the people of Paris, Du Camp neatly put the matter back to front. The Commune was less a rebellion than a struggle by Paris to survive as state authority vanished. The collapse of France's armies (July–September 1870) in an ill-chosen war with Prussia had finished off the authoritarian Second Empire. To seal victory and end the war, the Germans besieged the capital. As food supplies ran low in January 1871, the French sued for terms. In an electoral campaign, radical French cities vied with a conservative countryside for control of a fragile new republic. War-weary voters chose a right-wing government under Thiers, granting him a mandate to accept a harsh German peace.

In that election, radical candidates had swept the Paris parliamentary seats. In the poorer, more populous *quartiers* to the east, revulsion at the peace, dreams of fighting on, and anger at government help for creditors mingled with hopes for democratic rights and social reform. When regular troops began to fraternize with the Paris militia (March 1871), Thiers in some panic recalled the army and ministries to Versailles. Robbed of state authority, Paris elected a self-governing Commune of around ninety members, most of them minor professionals and self-employed artisans. Where radical Paris saw autonomy, conservative Versailles spied revolution. What to Versailles was restoring political order, the Commune took for class war by the rich.

Anarchist and Utopian talk rang in political clubs, but the Commune was neither proletarian nor revolutionary. Its goals were greater self-rule for Paris and the removal of burdens on craftsmen and small businesses. The Commune lasted seventy-two days, scant time to meet any goal, though time enough for Thiers to regroup and crush a spontaneous insurgency his government had done much to bring about. In May, 130,000 troops from the French regular army entered Paris from the western suburbs. Seven days later the army had killed perhaps 10,000 defenders, unarmed helpers, and hapless bystanders. Prisoners were shot out of hand. Of 36,000 people arrested, some 10,000 were executed, jailed, or deported.

With the skill of a prosecuting attorney, Du Camp drew from these muddled, terrible events one cause for blame: a "fourth estate" of radical troublemakers and left-wing intellectuals. They aimed to end privileges that "existed only in their imagination" and bestow government "by right of birth on those who learn nothing, know nothing, and want to do nothing." They were animated by envy "that primal vice" of "base people with suspect minds." This unrepresentative army of the disappointed included "déclassé petty bourgeois, workers in despair at not being bosses, bosses incensed at not making fortunes, newspapermen without newspapers, doctors with no patients, teachers with nobody to teach." The political lesson of giving in to this imaginary monster was for Du Camp quite general for Europe as a whole: "Collectivists, French communards, German social democrats, Russian nihilists . . . Different labels, same poison."

Where Du Camp was heated and direct, the American author and historian of the United States Henry Adams (1838–1918) was allusive and elegiac. A disillusioned progressive, Adams saw people en masse as well-intentioned but biddable. Political engagement was part, but not the larger part, of their lives. Without a vigilant-enough citizenry, his country's admirable democratic institutions had been captured by mon-eyed interests, which paid politicians to govern in the people's name. To Adams, it was a sordid bargain.

The grandson of one president and great-grandson of another, Adams was born to wealth and excellence in a country where the first was prized, the second mistrusted. Both were needed in a democratic com-monwealth, he believed, but he could not resolve how wealth, excel-lence, and democracy could cohere. The tension ran through his third-person autobiography, *The Education of Henry Adams* (1907) and through *Democracy* (1880), a fictional but ever topical satire of corrupt lobbying in Gilded Age Washington.

Looking back at the early United States as a historian, Adams treated it as special and fixed in character by the end of its second war with Britain (1815). It was in its time uniquely democratic. As he wrote in his account of the early republic, published 1889–91: "War counted for little, the hero for less; on the people alone the eye could permanently rest." Reflecting on his own time, Adams had little hope for democratic self-government, distorted as it was by private interests.

Disillusionment runs through *Democracy*, in which the plot—a mar-riage romance mixed with partisan intrigue—took distant second to Adams's play of ideas. The heroine is a do-good widow, come to Wash-ington to observe its ways. The antihero is the corrupt but powerful Senator Ratcliffe. Into Ratcliffe's mouth Adams puts a scornful view of mass suffrage and social reform: "No representative government," he intoned, "can long be much better or much worse than the society it represents. Purify society and you purify government." Adams, as a young progressive, had believed in social reform but lost his faith. The reader is hard put to know whether Adams is repelled by Ratcliffe's cynicism or attracted by his frankness. The same uncertainty occurs with the autobiography, when Adams writes of the real-life senator and political gamesman from Pennsylvania, Simon Cameron.

Though drawn to Ratcliffe, like Adams, the heroine rejects his advances. When she confronts him about his corrupt dealings, he replies that taking money from an unsafe steamship company for legislative favors was harmless so long as it helped his party, because his party did better for society than its rival, and doing well by society was his highest duty. The heroine finds Ratcliffe to be a "moral lunatic" but ruefully concludes that in rejecting him, "nine out of ten of our countrymen would say I had made a mistake." She leaves political Washington to do good works with "her paupers and her prisons, her schools and her hospitals." Adams never lost his belief in the ideal of popular sovereignty as the least bad way to organize politics but came to think that the people were too scattered, preoccupied, and weak to resist the concentrated power of money.

Adams was a hesitant, troubled conservative. H. L. Mencken (1880–1956), by contrast, was the knock-'em-down roar of a right-wing phrasemaker and balloon popper. Adams wished people to be wiser than they were. Mencken never doubted their stupidity. He teased his middle-class readers, which he called a "boobocracy," for pretentiousness and conformity. Yet those same readers enabled him to have a glittering career as the nation's favorite curmudgeon and sage. Mencken was a Baltimore journalist, critic, and editor, known as the guiding spirit of the magazines *The Smart Set* and *American Mercury*, which exposed political follies and mocked cultural striving.

Mencken's private prejudices—against blacks, Jews, almost all foreigners save Germans, the one people he admired—were unconfined and are no longer printable save when clearly flagged in quotation marks or as indirect speech. A brief selection, from published and unpublished writings, gives their acidulous flavor: "Mysogynist, a man who hates women as much as women hate one another." "The educated negro of today is a failure, not because he meets insuperable difficulties in life, but because he is a negro. He is, in brief, a low-caste man, to the manner born, and he will remain inert and inefficient until fifty generations of him have lived in civilization. And even then, the superior white race will be fifty generations ahead of him."

Government, the common citizen, and the public's intelligence came in equally for Mencken's scorn: Democracy was "the art of running the circus from the monkey cage." "All government, in its essence, is a conspiracy against the superior man: its one permanent object is to oppress him and cripple him." Mencken made sport of inciting readers to violence: "Suppose two-thirds of the members of the national House of Representatives were dumped into the Washington garbage incinerator tomorrow, what would we lose to offset our gain of their salaries and the salaries of their parasites?" "I propose that it shall be no longer *malum in se* for a citizen to pummel, cowhide, kick, gouge, cut, wound, bruise, maim, burn, club, bastinado, flay, or even lynch a jobholder."

As for the moral and mental capacities of the common citizen, Mencken wrote: "The average man's love of liberty is nine-tenths imaginary, exactly like his love of sense, justice and truth. He is not actually happy when free; he is uncomfortable, a bit alarmed, and intolerably lonely." The ordinary, devout American was credulous, for "religion, generally speaking, has been a curse to mankind." He or she was unable to reason clearly. Citizens never formed a deliberative whole but remained an unthinking herd. "When a candidate for public office faces the voters, he does not face men of sense; he faces a mob of men whose chief distinguishing mark is the fact that they are quite incapable of weighing ideas."

Nor were the intelligent classes much help. The nation lacked an "intellectual aristocracy—sound in its information, skeptical in its habit of mind, and above all secure in its position and authority." Those who should serve as ethical and cultural authorities failed laughably at their task. The typical college president was "a perambulating sycophant" engaged not in "the battle of ideas, the pursuit and dissemination of knowledge but in "the courting of rich donkeys and the entertainment of mobs."

Mencken was widely, though not universally, revered in his day as a wit and scourge of conventional opinion. Walter Lippman in the 1920s judged him "the most powerful personal influence on this whole generation of educated people." By the 1930s, the reading public's mood had changed. Mencken came to sound tired and old hat. Without positive opinions of his own, he became a grumpy, out-of-touch conservative who treated Roosevelt as worthier of condemnation than Hitler.

His sallies relied on more than spleen. He read and wrote a study on his favorite thinker, Nietzsche. Like George Orwell and Victor Klemperer, Mencken grasped the politics of the words we choose. In *The American Language* (1921), he defended the inventiveness and demotic vitality of American speech against the stuffiness of "proper usage." Yet Mencken himself threw damaging words about with abandon.

Defenders have pled for Mencken that he was never pompous or self-righteous. His prejudices were so over the top as to mock prejudice itself and, as his recently published diaries showed, indiscriminate in their targets. Mencken's contempt for human folly was not selective, it is insisted, but universal; that is, he derided humans and their failings whatever their creed or kind. Furthermore, no one fought harder than he did for his one overriding principle, free speech, as he himself proclaimed in *What I Believe* (1930) Finally, enthusiasts spied in Mencken's dread of people en masse a warning against unfiltered democracy of a populist kind to which, he feared, his country was prone.

Mencken's reputation serves as an informal litmus test of the political climate—having plunged in the 1930s, it recovered in the 1980s, when a coarsened Menckenism became popular on American right-wing media and liberals were pilloried for political correctness. In Mencken's spirit, the German and French hard right in the 2010s made a defining cry of bravely saying what, as they claimed, they were "not allowed to say." Mencken's disbelief in the capacity of democratic electorates to make wise choices has echoes among present-day right-wing American scholars who are advocating, in effect, the disenfranchisement of stupid or ignorant voters.

Responses to Mencken depend in part on whether it is thought regrettable or a good thing that people once learned the lesson of not talking in public as Mencken wrote. They depend also on how convinced people are by Mencken's know-all tone. It relied on the specious argument: "*p* is commonly believed; common beliefs are often wrong; therefore not-*p*." Mencken was a deep, uncritical admirer of Nietzsche's writings on morality. As a moral skeptic, Nietzsche's problem was that to knock down morality, you needed to leave some of it standing. As a conservative oppositionist, Mencken always seemed to know which opinions were wrong. But he rarely, if ever, could say which were right.

Of the thinkers and writers in this chapter, Georges Sorel (1847–1922) was the most openly political but also the hardest politically to pigeonhole. He imagined the people as the working class and the working class as a condign weapon for use against liberals and parliamentary democrats. Because neither picture was wholly true or wholly false, Sorel's work has remained a critical rummage box for all who think of liberal democracy as unredeemable. Sorel was typed as an eccentric Marxist and herald of fascism. The clearest thread in his thought was contempt for liberalism. It made him companionable for the radical left but also for the unreconciled right, which earns him a half place in a history of conservatism.

Sorel wrote prolifically, but he is remembered chiefly for *Réflexions sur la violence* (*Reflections on Violence*, 1906) and *Illusions du progrès* (*Illusions of Progress*, 1908). The first was a collection of essays on liberalism and socialism, the second a history of *progress* as a political idea. They shared powerful common themes: politically, the derision of liberal-democratic trust in public reason, elections, and parliamentary government; and socially, the castigation of middle-class flabbiness on which liberal-democratic politics rested. In the hostility of the working class, Sorel saw both a means for unmasking the liberal-democratic sham and an energy-source to reinvigorate a decadent society.

Liberal society had lost the productive energies it once drew from capitalism. With the early vigor gone, there prevailed instead a decadent, pacific ethic of consumption. Politically, that ethic found expression in the suffocating sham of liberal democracy. It smothered social vitality in procedures, talk, and palliative reform. Sorel looked to working-class hostility to expose the hypocritical shortfall between the liberal pieties of egalitarian progress and the actual condition of class-divided liberal society.

In denying that reason and argument guided collective action, Sorel followed Le Bon and Tarde, both of whom he admired. Whereas they concentrated on *how* people en masse thought (like a crowd, and by imitation, respectively), Sorel focused on *what* they thought. Social behavior, Sorel wrote, was guided by myths. They were pre-reflective, unreasoned, and irrefutable. To that extent, they were irrational. Yet myths were not thoughtless. They had content and were about something. Myths pictured how society was and ought to be. As such, they served as collective norms, much like the "authorities" that the conservative Le Play (whom Sorel also admired) thought were essential to social order. Myths for Sorel were deep and imperative. They expressed a people's strongest commitments.

Sorel distinguished revolutionary myths, which were genuine and popular, from Utopias, which were spurious and made by intellectuals. Popular myths had the necessary wherewithal to endure, which intellectual myths lacked. Popular myths were in a sense grounded and credible. Intellectual myths were factitious and deceptive. Among the intellectual-made Utopian myths, none was weaker than the liberal myth of self-organizing market society. (Sorel might have added a later liberal myth, the myth of the end of myths.) The myth of socialism was part revolutionary and part Utopian. It was "serious, formidable, sublime." It had a more truly revolutionary competitor in the myth of syndicalism, which advocated a general strike. Socialists wanted to replace those running the state. Syndicalists wanted to replace the state itself.

By "violence" Sorel meant not the smashing of shop windows or the butchering of the rich but the readiness to turn one's back on liberal and democratic norms in an abrupt clean break. Political violence, so understood, included all radical actions, unhemmed by law, to overthrow the old order. It was undertaken without hatred or the spirit of revenge and was conducted dispassionately, like a military operation. A general strike would be violent in this sense. Readiness to overturn social norms was endemic. Violence so understood would never be outgrown. The only open question was whether violence was to be bestial or noble.

Physical violence was but one form, a defensive extreme when facing the state's police.

Sorel was not strictly conservative, because he belonged strictly in no political camp. As a Dreyfusard, he turned against liberal politicians who misused government to further their principles and make their careers. Then as a radical syndicalist, he championed Marx in France and supported the strike wave of the early 1900s. His Marxism was more ethical than economic. Marx, for Sorel, suffered from the same reductive failing as the political economists Marx himself criticized: both rested ethics on economics, whereas for Sorel it was the other way around. Workers, Sorel thought, were to kick out the bourgeoisie not because the bourgeois had money but because they were feeble and weak-willed. After the First World War, he flirted with the anti-liberal right and turned anti-Semitic before ending as an admirer of Lenin.

Sorel's criticism of Marx stretched to a general dissatisfaction with narrow ideas of human progress. More knowledge, more material goods, and more leisure did not, he wrote at the end of *Illusions of Progress*, reliably make people happier. The mistake of thinking that they did was inherited from enlightened eighteenth -century reformers. It arose from a soft "ethic of consumption." Happiness, Sorel suggested in a brief passage that echoed Mill's own bow to immemorial wisdom on the topic, depended heavily on being active and having satisfying work. Sorel's contrast between the ethic of production and the ethic of consumption was heard again in post-1945 anxieties about capitalism's power to sap its own vitality.

Sorel's thought had clashing elements: cycles of rise and decline as well as advancing historical stages marked by sharp ruptures; social myths as class weapons that were neither true nor false, as pragmatic social norms apt in their time, or as illusions and deceits (in the wrong hands) and emancipating truths (in the right hands); certitude about the flaws of a system in plain view (liberal democracy) with virtual silence about its yet-to-be-seen replacement. For someone convinced (and glad) that democratic liberalism is dying, Sorel's writings provide rhetorical ammunition. For critics of democratic liberalism who hope to reform it, Sorel's work is a useful lesson in the failures of overkill.

Sorel's lodestone was a critical contempt—for both liberal democracy and palliative reform. For him, they served only the bourgeoisie, together with its political and intellectual helpers, while gulling and distracting the masses. Sorel's contempt for elections, parliaments, and never-ending argument ran with electric charge deep into the twentieth century. Mussolini claimed to keep Sorel's writing by his bed. Over Schmitt's executive "decisionism," Sorel's celebration of nonrational action and disdain for parliaments hovered. His picture of the people as a homogeneous mass united by contempt for liberal elites echoed loudly in the rise of the populist hard right in the 2010s.

iii. Cultural Decline and Ethical Anomie: Jünger and Other Germans, Drieu la Rochelle, the Southern Agrarians, and Eliot

Damage to liberal-democratic self-confidence from the 1914–18 war re-energized unreconciled conservatives. It gave them ample opening to disparage liberal societies they found debased, without aims, and spiritless. Mutual slaughter among prosperous, open nations that ought on liberal theory never to have taken place had shaken liberal certitudes. Colonial domination of "lower" peoples and imperial rivalries that smoothed the path to slaughter had exposed liberal talk of progress and equality. Rapturous popular support for war when it began turned to mutiny, rebellion, and revolution as war ended, darkening liberal trust in electoral democracy.

The shaken liberal mood was caught with near-despair in an article by the economist John Maynard Keynes in 1923: "We are today the most creedless of men. Every one of our religious and political constructions is moth-eaten." Keynes did not mean "liberal" in a party-political sense. He was talking of a liberal world that conservative governments had done much to create. In fixing the blame for the 1914–18 war and the harsh peace that followed, mainstream conservatism took a large share, not least from intellectuals on the right.

Like the French Revolution, which its critics treated as symptomatic of graver flaws, the First World War gave the unreconciled right in the 1920s and 1930s decisive-looking evidence of failed liberal orthodoxy. Some stayed in politics, working as militants from the edges to change the mainstream. Others, chiefly writers and thinkers, withdrew to higher criticism of a spiritually empty liberalism and a coarsened democratic culture. The line between them could be fine. Maurras in France and, for a time, Ernst Jünger in Germany played both roles. The Anglo-American poet Eliot was a pure case withdrawal to countermodern criticism. All drew critical energy by contrast with the pragmatic excuses and weary, "it-could-be-worse" defenses from writers of the conservative mainstream. The tumult of right-wing opinions echoes in the intellectual confusions of conservatism now, with bold attacks and big claims from fiery malcontents on one side and weary-stubborn defenses of right-wing liberalism on the other.

The tumult of the 1920s and 1930s varied in pitch and volume. The Germans Oswald Spengler, Arthur Moeller van den Bruck, and Ernst Jünger spoke in their different ways for a "conservative revolution." Southern Agrarians in the United States championed farms and country as a more elevated life than factory work in cities. The right-wing French writer and fascist sympathizer Pierre Drieu la Rochelle met the liberal enfeeblement he saw around him with a cult of personal action. Against the anomie of liberal modernity, the great modernist poet Eliot, an American become British, argued as if echoing Coleridge for a high cultural canon embedded in Christian tradition. Each was a political outsider. Their criticisms of the intellectual climate of democratic liberalism were openly ethical and cultural. As conservatives, they took their critique to matter politically.

The phrase "conservative revolution" was given currency by an eminent German conservative, Armin Mohler, in a book of that name published in 1949. Looking back to the early Weimar Republic, Mohler parsed the intellectual ferment on the German right after 1918 into five types: the Young Conservatives, the *Völkisch*, the joiners of various anti-Weimar leagues, the Agrarians, and the National Revolutionaries. The detail and accuracy of Mohler's typology, which he later changed, mattered less than its broader historical purpose: to find a purer strain of conservative anti-liberal radicalism in the 1920s for which fascism and Nazism might be treated as contaminations or as nonconservative movements of an altogether different kind. What thinkers of the conservative revolution shared, on Mohler's account, was a sense of liberalism's inability to recognize its incoherences, together with contempt for liberal hypocrisy: professing universal good will while serving class and wealth; affirming faith in progress while ransacking the world and plunging its peoples into war.

At the distance of a century, three writers from Germany's "conservative revolution" stand out: Oswald Spengler, author of *Decline of the West* (1918); Arthur Moeller van den Bruck, who wrote *The Third Reich* (1923); and Ernst Jünger, a long-lived and controversial writer for whom Mohler worked as literary secretary (1948–52).

Had Spengler's vast study of the rise and fall of civilizations been known by its subtitle, *Outlines for a World-Historical Morphology*, it is a nice question whether it would have sold over a hundred thousand copies in the eight years after its publication. Many Germans took it by repute for a study of national defeat and the humiliation of the Versailles Treaty, although Spengler had begun mapping his panorama in the early 1910s, a period of relative détente and liberal hopefulness. The son of a ballet master and a dancer, Spengler (1880–1936) studied under eminent economists and philosophers before inheriting money on his mother's death, which allowed him to live as a gentleman scholar.

Like a high Gothic master builder, Spengler aspired to structural clarity and comprehensive symbolism. He offered to span great historical spaces in lucid, overarching categories arranged in intelligible sequence. About every aspect of human life was found to have symbolic meaning and fitted into the whole. The modern present might be chaotic and bewildering. Superhistory in Spengler's hands promised the present its place in the world's order. The news for Western moderns—by which Spengler meant progressive liberals—was discouraging. It was comfort of a kind that the liberal West had played a due part in the world-historical scheme. Less comforting was Spengler's topical message that the West's part was over.

High cultures, according to Spengler, arose, came to prevail, and then declined in cycles of roughly one thousand years. The West had emerged from the last three of the eight "high" cultures Spengler identified: Apollonian (Greece), Magian (Semitic-Paleochristian-Islamic), and Faustian (late Christian). Every culture was a living, self-reflective whole. None was embodied in a supposed race or ethnic group. Cultures united the classes, and cultures fused faith, custom, and arts. In pure, early form, cultures were rooted, organic, and rural. They grew, along with cities, but bearing seeds of decay—overthinking, neglect of instinct, loss of intimacy and naturalness. In expanding, high cultures "mummified" and became civilizations. On view in Spengler's scheme were the familiar anti-modern contrasts of Romantic conservatism—country against city; feeling against reason; whole against part, together with the running presumption that city dwellers, critical thinkers, and liberals were on the wrong side of the contrast.

The West had passed from strength to weakness, from culture to civilization. Its mummification was evident in politics. Free institutions of democracy and money were weapons used against the nobility by the bourgeoisie, aided by the press. Freedom enabled ingenuity to create machines that both benefited and enslaved. Money led to the marketization of all values. In a "last battle," the dictatorship of money would be ended by Caesarism, and the historic cycle would start again.

Spengler's political point was graspable without the overblown history or Romantic anti-modernism. He made it clear in *Preussentum und Sozialismus* (*Prussianness and Socialism*, 1919): Germany needed neither Marxism nor liberalism but a "Prussian socialism," a wished-for hybrid that would combine social well-being and popular approval under conservative control.

Arthur Moeller van den Bruck (1876–1925) also pled for the reconciliation of opposites in *Das dritte Reich* (*The Third Reich*, 1923), his vision of a conservative Germany to come. Moeller was the autodidact son of an architect who named him Arthur after the philosophical pessimist Schopenhauer. His architectural study, *Der Preußischer Stil* (*The Prussian Style*, 1916), found, like Ruskin, moral significance in architectural form, though with nakedly chauvinist purpose. Moeller contrasted the "manly" values found in Prussian tradition of matter-of-factness, dutifulness, respect for authority, and self-restraint with the "feminine" values of dreamy universalism and sensuous exuberance found in Baroque and Romantic architecture elsewhere in Germany.

Politically, Moeller, like Spengler, was chiefly negative. He knew best what he was against: the present day. The new Germany as wished for in *The Third Reich* would be neither progressive nor reactionary, neither absolutist nor constitutional. Its hazily specified values would be timeless and conservative but with the modern courage to live "with contradiction." Its socialism would be "organic," that is, grown out of the national character. The new Reich would be ancient but modern. Above all, it would not be liberal or parliamentary. "Liberalism," Moeller wrote, "is the death of nations." The American historian Fritz Stern justly called Moeller's style of argument "annihilation by labels." Moeller's wish to be at once modern and traditional echoed in Nazi speeches and doctrines. His mix of anger, grievance, and pseudo-learning typified the welcome given to unreason in public argument among large parts of the German right in the 1920s—an abasement with echoes in the hard right of the present day.

The long-lived and controversial Ernst Jünger made his military name in the 1914–18 war as the youngest officer to win his country's top honor, the Pour le Mérite. He made his literary name with *Storm of Steel* (1920), a best-selling record of trench fighting written up from war diaries. British war memoirs tended to be elegiac, self-deprecating, even comic. Jünger was different. As edited later and expanded on in further essays, notably "Battle as Inner Experience" (1922), Jünger's book stressed war's moral opportunities. Courage in the face of horrors, Jünger suggested, could elevate humdrum lives.

Jünger's wartime lesson generalized in his later writing into an ethic of redemption through disengagement. Everyone was crushed in mass society, whether its forces were chaotic (liberalism) or organized (totalitarianism). But, as Jünger reflected of his shrunken unit at war's end, crushed did not mean conquered. Personal self-respect was salvageable by tactics of refusal: politically, in the rejection of conventional party-political work; culturally, in the forswearing of admiration and enthusiasm in favor of detached observation (Jünger was an expert on beetles); ethically, in the avoidance of big ideas and doing your duty by colleagues and family. Though no thinker, Jünger saw himself as a conservative enemy of moral nihilism, thought to plague liberal modernity. His search for a resting point passed through "conservative revolution" in the 1920s and inner emigration in the 1930s to end after 1945 not far from Oakeshott's quiet dutifulness in Britain: stoical service in war, avoidance of political torment in peace.

In the 1920s, Jünger joined the Conservative Revolution, dashing off books and pamphlets against the Weimar Republic for trying to achieve liberalism and democracy, which Jünger detested. For the civilizational ills of modern life, he blamed bourgeois liberals. Of democracy, he wrote in 1925, "I hate it like the plague." He tried in these years to create a right-wing worker's movement with equally hard-to-label friends, such as Ernst Niekisch, but grew tired of the factional infighting. Jünger's openly political ideas had fullest expression in *Der Arbeiter* (*The Worker*, 1932), a blurred vision of an assembly-line society guided by elite artist-soldiers. It was hard to tell from Moeller's "Prussian socialism" and critics aptly called it right-wing Bolshevism. After Hitler took power, Jünger, who was not a Nazi, fended off efforts by admirers in the party to make him their literary star and withdrew from public life. *On the Marble Cliffs* (1939), his fable in crystalline prose about peaceable lake dwellers crushed by demon-led ruffians, was widely, but not universally, read as quiet resistance. For some, it was a veiled attack on Hitlerism, for others a neo-Nietzschean protest against mass society for crushing excellence and daring.

Jünger, the political conservative who scorned modernity's disorder, wrote a very modern, unconservative prose. André Gide, Bertolt Brecht, and Jorge Luis Borges were admirers. In 1939, on volunteering again, he began a second wartime diary as an officer in Germany's invasion force, in occupied Paris, and on the Eastern Front. Aphorisms, philosophical half-thoughts, and religious musings jostle with odd, though seldom funny, dreams. Small pleasures flank sudden horrors. Jolting images appear and vanish as if on the surface of a lake. The German critic Karl-Heinz Bohrer aptly called Jünger's "the aesthetic of shock." None of it adds up. No line is drawn or balance struck. Admirers found his cool, detached writing true to the disconnections of modern life. To doubters, it was mannered and amoral.

On a country walk along a bomb-strafed road near his home late in 1944, Jünger indulged a moment of conservative relish, which he recorded in his diary. As he strolled, he told himself that it was the liberals who were to blame for what had befallen. How wonderful it was, he wrote, "to watch the drama of the old liberals, Dadaists, and freethinkers, as they begin to moralize at the end of a life devoted completely to the destruction of the old guard and the undermining of order." "Blame the liberals!" was conservatism's charge at birth. It hobbled the Weimar Republic and bedevils politics in our day. Not to pity Jünger for his personal travails—one son killed in action, his other a suicide—would be defective. Not to respond to the prose would be deaf. Politically, it was as if he had learned nothing.

After 1945, Jünger abandoned work on his "Appeal to the World's Young." Though semimystical in tone, its vision of Christian understanding among peaceful European nations was widely shared by German conservatives reconstructing a liberal-democratic right after 1945. From that task, Jünger stood aside. In often allegorical writings, he shared with the postwar intellectual right in Germany many criticisms to be returned to in part V: the unjust balance of war guilt, the unchecked power of the modern state, the global erosion of locality and tradition, and the mindless global spread of uncontrolled technology.

Jünger once wrote that conservatives conserved their enemies. His point was that, as he saw it, conservatism was a creed of resistance. In like spirit, he described it elsewhere as anarchistic. A conservatism of such kind was largely negative, a turning of the back on democratic society and culture, the only constructive advice being personal escape, a course of action recommended in Forest Passage (1951). Such an "individualistic" conservatism of personal salvation had a second coming, as will be seen, after 1980 among cultural and philosophical critics who urged a principled withdrawal for conservative minorities who saw no room for compromise with liberal modernity.

The 1914–18 war came also to the French writer Pierre Drieu la Rochelle (1893–1945) as a liberal suicide. Unlike for Jünger, however, Drieu's veterans were not heroes but cynics. In Drieu's view, furthermore, worse calamity was waiting to happen. Like others on the French right, he was preoccupied by social decadence and national decline. Alarm at France's condition was shared, it should be stressed, across politics. Concerns focused on France's late industrialization, war losses (more than 10 percent of active men), a falling birth rate, depopulation of the countryside and its small towns, retreat of the French language, and the invasion of American culture, above all film, which France had pioneered. Added together, these fears tended to cancel and paralyze. For example, more factories and towns were required, but the land needed sustaining and people in towns had fewer children. Or again, the French both had to work harder and take more time for culture. No matter, the gospel of decline was popular and hard to reply to.

If France was stuck, to where outside should it turn? Moderate conservatives like Tardieu, as earlier noted, looked to the United States as a model of bipartisan modernity. French cultural conservatives, by contrast, tended to view Americanism as a civilizational disease, a mixture of liberal spinelessness and popular self-indulgence. In *Scenes from Future Life* (1930), Georges Duhamel pictured the contemporary United States as an anti-France of moronic films, savage jazz, industrial food, and barbarous sport. In contrast to the humane, rooted French, *déraciné* Americans were slaves to conscience who spent their few hours freed from routinized work on punishing self-improvement. American culture, Duhamel judged, promoted "reversible"—that is, changeable— values, whereas a country needed "nonreversible" values. A comparably summary dismissal came from Robert Aron and Arnaud Dandieu in *The American Cancer* (1931).

Drieu's gaze was drier and less excitable. He could not believe in technocratic renewal, and cultural carping struck him as beside the point. He looked South and East, to illiberal, collectivizing, one-party modernity in Rome, Berlin, and Moscow. All attracted him, but he could not settle on which. Instead, Drieu wandered through the political fringes looking for a nonliberal space that was neither communist nor fascist.

His vagabondage makes a rough map of France's interwar hard right. First left-wing Surrealism (appeal: unreason), then Action Française (appeal: authoritarianism, though the Christian moralizing repelled him). Drieu's *Socialisme Fasciste* (1934) read as a traffic jam of "isms," none of which worked for France: capitalism (exhausted), Marxism (too narrowly economic and not Nietzschean enough), nationalism (not fascist enough), fascism (needed a charismatic leader, but none were available in France). Drieu turned to Doriot's anti-parliamentary Parti Populaire as an alternative to other one-party paths, only again to pull away. After the German occupation, Drieu took on the editorship of the *Nouvelle Revue Française* and collaborated with his Nazi censors. After the liberation of Paris, Drieu shot himself in disgrace.

Drieu's masterpiece was *Gilles* (1939), a semiautobiographical novel of self-loathing and despair with politics set in prewar Paris. Drieu's seductive antihero, Gilles, wounded, like Drieu, in the trenches, drifts through the city, despising himself, his rich Jewish mistress, his Marxist-Bohemian friends, and France's besieged republican liberals. Gilles combines well-turned hate speech and loathsome ideas with small acts of decency—or rather urges to act decently, for torpor and self-disgust habitually get in the way of action. Ineffectuality was Gilles's problem, as it was the problem, to Drieu's mind, of France. Drieu's fictional way out was for Gilles to martyr himself as a hapless, unprepared, and unbelieving volunteer for the anti-Republicans in Spain's civil war. Well before France's military defeat (1940), national submission of like kind was, for Drieu, France's only practical choice—a despairing, overdrawn conclusion that underlines his intellectual exhaustion. His rejection of France's liberal-democratic orthodoxy was so sweeping as to leave him unable to imagine any alternative. He said he was "fascist without knowing it." A better label would be right-wing nihilist. "The only way to love France," Drieu wrote, "is to hate it in its present form."

The entry of the United States into the European war (April 1917), and the Bolshevik revolution (November 1917), changed the script for American conservatism. The rise of the Soviet Union turned a once revolutionary nation into a counterrevolutionary world power, as Patrick Allitt nicely put it in *The Conservatives: Ideas and Personalities throughout American History* (2009). Anticommunism no longer distinguished the American right from the left. Foreign war, by contrast, divided the American right. Conservatives split, as seen, on the terms under which the United States would use its world power: either with others or alone. In international high politics, Republicans divided into multilateralists and unilateralists, known more familiarly, if misleadingly, as isolationists.

The line of engagement or disengagement divided conservatives over politics at home. Mainstream conservatives stayed in the game, competing and compromising with democratic liberals. Vocal minorities on the American right stayed aloof. They criticized contemporary society, as it were, from the outside the familiar party contest. The outstanding conservative example in the 1930s was Southern Agrarianism.

The Agrarians, Southern writers and intellectuals linked to Vanderbilt University, set out to defend the cultural aims and ideals of their region against the prejudices of the North. A book of their essays, *I'll Take My Stand* (1930), stood up for the "Southern way of life" against the "American or prevailing way." It took the contest to be "Agrarian *versus* Industrial." An agrarian society, being immemorially familiar, did not need definition. It had use for industries, professions, scholars, and artists, even for cities. Yet agriculture was "the leading vocation" and the most rewarding labor, whether pursued for wealth, pleasure, or prestige. The "culture of the soil" was "the best and most sensitive of vocations," hence it should have "the economic preference and enlist the maximum number of workers."

A celebration of Southern writing, the book was a delayed rebuke to Mencken's "Sahara of the Bozart" (1917), a squib (punning on "beaux arts") that dismissed claims to cultural superiority in the New South—"a gargantuan paradise of the fourth-rate"—and teased white Southerners with a racialism of its own for being mostly half-breeds. In the lead essay in *I'll Take My Stand*, John Crowe Ransom took counter-aim at the liberal pieties of progress, hard work, and innovation. A historian attacked Northern hypocrisy in rewriting the Civil War as a crusade against slavery. In truth, he argued, the war was a contest of industry against farming (weakening his case with racialistic denigration of blacks). In his contribution, "The Briar Patch," Robert Penn Warren made a vivid but tangled defense for segregation and the doctrine of "separate but equal." It was all right, he suggested, for a black Southerner to expect as comfortable a hotel bed as one offered to a white Southerner, but not to demand to stay at the same hotel—thus sidestepping the simple point that discrimination's harms turned not on comfort but on dignity.

Like the English conservative Catholics Hilaire Belloc and G. K. Chesterton, the Agrarians favored a "distributivist" apportionment of land to people on which to farm in small communities. The "back to land" plea was over-hopeful. The writer Allen Tate, who had inherited his farm from a rich urban brother, quickly found the work too hard. The worldlier contributors saw that the disruption they called for was radical, if not Utopian. Reluctantly, they accepted industry, but on Southern terms, and not imposed or run by Northerners.

Objections to the business civilization of the United States were not unique to the Agrarians. They were common in social criticism to left and right. The cultural left derided American consumerism and materialist shallowness in the name of personal liberation and richer lives. The cultural right, represented by figures such as Irving Babbitt and Elmer More, did the same in the name of higher, humane values. The Agrarians shared some of that cultural elitism but attacked "business civilisation" in a further way: on behalf of the South and its special ways. They asked, like Calhoun, to be left alone. How conservative were the Agrarians? Separatism and regionalism themselves are neither right-wing nor left-wing, or conservative or nonconservative. However, as with Calhoun, the local values and attitudes the Agrarians defended were well to the right, undemocratic, and illiberal.

An American who had long since abandoned his native Midwest, gone to Europe, and become a preeminent literary modernist was T. S. Eliot (1888–1965). Eliot was poet, playwright, publisher, critic, and conservative dissenter from liberal modernity. What stable institutions were to the conservative political mind, cultural tradition was to Eliot's literary mind. Tradition answered modernity's spiritual emptiness, which was explored poetically in *The Waste Land* (1922). Traditions were not inherited but had to be worked at and upheld, Eliot explained in *The Sacred Wood* (1920). His essays aimed to fix a poetic canon and establish, neither puritanically nor didactically, poetry's distinctive moral value as "truth seen in passion." Without a central tradition, writers and thinkers became cramped, deprived.

Eliot reached into social criticism in *The Idea of a Christian Society* (1939). This was the year he closed down *The Criterion*, which he had edited since 1922. His diagnosis of modern society, which religious conservatives nowadays may find agreeable, was bleak. He contrasted a religion-minded society, "in conformity with nature" against a pagan society, out of conformity with nature, based as it was on "private profit," "public destruction," and "exhaustion of natural resources." At present, liberalism was failing, but no alternative was clear. Although reconciling authority and community, fascism was flawed by paganism. To resist the advance of paganism and materialism, Eliot looked instead to the "prospect of a Christian society." The idea, he allowed, would not appeal to the majority. Yet what were the alternatives? Either "apathetic decline, without faith and therefore without faith in ourselves, without a philosophy of life, either Christian or pagan, and without art." Or "totalitarian democracy," with the "regimentation and uniformity" of a "hygienic morality in the interest of efficiency." In the meantime, leading a Christian life in a non-Christian society was growing ever harder, because Christians were implicated in a "network of institutions" no longer neutral, but non-Christian, from which they could not extricate themselves. It was not good enough for Christians to be a tolerated minority. Indeed, it might "turn out that the most intolerable thing for Christians is to be tolerated."

Eliot's postwar view was more hopeful. In *Notes towards a Definition of Culture* (1948), he argued that high sensibility might yet "permeate" the broader culture. The term "culture" could not be neatly defined, Eliot allowed, but culture could be recognized and characterized. Among things he stressed about culture was that it was passed down primarily through the family. Hierarchy was another element: "In a vigorous society, there will be visible both class and elite." It was wrong, above all, to think there could be culture without religion or to think, with Arnold, of culture as religion. You could not, Eliot wrote, make a religion out of a culture.

Eliot was versed in the counterliberal past. He admired Coleridge's insistence that conservative intellectuals should have clear views on political and social matters. His own university thesis was on Bradley's ethical thought. Eliot believed, as did Bradley, that personal liberty, duties to others, and social order were not disentangleable. Nor, he thought, could social order be separated from culture or culture from religion. In an early essay on *Democracy and Leadership* (1924) by Irving Babbitt, his Harvard teacher, Eliot contrasted support for humanistic learning, which he approved of, with humanism, in the religious sense of secularism, which he disapproved of. Babbitt had argued for all-round humane education in universities as a necessary counterbalance in a democratic culture. He opposed Charles Eliot Norton's electives, which gave undergraduates too much choice, and graduate research for graduates on the German model, which produced narrow specialists. Eliot favored Babbitt in that debate but balked at Babbitt's attempt to "line up" humanism "in battle order with religion against humanitarianism and naturalism." What Eliot meant was that, as far as a religion-minded conservative was concerned, the humanist (that is, cultivated secularist), the humanitarian (the secular, do-good liberal), and the naturalist (the science-minded denier of religion) were all on the wrong side of the line. Babbitt, in Eliot's view, was making the same mistake Arnold had made about culture, of trying to turn culture into a religion. "You cannot make humanism itself into a religion." Eliot was stern: "The humanistic point of view is auxiliary to and dependent upon the religious point of view." With characteristic eloquence, Eliot summed up his cultural conservatism in the following high terms: "The conservative response to modernity is to embrace it, but to embrace it critically, in full consciousness that human achievements are rare and precarious, that we have no God-given right to destroy our inheritance, but must always patiently submit to the voice of order, and set an example of orderly living."

iv. Funeral Oratory for Liberal Democracy:
Schmitt and Maurras

More direct damage to liberal democratic self-confidence came in the 1920s and 1930s from political discredit. To the left were writers looking for a gap between liberalism and Stalinism. They hoped to rewrite the Marxian grand narrative of historical progress toward an emancipation in which human conflict would end. To the right, radical conservatives harped on liberalism's inability to rally popular passion and on the representative democracy's failure to govern and make decisions. Outstanding examples were Carl Schmitt in Germany and Charles Maurras in France. Neither had clear alternatives. Both were at conservatism's outer edge, and both detested liberalism. When crisis came, Schmitt embraced Nazism, and Maurras militated for authoritarianism.

Outside his native Germany, there was something of the sea monster about Carl Schmitt (1888–1985), much reported and seldom seen though assuredly deep and alarming. He was a conservative anti-liberal, a Roman Catholic, and a Nazi (1933–45). His long engagement with Hitlerism hampers impartial treatment of Schmitt's thought, yet as a public lawyer, he wrote a standard work on constitutional law. As a political essayist before 1933, Schmitt questioned liberal-democratic assurances in short, caustic books.

Schmitt put disconcerting questions about the nature of the state, political authority, and democracy in charged, suggestive epigrams: "All significant concepts of the modern theory of the state are secularized theological concepts." "Sovereign is he who decides the exception." "Dictatorship is not antithetical to democracy." "When you talk of humanity, you are lying." The style of this singular jurist was likened to the momentary illumination of the flashbulb. His biographer Paul Noack described Schmitt as arguing in "concept-packed myths."

Schmitt's best-known epigram, "The distinction specific to politics . . . is that between friend and enemy," was intended to stun. Like many good epigrams, it contained enough truth to distract from its overall falsity. On encountering *The Concept of the Political*, Ernst Jünger dashed off a letter to Schmitt in October 1930 congratulating him for "a mine that silently explodes." Under the gown of a legal scholar, Jünger had spotted an ideological sapper.

In the Weimar years, Schmitt's expertise engaged him in constitutional disputes that marked the republic's short life. Like many across politics, Schmitt wanted a stronger presidency. As a conservative concerned for social order, Schmitt feared the anticonstitutional right and left. His *Legality and Legitimacy* (1932) set out the case for banning the Nazis and Communists.

Whereas in 1933 many German conservatives accepted Nazism as the lesser evil, Schmitt became an enthusiast. He joined the Nazi party, encouraged by Martin Heidegger, and helped draft laws Nazifying the German states but remained wary of Hitler, until in 1934 the Führer had his rivals bloodily eliminated, including Kurt Schleicher, Schmitt's patron. In a notorious article, "The Führer Protects the Law," Schmitt sought to justify the slaughter. Despite his ambition and adaptability, however, Schmitt was too scholarly and not crude enough to become the Nazis' "crown jurist." Sidelined, he withdrew into academic life, though not far enough to escape disgrace after 1945. Unlike Heidegger, who largely fell silent after early pro-Nazi encomiums, Schmitt's engagement with Hitlerism was long and open. He sanitized his writings by cutting back references to Jewish or left-wing thinkers and adding anti-Semitic asides. In 1936 he lectured, on "German law in the fight against the Jewish intellect," ending with Hitler's words, "By fending off the Jew, I struggle for the work of the Lord." After 1940, he gave talks in occupied Europe on Nazi legal and cultural policy. Interrogated and released by the Americans after 1945, Schmitt turned to geopolitics, writing *The Nomos of the Earth* (1950), a power-political history of American gradual domination of international order.

Schmitt's pre-1933 work, for which he is chiefly remembered, focused on political power and the unity of the nation. More critic than constructor, Schmitt worried away at liberal democracy's weaknesses. In unusually large measure he shared the conservative belief in people's inability to govern themselves, in the vulnerability of institutions, and in the consequent need for a decisive, strong hand in government. Liberals and democrats got all three wrong, Schmitt thought. Popular passions routinely caught liberals off guard, and they were slow to defend their institutions and values against enemies. Representative democracy was vain in mass society, where popular myth trumped reasoned argument among the well-informed.

A first move of Schmitt's against liberal democracy was to decouple democratic representation from liberal restraints on power. Though jewels of liberal theory, parliaments were neither points of sovereign decision nor places of informed argument, so Schmitt argued in *The Crisis of Parliamentary Democracy* (1923). Either parliamentary decisions were made by brokering deals (not democratic), or decisions were put off in unending talk (ineffective). Limits to arbitrary rule vital for liberals—division of powers, independent courts, an effective, law-bound executive—were possible without elected parliaments. On the democratic side of the link that Schmitt hoped to break, elected parliaments were a fudge. Popular sovereignty invoked an identity of governors and governed that had no workable expression. Plebiscites and referendums could make parliamentary government more democratic, Schmitt admitted. But he had a low opinion of voters' knowledge and wisdom. Besides, direct democracy was equally open to manipulation by party politics, Schmitt's bugbear.

Liberal democracy's other main failing was its inability to touch the mythic element. That was a bow to Sorel, whose work Schmitt liked. Myths could be rational or irrational; Marxism, for example, offered the "rational myth" of proletarian self-rule. Yet class myths, Schmitt thought, were contingent and weak. They turned on shifting calculations of economic interest. As the working class grew richer, the pull of the proletarian myth was bound to slacken. More powerful were "irrational" myths. Only they could engage and hold people in large number, Schmitt believed. The one myth suited to the present was the nation.

Belonging to a nation did not involve ifs and buts. It was a brute fact or an unreasoned engagement, like an act of faith. Either way, devotion to nation offered the required cohesion that Marxism and liberal democracy lacked. (Marxist cohesion was unlikely to last; liberal democracy had none to start with). The democracy that suited the present, Schmitt concluded, was neither parliamentary nor plebiscitary. Rather, it would be the word of a nation willingly mobilized under a charismatic leader. Schmitt was reminding readers of the ample room to be found in conceptual space for illiberal democracy. From there to fascism or Nazism was barely a step.

The nation might bind the people, but what bound the nation? Schmitt's answer came in the *Der Begriff des Politischen* (*The Concept of the Political*, 1927). In sixty pages, Schmitt touched on political obligation, sovereignty, group identity, and life's purposes. To tie those disparate topics together Schmitt used a single emotive term, "the enemy." The presence of an enemy, he wrote, engendered the nation, bound people to the state, created need for a sovereign, and lifted politics out of the mundane. So rich and compressed was his essay that Schmitt was variously taken to be arguing as a Hobbesian "realist," a Hegelian nation-state venerator, and an Augustinian pessimist. The Hobbes parallel offered most light, but unlike Hobbes's rivalrous neighbors, Schmitt's enemies were external. The enemy, for Schmitt, was any outsider against which the nation might define itself and perhaps fight to survive. (The circle was evident: no enemy, no nation; only a nation could spot the national enemy.) Schmitt stressed that the binding enmity need not be reasonable or passionately felt. Foes did not have to be economic or geopolitical rivals. They need not even be hated. They had simply to be the nation's Other.

As the philosopher Bernard Williams remarked of it, Schmitt's friend-enemy claim is in one way banal and harmless. All politics involves parties and camps. All politics involves competition and conflict. In another way, however, Schmitt's claim was neither banal nor harmless, for it appeared to turn politics into a special kind of conflict, namely, warfare. If politics inevitably sets friend against enemy, civic unity would require not shared principle but an external foe. Civic diversity would have to be thought of not as a clash of bargainable interests and containable arguments but as low-grade civil war.

A pure enmity drained of rational aim or hostile feeling was mysterious enough for Schmitt to soon add (in a revised edition) an instrumental reason for defensive vigilance: keeping up a guard against an outside enemy gave politics an urgency and decisiveness that liberal democracy could never match. Despite the change, Schmitt continued to treat his friend-enemy distinction in quasi-spiritual manner. If given into, he seemed to say, enmity enhanced and intensified life. Like cultural conservatives before him and after, Schmitt was also disturbed by the apparent loss of compass and bleak purposelessness in liberal modernity. The oddity, for a conservative, was Schmitt's looking to politics to fill the gap. A more natural filler—one sought by Newman, for example—was an authoritative religion. Schmitt's correspondent and interlocutor, Leo Strauss, pointed that out to Schmitt, who acknowledged the religious element in his thinking.

Schmitt tended to argue in arresting but false alternatives: liberals were ineffective weaklings or hypocritical manipulators; true democracy was either a continual plebiscite or a permanent dictatorship; politics was wholly amoral or the highest morality. He was right that, when defending its life, liberal democracy was bound to injure some other high value, but injury was still to be limited where possible, even in extreme conditions. Circumscribed emergency powers watched over by courts were one thing. Unlimited "commissarial" dictatorship, even if temporary, which Schmitt favored, another. Liberals, contrary to his repeated suggestion, did not ignore loyalties, passion, and myth. Because liberals understood their power, they insisted on nondiscrimination, church-state separation, and not intruding on people's deepest beliefs.

Visible in Schmitt's close threadwork was a recurring pattern. As a political anti-liberal, Schmitt put a high value on social unity and common purpose. Liberal pluralism, competition, and diversity alarmed him. Morally, modern life, much as Taine had described it, struck him as private and aimless. Liberalism, in Schmitt's view, was accordingly twice to blame and a post-liberal politics offered a double cure. Schmitt could not see how political authority could survive party competition and public argument. He could not see how moral authority could survive personal judgment and the discredit of tutelary guides. He looked confusedly to unchecked power to restore both authorities, political and moral. As Jan-Werner Mueller neatly put it in *A Dangerous Mind: Carl Schmitt in Post-War European Thought* (2004), Schmitt asked "too much of politics in terms of meaning and too little in terms of morality."

Charles Maurras (1868–1952) was the intellectual force behind Action Française, the leading monarchist party, a tireless critic of the Third Republic, and a disbeliever in both liberalism and parliamentary government. In cool epigrams he welcomed the morally repugnant and nudged followers to violence, denying responsibility afterward. His favorite target was "the stranger within," a wanton term of his for French Protestants, Jews, Freemasons, and not-yet-French immigrants.

Maurras's mental outlook had three fixed points. One was a sunlit classical past, rooted in the Mediterranean world, where he was born at the port of Martigues, just north of Marseilles. He read the classical authors to relax and wrote a limpid, daylight prose that hid little in shadow or irony. Least of all did Maurras allow democratic courtesies to hide his disdain for the crowd. He thought of authority, like beauty or intelligence, as a gift of nature, recognized and respected where found, and that human virtues or excellences, though unmistakable, were rare. "I am Roman," he said, "and I am human. These to me mean the same." His respect for Roman values as he imagined them extended to Rome's heir, the Catholic Church, the second point of his intellectual triangle. Maurras was not a religious believer but saw in the Church, its rites, and its traditions a source of ethical order that liberal modernity, as he took it, had undermined.

The third element of his outlook was the "positivism" of Auguste Comte. Maurras shared neither Comte's belief in human progress nor his faith in the rational organizability of society. He followed Comte all the same in rejecting mystical or irrationalist approaches to politics. To Maurras, a political outlook should grow from an understanding of the facts of human life, which began with the particular character of the tradition people found themselves in.

Maurras's chief objection to liberalism was that any picture of society as an assemblage of personal units cooperating with each other and consenting to authority by choice was fantastical, a blatant denial of visible facts. Maurras also followed Comte in thinking that society needed a binding glue of shared belief. The content did not matter. Calling for a faith appeared to clash with the "positivist," science-minded rejection of metaphysics and respect for social actualities. The objection did not trouble Maurras. For Roman Catholicism to his mind was rooted in French tradition. That, too, was an observable truth. Catholicism served well as the common faith a healthy society needs. His Comtean "positivist" outlook set Maurras off from irrationalist streams on the French far right.

In thinking about society, Maurras paid more attention to the past than to the present. His liberal enemies might feel nostalgia for the nineteenth century, but Maurras pined for the Middle Ages. The nineteenth century was to him an age of moral and intellectual anarchy that had its roots in the Protestant Reformation. His golden age had ended with the collapse of Christian universalism.

Maurras had no quarrel with authority, nor indeed with power as such, treating domination and submission as natural and inevitable parts of social living. He did not believe in progress in any general sense, only in local improvements. Liberals who likened progress to natural change, Maurras noted, seemed to forget that in nature birth and growth led to decay. Humanity was not a person, he added, but if liberals insisted on thinking of it as one, they were surely wrong to treat its potential for improvement as boundless. Liberals treated humanity as a god. Why could liberals simply not accept, Maurras asked, that when they spoke of progress, what they meant was hope?

Maurras took liberal respect for people whoever they were as a flimsy mask for commercial interests. The liberal search for order was bound to fail. By railing against power, insisting on endless reform, and overemphasizing respect for personal choice, liberals poisoned the only sources of order that were genuinely available in society: respect for authority, respect for continuity, and respect for the fabric of collectivities out of which society was composed. To Maurras, "liberal" and "anarchist" were different words for the same thing. He could see little or no middle ground between liberalism and libertarianism.

Those arguments of principle against liberalism shared houseroom in Maurras's outlook with violent prejudices. The weakness of the Third Republic in Maurras's eyes owed much to its dependence on inside-outsiders whom he despised: Protestants, Jews, Freemasons, and immigrants. Together the four formed a standing conspiracy by the "legal country"—a largely fictional entity, the nation in law—to exploit and manipulate the "real country," the actual nation of ordinary men and women, villages, towns, associations, and parishes. Maurras's answer was monarchy, "the least imperfect" form of government. Restored to France, it would stand for tradition against modernity; for heredity against elections, a more hazardous way than birth to pick good leaders; for authority against the indecision and paralysis of parliamentary government; and for the decentralized liberties of communes, regions, and associations freed from the suffocating hand of the Jacobin-Bonapartist state.

Confusions in Maurras's practical suggestions stood out. Despite his insistence that outlooks and policies should grow naturally from their surroundings, his monarchism was radical, indeed revolutionary—a Utopian attempt to overturn a republican form of politics that had spread wide roots and grown strong over a hundred years. His anti-liberal hatreds were clearer than his suggestions for actual change. How Maurras's decentralized monarchy was supposed to run was, it seemed, too prosaic to pursue. His passionate, exclusive love of France sat ill with his Romano-Christian universalism. As much as he hated France's inside outsiders, he also hated Germans and Germany. "They are barbarians," he wrote, "and the best Germans know it." Nations, Maurras thought, were no more equal than people were, and none was superior to France—the "real France." that is, and not the "legal France" that was already as good as in enemy hands.

Maurras's following in the monarchist "street" cared less for winning arguments than for making trouble. Maurras cared for both. He stirred up right-wing street fighters with violent prose in the newspaper he edited, *Action Française*, and then disclaimed responsibility for the damage they caused. In 1934, for example, right-wing rioters egged on by *Action Française* attempted to storm the parliament in Paris. During the Popular Front government of 1936–38, Maurras's paper called on followers to "cut down" the prime minister, Léon Blum, a Jewish socialist. The same paper accused Blum's minister of the interior, Roger Salengro, of desertion in the 1914–18 war. Salengro was in fact a prisoner of war, but the slander contributed to his suicide. The liberal center of French politics just about held, but poison of the kind hung in the air, to narrow and worsen French choices after 1940.

In the event, Maurras's hatred of the Third Republic narrowly overcame his hatred of Germany. The fall of France was for him a "divine surprise," and he welcomed Marshal Pétain as an authoritarian second-best to monarchy. As if to confirm that doctrinal zeal does not save people from hard choices, Maurras's followers split. Some collaborated with the Germans, some joined the anti-German resistance, some did neither. Characteristically at odds, Maurras opposed both collaboration and resistance. After the war, he paid the price for his motivated subtleties. A French court sentenced him to life in prison for treason. He served until 1952, when he was released for his health. Maurras had accepted the Catholic faith, he claimed in earnest, and died soon after.

The thought and careers of Schmitt and Maurras serve to mark an outer border for the political right that puts conservative authoritarians inside, and nonconservative fascists outside. The differences in practice may be small and the human costs of both high, murderously high, nevertheless, they are not the same. Fascism, to schematize, is a form of totalitarianism. It imposes control on every aspect of the state, society, economy, and cultural life. It works through a single party with an all-embracing ideology commonly under a charismatic leader claiming to speak for the people. Its enemies are pluralism and diversity. Fascism stifles opposition by violence and fear and stabilizes itself by mobilizing popular engagement. Authoritarianism, by contrast, allows independent economic and social bodies, forms of limited representation, and a degree of freedom for religion. Its enemy is democratic participation. It also stifles opposition by violence and fear but stabilizes itself by relying on passive acquiescence in a trade-off of social quiet for loss of political role. The fascist is a nonconservative who takes anti-liberalism to extremes. The right-wing authoritarian is a conservative who takes fear of democracy to extremes.

If taken as the promise of liberalism's boons for all, democracy offered conservatives a double target. Conservatives could fault the scope of the promise or its content. They could object to the democratic guest list or the liberal menu. One guest-list problem was distributive overreach. Liberalism promised people civic respect and protection from power, whoever they were and whatever their merits or capacities. The snag was the cost of universal delivery. Understood democratically—for everyone—liberal protection and respect were too expensive, counterproductive, or unachievable. The criticism was more pragmatic than principled. They were silent on the worth of liberal aims themselves. Such complaints, when bundled into the all-purpose claim that democratic liberalism overburdened government, became common currency on the right after 1945.

A different guest-list objection from conservatives raised matters of fact and principle bearing on equality. The trouble was that liberalism's menu was too rich to suit all. Respect was due to merit and excellence. Few had either. Nobody as such deserved respect, save as equals at law or in the thinnest, quasi-religious sense. Further, if everyone, as liberals insisted, could say "no" to power, be it state, wealth, or social convention, then everyone would need to be self-governing, economically self-reliant, and ethically self-guiding. But such people, if they existed, were vanishingly rare. Charitably, then, liberalism might work for a few. It could never work for everyone. It might work among equals, but not everyone was equal. To conservatives, democratic liberalism—liberalism for all—was bound to fall short or fail.

Yet deeper for conservatives was liberalism's menu problem. It was not just that liberalism's promises were undeliverable to all. Taken together, they were deliverable to none, for they were incoherent. Liberalism promised respect for each last citizen and progress for society, but it was unable to say which mattered more. It claimed to provide for social order but treated moral and material conflict to be inevitable, indeed, to be encouraged. Liberalism, worst of all, fantasized about people rather than taking them for how they were: passionate, unreasonable, eager for guidance, and in need of roots. It scattered freedoms and choices while neglecting people's needs. If that is correct, "liberal conservative" labelled, at most, a conservative suspension in which liberal bits floated, not a solution in which they blended. For a sincere conservative, on such an understanding, compromise with democratic liberalism could never be more than tactical.

PART V

Conservatism's Third Phase (1945–80)

Political Command and Intellectual Recovery

The Year 1945

The most destructive war in living memory came to an end, having taken the lives of more than twenty to thirty million soldiers and fifty million civilians. American atomic bombs obliterated Hiroshima and Nagasaki in Japan. The British and Americans firebombed German cities, killing hundreds of thousands. Six million Jews died in a German genocide. Uncounted prisoners of war died in Russian hands. American, British, French, and Soviet troops occupied a defeated Germany, now divided into a Soviet occupation zone in the east and three Western zones.

Amid anti-colonial resistance, French forces killed several thousand Algerians and many hundreds of people in Syria, where Damascus was shelled. In Vietnam and the Dutch East Indies (later Indonesia), now liberated from Japanese occupation, British troops stifled moves for independence, enabling the French and Dutch to retake colonial control.

In France, Pétain and Laval, leaders of the collaborationist Vichy regime, went on trial for treason. Pétain was spared because of his age; Laval, executed. De Gaulle, the leader of the Free French, continued as head of a provisional government, which soon split over the drafting of a new constitution. In Britain, the Conservatives were crushed by the Labour Party in a July general election. In the United States, President Roosevelt died. His successor, Truman, began the Democrats' thirteenth year in the White House.

Only five thousand American homes had television. In adjusted dollars, a gallon of gasoline in the US cost about what it costs now. Staple foods like bread and milk were twice today's prices. An early computer, ENIAC, was set running. The new microwave oven and the first successful ballpoint pen went on sale. The science-fiction writer Arthur C. Clarke suggested in a magazine article that artificial satellites might one day be used for communication. *Ebony* magazine, aimed at African-American readers, began publication in Chicago.

Babies were born who, unknown to the world, would grow up to reshape ethical and cultural proprieties in the 1960s: Daniel Cohn-Bendit (student politics), Eric Clapton and Pete Townshend (rock music), and Rainer Werner Fassbinder (film).

7

Parties and Politicians
RECOVERING NERVE AND REWINNING POWER

For conservatism, 1945 was the year zero. There was nowhere to go but up. The political right had governed in much of the past half century, but fairly or unfairly, it now paid the price for economic slump and war. Social-minded liberalism had the high ground. To recover, the right had little choice but to adapt. Given adaptation, the right's recovery proved swift. By the 1950s, parties of the right had returned to power or, in France, were sharing power. They governed at the center as right-wing liberals. Helping to anchor them there was the vanishing of illiberal and authoritarian options.

Though swift, the recovery on the right itself was neither smooth nor uncontested. Mainstream conservatism accepted and soon mastered a new liberal-democratic status quo. On the party margins, right-wing resistance continued to burn. Intellectually, a recovery of conservative self-confidence was under way. Success, again, was double-edged. The more conservative thinkers accepted prevailing views, the less distinctive they became and the more blurred their outlook. The more they rejected liberal-democratic orthodoxies, the less relevant they sounded to party politics and government.

As demands made by democratic liberalism grew, so the costs of conservative compromise rose. The old question—Chamberlain's "What ransom for property to democracy?"—came back in new guises. How far would conservatives accept welfare capitalism? Concern for property and free markets pushed them one way, paternalist concern for the market's harms another. How far would conservatives accept integration and multilateralism? Again, free-trading internationalism gave conservatives one answer, attachment to nation and autonomy another. As for society's rapid shift toward cultural and ethical laissez-faire (1950s–1960s), conservatives also divided. Some acquiesced in prudential spirit to fighting only winnable wars. Others resisted in the spirit of principle on behalf of older, stricter values.

For four decades after 1945, mainstream conservatives broadly met those costs of compromise. They did it slowly or with regret—but they did it. The reward was office, which came with a price. Mainstream success stored up inner-party trouble for later. A resistant fringe found the costs of compromise too high: welfare was ineffective and morally corrosive; the nation was short-changed; letting go the ethical reins was an irrecoverable loss. Although those disparate charges did not add up to a tidy package, each was strongly felt enough to run together after 1980 into a hard-right insurgency against the old conservative mainstream.

National patterns varied. In Germany, conservatives after 1933 had fallen silent or given in to a totalitarian perversion that brought moral ruin, military occupation, and national division. The self-inflicted damage was so comprehensive as to offer postwar German conservatism a clear site on which to rebuild using pre-1933 elements, notably the Christian-social tradition.

The French right's prewar parties were tarred in turn with military defeat and collusion in Vichy's authoritarian experiment. Rebuilt, in the 1950s they shared without controlling power. Tarred by neither defeat nor collusion, De Gaulle united France's conservatives and took charge of government in the 1960s, and when, in the 1970s, that mainstream again divided, the gap between the liberals and Gaullists was small enough for durable alliances.

In 1945, Conservative outs in Britain and Republican outs in the United States shared credibly enough in celebrations by the winning side. Although they were blamed, and not just by the left, for previous economic failure (1930s) and for not standing up earlier to Germany and Japan, both parties were nevertheless soon back in power under former wartime leaders, Winston Churchill and Dwight Eisenhower. As in France, vain efforts in Britain to hold a broken empire split the parties within themselves rather than cutting across party lines. That communists, not just liberal democrats, had won the 1939–45 war was finessed. Soon the Cold War provided a Free World versus Communist frame that limited the right-left contest in the name of greater Western unity. Multilateralists and unilateralists continued to split the American right. The unilateralists lost (1945–80) but returned in growing strength at the end of the century and into the next.

After 1945, conservatives coped with rather than made the social weather. As economies changed and knowledge spread, the old inequalities etched into the conservative understanding of social order and authority began to crumble: men over women, white over black, old over young. (Disputes over the binary-nonbinary inequality itself were yet to come.) Conservatives troubled by the ethical and cultural upheaval brought on by such shifts in society were unsure how to respond. In conservative tradition, the family was a cell from which social order grew. Yet women were now working and going to college. When conservatives pictured society, motherhood no longer typified womanhood. The change might be irreversible, but for many on the right it was still unacceptable. Cultural conservatives found themselves in the awkward position of not feeling at home in a world that political conservatism had done much to create.

As ethical and cultural hierarchies flattened, a general anxiety spread. Did it matter in the end *who* stood up for ethical and cultural standards, so long as somebody did? Holding the line against an ethical free-for-all and a democracy of taste could in principle be done by anyone. The arbiters did not have to be male, white, or old. What mattered, surely, to a liberal-minded conservative was that there should be standards and that they should be kept to. The distinction between required roles and who performed them is easy to state, but in the smoke of the culture wars from the 1960s on, it was often easy for cultural conservatives to forget.

i. Normality, Pride, and Rage in France: Pinay, de Gaulle, and Poujade

In post-1945 France, the choices offered to conservative voters were normality (growing prosperity in a consumer society), pride (national grandeur as France decolonized and Europeanized), or rage (the frustrations of the hard right).

Antoine Pinay, the hero of normality, led the Centre Nationale des Indépendants et Paysans (CNIP), heir to the prewar economic liberals of the rural center-right. Charles de Gaulle, the voice of national pride and honor, led the party movement of various names that formed under him (1958). Pierre Poujade, speaking for rage, rallied the scattered elements of France's far right around his tax-protest party (founded 1953), creating a party-political space eventually taken in the 1970s by the anti-mainstream National Front. Parties were fluid and pairings were possible. Rage was compatible with pride (Poujade, the hard right) as was pride with normality (Gaullism).

The party contest played out in successive institutional frameworks: a provisional government (1944–46), led by de Gaulle until he failed to win his way on a new constitution and retired; the Fourth Republic, with a strong parliament and weak president (1944–58); and the Fifth Republic (from 1958), when de Gaulle won his way for a new constitution with a strong president and weak parliament.

Gaullist (and Communist) legend belittled the Fourth Republic, though its achievements were considerable. Amid early hardships of shortage and cold winters, war-damaged France faced national reconstruction. A third of the workforce was still on the land, beaten down by agricultural depression that had lasted on and off since the 1880s. Large industrial areas of the northeast were pillaged or destroyed. The government was as good as broke, France in debt, and the franc weak.

From that bleak start, France rapidly recovered in the next three decades, a period that was looked back upon after as the "trentes glorieuses." France's economy grew annually on average 4–5 percent (1947–73). By the early 1960s, it was bigger than Britain's. In 1945, the average French person earned half as much as the average American. By the 1970s, the gap had closed to four-fifths. The burst of growth, not known before or repeated since, was partly catch-up from the economic slump and war. Nor did France do it alone. Aid from the United States, keen for a stable Europe and alarmed at the strong French Communist Party, helped start France's recovery.

As France stabilized and modernized, normality without rage or pride became popular with voters on the right. A politician for whom stable prosperity was aim enough for conservatism was Antoine Pinay (1891–1994), who called himself Mr. Consumer. Judicious in approach and simple in speeches, Pinay appealed to conservatives in France who wanted a quiet life. They were glad to have a choice on the right besides moral crusade and social war (Pétain, with the contemporary example of Franco in next-door Spain) or national *ralliement* of stirring but uncertain aim and authoritarian coloring (de Gaulle). By championing universal concerns of shoppers and taxpayers, Pinay deflected the class-based calls of the left for redistribution and workplace democracy.

The son of a hatmaker from St. Symphorien, a small town in the central southeast, Pinay embodied the values of his CNIP party and its voters. "Money," he liked to say, was "an image of the nation." Fiscal discipline, economic health, social order, and moral probity were for Pinay interdependent. He was, in a sense, a values conservative, the values in question being good housekeeping and sound finance. (In charge of national finances, he twice killed inflation.) He favored Moroccan independence and, while wary of self-determination for Algeria, frowned on Algérie Française die-hards. Pinay had none of de Gaulle's conservative anti-Americanism. Nor was he anti-European. Neither lawyer nor intellectual, Pinay disliked Paris and posed as a simple Frenchman, suspicious of spendthrift governments and tax collectors. He was the hope of the non-Gaullist center-right for the presidential election (1965), but declined it without explanation, it was claimed for fear of exposure in a personal scandal.

Pinay's was a center-right conservatism of the everyday, light on doctrine and grandeur, little concerned with social justice or people's morals, and promising only to keep the boat steady and allow for a quiet life. Such an outlook appealed to the CNIP's rural electorate of local-minded small farmers and small shopkeepers. If Pinay's "normality" is extended back in time, it appears in the Orleanist economic liberalism of the July Monarchy. It reappears in the lay-urban hard-money Alliance Démocratique of Poincaré (to which Pinay had once belonged) and in the rural-Catholic Fédération Républicaine of Méline and Marin in the Third Republic. Extended forward, Pinay's "normality" divided in its legacy.

Its fiscal tightness continued with Valéry Giscard d'Estaing (1926–), who offered a new version of quiet-life conservatism.

Twice minister of finance (1962–66; 1969–74) and president from 1974 to 1981, Giscard held that "two Frenchmen in three" were socially and economically liberal but hostile to the socialist left. Giscard believed in technocratic economic and fiscal management, ideally undisturbed by democratic pressures. Like the old CNIP, he thought the Fifth Republic overcentralized. His government devolved powers to the regions, strengthened parliament, and freed the media from government oversight. Unlike the old CNIP, his party was socially, not just economically, liberal. His government eased France's restrictive laws on contraception, abortion, and divorce. A pro-European, Giscard strengthened Franco-German ties and promoted the evolution of the European Economic Community into a closer union. After de Gaulle sacked him from the government in 1966 for his pro-Europeanism, Giscard formalized his center-right following into the Independent Republicans. Renamed the Union pour la Démocratie Française (UDF, 1978), it became Giscard's vehicle for consolidating his presidency in 1978.

For Charles de Gaulle (1890–1970), politics was not about brokering interests or managing the everyday, but about the proper use of national power. A career soldier, president, and statesman, he exemplified, like Churchill, whom he never got on with, the force of will and myth in political life. De Gaulle's vision of politics combined a strongly plebiscitary view of democracy, a suspicion of parliament, and a closeness between leader and people that led opponents to think him authoritarian. Finding a category for him in French tradition was difficult. He quickly acquired his own "ism," as if to suggest, try as people did, that he was not categorizable. Like his times, de Gaulle was out of the ordinary.

A veteran of 1914–18, de Gaulle pled in vain as a staff officer afterward for army mechanization. On German occupation (1940), after his tank units made a bold but unsuccessful stand, he left for London and made himself the personal embodiment of a ghostly Free France. As liberation neared in 1944, he strove successfully to avert Allied occupation of France, secure French occupation in Germany, and win France a seat at the tables of postwar peace. As the leader of the provisional government from 1944 to 1946, his priorities were to restore the economy, rein in vengeance against collaborators, regain French colonial control in Indochina and Algeria, and establish a strong presidency. Rebuffed, he began a long "crossing of the desert" but returned in the Algerian crisis in 1958. Pressure on France from the Americans and others to negotiate with Algerian independence forces split the government, provoked rebellion from French Algerians, and threatened, many feared, civil war. Opponents called his ascent to power a coup, but formally speaking, de Gaulle was named premier by President Coty and confirmed by parliament. To the suggestion that he had seized power, he scoffed, "How could power be seized? It had to be swept up." He promoted a strongly presidential constitution, which was massively approved in a referendum in 1958, as were the truce and cession of Algeria soon after.

De Gaulle then oversaw independence for French Africa, the development (with American know-how) of France's own nuclear arsenal, and France's commitment to European integration. Whether his contrary gestures of national pride—pulling France from NATO, obstructing the European club, blackballing Britain, appealing to the Third World as a Cold War middle choice—were theatrical or sincere, all were reversed in time, France remaining at root Atlanticist, anti-Soviet, and European. The ups and downs of Gaullism can be traced in the votes in his referendums: constitution (1958), 83 percent; Algerian self-determination (1961), 75 percent; peace and independence (1962), 91 percent; direct election of president (1962), 62 percent; and senate and regions (1969), (rejected), which prompted his retirement.

Gangly, aloof, and self-possessed, de Gaulle was mocked throughout his life, but made himself immune to mockery. He detested party politics and, though hard to label more finely, belonged squarely on the right. Autocratic in style, he was convinced and able to convince others of his providential duties to France. When thwarted, however, rather than trying to reimpose his will, he walked away (1946; 1969), which belied the authoritarian charge. A traditional Catholic, he took restrictive laws on personal morality, when he thought of them at all, to be familiar, comfortable furniture that there was no reason to replace.

Politics did have a moral imperative, on his view: to uphold the independence and security of the nation.

That the man himself was *hors catégorie* left the task of categorizing Gaullism. Was it an idiosyncratic modern alternative to liberal democracy in the local tradition known as Bonapartism? Or a return, by abnormal means, to liberal-democratic norms when those norms were endangered or thrown aside? A clue to the answer, that it was more the second than the first, lies in the Third Republic's conservatism, which de Gaulle tried to defend, and in the Gaullist conservatism of the Fifth Republic he left behind. Only military rout pulled Third Republic conservatism over the line from liberal democracy into illiberalism and autocracy. By the time de Gaulle left for good (1969), Gaullist conservatism was taking more liberal, more parliamentary, more diverse paths. Stubborn and uncategorizable as was the man, Gaullism itself belonged to the conservatism of compromise.

After de Gaulle, Georges Pompidou (1911–74) helped turn Gaullism from a personalized, transitional movement into a pro-European center-right party that blurred in time with its Giscardian rival, the UDF. While campaigning, Pompidou, who was prime minister and later president, from 1969 to 1974, played up his Auvergnat roots although he was a *Normalien* ex-banker. A worldly conservative, he believed neither (with the doctrinal left) that humans were good and society evil nor (with the doctrinal right) the opposite. A defender of vigorous capitalism and a strong state, Pompidou took, like Giscard, the high line of right-wing liberalism running from the July Monarchy through the Third and Fourth Republics to the present.

After Pompidou, the Gaullist succession passed to Jacques Chirac, who founded the Rassemblement pour la République in 1976. In speeches and symbols, it called on a Bonapartist repertoire of people, leader, and nation. It was in its core electorate more provincial and more middle-class than Giscard's center-right UDF, which appealed to urban, professional voters. The party contrast was more personal and historic than programmatic. They shared government and by the 1990s had amalgamated, only to fall back again two decades later in disarray against the successes of the hard-right National Front.

Anger's postwar mouthpiece was Pierre Poujade (1920–2003), the original begetter of France's post-1945 hard right. A teenage follower of Doriot disillusioned by Vichy, Poujade escaped France for Algiers. On his return, he became a traveling salesman for religious books before opening a book-and-stationary store in his home department, the Lot. Experience as a small shopkeeper led Poujade to politics. In 1953, he founded a tax-protest party to defend shopkeepers and small businesses against big chains and the fisc. His movement stunned the mainstream right three years later by winning 13 percent of the vote and over fifty seats, including one for a young Jean-Marie Le Pen, later the founder of the National Front. Poujade's movement was a fluid coalition of apolitical tax protestors and malcontents of the right, themselves a motley of pro-French Algerians, monarchist relics, and Vichyite revanchists. Tying that motley together was angry contempt for parliament ("the biggest brothel in Paris," as Poujade called it), parliament's deputies ("pederasts"), government technocrats (the source of all trouble), and the French state ("thief and villain"). The Poujadist wave passed, only to return with gathering force after the 1970s. Pompidou affected to listen to Poujadisme, but Giscard turned a deaf ear. Consistent in his contempt for the mainstream center-right, Poujade endorsed the socialist Mitterrand (1981). Poujade and Le Pen's hard right shared with Gaullism the rhetorical themes of people and nation, but they used them differently, in an angry, exclusionary, and anti-elitist way. Gaullism aimed to stabilize, the hard right to disrupt.

ii. Tory Wets and Dries in Britain: Macmillan to Thatcher

Although Britain's right in 1945 did not need a new party home, the old residence was roofless and flooded. In the general election of July 1945, the Conservatives lost half their MPs, winning the fewest number of seats since 1906. The party's organization had evaporated during the war as local offices closed, social activities ceased, and fundraising halted. The Conservatives' one electoral hope, Churchill, proved an electoral dud. His likening of Labour—the Conservatives' wartime partner in government and now popular rival for office—to the German Gestapo was laughed at. Though grateful for his wartime leadership and conscious of what Britain had suffered, people grasped that the Russians and Americans, not Britain, had done most to win. Voters on the left suspected that the Conservatives, Churchill included, had entered the war less to defeat fascism or defend working Britons than to preserve empire. War had shelved an agenda of popular, liberal-inspired social reforms that voters now wanted and that Conservatives seemed tongue-tied or divided about.

Beaten as they were, the Tories soon demonstrated their formidable self-righting capacity. Their total vote (with the National Liberal and National Labour allies) of over 39 percent was only just less than at the previous election, ten years before. The party organization was rapidly revived. By the early 1950s, it had close to three million party members, nationwide, triple the number of Labour Party members. Under R. A. Butler, the Conservative Research Department turned out policy papers and programs that restored intellectual confidence and gave back the party part in public argument.

The party, as before, was also arguing with itself. Some conservatives would follow Labour on its path of social reform inspired by the Liberal Party. They were, loosely, in the conciliatory line of Disraeli-Baldwin One-Nation Toryism, led in the 1950s by Macmillan, who was content to accept a mildly reformist liberal conservatism. Other conservatives took a sterner line in the radical tradition of Peel and Chamberlain. Both earlier politicians had seen Tory support for prevailing orthodoxies as symptoms of party exhaustion and national decline. The clearest of the 1950s naysayers who rejected middle-of-the-road conservatism was Enoch Powell, early herald of the hyper-liberal yet nation-first hard right that later took over the party.

Each stream had its clubs and pressure groups. In 1951, the conciliators founded the Bow Group, called by one self-mocking member an effort at making Toryism acceptable to *Guardian* readers. In 1961, the resisters founded the free-market Monday Club. Later, once radicals got the upper hand in the 1970s, the sides became known as the Wets and Dries. Like other "binaries," the contrast was disputed. Many Tories were part both, or once one, later another. Still, Wets and Dries marked opposite ends of a common tent.

At first, Conservatives flanked Labour in adapting, rather than opposing, liberal-social reform. They promised not alternatives to welfare capitalism but better-run, less wasteful, and though they did not shout it, less generous welfare capitalism. The right's support for a national health service, for example, was won with the concession from Labour that doctors in the new free service could continue also to practice privately. A mild Keynesianism was adopted in economics, set out in the *Industrial Charter* (1947), which made full employment the aim of policy and deficit budgeting the means. There was scant daylight with Labour on foreign policy. The Conservative Party Conference Statement on Foreign Policy (1949) was, like Labour, strongly anti-Soviet and spoke delphically of an empire in "constant evolution," that is, not to last in its present form. India and Burma were already independent, let go under Labour, which had lost control of events. On rewinning power, the Tories had to learn painfully that they lacked the will and capacity to hold the rest.

Labour's travails contributed to the Tories' swift recovery. Labour's leaders—in office alone or in wartime coalitions since 1940—were tired and ill. Britain was indebted and financially overstretched. Defending a weak pound in the Bretton Woods fixed-parity system became a running national drama. In the general election (February 1950), Labour's majority was cut to five. It limped on for another eighteen months, when the Tories won a clear victory, staying in office for the next thirteen years. Retreat from empire, a chastening in the Middle East (Suez Crisis, 1956), and Britain's relative economic decline against renascent France and Germany shook the Tory political classes more than it shook voters. Through the 1950s, Britain's housing stock increased, the economy grew, the standard of living rose, and governments raised spending without much affecting taxes. At each of the next elections (1955; 1959), the Conservatives increased their majorities. At the second, people responded to the Conservatives' cheery claim—pinched from the losing Harry Truman in 1952—that they had "never had it so good" and won just under 50 percent of the popular vote.

The beneficiary was Harold Macmillan, prime minister from 1957 to 1963. Macmillan (1894–1986) was a publisher and politician who sat before 1945 as an MP for Stockton in the jobless north and afterward for suburban Bromley in the prosperous southeast. Before the war, Macmillan spoke for the Britain that Baldwin conservatism had neglected, looking to government to help. His book, *The Middle Way* (1938), was a Keynesian bible for statist Tory Wets. Afterward, without abandoning welfare or intervention, Macmillan looked, in economically liberal fashion, to rising prosperity to take care of society's health. Foreign affairs preoccupied him. He sped the end of British Africa, completing a withdrawal from empire. He half-persuaded his party that Britain's future now lay in Europe, but de Gaulle rebuffed his application to join the European club.

Prosperity rose but did not keep rising as fast or as reliably. Tory election agents sent warnings that poor by-election results during 1955–58 were early signs of middle-class impatience with an aid-granting, interfering state that seemed to grow as fast as, or faster than, the economy. A fiscal crisis in 1958, in which Macmillan refused large budget cuts, led to Treasury resignations, including that of the radical free-market Powell, then a junior minister. Intellectually, the Tory right was quiet but nevertheless active in the background. The Monday Club joined the old Aims of Industry and the League for Freedom as forums where unreconciled Tories could think out alternatives to the Macmillanite middle way.

By the early 1960s, at head of a government beset by scandal, Macmillan was old and ill and had caught the wrong side of a cultural change in which deference to age and authority were at a discount. After an interlude under an old-school Tory standby, during which Labour regained power, the party's soul was fought over by an old centrist, a radical marketeer (Powell) and Edward Heath, who split the difference and won the leadership contest in 1965. He was the transitional choice between an older compromising, consensual Toryism and a new, unreconciled and conflictual kind soon to be known as Thatcherism.

Heath (1916–2005), who led the party till 1975 and was prime minister from 1970 to 1974, was remembered by admirers as the forerunner of Thatcherism and by detractors as a failed Wet. Radical scare words—"compromise," "fudge"—were hurled against him. In fact, he shared many of the radicals' aims: less regulation, more competition, ending government efforts to control wages and prices, curbing unions (as had Labour tried), less direct and more indirect taxation, and "targeted," that is, less generous, welfare. The Tory right, however, never forgave Heath for shepherding Britain, at last, into Europe (1973). Heath had bad luck (a third Arab-Israeli war, an oil crisis, and global stagflation). He also had undue trust in people's reasonableness over deep, long-running conflicts (unions, Ireland).

An intellectual Tory who lived out those party changes in person was Keith Joseph (1918–94), a Conservative MP from 1956 to 1987. A Macmillanite junior minister, he backed first Heath, then Thatcher. In the 1960s he had no time for the party's right, when he voted to end the death penalty and debate decriminalizing homosexualty. His conversion to the radical right came in the 1970s, when he put his brains and gift of phrase to creating Thatcherism. Private enterprise had not failed in Britain, Joseph said; it just hadn't been tried. Britain was "over-governed, over-spent, over-taxed, over-borrowed and over-manned." He founded the Centre for Policy Studies in 1974, as a base for his own (failed) leadership hopes and more lastingly for an overhaul in Tory thinking.

Joseph's book, *Reversing the Trend* (1975), played to a widespread belief among conservatives that Britain was on the road to perdition. Invoking the right's classic theme of decline, Joseph knitted discrete problems—subsidized transport, public housing, single parents, for example—into a compelling picture of a failed society in need of rescue. Strong values and a clear picture of social health mattered in politics more, Joseph believed, than narrow economic rationality, which was needed, but alone was not enough. A sound economy and social health were connected all the same by the expedient virtues of responsibility and hard work.

Had they existed in Britain, Joseph would have been a neoconservative. Like his American and German counterparts (soon to be described), Joseph grasped political essentials in a detached, thorough-going manner without the least feel for popular democracy. He endowed Thatcher with ideas, but she chimed with Tory voters in a way Joseph—liberal, subtle, non-jingoist—never could. She thrived from his ideas, but she knew also how to be—or sound—illiberal, blunt, and nationalistic. Joseph, in that regard, was Thatcher's good godparent; Powell, her bad. Joseph spoke for an economic radicalism that accepted democratic liberal limits. Powell, as will be seen, heralded an altogether more disruptive and populist hard right.

iii. Remaking the German Middle Ground: Adenauer and Christian Democracy

In 1945, little a sincere German conservative believed in was untouched by the ruin that Germany had visited on itself. The familiar elements of a conservative outlook—social unity, the authority of custom, unreasoned loyalties—looked sullied. Loathing for Germany's occupiers, Soviet and Western alike, was poor substitute for the sentiment, vital to conservatives, of national pride. Germany was defeated, shorn of territory and divided. Many cities were shattered. Millions of people were displaced or on the move. In the winter of 1946–47, disease and hunger spread. In the West, the economy's capital stock had, remarkably, survived the war and Soviet pillage, but industry, supply chains, and commerce were all badly dislocated. The self-inflicted catastrophe of war and the enormity of the Holocaust had to be explained and accounted for. Many conservative Germans had seen the war as a campaign for the West against Bolshevism. Germans of all opinions bridled at foreign occupation.

For German politicians of the postwar right who took responsibility for repairing that collective wreckage, the strategic tasks loomed of economic reconstruction, restoration of political sovereignty and national unity, and recovery of Germany's moral reputation in the world. Each was achieved, though not in sequence or at an equal pace. All were fought over within the right. First, a new political framework was required. It included a provisional constitution for Western Germany, known as the Basic Law (1949), and new conservative parties: the Christian Democratic Union (CDU) and its Bavarian "sister" party, the Christian Social Union (CSU).

A tempting but false view was that victorious Western allies airlifted liberal democracy into a broken, unwelcoming Germany. On that picture, the Basic Law was a foreign imposition, alien to German tradition, where the left was not liberal and the right not democratic. In truth, Christian Democrat and Social Democrat lawyers combined to draft, without foreign bullying, a model liberal-democratic charter. Its overriding aim was summed up by the Christian Democrat lawyer Adolf Süsterhenn as avoidance of the "concentration of power in any one place," a liberal principle with which many conservatives were now happy to agree. Catholic political tradition echoed in the first article: "Human dignity shall be inviolable," which all state authority was obliged to respect and protect. Further, citizens had a duty to resist tyrannous government. With an eye on Western communists but also on its own troublesome far right, conservatives accepted that the highest court could ban "anticonstitutional" parties.

Left-right disagreements as well as regional differences within the right were brokered away. Christian Democrats wanted less centralized taxation and revenue-sharing than did Social Democrats. Catholic Bavaria, which wanted greater regional autonomy, was joined by Baden and Württemberg, where liberal localism of small farming and craft industry was strong. When sent for ratification to the *Länder*, Bavaria voted against the new federal republic but agreed to join if two-thirds of the other *Länder* assented, which they did. Although Bavarians clung to old suspicions of a domineering, Protestant North, the weight of Catholicism had grown among conservatives when Protestant Prussia was shorn from the West in the division of Germany at Potsdam.

The heartland of the new Christian Democratic Party (CDU) was the Rhine-Ruhr. The region was industrial and rural, as well as Protestant and Catholic. The CDU was correspondingly a big tent. Centrists at the party core wanted to foster business and social peace. To the right were the national-conservative descendants of Weimar's old DNVP. The party to the left spoke for the Catholic workers' movement. Social Catholicism stamped, for example, the party's Ahlen Program (1947), which declared: "The capitalist economic system has not lived up to the state and social interests of the German people."

The Christian Social Union (CSU), in rural, tradition-minded Bavaria, was cool to economic recovery rooted in industrial peace and social welfare. Much as the CDU claimed the mantle of the pre-1933 Catholic Zentrum, so the CSU claimed descent from the old Bavarian People's Party. Like its predecessor, the CSU guarded its Catholic identity and conservative independence. Formally, the CSU was a distinct party, allied to but not merged with the CDU.

A third element of post-1949 mainstream conservatism was the Free Democrat Party, known as Liberals. A hinge party, the FDP had a permissive, social-minded wing, which allowed for coalition with the Social Democrats (1969–82), and a more conservative, free-market wing, which enabled coalition with the Christian Democrats (1949–56, 1961–66, 1983–98, 2009–13). In the 1950s, as a middle-class party strong on civil liberties and popular with civil servants, the FDP, together with the All-German Bloc, pled the cause of former officials sanctioned for having served the Nazi state.

Flanking the parties of the mainstream right were several unreconciled outsiders. The largest was the German Party (1947–61), which was strong in Lower Saxony. It sheltered right-wing discontents and refusals that were muffled or ignored by the CDU: monarchism and Hanoverian regionalism, as well as free-market opposition to social welfare and trade unions. Flying under the red-white-black colors of the Wilhelmine Reich (and the Nazi party), its prevailing tone was popular-nationalist. It won a few seats in the Reichstag (1949; 1953; 1957). The All-German Bloc of Expellees and Rights-Deprived rallied refugees from East Prussia and civil servants barred from work because of service in the Nazi period. Its strength encouraged an addition to the Basic Law, which was amended in 1953 to require to require parties to win at least 5 percent of the party-list vote to be allotted party-list seats.

The change speeded a consolidation of the German party-political right into a single large alliance, the CDU-CSU. A lesson from the

Weimar period was that party divisions and confusion of aims had weakened forces on the right that might have deflected the Nazi assault on power. In 1949, ten parties won Bundestag seats. The CDU had only 31 percent of the vote; the FDP, 12 percent; and the German Party, 4 percent. By 1957, the field of parties was down to four. The CDU-CSU received 50.5 percent of the vote.

As the new West German framework stabilized and prosperity grew, the appeal of edge parties faded. The CDU offered space for their concerns as well as a chance of government posts. By the end of the 1950s, the German Party's politicians and voters were blending into the CDU-CSU, and in 1961 the party itself disbanded. The poor fortunes of such fringe groups did not mean that the hard right had vanished from party politics. It revived and died several times before returning in strength after unification, in 1990, rooted in the old East, to harry and weaken the center-right, as will be seen in chapter 9.

For the recalcitrant right, the Germany of the 1950s was not the country they had hoped for and expected to love. A new currency, a new constitution, and even a divided country came to be accepted, if not normalized. It was irksome for conservative anti-moderns and other refuseniks of the right to acknowledge that the Federal Republic was capitalist, liberal, democratic, and Western. It was prosperous, unexpectedly stable, and, by the coarse test of electoral results of its conservative champions, popular. The combined scores of the CDU-CSU and liberals in the first five elections in federal West Germany were 43 percent (1949), 55 percent (1953), 58 percent (1957), 58 percent (1961), and 57 percent (1965).

Criticism of the Federal Republic continued from the right among thinkers and in small magazines, as will be seen in chapter 8, on the ideas of the right from 1945 to 1980. It echoed familiar charges against liberal modernity from unreconciled conservatives, charges now redirected to the conformity and materialism of consumer society, the lack of German national pride, and the loss of faith in any but "instrumental" public values of economic well-being and social quiet. The subtler, more interesting critics of the right pressed some of those objections while rejecting others, opening lines of intellectual compromise with liberal-democratic orthodoxies.

The leader who presided over the normalization of West Germany and the consolidation of the German right was Konrad Adenauer (1876–1967). He was chancellor from 1949 to 1963) and led the CDU from 1950 to 1966. Adenauer's sober politics of recovery and repair had little room for enthusiasms or extremism. "No experiments!" read election posters in 1957. The slogan summed up Adenauer's conservatism as well as his careful, stubborn pursuit of Germany's postwar tasks, which had to do with the economy, national sovereignty, and moral repute.

Adenauer fixed his tone in an opening address as chancellor in September 1949. It stressed personal freedoms and responsibilities, efficient markets, and social provisions to assure well-being. Brushing off claims of German specialness, Adenauer placed Germany squarely in the Western world and acknowledged the nation's debt to the United States (the Soviet debt was glossed over). The nation's moral roots he placed in a "Christian-Western" political culture of respect for law and for people's intrinsic moral worth. On Adenauer's lips, the theme of Christian-Westernism blended enlightened ideals with Christian tradition. Liberals and Christians, the suggestion ran, had little to fear from each other.

The Christian-Western theme had blunt campaign uses. The grip of Stalinism across Eastern Europe, the crushing of an uprising in East Germany in 1953, and the flow of Easterners to the West helped conservative voters accept the CDU's Cold War picture of a civilizational struggle between totalitarian despotism and Christian-Western freedom. CDU campaigning blackened the Social Democrats as dangerous Marxists. Of the Social Democratic leader, a CDU poster from the 1950s read: "What Ollenhauer sows, Stalin reaps." Against images of a cross and a medieval saint, another admonished, "Save Western culture!"

Mindful of the damage a divided right caused in the Weimar Republic, Adenauer established the Christian Democrats as a dominant, all-embracing party of the center-right. Besides absorbing radical fringes, the CDU maintained its often rivalrous alliance with the more right-wing CSU, led from 1961 through the next three decades by Franz-Josef Strauss (1915–88). A Munich-born butcher's son and Eastern Front veteran, Strauss was scourge of the left and thorn of the center-right, although quieter behind the scenes than his hard-right public face often made him appear.

Against the German revanchist right, Adenauer accepted the heavy loss of national territories and oversaw the return of several million expellees and refugees. Against a neutralist left, he resisted pressure for unification (dangled by the Soviets in the early 1950s), preferring to restore and fortify the Federal Republic under a United States shield (which also brought grousing from anti-American conservatives). With an ear open to the All-German Bloc, Adenauer replaced punishment of perpetrators (denazification) with reparation for victims. He gave scarce encouragement to a national reckoning over Hitlerism and the Holocaust. Germany's recovery of moral repute, Adenauer believed, was better served by decent behavior and respecting friendships. In the 1960s, it fell to a Social Democrat successor, Willy Brandt, as well as to historians and thinkers, to fill in the silences that Adenauer's postwar approach had left.

Adenauer, however, had squarely faced the lingering question of Catholicism's place in politics and role of the party in Catholicism. A Catholic Rhinelander, Adenauer shared his family's suspicion of Prussia and bitterness at Bismarck's Protestant-led *Kulturkampf*. He was Cologne's mayor for the Catholic Center Party (1917–33) and hostile to the Nazis, although he proposed a local coalition with them against the left, which they refused. Twice imprisoned, Adenauer became mayor again in 1945. In the 1920s, he had belonged to the wing of the Center Party that pressed to take it "out of the tower" (that is, to abandon its primary Catholic loyalties) and become cross-confessional, an aim which he now achieved.

When conservative critics chided Adenauer for sacrificing eastern lands, bowing to American interests, and cementing the division of Germany, he answered that a self-confident, prosperous West Germany would prove in time too attractive for the East to resist. Prosperous, West Germany became. Guided by his economics minister, Ludwig Erhard, the German economy rapidly recovered. During 1950–63, real wages doubled, working hours fell, and unemployment dropped from 8 percent to near zero. It took another quarter century, but East Germany did eventually collapse into West Germany's arms. For the embrace, when it came, to be so swift and peaceful, it also took the Social Democrats' diplomatic opening to the East and reduction in mutual suspicion (in the 1970s) that the German right, led by Strauss and the CSU, hotly opposed.

Like de Gaulle, Adenauer was conservative in social-moral matters, treated elections as necessary but regrettable, and governed high-handedly. He governed from the center-right, with conservative qualms about liberal modernity. Against mass society, materialism, and atheism, the best arms, he believed, were the civic virtues of patience, accountability, and courage.

He left a party whose strategic aims were never to cross the Americans on the Cold War, to keep its own Germany-first revanchists in line, and never to miss chances for better ties with East Germany. In Europe, the aim was French-German rapprochement and creation of a closer European union. Adenauer's successor, Helmut Kohl, continued that path. He became party chairman in 1973 in a period when the CDU was losing elections. The SPD had dropped its last Marxist pretenses at Bad Godesberg in 1959 and was now governing with the Liberals. Kohl set out to steady the party, grow its membership, and win back the Liberals. He saw off a bid for party leadership from Strauss, who sought and failed to remake the CDU as a majority, stand-alone party of the right. When the CDU-CSU chose Strauss to lead their ticket in 1980, he lost, opening the way for Kohl. In 1982, the Liberals again switched allegiance, so abandoning the Social Democrats and handing Kohl the chancellorship. The solid center of German politics won itself another three decades of life, but as will be seen, it was then shaken by the upheavals of a new century in a post–Cold War world.

iv. The US Right Divided: Eisenhower–Taft, Rockefeller–Goldwater, Ford–Reagan

"Well, this means eight more years of socialism," a conservative Republican sighed in dismay on watching Dwight Eisenhower win the party's nomination for president (1952). The favorite of the party right, Robert

Taft Jr., had gone down to defeat against a nonpartisan military hero widely treated by a mistrustful party as a closet New Dealer. Taft rallied a new generation of conservatives refighting the battles of the 1930s and 1940s, proud to uphold the warrior traditions of America Firsters and the anti-Roosevelt Liberty League. They were not enough. Eisenhower, who went on to win the White House, was the choice of Republicans content to live in the present and compromise with the United States as it had become under twenty years of reforming Democratic rule.

Without having heard of any of them—Gentz, Chateaubriand, or Stahl—Eisenhower Republicans were applying a lesson from those prudent nineteenth-century accommodationists: don't try to unmake one revolution by starting another. Their victory, however, was only the beginning and little guide for what was to come. A fight for the Republican tradition went on between moderate right-wing defenders of the liberal-democratic status quo and conservative insurgents who wanted radical change. The story of American conservatism over the next three decades, ending in the election of Ronald Reagan, may be thought of as a long revenge for 1952.

Robert A. Taft (1889–1953) was an heir apparent: Ohio-born, son of a president from the Middle American heartland, leader of the Republicans in the Senate, and foe of big government as it had grown under the New Deal and war. Taft had opposed Roosevelt's wary preparations for war during 1939–41 and Truman's anti-Soviet engagements across the globe. He treated international law and multilateral statecraft as the wrong tools for a proud, self-sufficient nation. He questioned the legality of the Nuremberg tribunals and opposed NATO, on his view a burdensome device created to meet an exaggerated threat. Taft criticized Truman for preaching peace but making war and for masking the American engagement in Korea as a UN-sponsored operation.

As a defender of business freedoms, Taft shaped labor-management relations. In response to a wave of strikes triggered by postwar layoffs and a sharp jump in inflation, Taft cosponsored the Taft-Hartley Act (1947), which curbed union freedoms and was passed over Truman's veto. Although the act did not touch broad rights to unionize and strike, which were underpinned by the New Deal's Wagner Act (1935), it forbade wildcat strikes, secondary picketing, and sympathy strikes, as well as jurisdictional strikes over who did what job, a measure ensuring management control of the shop floor. The act also banned or restricted arrangements that made union membership or the paying of union dues a condition of employment. States in the South and West followed with restrictions on unions of their own known as "right-to-work" laws. Anti-union legislation of the kind played its part in the appeal of the Sunbelt to northern business and in the growing strength of the Sunbelt in national politics.

Although derided by Democratic liberals as a golf-playing do-nothing and by Taft's followers as a risk-blind globalist, Eisenhower (1890–1969) presided as a skillful chairman over the post-1945 consolidation of American economic and strategic power. As former Supreme Allied Commander in Europe and then US president from 1953 to 1961, the changes he made to New Deal tradition were more in pace than direction. He pursued "containment" of the Soviet Union (that is, no further expansion, whereas Cold War hawks wanted "rollback"); accepted a draw in Korea, recognizing that the US could not win; sat quiet over the Soviet invasion of Hungary, in 1956; and sought détente with Khrushchev. He countermanded the ill-conceived Franco-British intervention at Suez but approved an American-directed invasion of Cuba (later bungled under Kennedy), as well as signing off on American-backed coups in Guatemala and Iran. Faced by the out-of-control, red-baiting Joseph McCarthy, rather than speak out against a fellow Republican, Eisenhower waited for McCarthy to ruin himself. Quiet also on segregation, Eisenhower nevertheless made Earl Warren chief justice and in 1957 ordered federal troops in Arkansas to enforce the Warren court's desegregation ruling, which had been resisted in a decade-long campaign of obstruction across the South. He spoke for small budgets, sound money, and letting the economy pull itself out of recessions, but he made no serious attempt to prevent Democratic Congresses from heavily raising government spending. His federal highways program contributed to the creation of suburbia, which drew the middle classes from cities and helped turned party-political differences into socio-geographic divisions.

In his farewell address, Eisenhower warned the nation against over-growth of the "military-industrial complex," yet much of the spending he had failed to rein in was on the armed forces. On faith and morals, Eisenhower was conventionally conservative, with scant sense of the cultural conflicts about to engulf the country. Careful with constitu-tional proprieties of church-state separation, he opened his first inau-gural address, before addressing his "Fellow citizens," with a personal prayer for "My Friends." The state might be debarred from intervening in religion, but religion was still part of public life. His second inaugural was a lyrical invocation to "America the Bountiful" with a warning not to expect too much from government action. Life for many Americans improved in the Eisenhower years, which amid later turmoil were looked back upon as a time of certitude and well-being. The judgment was seductive but selective. Conservative Republicans tolerated, more than warmed to, Eisenhower. He had a talent, often claimed as prudent conservatism, of not fighting battles he could not win and leaving them to successors.

One of those battles was for the soul of Republicanism. Scattered, out of sight, both in and out of politics, the forces of rollback were gathering. From around 1960, Eisenhower's last year in office, the Republican right began its slow return to power. Loose movements of resistance formed that rallied conservatives: to post-New Deal social reformism, to government-enjoined civil rights, and to the spread of a newly confident secular-modernism. The first was primarily economic. It drew on big-business lobbies that had opposed the New Deal and were now oppos-ing the Democrats' Great Society, as well as on the disgruntled, middle-class tax payer, Sumner's "forgotten man," who was fed up with paying, as they saw it, to help shirkers, unwed mothers, and others of the "un-deserving" poor.

The second element of resistance from the right was white backlash against desegregation and civil rights. It began in, but was not limited to, the South. By the late 1960s, after civil-rights acts had made open obstruction futile, resistance to integration was continued with changes of terms in the name of "suburban rights" for control over local taxes, neighborhood schools (that is, no busing), and residential zoning. The success of the racist ex-governor George Wallace among Northern union workers in the 1968 primary elections was a warning sign of which Nixon took note. Resistance came also from middle-class white liberals, who silently isolated their homes and their children, so deepening the contempt felt for liberals by conservatives readier to admit their fears and prejudices. A third wave of resistance on the right swept up Christian conservatives alarmed at moral permissiveness, indifference to religion, and a more liberal interpretation of the constitutional separation of church and state, as exemplified in the Supreme Court's 1962 ruling that banned official prayer in public schools.

Those several causes—opposition to big government, civil rights, and irreligion—had no obvious common thread. Still, they could come together, as in the Republican right's 1950s seedbed, Southern California and the Southwest. Migrants from the rural Midwest and South in the 1930s and 1940s had brought simple faiths and distaste for cosmopolitan attitudes. The religious right used local television to grow its churches. Law schools taught counterliberal ways to read the law. The spirit of local enterprise—ranching, small business—was self-reliant and anti-government. Agribusiness, dependent on Mexican-American workers, evaded federal regulation and unions. Defense was a big employer, paid for by big government, but in the good cause of standing up to communism. This was territory in which Barry Goldwater grew and flourished.

Goldwater (1909–98) formed a bridge between the old Taft wing of the Republicans and the party under Reagan, from which, after 1980, liberals were rapidly excluded. Arizona-born, Goldwater earned a pilot's license, flew air transports in Asia in the Second World War, broke into Phoenix politics, and, on Eisenhower's coattails, beat the Democratic majority leader in Arizona's US Senate race in 1952. Goldwater promoted further anti-union laws and pressed the investigation of union racketeering.

His breakthrough into national politics came in 1960, when he turned against Eisenhower Republicanism for a domestic agenda he called "a dime-store New Deal." Richard Nixon, Eisenhower's vice president, relied on East Coast liberals in the party to win the 1960 nomination, and made one of their grandees his running mate. Aggrieved Southern and Western Republicans determined to take over the party and made Goldwater their standard bearer.

For the Republican right, Nelson Rockefeller (1908–79), grandson of the oilman, governor of New York, and leader of the liberal Republicans, represented all they disliked in what they contemptuously called "the East Coast Establishment." He was pro-abortion, pro-Green, pro-UN, and for a bipartisan foreign policy, all things the Republican right disapproved of. His loss to Goldwater at the Republican convention in San Francisco (1960), when he was jeered from the floor, marked the beginning of the end of liberal Republicanism. Though some who loved Goldwater were bigots, Goldwater himself was less bigot than libertarian, approving in old age, for example, gay marriage. He nevertheless united the various streams of the hard right into a force with which Nixon and Ford had to deal and which won the Republican Party after 1980.

The presidency of a "hinge" Republican, Richard Nixon (1913–94), marked a double shift in the Republican center of gravity from the East Coast to the South and West and from Eisenhower's middle-of-the-road approach to the anti-liberal partisanship that came to prevail after 1980. Southern California launched Nixon, where he began as a zealous red-baiting lawyer. Eisenhower picked him for vice president to appease the Republican right, just as Nixon in 1964 picked a Boston Brahmin for his running mate to appease the moderates. Nixon lost, but liberal Democrats and liberal Republicans now faced backlash against civil rights, the Vietnam War, and in the culture wars. On those angry tailwinds, Nixon twice won the presidency (1968; 1972). Nixon campaigned from the right but governed (with a Democratic Congress) from the center. His administration brought in affirmative action in federal hiring, big increases in spending and borrowing, wage and price controls, a dollar devaluation, détente with Soviet Union, and the opening of China, as well as disengagement from Vietnam, however grudging and brutal. Nixon's career ended in scandal—campaign criminality concealed and lied about by the president. He resigned in 1974 to avoid almost certain conviction in Congress. A transitional figure, Nixon left a party divided between moderates in decline and radicals whose skills and confidence were growing, served well by counterliberal think tanks and generous conservative donors.

A messenger of change was the ex-broadcaster and US senator for thirty years from North Carolina (from 1973), Jesse Helms. As gifted spokesman for the hard right, Helms (1921–2008) played a role not unlike that of Enoch Powell in Britain. Moving in from the edges, Helms did much to make Republicanism's Southern voice its national voice. Proudly anti-liberal, he opposed civil rights, busing for desegregation, banning school prayer, decriminalizing abortion, extending the deadline for the failed amendment granting equal rights to women, and promoting gay rights. Helm depicted liberalism as both ineffectual and corrosive, which was not coherent as a charge but widely persuasive. Helms helped create an enemy in the so-called cultural left, turning it from a hate object of shout radio into one of the conservative right's primary targets. Although a failed competitor for leadership of the right, Helms's campaigning smoothed Reagan's ascent to the White House in 1980 and the Republican winning of the Senate that year—a victory that the Watergate scandal had merely delayed. The Republicans, in a sense, were pushing at an open door. Stagflation in the 1970s and the Second Cold War (1978–86) had broken the post–New Deal consensus (welfare Keynesianism plus containment-détente). Midwestern Taft Republicanism had returned as Reagan conservatism rooted in the South and West. Nor was the seismic shift purely within party politics. As chapter 8 will show, the unreconciled, counterliberal right had strong intellectual sources as well.

8

Ideas and Thinkers

ANSWERING LIBERAL ORTHODOXIES

Surveying the postwar intellectual scene, the American literary critic
Lionel Trilling wrote in *The Liberal Imagination* (1950) that there was no
longer "serious and intelligent" conservatism for liberals to argue with.
Trilling was thinking of the United States, but his dismissive judgment
was widely shared in Europe. The common rewards for thinkers of the
right on both sides of the Atlantic in the years after 1945 were obscurity
and neglect. Quiet, persistent work that questioned liberal-democratic
orthodoxies nevertheless soon restored the right's intellectual
confidence.

Trilling's charge was not readily answerable as it stood, for what
counted as "serious" conservative thought? Conservatives, after all, directed thoughtful fire at prevailing liberal policies: social reform, regulation of markets, and the state's growth. More broadly, many questioned
how the liberals' picture of open, competitive society led them to underplay its moral harms. Some even sought distinctively conservative
principles to back up those criticisms, but none offered an alternative
conservative orthodoxy. If such a lack is what Trilling meant by the absence of "serious and intelligent" conservative thought, he was setting
an unduly high bar. Setting aside that exacting standard, postwar thinking on the right was spirited and soon had party-political impact.

The mainstream right profited from a clarifying frame of thought in
Cold War anticommunism and economic liberalism. Support for the
one came from *The Open Society and Its Enemies* (1945), a critique by a
centrist philosopher of science, Karl Popper, of historical determinism
and totalizing thought in the Hegel-Marx tradition. Popper's work
added antitotalitarian ballast to geopolitical reasons that liberals, left or

right, had for pursuing the Cold War. Economically, the social theorist Friedrich Hayek's influential thoughts on the wisdom of markets and spontaneous social order (toughened by economist colleagues at the University of Chicago) served an economic liberalism of business freedoms and limited government.

Michael Oakeshott added second-order thoughts about the style of political action to be preferred. His "anti-rationalist" pleas for intellectual quiet and political modesty were taken by some (in non-Oakeshottian spirit) to epitomize a genuine conservatism and by others, topically, as a gloved polemic against left-liberal social reform. A different reading of Oakeshott would put him squarely in no partisan box but hear him as calling for moderation against zealotry, system-think, and extremism, whatever their stripe, which Oakeshott had seen much of during the 1920s to 1940s.

In Britain, a herald of the twenty-first-century hard right, made himself heard. Enoch Powell set himself and his career against the state-friendly centrism and multilateralism that attracted Toryism in the 1950s and 1960s. A powerful, unyielding mind, Powell was an early framer of a popular counter-faith in the unstable dual monarchy of the free market and nation that before long captured the right across Europe and the United States.

Liberal disregard of social and cultural authority was a favorite target of conservative criticism. In Germany, Gehlen set out a philosophical anthropology that pictured people as anxious and bewildered and without disciplines and institutions to guide them. Others attacked the ethical shapelessness of liberal society from different points of view. Working in London, the Austrian émigré philosopher Aurel Kolnai contrasted the ethico-cultural free-for-all of liberalism with respect for excellence and "social nobility"—an open, nonclass idea—that alone could head off "qualitative egalitarianism" in which no attachment or belief was worth more than any other. The French thinker Bertrand De Jouvenel refreshed for latter-day readers the nineteenth-century complaint that by isolating people from each other and weakening the middle-ground of civil associations, liberalism overempowered the central state. The philosopher-historian R. G. Collingwood pled on conservatism's behalf the cause of historical knowledge. History was vital, he believed, to understanding politics, which liberalism, in the Utilitarian spirit of cost-benefit calculation, was squashing into economics and social observation.

American universities gave shelter to speculative outsiders with imposing, lapsarian stories of liberalism's flawed origins. Eric Voegelin, another Austrian émigré, dated the Utopianism of liberal modernity to a wrong turn by idealistic early Christians who thought fallen man redeemable by worldly means. A conservative historian of ideas in Chicago, Richard Weaver, dated humanity's fated lapse into liberal modernism to scholastic theologians of the fourteenth-century who displaced what is naturally good for people from morality's driving seat and put there instead whatever people choose to want. With sharper bite and later historical focus, Alasdair MacIntyre, a British émigré to the United States, disputed liberalism's ethical groundwork in *After Virtue* (1981) and other works.

American conservatives listened also to worldlier thinkers. Both felt engaged in a *psychomachia* for the national soul. Each had a clear ethico-cultural outlook and weapons to fight with. William Buckley, a Catholic conservative and founder-editor of the *National Review* (from 1955), rallied the right's scattered forces, restored their confidence, and gave them a platform. Irving Kristol, a Jewish ex-Marxist, guided the neoconservative assault that from the late 1960s shook left-liberal orthodoxies. Both were New Yorkers who by the 1980s had planted their victory banners in the US capital.

i. Herald of Britain's Hard Right: Powell

If one thinker is to be credited with starting the long rightward shift in British conservatism from the 1980s onward, it is Enoch Powell (1912–1998). In a period of centrist compromise, Powell heralded Thatcherism, but he also did more. In elevating the market, Thatcherism, if not Thatcher herself, was at root global and multilateral. Powell revered the global market but wanted to return politics to the nation. At once economically globalist and geopolitically unilateralist, Powell was the herald of British conservatism's turn against Europe.

When sacked in 1968 from the shadow cabinet for an inflammatory speech on immigration, a shrewd Tory editorialist who sensed Powell's appeal wrote that containing Powellism would occupy his party for the next decade. The editorialist was off by a factor of five. Containing Powellism would occupy the party for the next half century and, in the 2010s, it would finally fail.

In the early 1950s, Powell had been a right-wing member of the One Nation group of young Tory MPs. Though the name recalled the social-unity Toryism of Disraeli and Baldwin, the group had, besides social-minded Wets, divisive, market-minded Dries like Powell. Instead of a welfare state, he proposed in 1953 that local authorities and voluntary bodies cover basic social and health needs. He pressed for lower taxes.

Powell hardened the loose, sentimental slogan "One Nation" into interlocking geopolitical, sociopolitical, and national claims. First of all, postimperial Britain was alone in the world; the Commonwealth was a sham; the United States was a bully, not a friend; Europe was a trap. Second, the postwar liberal British state was at odds with an alienated British society. Last, Britain was special and unique. Each idea— aloneness, alienation, and specialness—came into its own on the British right after 2010.

Powell was confirmed in his sense of Britain's aloneness by three postimperial epiphanies. On hearing of Attlee's plan for immediate Indian independence in 1947, Powell reported that he walked confounded through the streets all night. Next, Powell took American intervention to halt Britain's misadventure over Suez in 1956 to be a betrayal that confirmed British folly in depending on its hugely more powerful former ally. Last, Europe's federalist direction turned him against a venture he had once supported and he became a ferocious anti-European.

As for the "dangerous estrangement" Powell saw between society and government, experience in his Wolverhampton constituency convinced him that British governments failed to grasp the social effects of immigration from ex-colonies. It was wrong, he thought, for politicians to lose contact with their constituents. "Of the great multitude, numbering already two million, of West Indians and Asians in England," he wrote in 1972, "it is no more true to say that England is their country than it would be to say that the West Indies, or Pakistan or India are our country. . . . They are and remain alien here." As if trying to see how many mistakes to pack into one aphorism, Powell said soon after, "Skin colour is like a uniform" (1978). Powell was claiming to speak for the people, and in a special way. He claimed, in populist spirit, to be saying what "the people" knew to be true but feared to speak aloud because "elite" orthodoxy forbad them.

The specialness of the British nation for Powell was indexical. Britain was his "here." It was special to him because it was his. He did not try to distil an essence of Englishness in the manner of Disraeli or Baldwin. He scoffed at nostalgic "myths" with which fellow conservatives pictured the nation's past, particularly the golden Victorian times of industry and empire. Nor did Powell defend supposedly British values against foreign values. In that, his nationalism was not chauvinist. A polyglot translator and Cambridge scholar of Greek paleography, whose first intellectual love was German thought and writing, Powell was, culturally speaking, a cosmopolitan universalist. He defended Britain as it was, much as the Romano-cosmopolitan Maurras had defended France because he was French. Powell's patriotism, though contingent, was absolute and unconditional. Echoing Maistre, who claimed that he would honor the devil if so ordered by the Pope, Powell insisted, "I would fight for this country even if it had a communist government." His One Nation was neo-Hobbesian in its monistic vision of authority: the United Kingdom was indissoluble; the nation was indivisible; parliament was sovereign, being unbindable by any law or treaty.

An intellectual in an avowedly unintellectual party, Powell began as an atheistical Nietzschean skeptic and ended as an unflinching believer in the English nation and its national church. What survived the change were a ferocious mind, passionate temperament, and biting tongue. Powell was omnicapable and hardworking but too much his own man to be at home or effective in party politics. In brains and talent, he outshone rivals, yet spent all but three of thirty-seven years in parliament on the back benches. Pride fought with principle. He turned down posts he thought beneath him. He resigned rather than follow a line he could not accept. After 1968, he was finished in the then Tory Party. Although an effective minister of health, contemporaries judged him a maverick or an opportunist. Powell was one of two right-wing thinkers whom the Tory Wet Ian Gilmour savaged in his study of conservatism, *Inside Right* (1977). Hayek was the other. His flaw was dogmatism. Powell's was inconstancy, as shown according Gilmour by his U-turns: on immigration, Europe, Egypt, defense, and Ireland.

Powell's vehemence disguised it, but he believed in the "delicacy and vulnerability which sustains society." In Burkean spirit, he proscribed disruptive experiments. Yet amid centrist conciliation, he was a disruptor. His Christian faith was Augustinian and unsentimental. It chimed politically with disbelief in liberal progress or this-worldly equality. Christianity was not, Powell said in Salisburyish tone, a "story with a happy ending" told to please the "sugary mentality" of the modern age. Humans were open "to ignorance, incapacity, perversity." and "sheer human propensity to error" was "sufficient to ensure a high failure rate." Neither success or failure in life were due to merit. The poor were not deserving or the rich guilty. That said, everyone had duties to family and community.

How did Powell reconcile his populism with his parliamentarism? His radical vehemence with respect for settled values? Gilmour put Powell's reputation down to oratory, which he meant as a criticism. The charge missed its mark. Oratory was Powell's prophetic gift. People listened to what he said, and as they listened and repeated, Powell helped create a new climate on the British right.

ii. Our Conservative Second Nature: Gehlen

For a liberal, and that includes liberal conservatives, the trouble with Powell's Hobbesian vision of legitimate authority was to make its exercise too willful, too strong, and in the end without constraint. It was the trouble that foxed Schmitt. Whoever or whatever exercised legitimate authority in Powell's constitutional vision—parliament, nation, people, or some imagined combination—a liberal would want to know how authority could in practice be stood up to and gainsaid. Even allowing that supremacy and indivisibility were necessary for effective authority, they were not enough, in liberal eyes, for legitimate authority. For liberals, it also mattered how authority was exercised. Powell, by contrast, often sounded as if effectiveness were all that mattered.

A social version of that problem arose for the conservatism of Arnold Gehlen (1904–76), among postwar Germany's most searching thinkers on the right. He chose a naturalistic way to talk of an element that had always lain at the core of the conservative outlook: stable institutions. They were needed and valuable because of how humans were. Without stable, commonly accepted institutions, people had nothing to guide them or shape their purposes. By "institutions," Gehlen meant social norms and customs in a large sense. Without them, people were directionless, unable to say what they wanted, and at a loss. The social rootedness of ethics was familiar in the conservative tradition. So was the requirement that there be an accepted social ethic. Gehlen explained both by the vulnerability and dependence of the human animal. Left unexplained was whether some norms were more acceptable than others. Or was what mattered simply that a norm prevailed?

His conservatism was neither national nor chauvinist. The need for norms on Gehlen's account was universal, their content relative; that is, how norms were shaped and experienced varied from culture to culture. No society had a vantage point for judging others better or worse. Nor had Gehlen's cultures anything that smacked of race, an idea he took for bogus. His appeal to human biology was negative. Biology, on Gehlen's picture, told us much about the initial human make, little about the humans that life in society made.

According to Gehlen, we were, in Nietzsche's phrase, "incomplete animals." Early helplessness, long maturation, and a physical underspecialization unique among higher animals were elements of openness that by creating anxiety and tension left us craving a frame of order. We were born with undeveloped organs and unspecific instincts adaptable to an open range of tasks but were preadapted to none; with unusually broad sensory equipment, leaving us open to the world, "unstable and at risk, overburdened by affect"; and with an excess of energy that had nowhere particular to go. Institutions, which were understood to include norms, customs, and social frameworks, offered guidewheels, thus releasing us from overstimulated, anxiety-causing openness. Norms came to be felt as natural. Following them created "a feeling of beneficent certitude, a vital unburdening." Energy freed from anxiety and choice could then "rise upward, so to speak," becoming "available for particular, personal, unique and novel purposes." Personal variety and originality were thus possible, but only within prevailing norms. Anyone who sought distinctiveness regardless of them was bound to fail.

The technocratic character of liberal-modern society did not worry Gehlen. Technocracy—the neutral rule of expertise and management— was stabilizing, hence legitimate. Technocracy was not romantically to be bemoaned by conservatives but handled in a spirit of "realism," a line of thought linking Gehlen with Schmitt and, before him, Gentz, both of whom stressed the primary need for conservatives to manage actual circumstances, for good or ill.

The liberal character of modernity, on the contrary, did worry Gehlen. He criticized overambitious "humanitarianism," as well as the growing liberal tendency to confuse the personal and the political. He shared conservative anxieties about social indiscipline. He feared that without semireligious feelings of awe, sacredness, and taboo, social norms became perilously exposed, a thought pursued by Catholic conservatives in the United States and by Scruton in Britain.

Institutions could decay or be disrupted in several phases, on Gehlen's view. Norms we grew overaware of were "shaken," lost their sense of naturalness, became open to question, and were treated as optional conventions. Subjectivism could rear its head. People might experience "fortuitous predispositions" as if they carried "super-personal import." In "well-functioning institutions," "individual sensitivities and subjective frictions" were "neutralised" because people made sense of themselves "on the basis of external realities." By contrast, present-day society seemed to be failing. "Never," Gehlen wrote in 1960, had people "been more decisively thrown back on the limited reserves of their fortuitous dispositions than today." At the same time, those same fortuitous dispositions had never been so vulnerable.

The thought that unguided personal choice, far from liberating people, threatened to enslave them to the powers of state or social

convention was hardly new, being a commonplace ever since Tocqueville and other nineteenth-century worriers about cultural democracy, including Mill. Gehlen drew, however, a fresh lesson. In such "subjective" conditions, public argument decayed. As "irritated sensibilities"
emerged, each at odds with some aspect of society, they could not be
"relieved" through open discussion. As Gehlen put it: "The more people
make use of the fundamental freedom to speak their minds, that is to
say, to profess their subjectivism, the less authentic contact results." The
left-liberal Jürgen Habermas, who took Gehlen's work seriously, agreed
with him about the decay of public argument, though not its cause.
Habermas blamed the problem on domineering institutions. Gehlen
blamed it on us for asking too much on our own behalf.

Gehlen's conservative anti-liberalism was sophisticated and deeply
thought out. Liberal ideals both undercut customary norms yet imposed
impossible tasks on people. With dialectical skill, Gehlen turned the significance of human liberty, in Hegelian manner, on its head. Far from a
gift of nature, liberty was, to begin with, our curse. Lockean natural rights
twinned with an empty-slate picture of the mind showed us a helpless,
pitiable captive. We needed freeing from our primal liberty by familial
nurture and social rules. The preliberals of classical Western thought
looked to political authority to secure people's natural liberty and keep
them safe from each other. Gehlen looked to society to rescue people
from their natural liberty and make them safe from themselves.

Gehlen's counterpicture was bracing, the reasoning ingenious. There
were difficulties, however, and they were connected. From Gehlen's impressive schematism it was hard to draw practical advice not just because
his angle of approach was so steep but because any principle of choice—
whether fairness or well-being—was missing. Powell, it may be recalled,
fell short by not saying what principled limits there were, if any, to the
exercise of legitimate authority. Gehlen fell short by giving little principled guidance about which institutions or norms rescued us better
from bewilderment and gave us better shape to live by.

Gehlen was among other postwar German intellectuals of the right
faced with rethinking conservatism. They had the choice that conservatives faced everywhere: finding and defending distinctive conservative

values or, in a pragmatic, post-ideological spirit, turning conservatism into a political style or tempo marking: moderato, andante. They also had a particular question about German conservatism's immediate past. Save among a fringe of malcontents, it was agreed that the German right's attachments and commitments—social unity, suspicion of philosophical reasoning, sense of human imperfection—had to be recast. They had to be purged of the national chauvinism and pagan irrationalism that had blighted the German right in the past half century. The question was how. One approach took the long view. It rethought conservatism as the modern political expression of Christian-Western tradition. A second approach took the recent view. It rethought conservatism as an acknowledgment that the twentieth-century German right, Hitler's crimes notwithstanding, was the virtuous party. It had gone to war against Bolshevism. It had defined itself in the fight. Long-view, Western-Christian conservatism flourished on the intellectual right in the 1950s and died away, before returning among young German rightists in the 2010s. The recent-view approach—modern conservatism as anti-Bolshevism—exploded in the *Historikerstreit* (1980s). That politico-academic dispute over the historic roots of Nazism also died away to return in the new century as part of the hard right's vernacular of "saying what cannot be said."

A temptation was to recast Western-Christian conservatism in a Catholic and aristocratic spirit. Protestant Prussia was now in East Germany. The Catholic presence was accordingly stronger in the Federal Republic. One focus was an erudite group, Neues Abendland (New Occident or New West), backed by a rich, upper-class Bavarian. Its journal, which was published from 1946 to 1958, took the same name. It favored European integration not for trade or security but for re-creation of the *Abendland*, an imagined cultural unity of premodern Europe. The group was tepidly democratic, with authoritarian leanings. *Neues Abendland* held up Franco in Spain and Salazar in Portugal as contemporary models of Christian leadership. The ills of modernity—secularization, loss of moral compass, social conflict, and national rivalry—were set against the premodern virtues of unity, stability, and faith. Nazism was blamed on a fatal metastasis of modernity's vices: liberalism, Marxism, Nietzschean individualism, and Darwinism. A second journal, *Merkur*, founded in 1947 under the early editorship of Hans Paeschke, gave space to right-wing views of the kind, although also to counterviews from across the left-right spectrum.

The stronger vein of thinking on the German postwar right was pragmatic. Civilizational worries, fears of mass culture—particularly American culture—and grumbles about urban life (Greenism was yet to appear) dropped away in the 1950s. The right saw prosperity and national security as better paths to social order than ethico-cultural will-o'-the-wisps. Germany's pragmatic conservatism was a pursuit of normality in abnormal conditions of national division and recovery from historic shame. When the magazine *Der Monat* in 1962 asked German writers and thinkers "Was ist konservativ?," most contributors took conservativism for a contented if underspecified blend of liberalism, caution, and undemanding Christianity. Only Mohler, Jünger's ex-secretary, spoke out openly against liberalism and its flaws.

Appetite for principle did not die. By the 1960s, Germany's intellectual right was girding once more against liberalism. Two topics—dispute over Germany's recent past and the outburst of student protest—gave the right new targets and energy. The journal *Criticón* (1970–98), founded by Caspar von Schrenck-Notzing, made its hallmark *Unbefangenheit* (roughly, "unselfconsciousness") about Germany's Nazi past. *Criticón* helped ignite the *Historikerstreit* between conservative and left-liberal historians over the adequacy of German scholarly reckoning with the Nazi period. Political protest twinned with countercultural exuberance in the 1960s rekindled conservative anxieties about liberal modernity. Together, as with neoconservatives in the United States, they prompted calls for social disciplines that successful consumer capitalism seemed unable to provide.

iii. The Liberal Moderns' Fall from Grace: Weaver, Voegelin, and MacIntyre

In a mesmerizing speech at Harvard University (June 1978), the Russian author Alexander Solzhenitsyn told listeners that the West had lost all courage and that its politicians and intellectuals were slumped in depressed perplexity. An irresponsible media spread misinformation, fed "strong mass prejudices," and shut out unfashionable views. Moral harms went unanswered in the name of personal liberty. A people tyrannized by material interests was no longer willing to die for ideals. The common source for those ills was the West's abandonment of spiritual values and consequent surrender to the "corrosion of evil."

Solzhenitsyn's philippic divided opinion. It was broadly welcomed by American conservatives, alarmed as they were by Soviet pressure at the onset of the Second Cold War and troubled by evidence as they saw it of their nation's moral decay. To nonconservatives, the speech was partisan, selective, and overdrawn. A fortnight afterward at a public appearance in Washington, Rosalynn Carter, the president's wife, responded: "Alexander Solzhenitsyn says we can feel the pressure of evil across this land. . . . Well, I do not sense that pressure of evil at all. . . . The people of this country are not weak, cowardly and not spiritually exhausted."

Two imaginative pictures of a nation's civilizational health were here in competition. Solzhenitsyn's picture of a spiritless West came from an imposing gallery of conservative modern masters. The gallery opened with nineteenth-century Russians—notably Fyodor Dostoevsky and Konstantin Pobedonostsev, the reactionary Tsarist adviser—and ran on through Spengler and other modern declinists, to be refreshed at mid-century in the United States by conservative thinkers reworking a now familiar idiom of moral perplexity and decay.

The three mid-twentieth-century master painters of liberal disorder considered here—Richard Weaver, Eric Voegelin and Alasdair MacIntyre—all worked in the United States. Voegelin and MacIntyre were European emigrés. They wrote with a historical and geographic broad sweep. By the "West" they meant, willy-nilly, the classical Mediterranean world, medieval Christendom, and present-day rich, non-Communist nations. All took for granted a pervasive spiritual decline. None focused topically on this or that particular social harm or its solution. They wrote as if Western troubles were, if not of one kind, at any rate from a common source in a collective moral disorder. The scholastic and historical detail was imposing. With Voegelin, it was overwhelming. Despite the detail, however, the appeal of the picture lay in its simplicity and familiarity. Each told a time-honored story of Luciferan pride and fall. What liberals saw as progress, these thinkers took for ruinous and merited decline. Reversing decline, supposing that reversal were possible, was a matter of morals and how to think about morals.

Each had a social diagnosis, a historical story, and a suggested cure. On the diagnosis, they concurred. We were suffering from liberal modernity. On the timing of its onset they differed: the twelfth century, perhaps earlier (Voegelin); the fourteenth century (Weaver); eighteenth-century Enlightenment (MacIntyre). The suggested cure was to rebuff liberal efforts to privatize morality and put morality back into politics and public life. Weaver, Voegelin, and MacIntyre opened paths toward present-day "values" conservatism. They pointed to a sphere of politics that conservatives might hope to claim as their own.

Richard Weaver (1910–63) was a North Carolina–born scholar who studied at Vanderbilt University, where he came into contact with the Southern Agrarians, and later taught at the University of Chicago. His best-known work was *Ideas Have Consequences* (1948). It opened wryly with a nod to the conservative cultural pessimists of the 1920s and 1930s such as Spengler, Moeller, and Duhamel: "This is another book about the dissolution of the West." There followed a 187-page jeremiad against the sins of liberal modernity. As Weaver saw it, the mistake was to abandon a view of the world in which everything had its proper purpose, hence a value, whether humans liked it or not, to a view in which everything was pointless until humans gave things value for their own purposes. "Man in this world," he wrote, "cannot make his will his law without any regards to limits and to the fixed nature of things." Unities of faith and society, and morality and nature had existed in the Middle Ages. They were now lost. Among the dead or missing in the contest of unity and modernity that Weaver described in successive chapters were the "unsentimental" sentiment of wonder, respect for hierarchy, a sense of purpose in nature, art without ego, the iron linkage of personality and property, and unsullied, truthful public discourse. The most grievous loss was piety, an attitude of untroubled respect that admitted "the right to exist of things larger than the ego." Freed from profound error, modern people might yet return to respect for property, to new care for political language, and to piety toward nature, community, and the past.

Weaver's celebration of the Middle Ages reflected a shift in historians' attitudes toward the premodern past that was already familiar in the previous century. No longer was the medieval period caricatured as stagnant and dark. Historians, however, could acknowledge the intellectual achievements of premodern times without, like Weaver, denigrating modernity. A further problem was Weaver's eccentric singling out of William of Ockham, the fourteenth-century Franciscan theologian, as the serpent who had prompted our fall into modernity. Ockham, on Weaver's account, had cunningly tempted us with the apple of nominalism, one of the standard philosophical accounts of the nature of universals, which certain Ockham scholars deny he even held.

Quirky as it was, Weaver's book had a message for the right. By the 1940s, ideology of any kind had acquired an intellectual bad odor. Ideology, it was insisted, traded in Utopian ideals, and Utopian ideals, as the experience of the 1920s through 1940s showed, heralded collectivist tyranny. Grand ideas were out. The prevailing custom was to treat political studies as a neutral, fact-based science. In Germany, the anti-ideological custom attracted conservatives such as Gehlen and Odo Marquard. Weaver, however, told conservatives to disregard the custom of the day. Rather than accept the prevailing intellectual mood, he urged them to become ideological.

Weaver followed up with a better book and a plan of action. His *Ethics of Rhetoric* (1953) was a necessary reminder that politics is practiced in norm-laden words, above all in speeches and public argument. Weaver recognized that ideas and terms took rough handling in politics. He was notably suspicious of the "rhetoric of social science," which, he judged, disguised unavoidably normative talk in the borrowed, ill-fitting clothes of natural science. It was vital, however, to guard against the abuses of rhetoric. Weaver was writing in the same monitory spirit as Orwell's "Politics and the English Language" (1946) and Victor Klemperer's study of fascist discourse, *Lingua Tertii Imperii* (1947). Taking their speeches as his material, Weaver disapproved of Burke's rhetorical overkill, argumentative fluidity, and sense of expediency; he praised Lincoln's lawyerly insistence on clearly stated definitions and principles.

Weaver's other contribution to the post-1945 right in the United States was an intellectual battle plan. In "Rhetorical Strategies of the Conservative Cause" (1959), Weaver laid out a Gramscian program of dialectical warfare: sharpen arguments; aim them at the most vulnerable targets; and defend them in well-financed colleges and think tanks. By the 1980s, the conservative campaign Weaver had called for was under way and promising to sweep the opposition from the field.

Altogether more speculative was a grandly historical approach to political discourse of Eric Voegelin (1901–85), a German-born American scholar and social thinker. He had studied and taught in Vienna, working as an assistant to Hans Kelsen, the theorist of legal positivism. Hounded by the Nazis for dismissing racial theory as bogus science, Voegelin immigrated to the United States in 1938. He found shelter to teach the history of ideas at the whites-only Louisiana State University (beginning in 1942), which was then recovering from an embezzlement scandal that had put its former president and several state officials in jail.

Voegelin's was a lapsarian story, like Weaver's, but told with a deeper knowledge of languages and the past. The timescale ran from preclassical times to the present. He elaborated an overarching tale of humanity's fall into modernity in many essays, in an eight-volume history of political ideas written for college use, and in his main work, the five-volume *Order and History* (1956–87). For Voegelin, the "ismatic" apple that prompted our fall into modernity was not nominalism but gnosticism. By "gnosticism," he meant a corrosive error about the nature of social norms, made originally by puritanical, mystic religious sects—the Gnostics—in the early Christian period. The gnostic error on Voegelin's telling became pervasive in later myth, religion, and politics. The error was to confuse norms binding together present society with idealized depictions of a hoped-for future society. To that simple-sounding thought— that aiming to remake society was chasing a fantasy—Voegelin gave rich historico-philosophical clothing.

Religion and politics, on Voegelin's telling, were once indistinguishable. The authority of kings and priests was one. Divine order and social order were not distinct. Then, helped by Christians, the spheres were separated. Kings no longer had to be priestly, and people became governable without God. To cap the separation, people sought to govern themselves without kings. On Voegelin's telling, however, the unity of politics and religion was only suppressed, not overcome. Religion reentered through the back door in disguise. Self-governing people, ill adapted for the task, searched about for a missing divine authority. Unable to find one in secular, naturalistic times, they divinized themselves. The contrast between their imagined godly selves and their actual selves was too stark, and gnostic modernity was a sequence of bad tries at resolving the conflict. All took the form of impatient attempts to cash the redemptive promises of Christian revelation in this world.

In *Order and History*, Voegelin tracked the error from gnostics at the birth of Christianity, through reappearances in mid-to-late medieval thought, to its triumph in liberalism. Late moderns suffered a notably grievous form. On the one hand, they took the actual world for all there was. (Nothing for them, to invoke an unstable distinction, was "transcendent"; everything was "immanent.") On the other hand, late moderns were still gripped by visions of progress toward an ideal: an "eschaton," or final state. Voegelin's warning against liberal modernity was caught by the slogan, "Don't immanentize the eschaton," which it is said students wore on T-shirts.

In gnosticism, Voegelin believed he had a diagnosis of modernity's familiar ills: too much individuality twinned with the "massification" of society, which together raised the specter of total control. By confusing descriptions of hoped-for society with standards by which to judge present society, modern liberals denied human limitations. They asked for failure, disappointment, and worse.

Voegelin fitted into no obvious partisan or intellectual pigeonhole. His underlying point about the hollowed-out middle of liberal-modern society was not original. Tocqueville, speaking a century before as a conservative liberal, had worried about the unhealthy coupling of undue personal liberty and collectivist tyranny. The thought was common currency for midcentury conservatives such as Jouvenel, Kolnai, and, in a quieter vein, Collingwood. Nor was Voegelin's antipathy to ideology distinctive.

Voegelin's approach to history was both appealing and off-putting. The appeal was its anti-positivism. Without sympathetic engagement, Voegelin thought it impossible to grasp the sense of a people's history. Knowledge of the past required not the finding and confirming of causal laws; rather, it required imaginative understanding with how people thought about and symbolized their historical experience. Collingwood and Oakeshott would have agreed. Voegelin's way of realizing that approach was, however, unconstrained and hard to follow. His all-enveloping story harked back past Toynbee through Spengler to Hegel's lectures on the philosophy of history (1822) and Schelling's *The Ages of the World* (1815). Then, against that, in an open-minded spirit toward the end of his career, Voegelin recognized the limits of such epics. He dropped the idea that history was following a single path, whether upward, as dogmatic progressives insisted, or downward, as conservative pessimists claimed.

How conservative was Voegelin? If all "isms" in politics shared the gnostic fault of confusing the actual with the ideal, how was conservatism itself not guilty? To answer that abiding puzzle, Voegelin took the familiar step of insisting that conservative ideas were not of the first-order, overambitious kind that conservatives proscribed. Conservatism, for Voegelin, was a "secondary ideology." It knew what it was against. It countered and dismissed overhopeful ideals and unachievable plans. Such a second-order conservatism is often called "negative" and is without "positive" or "substantive" claims of its own. Repetition of this claim from Burke onward has not made the puzzle go away. The answer has the air of a dodge. Negatives can always be reexpressed as positives and vice versa. Is a secondary ideology an ideology or not? Is the persistent, comprehensive refusal of large ideas in politics itself a political large idea? Anti-ideological conservatism has rarely given a clear or stable answer.

Faced by Voegelin's critique, the poor liberal might feel they could not win. Liberalism, Voegelin charged, was both trapped in mythic thinking and deluded into believing that it had escaped mythic thinking. The charge against liberal modernism was common to post-theological thinkers such as Heidegger and Strauss. Of Voegelin's many characterizations of a distinctively modern outlook, one of the sharpest was the tendency of modern thinking to undermine itself. "The essence of Modernism," he wrote, "lies, as I see it, in the use of the characteristic methods of a discipline to criticise the discipline itself." That more graspable thought underlay the anti-modern critique of the third lapsarian here, Alasdair MacIntyre.

In lectures and writings in the 1970 that culminated in *After Virtue* (1981), MacIntyre objected that political liberalism rested on a flawed picture of morality. Liberals assumed that what people happened to want fixed their values and ideals, whereas in truth, values and ideals fixed what people ought to want. Values and ideals grew out of shared practices in society. Such practices alone gave people a purpose in life. Liberal modernity had dislocated society and shattered its practices. Without shared practices that gave people purposes and "narratives"— that is, ways to understand their practices—any talk of values and ideals was a kind of nonsense, an echo of moral discourse that once, but no longer, had coherence.

Moral incoherence was, to MacIntyre, liberalism's original sin. The stain passed down to Marxists and liberal Utilitarians alike. Liberalism, for MacIntyre, closed off ways of life. Far from being a philosophy of freedom, liberalism was a doctrine of constraint. Liberals had inherited its fatal flaw from the eighteenth-century Enlightenment, "a machine for demolishing outlooks." By abandoning an Aristotelian picture of man as finding purpose in his social nature, the Enlightenment had broken the link between morality and society, and moral discourse since had fallen into disorder.

The symptoms of disorder were abstractness, a lack of social anchorage, impersonality, and indecisiveness. Morals were supposedly authoritative, but, MacIntyre held, liberal argument about them was interminable. The only guides left in private morality were "the aesthete" and the "the therapist." Public life was overseen by "the manager." Under "managerialism," political society's primary task became the impartial, cost-effective balancing of people's wants. Although emptied of purpose, moral talk continued under liberalism in characteristic forms: claims to rights, which MacIntyre likened to the posting of "no trespassing" notices by squatters on common land; the unmasking or exposure of true interests behind their moralistic disguise; and protest, which was all that was left to dissent now that civil war was no longer an option and hope of persuasion by argument had gone.

In his personal convictions, MacIntyre moved from left liberalism to anti-liberal Marxism and thence to anti-liberal, left-wing Catholicism. What struck some as fashionable vagabondage struck others as an authentic search in the spirit of Mill's experiments in living. Friendly critics suspected that MacIntyre was, in effect, a closet liberal. Allowing for his concessions and provisos, the virtuous society MacIntyre envisaged was not radically different from the sort of place liberals such as nineteenth-century German cooperativists committed to local control and the small scale had once hoped for, although probably with more mental conformity than liberals as a rule have been happy with. Nobody, on MacIntyre's view, was to be harried or bullied to a less liberal, more virtuous life. Instead, MacIntyre hoped for an ethic of "moral resistance" from post-liberal minorities who would withdraw into "small communities," for example, self-managed societies or confessional universities. His ideas passed down to later conservatives after 1980, when a kind of MacIntyrean passive resistance became popular on both sides of the Atlantic among twenty-first-century "values" conservatives.

MacIntyre's critique of liberal modernity was less callow than Weaver's and easier to follow than Voegelin's, yet it shared faults with both. The charge of what was present (moral disorder) and what was missing (moral order) was presented at an almost content-free level of generality that made their plausibility hard to gauge. Those who enjoyed their sermons dark were likely to agree; those who preferred them sunny, to disagree. When pressed, it could be hard to find from MacIntyre particular arrangements and attitudes to which he objected. The intellectual history, with its widely varying dates, was overgrand and fluid. Humanity's fall into modernity, with its widely varying dates, recalls the postcard drafted to Heidegger by the antihero in Saul Bellow's novel *Herzog*: "What is the fall into the quotidian? Where were we standing when it took place?"

There was, besides, a tension in the picture of premodern times. Its intellectual unity was exaggerated. If, as historians had taught since the nineteenth century, reasoning and argument were vigorously alive in the Middle Ages, then not everyone agreed with each other or believed the same thing. The MacIntyre of *After Virtue* seemed to have forgotten his own fine *Short History of Ethics* (1966), in which the deep, enduring conflicts of Platonism and Aristotelianism, Stoicism and Epicureanism were lucidly accounted for.

If, as critics such as MacIntyre held, liberal society was awash with personal rights, it was awash too with counterpart duties. Far from an abandonment of morality, the modern web of civic rights and duties might be seen as a new morality in politics, the expression of the political community's shared outlook. Antidiscrimination rules in all their variety are a good example. They are irksome, indeed, to parts of the right. They are stigmatized as the liberal state's interferences with people's liberties or the suffocating imposition by society of political correctness. The charges are overheated, but even if true, they would hardly be evidence of liberal amoralism or modern anomie.

To leave it there, however, would be to underplay the critic's doubts. MacIntyre's were the most pointed. Why, he wanted to know, was liberal society so rich in unrealized dreams of its own and so full of damage to things of value that everyone, liberal or not, ought to cherish? Why, he wanted to know, was liberal society so effective in ruining collegial institutions, eroding excellence, commodifying culture, and marginalizing the needy? Such ills, MacIntyre suggested, were not failures to meet liberal ideals. They arose as predictable consequences of liberal ideals. The liberal sin, to MacIntyre, was urging society to let go of people and encouraging people to go their own way.

To liberals who objected that MacIntyre overplayed the ills of modern society and ignored its achievements, he replied that liberals were so confused by their "moral individualism" that they could no longer see the faults. MacIntyre pictured liberal society as a kindergarten of self-interested, isolated selves no longer able even to recognize the collective goods they were destroying. In blaming liberalism's flaws on "moral individualism," MacIntyre offered a way out he himself chose not to take. MacIntyre's entire attack tied political liberalism tighter to a contentious picture of morality when equally he could have broken the link. Many political liberals could agree with MacIntyre's charge that liberal modernity neglected and left to die too many things of shared or intrinsic value, but they could disagree as to why. MacIntyre made the failure moral. For liberals, at least liberals of a social-minded kind, the failure was different. In asking themselves why late-modern society had failed to protect what should be protected, liberals of the kind did not have to appeal to personal indifference or moral blindness brought on by a civilizational failing. The more obvious causes of liberal democracy's underperformance were more down-to-earth: lack of spending capacity and loss of political will.

iv. Winning the US Stage: Kirk, Buckley, and Kristol

Striking as were Miltonic tales of the moderns' fall from grace, most American conservatives argued nearer street level. Market economics, anticommunism, and civic morality defined the broad plane of maneuver on which the postwar American right rewon its intellectual confidence. Gathered to fight were old critics of the New Deal from the 1930s and 1940s in the name of economic liberalism and, before long, new critics of the Great Society from the 1960s; anticommunists, turned outward against the power and pressure of the Soviet Union, as well as inward in a hunt for collectivists in an anti-collectivist society; and, variously labelled, "values" or "cultural" conservatives disturbed by liberal democracy's ethical permissiveness and disregard for shared norms of common civility.

It was easiest after 1945 for American conservatives to combine anticommunism with economic liberalism or with "values" conservatism. It was difficult, however, to combine "values" conservatism with economic liberalism. Despite efforts at "fusion," no American conservatives were good at combining all three.

Begetter of the postwar "tradition" tradition was Russell Kirk (1918–94). The son of a Michigan railroad engineer, he had been stationed during the war on a chemical-weapons site in the Southwest, run a bookshop, become a college instructor, and befriended Richard Weaver, who encouraged him to write. Kirk studied under John Hallowell, a force for conservative thought at Duke University, who had himself learned from Gerhart Niemeyer of the University of Notre Dame. Those influences on Kirk wedded a high-church Christian faith (Episcopalian or Catholic) to thoroughgoing rejection of political liberalism. Kirk's contribution was to shepherd the pairing out of the university. Almost single-handedly, Kirk created in *The Conservative Mind* (1953), a canon of ideas and thinkers that served as an opening answer to Trilling's claim to find no serious conservatism in the United States.

Kirk's Adam was Burke, and Burke's conservative progeny were almost entirely Anglo-American, moderate in style, and largely reconciled to liberal constitutionalism and, with reservations, to electoral democracy. The canon excluded authoritarians, anti-parliamentarians, and anti-democrats, as well as economic liberals and libertarians. Kirk's rationale for excluding them was that they failed on one count or other his six-part test for true conservatism: belief in transcendent order, acceptance of mystery, recognition of social order based on class, interdependence of civic freedoms and ownership, trust in custom, which innovation, though welcome, must respect, and recognition of prudence as a supreme practical value in politics. Though narrowly applied by Kirk, his tests for conservatism were generously loose. With a negotiated change or two—moral objectivity for transcendent order; modest skepticism for acceptance of mystery; merit, not equal outcomes for social order based on class—an American liberal on the economic right could pass for a Kirkean conservative.

Kirk offered defining help in negative by identifying conservatism's foes: eighteenth-century *philosophes*, political Romantics in the tradition of Rousseau, Benthamite Utilitarians, science-minded positivists, and Marxists. Their common flaw, Kirk held, was overrationalizing, ideological thought. The attack on ideology was, as noted, itself a commonplace of the day. As did Weaver, Kirk aimed to reject political ideology without lapsing into scientism. What conservatism's foes all misused or failed to use was "moral imagination," our shared, intuitive sense of right and wrong. The appeal to imagination harked back to Burke, made contact with Europeans like Gehlen (who wrote, "Imagination . . . is the fundamental social organ"), and looked forward to cultural conservatives such as Scruton.

Kirk's immediate influence was slight; he was an outsider in too many ways. Although personally generous and attentive to the needy, his conservatism was felt to be precious and out of touch in its detachment from party politics and government policy. A Tridentine Catholic, he favored the Latin mass at a moment when the Church was modernizing itself and turning liberal. His American conservatives—Fisher Ames, Rufus Choate, John Randolph, for example—were never likely to win their time on shout media or in graduate seminars. It fell to others with more feel for the intellectual contest to revive a less detached conservatism. One was William Buckley and the writers with him at the *National Review* (founded 1955). The others were neoconservatives, grouped around the *Public Interest* (founded 1965) and *Commentary* (founded 1945).

William Buckley (1925–2008) took to heart Schumpeter's warning, "The capitalist order shows unwillingness to control its intellectual sector effectively." Doctrinal clarity mattered less to Buckley than winning opinion for the causes of the right. As a forum for conservative ideas, the *National Review* played as strong a part in the right's midcentury revival as the *New Republic* had played in the liberal-progressive tide forty years earlier. On his public-television talk show, *Firing Line*, bienpensant left-liberal guests could be surprised to meet a well-informed, dialectically formidable adversary. Undogmatic and strategic, he held together his fractious army of cold warriors, moral conservatives, and economic liberals. He opened a middle way for thoughtful American conservatives between Eisenhower centrism and the far-right fringe.

Buckley's fellow writers included the Cold Warrior, James Burnham, and the CIA man–cum–Yale professor, Willmoore Kendall. Burnham, an ex-Catholic and ex-Trotskyist, thought in sweeping, strategic terms, though given to sudden volte-faces, which he explained as tactical cunning. In *The Managerial Revolution* (1941), he argued that managers now controlled Western society, and in *Suicide of the West* (1964), that liberalism had won control of the managers. In between, Burnham argued as a hawk for "rollback" against the Soviet Union rather than "containment," the position of Democrats and moderate Republicans, though he later changed his mind. Kendall, who taught political ideas, disregarded Burke and saw in his hero Locke a defender not of natural rights as commonly thought but of popular sovereignty and, as such, the herald of modern populism.

The *National Review* was ignored by liberals and disdained by many conservatives. Kirk found it juvenile. Hayek disliked its personalizing style and cancelled his subscription. The magazine barely lived out its first year and went biweekly in 1956. However, by a double movement from inside the magazine and from outside in the awakening of the Republican right, the *National Review* survived its early trials and by the early 1960s had a circulation of over sixty thousand.

Money from his father, a Southern oilman, launched Buckley, but in ways, he succeeded despite his background. He was an untypical American conservative: not Main Street, not Protestant, not Midwestern. He had smart liberal friends, including John Kenneth Galbraith and his wife, with whom he partied in Gstaad. He kept in touch with a bogeyman of the Republican right, Henry Kissinger, whose memoirs he helped edit. He was, he said, a conservative less from temperament than from conviction.

The convictions were well to the right. In *God and Man at Yale* (1951), Buckley wrote that Yale University was paid for by Christian individualists whose sons learned there to become socialistic atheists. The university should drop its pretense of academic freedom, let the trustees decide what was to be taught, fire teachers who disagreed, and rededicate itself to the university's original mission, which was to promote "belief in God and a recognition of the merits of our economic system." In *Up from Liberalism* (1959), Buckley argued against democratic extension of civil rights to all and defended segregation and Southern resistance to court-ordered desegregation of schools. Much as Calhoun had argued over slavery, Buckley said of segregation: that wrong or right, it was too rooted in local custom to be quickly changed. Buckley was consistent at least in saying the same for Social Security. He opposed it but thought it also too widely accepted to be replaced. Rather than abolish segregation or Social Security, people first had to be persuaded that both should go.

Despite his manner and money, Buckley had a feel for popular opinion. In 1960, he founded the Young Americans for Freedom. It was a conservative action group drawn from college students, as was the left-wing Students for a Democratic Society, which had been founded the same year. These were respectively the right and left avant gardes of the coming decade's youth movements. A study in 1970 noted their social differences. Whereas 55 percent of the left-wing SDS members had upper-middle-class parents, only 28 percent of the YAF's did. Of the SDS, only 17 percent had working-class backgrounds, where the share in the right-wing YAF was 39 percent. Buckley played the patrician but was oddly closer to the masses.

When in 1960 Buckley asked Burnham to review where on the right the magazine stood, Burnham reported that it appealed to "libertarianism, isolationism, hardline anti-Communism, traditionalism, McCarthyism, laisser-faire, DARism, states-rightism and various semi-crackpotisms." For Burnham the ideological warrior, the *National Review*, in other words, had no single point of view. When he urged Buckley to push the magazine to the center in a hunt for readers beyond the conservative core, Buckley listened, aware as he was of their status as underdogs. Kendall spoke darkly of the magazine as engaged in "asymmetric warfare." More playfully, Buckley tended to see it as conservative jester to a liberal monarch. Few if anybody saw it as a promise of the future. Of the prospects for conservative thought generally, Niemeyer judged that liberals were in, conservatives out; that both had uniform, unchanging views; and that conservatives were not likely to be in any time soon. Niemeyer's timing was off. The *National Review* became a flagship for Goldwater Republicans in the 1960s and soon for

Reagan Republicans in the 1970s. The outsider was fast becoming the insider.

When introducing Buckley on a television interview in 2005, the conservative columnist George Will said this: "Without Bill Buckley, no *National Review*, without *National Review* . . . no conservative takeover of the Republican party. Without that, no Reagan. Without Reagan, no victory in the Cold War." Will's rhetorical exaggeration of the American—let alone the Reagan administration's—part in ending the Cold War is obvious, but Buckley's role in the rise of the Republican Right was large and undeniable. Yet even there, he was not alone. The American neoconservatives also played their part.

Many neoconservatives were ex-Marxists and all were liberals, albeit conservative liberals who had been "mugged by reality," in the well-known New Yorkism of Irving Kristol, one of their original circle. Kristol meant liberals who had given up their dreaminess and accepted certain social facts. Democrat by party allegiance, the neoconservatives first cohabited with Nixon Republicans and then with Reagan Republicans. When in the new century Republicans went off to the hard right, neoconservatives mostly gave up on the party.

The neoconservatives gathered around the *Public Interest* (1965), a magazine started by Kristol together with Daniel Bell, the profoundest of the group, and *Commentary*, edited by Norman Podhoretz from 1960 to 1995. The Democrat professor and US senator for New York, Daniel Patrick Moynihan spoke for them in Washington from 1977 to 2001, and Robert Bartley, the opinion-page editor at the *Wall Street Journal* from 1972 to 2002, opened his columns to the group. Bartley sensed that, though suspicious of intellectuals, business readers disarmed by the congenial antistatism would listen also to the neoconservatives' ethical and cultural opinions.

The neoconservatives earned both elements in their name. They held to the traditional conservative picture of social order as resting on discipline and respect for property. They were anti-liberals, although the liberalism they fought was not the liberalism resisted by the first conservatives but instead a social-minded liberalism captured by present-day big government and a dissident left.

They were also "neo." They were untraditional and rooted in the "now." Neoconservatives accepted pluralist openness and social mobility. They worried about capitalism's cultural toll but took its economic costs and benefits largely as they came. Like Gehlen and other postwar conservatives in Germany, the American neoconservatives looked to the present, not the past. They had no canon of great thinkers. They did not argue by selection from an invented tradition; history for them did not illuminate the present. Podhoretz, for example, once claimed that the American Civil War was as remote for him as the Wars of the Roses. They took themselves to be anti-ideological, pragmatic, and "realist." They had little conservative gloom about human nature or human prospects and made no pretense, in the English style, to be able to do without large ideas. Kristol described the neoconservative temperament as "cheerful" and "meliorist." Neoconservatives, that is, shared faith of a kind in progress. Rather than backing off into a hostile, anti-modern sulk, meliorists sought to improve and repair the world they lived in on the theory that "you can't beat a horse with no horse." Kristol was echoing the old plea of Stahl and Thiers not to make conservatism a counterrevolution.

First, however, the neoconservatives had to move rival improvers out of the way. Those were the defenders of welfare capitalism—latter-day New Dealers who by the 1960s were pushing for the Great Society— and the activists of civil rights who transformed a liberal campaign for nondiscrimination and equal rights into, in their critics' eyes, a nonliberal campaign of racial quotas and "positive discrimination." Welfare and affirmative action together provided ample targets. Politically, the neoconservatives were responding to the protests of the middle classes pressed by taxes and of northern white suburbanites—often one and the same—wary of "mixed" (that is, black and white) schools and hostile to busing for desegregation. Intellectually, the neoconservatives reconfigured what their liberal opponents saw as social need and civic exclusion (to be corrected by government) as undue demands on society and refusal of personal responsibility (to be disapproved of, then ignored). Welfare, their critique ran, overburdened government and dispirited its recipients. Affirmative action was illiberal, unfair, and counterproductive.

If liberal activism in government gave the neoconservatives one target, they found another in liberal inactivism over personal indiscipline, moral permissiveness, and what was misleadingly called cultural relativism. The *Public Interest* and *Commentary* ran essays against what they took for the most visible symptoms of a disturbed and weak-willed society: the spread of pornography; sexual license; family corrosion; progressive, or "child-centered," education; avant-garde art, especially when paid for with public money; professorial indulgence of badly behaved students and a growing readiness to silence uncomfortable thoughts in the name of what became known as political correctness. Against that Hogarthian vision of decline, the neoconservatives contrasted the social virtues of civic responsibility, reward for merit, and acceptance of social mobility (down as well as up, though the snakes were less dwelt on than the ladders).

The neoconservatives nevertheless were at home in late liberal-modern society in ways that other American conservatives were not. They had no time for Kirk's bookish romances with an embellished past or excursions into remote traditions, no time for Southern nostalgics, and no time for libertarians, whether asocial libertarians like Randians or dogmatic libertarians like Hayekians. Kristol, who claimed never to have read *The Road to Serfdom*, suspected that Hayek's "rationale for modern capitalism" could not "be believed except by those whose minds have been shaped by overlong exposure to scholasticism."

So long as they wrote and criticized, the neoconservatives displayed a kind of practical wisdom. They wanted to limit and improve, not cripple or disempower government; to promote not a society of equals, but an open, inclusive, mobile, and pluralist society; to temper without gelding capitalism. They were liberal conservatives or conservative liberals. Yet they remained intellectuals, concerned above all to fight other intellectuals.

Having won many of their arguments by the end of the 1970s, a younger generation went into government—Richard Perle, Elliott Abrams, Paul Wolfowitz, for example, all of whom served the Reagan or Bush administrations (1981–93). Their battle was not against liberal intellectuals of the Great Society, but against Washington's think-tank-or-university doves in the Second Cold War. Having convinced themselves of the same complacent end–of–Cold War history that underlay Wills's over-the-top Buckley tribute, these second-generation neoconservatives entered the post-Soviet world in the grip of an intellectualist illusion: they believed that the Soviet Union fell apart because of American pressure, that American pressure came from the Reaganite recovery of American self-belief, and that neoconservative writers had played a large part in that recovery. As with Buckley, the neoconservatives were correct about the role of argument and ideas in the rise of a buoyant Republican right. To leap from there to national self-confidence and fresh geopolitical capacity, let alone to a kind of historical omnicompetence, was to think magically. Support from those younger neoconservatives for the war against and subsequent occupation of Iraq was the movement's nemesis, much as the Vietnam War had been for post-1945 reform liberalism. An erstwhile neoconservative, Francis Fukuyama, wrote a damning obituary of the movement in the *New York Times* (February 2006). He likened to Leninism the neoconservative belief in the power of ideas backed by strong will. The Bolsheviks "believed that history can be pushed along with the right application of power and will. Leninism was a tragedy in its Bolshevik version, and it has returned as farce when practiced by the United States."

Other aspects of neoconservative intellectualism inhibited its achievement of the orthodoxy on the American right that its credo and grasp of the social facts in other respects deserved. One was religion. Try as they might, neoconservatives could never sit down at ease with Christian conservatives, although tactical harmonies were heard between themselves, the Israeli right, and the religious right in the United States. Nor, as highbrows, were they ever at home in a demotic culture, where few people had read as many books or had such a gift for argument.

An early historian of the movement, Peter Steinfels, reissued in 2013 an updated edition of his classic study, *The Neoconservatives: The Men Who Are Changing America's Politics* (1979). He resummarized the movement's achievements in the following terms. As conservatives, they attended to the cultural and moral foundations of society that liberals tended to ignore. They eyed well-meant government ventures critically with a view to perverse outcomes. They tempered their progressive leaning to activism with Burkean gradualness. They came with no conservative baggage of Kirk's traditionalist kind and—one could add—treated doctrinal free marketry with derision. They accepted both the welfare state and the "functional rationality" of corporation-led capitalism, hoping somehow to balance both with family life and a buffering of unions, churches, and neighborhoods. They spoke for "a culture dutifully patrolled by conservative intellectuals." The American neoconservatives were disenchanted in a Weberian way. Theirs was a Stoical ethic of modest liberty, hard-won, uncertain comfort, and "avoidance of Utopian fevers."

There was a link here, which Steinfels himself did not make, between American neoconservatives and their German counterparts, who also wearily accepted the limits and inevitabilities of complex, technocratic society. To American reform liberals, neoconservatism was too cramped and scared about what government and society could and should do. To fellow conservatives, neoconservatives were too liberal, too intellectual, too detached from the indispensable national myths of American greatness and goodness. Their vision, all the same, was in Steinfels words, "serious and plausible and unmistakably grounded on the realities of contemporary America." To conservatives who strove to start with social facts, even if not all the social facts, that was praise. Neoconservatism's encounter with responsibility and government was, however, sobering. Their troubled passage from conservative criticism to conservative ownership of a liberal-modern present was a microcosm of the right's broader story after 1980.

PART VI

Conservatism's Fourth Phase
(1980 to the Present)
Hyper-liberalism and the Hard Right

The Year 1980

The Second Cold War intensified. In Afghanistan, Soviet forces made no headway against antigovernment rebels, who controlled the countryside and were beginning to get American covert aid. The Solidarity movement spread from strikes in Gdansk shipyards to outright opposition to communist-only rule in Poland. The dissident physicist, Andrei Sakharov, was arrested in Moscow. The US embargoed grain sales to the Soviet Union and boycotted the Moscow Olympics. In China, Deng Xiaoping pursued the introduction of capitalism.

In April, a US airborne attempt to rescue American diplomats and others held hostage in Teheran failed short of its target, with loss of life. In November, the Republican Ronald Reagan defeated the incumbent, Jimmy Carter, winning the presidency with more than half the popular vote and forty-four states.

In Germany's federal election, the Bavarian Franz-Josef Strauss won the CDU-CSU most seats, but the Social Democrats, in coalition with discontented liberals, kept Helmut Schmidt as chancellor.

In Britain, where Margaret Thatcher entered her second year as Conservative prime minister, inflation hit 18 percent a year. State benefits to strikers were cut in half.

In New York, a deranged young man shot John Lennon dead. A right wing terrorist attack killed thirteen people at the Oktoberfest in Munich.

Roland Barthes, Alfred Hitchcock, Oswald Mosley, and Jean-Paul Sartre, died. Venus Williams, Ryan Gosling, and Kim Kardashian were born.

The Rubik's Cube went on sale. In medicine, the full-body MRI scanner was introduced for regular hospital use.

Tim Berners Lee began work that would lead to the World Wide Web. Bill Gates agreed with IBM to make an operating system for the personal computer.

9

Parties and Politicians

LETTING IN THE HARD RIGHT

For three decades after 1980, a self-confident, economically liberal right came to command government office and public argument only to find itself in the trap of success. Having bested, as it seemed, the historic left, it was without immediate opposition, a treacherous place. Outwardly, party competition ran on. A mainstream center-right in Europe and the United States traded office with the center-left. Slogans, symbols, and party loyalties aside, they pursued broadly indistinguishable agendas framed by promotion of the free market and a reining in of government. The end of the Cold War (1989–91) encouraged a fond belief that geopolitical rivalry itself would end as liberal prosperity spread. At home and abroad, liberal conservatism's triumph was widely felt to be complete.

For a time, it looked as if mainstream conservatism was achieving its post-1945 goal of establishing a liberal, business-minded status quo as the common frame of politics. The more satisfied with itself the mainstream became, however, the more dissent grew to its right. Geopolitics did not vanish but worked on in new guises, all the harder to think about for the right, which had grown geopolitically lazy in the Cold War.

At quickening pace in the 2010s, an illiberal hard right took away voters from the conservative center. Either new parties ate into the mainstream right from the outside, or as in Britain and United States, the spirits and complaints of what once had been the edge captured the center. In terms of ideas, the center-right found itself paying a high price for its earlier complacency in terms of lost self-confidence and uncertainty as to what it stood for. It had coasted, rather, on a right-wing economic liberalism that appeared indifferent to local and national needs and that was notably vulnerable to economic crises, as the crash

of 2008 showed. The mainstream right, to put it simply, had not translated post-1945 party-political success into a distinctive conservative
orthodoxy, and into that gap poured the uninhibited warriors of the
intellectual hard right.

The right-wing liberalism that the insurgents objected to was nicely
labelled *bougisme* by the French thinker Pierre-André Taguieff. His prescient book was called *Résister au bougisme* (Stand up to bougisme,
2000). *Bouger* in French means "to move," "to budge," "to shove over."
Taguieff's coinage expressed the core complaint of the countermodern
resisters: the *fact* of ceaseless turmoil in market society was turned by
its celebrants into a supposedly authoritative *command*: "Bouge!"
"Shove over!" "Get on your bike!"

Taguieff's prescience was to sense that yelling at people to do what
they did not wish to do or what was not in their power to do would, over
decades, provoke a mulish digging in of heels and, in time angry, open
resistance. Twenty years on, the mainstream center parties found themselves struggling with that obstinate refusal to budge. Taguieff was giving a merited *bras d'honneur* (a middle finger) to the *bougistes* of politics,
who were, as he saw it, forever proclaiming with long words and clever-
seeming theories that change was good for people, especially when
change was not guided or interfered with but left to its aimless self. The
objection to hyper-liberal orthodoxy was less to restless change itself
than to the *bougistes* of change, who made restlessness a boon or virtue
of its own.

i. The Center-Right in the 1980s and 1990s

Among the first and most eloquent of the *bougistes* was Margaret
Thatcher, leader of Britain's Conservatives (1975–90) and prime minister (1979–90). "What's the real problem with the Conservative Party?"
Thatcher in retirement asked the political writer George Urban (1993).
Answering her own question, she went on: "The name of it. . . . We are
not a 'conservative' party; we are a party of innovation, of imagination,
of liberty, of striking out in new directions, of renewed national pride
and a novel sense of leadership. . . . That's not 'conservative.' The name

is all wrong." The party's troubles, however, were not to be met by a change of brand, try as later leaders did to fiddle with slogans and images.

The right's problem in Britain was a local version of a common difficulty in Europe and the United States. For all its successes, economic radicalism had, locally speaking, served its time and was becoming inept. A second "real problem" was that, after 1990, the Conservative Party no longer had Thatcher; that is, it lacked a leader who could be both radical and moderate, *bougiste* and resister, globalist and nationalist at the same time. The party lacked a unifying presence that could hold those conflicts in check and turn them outward against external enemies—trade unions, local government, the civil service, the Soviet Union—rather than inward against each other.

Command of words and her brief were vital to Thatcher's rise in the party, her appeal to British voters, and her reputation in the world. Courage and fight in a world of male condescension also counted to her success. Yet her domination of Britain's Conservative Party owed most to the fact that she obeyed the historical pattern that successful Tory leaders—Salisbury, Baldwin, Churchill—managed the party's inner divisions. Thatcher was a Cobdenite, middle-class liberal who believed in open markets, free trade, and limited government that did not interfere with people's personal morals or beliefs. Unimpressed by class or status, she was keen for men and women of initiative to get on without envy or vested interests in their way. At the same time, unlike the pacifistic Cobden, she was a flag-waving patriot who derided appeasement, embraced the risks of war (Argentina, Iraq), and took a "strength-first" view of the West's best strategy in the Second Cold War.

Far from resisting or dispersing power, Thatcher concentrated and monopolized power. Her governments broke the power of industrial trade unions, of closed-shop British banking, and of local councils. They broke the esprit de corps of the ministerial departments. Claimed as a victory for workers' freedoms, the changes instead took power away from the unions and returned it management. The changes concentrated economic power in large banks and enterprises, often foreign; government power in the central administration at Whitehall; and

Whitehall power in the prime minister's office. The Thatcherite claim of saving the economy (or avoiding worse) was plausible at the time and widely believed, though open to later historical revision. Many of Britain's deeper economic problems—low productivity, low wages, low savings, and low investment—remained four decades on.

The "real problem" for post-Thatcher Conservatives was not the party's name but that by the 1990s it was running out of dragons to slay, state assets to sell, and new directions to strike out in. (Its last privatization—of railways after Thatcher (1994)—soon unraveled into stealth renationalization.) The economic legacy of Thatcherism itself was mixed. The innovation of using market-thought to make government more effective was judged successful and widely copied, although unintended costs showed up in time. Creating a "property-owning democracy" faltered. The proportion of British people personally owning shares in 2020 was half what it had been in the 1980s. Home ownership, another Thatcher aim, came to look beyond most young people's reach. Such costs and failures became visible in time, but seeing them was delayed by New Labour's part-embrace of Thatcherism after 1997.

On Europe, Thatcher grasped that her party combined opposite traditions in the foreign outlook of Britain's governing classes, as caught in the late eighteenth-century tag phrase: "Whigs for the Continent, Tories for the Shires." She was at once Whig and Tory, pro- and anti-European. She criticized the direction of the European Union, which she or her party did much to set. Conservatives pushed for rapid expansion of the European Union after 1989. They promoted a European single market in which goods, services, capital, and people moved freely, but they resisted the Europeanization of social and labor rights put in place to balance those market freedoms. She thwarted pro-Europeans in her party keen on European monetary integration, which led to her downfall in November 1990.

Blurring her Cobdenite liberalism was a sense of nation, particularly the English nation. Save for the United States and old Dominions, she mistrusted foreigners, especially the Germans, whom Cobden admired, and the French, Mill's love. Thatcher's English epic was a beguiling tale of rescuing the nation from the decline brought on by foes outside and doubters within. It drew on the inventions of nationalist nineteenth-century British historians such as the Tory Round and the Liberal Freeman, it echoed Enoch Powell's dark visions, without his fatalism, and it looked ahead to the popular chauvinism of the Brexiteers. Thatcher could also speak, in Baldwin's manner, of England's rare moderation and good sense.

She relied on more than speeches. Thatcher's hardheaded sense of what was doable as opposed to sayable rarely left her. On Ireland and southern Africa, ex-imperial points of Tory neuralgia, she balanced sentiment and sense. "Never negotiate with terrorists," she proclaimed in public. Secretly and successfully, her officials talked on her behalf to "terrorists" in Ireland and southern Africa. She was ultra-hawkish toward the Soviet Union in the Second Cold War but saw through the facade of military strength to the broken system behind and welcomed its reformer-destroyers, notably Mikhail Gorbachev.

By 1990, success was behind her. She gave in to junior ministers pressing for a radical but ill-thought-out reform of local taxes that provoked riots and was later withdrawn. Her tepidity to Europe was out of keeping with the pro-Europeanism then prevailing in her party, within business, and in the country. When her weakening leadership threatened the party's standing in the polls, she was driven out, as is the Tory wont. The anti-Europeans in the party soon exacted revenge. A party used to internal fighting—over tariffs and free trade, over Ireland, over empire—turned its zest for combat to Europe. Thatcher had balanced the party's factions. With her gone, a party without clear goals or ideas began its drift to the nation-first hard right.

Sensitive to conservative recklessness after 1918, the post-1945 German right made a point, dwelt on earlier, of gradualism and continuity. Helmut Kohl (1930–2017) began his twenty-five-year leadership of the Christian Democrats (1973) and his sixteen-year chancellorship (1982) when the swing-party Free Democrats pivoted to market liberalism from the social-minded liberalism of Germany's Brandt years. Flawed but underrated, Kohl was dismissed on all sides as a provincial Rhinelander and party fixer of limited vision. The left painted him as a market radical in thrall to business (although changes to Germany's "social-market" model proved less than the left feared). The Christian right doubted his conservative credentials. The cultural upheavals of 1960s and 1970s had disturbed them, and they disbelieved Kohl's claims, as an unzealous Catholic, that the new coalition would deliver on its promise of "moral and intellectual change." The party right wing objected too, in the name of Germany, about Kohl's seeming indifference to national sovereignty and national pride. Kohl kept the party tied to Adenauer's Westernism, he bowed to American pressure for a renuclearization of Europe in the Second Cold War, and he promoted Franco-German ties while doing little or nothing to end the division of Germany.

Kohl appeared to have the last laugh. In a torrent of events almost nobody had seen coming, Soviet communism dissolved and East Germany collapsed into West Germany's arms (1989–90). As ever more arguments flew in Germany as to what to do, Kohl made clear decisions, for which he then won broad support: the Germanys would be one, not in stages, but at once; not after negotiation between states with perhaps a new constitution, but by reabsorption under the western constitution of 1949; not as separate economies, but as a single economy with one currency and Easterners' savings in East Germany's old, near worthless currency exchanged for West Germany money at one to one. Fiscal-minded disciples of tight money moaned. Westerners griped at paying more in taxes. Eastern enterprises worried that on equal financial terms Western competitors would quickly sweep them away, as many did. Kohl, nevertheless, prevailed. Easterners, he insisted, were not to join Germany as paupers.

While grumbling at the cost, most Germans recognized unification as a success and grounds for pride. What, however, unreconciled conservatives had longed for since the 1950s and insisted that the mainstream right had only mouthed support for—unification—proved a disappointment. To Kohl's national-minded critics, unification absorbed old East Germany into a Westernized Bundesrepublik, a liberal-democratic "establishment," and a web of alliances that semisovereign West Germany had agreed to under what amounted to historical duress. Geopolitically, the critics had dreamed of an unburdened return to national sovereignty, a shouldering of world responsibility, and a freedom of maneuver that neither German capacities, great as they were, nor the geopolitical context permitted. Culturally, the critics had hoped for a celebration of Germanness as they understood it, freed from inhibiting shame and supposed rules about what could not be said. Arguments of the kind merged in time with economic grievances in the old East Germany, the two together fueling the stunning rise of the hard right in the 2010s.

Unification under Kohl came in peace and with scant disturbance to the neighborhood, thus removing a potential for conflict that had hung over a now peaceful but war-prone continent for forty-five years. In the eyes of the true-conservative, national-minded right, strategic gains mattered little against the costs of unification as achieved under Kohl: further Europeanization and Westernization of Germany, further loss of distinctiveness, and steady abandonment of German pride. Rather than recreating Germany, unification became another unhappy stage in the disappearance of Germanness.

Kohl might reasonably be expected to appear in any historic canon of the German right. Tellingly, he is missing from the indispensable but selective Almanac de Gotha of the European right since the eighteenth century, the *Lexikon des Konservatismus* (1996). It was edited by an erudite guardian of conservative Germanness, the former *Criticón* editor, Caspar Schrenck-Notzing. Bismarck the unifier (1871) and Adenauer the savior (1949) made Schrenck-Notzing's cut, but not Kohl the unifier (1990). Was it that, to win inclusion, Kohl was too plodding, too middle-class, too easy with political donations, and too preoccupied with lowly party management and government maneuver to raise his eyes to conservative ideals? One strain of the German right never accepted Kohl as a true conservative. He did not care enough about high culture and, though he oversaw unification, he never sounded proud enough about Germany. Worst of all, he seemed to agree with his social-democrat rival, Helmut Schmidt, that someone with visions I needed to see an oculist; that is, Kohl denied conservatism's need for large ideas. To his mind, performance in politics counted, not vision. His successor, Angela Merkel, believed much the same. That left a space on the German right where visions could be searched for.

Like Kohl, Ronald Reagan (1911–2004) was widely derided and dismissed before twice winning the presidency with ease (1980; 1984). Even in his own party, he was thought of as an underprepared hick with weak jokes and extreme views. That Reagan had twice won the governorship of the nation's most populous state, California, was discounted: the state's Republicans owed their victories to Southern California, where the right was well known to be unhinged.

Reagan had the better of his detractors, partly from shrewdness and talent, partly from practice (he turned seventy during his first month in office), much from luck, and not least for keeping the discordant families of American conservatism together in a workable coalition. As with Thatcher, when Reagan retired a control was removed on the American right, and its factions became freer to return to war with each other.

Reagan pulled together the Republican Party's free-market optimists, ultraright libertarians, family-values moralists, and America Firsters. As had Nixon earlier, he won the votes of disappointed ex-Democrats disturbed by urban crime and resentful about stretching the aims of civil rights from nondiscrimination to corrective preference. Aided by superior speechmakers, Reagan had a fine ear for a divided country that relished partisan conflict while longing to feel good about itself as a nation. He appealed to both the left and right wings of American liberalism: New Deal Democrats and tight-money, big business Republicans. A divorced, nonchurchgoer, Reagan could tell a fundamentalist Christian audience with apparent sincerity that everyone was "enjoined by scripture and the Lord Jesus" to oppose "sin and evil." He made the gospel of American liberty ring for latter-day Jeffersonians and Jacksonians across the West and Midwest proudly convinced of their self-reliance. He made it ring for whites in the South disturbed by do-gooding liberal Northerners intruding once again on a society, it seemed, they did not understand, as well as for clever young libertarians scattered across the nation in its graduate schools.

A good ear alone was not responsible for Reagan's success. A thematic umbrella under which the factions of the right could gather was hostility to government. Reagan rocked audiences with jibes at the expense of "big government" so skillfully that they forgot that big government was what he was asking them to let him run. He spoke out against government spending and waste but watched deficits soar, boasting that he might be old but was not stupid, and never once sent Congress a balanced budget. No matter. In the antigovernment gospel, the right under Reagan found a thematic unifier that it had lately lacked. For each of the right's factions, a convenient villain was big government: for business and banks, with its credit, work-safety, and consumer and environmental regulations; for moral conservatives, with ever greater liberal permissiveness of the law; for America Firsters, with its ruinous war in Vietnam, its foreigner-coddling multilateralism, and its boneless on-off flirtation with Soviet détente.

Reagan's success owed less to luck as such than to recognizing and using luck. He inherited a defense buildup started under his predecessor Jimmy Carter as well as a burst of high-tech creativity which that buildup nourished. In Paul Volcker he inherited a head of the Federal Reserve who had pushed interest rates to double digits a year before Reagan took office, a brutal recession-causing step that by early in the new presidency had cut inflation to 3.5 percent, so clearing a path to the long economic boom that lasted into the new century. Reagan inherited a superpower rivalry that the United States was on course to win as its Soviet adversary, mired in its own failures and shadowed by a rising China, began to implode. With practiced grace and skill, Reagan made the most of those opportunities. He knew when to push at an open door, calling out dramatically in Berlin in June 1987, "Mr. Gorbachev, tear down this wall."

Reagan left office (January 1989) at a moment of American contentment and strategic success that would have shone credit on a lesser politician. As it was, skill, luck, and timing confirmed him among contemporaries as a historic figure. On the American right, all factions could claim Reagan for their own. By contrast, Republicans who later followed him in the White House, George W. Bush (2001–9) and Donald Trump (elected 2016) divided their own party as successfully as they held off the Democrats.

In France, the political tide appeared to be flowing in countercurrent. François Mitterrand, the leader of the Socialist Party, won the presidency (1981) with Communist support. A Socialist ministry took office with several Communist ministers. There followed a brief experiment with state-led attempts to stimulate a flagging economy. The experiment ended, as economic liberals had predicted, when a weakening franc and rising inflation prompted a U-turn and fiscal retrenchment. In modern conditions of currency exposure and European integration, go-it-alone "Albanian" policies were, it was concluded, no longer possible. In 1985, a quarter of a century after the German Social Democrats at Bad Godesberg, the French Socialist Party at Toulouse formally dropped from its platform the remnants of state-directed socialism. The doctrinal shift reflected changes in society. In 1930, the French workforce was still divided almost equally among farming, industry, and services. It was now overwhelmingly in services. Almost nobody worked on the land, and only 20 percent of French people lived in the countryside. The industrial workforce had also shrunk. Despite the reputation of France's "street," by the end of the twentieth century the country had one of the lowest rates of union membership in Europe. Far from a breakthrough for the hard left, Mitterrand's two terms as president (1981–95) marked a consolidation of the French political center. By marginalizing the Communists and stifling the radicals in his own party, Mitterrand united and moved France's left rightward.

France, so seen, was less an exception to the right's post-1980 dominance than it looked. Mitterrand's presidency belongs also in the conservative story because it helped unite France's center-right, which formed a single opposition against him. The task in any event was made easier as the social, confessional, and symbolic differences between Gaullists and right-wing liberals were rapidly weakening. After 1981, they fell away to the point where the Gaullist party and the liberal UDF could fight the parliamentary election of 1986 on a common program. Edouard Balladur, a free-market Gaullist, urged the parties of the center-right to merge, arguing that, though distinct, they were no longer different. Balladur's proposal was premature, but the parties did eventually merge as the Union pour un Mouvement Populaire (UMP) in 2002.

Another contribution of Mitterrand's to French conservatism was not to the mainstream parties but to the hard right. In order to limit the center-right's gains at the polls (1986), Mitterrand had the rules for elections changed to proportional allocation. The right's vote was split, and the National Front won thirty-six seats in parliament. Mitterrand's gambit failed to deny the center-right victory and he was obliged to "cohabit" with a conservative government. The National Front, nevertheless, had broken through from the margins. French conservative voters now had a hard-right option at the polls. As the center-right grew foggier about what it stood for, the hard-right grew more attractive. The National Front built on its success in the 1980s, winning reliably 10–15 percent of the vote in elections and surviving a potentially damaging split (1999).

For insurgents on the right in Britain, Germany, and the United States, by contrast, the 1990s were harder times. In Britain, Thatcher's successor as Conservative prime minister, John Major, brushed off a bid to unseat him as leader (1995) by the ultra-free-market, anti-European John Redwood. The Germans were preoccupied with absorbing East Germany, painfully but effectively, and without disturbing the neighborhood. Kohl and his party were embroiled in financial scandals (a consequence in part of worthy but easy-to-breach rules designed to keep big money out of electoral politics). The German hard right seemed to be where Adenauer had quarantined it in the 1950s: beyond the margins of responsible politics. Beginning to stir in small magazines, however, conservative intellectuals criticized Germany's democratic laxity in ethics and culture, much as the American neoconservatives had two decades earlier. The Federal Republic, in conservative eyes, was provincial, dampening to the German spirit, and "boring."

In the United States, a fractious Republican majority in Congress under Newt Gingrich bungled its campaigns of obstruction against President Clinton. A centrist Democrat, Clinton cut welfare as federal budget deficits vanished. As Democrats achieved what Republicans had long tried and failed at, Republicans turned to institutional warfare (shutting down the government) and moral harassment (exploiting a presidential lie about sexual misconduct). With a strong campaigner, Democrats might have won a post-Clinton third term in the White House (2000), but a hung vote in a single decisive state (Florida) was given to the Republicans by a Supreme Court that voted 5 to 4 on conservative-liberal lines.

Local differences aside, by the 1990s, a pragmatic, economically liberal centrism that judged itself by results more than by principles was now conventional on the right. The conservatism of accommodation, it seemed, had bested the conservatism of resistance. The unreconciled right was only waiting its moment. The arrival of a new century scrambled assumptions and shook the conservative center. In fact, the new century arrived for the right-wing liberal mainstream three times: in 2001, 2008, and 2016–17.

Geopolitically, the terror attacks on the United States (2001) and the divisive American-led wars that followed in Afghanistan and Iraq threw the unity of the postwar West into question. Economically, the worldwide financial meltdown (2008) and the austerity that followed threw unchecked global capital into question. Politically, the rise of a hard right, evident in electoral successes (2016–17), threw liberal-democratic centrism into question.

ii. The Rise of the Hard Right: The Le Pens, AfD, Brexit, and Trump

The electoral rise of the hard right after 2000 was not smooth or uniform. Local differences were large and telling, yet something common was afoot. An early warning came in France, where the National Front broke into the second round of the presidential election (2002). In the United States, the insurgent Republican Tea Party organized a tax-payers' march on Washington (2009). In Britain, the anti-EU, United Kingdom Independence Party (UKIP) panicked the Tories with successes in the local and European elections (2013–14). In Germany, an alliance of free-market professors and anti-immigrant campaigners founded a new right-wing party, the Alternative for Germany (AfD, 2013).

An eighteen-months' payout for the hard right came soon after. In 2016–17, established parties in Europe and the United States suffered electoral reverses that exposed the liberal center's discredit. In June 2016,

51.9 percent of those voting in a nationwide referendum called for Britain to leave the European Union without specifying an alternative to membership and despite the near-unanimous collective finding of mainstream politicians left and right, business leaders, economists, historians, scientists, military specialists, and foreign-policy experts that withdrawal would prove an economic, social, and strategic blunder. In the US presidential election (November 2016), the New York property developer and television showman Donald Trump, running a right-wing "America First" campaign as a maverick Republican, won the presidency with a minority of the popular vote but a large majority in the electoral college. In France's two-round presidential election (April–May 2017), Marine Le Pen at the head of the National Front advanced to the second round, beating conventional parties of center-left and center-right. Although she lost the run-off, Le Pen won 34 percent of the second-round vote, a popular breakthrough for a party previously held at the margins. In Germany's national elections (September 2017), the hard-right AfD won ninety-four seats in the Bundestag, a seventh of the total. Not since the early 1950s had Germany's hard right won national representation and never in such strength.

Here at its breakthrough was a hard right that had resurfaced and established itself in the Western political mainstream. Its starkest elements were exclusionary nativism, doctrinaire libertarianism, and perverse appeal to the popular will. Though visibly ill-sorted and at odds with each other, those elements together threatened democratic liberalism, or to use the standard label, liberal democracy.

In describing these movements, the term "hard right" is to be preferred to "new right" because the slogans, themes, and appeals are old. They go back through the twentieth and nineteenth centuries to historic splits on the conservative right, back, in fact, to conservatism's never-resolved ambivalence about capitalist modernity and hence to its original quarrel with political liberalism.

The term "hard right" is also to be preferred to the "far right" because "far" suggests fringe and the hard right has left the fringe to become a normal part of the political contest. The hard right entered office in Britain in the guise of a UKIP-spooked Conservative Party from which moderates fled or were driven out. In the United States, a radicalized Republican party controlled (2016) the three branches of federal government, thirty-two of the fifty state legislatures and thirty-three governorships. It lost its majority in the House of Representatives, as well as control in several states, in 2018, but the right's grip on the federal judiciary, including the Supreme Court, tightened. Although successfully barred from government, the hard right in France and Germany had broad and, it seemed, growing popular support. The Front National, now renamed the Rassemblement National (National Rally), and the German AfD drew away voters from mainstream conservative parties, facing them with a choice of standing their ground or themselves moving rightward.

A normal pathology had become a pathological normality, as the Dutch expert on the hard right, Cas Mudde, sharply put it. An American writer, Clay Shirky, watching the 2016 presidential campaign, made a similar point in terms of the hard right's popular support: "Trump is the voice of angry whites. He wasn't on stage because he has unusual views. He was on stage because he has the usual ones, loudly." The hard right, in sum, was not weird or extreme. It was popular and normal. Indeed, it was alarming because it was popular and normal.

Lest the term "hard right" here sound loaded, and the account of events overdrawn, the passion and dismay with which mainstream conservatives themselves reacted needs recalling. They did not, in detached spirit, dwell confidently on the hard right's visible weaknesses and incompatibilities. They did not ask if there was here a pantomime villain got up by the liberal left. They reacted with shock and grief as if a comrade had been lost or a treasured possession snatched away. They were fighting for a tradition and realized in shock that they might be losing. From Trump's victory onward, the newspaper columnists George Will, David Brooks, and Ross Douthat—representative voices of conservative opinion from three successive generations—anathematized Trump-seized Republicanism in their many newspaper columns. The liberal-conservative *Economist* was as harsh in its judgment of Brexit-seized Toryism. Before the December 2019 election, it called the Conservative leader, Boris Johnson, "indifferent to the truth," judged his close adviser, Dominic Cummings, a "Machiavellian ideologue," and urged voters to choose instead the centrist Liberal Democrats.

Allowing for national differences, four general things may be said about the hard right. First, it had a common character. The hard right combined economic libertarians and aggrieved nation-firsters, united in opposition, as they saw things, to self-serving, out-of-touch elites that had perverted true conservatism. The hard right showed a radical willingness, where in power, to upset familiar norms and arrangements all at once. In or out of power, the hard right used a shared repertoire of rhetorical appeals that skillfully disguised its inner tensions.

Second, it was characteristic of a historic strain in conservatism. For the hard right was not new and drew for its critical themes and its supporters on the long tradition of unreconciled conservatism. Although it is common on the moderate right to distinguish conservatism (good thing) from the hard right (bad thing), the hard right is integral to conservatism and not an alien presence threatening conservatism from without. At times the hard right was quieter and contained; at others, as now, it was louder, larger, and more confident. It was always there, a shadow or conscience, to remind conservatism of its original ambivalence toward liberal modernity. Third, the hard right is wrongly called "fascist" in any historical sense of the term. It is rightly called "populist" or "nationalist" only on a careful understanding of those misleading labels. Fourth and last, the resurgence of the hard right had help from various factors—anger over immigration, the financial crisis, weak mainstream candidates—that mattered more in some places than others. The deeper reason was a common failure by the liberal center, right and left, to honor the promises of democratic liberalism and keep it in good repair.

The origins of the present-day hard right lay in a strange pairing of small-government, socially permissive, border-blind libertarians who favored economic globalization and nativist conservatives preoccupied with cultural identity and national decline. Both claimed to speak for that imagined being, the people, against what they called the elites. The libertarian right claimed that the people would be better off once freed from the grip of a big-government political class. The nativist right claimed that the people would be better off once freed from the grip of out-of-touch, foreigner-friendly cosmopolitans. Libertarians of the right and nativists of the right alike were abandoning the liberal center but pressing in different directions. Each took one element of conservatism—defense of property and markets; allegiance to the nation—and supercharged it to the neglect of other values and concerns. Tying that odd couple together were a common enemy—the liberal center—and a bewitching set of themes and appeals.

The hard right's rise is often thought of as driven by popular anger after the crash of 2008 at economic hardship, decaying public services, and government neglect, all of it compounded by long-standing discontent with seemingly uncontrolled immigration. By undermining the center-right's claim to competence, those factors, it is true, opened a space for the hard right. But though its rapid growth relied on an upwelling of popular anger, the hard right actually began with a downwelling of cash from conservative businessmen and bankers. Party vehicles were created and financed from above that later gained the pulling power of voter support. The finances of France's National Front are opaque, although rumors that Jean-Marie Le Pen borrowed from Russian backers have lingered, and he started the party's political ascent in the 1970s with a legacy from a conservative cement magnate. Although once in the Bundestag, Germany's hard-right AfD was subsidized with public money, it was helped at the start, according to the magazine *Der Spiegel*, with money from the billionaire August von Finck and his asset manager, Ernst Knut Stahl. Of the £24 million donated to the two main Leave campaigns in Britain in 2016, an estimated £15 million was given by seven rich donors. Billionaire Republican contributors in 2016 included the founder of PayPal, Peter Thiel; the Las Vegas casino owner Sheldon Adelson; the Johnson and Johnson heir Woody Johnson; and Carl Icahn, a corporate raider and conglomerate owner. To note that backing is not conspiratorialist. All parties depend on someone else's cash. The point here is that, although various voters for various reasons were fed up with the centrist major parties, it took money, intellectuals, and politicking to give that anger a solid platform and a purposeful focus.

The hard right's vote comes from many sources: first-time voters, disgruntled left-wing voters, and, for the most part, disgruntled conservatives. They are socially mixed and some are economically distressed, but one marker of the typical hard-right voter is the lack of a higher degree. In the United States in 2016, Trump equaled or bettered his Democrat opponent, Hilary Clinton, among voters in all educational categories except those who had completed college. In Germany, the hard right AfD won close to 13 percent of the vote nationally but had only 7 percent support among graduates. The hard right may be paid for by wealthy donors, but in all four countries, the hard right had strong appeal to lower-middle-class and working-class voters.

Age is a factor in some countries, not others. In Germany, the AfD appealed strongly to first-time voters. Among previous voters, most were disappointed conservatives, although some were ex-left. In the second round of the French presidential election (2017), almost none of the Socialist left's voters switched to the National Front. Of the new-left vote for Jean-Luc Mélenchon's Les Insoumises, half went to Emmanuel Macron, two-fifths abstained, and fewer than a tenth went to Le Pen. By contrast, most of Le Pen's three million second-round gain came from voters for the mainstream conservative, François Fillon. It is no truism to stress that the hard-right vote is a right-wing vote. The hard right has grown out of a conservative electorate.

The peak age for the hard-right vote varies. Britain's Brexit campaign was unpopular among the young, popular with the old. A similar pattern appeared in the American election. Trump's popularity grew steadily with age over forty, dropped steadily under forty. By contrast, the core strength of the hard right in France and Germany was among middle-aged men. Young voters in both countries tended to vote hard-right somewhat more than the national average. Support for the AfD tailed away to vanishing among the old in Germany, perhaps because they were closer from experience to the illiberal past, Nazi or Communist.

Underlying those variations is a broader constancy. Voters for the National Rally (ex–National Front), Brexit, AfD, and Trump were, in the majority, not voters from the left but from the right. Focusing on where they lived, how old they were, when they left school, and how

much they earned in the hope of establishing a convincing social ste-
reotype missed a political point. Voters for the hard right were, at their
core, conservative voters disappointed by present-day liberal-minded
conservatism. Some were working class, it is true, but the left had been
losing working-class votes for decades. The alliance of property and
right-wing working class was a historic part of successful conservatism's
electoral playbook.

If the liaison between property and discontent was new, the content
of the hard right's message was old. It took the historic elements of
conservatism—defense of property, celebration of the nation—and
supercharged each. Economic liberalism and nationalism point, intellectually, in opposite directions. The first is open-bordered and global;
the second, sheltering, exclusive, and shut-in. Both, however, when supercharged as "hyper" and "ultra," serve to abandon right-wing centrism. Right-wing libertarians want to be done with tempered capitalism, to deny responsibility of markets to society, and to throw off
social-minded conservatism. Ultranationalists want to turn back globalism and shut the door on liberal openness. Each was moving to leave
the liberal center, but by different exits. They shared a destructive common purpose strong enough to conceal their differences but with no
promise of a stable alternative. Their larger interests—global and national, corporate and communal—diverged. Given the hard right's incoherences, its favored modes were party-political disruption and intellectual improvisation.

The German AfD arose as an unstable mixture which allied libertarians
and skinheads, ex-bankers and disruptive radicals, ex–Christian Democrats and previous nonvoters. One of the AfD's two parliamentary leaders, Alice Weidel, worked for Goldman Sachs and the state-owned Bank
of China and speaks Mandarin. Weidel was a new kind of unreconciled
conservative whose objections to the prevailing state of affairs were
topical and practical, not moralizing or hortatory. Greece should leave
and Germany should stay in the EU, she thought, but abandon the euro.
The EU should limit immigration while investing in the Middle East to
discourage out-migration. Weidel, who was widely reported to live part
of the year in Switzerland with her woman partner and their two

children, favored civil partnerships but not gay marriage. The AfD's other leader in the Bundestag was Alexander Gauland, an ex-CDU lawyer-publicist and author. In well-mannered writing, Gauland has rehearsed old conservative anxieties about the mainstream right's embrace of technology, the neglect of German character, and indifference to family, homeland, and high culture.

By contrast, a leading AfD radical, Björn Höcke, followed the tactic of speaking to shock. Of the Holocaust Memorial in Berlin, Höcke said: "We Germans are the only nation in the world to have planted a monument of shame in the heart of their capital." In like vein, a Thuringian party colleague, Stephan Brandner, campaigned with such crowd-pleasers as "Merkel should go to jail" and "The typical family of refugee Syrians is a father, a mother and their two goats." Höcke stunned Germany in 2019, when the AfD under his local leadership came second, with 24 percent of the vote, in Thuringia's state election.

In France, the National Front, founded in 1972, combined xenophobia that attracted bigots, and free marketry that attracted small businesses. For thirty years, its first leader, Jean-Marie Le Pen kept his rackety vehicle on the road, swerving from triumph to disaster and back. After the NF's first electoral coup (2002), there followed a decade of splits and drift. A cash-strapped party under an aging founder watched as the mainstream right under Nicolas Sarkozy echoed its themes and stole back voters.

When Le Pen's daughter, Marine, took over the party (2011), she set out to "dedemonize" it by toning down the bigotry. She talked up wages and welfare to win working-class votes, and better security amid terror to win center votes, while continuing to appeal to the prejudices of the party's base in code. She dropped her father's overt racialism, made pro-Jewish gestures, gave up lecturing voters about family values, and replaced a narrow, pro-business, anti-labor line with welfarist calls for the "état protecteur" (protective state) to ensure economic equity for all. "Ethnicity" replaced "race" in her speeches. Her father's "national priority" (for French citizens in receiving government services) became "social patriotism." She changed the name of the party to the National Rally, but fine ears could still hear the National Front's old music of anti-immigrant hostility. As with the AfD in Germany, success at the polls brought out rivalries among leaders (after 2016, her deputy quit) as well as conflicts over character and aim. Her formula worked well in the presidential contest, poorly afterward in first-past-the-post elections to parliament, which punished small parties. She fired her right hand, Florian Phillipot, who wanted to cut the party loose from its bigots and move without baggage to win the mainstream. Le Pen preferred her previous strategy of triangulating the party's proven appeal: to the old hard-right base with coded prejudice, to the disaffected left with social justice, and to floating voters of the center alarmed about terrorism and insecurity. Intellectually, Marine Le Pen's National Front–National Rally remained a job lot of welfare advocacy, right-wing Catholicism, cross-party anti-Europeanism, and oracular geopolitics of a kind favored on the hard right since Spengler and before.

A third-generation Le Pen, Marion Maréchal (1989–), the founder's granddaughter, wants to raise the party's mental game. She is the director of a still small training school–think tank in Lyon, the Institute of Social, Economic and Political Sciences, which is financed by local businesses. Like Steve Bannon, an American ally, she seeks to reach out in Europe and the United States to young conservatives disappointed both with the old right and with liberal centrism.

Maréchal has the family's feel for words. To distance herself from her grandfather and aunt, she dropped the family name and took her mother's, which for those who recall Marshal Pétain has its own hard-right echoes. She can be provocative: "France is in the process of passing from the eldest daughter of the Catholic Church to the little niece of Islam." She can be reasonable. She raises difficulties about Muslim-majority communities in France that multicultural liberals find awkward to face: "Women's rights are losing ground in those neighborhoods." She touches counterliberal themes that occupy other young rightists: about the family and sexuality, organic community, dislike of neoliberalism, and suspicion of tech giants.

Open and improvisational as Maréchal may sound, her core watchword comes from the hard-right French tradition of Barrès and Maurras, *enracinement* (rootedness). The term is ambivalent. Rootedness is desirable; rootlessness, by implication, undesirable. It sounds, and is in many ways, banal. Rootlessness can be talked of inclusively and sympathetically as a condition that weary moderns have broadly learned to put up with, even turn to advantage. Or it can be talked of in a hostile, exclusionary spirit. Maréchal does not have to spell out that when she speaks of the rootless, the people she wants listeners to think of are secular liberals without roots in principle, Muslims without roots in a Christian world, and scary migrants without roots of any kind.

In the United States, Trump's diversionary theatrics and early failures in Congress kept off the front pages a bonfire of social and environmental regulations as well as a purge of liberal judges from the federal bench that continued in the background with little resistance and that promised to play out for decades. When thwarted by Congress, Trump resorted to executive orders and emergency powers, as had presidents before him, though with a radical, institution-shaking appeal in justification "to the people" rarely heard since the New Deal. Internationally, the unconservative revisionism of the hard right was evident in Trump's questioning or pulling back from previous American commitments— the Iran nuclear deal, world climate accords, the Western alliance itself. Rather than standing up for liberal democracy and universal values, he praised authoritarians: China's Xi, Russia's Putin, Saudi princes, the Philippines' Duterte. Rather than follow every administration, Democrat or Republic, since 1945 and align Americanism, Westernism, and universalism in an avowedly virtuous trinity, the Trump right detached Americanism as justified and defendable on its own.

In Britain, hard-right revisionism packed itself into the single, self-destructive nuclear option of Brexit. From the 2000s, anti-Europeanism was pursued with skill and determination by the upstart UKIP party (founded 1993) and among Conservatives by the old, unreconciled, Britain-first rump, perhaps a third of the parliamentary party. Shaken by diplomatic failures with his European partners and spooked by the rise of British anti-Europeanism, David Cameron, who was prime minister from 2010 to 2016, called a referendum on British membership of the EU, which he expected to win. On narrowly losing, rather than play for time a shaken Cameron announced within hours that "the instruction" of "the people" should be "delivered." He resigned, leaving to his successors, Theresa May and Boris Johnson, an anti-liberal, populist discourse of people against elites, democracy against parliament, which May nibbled at and Johnson swallowed whole.

Calling Johnson's radicalism "hard right" might sound overdrawn. He did not set out to lead the party further to the right or, indeed, to lead it anywhere. His primary aim was to lead the party. Finding a label for his outlook is accordingly in one way pointless. Like Trump, he has no settled outlook. Nor is he unique in that regard among British Conservatives. Since the end of the Cold War and the collapse of Thatcherism, the Conservative Party has had no clear viewpoint. Anti-Europeanism, which appeared to fill the gap, was negative and temporary. Lacking aims or content of its own, Johnson's radicalism lies in his forceful, hard-right style, with its disregard for familiar liberal-democratic norms and its claims to speak for "the people" against the elites and institutions. As a superbly skilled "trimmer," Johnson is suited to improvisation by character and driven to it by predicament. Britain's divided hard right, which he took over and found himself having to manage, promised implausibly to please both global-minded business and voters fed up with neglected public services, insecure work, and lack of housing.

iii. The Theme Music of the Hard Right: Decline, Capture, Enemies, and Victimhood

The rhetorical themes played on by the hard right are shared and traditional. Decline is one of them. The hard right sees deterioration in social and moral health everywhere. A once strong nation, we are told, is in decay. A once cohesive society has been fractured. A once virtuous people has grown decadent. Decline was presumed in Trump's slogan "Make America Great Again." An appetite for tales of national ruin made best sellers of Eric Zemmour's book *The French Suicide* (2014) and *Germany's Destroying Itself* (2010), by an ex–central banker, Thilo Sarrazin.

The venerable theme of the West's civilizational decline, heard since the early twentieth century from Spengler and others, resurfaced.

According to the narrative of national decline, politics and government had been captured by self-serving elites who neither understood nor spoke for the people. Trump promised to "drain the swamp." The National Front blamed France's troubles on a corrupt *classe politique* in Paris. The AfD posed as the necessary replacement for unrepresentative, exhausted parties of center-left and center-right that were letting Germany fall apart. In Höcke's words, the party's promise is to "bring back our Germany, piece by piece."

Decline and capture were cleverly run together in the Britain's Brexit campaign. Europe had sapped and manacled a once proud nation, and aided by Britain's Europeanized elites, the EU had taken its constitution prisoner. In Britain, the headline writers of the populist, anti-EU *Daily Mail* excelled at lining up a devil's party of elected parliamentarians ("House of Wreckers"), high-court judges ("Enemies of the People"), and their European masters ("EU war on Britain") against traduced, virtuous islanders ("Now *You* decide, Britain!"), the latter being a masterly, deceptive elision of *Daily Mail* readers, voting electorate, and nation.

The flipside of capture was deliverance. The true nation or—to give it the name the hard right used interchangeably, "the people"—were unspoken for at present and powerless. The common institutions of state and society—government, media, universities, courts—had fallen into unrighteous hands. If the nation could free itself from hostile elites, a redemptive liberation awaited.

Those enemies of the nation, inside and out, provided a final theme. The inner enemies of the nation were liberals, right or left. They worked for themselves, not for the people or nation. The defining moral flaw of the liberal might show itself as greed, godlessness, or lack of patriotism. The liberal was self-interested to the point of amorality, deaf to the call of faith, and without robust attachment to much beyond his or her aims and preferences. The picture of the typical liberal was a caricature, but as the next part shows, had eminent philosophical defenders.

The captors without were other nations, foreign entanglements, and international commitments. "Our nation first" was so common a cry that the hard right was often called nationalist, though that was a misnomer. Nationalists in a strict sense familiar from the nineteenth century wanted to defend or create a modern nation-state and make of its aims the highest, overriding aims in politics. That sense caught the hard right's attitude to national power partially at best.

Geopolitically, the hard right grasped that the nation-state was in the world and must work with the world. It was, to that extent, internationalist. What distinguished the hard right was that it wanted the nation to work in the world on the nation's terms. The hard right, that is, abandoned multilateralism for unilateralism. For a weak power like Britain, unilateralism is a fantasy. For strong powers like the United States or China, it promises autarchy and disruption.

Nor was the hard right nationalist in the nineteenth-century sense of putting duty to nation above other public duties, especially in Germany and Italy, for example, where the nationalist's first duty was to create a nation-state. Hard-right politicans, by contrast, talk less about what citizens owe their nation than about who belongs in the nation and who should be kept out of the nation. They cling, in that way, to an exclusionary idea of the nation as *ethnos*, not demos—to an idea of nation as birthright, shared origin, and historical continuity—not of nation, understood inclusively, as common citizenship and shared commitment to a necessary minimum of civic norms. In practice, it is true, defending nationhood under that inclusive conception might well require steps to limit immigration, and discrimination between citizens and foreigners in the provision of public services, as well as insistence on respect for liberal norms. There is still a difference that matters of how steps of the kind are defended—inclusively or exclusively, liberally or illiberally.

Victimhood was the hard-right theme that tied its others together. Like the nation that the hard right defended, the hard right itself was victimized by usurping forces. The hard right spoke for the people, but without being heard. The majority was silenced, for only a minority spoke—unrepresentative liberals, the media, and universities. In weakness, however, lay strength, for oppression defeated itself and virtue in the end prevailed. The idea of righteous suffering that promised future vindication had a venerable religious pedigree. "In this wicked world, and in these evil times," Augustine had written in the *City of God*, "the Church through her present humiliation is preparing for future exaltation." That profound claim became a bass note of Christian conservatism, consoling the weak and reassuring the strong. However, the theme of victimhood was not limited to Christian conservatives. Victimhood served the hard right generally to bridge the divide in its two bodies of support: privileged connection, social advantage, and wealth on one side, resentful dispossession, cultural or economic, on the other. Both sides of that unnatural coalition could be presented as victims: those who were victims of a grasping, intrusive state that took away what belonged to others and interfered in matters it misunderstood; the others, victims of hypocritical, indifferent liberals, who did nothing for the poor and imposed a permissive ethic despite claiming to have no ethic of their own.

The hard right's scorn and vituperation is more shouted and more tweetable, but it draws on a fine tradition of invective against liberal moderns that goes back to Mencken, Nietzsche, Baudelaire, and Maistre. The hard right is vehement, hot, and angry, qualities that cause it pride, not shame. When liberals quail and fall silent before its bellowing, the hard right doesn't think it has lost the argument. On the contrary, it senses it has won.

Despite near-universal surprise at the post-2010 rise of the hard right, none of its themes or appeals was new or original. Its awkward alliances, stock themes, and taste for radicalism were all traditional on the right. They harked back through the 1960s and 1970s, 1920 and 1930s, and 1890s and 1900s to conservatism's original struggle to reconcile itself with capitalism and democracy.

Hard-right themes were heard in the 1960s and 1970s. Recall from chapter 7 Nixon's use of them when winning back George Wallace voters. Nixon's appeal to "the silent majority" created Nixon Democrats, who became Reagan Democrats, and who were then rediscovered in amnesiac surprise as Trump Democrats. Recall Enoch Powell, that

British free marketeer and imperial nostalgic who combined polyglot high intellect with a perfect ear for English unreason and who noted with justification that Conservatives in the twentieth century had "a grand sense of where the votes are."

The hard right's themes were heard in the 1920s 1930s. Trump's "America First" slogan was itself borrowed from the noninterventionist America First Committee of 1939. The rabble-rousing governor of Louisiana, Huey Long, and the right-wing Catholic radio priest Father Coughlin, promised, as do Republicans today, to help the little guy without hurting the rich. In the 1920s, a tidied-up, sanitized Ku Klux Klan marched in Washington for discriminatory immigration laws. In Germany, Moeller told disoriented readers that liberalism was the played out "death of nations" and called on the young to embrace an exhilarating but unspecified collective alternative.

The hard right's themes were heard in the 1890s and 1900s. Playing on the ethnos-demos distinction, the French ultrarightist Charles Maurras wrote of the "legal nation" and the "real nation." Recall that, as Maurras had it, France's legal nation had been captured by enemies within: liberals, Jews, Freemasons, and *métèques*, an old offensive French term like the English "wop" or "wog." Genuine members of the French nation, he believed, were monarchists and Catholic heirs of Greco-Roman civilization. In Germany in the same period, the ultraconservative Prussian newspaper, the *Kreutzzeitung*, stigmatized the anticlerical liberal—often Jewish, it noted—as an enemy within who had undermined what previously bound together the nation, namely the Christian faith, albeit Lutheran, not Catholic. In the United States, the hard right was less bookish and doctrinal but no less fierce. Campaigns against Freemasons, against Catholics, and against Jews were a feature of nineteenth- and early twentieth-century politics, not to forget pervasive antiblack racialism, whether legally encoded or socially prescribed, in the North as well as in the South.

That the hard right has old and nourishing roots is to be expected. Its present resurgence is the latest manifestation of the right's original and unresolved ambivalence about capitalist modernity. The resurgence of the hard right, with its historic ambivalence toward democratic liberalism, is alarming because democratic liberalism is in disrepair and repair can succeed only with the help or acquiescence of a liberal-minded right.

iv. What Populism Is and Isn't

Populism, historically speaking, arose late in the nineteenth century on the left and right, when political outs, discontented with the ins, made demands in the name of the people. On the right, as mainstream conservatives adapted to liberal-democratic ways, a disruptive, radical fringe turned old conservative attachments—social harmony, national unity—to exclusionary purposes. Claiming to speak for the "nation" or "people," they contrasted themselves with unrepresentative, divisive elites. The disruptors put a beguiling Romantic tale of national deliverance to villainous political use; in Germany, with ruinous consequences. The tale went like this: the nation is ailing because it is morally split. It cannot heal itself but needs a visionary guide who can restore it to health in redemptive unity.

Such a tale, well known to students of the apocalyptic mind, is bound in the context of twentieth-century history to bring fascism and Nazism to mind, but it matters to be very clear about what is not being said. The hard right is not fascist or, save on the fringes, protofascist. Fascism was nourished by the themes and anger of the unreconciled right in the 1880s and 1890s but was itself historically specific. Although of the right, fascism is not on the right, being outside the left-right spectrum of the liberal-democratic world. It sprang up in Italy in the 1920s, after a ruinous world war without European winners. It relied not only on a cult of the charismatic leader and a totalizing vision of society, but also on a unifying Bolshevik enemy and a single, mass party. Unlike the conservative authoritarian, the fascist, as earlier noted, aims to stifle all independence and diversity. The authoritarian relies for control on fear and acquiescence; the fascist, on fear and popular mobilization. Although fascism won power through the ballot with the aid of irresolute constitutional authorities, it embraced illegality and violence as routine and acceptable methods in politics. Nazism in Germany added the toxic element of anti-Semitism.

Nowhere in the four countries here are those historic elements to be found together or, as yet, in dangerous strength. That is not to say that the hard right could not become a latter-day, cleaned-up, and softer variant of fascism. What should be stressed is that the hard right need not be protofascist to cause alarm. There is more here than historico-conceptual quibbling. The complacency is often heard that, frightening though it looks, the threat from the hard right is exaggerated, because the hard right is not fascist. In arguing for their place in the mainstream, apologists for the hard right lean heavily on "Not fascist, ergo acceptable." Well, yes to the first, but not to the second. The hard right can threaten liberalism and democracy without being fascist in any historical sense. Fascism is not the only way liberal democracies weaken or end.

The label "populist" is more apt, but it is open to misinterpretation. Populism, properly understood, is not a mass movement, an institutional arrangement, or a form of democracy but instead a style of political self-justification. To use its own contentious language, populism is an elite phenomenon. It involves not a contest between people and elites but a contest among elites in which one side, the populist side, claims to speak for the people. Marion Maréchal, the clever member of the Le Pen clan, made the claim neatly (January 2019), "Behind the word 'populism,' there is first off the word 'people': the people abandoned, the people without representation"—by which she implied without representation save by the hard right.

Right-wing populists claim to defend a virtuous nation, often ethnically imagined, against corrupt establishments and menacing foreigners. Left-wing populists claim to defend the working people against corrupt establishments and the rich. Right or left, populists tend to be political outs exploiting electoral odium against the ins. As insurgents, they often upset familiar party patterns, lending force to the sly definition of "populist" as what losers call winners after an unexpected electoral defeat or sudden collapse of a well-established party. Populists may form a new party or capture an existing party, as in Britain the Brexit minority did to the Conservatives and Corbyn's hard-left backers did to Labour, or in the United States as hard-right insurgents did to the Republican Party. Whichever populists do and however loudly they speak for that mythical being, the people, they are activists, usually of the same background and education as the rivals in power they aim to displace.

Even if they win at the polls, populists' claims to speak for "the people" are exaggerated and overdrawn. In competitive, multiparty democracies, elections give winners temporary license to govern. No electoral majority is stable, none are immune to reversal at the next election, and, when misleadingly taken as expressing a coherent point of view—as opposed to an arithmetical result on a narrow ballot choice—all are statistical constructions from discordant opinions and particular judgments. In office, populists tend to bully critics, favor cronies, attack judges whose rulings they dislike, and go easy on the excesses of other populists. Once that is grasped, it is fair to say that Trump together with the British Tories May and Johnson have behaved like populists.

Asked about remarks of his that had seemed to favor Germany's hard right, Trump's ambassador in Germany replied on social media (June 2018) with diplomatic correctness: "The idea that I'd endorse candidates or parties is ridiculous," but added, "I stand by my comments that we are experiencing an awakening from the silent majority—those who reject the elites and their bubble." On taking office—chosen as his party's leader, hence prime minister, in a ballot of 120,000 Conservative members—Johnson called on "the people of Britain" against parliament. Crushing victory in a general election soon after gave him command of parliament, allowing for conventional government without appeals against the institutions, although the populist urge remained in proposals to curb the judiciary and reinsulate British law from European protections of human rights.

Populism is easy to confuse with direct, or participatory, democracy, in contrast to the representative kind. That is wrong, however, as Jan-Werner Mueller made clear in *What Is Populism?* (2016). Populists are for representative government, he noted, so long as they are the representatives. Once elected to power by representative means, they resort on Mueller's account, to plebiscites or referendums to confirm courses of action already decided on. Populists are ill at ease with multiparty competition or coalition government and happiest when the elected opposition is demoralized and ineffective. Populists act as caretakers of the people's will, claiming to know it better than their competitors. Jealous of their authority, populists are indifferent or hostile to countervailing powers within the state and society.

As a justificatory description of how politics and government work in large, constitutionally intricate democracies, populism is inept. To the liberal mind, left or right, there is strictly no such thing as the will of the people, hence nothing for elected power to know or speak for. Popular sovereignty, as Madison and Guizot understood, involved a refusal—the denial of sovereignty to any single interest or class. In speaking for the people, sovereignty spoke for the citizenry and answered to the citizenry. In speaking for all, sovereignty spoke for no one in particular. Sovereign decisions resulted not from intuition or divination but from often frustrating constitutional procedure. To the populist mind, by contrast, the will of the people was single, undivided, and authoritatively intuited by power. The people were not the citizenry but a blend of cultural nation, which distinguished it from foreigners, and common folk, which distinguished it from elites.

Populism has its own history in the United States. The American Populists were prairie radicals of the 1890s, the working-class half of a movement whose other half was middle-class Progressivism. Because the term "populist" was spoken for, to call the Republican tide of 2016 "populist" was misleading without more to say. In a farsighted article written before Trump entered national politics, Walter Russell Mead had made a case for the apter label "Jacksonians." A Jacksonian, on his account, is a distinct type of voter who by class or education alone might once have been a loyal Democrat but who since the 1960s had tended to vote Republican. As characterized in "The Jacksonian Tradition" (1999), such voters are commonly white and lower middle class. They disliked federal government, do-gooding at home or abroad, and taxes so long as the programs that favored them—such as Medicare, mortgage deductions, and Social Security—were not jeopardized. They believed in honor, military virtues, and equality with those above them, an ethical code, Mead suggested, that many black Americans shared.

White Jacksonians were recognizable at Trump's rallies, in Trump slogans, and in Trump speeches, but they were not his only voters. Powerful as Mead's ideal-type portrait was, the Trump voter could not be neatly typified, save tautologically and unhelpfully as a typical Republican. The same was true across Europe, where hard-right voters were a motley, not a single type: anti-immigrant nativists, moral traditionalists, anti-EU libertarians, and defenders of Western-Christian values against the feared encroachment of Islam.

As an explanation of the American and British votes, the Forgotten White Democrat and the Disgruntled Labour Voter won due attention. That the liberal left did not own the working-class vote should have surprised nobody. A segment of the white working class previously loyal to the Democrats had been voting Republican since the late 1960s. Labour's share of the working-class vote had already fallen from a historic two-thirds to a half in the 1970s.

In Britain, it is true, the hollowing-out of the old working class and its institutions has accelerated in recent decades. "Working class" is in ways becoming a callous misnomer for "non-working class." It was estimated that the proportion of unskilled working-age men not active in the labor force rose from 3 percent in the 1990s to 30 percent today. The typical union member now is a woman in her fifties working in the public sector. A recent sounding suggested that nearly 80 percent of Labour Party members were in the top three (ABC1) social groups, that is, comfortably middle class. In short, the once typical Labour voter—a white, working male—has been left behind on three fronts: economic, social, and party-political. The character of the present Labour Party reflects that change. Its members are predominantly public-sector professionals, ethnic minorities, and university-educated but frustrated millennials priced out of affordable homes. If a one-factor explanation is insisted upon for the Brexit result (2016), it was not class but age. Young voters were heavily pro-Remain and turnout among them was, at 65 percent, only just below the national turnout of 72 percent. However, among voters over sixty-five years of age, who were heavily pro-Brexit, turnout was around 90 percent.

The Forgotten White Democrat was, equally, a weak way to explain Trump Republicanism. In 2016 Trump carried three large states that contributed to his electoral college victory—Michigan, Pennsylvania, and Wisconsin—by less than eighty thousand votes in all. These were commonly and misleadingly described as Democratic states, whereas all had gone Republican in the Nixon (1972) and Reagan landslides (1984). In the 1940s and 1950s, Wisconsin voters had twice sent to the US Senate a red-baiting Republican bigot, Joseph McCarthy. If a one-answer explanation was insisted on for the presidential result, an equally plausible candidate was the sharp drop in the Democrats' black turnout.

Religion, certainly, played a part in hard-right Republicanism after 1980. Many white Protestants, it is claimed, are distressed at a nation, which statistically pictured, is ever less Protestant and less white. The sociology is questionable. For "white" and "Protestant" are too coarse as categories. There are liberal as well as conservative Evangelical Protestants. Many of the writers and thinkers of the right-wing revival in the 1970s and 1980s were Jews or Catholics. Even with finer categories, the explanation is fragile. It buys into the populist outlook by assuming that resentment is felt by "people" for "elites." A better explanation looks for resentments among competing elites.

A suggestion of the kind was made decades ago by Daniel Bell in "The Dispossessed," an essay from the collection *The Radical Right* (1962). Bell described a "status discrepancy" he detected among outside-insider Americans—midsize-business managers, army officers, small-town worthies. They were an "elite" within their sphere, but their spheres were too small to have a say in argument or policy nationally. Often they knew more about their businesses, military tasks, or towns than bankers on Wall Street or policy makers in Washington. Local knowledge of such kind, however, traded at a discount in centrally run organizations, state or corporate. There was a mismatch, Bell judged, between the authority that outside-insiders enjoyed in their local sphere and "their power and prestige in the nation as a whole." Resentment, for Bell, had more to do with social geography than with social class.

That fruitful line of thought might be stretched to include a resentful feeling that involves what can be called cultural geography. Among the writers and thinkers of the hard right, as chapter 10 will suggest, one clear message is an angry conviction of being somehow shut out of the national argument and having deeply felt concerns and strongly defended principles simply ignored. That feeling of neglect, as the story so far has amply shown, is nothing new. The right has never got into balance its unquestioned command of power and nagging sense of intellectual inferiority.

Liberal-democratic society suffers grievous ills that need urgent repair. Populists of the hard right claim to be messengers of that grievance, but their credentials are thin. They speak for interests that cannot obviously be reconciled: globalist liberals and national-minded locals; border-blind capital and left-behind neighborhoods; businesses that want less regulation and the religious faithful who want more moral controls. To repair society, the hard right promises money from taxes, but which the left-behind earn too little to owe and which business and the rich either cannot or will not pay. Populists claim to speak for "the people" but serve discordant interests. They should be asked, to echo Thomas Mann, where they find the incredible gall to confuse themselves with their country.

That is easy to say and makes for a good debating point, but the hard right will not so easily be pushed back. To conceal its own conflicts and square the divergent interests it serves, the hard right makes a powerful and seductive appeal. Like authoritarians and fascists before them when faced by widespread disillusion with the prevailing status quo, the hard right promises security. To global business, it promises security for restless wealth that will move without compunction if the local neighborhood becomes unfriendly and too demanding. To ordinary people shaken by a hurricane of social change that nobody yet understands, the hard right promises a longed-for security of life, imagined as a common shelter, whether neighborhood, community, nation, or national people.

Missing from the hard right's appeal or well down its list of promises are liberalism's twin demands for protection from power and respect for all, whoever they are. Order and security have always mattered to conservatives, but for liberal conservatives, not at any price. For the hard right, security in turbulent, bewildering times is offered as a value that overrides others. Conservatives face a stark choice between two different versions of their tradition. They cannot have both.

10

Ideas and Thinkers
YES OR NO TO A HYPER-LIBERAL STATUS QUO

In the *Confessions of a Conservative* (1979), a late convert to liberalism, Garry Wills remarked that the modern American right was "stuck with . . . a philosophy of conserving and an actual order it does not want to conserve." Not long after, the Conservative thinker-politician David Willetts ruefully noted a British version of that same tension. In an election pamphlet, "Why Vote Conservative?" (1997), Willetts had boasted that for two decades Conservative governments had ploughed like an icebreaker through "frozen wastes of state control." When canvassing in his safe Hampshire constituency, however, he found Tories for whom conservatism meant more than free marketry and government bashing. Knocking at a Tory door, Willetts was cheerfully greeted by the householder who told him that the party she had long supported was no longer conservative and should be renamed "the demolition squad."

In the years after 1980, thinkers of the right faced an intellectual version of the trap in which conservative parties now found themselves. The right had won. Its old enemies had given in. The left was everywhere in disarray or had run away with the right's clothes. Conservatives were facing the difficult truth that, as the American scholar Harvey Mansfield put it, they were "no longer the hardy few." Used to presenting themselves as intellectual outs, conservatives were now the ins. How, though, would conservatives know who they were and what they stood for without an orthodoxy to oppose? Who was the right to argue with?

Conservatives no longer had a strategic opponent to the left against which to define themselves or their outlook. Liberalism had served conservatism as such a definitional foe early in the nineteenth century. Later, it had electoral democracy and soon economic democracy. After

1945, a now liberal conservatism had two Others on its left against which to define itself. One was left-liberal, government-tempered capitalism. Variously labelled statism, Keynesianism, New Dealism, social reformism, or welfarism, that Other was driven from the field in the 1980s. Liberal conservatism's second Other, world communism together with its Western supporters, real or imagined, then vanished in turn, with the collapse of the Soviet Union and China's embrace of one-party capitalism.

For the dissidents of the right, that loss of a double frame was in ways an intellectual liberation. It released talents and energy, and it revived old conservative attachments that had come to look marginal or quaint. The recent failings of the mainstream right in government were themselves a kind of gift to the critics. In blindly overshooting, hyper-liberalism gave conservative dissenters an economic target. In accepting an end to moral policing in the new climate of permissiveness, mainstream conservatism had given them an ethical and cultural target. Last, in promoting neighborhood-blind globalism, the mainstream right had given the hard right a national cause of strong appeal: protect and repair our national shelter! How that might add up to a post-liberal orthodoxy, none on the hard right could say. The search, still, was exhilarating. It was, for the searchers, livelier and more honest than repeating poor arguments for a suffocating liberal-conservative orthodoxy.

In the eyes of the hard right, the mainstream had only two things to say for giving in to the present, neither persuasive. One was "markets work; government doesn't." The other was that giving in was tactical, not strategic. Markets had been extended into fields of life—education, health, the arts—that the state had shielded from commercial pressure on behalf of society. Government had been shorn of even minimum paternalist duties to society. Energy directed at the tempering of capitalism and the moralizing of people had been turned inward to restraining government's own appetites, shrinking its responsibilities, and losing weight. The liberal right had encouraged the growth of privileged castes with the triple protection of untroubled wealth, social approval, and political indulgence. It had thrown away traditions, neglected people's need to belong, and torn down one authority after another. Mainstream conservatism, in short, had not compromised with liberal modernity. It had surrendered. So the critics from the hard right argued.

The unreconciled right had been saying as much about liberal modernity since the early nineteenth century. It repeated the lesson after 1945 to deaf ears. After 1980, the dissidents were determined to make themselves heard. A house thinker of Germany's AfD, Marc Jongen, summed up the radical discontent. Right-wing and left-wing liberals were both "reactionaries," he thought. What they defended was discredited and unrescuable. Echoing the malcontents of the 1920s, conservatives were, for Jongen, "today's revolutionaries."

i. Right-Wing Liberals, Antiglobalists, and Moral-Cultural Conservatives

The American "paleoconservative" Paul Gottfried summed up the unreconciled right's attitude to the liberal status quo in *Conservatism in America* (2007). Unlike the neocons, who tended to ignore the past in favor of present-day social observation, Gottfried argued for anchoring a conservative politics in a grasp of the nation's history and culture. The American right's historic task, Gottfried wrote, had been to offer "ideological opposition." Conservatives, in Gottfried's terms, were one part of the right, the truer part. They believed in preserving custom, standards, and hierarchy. True conservatives, however, had lost the battle on the right. The victors had made themselves "talking partners of the left." They acknowledged the local costs of global progress. They made placatory concessions to conservative traditions about people's need for belonging, the worth of nationhood, and the need to respect nonmarket values, but they would not be budged from commitment to economic globalism and cultural liberalism. For liberals of the left and right alike, on Gottfried's telling, liberal democracy ran to the horizon. As the new hyper-liberal right continued to call itself conservative, Gottfried bowed to usage and coined "paleoconservative" as a term for true believers.

Gottfried's picture of the struggle within the right had counterparts outside the United States. A French example was François Huguenin's

Le conservatisme impossible (Impossible conservatism, 2006). Huguenin, a social-minded, anti-liberal Catholic who writes for the social-Christian *La Vie*, described the historic failure in France of a distinctively conservative anti-liberal tradition to take form and endure. A similar fracture was identified, as will be seen, by German conservatives and, in Britain, by the late Roger Scruton.

To the unreconciled right, status quo conservatism was blind to its own failings. Viewed with open eyes, it promised economic and cultural perdition. Its globalism was Utopian; its lenience, corrosive. There agreement tended to end. Priorities were disputed. Some were geopolitical antiglobalists, who wanted to put the nation first. Some were "cultural" conservatives, who would cure or abandon a sickened culture, thought of in a broad way to include morals and ideas about good ways to live. None of the dissidents had clear alternatives.

Antiglobalists believed that the costs of international openness outweighed the benefits. They sought to leave or limit an open international order by putting the nation first, socially and economically. Defending liberal democracy by promoting it across the world, let alone fighting for it, was in their eyes a doomed and irresponsible folly. For cultural conservatives, political and social problems were at root spiritual. In their contemporary, secular climate, cultural conservatives saw rootlessness and blight. Untimely and unreconciled, they aimed for restoration or abandonment. The two kinds of conservatives had points of connection. In their different ways, each was preoccupied with the nation. On both their accounts, liberals sold the nation short. Economic globalism hollowed out the nation socially. Ethical and cultural democracy undermined the nation morally. Either cause made unreconciled conservatives, to use the proud phrase of the German quarterly *Tumult*, "consensus disruptors."

Disruptors they might be, but the damage they were doing was open to question. Criticizing an orthodoxy is one task, providing a replacement is another. The German political historian Martin Greiffenhagen nailed the general problem more than forty years ago when describing the difficulty that faced present-day conservatives who continued to resist liberal modernity. He had Germany in mind, but his point applied more widely. In "The Dilemma of Conservatism in Germany" (1971), Greiffenhagen wrote: "The difficulty after 1945 for conservatism was to revive enthusiasm for its ideas—unity of society, anti-materialism, national feeling—in a post-ideological climate where prosperity depended on industry and internationalism, two things conservatives were supposed to suspect." The task of creating a counterliberal orthodoxy was all the harder since "post-ideological" liberals were clever at denying the need for orthodoxies.

To expect new orthodoxies or grand narratives from disruptive conservatives since 1980 is accordingly to ask a lot. There are noble exceptions, who think on a big scale. Exemplary figures of the kind (to be discussed below) are John Finnis at Oxford and Notre Dame, a moral rigorist and skillful defender of the Catholic natural-law tradition, which has influenced conservative American law schools and courts in the turn against liberal permissiveness; the just-metioned Scruton, who has worked up over decades a compelling picture of a culturally attentive, anti-liberal conservatism; and the hard-to-pigeonhole German provocateur Peter Sloterdijk, who prods readers with encyclopedic chutzpah to think and feel their way out of the liberal-democratic bubble. Each has gathered materials for an alternative picture of society and culture, and each has damaged liberalism's defenses. But none has gathered those materials into an alternative orthodoxy, and none has won and held intellectual high ground.

Lightly occupied only forty years ago, the midlevel of public argument is now dense with small journals, little magazines, and Webzines that question liberal orthodoxies. Besides the conservative flagship daily *Figaro*, France has *Valeurs Actuelles*, *Eléments*, and *L'Incorrect*. In Germany, there is the weekly newspaper *Junge Freiheit*, which serves as a hinge between the hard right and center-right, as well as *Tumult*, a quarterly for "disrupting the consensus" and a magazine that announces counter-orthodox aims in its name, *Sezession*. Disruptive conservatives in the United States have a range of thoughtful outlets that undercut the claim that liberalism, right or left, monopolize public argument. They include the Catholic but ecumenical *First Things*, which castigates political liberals and preaches moral rigor; Patrick Buchanan's antiglobalist, pro-Trump *American Conservative*; the hard-right *Breitbart*; the counterliberal *Claremont Review of Books*; and aggregation sites like the Hoover Daily Report, which posts well-argued anti-liberal articles from across the conservative spectrum.

Prominent counterliberal names in public argument—Patrick Buchanan, Götz Kubitschek, Alain Finkielkraut, Alain de Benoist—use the vehicle of the short essay, the article, talk radio, and the podcast. Instead of treatises, they publish collections of small pieces. When writing as a provocateur rather than a philosopher, Scruton was adept at the mode. Reflecting on that essayistic genre of right-wing disruption at the turn of the century, the French liberal Pierre Rosanvallon wondered if there was more to the hard-right ferment of ideas than a "common front of denials and dislikes." The implication behind his pointed question was that that was all there was.

The unreconciled right, it is true, cannot be said to have a coherent, thought-through critique of present-day liberal orthodoxy, let alone a positive conservative orthodoxy. It has, all the same, a powerful set of rhetorical themes, just noted—decline, capture, national enemies in and out, deliverance—that play well in public argument. If the hard right is to be believed, the Western landscape is bleak: nations in decline; spiritual and cultural values trampled; liberal enemies within; unassimilable immigrants pressing from without. The ruination is in plain view, save to liberals, who are blinded by an orthodoxy that overvalues choice, disprizes merit, subverts standards, and, worst of all, stops conservatives from telling the truth about a desolate state of affairs. Deliverance can reclaim the desert but about how or when that will occur, little tangible can be said. Like any persuasive gospel, no element is without some small truth. Taken as a whole, the radical gospel sets itself as at war with a conservatism of prudence and moderation.

ii. The Hard Right in the American Grain: Buchanan, the Paleos, and Dreher

Much as Enoch Powell in the 1950s heralded Thatcherism in Britain thirty years later, so Patrick Buchanan in the 1990s heralded Trumpism in the present-day United States. Buchanan was champion of the paleoconservatives, a loose pre–Tea Party movement of hard-right Republicans who refused to share the good cheer of the times. A booming economy was shriveling public deficits. The end of the Cold War had left the United States, as it seemed, without a foe or rival in the world. Unimpressed, the paleos grumbled about immigrants. They saw costs in the new world-trade order, not benefits. They railed against big government for spending too much at home and for futile overstretch abroad. They lamented cultural poverty and lax morals. For culprits they looked to a self-serving Washington that failed to put Americans first, unsure who there was worse, the ever-contemptible Democrats or the pseudo-Republicans, who had sold out the conservative cause. Special odium was reserved for the neoconservatives, who proved their treachery by subverting and discrediting the administration of Bush the younger.

Of mutual hostilities on the right, none was greater than that between the paleocons and neocons. Among the paleos, none had a better ear for the moods of the American right than Buchanan (1938–). He had written speeches for Nixon, directed communications in Reagan's White House, and set a new industry standard for televised party-polemic on CNN's *Crossfire* (1982–91). Few were as skilled at framing arguments in simple terms that all but his liberal opponents, as it seemed, could understand. If *Paleo* were a movie, Trump would star and Buchanan would get the writer's credit.

The label "paleo" was a retronym coined in the 1990s, but the strain in Republicanism was old. It was noted earlier in Taft and Goldwater, heroes whom the Republican right had watched their party sacrifice to East Coast multilateralists and big spenders. Reagan, for all his skills as a party unifier, had disappointed the paleos. He cut taxes, it is true, but ballooned deficits and did little of the moral crusading that Catholic and Evangelical conservatives hoped for from a president of the right. In paleo eyes, George W. Bush's "big-government conservatism" was even worse than Reagan's: more Medicare, more government spying, more federal-bank bad-debt buying to rescue banks.

Many of the best-known paleos, starting with Buchanan, were Catholic. The confessional mix was part of the mutual suspicion paleos and neocons held for each other. Many neocons were Jewish. Whereas Jewish pride on the neocon side was compatible with the liberal refusal to pigeonhole and stigmatize, the same could not be said for the paleos. They tended to be free with anti-Semitic suggestion and abuse. To give a feel for the prose, one overexcited paleo writing in *The Imaginative Conservative*, a right-wing Webzine devoted to the American Burkeanism of Russell Kirk, described the neocons as "ex-Marxists who, like the town whore, get religion and after teaching choir want to write the vicar's sermon." In the annals of paleo martyrdoms at the hands of the elites, few are as bitterly remembered as the sacking of Joseph Sobran in 1993 from the *National Review*, where he had written for twenty-one years. Sobran's villainous anti-Semitism had become too much for Buckley. To Buchanan, Sobran was among the best columnists of the day. The paleos were playing as outside-insiders, invoking the people against intellectual elites. In truth, they were in the intellectual elite, fighting with others over its spoils.

Buchanan ran for president twice in the Republican primaries, in 1992 and 1996, failing with about a fifth of the gross vote each time, and once as leader of a breakaway Reform Party, in 2000, winning less than 1 percent in the general election. He started the *American Conservative* (2002), a bimonthly magazine that concentrated fire on the administration of Bush the younger from various redoubts on the right: libertarian, unilateralist, and paleo-Catholic.

Buchanan's books announced his themes: *A Republic Not an Empire* (1999), which was against foreign intervention and multilateral engagement; *The Death of the West* (2002), a cry of alarm at the demographic decline of white peoples and a call for them to have more children; *Where the Right Went Wrong* (2004), which took aim at the neocons who, in Buchanan's eyes, undercut Reagan and later captured the younger Bush. Americans were fighting, Buchanan objected, where they had never fought before and where they had no interests. Echoing the French appeaser Marcel Déat's "Mourir pour Dantzig?" (1939), Buchanan asked in 1990 "If Kim Il Sung attacks, why should Americans be the first to die?" An early defector from free trade, Buchanan held that the world-trade order served only Wall Street bankers; NAFTA had sold out

American workers. Immigrants were overrunning the country, breaking its laws and bankrupting states from California to Florida. The "eternal truths" of the Old and New Testaments had been "expelled" from the nation's schools and a fight must be waged to get back "the soul of America." The growing hardship of "forgotten men and women" was ignored by big government. With the "ice of indifference," it listened instead to foreign lobbyists and Fortune 500 donors.

In Buchanan's books, conservative reviewers saw muddle and overkill, as well as white nativism and anti-Semitism. No matter. Buchanan never thought he was talking to eggheads. He wanted to connect, like Trump, to the right-wing base, with a usable catechism of simple ideas. Although Trump leaned less on confessional loyalties than Buchanan did, he replayed Buchanan's leading themes with little more than a change of words.

Disconnected as they might look, Buchanan's themes could be bundled together in opposition to a common foe. Much as Reagan, in terms of policy, led the factions of the American right to aim not at each other but at big government, so Buchanan, in public argument, urged fellow polemicists to stop quarrelling among themselves and aim together at the liberal media. Buchanan coined for Nixon the term "silent majority" with its false but bewitching suggestion that righteous popular opinion was being stifled. He wrote Spiro Agnew's Des Moines speech of November 1969, which served as the anti-liberal right's opening salvo in its ongoing war of the word. Agnew spoke of a "form of censorship" in which "the news that forty million Americans receive each night is determined by a handful of men responsible only to their corporate employers and filtered through a handful of commentators who admit to their own set of biases." Buchanan was still proud of that speech close on half a century later. Nixon and Agnew, he told a reporter in 2016, had shown people how the mainstream press and television were "vessels flying flags of neutrality while carrying contraband." The message was accepted to this day, Buchanan believed, because "people know it's true."

Although anti-intellectualism of Buchanan's kind is not a monopoly of the American right, right-wing suspicion of liberal media and of universities that supply them with staff and ideas is angry and deep. According to a Pew Research Center study of July 2017, a majority of Republicans and right-leaning independents think higher education has a negative effect on the country. Discredit of colleges and universities, Pew reported, had grown since 2010, when negative perceptions among Republicans was measured at 32 percent. Seven years later, they were 58 percent. Trump's biggest advantage, according to educational category, recall, was among whites without college educations (67 percent to 28 percent). In 1970, the best predictor of high conservative alignment in voting was a college education. Now, it is the reverse. Republicans still win the votes of the well-off but rely more and more on those of white non-college-educated Americans. Popular distrust of higher education on the right is accordingly encouraged by conservative politicians. In 2016, Trump mocked universities for taking $200,000 of parents' money to teach their children "zombie studies" and how "to hate our country." The website Professor Watchlist lists university and college teachers who criticize conservative ideas and, it claims, discriminate against conservative students. Scorn for settled opinion in higher learning has stretched in recent years from politico-cultural topics to the credibility of natural science, including results in stem-cell research, climate change, evolution, and epidemiology.

Skilled as he was with words, Buchanan was always going to be on the defensive against a semi-articulate manipulator like Trump. In compensation, Buchanan watched Buchananism pass down a generation and flourish on the Republican right. Recognized or not, he could justly claim a pair of political godsons, both Catholic: one profane, Steve Bannon; the other sacred, Rod Dreher.

Bannon is a former naval officer, banker, news executive, and ex–Trump aide who has tried to build bridges between the American hard right and the hard right in Europe. Siding with the little guys, he opposed free trade and immigration without otherwise threatening the rich. Bannon's gospel reprised Buchanan's. Popular discontent came from exporting jobs and from the undue power of banks. The US offered "socialism for rich and poor," "Darwinian capitalism" to everyone else. Free-market liberals were the people's enemy. Left liberals, who claimed to speak for the people, were either interfering busybodies or out-of-touch "pussies." Bannon called himself a "right-wing populist" who would put the nation first and "maximize citizen value." Let go from the Trump White House, Bannon proselytized in Europe in alliance with Maréchal Le Pen and a British Catholic rightist, Benjamin Harnwell. At the end of 2019, he and Bannon were fighting eviction by the Italian state from a former Carthusian monastery southeast of Rome, where they had set up a hard-right think tank and university, the Dignitatis Humanae Institute.

A stalwart of Buchanan's *American Conservative* and prominent author is Rod Dreher. He shares the magazine's geopolitical misgivings about foreign interventions but is best known for a despairing moral picture of American culture. As to what ails the culture, contrasting stories long circulated among American conservatives, one hopeful, one bleak. The hopeful story told of liberal capture. In the 1950s and 1960s, an unrepresentative secular, liberal elite seized the churches, universities, media, and courts of a fundamentally God-fearing and virtuous people. The task for conservatives was to win them back. That aim inspired the Christian right in its fight for the soul of the Republican Party. At its peak in the Reagan-Bush years of the 1980s, the Christian right came close to believing that it had realigned America's political majority with an underlying moral majority.

Dreher's was the bleak story, which he told in *The Benedict Option* (2017). Secular decadence was too seductive not to prevail; America now had an immoral majority. Neither businesses nor politicians cared what people did in bed or if they said their prayers beforehand. A violent, godless, and sex-obsessed culture could not be cured, only abandoned. Dreher recommended that American Christians drop their frontal resistance and save their families from the spiritual ravages by retreating to small, self-isolating communities where proper, godly tradition could be preserved and handed on. Dreher's title gave a nod to Benedict of Nursia, a leader of Christian monasticism as the Western empire broke up in the sixth century. A more recent and more direct inspiration was Alasdair MacIntyre. As seen earlier, the Catholic, anti-liberal

MacIntyre looked forward to an archipelago of teaching institutions that might spread counter-orthodox traditions. Not only was MacIntyre's philosophy rich and Dreher's thin, Macintyre's vision was social and Dreher's personal, as if he himself could not escape the self-involvement and social fragmentation he decried. Dreher attacked liberal pluralism and toleration of diversity, but it was thanks to those things that safe spaces were available for the kind of retreat Dreher proposed. Dreher's suggestion of spiritual withdrawal free rode on the liberalism it claimed to oppose.

The hard right's claim that liberal orthodoxies stifle and censor what people may say has a popular and historical version. The popular version of the soft-censorship charge is common in the United States. It is, in effect, that orthodoxy silences what "the people" know but may not speak. The historical version is commoner in Germany and France. There the claim is that liberal orthodoxy silences the past. The shame over 1933–45 in Germany and over 1940–44 in France prevents, it is held, an honest, undistorted sense of national history. Further, since a nation is united by a shared sense of the past, amputating the past in effect undermines or denies the nation. After 1945, it is true, the German Neue Rechte and France's Nouvelle Droite had to absolve pride in the national tradition from the charge of neo-Nazism or crypto-Pétainism. That task, however, was accomplished. Past disgrace, the hard right accordingly argues, can no longer be allowed to cloud present controversies.

According to its own picture of how things were, the hard right had truths to tell but was silenced by liberals, who were tongue-tied by historical conscience and too quick to attach opponents to a shameful past that was not the opponents' doing and that opponents had never stood up for. The right complained that it could not, for example, raise doubts about immigration without being heard to advocate biological racism or exclusionary Catholicism. The German Neue Rechte and the French Nouvelle Droite worked hard, on their own account, to distinguish themselves from the right of the 1930s and 1940s. It was, they insisted, liberal mudslinging to blame them for a past from which, in their eyes, they were wholly free.

iii. The New Voices of the Right in Germany and France

Unlike post-1945 conservative German thinkers such as Gehlen or Marquard, who responded to the cultural upheavals of the 1960s and 1970s in philosophical mode, the thinkers and publicists of the German hard right are more openly polemical. A German quick to deny the right's links to a discredited past is Götz Kubitschek (1970–). He has a small think tank, the Institut für Staatspolitik, at Schnellroda Manor in Saxony-Anhalt and a publishing arm, Antaios. He edits *Sezession*, an online magazine of the Neue Rechte, staffed by writers with university backgrounds in history, philosophy, and the arts. Too young to be refugees from earlier centrifugal movements—neo-Nazi nostalgia (1950s–1960s) or disaffected neo-Marxism (1960s–1970s), these members of the right are hard to place.

Kubitschek is wary of political labels. A Catholic, he thinks ethical and cultural values matter more. He and the American Dreher would have much to say to each other. Modernity's ill are spiritual, in Kubitschek's eyes. They include a mechanistic view of life, consumerism, and loss of Christian faith. Liberalism apologizes for too much, blames itself for the wrongs of others' or of nobody's making, and is woefully timid about national pride. Not that Kubitschek's patriotism is notably liberal or inclusive. In a diverse nation that has been arguing with itself about Germanness since before unification in 1871, Kubitschek has few doubts about which region is the most German. Western Germans, in his view, are hypermoral (meaning bossy and idealistic in the wrong way), too easy on immigrants, and soft, whereas in eastern Germany, where there is less immigration, "Germany is still Germany."

Although national under-confidence takes its own form in Germany, the lack is common elsewhere in Europe and the United States and is getting worse, in Kubitschek's view. In Spenglerian mode, he wonders if the West has the will to survive. In 2017, *Sezession* published the special issue "Finis Germania," a collection of posthumous essays by Rolf Peter Sieferle that was a succès de scandale on publication by Antaios. Sieferle's pieces in "Finis Germania" covered the familiar hard-right themes of unburdening the German conscience, the irresponsibility of a nation unwilling to shoulder power in the world, the dull conformity of the Bundesrepublik, and, more generally, the intellectual failings of liberal democrats. Kubitschek is a friend of Höcke's (mentioned in chapter 9). Together they represent the Flügel, the wing of the AfD concerned above all with immigration and national identity and which soon after the party's founding engineered the removal of a free-market economist as its leader.

Is *Sezession* the seed of new conservative orthodoxy or a dandyish indulgence? On the masthead of *Sezession* is the Latin tag "Etiamsi omnes ego non" (Even if everyone else, not me). It was the motto of Stanislas de Clermont-Tonnerre, the constitutional monarchist killed when a Paris crowd stormed the Tuileries on the fall of the crown in 1792. *Sezession* promotes not a "Europe of the fatherlands" but a Europe that is "skeptical of capitalism" and beyond all national chauvinism. It calls for "intellectual struggle" and "metapolitics," that is, talking about how to talk about politics and, immigration aside, seems detached from the pressing questions of government or policy. *Junge Freiheit*, a weekly newspaper now also online, explores similar territory in more everyday tones. Founded in 1986 by Dieter Stein, it serves as a hinge between the AfD and the mainstream right.

A taste of the AfD's tone and way with words can be had in a short "manifesto" written by Marc Jongen, an intellectual spokesman for the insurgent party, and published in the politico-cultural magazine *Cicero* (January 2014). The hard right's familiar themes were there but expressed without apology in the language of "revolutionary conservatism" from the 1920s to the 1930s. The party had a "historic mission" to offer Germany an alternative to "modernity run riot," in which "everything stable" was open to "permanent evaporation." Though spurned and despite all attempts to silence the party, the AfD was now recognized as "a power." For Marx, the bourgeois and proletariat were mutual foes. The interests of "finance capital" and the bourgeoisie had since split apart. The AfD spoke for a "bourgeois middle class" that had suffered "proletarianization" and was accordingly the new "revolutionary class." Its enemies were "bourgeois liberalism," which strove to silence opposition, and its financial ally "banking socialism." Under a self-serving "nomenklatura," the European Central Bank, by buying up bad debts of "bankrupt states," was threatening to despoil German savers. The "central monster of structural corruption"—the European Union—must be freed from its "hybrid" status as neither a loose confederation nor political union and radically reformed by "good Europeans." Germans who do the work and preserve the culture must free the nation from the welfare burden below and the financial elite above. They must stifle bad conscience, defend national values with confidence, and stand proud in the world. Immigrants "willing to integrate," Jongen threw in, would not wish to live in an apologetic country unsure of what it stood for. The quarrel between radicals and moderates in the AfD, he added, was an invention of the press. Jongen's home brew is cooked up from familiar twentieth-century sources of disaffection and resentment, previously noted in the conservative story. At one taste, most centrist German conservatives would spit it out, but Jongen proved to have known his minority market.

In France, the antiglobal plea for a cultural shelter found eloquent expression in Alain de Benoist, a leader of what became known as France's New Right after the upheavals of 1968, and in Alain Finkielkraut, who turned against Marxist universalism soon after. Benoist thinks more in terms of Europe, Finkielkraut more in terms of France, but in a country where Roman universalism and French nationalism have often blended, there are similarities between them as well as differences.

As thinker and cultural critic, Finkielkraut (1949–) has defended French tradition against what he takes to be the corrosions of multiculturalism and moral relativism. For three decades as essayist and controversialist, Finkielkraut has journeyed from the left, bashing or abandoning one progressive idol after another: French communism, sexual liberation, postmodernism, identity politics. Finding the French Communist Party timid and domesticated, he was a Maoist in the 1960s. Unimpressed by Herbert Marcuse's gospel that even if good for civilization, checking the libido was bad for each of us, he wrote with Pascal Bruckner *Le nouveau désordre amoureux* (The new love disorder, 1977). Free love, far from liberating, harmed women. In *La défaite de la pensée*

(*The Defeat of the Mind*, 1987). Finkielkraut's lamented the "theoretical" left's skeptical anti-humanism and faddish embrace of popular entertainment at the expense of cultural worth. In the 1990s, Finkielkraut turned from iconoclasm to defending his vision of what France should be preserving: a nondiscriminatory secular state and a common culture shared by patriotic citizens. The label "right-wing" for Finkielkraut is not his, since it is the liberal left and hard left that have disowned him.

Reconciling the elements of a picture loosely called neorepublican has not been easy. Finkielkraut's detractors, who are many, have tended to seize on one element—the hostility to multiculturalism and suspicion of cultural relativism—while ignoring the insistence on nondiscrimination and civic values. Daniel Lindenberg named Finkielkraut as one of France's "new reactionaries" in his essay, *Le Rappel à l'ordre* (2002), along with a motley of others that included Michel Houellebecq, the novelist; Pierre-André Taguieff, the historian who besides coining *bougisme* as tag for neoliberal orthodoxy has written in alarm on the return of anti-Semitism in France; as well as the very liberal editor of the centrist journal *Débat*, Marcel Gauchet. Lindenberg's short book, whose title reprises a collection of pieces by Jean Cocteau in 1926 calling for artists and musicians to abandon the avant-garde and return to classical traditions, prompted a taking of sides. By France's law of the politically excluded middle, Finkielkraut was now widely anathematized on the left and celebrated on the right. For the left, he was a pseudo-thinker with a chip (Pierre Bourdieu called him a "cultural poor white") and a herald for the anti-immigration National Front. For the right, Finkielkraut was a thinker of clarity and courage who said things the left did not want to hear.

Schools and teaching are at the core of Finkielkraut's thinking about culture and assimilation. Opponents treat his insistence on secular schooling, defense of the French language, and pride in France's cultural traditions as forms of neocolonial bullying and anti-Muslim prejudice. Finkielkraut replies that he called for European intervention against Serbia in its attacks on Muslim Bosnia in the Yugoslav wars. His opponents, he insists, duck the sociocultural challenges of Muslim immigration and ignore growing anti-Semitism. *L'identité malheureuse* (2013) repeated his concerns at what he took for France's failure to absorb Muslim immigrants into French republican ways and his lament for the decline in French schooling. The book sought a narrow path between welcome and exclusion. Finkielkraut, a child of enlightenment, thought French identity to be complex and held that no tradition should be demeaned or denied. However, foreign tradition should not be implanted and imposed on France: "For the first time in the history of immigration, the newcomer (*l'accueilli*) refuses to let the host (*l'accueillant*) embody the country of welcome." The historian Pierre Nora, who later gave the speech of sponsorship on Finkielkraut's induction into the Académie Française, remarked of the book on publication that French identity would be problematic even if France had not a single immigrant.

Finkielkraut's civic republicanism and his stress on *laïcité* might seem at odds with his own Jewish sense of himself, his critical affirmation of Israel, and his tireless warning against the resurgence of French anti-Semitism. To his critics he seemed to be attacking identity politics while celebrating his own identity. As child of Polish refugees from Nazism, Finkielkraut has a ready reply. Because he understands ethnic and cultural persecution, he insists on secular nondiscrimination. Only in such a society can passionate allegiance to one creed exist side by side with passionate allegiance to another. His critics have replies in turn. They may say something like this: where, as in France and elsewhere, those with a minority allegiance are markedly worse off than those with a majority allegiance, the neutrality of a secular state between the two deepens the exclusion of those less favored. Or, again, critics may say that secularism demeans the faiths and cultures that it claims to be protecting. The dialectic is familiar. The liberal argues for neutral nondiscrimination on matters of faith or ethnic allegiance. The left then charges the liberal with hypocritical neglect of social disadvantage, the right with humbling disregard for the faith of others while imposing a faith of the liberal's own. Caught in the toils, Finkielkraut, a would-be liberal, has been pulled further to the right.

A controversial eminence in his seventies, Finkielkraut is now looked up to by a new generation of Catholic rightists that includes the Canadian Mathieu Bock-Côté and Bérénice Levet. They applaud him for reviving, as they see it, a conservatism with principles, or perhaps with one rather Burkean principle: the "singularity," or specialness, of France for the French, with their common culture and tradition. Bock-Côté shares Finkielkraut's concerns about multiculturalism and the erosion of a French ethos in education. Levet is a leading antifeminist, whose books blame feminist-inspired reforms of recent decades for harming women and the family. How far Finkielkraut's French republicanism would blend with their religiously based moral appeals is another matter. Bock-Côté, Levet, and young militants like them carry on a tradition of active engagement in politics, as seen in the 1980s when the Socialists were obliged to withdraw a school reform in face of mass Catholic protest. In 2013, the younger generation took to the streets of Paris in La Manif pour Tous, a protest organized against recognition of gay marriage, though this time with no result save the creation of a politico-moral movement that continues under the same name. That mixed outcome was telling. Moral conservatism in France, it seems, has limited strength in politics save when tied to other movements or parties. Even then, the yield in change to policy is small. The career of Christine Boutin, a right-wing Catholic and antiabortion crusader, is a fair example. She won 340,000 votes for president running alone in 2002. Nicolas Sarkozy, who later won the presidency, rewarded her support by making her, not health, but housing minister. Boutin later backed Le Pen and left politics. France's permissive abortion laws remained in place. A remnant of earlier prohibition, the mandatory week's waiting period, was abolished in 2015.

The younger generation of militant right-wing Catholics talks of changing mentalities and escaping from liberal orthodoxy. In practice, they mean local changes within the system, mostly to do with schools and sexual ethics. They have no grand strategy to offer for overturning the present liberal state of affairs, let alone what kind of society might take its place.

The journey of Benoist (1943–) to France's New Right, as it was then called, began precociously in the lost campaign for French Algeria. Less of a public figure than Finkielkraut but more focused in argument and equally prolific, Benoist founded the right-wing think tank Groupement de Recherche et d'Etudes pour la Civilisation Européenne (GRECE). The name and its bearer announced Benoist's intent: to set up a "cultural counterpower" that would defend European values. Benoist, who was never easy to pin down politically, was clearer about what his pro-Europeanism did not include than what it did. He took Christian universalism for suffocating and "totalitarian," a fault shared by the other great monotheisms, Judaism (which he took for intolerant, fanatical, and enslaved to the deity) and Islam. His "new right" was accordingly new in turning its back on Christian conservatism. Unlike neoconservatives in the United States and Germany, his "new right" was not trying to close the cultural stables thrown open in the 1960s. His intellectualism and fascination with doctrine—*Vu de droite* (1977), a micro-scrutiny of three dozen motley thinkers, including Clausewitz, Mao Tse-Tung, Popper, Gobineau, and Gramsci—made him out to be a *marxisant* '68er with the signs changed. Benoist's European values did not include liberal values. He denounced free-market globalization, democratic equality ("levelling down"), and human rights ("law contaminated by morality"). He detested the two main philosophies on which political liberalism might be held to rest, the "philosophy of efficiency" (Utilitarianism) and rights-based liberalism, especially when stretched to defend universal rights. Benoist was not a France-firster or hyper-patriot. Unlike many conservatives, he disbelieved in the nation as a cultural ethnos and on that ground alone thought immigrant communities should be discouraged from living cut off in a micro-ethnos of their own. His Europeanism had nothing to do with the European Union, which he took for an undemocratic, free-market facilitator. Benoist's Europe would be one of regions with their own distinct but overlapping traditions. When the mainstream parties of the French right made their peace with globalizing capital in the 1980s, Benoist saw his years of unsung Gramscian toil rewarded as a space opened between the National Front and the mainstream center-right of the UDF-RPR.

Benoist differed from France's Catholic right in his "transhumanist" interest in biogenetic engineering and the possibilities of biological improvement of the species. Although claimed by some as its apologist, he said in 1992 that the National Front turned his stomach. Benoist admired the thinkers of Germany's conservative revolution, such as Jünger and his secretary Mohler, who gave it a name and carried certain of its ideas into the late twentieth century. Benoist's positive ideas, in contrast, were hard to pin down. He was omnicurious about history and ideas but incurious about institutions and policy. Perhaps his largest idea was negative: "inegalitarianism." The egalitarianism of equal respect to which liberals were committed Benoist took for a delusion. In Comte-Spengler mode, he saw the myth as having had distinct phases, each now exhausted: mythic Christian equality, philosophic Enlightenment equality, and scientific Marxist equality. The time had come, Benoist held, for recognition of inequality in a society that was neither "individualist" nor "collectivist."

What Benoist's "ni-ni" added up to was uncertain. Over time, his opposition to liberal democracy shifted. What started as civilizational defense of the West morphed into loathing of the "economic man" of American capitalism. Benoist's later anti-Americanism put him alongside similarly disaffected spirits on the French far left. Recent books included *Le moment populiste: Droite-gauche, c'est fini!* (2017) and *Contre le libéralisme: La société n'est pas un marché* (2019). He still understood the right's tasks as resisting liberal democracy, exposing its hypocrisies, and deriding its pieties, yet he had barely a sketch of an alternative and little sense of the values, besides scorn for the present, that such an alternative would embody.

Whereas in books and his magazine, *Eléments*, Benoist patiently gathered arguments and material to explain why today's conservatives should reject liberal democracy, the newer *L'Incorrect* uses sarcasm and mockery to the same end. The name, a play on "political correctness," flaunts resolve to say what supposedly cannot be said. In the pages of *L'Incorrect*, recent French history is a parade of left-wing villains and clowns, beginning with the "corrupt enchanter" Mitterrand. Given its twentieth-century crimes, the left's moralism should be thrown back in its face. Old Europe is dead and the new Europe dawns in Poland and Hungary, where Christian Democracy is being reinvented. Liberal democracy is done for: aimless, without authorities, its suburbs in flames, and, demographically, in suicidal decline. Reading *L'Incorrect* is not unlike listening to shout radio. You put it down impressed not by the argument but by the rage.

It is looking as if Pierre Rosanvallon's question—was there more here than shared "denials and dislikes"?—has to be answered "no, not yet." Finkielkraut's entreaties on behalf of French culture and language are made in a liberal vein by appeal, in the end, to a local embodiment of universal, Enlightenment values, notably mutual forbearance and civic respect. Despite the angry tone and provocative words, hard-right pronouncements about threats to the nation or the costs of immigration are not, as presented, anti-liberal or anti-democratic. They pay homage to liberalism by disavowing ethnic prejudice and biological racism. On the liberal side, only the dogmatic, universalist libertarians deny the link between democratic allegiance and national feeling.

A complacent liberal, right or left, who surveys this hard-right ferment might sigh with relief. Beyond well-known anxieties and erudite posturing, there was little to keep defenders of the liberal consensus awake at night. There was little to give the hard-right intellectual coherence, as opposed to tactical points of connection. Against geopolitical threats made by nonliberal competitors and planetary threats created by liberal modernity itself, the intellectual complaints of the unreconciled right looked more like a local nuisance than a source of serious concern. It was replaying themes and postures familiar since the 1890s, ever revived, ever discredited: an apocalyptic vision of Western decline, a false contrast of people and elites, inattention to government or policy, and a bootstrapping attempt to break out of liberal orthodoxy that found itself back in despite grand-sounding projects such as the pursuit of "metapolitics."

An uncomplacent liberal could agree with all that yet still worry. Few of the hard right's criticisms added up to a whole. Nothing cohered into an alternative orthodoxy. And yet, given the evident flaws and unfulfilled promises of democratic liberalism and given the loss of outspoken, lucid defenders at the political center, each of those points from the hard right appealed to someone, somewhere. When a person has several minor infections, each is treatable. None is dangerous on its own. Left untended, they threaten to run together and become systemic.

iv. Three Unreconciled Thinkers: Finnis,
Scruton, and Sloterdijk

As critics of liberal-modern orthodoxy, the mode chosen by John Finnis, and by Roger Scruton and Peter Sloterdijk when arguing seriously, is more philosophical than polemical. Finnis is a legal philosopher; Scruton, who died in January 2020, was a philosopher of aesthetics; and Sloterdijk is a hard-to-categorize speculator. All three have faulted political liberalism for trying to get by without a defendable picture of what humans are and what is good for them.

Against banishing goodness from the concerns of politics, Finnis as a neo-Thomist thinks we can reason out from human nature what is good or bad for people. As an upholder of a natural-law tradition favored in conservative Catholicism, Finnis thinks law and politics should promote good ways to live and discourage or forbid bad ways, especially to do with sex and the family.

Scruton's human being is a socially rooted person, rich in sentiments that liberalism neglects: allegiance, piety, a sense of sacredness, and guilt. A British cultural critic in a line of conservative descent from Coleridge and Eliot, Scruton looked to a restoration of values that liberalism ignores. In liberal spirit, he thought, we ourselves, not politics or law, should bring that restoration about.

Sloterdijk is a prolific, omnicurious professor at the Karlsruhe University of Arts and Design. For many years, he had a philosophical talk show on German television. Part thinker, part intellectual entertainer, Sloterdijk says too much about too many things to answer clearly who humans are and how they should lead our lives. Unlike political liberals, he considers the question to be sensible and urgent. His human is an inventive toolmaker in a cluttered space. In long, chaotic books, he muses about how we are to "immunize" and shelter ourselves from present-day chaos.

Finnis's approach to morality, law, and politics comes from medieval tradition and from the climate of his times. The scholastic rationalism of Thomas Aquinas is one focus. The liberalization of laws to do with personal conduct and morality during the 1950s and 1960s is another. A century after Mill had pled for such changes, restrictive laws on personal conduct began to be lifted or lightened, and once begun, change came in a rush. The forbidden was allowed, the unspeakable was spoken about, and what law had banned and punished became not just legally blameless but in a growing body of opinion morally innocent: divorce by consent, contraception, homosexuality, abortion, single-sex marriage. Within a generation or so, a familiar moral dwelling in which conservatives—including free-market conservatives—had felt comfortably at home fell into ruin. The public sphere shrank; the private sphere grew. Law and to some degree society itself were pried out of personal morality.

Democratically, public opinion welcomed the changes and has not since changed its mind. Intellectually, a conservative fightback began. A conservative resistance refused to accept that law had no say over private conduct. On the right, the ghost of Fitzjames Stephen prevailed over the ghost of Mill. Law, it was insisted, should mark out what was good and reasonable for people to do and forbid or discourage what was bad and unreasonable. A favorite weapon in the fight was natural law. In moral rigor's van was Finnis.

In distinguished retirement at eighty, Finnis made the news in 2019 when a petition circulated briefly at Oxford University, where he had long taught, to strip him of academic honors. The question was Finnis's views on gay sex. It was morally wrong, Finnis believed, for undermining the family and open to government to discourage. The petitioners were younger scholars who saw Finnis's work as a cloak for bigotry. Older scholars, who disagreed with Finnis's moral conclusions but praised him as a philosopher, stood up for his academic freedoms.

In legal philosophy, much of what Finnis has had to say is said also by legal philosophers of liberal outlook. Take the claim, for example, that there are moral facts bearing on law that can be known and reasoned about. A conservative and liberal can agree to that yet disagree about how far law should intrude on morality. A liberal, that is, could accompany Finnis, the legal philosopher, some way into the jurisprudential forest. The puzzle is Finnis, the moral rigorist, who comes out the other side.

Morality, to Finnis, bore on what was good or bad for people. Goodness did not depend on choice or convention. There were facts here that we could learn (and forget). Factual, though, did not mean simple or obvious. Good was complicated. Finnis picked out seven basic goods in human life. They were "states" (these included activities and capacities) to aim for and cherish: life and health, knowledge (for its own sake), friendship, play, aesthetic experience, practical reasonableness, and religious faith. (Purposeful work was oddly missing, although work appears on other lists of basic goods in the modern natural-law tradition.) No item on the list was reducible to any of the others. In that framework and with dialectical skill, Finnis defended a strict personal morality at odds with prevailing norms, notably on sex and marriage.

Finnis accepted the secular climate of liberal-modern public argument, as noted earlier. When defending his moral positions, he did not directly invoke religious faith and thought other moral conservatives in the liberal West should do likewise. In reworking the natural-law tradition, Finnis drew first on nontheological elements in Aquinas. Finnis, that is, aimed to justify moral maxims either by appeal to universal standards of human reasonableness (given that humans are rational creatures) or by appeal to what will, as a matter of fact confirmed by experience, most foster human well-being overall. Given that outcome, fellow scholars have spied in Finnis's methods Kantian elements (the universality of the maxims) and Utilitarian ones (the common good as shared aim of morality and law). Finnis's morality of law has, accordingly, a double aspect. In arguing as a secularist, Finnis on the one hand had to use a lot of liberal rope. On the other hand, to reach his illiberal maxims, notably on sexual morality and criminal punishment, he had to stretch what counted for human well-being overall well beyond what most liberal-minded people would agree was needed for their own good. Finnis, in riposte, chided liberals for failing to follow through with their own methods and instead reaching the conclusions they wanted. Each side suspected the others of deducing the moral intuitions they began with.

At the high end of the argument, not all religious conservatives follow Finnis in bowing to the secular-reasons-only rule. Valiant appeals to faith can be heard from *First Things*, a Catholic magazine that opposes liberal arguments that its late founder, John Neuhaus, described as based on a false belief in the "naked public square." Its main aim, the magazine announces, is "to confront the ideology of secularism, which insists that the public square must be 'naked,' and that faith has no place in shaping the public conversation or in shaping public policy." The statement of aim is stirring but equivocal. If it means the faithful should have an equal place in public argument, well and good. If it means that reasons of faith should have an equal place with non-faith reasoning, that is problematic. For which faith is that to be? The magazine, which is open-mindedly ecumenical, acknowledges that many faiths coexist. It recognizes, in another equivocal phrase, a "religiously pluralistic society." If faiths disagree on the topic at hand, their disagreements can be resolved by considering nonreligious reasons that separate them. But then they are arguing nonreligiously, not as faiths. But if, as *First Things* appears to want, they argue as faiths, religious reasons cannot settle their differences. Public argument offers no resolution. Religion's schismatic history repeats, and the "public square" becomes a space of private chapels. If, against that, it is insisted that discordant faiths nevertheless share a core of religiously rooted morality that nonbelievers cannot share, the claim may again be split into two. Unless the moral core is very odd, nonbelievers will mostly be able to agree with its content while disagreeing with the faithful about morality's religious sources. Once again, religious reasons drop out of the argument.

Besides avoiding theological premises and using secular arguments, Finnis himself made a second self-denial. Unlike the Victorian rigorist Fitzjames Stephen, for example, Finnis did not ask, "What does the public think?" Stephen appealed to conventional views of what is moral or immoral and what the state, as the guardian of order, should accordingly permit or forbid. Finnis acknowledged the prevailing laxist climate but rested his rigorism on a philosophical view of human needs. Laxists have had the wind of opinion behind them for half a century, it is true. What if opinion changed? It might do so in smaller and larger ways. It might shift from laxity to rigor within an unchanging climate of secularism, which debarred religious reasons from public argument. Or it might shift against secularism itself, allowing rigor the support of religion.

Neither shift looks probable for now. In the United States, for example, opinion on abortion seems stable. According to the Pew Research Center, poll figures for allowing (58 percent) or forbidding (37 percent) "all" or "most" abortions figures have barely shifted since the 1990s. That has not discouraged conservatives from the fight, in Europe, as earlier noted, or in the United States, where Republicans have pressed antiabortion bills in state legislatures in language that is at once party-political and religion-tinged. Defending such a bill in Ohio, one state lawmaker declared in December 2019: "The time for regulating evil and compromise is over."

If Finnis represents the high end of the modern natural-law tradition, the popular end is served by Patrick Deneen, an American scholar, who drew notice with "Unsustainable Liberalism" (May 2012) in *First Things* and developed that attack in *Why Liberalism Failed* (2018). Liberalism's deep flaws, for Deneen, were "anthropological individualism" (in aiming to free people "from constitutive relationships, from unchosen traditions, from restraining custom"); a voluntarist conception of choice (which "dismissed the idea that there are wrong or bad choices"); and a separation of people from nature (understood as a universal order that included norms of what was good and bad for people). Deneen was here guilty of what Stephen Holmes in *Anatomy of Antiliberalism* (1993) called "antonym substitution," a rhetorical device of stripping what liberals oppose from its context and substituting for that something which they, conservatives, favor. Liberals do not contrast personal choice with the moral choice but with the choice that an arbitrary authority claims is moral. They do not contrast personal liberty with acknowledgment of authority but with submission to arbitrary, unchecked authority. They do not contrast a person's sense of themselves with their roots in a community but with unchosen, often subordinate membership in a clan or social group. Liberal reluctance to use coercive law in the enforcement of morality is not a denial of morality.

While waiting for opinion to shift, moral rigorists, notably in the United States, also place hopes in a top-down approach from the heights of law. Two of Finnis's Oxford pupils are well known in the world of American law. Neil Gorsuch, who studied under him, is a justice on the US Supreme Court. Another ex-pupil, Robert George, a professor of law at Princeton, wrote the Manhattan Declaration. It called for resistance by churches and charities against laws that embroiled them in tacit support for abortion, same-sex marriage, and embryo-destructive research. More vocal in conservative polemic than Gorsuch, George holds that liberals are slave to a "secularist orthodoxy" of "feminism, multiculturalism, gay liberationism, and lifestyle liberalism."

Both Gorsuch and George belong to the Federalist Society, a lobbying club of conservative and libertarian lawyers. The society was founded in 1982 with its first chapters at Yale University and the University of Chicago. The aim was to win back the federal bench from "activist" liberal judges. The society's vice president, an influential Washington fixer, Leonard Leo, is reputed to have given Donald Trump names of Supreme Court nominees acceptable to the conservative right, including Gorsuch and Brett Kavanaugh. Four other present justices, including the chief justice, are also members. Judges the society favors tend to be against gun control and abortion but for the right to bear arms and the duty to bear children. In its determination to overturn forty to fifty years of constitutional decision-making, the *Federalist* approach has been criticized for judicial activism, that is, for judges taking the making of law out of democratically elected legislatures' hands, a charge made in the 1960s and 1970s by conservative jurists against liberal judges. Its statement of purpose from 2015 rises above those tensions. The aims were to "promote the principles that the state exists to preserve freedom, that the separation of governmental powers is central to our constitution, and that it is emphatically the province and duty of the judiciary to say what the law is, not what it should be."

The largest puzzle about Roger Scruton is how there could be only one of him. A philosopher, journalist, and novelist, who once said that if he did not write four thousand words a day, he felt unclean, Scruton published more than fifty books, edited a political magazine, wrote many scholarly articles, and enraged liberal readers over the course of forty years with countless short squibs in the press. His range was daunting.

He wrote on morals, the philosophy of personhood, political thought, aesthetics, music, architecture, morals, wine-drinking, sexual morality, and care for the environment. His philosophical learning was deep, and his skills as a lucid expositor, on show in *Kant* (1982) and the *Dictionary of Political Thought* (2007), unsurpassed. He wrote simply and accessibly in once common fields now closed to nonspecialists. Although Scruton's tone was provincial by adoption, his range of learning and languages was cosmopolitan. He could be a serious philosopher or a philosopher-provocateur. As a British eminence, he was a local counterexample to the hackneyed falsehood that conservatives are afraid of ideas.

Scruton, who was schooled in science and math, never lost trust in either as bankable knowledge. Philosophically, in the spirit of Collingwood and German idealism, he resisted conflating natural science with all knowledge or the only model of knowledge. Resistance to scientism and its cousin "clairantism"—erroneous trust in demystifying explanation that left what was obscure unexplained—became intellectual leitmotifs. Convinced that "conservatives needed to think more," he founded the Conservative Philosophy Group in 1974, applied in vain for a Tory candidacy in 1978, and started with John Casey, the *Salisbury Review* (1982), a conservative quarterly taking its distance from the libertarian right in the name of traditional values, which he edited for eighteen years.

Scruton wrote several books that aimed to ground conservative politics in a philosophical outlook. That attempt alone sets him aside as almost unique in the present-day English-speaking intellectual world. For all his Englishness of manner and clarity of prose, he fits at a remove in German traditions of philosophical idealism. Looking back twenty-five years later, he called his first book, *The Meaning of Conservatism* (1980), "a somewhat Hegelian defence of Tory values in the face of their betrayal by the free marketeers." The description was apt.

Scruton grasped that mainstream conservatism in Europe and the United States was a right-wing liberalism. Celebrating market society ignored the damage free markets did to society. Worse, celebration was not philosophy. In the 1980 *Meaning* and later editions, Scruton aimed to fill the gap. He sought to distinguish a purer conservative outlook from the market-mindedness of Hayek. When Hayek looked to philosophy for vindication, it was to a workaday Utilitarianism. Scruton sought to draw out Oakeshott's cross-party intimations about limited social knowledge and the character of political allegiance, turning them to openly conservative purpose. Scruton later became friendlier to the free market, stressed people's essential freedom, and rejected "holistic" pictures of society that seemed to deny that freedom. He took to calling *Meaning* "a young man's book," yet its themes remained with him as the core of a philosophical conservatism.

Authority, institutions, and allegiance formed, for Scruton, an interlocking core of requirements for order in society. To preserve and hand on social order was for Scruton the overriding political task. The requirements worked together in chain: without authority, no order; without institutions, nothing with which authority could make its demands and save itself from arbitrariness; without allegiance, no institutions, for institutions required not prudent acquiescence but an unreflecting acceptance that Scruton spoke of as awe or piety. Order of that kind he called "establishment," and establishment was the "great internal aim of politics."

Order, or establishment, was not chosen by presocial people. Nor was it created in an act of constitutional foundation. Order emerged through habituation and by care for custom in unbroken tradition. The task of politics was guardianship of order. It had no guiding aim beyond that such as promoting greater equality or social justice—nor, it could be added, preserving greater hierarchy and privilege.

The institutions Scruton took to be needed for social order were familiar from the conservative canon. They included law, private property, and personal liberty. Here too requirements interlocked. Liberty required property, for without property, people lacked social personality—a capacity of one's own to act in society. What was unowned, further, was a source of unsettlable conflict. Property and liberty were each protected by law, above all by judge-made common law, for common law, unlike legislation, forswore any aim save justice—giving what was due—in the case at hand. Needed as they were for order, both property and liberty must be tempered and limited by a common spirit of allegiance, without which institutions foundered. Such allegiance would be to a social whole bigger than the locality, smaller than humankind. The most familiar such whole was the nation. Nations bound people not ethnically or religiously but by common culture, shared historical memories, and civic commitments. A healthy nation allowed for diversity and disagreement.

Scruton's picture of society and politics was drawn to distinguish it from contrasting pictures required, as he took it, by liberalism. Scruton's picture was not "contractual." It dispensed with any idea that social obligations arose from mutual consent. It balanced personal liberties with impersonal duties implied by the general requirement of allegiance. It was not "progressive" and it proscribed attempts to aim at improved patterns against which actual society might be judged and held not yet to have reached. It credited the idea of a human nature and took as empty liberal pictures that denied the needs and constraints of that nature, including passion for home, belonging, and stability.

Historically, Scruton's picture was of cosmopolitan parentage. It stood in the line of descent from Oakeshott and Burke. In denying politics aims besides preserving social order, or "establishment," Scruton echoed Oakeshott's proscription of "rationalism" in politics. In linking custom to "costume," Scruton adopted Burke's metaphor of social norms as clothes for our animal being. That thought of society providing people with a "second nature" was prominent, as seen with Gehlen, in post-1945 German conservative thought.

Scruton was at the same time proudly Kantian in singling out rationality—our capacity to give and take reasons—as at our nature's core. Arguing in Kantian fashion, Scruton laid out a chain: without self-recognition, no reason; without recognition of others no self-recognition; and without recognition of others, no mutual acceptance on which sociability and morality rested. Reversing the chain, reason was rooted in society and morality.

Reason, however, need not be universal. Scruton also echoed Hegel. For his "reason" had everywhere local and historical shape. The reasons we gave each other as guides and explanations in life came from inside the society we grew up in. Each society had custom-forming institutions—family, learning, law, property, and exchange. Such institutions took various shapes in different societies and formed custom in different ways. Our allegiance to custom must, accordingly, be relative. It had to be to the customs of our own society, not to those of others. Diversity might be recognized, even welcomed. We might believe it good to live in a world where other societies had other customs, but recognition of diversity was not allegiance. It did not involve acceptance of other customs. Recognition of other customs, like toleration of other faiths, still allowed for insistence that other customs were wrong.

Questions were many. What drove Scruton's striking reconciliations? Richer determination of key terms—"custom," "society"—were needed. Where did one society start, another begin? How uniform was national custom? In capitalist modernity, the division of labor and the easy movement of people and money had done their corrosive work. Societies were diverse. Customs coexisted within them. Conflicting loyalties jostled with shared loyalties. Faced by those facts, to insist that, within conflicted, liberal-modern society, one national custom prevailed looked like hectoring. To claim, at the other extreme, that each of us could choose a custom that embodied the nation looked like nonsense. Where in a diverse, present-day nation a conservative was to find unity was from Scruton unclear. An answer was available in Scruton's larger thinking about the "human kind," in his phrase, but it was indirect and not obviously conservative.

Scruton's *On Human Nature* (2017) was a far-reaching essay in philosophical anthropology. As with much of Scruton's work, it could be taken in either a more partisan or more neutral spirit. To characterize "the human kind," Scruton followed a categorical divide, one found sharply in German philosophical traditions, between natural science and humane enquiry. Science, particularly biological and neurological science, has explained ever better our animal being. But science explained "happenings" in our bodies. It could not explain our rational selves. It offered no account of what we did when we recognized each other as reason-guided creatures.

That mistaken idea—that science could tell us the whole truth about ourselves—was the first of three errors in a thin, distorted picture of human nature that, for Scruton, was now common and that distorted liberalism's picture of society. A second error was a misunderstanding of moral autonomy. We were each morally free in the sense of personally accountable for our choices. We were also morally bound by unchosen social ties that imposed duties and gave shape to our aims in life. We were free in the observance of morality, not free in what morality to choose. A third mistake in liberalism's picture of society was to treat everything of value as something that had acquired it by preference or consent. That error threatened to equate value with price and render everything that mattered open to trade. Many things, Scruton countered, mattered for themselves: for example, beauty, learning, the natural environment, the social community. Such "lasting things," including one's nation, needed to be cherished and protected. The proper attitude to them was not to ask "What is this for?" or "What are these worth?" That took beauty or learning, for example, as tools for tasks that might be served as well by other tools, traded at the right price. The proper attitude was to show "lasting things" what Scruton called piety, that is, unquestioning recognition, respect, and love.

The mistakes might be labelled, although Scruton himself did not do so, as scientism, libertarianism, and transactionalism. In liberal and secular societies that trio passed, on Scruton's account, as an adequate account of the human kind, as this-worldly, reason-guided, satisfaction-seeking beings. Each, however, was flawed and superficial. In their understanding of our moral nature they made no room for the ideas of pollution, defilement, or desecration. Their shop-counter picture of human motivation neglected the sense of guilt and longing for redemption. In a neutral spirit, fellow philosophers could question the reasoning while still admiring the synthesis. In a partisan spirit, the political liberal could ask what it was in Scruton's sought-for philosophical conclusions about the human make—the inescapability of shame and guilt, the unreasoned authority of the forbidden, the existence of moral facts—they were debarred by their politics from agreeing with.

Although theories are commonly fathered on liberalism en bloc, political liberals need not be Lockean contractualists, "individualists" in some sense of a cloudy, multitasking term, deniers of unchosen duties, or disbelievers in moral "objectivity." They need not be reductive in their scientific understanding of the human person or transactional in equating value with price. From those disputable conjectures, there are no straight, imperative lines to political liberalism, with its recognition of social disagreement about values (which is not a denial of value), its fears for how unchecked power may mistreat the human person, its faith in human improvability, and its respect for persons as such, whoever they are.

Nor need political liberals deny the unchosen value of "lasting things" such as beauty, learning, and undespoiled nature that Scruton, as a conservative cultural critic, movingly defends. Liberals can, and often do, find those valuable things, as Scruton finds them, disregarded and underprotected. In *Beauty* (2009), Scruton wrote, "Beauty is vanishing from our world because we live as if it did not matter." That was a half-truth. Set aside that Scruton framed his bleak picture of present-day culture to leave out not just the rich artistic achievements of its makers but also unprecedented modern routes of access to our cultural inheritance for lookers, listeners, and readers (for example, the camera, recorded sound, and Web libraries). Ignore, that is, the pessimistic selectivity of the picture. Much culture is coarse and ugly (and probably always was). Where Scruton fell short was in explaining cultural blight. His account is too narrowly intellectualist. It is also causally inept. Implausibly one-sided blame lies on disruptive, critical minds, notably modernists and anticlassicals, who have either the wrong standards or no standards. Missing from Scruton's guilty bench are social or economic factors. Present-day cultural blight is due also to profit-needy cultural industries, popular conservative media, and underfinanced schools, as well as management-think in universities and cultural bodies who put a price on humane values when their task is to defend them. Put in economic terms, Scruton's criticism exaggerates underdemand for culture worth keeping and ignores supply-side distortions in a money-governed cultural market. As a conservative defender of property, Scruton could fairly be asked a present-day version of Chamberlain's question (1880s) about paying for social reform: What ransom is property prepared to pay for cultural recovery?

Slippage between Scruton's philosophy and his politics occurred with a question, mentioned above, how is national unity to be found in diverse modern society? An answer is available in Scruton's rich account of the social imagination. They key is our imaginative ability to see one thing "as" another: a picture in a pattern of painted marks, a melody in a sequence of sounds, or aesthetic properties in a building that were not strictly there, such as grace, balance, or invitingness. The capacity of "seeing as" underpinned, for Scruton, not just our engagement with art but our sociability and our induction into morality. A primary step was to see each other as persons. That did not mean persons were fictions; seeing others as persons did not create things not there before. Interpersonal imagination was not normless, associative fancy. Far from discarding, it relied on knowledge, not least about responsibility, resentment, praise, and blame. Understood as a purposive act of mind, "seeing as" could be in some sense "objective": sharper or blunter, better or worse, open to argument and correction. On its judgments, people could converge to agreement. Once seeing each other as persons, we saw each other as family members, colleagues, friends. Without "seeing as," for Scruton, there would be no social world.

A natural extension of that thought offered Scruton an answer about where in diverse, modern society to find unity, a national whole. On his account of the social imagination, it would be open to a conservative to say we saw the national whole when we saw each other as fellow citizens. Without such recognition there was no shared society, with its varied customs and values that gave us each a sense of ourselves as belong to one nation. Such a thought could be, to a liberal mind, the beginning of an answer to reconciling national unity and social diversity. But perhaps not to Scruton. For his politics asked more of nationality than shared citizenship. It asked more than civic and political commitment. It asked much broader ethical and cultural allegiance, which in modern society is simply not there. Try as we may, we cannot see society as orderly or united.

Scruton made much of human anchorage in an implausibly steady and supportive society, too little of our anchorage in changeable living matter. His human person, not unlike Sartre's, often seems to be too much a free, active, and imaginative mind and not enough what humans universally share: a widely unfree, needful, and demanding body. The imbalance reappears in Scruton's politics. In sound conservative tradition, he is an anti-progressive who thinks we should take people as they come. Yet his scrupulously social, overthoughtful people are oddly more how liberals are supposed wrongly to imagine them: more Kantian, more like angels or clever Martians than like the needy, befuddled and imperfect fellow humans that political conservatives forever worry about how to govern.

A final worry about Scruton's powerful, attractive synthesis is the moral reliability of local custom. It is one thing for conservatives to forswear holy war against foreign custom in a spirit of live-and-let-live prudence. It is another for them to imagine themselves in a foreign society and ask of that society, What moral authority have its local customs? What makes them correct? That this is a problem for liberals does not mean it is not one for conservatives. It is a question conservatives have to face wherever and whenever. A classic conservative answer—derived from Hume through Burke—was that custom became morally reliable through endurance. By enduring, customary values became morally demanding values. Time, that is, creates value and tradition conserves it. The trouble is that time and tradition are not reliable; they conserve also disvalue. Tradition, for example, conserved slavery and the subjection of women. The "anti-rationalist" conservative could agree, yet still insist that society's arrangements can be judged only from inside, not from outside by extrasocial or universal standards. Slavery and women's subjection were rejected as Western society's self-understanding improved, as its recognition of personhood grew less confined and more universal. Hegel's ghost is speaking here. The reconciliation looks attractive. The difficulty is that such liberal "universalist" standards were proscribed by Oakeshott and Scruton under another description as "rationalist" and inapplicable. Yet they came from within Western society as it learned to see the world better. They were not an alien, extrasocial import.

Exaggeration is a fault in Scruton's critique of liberalism that tended to blunt its thrust. He exaggerated grandly and arrestingly, in the tradition of conservative exaggeration that took its first lessons from the flights of Burke and Maistre. Scruton, in addition, could squash, skewer, and deflate liberals with the cruelest of the right's satirists going back to Mencken, even Nietzsche and Baudelaire. Scruton's exaggerations are on show in *Fools, Firebrands and Scoundrels: Thinkers of the New Left* (2015) but haunt his political writing generally. Scruton was in an altogether higher thought class than Deneen, but he too was given to false contrasts. Liberals are not for unrestricted equality, as Scruton suggested, but for less inequality; not for despoiling wealth but for wealth paying a greater share; not for replacing capitalism but for containing capitalism; not for denying market values but for refusing to make them a unique and primary value.

When Scruton first wrote about conservatism in the 1980s, he was sharper in his suspicion of free-market radicalism. He was an unreconciled conservative. He had never met Margaret Thatcher, he was proud to say. He was a conservative with a small *c* but not a Conservative in a British party sense. With time, Scruton became friendlier to the free market. As source for the idea that society was too complex, subtle, and sensitive in its connections to understand or meddle with in service to political ideals, he began to cite not just the anti-rationalists, Burke and Oakeshott, but also the Utilitarian Hayek. The first two editions of *Meaning* (1980; 1984) marked off British conservatism from the American right. English freedom and "American Republican freedom," Scruton wrote, were different. "The concept of freedom . . . cannot occupy a central place in conservative thinking," he wrote then, and "no conservative is likely to think democracy an essential axiom of his politics." In later books, bold claims of the kind gave way to a picture of conservatism that right-wing liberals in the United States could feel more comfortable with. In *Conservatism* (2017), Scruton stressed that conservative philosophy had always cherished the "freedom of the individual" and rejected collectivist pictures of society fathered on conservatism as "an organic network bound by habit and submission." In age, contrary to the life-pattern claimed in folk wisdom according to which people become more conservative as they grow older, perhaps Scruton was becoming, in an economic sense at any rate, more liberal.

The German politico-cultural magazine *Cicero* reported early in 2019 the passing of a spiritual torch. Its February issue announced that the bête noir of Germany's liberal left, Peter Sloterdijk, had topped a reader poll ranking the country's five hundred leading intellectuals. Jürgen Habermas, the keeper of the nation's liberal-democratic conscience, had to content himself with second place. The poll had no official standing and was not a public honor, but in a country where intellectuals are respected, it was as if the congregation had booed the preacher and called instead for a jester.

Slotjerdijk's base is the design school at Karslruhe, where he was born (1947). He made his name with the 960-page *Critique of Cynical Reason* (1983), a masked assault on liberal Enlightenment by an enlightened post-liberal. He followed with the three volumes of *Spheres*: *Bubbles* (1998), *Globes* (1999) and *Foams* (2004). The trilogy was a free-ranging, speculative anthropology treating in turn, when rarely it paused for breath, the human person, its means of shelter, and its social being. Besides publishing several dozen smaller collections of pieces and interviews, Sloterdijk hosted, with the Nietzsche biographer, Rudiger Safranki, an ideas show on television, *In the Glasshouse: The Philosophical Quartet* (2002–12). Sloterdijk's message, in a sentence, is to shed liberalism's cramping moralism, stop fearing technology, and rethink our ethical homes.

For all their differences, Sloterdijk occupies a cultural space in Germany not unlike that of Scruton in Britain. Each reacted against the intellectual leftism of the late 1960s and early 1970s. Both experienced abroad a form of life quite different from the familiar world in which they had grown up. Following Schopenhauer in his fascination with Eastern thought, Sloterdijk spent formative time on an Indian ashram. Scruton, repelled by student protest in 1968 Paris, worked bravely with central European dissidents in the last years of Soviet communism. Both were outsider achievers in the academic world. Scruton irked universities for mocking, as he saw it, their liberal pieties; Sloterdijk, for ignoring scholastic disciplines. Neither were shy about making themselves part of their arguments, both sparkled in the press, and both wrote a book or more a year. Despite the knockers and belittlers, each became celebrities in their own countries and abroad. Both had a gift of phrase, although, whereas Scruton wrote simply and clearly, Sloterdijk's preference is for polysyllabic, ten-dollar words. Both have had something to say on just about everything, although Scruton was more careful than Sloterdijk not to aphorize about the natural sciences. Scruton, who said of the analytical philosophy in which he was trained that it was a tradition he could neither follow nor forget, argued clearly and simply. His vehicle was the lucid essay or short chapter. Sloterdijk, who seems to have read or dipped into everything written since the transcription of Homer, gives argument second place to metaphor, allusion, analogy, aphorism, neologism, and mock-scholastic classification, as well as to zany or eye-catching illustrations (particularly naked women and scenes of cruelty). Sense can vanish for pages. "I am," he once boasted, "never alone with my interior polylogue." Readers will wait in vain for a clearly stated claim or carefully reasoned conclusion. Never wholly lost is a preoccupying question Sloterdijk that shares with Scruton: what in the ethico-cultural turmoil of the present is a thoughtful person to shelter and preserve?

Like Scruton, Sloterdijk enjoys teasing the liberal left. In party terms, he wanted a liberal-CDU coalition in 2017. He derides the liberal-left "indignation activists" of the "pessimist international," who specialize in "importing misery" and transforming it into "high-quality reproach products." He rattles off familiar right-wing objections to the welfare state: "the modern state pillages its productive citizens" and tax is a "booty," making liberal democracies into "lethargocracies" and "kleptocracies." The interest in Sloterdijk as a counterliberal thinker lies, first, in his sprawling books.

The *Critique of Cynical Reason* was Sloterdijk's attempt to fence off the Enlightenment and so make room for genuine criticism of how we live. The false critics were "cynics," who had perverted the pursuit of truth in the service of power. They were familiar "unmaskers." Spinoza,

Hume, Voltaire, Nietzsche, and Freud headed the list. By exposing false ideas, they had pretended to shake society and its conventions. Instead, they buttressed society by robbing us of ways to think or talk about it. Sloterdijk's "cynics" had eight polemical strategies: revelation was empty; religion was illusory; metaphysics was vain; ideals masked self-interest; morality was groundless; self-knowledge was impossible; human nature was a myth; and the self was a delusion. We were left with the Christian hand-me-downs of self-reproach and discontent in our own world. Liberal-democratic society no longer even pretended to provide a rationale for itself.

Sloterdijk's cynics were conservatives in disguise. In robbing the liberal-democratic orthodoxies of justification, they blinded those within it to possible criticism from the outside. Such was a standard latter-day criticism of the Enlightenment, whether from Frankfurt School neo-Marxists or MacIntyrean anti-liberals. Sloterdijk's novelty was to introduce the cynic's opponent, the "kynic." The kynic was a genuine disruptor. Diogenes (of the tub) was the model kynic. Whereas cynics argued scholastically, from above, with reasons, the kynic jestered and clowned. Rather than criticize convention, they farted at convention. Their clowning had purpose. The kynics were trying to preserve themselves as rational beings in distorted, "semi-rational" societies. Western thought could be described—in his zany way, Sloterdijk described it—as a contest between cynics and kynics.

Which was Sloterdijk? Cynic or kynic? What Sloterdijk has had to say about our condition—and in page terms, it is a lot—swings between the roles. The aim of his twenty-four-hundred-page trilogy, *Spheres*, Sloterdijk grandly said, was to do for human experience in space what Heidegger had aimed to do for human experience in time. In *Being and Time* (1927), Heidegger had promised a truer picture of human life than natural science or "positivist" philosophy mimicking science could give. In their overdetached view, with their overgeneral categories, they falsified lived experience, as Heidegger argued. Art and literature caught life's graininess and particularity, although they worked by examples, whereas philosophy, being broader, could get closer to life's deeper truths. Here, however, Heidegger fell into the trap he blamed "positivism" for. His philosophical account of human experience became hyper-general and, where clear, self-contradictory. It was claimed that there was no human nature, no "essence" of being human, yet insisted that the essence of human life, in the simple sense of the fact that shaped everything else about us, was that our lives were limited in time. Unafraid to enter such territory, Sloterdijk opened *Bubbles* by announcing that the all-else-shaping fact about us was our being limited in space. What followed was less a further essay in hyphenated midcentury metaphysics than a pyrotechnic, free-associative meditation on the human need for material protection and shelter. Gaston Bachelard's poetics of space was here more guide than Heidegger. Sloterdijk's thread was "interiors," his running metaphor "immunity." "Only in immune structures that form interiors can humans continue their generational processes and advance their individuations." In simpler terms, we are bodily creatures with vulnerable insides who prefer to live sheltered in private.

Sloterdijk's quicksilver mind soon scampered free of anything as mundane as a house. *Bubbles* roamed over the amniotic sac, the Copernican revolution, which rendered "the immune system of the sky useless," Catherine of Siena's belief that Jesus had taken her heart and that she was living without one, the "emergence" of the human face, portraiture and physiognomy, eggs, ova, and twins. *Bubbles* did include a long riff on philosophical anthropology, "The Domestication of Being: For an Elucidation of the Clearing." In it Sloterdijk, siding with Heidegger, made neither biology nor language the source of our humanity but instead, toolmaking and shelter building.

Globes (1999) was, in Sloterdijk's description "a mausoleum for the idea of all-encompassing unity." It rambled over the symbolism of the orb, the making of maps, the nest building of the weaver bird, Girard's theory of our need for guilt-relieving scapegoats (turned into Sloterspeak as "the immune response of the sociosphere"), a potted history of philosophy ("The Ontological Proof of the Orb") that presented philosophy as a vain attempt to say something about everything, message carriers (from Hermes to the web), bureaucratic control, Fortune's wheel, and imperialist predation (analogized by Melville's division of whales into "fast fish" (those taken) and "loose fish" (those for the taking). That jumble of learning finally tumbled downstairs to unstartling historical conclusions. Schismatic conflict in the sixteenth and seventeenth centuries threw Europeans into modernity with the collapse of the "outsiderless, universal container." An "epochal trend towards individualistic life forms" showed "immunological significance" as "individuals break away from group bodies to disconnect their happiness from the being-in-shape of the political commune"; that is, how liberal societies may hold up as people go their own way is anybody's guess.

Foams (2004) traded familiar, contrasting metaphors for society—as an organism (conservative) and as a molecule of personal atoms (liberal)—for treating it as foamy. Foams were "multichambered systems of air-pockets within solid or liquid materials whose chambers are separated by film-like walls." In society as foam, "co-fragility and co-isolation of units" were "stacked in dense lattices." (Or, as Kant put it more simply, people enjoy being in society and being out of society.) Floating in the tub along with air-ballooning, gas warfare, and air-conditioning were brief accounts of how Plato, Hobbes, Simmel, and Rawls pictured society.

In a distracted moment of explicitness, Sloterdijk described the various types of "human immune systems," that is, social environments: absolute islands, space stations, and hothouses. Sloterdijk's favorite was the hothouse. Absolute islands shut out other peoples. Space stations shut out nature. Hothouses avoided either danger. Canonical hothouses in architecture were the Crystal Palace (London), Buckminster Fuller's geodesic domes, and Nicholas Grimshaw's Eden Project. Hothouses had drawbacks. They could overprotect (for example, the welfare state). Hothouses, all the same, were humanity's best hope.

To summarize a twenty-one-hundred-page fireworks display, Sloterdijk seemed to want to tell us this in *Spheres*: liberal-modern society had solved the main problems of material life. Now we had to focus on our social and natural environment. A short speech by a liberal-conservative German Green might say as much, but not so divertingly.

Sloterdijk believes too much in progress, especially technical progress, to be a good Heideggerian. His confidence in human improvability makes labelling him a conservative tricky. Conservatives, Sloterdijk has said, are political melancholics. They are "anti-modernists, religious fundamentalists, devotees of classical metaphysics, and owners of choice libraries and wine cellars. In other words, everyone who adheres to the metaphysics of perfection and believes more in decline than in progress." Conservative melancholy had its heyday in the nineteenth century in backward-looking resistance to liberal modernity. Twentieth-century horror made it impossible for conservatives to look back, and twentieth-century success made it impossible for them to cling to "hardship, misery-conservative Catholic and wealth-denying conservatism." With long words, hyphens, and digressions, Sloterdijk was again saying something simple. Conservatives had evolved into right-wing, economically minded liberals.

When, in a provocatively titled essay, "Rules for the Human Zoo" (1999), Sloterdijk likened politics to the domestication of animals, he was jumped on by left-wing liberals for raising ghosts of a racialist and eugenic past. Elsewhere, Sloterdijk has rhapsodized about the technical promise of improving humankind. In neither mode was Sloterdijk thinking of bioengineering as much as he was of "mental and spiritual technology." His "anthropotechnics," he has insisted, was not about prosthetics but about altering mentalities.

On how much needs altering, Sloterdijk blows hot and cold. In *Rage and Time* (2008), Sloterdijk wrote, earlier than many, that the characteristic political emotion of our time was rage. Its rival among the passions was pleasure, with which it was classically (and psychoanalytically) contrasted. As *thymos*, rage had been equated, variously, to passion, wrath, and spirited ambition. Its cousins were pride and demand for recognition. When offended or frustrated, rage soured into resentment. Rage, so seen, was a human universal. Managing rage was—yet another characterization of the topic—the historic task of politics. Jewish, Christian, and Communist traditions each had a rage-management strategy. Jews banked rage in God, who redirected it, without warning, either at the Jews' enemies or at the Jews themselves. Christians turned rage inward, making everyone angry with themselves. Communists brought rage out again and shared it evenly among the warring camps, capitalists and workers. In liberal capitalism, Eros (pleasure) got the upper hand. Rage was shared to all and discharged in shopping and fun. Liberal capitalism, it might seem, had tamed rage. The "rage" economy, however, was not efficient. Equal sharing was imperfect. Not all markets cleared. Disoriented, frustrated people remained with rage-holdings they could not discharge. Rage then broke out, unpredictably, in protest, rioting, and terror. *Rage and Time* is probably best read as Swiftian satire on intellectuals of all types—liberal economists, evolutionary biologists, neo-Marxists, Heideggerians, and Sloterdijk himself—who labor in vain with artful but bogus analogies to explain our liberal-modern confusions.

In a sunnier mood with *You Must Change Your Life* (2009; 2013), Sloterdijk showed confidence in the "human proclivity for self-transcendence." The book recommended a practical quietism—part Oakeshott, part Indian mysticism—of doing the doable, not straining as overscrupulous, reason-greedy liberals to remake society, and not forever worrying "why?" Scruton has spoken in that connection of the pleasure a wise conservative takes in not having to think of reasons. It is not a pleasure Sloterdijk often denies himself, one reason he is fun—and maddening—to read.

Sloterdijk's popularity marks a change in the German intellectual climate. He is dissatisfied with the anti-technology, Heideggerian critique of liberal modernity. He is disenchanted with critical theory and the Frankfurt School, led in its third generation by Habermas, who described the goal of "theory" as "self-enlightenment of socialised individuals about what they would want if they knew what they could want." Sloterdijk is against the hard right. He broke with its intellectual spokesman, Jongen, an erstwhile follower. He is not, however, frightened of the hard right enough to silence doubts about left-liberals and to call for a right-left alliance at the moderate center. Intellectual gatekeepers tend to ignore Sloterdijk or dismiss him as a charlatan. Like it or not, Sloterdijk operates successfully in a climate where gatekeepers and experts are widely disbelieved.

A conservative Catholic legal philosopher, a latter-day British cultural critic in the spirit of Coleridge and Carlyle, and a German post-Heideggerian post-liberal make an exemplary trio. As critics of a liberal status quo, they are looking for a footing amid the turmoil they sense we are in. Finnis looks to a morality rooted in an intelligible order whose grounding is extra-human. Scruton looked to ethical and cultural allegiances rooted in custom and tradition. Sloterdijk is latest in a long line of modern thinkers reaching, in his singular way, for whatever can be recovered for a humane understanding of life in a disenchanted world of science, secularism, and skeptical "unmasking." For all their strength of argument or fertility of metaphor, none have escaped the liberal climate they criticize. They argue, that is, to persuade liberals rather than to silence them, or in Mill's phrase, blot them out. To persuade liberals, their critics need and accept some common ground.

Finnis accepted that in present-day society his moral rigorism must be argued for with secular, not religious, reasons. Political liberals can share much of Scruton's cultural conservatism. Despite a provocative taste for bigoted utterances, his political conservatism has became, with time, more liberal. Sloterdijk's writing sparkles with unorthodox hints and suggestions. What his intellectual fireworks mainly light up, before the sky goes dark again, are perplexities—about late-modern society; about the planet's sustainabilities—which open-minded conservatives and liberals can share.

Could it be that the ideas and assumptions of the liberal status quo are for now too widely accepted even for unreconciled conservatives to escape from their hold? None seem to suggest that, in Hegelian spirit, they have caught where the world-mind will go next. None have shown a clear path between their philosophical outlook and the topical criticisms they have of political liberalism. None have laid out even the sketch of a counterliberal orthodoxy. Nor have their doubts and criticisms visibly shaken mainstream defenses of liberal conservatism, which continue to be spoken up for by thinkers on the right. It is striking, in fact, how little the two sides appear to talk to each other or reply to each other's arguments. Far from seeking to "think more," as Scruton urged conservatives when launching his *Salisbury Review* in 1982, it feels as if conservative defenders of the liberal-democratic status quo are eager to think less, or at any rate to speculate less, and concentrate instead on policy and practical repairs. A few thinkers of the mainstream do venture large ideas, but with varying degrees of confidence, they argue for a wised-up conservatism as least bad among the available political outlooks. They can be divided into the pragmatic, the via media, the ethically anxious, and the robustly "realist."

v. For the Status-Quo: Pragmatism, the Via Media, Anxiety, or "Realism"

Pragmatic conservatism relies on higher-level, context-free maxims of wise government. A distinguished recent defender was Anthony Quinton (1925–2010), who described the task of government as "driving a car along a narrow, winding road." His *Politics of Imperfection* (1978), though confined to the British tradition, was perhaps the best recent philosophical history of conservatism. It included religious traditions (Hooker, Burke, Coleridge, Newman) and secular traditions (Halifax, Bolingbroke, Hume, Disraeli), treating them as compatible expressions of a single outlook that takes politics as the management of human limitations. Quinton advised Margaret Thatcher (who made him a peer) but was not a dogmatic free marketeer, or dogmatic anything. A Utilitarian in ethics, an empiricist about knowledge, and a materialist about what there is, Quinton looked on philosophy as the challenging of assumptions, including his own, in the spirit of Hume, who once had asked Horace Walpole, "If you do not like argument and whist, what do you like?"

Quinton was rare among conservative thinkers in confronting a question that was often ducked: was conservatism's rejection of ideology not itself ideological? "The kind of theory that conservatism proscribes," Quinton wrote, "can be distinguished from the kind it exemplifies." Both proscribed theory and conservative proscription were general. The one rested tenuously on untested or a priori principles. The other rested on experience of misgovernment when bad theory is pursued. The distinction is vulnerable to a version of the riposte, previously noted, that the philosopher C. D. Broad made to the claim of unintended consequences against liberal reform. We had no evidence that all unintended consequences were bad, Broad pointed out. Similarly, not all reforms based on nonempirical principles (slavery is wrong, for example) prove bad. We also have experience of sound government when good theory is pursued.

A conciliatory via media is recommended by the political philosopher John Kekes. In "What Is Conservatism?" (July 1997) and *A Case for Conservatism* (1998), Kekes laid out reasons of prudence for the right to accept a liberal centrism. His method was to find unattractive alternatives and then recommend splitting the difference. Conservatism, for Kekes, was a "morality of politics," by which he meant a view about the proper way to think about politics and judge social arrangements. It was not a first-order defense of interests or values but a second-order outlook about wise and unwise political reasoning.

Conservatives, on Kekes's account, held that social arrangements were purposive. They endured by serving the purpose of fostering and encouraging good lives. The test of which arrangements succeeded and which failed was historical experience, not compliance with a presumptive social contract, meeting the ideal standard of a supposedly better society, or serving overall the good of humankind. Durable arrangements, according to a favorite conservative metaphor, "made a house a home." What lasted, however, was not necessarily what deserved to last. Also, people disagreed about what a good life was like. Conservatives, accordingly, needed to say more about reasons for favored arrangements and reasons for their conception of a good life.

Kekes picked out contrasting pairs of extreme attitudes about how to think of a good life and urged us then to steer between them. The first was a metaphysical appeal to a moral order beyond experience or skepticism about moral values. Neither had practical grip. The second was "absolute" (that is universal) or relative ("what works here") standards. Taking those pairs together, wise conservatives would reject both moral skepticism and universal standards. A few universal rules demanded everywhere a moral minimum; otherwise, local pluralism prevailed. People could still criticize their own societies so long as criticism was persuasive within that society. The third trap was overdoing the claims of autonomy (liberalism) or the demands of society (conservatism). Liberals could get the first wrong—some people liked obeying orders (monks; soldiers). Conservatives worried unduly that, released from moral policing, people reliably led bad lives. Kekes then divided local moral tradition into the intolerable (to be resisted and abolished); the tolerable (shown by experience not to foster good lives but best left to die out); and the sound (to be encouraged). From those high-level thoughts about how to reason about political morality, Kekes moved down to how a middle-way approach to politics would play out in practice. His moderate conservatism would favor limited government, forswear the pursuit of ideals, restrict itself to safeguarding social order and personal liberty, bow to law, and make its procedures clear.

In Kekes's defense of a sensible, liberal-sounding conservatism lingered the ghost of the Aristotelian mean. Kekes's mindfulness allowed for spotting flaws in liberal centrism and calling for correction. It gave the sensible conservative little grounds for quarrel with a moderately progressive Utilitarian or a cautious rights-minded liberal.

The worldly cheerfulness of Quinton's conservatism and the steer-down-the-middle moderation of Kekes might feel out of keeping with the turbulent spirits of the moment. A thinker more attuned to troubled times is Yuval Levin, a third-generation American neoconservative. He makes an anxious, ethically minded defense of right-wing liberal orthodoxy. In *The Fractured Republic: Renewing America's Social Contract in an Age of Individualism* (2016) Levin told a historical tale of conformity (1940s–1950s), frenzy (1970s–1980s), and anxiety (1980s to now). Levin was worried by social fragmentation, the neglected costs of technological change, and "hyper-individualism." He had no deep quarrel with market society but felt that the market should not be made supreme. He was dubious, however, about old social-democratic remedies. Neither social democrats nor libertarians got liberty correct, he believed. The ones mistook it for a power to act, the others for an absence of restraint. For a conservative, Levin wrote in Stoic mode, liberty was self-mastery, which required freedom from untamed passion. To promote self-mastery in a world of unmasterly selves were required better "moral formation," stronger families, more fulfilling work, and greater civic engagement.

For a conservative committed to not wrecking the household but sticking to what was prudently achievable, that was both a highly general but also daunting list. It was as if Levin had set out to defend the liberal state of affairs only to be appalled by what he found. When the first generation of neoconservatives attacked liberal orthodoxies in the 1960s, they were taking aim at restless, ill-considered liberal reform and its unintended bad social consequences. In repeating the charge half a century later, Levin was complaining about a late-modern society that conservative governments since the 1970s had done much to create. Levin's social analysis and political loyalties did not add up.

Levin's problem was shared by an eloquent values-minded conservative, David Brooks, a columnist for the *New York Times*. For Brooks, too, conservatism was rooted in a moral outlook. The Canadian-born Brooks had come from internship at Buckley's *National Review*, through posts at the *Wall Street Journal*, to become a public conscience of the American center-right. Appalled by the rise of Trump and his seizure of the Republican Party, Brooks has attributed his disquiet evenly to Trump himself and to Trump's popularity. In good, small *r* republican manner, Brooks addressed conservatism's moral demands first to citizens, only then to government. For a prudent conservative, as with Levin, the demands have often sounded overdemanding. Nothing less than moral regeneration was called for. Far from a managing of human imperfection, Brooks's conservatism can sound like a progressive perfectionism. Brooks detests national bigotry and the populist disdain for expertise, yet, like Levin, he has had little to say of why so much of what appalls him has happened on the conservative watch. His eloquence and passion for all that are unshaken. "If conservatism is ever to recover," Brooks wrote in monitory tones (2018), "it has to achieve two large tasks. First, it has to find a moral purpose large enough to displace the lure of blood-and-soil nationalism. Second, it has to restore standards of professional competence and reassert the importance of experience, integrity and political craftsmanship. When you take away excellence and integrity, loyalty to the great leader is the only currency that remains."

A more robust conservatism that saw its tasks as political, not ethical, was heard from the British historian and thinker Noel Malcolm. At a gathering of conservative freemarketeers held in the mid-1990s near London, Malcolm sketched elements of a "conservative realism." It marked a clear line of separation from the socio-ethical concerns of the kind that had exercised American and German neoconservatives. At the same time, it distinguished the economically liberal conservatism Malcolm approved of from the Christian-social traditions of continental Europe, which he disapproved of. Christian Democracy, in its French and German variants, had reawakened a European spirit of political universalism and deflected the European Union from its narrower, nation-to-nation purposes.

Many of the conference papers, published in *Conservative Realism* (1996), rued the present-day flatness and exhaustion of right-wing thought, frozen as it seemed between faith in the market and old conservative allegiances. Not so Malcolm, who in his paper, "Conservative Realism and Christian Democracy," made a stalwart conservative defense of the economically liberal status quo together with a tempered nationalism.

Malcolm's "realist" conservatism was skeptical about the improvability of human nature, mindful of "economic realities," and clearheaded about the limits of political action to alter those realities. Above all, the realist conservative, as opposed to the moral-minded conservative, recognized the special character of politics and the autonomy of the political sphere. "For a conservative (and especially for a conservative realist)," Malcolm wrote, "the existence of a nation state, implying both the existence of a genuine political community and the exercise on behalf of that community of the final political authority known as sovereignty, is not some easily adjustable contingent fact but a crucial—rather, the crucial—feature of our political landscape."

Malcolm (who among many distinctions is an eminent scholar of Hobbes) was presenting here a Hobbesian picture of politics in which the ideas *political community, nation state,* and *final authority (sovereignty)* interlocked: without final authority, no state; without a state, no community. Working backward up that chain, community implied a state, which implied sovereignty. For Britain to yield up supreme authority to the European Union would be to weaken the British state, and weakening the British state would undermine the political community. Britain, in short, formed a political community only to the extent that it was subject to a single, undisputed authority.

Conservative realism, on Malcolm's neo-Hobbesian account could maintain, whereas Christian Democracy could not, a "clear or workable distinction between politics and morality." By morality, Malcolm had in mind the social-justice thinking of Catholics such as Emmanuel Mounier and Jacques Maritain, which was given papal encouragement in the 1930s. When taking economic liberalism for an illness, the Roman church in the 1890s had judged socialism worse. The encyclical *Quadragesimo anno* (1931), by contrast, put "economic individualism and the collectivism of expropriation and state ownership," in Malcolm's words, into "deeply misleading" symmetry. The later encyclical, that is, took each as bad as the other. That falsified the facts in Malcolm's view. Reviled "economic individualism" in truth brought prosperity so long as everyone pursued their own economic interests in a frame of common rules and a "community of practices and law." Mass poverty arose when "economic individualism" was interfered with in the name of social justice or fair wages, and so made to malfunction. Malcolm's was a coherent defense of inegalitarian, national-minded free marketry with an untroubled conscience.

Malcolm made a discreet but telling concession to the demands of morality, in line with Hayek and Marshall before him, although the concession had an instrumental feel. The morals in question were useful to order and efficiency. To share its bounty, Malcolm argued, "economic individualism" had to function not only within a "community of practices and law" but also in a "frame of common rules for conduct." Bankers and business people, that is, had to behave well, at least to each other. They had to keep their word and not defraud. Whether "common rules for conduct" applied for what, if anything, bankers and business people owed to society, Marshall thought they did, Hayek thought they didn't. Malcolm here left the matter open.

He brushed back Christian Democratic hesitations about the Thatcher government's union reforms of the 1980s. It was no accident that Malcolm, who later became an eloquent Brexiteer, was speaking as Jacques Delors completed his ten years as EU Commission president. An ex-finance minister, Delors had led and secularized France's leading Catholic trade union. As head of the commission, Delors pushed through the charter of labor rights that irked Britain's Conservatives and provoked Thatcher's Bruges speech in which she said she had not rolled back the frontiers of the state only to see them reimposed by a European superstate.

Malcolm pressed his liberal conservative rejection of social-minded Christian Democracy further. Its picture of politics, he wrote, came down from premodern scholastic thought, which "envisage[d] a hierarchy—almost a continuum—of levels of human co-operation or 'community'—the family, the extended family, the circle of friends, the wider social group, the local community, the regional community, the nation, the family of nations, the world." Authority, on such schemes, was a mere tool for the common good, however big or small the commonality. On the medievalizing picture Malcolm objected to, there was "no *qualitative* distinction . . . between the authority of the chairman of a tiddly-winks society, who guards and promotes the common good of that association, and the authority of the president of a republic." That failure to recognize the distinctiveness of supreme authority in a political community was, to Malcolm's mind, the explanation of the "enthusiasm of Christian Democrats for extending authority upwards to a new, European level." For them, there was nothing special about any particular level in this hierarchy, such as the level of national government.

In democratic times, the political community exercised control over who exercised authority through elections. Europe's "democratic deficit" had arisen with a shift of authority upward without a corresponding shift in democratic control. Member nations were betwixt and between. They could press for democratic control in a European state, they could withdraw and recover the balance between sovereignty and democracy at the national level, or they could accept the present half-way house. In defense of that third option was a subtler view of the democratic deficit. Exercise of national sovereignty was indeed constrained by the membership of the EU. However, protection and freedom of maneuver vis-à-vis larger sovereign powers—the United States, China, for example—was greater for middle-sized nations in a larger whole. European voters did not have direct control over the exercise of Europe-level powers, but they did in its intergovernmental operation.

Malcolm's conservative appeal to democracy, like the appeal to corporate ethics, was instrumental, not a matter of principle. The concern of the conservative was for what served or disserved the health and stability of the political community. "Conservatism viewed in the most long-term historical perspective," Malcolm wrote, "is not necessarily tied to liberal democracy, but present-day conservatism values liberal-democratic institutions as the most reliable way of maintaining the health of a political community."

By contrast with Malcolm, the American conservative libertarian Jason Brennan was more direct and less forgiving about democracy, especially elections. A leading aim of politics, on Brennan's view, was to promote prosperity by promoting free markets. Electoral democracy, on Brennan's view, thwarted that aim. Versed in the study of elections, Brennan was troubled by how little voters know. In *Against Democracy* (2016), he revived doubts aired by Schumpeter about the compatibility of liberal capitalism with electoral democracy. Brennan was no longer confident that the rights to good and limited government enjoyed by each citizen were still adequately protected from ignorant majorities. Brennan defended "epistocracy," that is, competent government by those who knew what they were doing as opposed to incompetent government confirmed by voters who didn't know what they were voting for or why. He was open-minded about how epistocracy was to be applied. Local experiment, double votes, knowledge tests, and insulating economics from democratic control were offered in a spirit of open-minded suggestion. Brennan's sharply argued critique of electoral democracy may fairly be thought of as the scholastic side of voter-suppression movements. It has a long American pedigree, left and right, but has drawn most notice recently in Republican efforts to get poor voters off the registers.

There is no better thinker with which to end this brief survey of how conservatives defend right-wing liberalism than David Willetts. His intellectual journey exemplifies the trials of the reasonable conservative buffeted by anger and impatience on either side. Willetts began as a radical free-marketeer but turned, with age and experience, into a troubled centrist. Willetts worked at the Treasury (1978–84) and fed the government with novel policies, including paying for public works and public services with a mix of public and private financing. He was a Tory MP (1992–2015) and frequent author. Three books of his, *Modern Conservatism* (1992), *Is Conservatism Dead?* (1997), and *The Pinch* (2010), suffice to track his political path. The first was confident that Thatcher Toryism had to a degree cured postwar Britain's worst socioeconomic ills. The second, which appeared as Labour buried his party in an electoral landslide, worried about the conflicts between community and market. The third was a nonpartisan, future-of-our-children book about the problems of aging populations, taxes, pensions, housing, and social mobility through the cycle of life that all rich nations are facing. Willetts was too intelligent and experienced in politics to dismiss the force of large ideas or the need for framing narratives, yet he had grasped how in time a large idea and framing narrative—call it Thatcherism—had become desiccated and had outlived its usefulness. Rather than propose a new conservative large idea, Willetts has chosen to focus in nonpartisan spirit on present ills and unmet repairs that are needed in the prevailing frame. It is as if he saw that to reclaim intellectual high ground, conservatives would first have to re-earn its reputation for prudence and sound government. Nor was reputation all that was at stake. Without prudence and sound government, liberal conservatism would be further battered from within by an angry, unreconciled hard right.

Coda

Choices for the Right

We are living in an era of the right. But which right is that? For what tradition do conservatives speak? Which conservatives is it who are now to control the tradition? On one side are liberal conservatives, who did much to create and sustain liberal democracy after 1945. On the other is an illiberal hard right, an odd alliance of hyper-liberal globalists and one-nation conservatives claiming to speak for "the people."

The left is everywhere in retreat. The old center-left parties of Europe are rapidly losing support. The European left's commitment to socialism in any historically meaningful sense was abandoned half a century ago. That grand tradition survives at most in largely aestheticized form within the humanities departments of universities, including the United States, where socialism as a political movement never gained traction. Save when the economic system is threatened with collapse, American Democrats repeatedly prove wary of Keynesian, welfarist, or social-democratic policies, misleadingly called "socialist." In the absence of effective party-political or intellectual opposition from the left, partisan argument is being reshaped by a fight among conservatives for control of their tradition.

Drawing on critics of the French Revolution, the first conservatives early in the nineteenth century spoke for social unity and the authority of custom, both of which were under threat, as they feared, from capitalism and from its political champion, liberalism. They believed neither in liberal progress nor democratic equality. As heirs of aristocratic rulers who had been used to giving orders rather than explaining themselves, the first conservatives were impatient with public argument and slow to accept that they needed ideas and intellectuals of their own.

By the late nineteenth century, mainstream conservatives made historic compromises. They slowly accepted electoral democracy. To fend off economic democracy (socialism, unionism, social democracy, or welfarism in some combination and strength), they allied with right-wing liberals, who were equally afraid of the economic challenge from the left. Between 1880 and 1945, a new political animal, the liberal conservative (or conservative liberal) emerged. Mainstream conservatives organized themselves in parties of the center-right. They were flanked by two kinds of dissent from within the right: conservatives on the party fringes who refused to compromise with the liberal-democratic status quo, and conservative critics, outside party politics and often indifferent to policy, who found ugly or unethical the liberal-modern world that political conservatives were helping to create.

Under popular pressure, the center-right gradually accepted social reforms and welfarism, especially after 1945. When the social-liberal consensus overpromised, ran out of money, and came to grief in the inflation of the 1970s, the center-right adopted a zealous free marketry of liberty for business, small budgets, and open borders. That radical consensus in turn came to grief in the new century, leaving a party-political and intellectual gap on the right into which the hard right poured.

As an amalgam of populists and libertarians, the hard right, like the ancient chimera, ought strictly not to exist. The populists want more welfare for an exclusive, national "us." They want less of a voice for parliament and elected representatives and more say directly for themselves, with less for experts and so-called elites. The libertarians want to shrink welfare capitalism or drop it altogether and to give ignorant voters not more say but less. One side calls for the shelter of a national home, the other heeds the authority of global markets. Both promise security, although in different ways. Business and banks are promised the security of not being interfered with and being at liberty to move themselves and their assets where they wish. People are promised a longed-for familiarity of life— steady work, cohesive neighborhoods, the sense of a nation with clear borders—that many fear has vanished, perhaps for good. For politicians of the shaken center, whether left or right, to console themselves that neither promise is really deliverable and that each conflicts with the other would be complacent. The unreconciled right, as this book has shown, is resourceful at turning apparent incoherences to advantage.

When Schumpeter, the ironist, asked if capitalism could survive democracy, he answered his own question, "Yes, if," before listing, as was seen, several demanding conditions. In the present climate, Schumpeter's question can be turned around. Can liberal democracy survive capitalism? The question does not presume that there is at present a noncapitalist alternative. It assumes, rather, that capitalism is here to stay for now and that conservatives must accordingly make a choice. Do they side with the hard right and leave liberal democracy to the mercies of uncontrolled markets and national populism? Or do they look for allies with whom to rebuild a shaken center?

Appendix A

CONSERVATIVE KEYWORDS

CLOAKING AND UNMASKING: Society gives the naked, unfinished human a second nature that cloaks the animal character. "Society is founded upon cloth" (Carlyle). It is dangerous to rip off the "cloak of custom" (Burke). Unmaskers (for example, followers of Marx, Nietzsche, Freud, evolutionary psychology, natural-science reductivism) neglect the danger.

CONSERVATISM: Modern practice of politics dating from the early nineteenth century in competition first with predemocratic liberalism then with democratic liberalism, which conservatism reluctantly accepts but seeks to temper.

CONSERVATISM'S HISTORY: Gradual conquest of a liberal modernity in which conservatives cannot feel at home. The tension between accepting and resisting liberal modernity makes for an unending contest among conservatives for ownership of their own tradition.

CONSERVATISM'S OUTLOOK: Belief in social unity; trust in established power; doubt as to desirability or achievability of progress; disbelief in people's equality and respect instead for merit, rank, and property; low expectations of people, hence of political action. Schematically, the conservative outlook contrasts, point for point, with the guiding ideas of liberalism (see "liberalism's outlook"). Conservatives' disbelief in equality and low expectations of people underlies their suspicion of democracy, whether electoral, economic, or in ethics and culture.

DECLINE: Conservative deflation of liberal hopes for human progress can, without needing to, take historical form in the dismal claim that the present is reliably worse than the past, the present likely to be better than the future. Asked "How you doin'?" the conservative declinist replies, "Oh, average. Worse than yesterday, better than tomorrow."

DEMOCRACY: Liberalism's political promises extended to everyone, whoever they are. Political democracy promises everyone the protections of votes and voice against state power; economic democracy promises everyone protections against the power of wealth and the market (but see "economic democracy"); cultural democracy promises everyone a final say in ethical and cultural judgments, free of legal or tutelary interference. Democracy universalizes conservative doubts about liberalism: already suspect when made for a few, liberalism's promises are considered to be destructive or undeliverable when extended democratically to all.

ECONOMIC DEMOCRACY: Roughly, an economic stake for all. When extended to all, democratically, protection from wealth is of nonliberal (socialist) or liberal (reformist) kind. In nonliberal forms economic democracy denies protection *for* wealth. (At the extreme, the state or society owns all; there is no private property.) In liberal form, economic democracy protects everyone *from* wealth. It also offers protection *for* wealth from state and society. Since 1945, democratic liberalism has presumed economic democracy, though the strength of the latter (more market? more society?) is fought over. (See "hyper-liberalism.")

ECONOMIC LIBERALISM: Protections *for* wealth, capital, and enterprise from the interfering power of state and society. As wealth confers power, such liberalism also promises, or ought to promise, protections *from* wealth.

EQUALITY: People, to conservatives, are not and will not become equal. Talents, energies, and capacities vary. There is no entitlement to equal resources or equal social respect. People are of equal moral worth and should be treated equally at law, but equalizing rewards and outcomes misses its aim and disturbs social order.

ESTABLISHMENT: A familiar conservative chain of argument rests social order on authoritative power, authoritative power on established institutions (those that have stood a test of time), and established institutions on unquestioning, unstinting allegiance. If politics is held to forswear aims besides preserving social order, establishment becomes "the internal aim of politics" (Scruton).

EXPERIENCE: A philosophical cudgel for use against liberal intellectuals. For many conservatives, experience is a surer guide in politics than "theories" or "abstract" ideas. Experience, so understood, explains itself in a loop. Experience (political knowledge) comes not from repeatable lab experiments (impossible) or empirical data mining (deceptive) but from experience (past activity). Once old and repeated enough, experience (past activity) becomes custom (which embodies knowledge). Its origins, though not its content, are by then forgotten.

FAMILY: With law and property, a vital constituent of a stable, orderly society.

FASCISM, AUTHORITARIANISM, AND CONSERVATISM: As a totalitarianism, fascism is not on the right-left spectrum of liberal modern politics under view in this book. Authoritarianism lies on that spectrum, at its outer right edge. Authoritarians deny democratic representation but allow economic, and some cultural, diversity. They rely for control on fear and passive acquiescence. Fascists exploit one-party representation, deny all diversity, and rely for control on fear and popular mobilization. "Conservative fascist" is a contradiction in terms, unlike "conservative authoritarian."

HARD RIGHT: As distinct from center-right, a segment of conservatism that rejects one or more core elements of the liberal-democratic status quo. An unstable tactical alliance of free-market hyper-liberals and popular anti-liberals, the hard right claims to speak for "the people" against "the elites." It is called "hard," not "new," because its themes are old; and "hard," not "far" or "extreme," because since 1980, it has drawn off votes from the center-right to join the mainstream.

HAVES AND HAVE-NOTS: Like any political tradition, conservatism serves interests. Among the many interests it serves, property stands out. Conservatives, to that extent, are, first of all, the party of the haves. Since the forms property that can take are many and who owns property changes, identifying the haves and how to defend them is not always easy for the right. (See "private property.")

HUMAN NATURE: People, to conservatives, are imperfect and not much improvable. Their knowledge of themselves, society, and each other is limited. They are partial, undersupplied with fellow feeling and ill-suited to self-government. That unexalted, broadly dismal view of people is held to give conservatives an edge over opponents. "Human nature: We conservatives understood and understand it; the socialists didn't and generally still don't" (Margaret Thatcher).

HYPER-LIBERALISM: In economic life, radical denial or disregard of society's and the state's say over how wealth's power is exercised. Often used interchangeably with "neoliberalism." (See "libertarians.")

IMPERFECTION: Political action is imperfect because humans are, and neither is much improvable. Although conservatives are broadly happy with this dismal view, they are cautious in applying it to themselves. It sits ill with their claims to superior prudence. It is awkward in the democratic marketplace, where the "least awful alternative" is a poor sell.

INNOVATION AND CHANGE: Conservatives fight for tradition by seeking to pick out and hold on to established values in the rush of change. At the same time, they embrace capitalism, modernity's great engine of change. The contest of innovation and establishment runs through the conservative story.

LAND AND COUNTRYSIDE: For conservatives in Romantic, anti-urban vein, the countryside is a place of virtue, stability, and harmony. Early celebrants were William Cobbett and Wilhelm Riehl.

LIBERALISM: Modern practice of politics dating from the early nineteenth century opposed by conservatism and soon confronted by democracy.

LIBERALISM'S OUTLOOK: Society is diverse and conflicted materially and morally; power, even authoritative power, is to be resisted notably by countervailing power; social improvement (progress) is achievable and desirable; everyone deserves respect from state and society regardless of merit, rank or property. Liberals have high expectations of people, hence of politics. Understood as unending public argument, politics is needed and effective for stabilizing an open, competitive society. Resisting power and showing civic respect are, for liberals, correlates. One calls on people to support institutions and traditions that entrench protections from power. The other calls on state, wealth, and society to honor that forbearance.

LIBERAL MODERNITY: See "modernity."

LIBERTARIANS: Extreme liberals who deny society or the state a say in people's options and choices. If economic, they may be left (unwilling to defend property) or right (unwilling to impose on property). Cultural libertarians deny the state or society any ethical or cultural say.

LIMITS OF POLITICS: On a quietist picture favored by many but not all conservatives, the effectiveness of political action is limited, the scope of political responsibilities small, and the part of politics in a sensible person's life minor. "The man who puts politics first is not fit to be called a civilised being" (Quintin Hogg).

MODERATE-RADICAL: Distinction marking a style or manner of politics, not a political practice, outlook, or character type. Conservatives can be moderate or radical. The contrast is adverbial, not substantive. Radicals act zealously, with a view to silencing opposition in total victory. Moderates act temperately, with a view to compromise, able to live with failure. Neither manner works everywhere or always. Radicals can be overaggressive, driving change too far; moderates feeble and weak, failing to act when needed. "All that legitimists legitimize is revolution" (Metternich, on radical monarchists).

MODERNITY: Condition of society from late eighteenth century, marked by rapid growth of population, spread of industrial and then finance capitalism, division of labor, literacy, and mobility. Intellectually, a climate of ideas marked by secularization and enlightened thought.

Modernity cut loose natural science from the divine and the supernatural; philosophy from alone explaining the world; morality from the task of human redemption; law from the putative universal order of nature. Modernity entered political thought *via* Machiavelli and Hobbes, who lifted from rulers any duty beyond ensuring a safe, stable frame for people to flourish in and pursue worldly concerns. To liberals, modernity was a liberation, to conservatives a loss of anchorage and human shelter for which they blamed liberals, hence the term, "liberal modernity." "Many old works become fragments. Many modern works start out as fragments" (Friedrich Schlegel).

NATION: Of ways to tie together the ideas, *nation, society, state*, conservatives, with exceptions, tend to stick with that sequence. First, the nation is imagined ancestrally, as a distinct body of people with a common origin, or culturally, with common beliefs, attachments, and memories. The nation then forms a stable society, from which emerge states and citizens. "True politics can only be sustained by a great national existence" (Leopold von Ranke).

ORGANIC METAPHOR: Treating society "organically" as a "living whole" can make various points, mostly negative: society's origin is "natural," not made or planned; its pattern of change is slow and without sudden breaks; in composition, society and members are interdependent; as to purposes, society is not an instrument for its members several uses; society, rather, has ways of working and sustaining itself not fixed by interests or choices of its members.

PEOPLE, "THE PEOPLE": An imagined being, variously thought of as a citizenry, a populace, the common folk, or a nation.

POPULISM: A style of political self-justification. To use its own contentious language, populism is an "elite" phenomenon. It arises in a contest among politicians in which one side, the populist side, claims to speak for the people. "Populism is a permanent shadow of representative democracy and a constant peril" (Jan-Werner Mueller).

PRACTICE: As a historical practice, politics is pursued in various ways. Conservatism (like liberalism and socialism) are local, modern ways. Each has exemplary followers or "practitioners"—politicians, thinkers, think tanks, press, donors, voters—with an outlook of aims and ideals to guide them. Conservatism has an outlook but is not itself an outlook. Political practices could be called "traditions"; outlooks, "ideologies." It depends on ear. Political practices are invariably fought over by their adepts. They are, in the philosopher Simon Evnine's phrase "endemically contested entities."

PRESCRIPTION: In law, the defendable claim to a resource based not on explicit title of ownership but on long, uncontested use or possession. In politics, a way to justify prevailing arrangements. If "abstract" tests for norms or institutions (e.g., justice; social utility) are ruled out, then long, uncontested use may be held to legitimize, because, so it is held, survival indicates utility. Once a long-accepted arrangement starts to disserve social order, conservatives must decide if or not it should be kept. They have then to rely on intuition (hunch) or on a proscribed "abstract" test of present utility.

PRIVATE PROPERTY: Like law and the family, private property to conservatives is vital for social order. It averts a ceaseless war for life's resources. It creates duties for the haves and aspirations for have-nots. Requiring that there *be* property is consistent with changing particular *distributions* of property. As defenders of the haves, however, conservatives tend to accept prevailing distributions by default, arguing that redistributive interference is ineffective or destabilizing. (See "Haves and have-nots.")

PROGRESS: In sense of broad improvement to people or society, conservatives generally deny the achievability of progress. It is elusive, on their count, either because desired improvement cannot be made; because the change proves bad, not good; or because change causes something worse elsewhere. A conservative "is enamored of existing evils, as distinguished from the liberal, who wishes to replace them with others" (Bierce).

RIGHT-LEFT: Dividing line on the field of modern political competition, regularly declared redundant or hard to see but durable and seemingly indispensable. To start with, conservatives occupied the right of the field, liberals the left. When democrats joined the contest, some liberals moved rightward to blur with liberal-minded conservatives. In this book, "the right" and "conservatives" are used interchangeably. To start, "right/conservative" and "left/liberal" marked one divide. In time, there were right-wing liberals, hence conservative liberals, or to say the same thing another way, liberal conservatives. The term "liberal conservative" was recognized early and is neither confused nor a contradiction in terms.

SCORN AND RAGE: Scorn is what conservatives standardly feel toward callow reformers and idealistic dreamers. Its typical modes are vituperation and satire, literary genres at which the right shines. Rage may be felt by conservatives toward themselves, torn as they are by responsibility and shame for the condition of modern societies that they both sustain and spurn. "Conservatives start out frustrated, progressives end in frustration" (Niklas Luhmann). "Rage is the characteristic political emotion of our time" (Peter Sloterdijk).

SECOND NATURE: Nurture, education, and society give unfinished, vulnerable humans a "second nature." The thought, noted by Aristotle, is common property, but is open to distinct conservative uses: to deny, in Burkean style, a common human nature, hence to cast doubt on (liberal) universal rights; to stress the social rootedness of people's aims and character, hence to suggest limits to (liberal) self-assertion and autonomy. Far from imprisoning people (the left postmodern view), social norms "unburden" them (Gehlen) from bewildering dependence and vulnerability.

SOCIAL UNITY: A well-ordered society is, for conservatives, united and to a degree cohesive. It is not, as liberals are held to claim, an aggregate of isolable, "atomic," and competitive people, nor on the socialist picture, a battlefield of classes at war. Conflict of interests and ideas is acknowledged but framed, not just by respect for law, but by common allegiances and social duty. Liberal conservatives and anti-liberal conservatives argue over how tight that frame should be.

STATE: On the liberal right, the say of the state should be final, but in its proper domain. Supreme power, that is, can be effective and unchallengeable without being unlimited or comprehensive. Less restrictive views of state power are common on the nonliberal, populist or authoritarian right.

TRADITION: What, of established, lasting value, conservatives seek to identify and preserve amid turbulent modern change. In a different sense, a tradition or practice of politics, for example, conservatism. Conservatism is a struggle for tradition in both senses: a taxing search for what to preserve amid the creative destruction of capitalism, and a fight among conservatives for ownership of their common tradition.

Appendix B

PHILOSOPHICAL SOURCES OF CONSERVATIVE THOUGHT

Conservatism is not a philosophy of politics. To treat it as one involves a confusion of levels between outlooks in politics and philosophical reflection on how outlooks are talked about and justified. The conservative outlook was fed, all the same, by a great drainage basin of general ideas about people, morality and society. A useful contrast from which to start a brief overflight is the broad commonplace that for liberals (following Rousseau), people are good, society bad, whereas for conservatives (following Burke), society is good and only mischievous liberals thought otherwise. Good people, Rousseau thought, could perfect a flawed society. For Burke, society was needed to restrain imperfect people. So far, so simple.

Early sources of conservative thoughts and reusable arguments in their defense can be found throughout the Western canon. Plato disbelieved in people's equality and capacity for self-government. Aristotle stressed their natural sociability, the importance of property, and families. He preferred law-governed, constitutional arrangements to arbitrary rule and took ideal societies for illusory. Some forms of life, nevertheless, were superior to others. The highest form for Aristotle, a mixed life of ease, civic engagement, and contemplation, required a slave class, an early statement of the need for inequality.

Cicero took the Stoic view that the universe was orderly and intelligible, governed as it was by a natural law that fixed the operations of nature and hence guided human conduct (humans being by nature rational animals). The flourishing of critical thought in the Middle Ages produced lines of division later seized on by twentieth-century contestants as pre-echoes of their own disputes. Was the state a divine remedy for human wickedness and imperfection? Conservatives, looking back, tended to agree. Even if not divine, the remedial state was opaque to critical reason. Or was the state, as Occam and Marsiglio held, a human device shaped for human ends? Liberals, looking back, favored that thought, along with its suggestion that states could be fashioned by their citizens and that coercive law was the price people accepted for peace and order.

For Hooker, in the sixteenth century, natural law was a schema that different societies drew on in their own way, an idea looking forward to Montesquieu's anti-universalist view that apt political arrangements depended on climate, land, and people. Jean Bodin prefigured a "realist" conservative tradition of uncontested strong government that was nevertheless constrained by custom, law, and the requirement of toleration. Almost everyone accepted the immemorial wisdom that government relied on consent, but not everyone thought of consent in the same way. Some took the survival of institutions for evidence of consent, the burden of challenge resting with the challenger. For others, institutions needed to justify themselves in order to win consent. Möser, for example, attacked the centralizing reforms of a bureaucratic state justified by arguments from economic rationality on the ground that such arguments missed the hidden usefulness of seemingly pointless or outdated customs.

As for the question "Was x a conservative?," it is anachronistic of this or that philosopher before the nineteenth century, and often misleading afterward. Some have taken Hobbes to have been conservative because he stressed the primacy of lawful order and absoluteness of sovereignty. Others took him to have been no conservative at all but an authoritarian rationalist, if not a sinister, proto-Bolshevik. When Margaret Thatcher had the Gorbachevs to dinner at the British Embassy in Moscow in 1987, her Foreign Office brief described Raisa Gorbachev as a dedicated Marxist. In her memoir, Thatcher recorded what—half-jokingly?—she took for confirmation. On being shown the embassy's well-stocked library, Mrs. Gorbachev chose, from among the many fine books, to peruse Hobbes's *Leviathan*.

Hegel foxed twentieth-century thinkers who tried to pin on him a partisan or ideological label. To Popper, he was a totalitarian; to Rawls, "a moderately progressive reform-minded liberal"; to Scruton, a communitarian conservative. Hegel's heritage was disputed in his day by Right Hegelians, who took him to be saying that the march of freedom ended in a law-governed constitutional monarchy, and by Left Hegelians, who saw in the looming contest between capital and labor a continuation of history's motor struggle of master and slave. Between the left-socialist Hegel of class conflict and the right-liberal Hegel of person-blind unity in state-sanctioned law, loomed a third Hegel, that of appeal to ethical conservatives as source for their belief in the social roots of moral norms.

Kant, who wrote little directly on politics, was rarely placed in the conservative camp. In early-nineteenth-century German argument, he was suspected to be an enemy of established order. Kant took the British constitution for a despotic oligarchy and welcomed the French revolution. He was treated by some as a faith-corroding rationalist, even though he described his aim as setting reason's bounds to make room for faith and beauty. The German Neo-Kantians of the late nineteenth century divided into those whose first interest was securing Kantian foundations for natural science and those keener to defend the independent security of historical understanding. Later German-aware conservative thinkers (Collingwood, Scruton) stressed the irreducibility of history to natural science. When the anti-Utilitarian threads in Kant were revived in the twentieth century, it was by American liberals. Scruton, by contrast, found conservative consequences in Kant's emphasis on the imaginative, constructive powers of the human mind, especially as regards morals, art, and society.

As representatives of the haves, conservatives have never lacked for sophisticated high-level arguments for private property. They included Hegelian defenses of the institution itself. Property capacitated, Hegel thought, for without property people were not free to act nor were they fully responsible. William Blackstone had put a parallel brutally: the propertyless, having no defenses against the bullying of wealth and status, were easily bribed and suborned. Conservatives had also Hayekian prudential arguments against futile interference with the institution: successful redistribution of property presumed knowledge that was in principle unavailable. In Utilitarian spirit, conservatives could appeal to property's social benefits: private property served the public good by stabilizing society; it gave the haves a stake in the present order and the have-nots a hope of becoming haves. By giving life and content to civil law, property sustained a peaceable method of settling disputes that allowed society to be competitive without becoming explosive. If property was seen in Lockean spirit at its most general as whatever people owned by right, in a society without rights, every human interaction became in theory contestable, with the promise of unremitting discord. Historical experience, lastly, gave conservative inductive arguments for private property. Collective ownership, when tried at social scale, had not worked. It destabilized society without freeing or protecting its members. Private property proved better in the long run at increasing and spreading wealth.

A cautionary conclusion of that rapid overflight is that the labels "liberal" and "conservative" are political, not philosophical. The philosophers mentioned predated liberalism and conservatism. Few if any took themselves for strictly political thinkers. They all asked how statecraft, morality, and the nature of things might be fitted together philosophically, but not in ways that were liberal or conservative, although most at some time or other have been claimed by either side. Forcing past philosophers into present-day partisan boxes is a kind of intellectual ballot-stuffing.

Appendix C

CONSERVATIVE LIVES: A GAZETTEER

Politicians and Thinkers

1. Politicians

John Quincy Adams (1767–1848): US president (1825–29), secretary of state (1817–25), US senator (1803–8), and representative for Massachusetts (1831–48), American envoy to the Netherlands, Prussia, Russia, and Britain. A framer of the Monroe Doctrine, Adams stabilized his country's foreign position after renewed war with Britain and Spain's retreat from Latin America. Humorless, quick to anger, and self-disciplined, he kept a political diary for fifty years. A strict Calvinist, he believed God's grace was necessary to control his depraved nature. His father was president; a brother and two sons, all alcoholics, died young. As an early convert to anti-Federalism, Adams was wary of central government. As an anti-Jacksonian (after 1824), he came to fear popular democracy.

Konrad Adenauer (1876–1967): Catholic Rhinelander, Cologne's mayor for the Catholic Center Party (1917–33; 1945), and chancellor of West Germany (1949–63). Adenauer oversaw economic revival, Western integration, and reconciliation with France and Israel. He made Christian Democrats the dominant center-right party, kept Social Democrats at bay, and encouraged capital-labor peace in a "social-market economy." By ending nazification, he helped postpone a historical reckoning. Strategically, he broke recovering German sovereignty into stages: Western anchorage against Soviet pressure, ending allied occupation, reuniting the Germanys. To conservative critics, he sacrificed eastern lands, bowed to American interests, and cemented German division. A strong, prosperous West Germany, he answered, would prove too appealing for Easterners to resist. Socially conservative, he governed high-handedly and treated elections (despite four wins) as regrettable necessities. Reconciled to liberal democracy, Adenauer had conservative qualms about modernity. Against massification, materialism, and atheism, the best arms, he believed, were patience, public accountability, and civic courage.

Stanley Baldwin (1867–1947): Three times British Conservative prime minister (1923–24; 1924–29; 1935–37). Baldwin deflected the General Strike, deputized as government leader through the Depression, held off a noisy hard right, and, by stage-managing a royal abdication shored up esteem for the monarchy. Although a free trader, Baldwin gave in to high-tariff Tories, favored the richer South and Midlands over the poorer North, and failed (like others) on Hitler. He avoided confrontations (rebuffing, for example, Churchill's call for force against strikers), presumed adversaries were open to compromise, and, in radio speeches and popular writings, updated the one-nation image of conservatism as the commonsense, nondivisive creed for all classes. Baldwin's picture of an island people at ease with itself and insulated from the world belied the social and geopolitical facts but gave imaginative backbone to later Conservatives in disputes over Britain's strategic place. Less a buffer than depicted, Baldwin exemplified the conservative as a right-wing liberal.

Theo von Bethmann-Hollweg (1856–1921): Nonparty conservative from a family of high officials and professors; German chancellor (1909–17). Diplomacy and war occupied his time as chancellor. Bethmann sought to avert a war that his hesitations helped start. Britain's wish to stay ahead dashed his hopes for naval detente. He failed to restrain Austria from attacking Serbia (July 1914). The September Program drafted in Bethmann's office was, to critics, a long-planned strategy for domination; to defenders, a wish list to rationalize unwanted war. Against his advice, hawks rebuffed American mediation (1917). When a Social Democrat peace resolution passed the Reichstag, Bethmann resigned (July 1917), his career and world at an end.

Georges Bidault (1899–1983): *Résistant* and rival to de Gaulle as the postwar leader of the Catholic, anti-Vichy right, Bidault swung from France's equivalent of Christian Democracy, his Mouvement Républicain Populaire, to the obdurate far right defending the Organisation Armée Secrète, which fought Algerian independence with terror in France. A prewar contributor to the anti-fascist Catholic *L'Aube*, he had, unlike de Gaulle, no truck with the Maurrasian right. To escape prosecution for his OAS support, Bidault fled France, returning, amnestied but discredited (1968). Nevertheless, his MRP stamped the postwar French right, with its Catholic social engagement, strong statism, union rights, tempered Europeanism, and paternal colonialism.

Bernhard von Bülow (1849–1929): Together with his friend Phillip Eulenburg and his mentor Friedrich Holstein, sphinx of the foreign office, Bülow dominated policy making in the early 1900s. Foreign secretary (1897–1900) and German chancellor (1900–1909), Bülow replaced Bismarck's questioning view of colonies with frank imperialism, demanding Germany's "place in the sun." Politically, he sought a liberal-conservative bloc to shut out the Social Democrats. Although grain tariffs (1902) pleased the Junkers, they foiled Bülow's attempted tax reforms. Witty in private, he was blustery and provocative in speeches, telling the Reichstag (1899) that the "struggle for existence" required armed might and that the German people would now be either "hammer or anvil."

Henry Cabot Lodge (1850–1924): Aloof, learned, upper-crust Bostonian who foiled Wilson over US membership in the League of Nations. A party loyalist, Lodge backed the corrupt Republican Blaine against Mugwump reformers (1884) and the incumbent Taft against his own friend Roosevelt (1912). Conservative in outlook he opposed open immigration and progressive reform but backed a failed bill to protect black voters. His aim was to make America ("the world's best hope") a global power with a strong navy. Unilateralist, not isolationist, Lodge wanted a liberal world order on American terms without treaty commitments. He backed war with Spain and a commercial "open door" in China.

George Canning (1770–1827): The younger Pitt's most brilliant follower, epitomizing a new type, the publicist-politician. Canning's father failed at business, and his mother had been an actress. He rose by brains. His weekly *Anti-Jacobin* (1797–98) pilloried radicalism and beat the war drum. As foreign secretary (1807–9; 1822–27), Canning counselled against alliances, disengaged Britain from Europe, and promoted independence in Spanish America, opening it to British trade. Backing Catholic emancipation and parliamentary reform, Canning might have united liberal Tories and conservative Whigs, but he died suddenly (1827). His conservatism combined shrewdness with unreasoned attachment to nation: "We avow ourselves to be partial to the country in which we live."

Joseph Cannon (1836–1926): Congressman from Illinois (1873–1923, with gaps), and conservative holdover from the Gilded Age who as domineering Speaker of the House (1903–11) blocked reforms sought by Progressive Republicans. Small, unpolished, and pugnacious, "Uncle Joe" Cannon kept an iron grip on committee assignments to ensure that no reform bills pressed by supporters of President Roosevelt under George Norris in the House sneaked past his conservative Old Guard. Roosevelt's Republican successor Taft (1909) hoped to use Cannon, but Democrats allied with the Progressive Republicans united to break Cannon's power and the House's conservative veto on change, permitting in time the wide-scale reforms of Wilson's first administration (1913–17).

Chambord (1820–83): Henri d'Artois, known as Comte de Chambord, was a Legitimist intriguer against the Third Republic and the last of three claimants to a vanished French throne, the first two being the Orleanist, Louis Philippe's son, who died accidentally (1842), and the Bonapartist, Napoleon III's son, who was killed fighting Zulus for the British (1879). The "miracle child" Chambord was born seven months after the murder of his father, Duc de Berry, son of the last Bourbon king. After 1870, Chambord hoped to return from a forty-year exile. Calls for a legitimist coup went unheard. Obstinate and out of touch, Chambord believed that "monarchy always led the working classes." He was said not to know how to tie his shoelaces.

Winston Churchill (1874–1965): For the English-speaking right, Churchill occupies a party-political place like Burke's in ideas: exemplary, contested, and unassailable. First Conservative, then Liberal, then Conservative, Churchill held high offices of state from 1908 and was twice prime minister (1940–45; 1951–55). Blunder and failure dogged him in office, as did alcohol, depression, and personal debt. With luck and determination, he was never bested. Churchill won censure by the decade: military calamity (1915), mismanaging sterling (1925), imperial nostalgia and ambiguity on resisting fascism (1930s), and another military calamity (Norway). Once wartime leader (May 1940), he communicated an indomitable will to resist while leaning for strategy on military advisers and for home affairs on Labour ministers. As premier (1951–55), Churchill was chairman of the board, when Conservatives, learning from Labour, pursued social provision and house building in a fast-growing economy. Indifferent to party and impatient with doctrine, Churchill claimed always to have been a liberal.

Henry Clay (1777–1852): Anti-Jacksonian Whig, conservative nationalist, and promoter of the American System (tariffs, federal works, national bank). The Virginia-born, Clay inherited a Kentucky slave plantation. He was Speaker of the House, a US senator, or a representative from Kentucky (1806–52, with gaps). Favoring slow emancipation and return to Africa, Clay, like his party, failed the challenge of slavery. A border politician known as "Harry of the West," he was the "great conciliator" to admirers, a principleless dealmaker to foes. Of eleven children, all six daughters died early. Three sons were either mad or alcoholic. His favorite son died in the Mexican War for Western expansion, which he opposed.

Calvin Coolidge (1872–1933): In liberal demonology, a wooden totem in the do-nothing interlude separating Progressivism (1910s–1920s) and New Dealism (1930s–1940s). Vermont-born

Coolidge was president (1923–29) between the scandal-wracked Harding and the semiliberal Hoover. A small-government, pro-business Republican, Coolidge sent troops to end a
police strike when Massachusetts governor. As president he won income tax cuts and, amid
strong economic growth, revenues rose. Laconic in person, Coolidge in speeches suggested
unreflecting confidence in a providential nation, "reverence" for "great men," and placid
acceptance of wealth if it was taken for "means and not the end." Reagan hung Coolidge's
portrait in the Oval Office.

François Coty (Spoturno) (1874–1934): Corsican-born journalist and perfume manufacturer,
anti-Semite, and paymaster for far-right causes in the 1920s and 1930s. In 1922, he gained
control of *Le Figaro* and in 1928 launched *L'Ami du peuple*, a cheap newspaper aimed at the
working class. It attacked the political parties, spread anti-Semitic venom, praised Mussolin-
ian fascism, and called for a Bonapartist strong man to take control in France. Coty's scent
fortune supported for a time the Faisceau (1925). In 1933, he founded Solidarité Française,
a paramilitary body, which took part in the anti-parliamentary riot (1934). Together with
other militant leagues, both were banned by the Blum government (1936).

Charles Coughlin (1891–1979): Hard-right Catholic radio priest (1930s) heard across the nation.
Cut off by his network when the family homilies turned political, Coughlin was popular
enough to broadcast alone. He turned against the New Deal, railed against bankers (notably
Jewish bankers), and as an America Firster, helped kill American membership in the World
Court (1935). He backed a hapless right-populist against Roosevelt (1936) and opposed
entry into the war. Pro-Hitler broadcasts (1940) shriveled his following. His church de-
barred him from politics (1942), and his paper, *Social Justice*, was denied federal mails.
Coughlin remained pastor at Detroit's Shrine of the Little Flower until retirement.

Charles de Gaulle (1890–1970): French soldier and president exemplifying the political forces
of will and myth. After a brave failed stand against German forces (1940), he embodied, in
London exile, a ghostly Free France. On liberation (1944), he averted Allied occupation of
France and won a French sector in occupied Germany. As provisional government leader
(1944–46), his desired constitution was rejected, and he retired. Prime minister during the
Algerian crisis (1958), he introduced a new, president-strong constitution and ceded Algeria,
both approved by referendum. He oversaw African decolonization, creation (with US help)
of a nuclear arsenal, and French integration in Europe. Contrary gestures—against NATO,
the EEC, and Cold War Westernism—were reversed in time. Theater aside, Gaullist France
was Atlanticist, European, and anti-Soviet. Gangly and aloof, he detested party politics and
treated his ministers autocratically, although when thwarted he walked away (1946; 1969).
Hard to label, he was like much of France: right tinged but centrist.

Marcel Déat (1894–1955): Journalist convinced that decadent France was no match for energized
fascist nations. A clever pupil of liberal professors, Déat was a left-wing appeaser who turned
to the hard right. He called for accommodation with Germany, opposed intervention in
Spain, questioned the Franco-Soviet pact, and penned (May 1939) the piece urging France
not to honor its promises to Poland, "Mourir pour Dantzig?" Déat by then competed with
Doriot's PPF and Bucard's Francistes for pro-fascist support. In Vichy, Déat's party was more
Nazi in language and symbolism, and he was labor minister (1944) before fleeing to
Germany.

Jacques Doriot (1898–1945): A French migrant from Communism to fascism, Doriot, a metal-worker's son, was a popular deputy for St Denis, a working-class suburb of Paris (1928–38). Communist slowness in face of the Nazi threat alarmed him and he called for left unity. When the Communists themselves called for popular fronts (1934), Doriot was punished with expulsion for being right too early. Communism now became his main foe and he moved to the right, founding the Parti Populaire Français (1936). Sidelined in Vichy, he led a French "anti-Bolshevik" brigade in Russia. On escaping to Germany, Doriot died when an allied plane strafed his car.

Dwight Eisenhower (1890–1969): Supreme allied commander in Europe and Republican president (1953–61). A golf-playing do-nothing to Democrats and a New Dealer to Taft Republicans, Eisenhower presided over the post-1945 consolidation of American power. He pursued "containment" of the Soviet Union (when hawks wanted "rollback"), accepted a draw in Korea, sat quiet over Hungary (1956), and sought détente with Khrushchev. He countermanded the ill-conceived Franco-British intervention at Suez but approved a bungled American invasion of Cuba, as well as coups in Guatemala and Iran. Eisenhower let the red-baiting McCarthy ruin himself. Quiet on segregation, he made Earl Warren chief justice and ordered federal troops in Arkansas (1957) to enforce the court's desegregation ruling. A defender of small budgets, he let Democratic congresses spend. His federal highways transformed politics by helping create suburbia. Of the center-right, he cared little for party or doctrine but showed the prudent conservatism of not fighting battles he would not win.

Philipp zu Eulenburg (1847–1921): Aide and friend to "William the Sudden," Kaiser Wilhelm II, adversary of the more liberal post-Bismarck chancellors, and victim of a homophobic press campaign that brought about his fall (1908) in a libel trial more grueling than Oscar Wilde's. Eulenburg was a mainstay of the Kaiser's personal rule, notably in foreign policy, semi-formalized in the late 1890s, which Max Weber likened to driving a train at speed without knowing if the points ahead had been switched. With a household of 2,320, the court had little check on its actions or budget, which was higher than those of the chancellery, foreign office, and federal courts together.

S. J. Field (1816–99): Influential Supreme Court justice who upheld business freedom from regulatory and union demands but who left the legal-moral blight of racial discrimination untouched. An economic liberal and social conservative, appointed by Lincoln, Field in his thirty-six-year-term fashioned from the due-process clauses of the Constitution (Fifth and Fourteenth Amendments) a new doctrinal weapon, substantive due process, to use against social legislation by the states. Due procedure protected people from the wrongful exercise of law; substantive due process, from wrongful laws, albeit lawfully enacted, that injured people's rights. The weapon was two-edged, wieldable by conservatives for laissez-faire and by liberals for civil rights.

Pierre Flandin (1889–1958): As leader of the center-right Alliance Démocratique from 1932, a stubborn advocate of austerity and appeasement. From a family of well-off professionals, he trained as a pilot before 1914. Briefly premier (1934–35), he opposed French mobilization when Germany remilitarized the Rhineland, welcomed the Munich Agreement, and opposed war in 1939. Again, as briefly acting premier in the Vichy regime, he left for unoccupied Algeria (October 1942), where the Free French arrested and interned him. He was punished with the suspension of his civil rights (1946), which were returned to him seven years later, permitting him to serve as a departmental councillor in Yonne.

Robert Gascoyne-Cecil, Marquess of Salisbury (1830–1903): Erudite, patrician architect of a Conservative party that spoke for business and finance, honored old attachments (crown, Lords, church), and made itself popular enough among voters to become the leading party in Britain for much of the twentieth century. With its three premierships (1885–86; 1886–92; 1895–1902) and four turns as foreign secretary, Salisbury's career exemplified, besides European and colonial statecraft, Tory accommodation to modern capitalism and electoral democracy. To young Salisbury a wider franchise meant careerists, not better, more consensual government. His unsentimental Christian faith treated the Sermon on the Mount as a poor guide to policy. The poor were no less vicious than the rich, he believed, only more numerous. Old Salisbury and his agents modernized the party, introducing local offices, briefings for journalists, party manifestos, and shadow cabinets. His career was a conservative master class in playing a weak hand with a diffuse creed against apparently superior forces.

Gerlach Brothers, Leopold (1790–1861) and *Ernst Ludwig* (1795–1877): Reactionary core of a court camarilla that guided the changeable, underconfident Prussian king Friedrich Wilhelm IV. As Christian Pietists, the Gerlachs felt the draw of personal faith and service to community. Ludwig, the more political, later reverted to Lutheranism. Practical-minded conservatives like Radowitz took their Romantic constitutionalism—a dutiful king advised by respectful estates—for medievalizing fantasy. Bismarck envied their closeness to the king but characteristically had the last word. When a stroke incapacitated Friedrich Wilhelm (1857), his brother Wilhelm, Bismarck's ally, became regent. The Gerlachs were out. Leo caught cold and died soon after Friedrich Wilhelm's funeral. He reminded Bismarck of "old retainers who chose to die with their princes." Of Ludwig, Bismarck scoffed: "He sits on his column refusing to let anyone agree with him."

Newt Gingrich (1943–): US Congressman from Georgia (1979–99) and Speaker of the House (1995–99) who presided over an acceleration of the Republicans' rightward shift and the elimination of bipartisan compromise with Democrats. After his federal government shutdown (1995–96) hurt the Republicans, Gingrich cooperated with the Democrat president, Bill Clinton, to limit welfare. Gingrich's legacy, nevertheless, was making Congress a theater of partisan war, encouraged as it was by the twenty-four-hour combat news of MSNBC and Fox News (started 1996). In *To Renew America* (1995), Gingrich expressed the right's ancestral cri de coeur: the nation was going to hell, conservatism was the only alternative to decay, and there was "no middle ground."

Valéry Giscard d'Estaing (1926–): Liberal conservative politician in a France where two people in three, Giscard believed, were socially and economically liberal but anti-left. Twice minister of finance (1962–66; 1969–74) and president (1974–81), he strengthened Franco-German ties with Helmut Schmidt and promoted closer European union. His party, the Independent Republicans, a distant, made-over descendant of the CNIP, morphed into the Union pour la Démocratie Française (1978–2007). Giscard believed in technocratic economic and fiscal management, both undisturbed by democratic pressures, but was liberal in freeing the media of government's hand, strengthening parliament, devolving powers to regions, and easing restrictive laws on contraception, abortion, and divorce.

Barry Goldwater (1909–98): Party-political herald of the present-day American right. Goldwater bridged the old Taft Republicans and the post-1980 Reagan party, from which liberal Republicans were rapidly excluded. On Eisenhower's coattails, Goldwater won Arizona's US Senate race in 1952. He was anti-union, liberal on moral policing (in old age, he approved of gay marriage), and an America Firster in foreign policy. Goldwater made a national name (1960) by attacking Eisenhower Republicanism as "dime-store New Deal." Eisenhower's heir, Nixon, needed East Coast Republicans to secure the nomination and chose a liberal for his running mate. Goldwater took up the standard of affronted Southern and Western Republicans. He beat Rockefeller for the Republican nomination in 1964 but was trounced by President Johnson, winning only six states. The setback was temporary. Using the South and West for a base, the post-Goldwater right formed a Republican force that buffeted Nixon and Ford and after 1980 won the party.

Mark Hanna (1837–1904): Cleveland-raised businessman and Republican manager who ran President McKinley's campaign (1896). Hanna exacted more than $100 million in today's money from Standard Oil, the Morgan bank, and other interests, and kept McKinley at home in Ohio while Republican speakers talked up sound money and high tariffs to restore prosperity. Democrats and Progressives typed McKinley Republicans as the haves' party, a corrupt Gilded Age leftover. As Ohio governor, McKinley aimed at votes of "working Americans," coded to exclude Catholics, immigrants, blacks, and shirkers.

Hard Right in France before 1914: *Edouard Drumont* (1844–1917), author of *La France juive* (1886) and editor of the anti-Semitic *La Libre Parole* (founded 1892). Scabrous anti-Dreyfusard, Drumont parsed the prejudice into Christian-traditional (Christ-killers), anthropological ("scientific" racism), and politico-economic (anti-capitalism). After the 1890s, he was overtaken by Action Française, by which time, outside the hard right, anti-Semitism in France had died down. *Paul Déroulède* (1846–1914), soldier, poet, prisoner from the Franco-Prussian War, and hard-right skirmisher. Déroulède made his name with *Chants du soldat* (1872), a short book of ballads that lamented fallen comrades, called for revenge, and linked love of the countryside with impassioned mourning: "They're there in that dark wood. . . . There in our France." The Ligues de Patriotes, which he started (1882) as a pressure group on parliament became an anti-republican street force as he became an ever rowdier and soon derided figure. *Léon Daudet* (1867–1942), a mudsplatterer alongside Maurras of *Action Française*, playing Sancho Panza to his Don Quixote, Daudet wrote for Drumont on *Libre Parole* before leaving to found the Action Française's own newspaper (1908). During 1917 he attacked the "Bosch lovers," for example, Caillaux, who favored a negotiated peace.

Hard Right in France in the 1930s and Vichy: *François de La Rocque* (1885–1946), a general's son who served in North Africa on the staff of the military colonialist Hubert Lyautey. In 1931, La Rocque took over and politicized the Croix de Feu, which had begun as an association of decorated war veterans but which he opened to all-comers, winning it sixty thousand members by 1934. He organized *dispos* (paramilitaries) with money from Coty and others. When extra-parliamentary Ligues were banned (1936), the Croix de Feu became the Parti Social Français (PSF). *Marcel Bucard* (1895–1946), an avowed French fascist, founder and leader of the Francistes (1933), paramilitary streetfighters. From a family of well-off horse dealers outside Paris, Bucard was destined for the church until war intervened, when he rose to captain, was wounded three times, and returned with his own violent stamp on the "spirit of the trenches," writing of liberals and the left: "I love my revolver and will use it against scum and their newspapers." His Francistes emulated Mussolini's *squadristi* but numbered no more than eight thousand at their peak and served mainly as encouragement to the Blum government to ban them and other street brawlers. Revived after 1940, Bucard's Francistes aided Vichy's anti-resistance Milice. In 1946 he was tried for treason and executed. *Philippe Henriot* (1889–1944), a Fédération Républicaine politician, close to the Ligueurs of the early 1930s, who in Vichy used his powerful oratory in weekly radio broadcasts to press the ideas of the National Revolution. They were a hodgepodge of anti-republicanism, economic corporatism, Catholic social and family policy, help for farmers, cultural reaction, persecution of the left, and exclusion of unwanted foreigners. Laid out in Sixteen Principles of the Community, Vichy's ideas were sloganized, in counter to the republican "Liberty, Equality, Fraternity," as "Work, Family, Nation." In July 1944 Henriot was shot by a resistance commando.

Edward Heath (1916–2005): Conservative Party leader (1965–75) and British prime minister (1970–74), remembered by admirers as the herald of his successor Thatcher, and by detractors as a failed Wet consensualist. Thatcherite scare words—"compromise," "fudge"—were hurled against him. Heath and Thatcher in fact shared many aims: less regulation, more competition, ending incomes policy, curbing unions (as Labour had tried), less direct and more indirect taxation, and "targeted," that is, broadly speaking less generous, welfare. The Tory hard right never forgave Heath for shepherding Britain into the European Economic Community, the EU's forerunner. He had bad luck (global stagflation, Middle East) and undue trust in people's reasonableness over deep, long-running conflicts (unions, Ireland).

Karl Helfferich (1872–1924): Monetary expert, pro-colonialist, and post-1918 leader of the German conservatives (DNVP). Helfferich typified a hyper-qualified generation making government careers between the unifications wars and 1914, a period when Germany was confident, expansive, and successful. Helfferich had more technical prowess than practical wisdom or sense of democratic politics. At the wartime treasury he financed spending by borrowing, storing up postwar inflation. Afterward he focused on winning backing from business and landowners for a stabilized currency. What Germany needed was his party's backing for the republic. Hjalmar Schacht pipped him for presidency of the Reichsbank (1923). He died in a train wreck at Bellinzona.

Otto von Helldorff (1833–1908): A wounded veteran (1866) with four university degrees, Helldorff rallied Prussia's Conservatives into Bismarck's staunch defenders in the Reichstag. As leader of the Deutschkonservative Partei (DKP), he kept at bay both the last of the Christian-Romantic Ultras and the social conservatives led by Wagener. His task was complicated by Kleist, Bismarck's foe in the Prussian senate and by the *Kreuzzeitung* group, which feared that Adolf Stoeker was outflanking the DKP on the right. Helldorff's openness to compromise and unwillingness to oppose freer trade under Caprivi cost him the party leadership, his other posts, and in effect his career.

Jesse Helms (1921–2008): American broadcaster, Republican US senator from North Carolina (1973–2003), and hard-right spokesman of Southern conservatism. Helms did much to make Republicanism's southern voice its national voice. Proudly anti-liberal, he opposed civil rights (1964), busing for desegregation, banning school prayer, decriminalizing abortion, and promoting gay rights. Helms smoothed Reagan's ascent and his fundraising aided the Republican winning of the Senate (1980). Helm's caricature of liberals as both ineffectual and corrosive was incoherent but widely persuasive. Helms helped create an enemy in the so-called cultural left, turning it from a hate object of shout radio into one of the conservative right's primary targets.

Ernst von Heydebrand (1851–1924): Conservative leader and "uncrowned king of Prussia," who said "Prussian ministers must jump to my tune." A veteran against France (1870), he led the conservative majority in the Prussian lower house (1888–1918) and sat for the DKP in the Reichstag (1903–18). Brusque and difficult, he openly criticized the Kaiser, wrecked Bülow's financial reforms (1909), and thwarted Bethmann-Hollweg when he threatened Junker interests. The monarchy's collapse (1918) ended Heydebrand's politics. The postwar right was eager to dissociate itself from old elites because voters hated them for the war yet determined to obstruct the very republic that made popular electoral concern necessary.

Alfred Hugenberg (1865–1951): Conservative businessman and media baron who led the DNVP rightward (from 1928), hastening the Weimar Republic's fall. A Hanover politician's son who studied the German migrations, Hugenberg was an ex–National Liberal, enthusiastic imperialist, and 1914–18 annexationist. Business interests included arms making (Krupp) and newspapers and film (UfA). He aimed to strengthen Germany and resist socialism. Though himself neither monarchist nor anti-Semitic, Hugenberg's papers were often both. Alliance with Nazis (Harzburg Front, 1931) helped Hitler more than it did Hugenberg with right-wing voters. As Germany's economy slumped (1932), they blamed Weimar parties, including his. Like other conservatives, Hugenberg saw the danger of Nazism too late.

Boris Johnson (1964–): New York–born British journalist, author, Conservative MP, London mayor, foreign secretary (2016–18), and prime minister (2019–). Without settled aims or evident principles, Johnson is a leader of rare gifts, which include a gamesman's skill at inner-party maneuver, power of words, bold judgment, and strong public rapport. In 2016, his spirited campaigning, rich in seductive half-truths, helped tip a national referendum against the UK's staying in the European Union. First from inside then from outside May's cabinet, Johnson rallied Conservatives against further delay in leaving the EU, replaced May as prime minister, and won a landslide election victory (December 2019). Without effective opposition in parliament, Johnson now led a hard-right party of ill-matched hyper-liberal globalists and nation-first populists, from which liberal Tories had largely fled or been expunged. How the party's conflicts might resolve themselves and whether Johnson would command the party or the reverse, remained open.

Keith Joseph (1918–1994): Radical economic liberal, Conservative minister and MP (1956–87). His rhetorical gifts and focused mind helped create Thatcherism. Private enterprise had not failed in Britain, Joseph said; it hadn't been tried. Britain was "over-governed, over-spent, over-taxed, over-borrowed and over-manned." His overarching theme, a right-wing classic, was decline. Joseph knitted discrete questions—subsidized transport, housing shortages, welfare-dependent parents, student protest, moral permissiveness—into a compelling picture of a failed society needing rescue. Joseph's call to action prompted corrective steps, with mixed results. His concern for the ill, old, and disabled, for example, was profound, the scope for help, given fiscal stringency, limited.

Wilhelm Kardorff (1828–1907): Leader of the pro-Bismarck Free Conservatives (1880–1906) in the Reichstag and active in the Prussian lower house from 1866. Kardorff had large holdings in banking and heavy industry and in 1876 founded Germany's big-business lobby. Kardorff won local government for cities, freeing them of provincial control (1872), and protective tariffs for industry (1879) but failed to persuade fellow Free Conservative magnates like Stumm to accept cheap-money bimetallism. He opposed the liberalizing and free-trade reforms of Caprivi (chancellor, 1890–94) and backed the farm-protest Land League in the 1890s but turned against it in fear that popular energies were swamping an elite-led party.

Hans Hugo von Kleist-Retzow (1814–92): Like Britain's Salisbury, young Kleist brilliantly defended unsellable ideas. He later accepted the times and fell in with Bismarck, whose niece he married, only to revert after 1870 to the Christian-patriarchal right. In between, Kleist opposed liberals in the Prussian senate. A localist foe of the modern state and centralized churches, Kleist led the resistance to Reich-wide rules for police and administration in East Prussia (1872). As a German Conservative Party deputy (1877–92), Kleist defended his backward-looking ideas to an unresponsive Reichstag. He guessed rightly as a young man that his principles-or-nothing approach would bar him from success or high office.

Helmut Kohl (1930–2017): CDU leader (1973–98) and German chancellor (1982–98). Rhineland Catholic who benefitted from the Liberals' pivot from social-minded liberalism to economic liberalism (1982). Flawed but underrated, Kohl's moment was unification. As others planned and puzzled, Kohl's government decided. Germany was to become one at once; not as a neutral, but in Europe and the West; not after two-state negotiation for a new constitution but by reabsorption under the Basic Law of 1949. Blending the two economies would take decades but Germany was rich enough to speed the transition, Kohl believed. Unlike Bismarck's, Kohl's unification occurred in peace and, despite social and political costs, without wider disruption. Kohl then ran a successful, discreditable campaign in the old East, blackening Social Democrats as Communists. After retirement, it was confirmed that he had long dispensed under-the-table political money. Though without a distinctive outlook, Kohl's actions in 1989–91 showed confidence in a centrist Germany anchored in Europe.

Joseph Laniel (1889–1975): Center-right conservative from family of Normandy textile makers who after 1945 helped reconstruct a right-wing party for small businesses, shopkeepers, and farmers to support after the Vichy disgrace of the Fédération Républicaine. In the 1930s, with Tardieu, a soft-money supporter of devaluation, Laniel voted full powers to Pétain (1940) but joined the resistance, emerged with honor, and cofounded the National Centre of Independents and Farmers (CNIP). Indochina undid him as premier (1953–54). The hard-rightist Poujade was after the same voters. Laniel was pro-state and fended off Poujade. Pinay, Laniel's CNIP rival, was anti-statist and warmer to Poujade.

Pierre Laval (1883–1945): A migrant from the left to the right and dominant figure in the Vichy regime, Laval was son of an innkeeper from remote Auvergne. Politics for him was not dossiers but making deals. From labor lawyer, Socialist deputy, and mayor in the Paris "red belt," Laval became an anti-party authoritarian grown rich thanks to wealthy friends. He was pacifistic (against three-year call-up) before 1914 and afterward for reconciliation. Two premierships and a turn as foreign secretary in the early 1930s gave him personal experience at failing to solve crises. The collapse of the Popular Front convinced him that parliamentary government was finished. On defeat (1940), the Vichy right ensured it was. Unlike doctrinaires hoping for a "new order," the dealmaking Laval saw occupation as an opportunity for Franco-German rapprochement. Laval badly underestimated French weakness and misjudged the untreatable character of Nazi Germany under Hitler. In 1945, he was condemned to death in a controversial trial for treason and shot.

Andrew Bonar Law (1858–1923): Prime minister (1922–23) and Tory leader (1911–21; 1922–23), who marked the Conservative transition from the era of Salisbury and his nephew Balfour. Canadian-born iron merchant, and later banker, of Ulster-Scots origin, Law entered Parliament (1900), soldiered in the opposition, and, on Balfour's retirement (1911), inherited a party split over tariffs and Lords reform. Law hoped Irish Home Rule would unite the wings in opposition. Philistine, teetotal, and unpatrician, he had the "mind of a Glasgow bailiff" (Asquith). His moment was October 1922, when Conservatives, pushed by Baldwin, broke up their coalition with the Liberals and he became prime minister.

Jean-Marie Le Pen (1928–): A Breton orphan, Le Pen was born for a fight. The Free French rejected him at sixteen as too young. As a Paris law student, he passed out far-right leaflets, played rugby, and street-brawled. He soldiered in Indochina (for the army press department) and in Algeria (later accused of torture). Poujadism occupied him (1950s–1960s). He cofounded the Front National (1972) with money from a conservative cement heir. Marginal till the 1980s, Le Pen then dropped factional street brawling and appealed to right-wing voters conventionally. With Mitterrand's aid (making elections proportional to split the mainstream), the FN obtained thirty-five parliamentary seats. As the mainstream right won anyway and soon changed back the electoral law, the FN's stock fell again. In 2002, however, Le Pen stunned France by getting into the presidential second round. No longer of the far right, the FN was now threatening to enter the mainstream as a party of the hard right.

Marine Le Pen (1968–): When Marine Le Pen took over the Front National from her father (2011), she announced her aim as winning power. Alarmingly for the mainstream right, her goal was not absurd. She profited from disaffection with political orthodoxies and from her own "detoxification" of the party. She dropped her father's overt racialism, made pro-Jewish gestures, gave up lecturing voters about family values, and replaced a narrow, pro-business, anti-labor line with welfarist calls for the "état protecteur." Fine ears could, however, still hear the old music of anti-immigrant hostility. Success at the polls brought rivalries (after 2016, her deputy quit) and conflicts of purpose. The FN mixed oracular geopolitics, welfare advocacy, right-wing Catholicism, and anti-Europeanism. Le Pen made a triple appeal to the old right-wing base with coded prejudice, to the left with social justice, and to the center with concern for security amid terror. The party changed its name to National Rally in June 2018.

Harold Macmillan (1894–1986): There were two Macmillans: the pre-1945 MP for Stockton in the jobless north, advocating Keynesian remedies and writing *The Middle Way* (1938), a bible for statist Wets; and the post-1945 MP for suburban Bromley in the prosperous southeast, who as prime minister (1957–63) told Britain it had never had it so good and won the election (1959) in a landslide. He sped the end of British Africa, completing a withdrawal from empire. De Gaulle rebuffed his hoped-for alternative, membership in the European club. Fiscal trouble, scandals, and a new Labour leader who foxed him in parliament made him yesterday's man.

Otto von Manteuffel (1805–82): Civil servant schooled (as were Nietzsche and Bethmann-Hollweg) at the intellectual forcing house of Schulpforta in Saxony. Interior minister (1848–50) and premier-foreign minister (1850–58), Manteuffel held a balance in Prussia's government between moderates and ultras in a period of thwarted constitutionalism after 1848. In foreign policy, against Radowitz, Manteuffel deflected the creation of a Prussian-led German union, siding with counterreform Austria. Governmentally, against the Gerlachs, he pushed through a representative constitution for Prussia, promised since 1815, but subverted its terms, notably by a three-class franchise. On Wilhelm I's regency (1858), Manteuffel was dismissed, Bismarck's rise putting him among yesterday's men.

Louis Marin (1871–1960): An ultra-nationalist Lorrainer from the same lycée as Barrès, Marin joined the Fédération Républicaine (founded 1903) and became its leader (1925). His hyper-patriotism pulled hard rightists into the party, whom Marin was wary about. He tried to turn the party against appeasement but, leery of communism, opposed a Soviet alliance. He backed Reynaud, an anti-defeatist (May 1940) and honorably abstained with a small minority of the FR in the parliamentary vote at Vichy to kill the Third Republic. After resistance service, Marin rewon his Nancy seat (1945). For its equivocal 1930s and support for Vichy, the FR itself was heavily tarnished.

Jules Méline (1838–1925): Conservative defender of France's farming interest. A lawyer, Méline represented Vosges (1872–1925). He led the anti–free trade lobby from 1881 and pushed through the Méline Tariff (1892), raising levies on farm imports from 3 percent to 21 percent. He also promoted farm credit. He became premier (1896–98) after Bourgeois failed to secure an income tax. Méline became leader (1903) of the Fédération Républicaine, which was more Catholic and less liberal than the other pre-1945 main conservative party, the Alliance Démocratique. Representing a frontier region, Méline wanted a Franco-Russian pact to deter Germany. As premier in the Dreyfus affair, he stood aloof. His government prosecuted Zola.

Angela Merkel (1954–): Of the party she led for two decades, Germany's chancellor Angela Merkel once said, "I'm a bit liberal, a bit conservative and a bit social-Christian, and that goes for the CDU too." Born in Hamburg, she was taken as a baby to East Germany, where her father, a Lutheran minister, was offered a pastorate. A research scientist with a physics doctorate, she won a Bundestag seat after unification. She rose as Kohl's protégée, only to call for new leaders when Kohl was exposed in a party-funds scandal. On the CDU's victory (2005), she became Germany's first woman chancellor. Her Europeanism was strong but open-eyed. Europe could not defend its values without paying its bills. A favorite line of hers was that Europe had 7 percent of the world's population, 25 percent of its GDP, and 50 percent of its social spending. Principled and decisive, but not always wise, she provoked the Russians by pushing for Ukraine to join NATO. By letting in 1.5 million refugees ("We can handle this") in 2015–16, she facilitated a breakthrough into the Bundestag of the hard-right Alternative for Germany. In 2018, she announced that she would not seek reelection as chancellor in 2021, but her hand-picked liberal-centrist successor as party leader was soon driven out by the CDU faction that favored an opening to the hard right.

Oswald Mosley (1896–1980): Mosley's rapid rise and fall as herald of British fascism in the 1930s was testimony, among other things, to a common British belief in the power of mockery. Son of Staffordshire gentry, Mosley was by turns a Conservative, independent, and Labour

MP. As minister (1929–30), his Keynesian proposals against unemployment were ignored. After resigning, he founded the British Union of Fascists in 1932. It failed to win a seat and was proscribed in 1940, when Mosley was interned. Citing Mosley as evidence of British conservatism's immunity to extremes is complacent. Fascism is not the only way conservatism can lurch toward unreason or the hard right.

Albert de Mun (1841–1914): Social Catholic who hoped in the 1880s for a Catholic party like the German Center, though was dissuaded by Pope Leo XIII, who was loath to envenom church-state relations when compromise looked possible. A royalist and managing agent for the legitimists, Mun nevertheless took Chambord's hopes for absurd. In 1892, he accepted the Vatican's call for a *ralliement* by French Catholics to the Republic. Though partyless, Mun pursued social Catholicism with workers' and young peoples' associations, advocating social insurance, income, and state employees' right to strike. He was an anti-Dreyfusard and, when the church-state controversy burst in the 1900s, a ferocious anti-liberal.

Richard Nixon (1913–94): A "hinge" Republican. Nixon's presidency (1969–74) marked a double shift in the Republican center of gravity from the East Coast to the South and West and from Eisenhower's middle-of-the-road approach to post-1980 anti-liberal partisanship. Civil rights, Vietnam, and the onset of America's cultural wars resharpened party divisions in the 1960s. Nixon campaigned to the right but governed (with a Democratic Congress) from the center (affirmative action in federal hiring, more spending and borrowing, wage and price controls, dollar devaluation, detente with the Soviet Union, disengagement from Vietnam). Nixon's party and governmental legacies diverged, the one mainstream, the other pointing without resistance toward a Republican hard right.

Elard von Oldenburg-Januschau (1855–1937): A blunt Junker die-hard remembered for telling fellow deputies in the Reichstag (1910), "The Kaiser should be always be on standby to send a lieutenant and ten men to close this house." As an owner of East Prussian estates, Oldenburg moved up the political ladder from provincial assemblies to the Reichstag and Prussian senate. He never finished high school, loved his time in a cavalry regiment of the Uhlans, and despised democratic politics. Hostility continued into the Weimar Republic, when he urged his friend President Hindenburg to rule by decree and supported Papen in his coup against the Prussian government (1932).

Parti de l'Ordre: Informal grouping of the French mid-nineteenth-century right that met at the Rue de Poitiers in Paris in May 1848 to resist radical republicans and democrats under the banner of "Order, property and religion." It included ex-ministers and July Monarchy grandees, provincial legitimists from the West and local notables who had come up in the February Revolution that got rid of the Citizen King, Louis Phillipe. The grandees included right-wing liberals (Thiers, Tocqueville, and followers of Guizot), an early core of the French center-right that reemerged in the Third Republic as the Union Républicaine and after 1918 as the Democratic Alliance.

Robert Peel (1788–1850): Twice prime minister (1834–35; 1841–46) and, in Salisbury's jibe, twice betrayer of his party (over Catholic emancipation and free trade). Peel represented the business-minded half of British conservatism's divided soul. The brainy, devout son of a newly rich calico maker, Peel was a reforming home secretary (1820s). Under him, criminal law grew less savage and civic disabilities for Catholics were lifted. He supported the Reform

Bill of 1832 to avoid "a perpetual vortex of agitation." In opposition, Peel organized and wrote the Tamworth Manifesto (1834) for the newly named Conservatives. On return to office, Peel introduced an income tax (1842) and won repeal of the Corn Laws (1846). The anti-Peel majority kept the "Conservative" name. The minority, Peel's supporters, became Liberals after his death (crushed by his horse while riding on Constitution Hill in July 1850). He is remembered admiringly as a creator of liberal conservatism and unadmiringly as a faith-justified, free-market dogmatist.

Antoine Pinay (1891–1994): Post-1945 France's "hero of normality," Pinay was a center-right politician of the everyday, light on doctrine and suspicious of grandeur. Self-labelled as "Mr. Consumer," Pinay saw his job as deepening and widening economic prosperity. As premier (1952–53) and finance minister (1958), Pinay twice stabilized the franc. Despite his prewar indulgence to the hard right (1930s) and a controversial time in Vichy, Pinay recovered credit for the conservatism of small shopkeepers and farmers, gathered into one party as the postwar CNIP. Though more liberal on socio-moral matters, Giscardism later realized Pinay's hopes to create a non-Gaullist, pro-European, economically liberal party of the center-right.

Raymond Poincaré (1860–1934): A Lorrainer, lawyer, and conservative republican in the Alliance Démocratique, Poincaré held all the top offices in a long career, speaking for the middle-class values of work, thrift, and honesty. He and his rival Clemenceau agreed on an implacable anti-Germanism. When French forces mutinied (1917), Poincaré as president made Clemenceau, the "soldier's friend," premier. Poincaré demanded a hard peace, sending French troops to the Ruhr to exact reparations. Banking's hard-money man against industry's soft-money Tardieu, Poincaré stabilized a nose-diving franc (1926). Aloof and narrow, he was remembered with more respect than fondness. Poincaré thought Clemenceau unprincipled; Clemenceau thought him a prig.

Georges Pompidou (1911–74): Gaullist prime minister and president of France (1969–74), Pompidou helped turn Gaullism after de Gaulle from a personalized movement of transition into a pro-European center-right party that blended in time with its Giscardian rival. On campaign, Pompidou played up his Auvergnat roots but was a *Normalien* ex-banker. A worldly conservative, he believed neither (with the left) that humans were good and society evil, nor the opposite (with the right). A defender of vigorous capitalism and a strong state, Pompidou took the high line of right-wing liberalism that ran from the July Monarchy through the Third and Fourth Republics to the present.

Post-Thatcher Toryism: Two intellectual British Tories from 1980s exemplified divergent paths in post-Thatcher conservatism, social rigor and social policy: *John Redwood* (1951–), an Oxford historian, right-wing Tory MP, and longtime anti-EU campaigner. He ran Thatcher's policy unit (1982–87), swept up the Poll Tax mess, and twice failed to win the party leadership. He called for a strict, social conservatism. He opposed gay marriage and wanted capital punishment back. He summed up his conservatism (1996) as limited but effective government, defense of a strict moral code rooted in the traditional family, and confidence that the state will charge and punish wrongdoers. *David Willetts* (1956–): worked at the Treasury (1978–84) and fed the government with policy ideas, notably public-private finance. An MP (1992–2015), he was a Thatcher radical turned concerned centrist; three books, *Modern Conservatism* (1992), *Is Conservatism Dead?* (1997), and *The Pinch* (2010) marked the change.

The first showed confidence that Thatcher Toryism had largely cured postwar Britain's worst ills. The second, appearing as Labour buried his party in a landslide, worried over community-versus-market tensions. And the third was a nonpartisan, future-of-our-children book about the problems of aged populations, taxes, pensions, housing, and social mobility that vex all rich nations.

Pierre Poujade (1920–2003): The original begetter of France's post-1945 hard right, Poujade was a teenage follower of Doriot but later disillusioned by Vichy and who escaped to train for the RAF. Poujade afterward championed shopkeepers and small businesses against big chains and tax collectors. His tax-protest party (founded 1953) stunned the conventional right with a 13 percent vote in 1956. It was a fluid coalition of apolitical tax protestors and malcontents of the right, themselves a motley of pro-French Algerians, monarchist relics, and Vichyite *revanchards*. The wave passed, only to return later. Pompidou affected to listen to him, but Giscard held him at bay. Poujade endorsed Mitterrand in 1981.

Joseph von Radowitz (1797–1853): Conservative constitutionalist from a Catholic noble family in Brunswick who accepted accommodation, rather than reaction, as the surer strategy for social order. Charged with foreign affairs (1848–51), Radowitz failed to win support for German unity under Prussian leadership. Like the Gerlachs, he was close to Friedrich Wilhelm, the wayward king from 1840. Unlike the brothers, Radowitz learned from events. In the 1830s, he had argued for church and crown against reform. By the straitened 1840s, Radowitz wrote in *State and Church* (1846) that government should act to reduce poverty. Conservatives were foolish, he believed, to shut out liberals when the threat was working-class radicalism.

Ronald Reagan (1911–2004): Reagan united the party's discordant conservatives—free-market optimists, family-values moralists, and America First nationalists—and, while appealing to the political center (twice elected president with ease (1980; 1984) led a party from which moderates and liberals were slowly excluded. He had superb ear for a divided country that wanted to pursue brutal partisan conflict while feeling good about itself. He rocked audiences with jibes at big government so skillfully they forgot big government was what Reagan was asking them to let him run. Graced by charm, luck, and remarkable political talents, Reagan made the most of his opportunities. He appealed to the left and right wings of American liberalism, to New Deal Democrats, and to tight-money, big-business Republicans. He knew how to appeal as well to illiberal Bible Belt Christians and to beyond-the-liberal-fringe libertarians. After Reagan, Republicanism moved to the hard right as an amalgam of America Firsters, libertarians, and religious conservatives.

William Rehnquist (1924–2005): US Supreme Court justice (1971–2005) and chief justice (from 1986). The Rehnquist court began a right-wing "rollback" of liberal rulings over the previous three decades, which spoke both to a conservative public mood and to conservative legal scholars who argued that the 1950–70 courts were not "restrained" enough but too "activist" as, in effect, policy makers. Neither theoretically nor historically does the dispute over the proper approach to interpretation between the "original intent" and "law as it is" schools match the conservative-liberal divide. Late nineteenth-century conservative courts were activist. The dispute nevertheless is commonly fought across a right-left divide, to the puzzlement of nonlawyers and foreigners.

Paul Reynaud (1878–1966): A rare anti-appeaser in the Alliance Démocratique, Reynaud is remembered as the premier (March–June 1940) during the fall of France and, though linked with defeat, was not himself defeatist. Tiny and cocksure (nicknamed "Mickey Mouse"), Reynaud struggled to rally resistance. Judging France lost, Churchill refused military aid. Judging Britain lost without France, Reynaud pleaded for aid despite the risks. Churchill proposed instead political union. Before Reynaud could plead for it in the cabinet, France had capitulated. Pétain had Reynaud arrested and sent to prison in Germany. De Gaulle's patron in the 1930s, Reynaud backed him again in 1958 but opposed his direct election for president.

Henri Rochefort (1831–1913): Anti-parliamentarian publicist, son of a legitimist nobleman, first left, then right, scourge of the Second Empire, Communard, extreme nationalist, Boulangist, and anti-Dreyfusard. His gossip-and-satire *La Lanterne* began publishing when press restrictions were eased in 1868 and was soon selling 120,000 copies but was closed again after eleven issues. There followed prison, escape, quarrels in the Commune, and a second exile, after which Rochefort returned to Paris as a rightist. Promoter of the unreliable General Boulanger as France's supposed soldier-savior, Rochefort's plea for a coup went unheard. He fled again. In his second paper *L'Intransigeant* (1880), Rochefort called Dreyfus the "Judas of Devil's Island" and the Socialist Jaurès, a "mouthpiece for traitors."

Edward Stanley, Lord Derby (1799–1869): A leading mid-nineteenth-century Conservative, Derby left the Whigs over Irish church reform (1834) and led Tory opposition to Corn Law repeal. A landowning Lancashire grandee working from the Lords, he was seconded by Disraeli in the Commons. Derby aimed to stifle radicalism by political concession and social alleviation. Prime minister three times (1850s–1860s) and Tory leader (1846–68), Derby took electoral democracy to be an unavoidable "leap in the dark." Progress's boons came with harms. Railways, for example, destroyed working-class housing. From the unstoppable "machine" of change, good might come with "a skilful hand" but if "recklessly accelerated," "overwhelming wreck" was inevitable.

Adolf Stoecker (1835–1909): A destructively influential German Lutheran minister, Stoecker preached that respecting Jews was un-Christian. Of lower-class background, Stoecker shone in the pulpit, won notice for a patriotic sermon (1870), and became chaplain at court. Claiming to serve the poor, he founded the Christian Social Party (1878). With the nationalist historian Treitschke, he proposed halting Jewish immigration. Stoecker scared the German Conservative Party into adopting its anti-Semitic Tivoli Program (1892). Anti-Semitism's popularity died, only to return after 1918. Stoecker turned Christian Pietism's original appeal (resist governmental and clerical centralization) into an exclusionary call to voters looking for purpose and belonging in big cities.

Franz-Josef Strauss (1915–88): A Munich-born butcher's son and Eastern Front veteran, Strauss was for three decades scourge of the left and thorn of the center-right. Head of the Christian Social Union in Bavaria from 1961, Bavarian premier (1978–88), and federal minister (notably for defense and finance), Strauss was ferocious in public but quieter behind the scenes when the menaces tossed down and hard-right postures struck were often put aside. He opposed, without deflecting, *Ostpolitik*. In Strauss's time, Bavaria became a German California, and scandal—aerospace kickbacks, press spying—marred his career. Under Strauss, the CDU-CSU almost won the federal election (1980), but Kohl afterward outmaneuvered him for party control.

Robert A. Taft (1889–1953): A pro-business, unilateralist Republican and son of a president, Taft opposed the New Deal, doubted the communist threat, and ceded to Eisenhower the

Republican nomination in 1952. He sponsored the Taft-Hartley Act (1947), which was
passed over Truman's veto, limited trade-union strike rights, and permitted state "right to
work" laws, which were soon passed across the South and West. He attacked Truman for
involving the country in war while professing peace, even as he himself insisted that "we
should stay out of the war unless attacked" but still "build up our defense to meet any possible threat of attack."

André Tardieu (1876–1945): A conservative French republican with corporatist and anti-
parliamentary leanings, Tardieu was three times prime minister during the onset of economic crisis (1929–32). His watchwords were patriotism, social modernization, and an effective state. A defender of the Versailles peace, Tardieu was a leader in the politico-business
campaign for national "recovery" that proposed reforms to strengthen the executive, all of
which presumed exclusion or deflection of the left ("Le socialisme, voilà l'ennemi"). A Parisian bourgeois and tireless author-journalist who admired the United States, Tardieu
looked ahead to the technocratic approach to politics and government that marked much
of France's center-right after de Gaulle.

Margaret Thatcher (1925–2013): Conservative leader (1975–90) and prime minister (1979–90).
Thatcher owed her rise in the Tory Party, her success with British voters, and her reputation
in the world to several strengths: knowing her brief, a command of words, courage, and
decisiveness, as well as the ability to combine a liberal and nonliberal conservatism. A Cobdenite liberal in economics and a Millian liberal about policing morals (for abortion; for
decriminalizing homosexuality), she was keen for men and women of initiative to get on
without envy or vested interests in their way. Nonliberally, she broke noncentral powers
(unions, local councils) to concentrate central power. Her national feeling, above all for
England, expressed itself in distrust of foreigners (Americans excepted), especially of French
and Germans. She told a beguiling story of rescuing Britain from national decline brought
on by foes, inside and out. More flexible than she sounded, she intoned in public "Never
negotiate with terrorists" in public as her officials successfully talked for her behind the
scenes with "terrorists" in Ireland and Southern Africa. She was "assassinated," according to
party tradition, when her uncharacteristically wavering leadership imperiled its election
prospects. Her anti-Europeanism was out of step with the prevailing pro-Europeanism of
the country. Conservative anti-Europeans soon had their revenge.

Adolphe Thiers (1797–1877): Journalist, historian of the French Revolution, and political leader
whose long career mapped the nineteenth-century French right's halting progress toward
acceptance of democratic republicanism—in other words, liberal democracy: liberal nemesis of the last Bourbons (1830), ally then foe of Louis-Napoleon, crusher of the Paris Commune, conservative defender of the Third Republic. Clever son of a failed businessman from
Aix, Thiers escaped the provinces for Paris, where he fell into the literary world and was
taken up by Talleyrand, who called him "an urchin of genius." A leader of the July Revolution
(1830), Thiers moved right at the 1848 Revolution. On Napoleon's coup d'état (1851) he was
sent to foreign exile but allowed to return, when, elected to the National Assembly, he spoke
out against Bonapartist autocracy, French adventurism, and Germany's growing power.
After France's military collapses in the Franco-Prussian War (1870), Thiers gave in to Bismarck's terms for a punishing peace: heavy indemnity and loss of Alsace along with part of

Lorraine. Thiers sent MacMahon's army to crush the Paris Commune (May 1871) and became the Third Republic's first president (1871–73). When his successor, MacMahon, moved against the government on behalf of the monarchist right, Thiers, at eighty years of age, stood by the republic.

Tories and Whigs in Britain: Party division in the predemocratic British parliament (late seventeenth to mid-nineteenth century) when oligarchic grandees were divided over confessional-dynastic quarrels (Protestant versus Catholic; Orange-Hanoverian versus Stuart) and over institutional primacy (crown, ministers, or parliament). "Tory" was from *toraigh*, Irish for "bandit" or "bogtrotter," used by Court Protestants against supporters of the suspected Catholic James II; "Whig" was from "Whiggamors," Scottish Protestant protesters (1640s) against the English church, used by James's camp against his Protestant foes. Whigs and Tories disputed influence at court until the Hanoverian succession of George I (1714). Contending Whig cliques alternated in ministries until the 1760s, when war debt and colonial unrest taxed government capacities. George III (acceded 1760) sought to free government from faction and win the crown more power. His supporters were Pittite Whigs; his opponents, Rockingham Whigs, spoken for by Burke. Radicalism and revolution brought a new division, from which the modern parties formed. The Rockingham (now Portland) Whigs split over the French Revolution (1794). Fox was for; Portland, who joined Pitt the younger, against. The Pitt-Portland Whigs became Tories, the Foxites keeping the Whig label. In the new conditions of capitalist modernity, the still blurrable parties of order and hierarchy, change and equality were relabeled "Conservative" (1834) and "Liberal" (1859).

Donald Trump (1946–): "I don't think it's about any specific set of policy positions, but it's about somebody being a warrior for folks," was a Mississippi Republican's explanation for Trump's rise from an inherited New York real estate business via an NBC reality TV show to the White House (elected 2016). Trump benefitted also from a long democratic tradition in which bankruptcy and ridicule were no bar to high office, as well as from opponents of both main parties who foolishly underestimated his talents and popular appeal. Trump's *Apprentice* show revived a failing television network, won twenty million viewers, and was notably popular among blacks and Latinos. He could have run as a centrist but chose the playbook of Republican campaigns since the 1960s: win small but adequate numbers of discontented white working-class Democrats in swing states. Unburdened by settled thoughts, political doctrines, or party attachments, Trump's politics is improvisational and opportunistic. Dismayed conservatives who found him incoherent, unprincipled, and unanchored missed his strengths. If it is true that he was shell-shocked to wake up president-elect, he quickly grasped the interests, high and low, a Republican president was expected to represent: big business and finance (lower taxes; less regulation; no climate anxiety), as well as folks convinced they were put upon and who wanted their own warrior.

Vichy's National Revolution: A hodgepodge of anti-republicanism, economic corporatism, Catholic social family policy, rural aid, persecution of the left and Jews, cultural reaction, and exclusion of unwanted foreigners, laid out in the Sixteen Principles of Community and sloganized in the counter-triplet to "Liberty, Equality, Fraternity" as "Work, Family, Nation." The National Revolution drew on two leading streams of right-wing anti-liberalism: the hyper-national authoritarianism of Maurras and the "national recovery" movement among business elites convinced of France's economic backwardness. Both played on the claim of national decline requiring radical change under a galvanic leader, a classic right-wing cry from the early nineteenth century to this day.

Hermann Wagener (1815–89): An ex-churchman and conservative publicist, Wagener was from the "most Prussian of Prussian towns," Neuruppin, in lake country near Berlin, where the old state's literary memorialist, Theodor Fontane, was also born. Hostility to freethinking irked his liberal church and he turned from the pulpit to the press, helping start the ultraright *Kreuzzeitung* (1848). Its target was liberal modernity, which destroyed moral authority and cruelly preyed on the poor. Wagener answered the massive liberal *Political Lexicon* with the thirty-two-volume conservative *Political and Social Lexicon* (1859–67), which was for social welfare and against free markets. He was disgraced when exposed, by liberals, in a stock-market scandal (1873).

Daniel Webster (1782–1852): An anti-Jacksonian Whig and US representative or senator from Massachusetts (1823–50, with intervals). He and John Adams opposed wider franchise in Massachusetts (1820). As lawyer, he argued before Supreme Court to uphold private contract and federal commerce-banking powers. He opposed Clay's high federal tariffs and Calhoun's state campaign to nullify them (1830s). Webster feared that annexing Texas would destroy the North-South balance, and he opposed the Mexican War (1840s). Like Clay, and later Douglas but unlike Lincoln, he wanted Western expansion of slavery left to "popular sovereignty" (voters in new territories). Rich from a second wife, Webster was ruined in Western land speculations.

Alice Weidel (1979–): Co-leader of the Alternative for Germany. Her party won ninety-four Bundestag seats in 2017, the hard-right's first breakthrough since 1949. An ex-banker who lives with her woman partner and their two children, Weidel is a new kind of conservative, more given to challenging than upholding the present order: Germany (not Greece) should stay in the EU, though leave the euro and limit immigration, while investing in the Middle East to discourage outmigration. She favors civil partnerships, not gay marriage. As with France's National Front and Britain's Brexiteers, the AfD has no single message but appeals to a variety of powerful discontents.

Kuno von Westarp (1864–1945): German conservative naysayer in the Weimar Republic, when it needed conservative support. Veteran of the pre-1918 Land League and a war hawk in 1914–18, Westarp afterward cofounded the German National People's Party (DNVP). It united conservatives, torn as they were between dissociating themselves from old elites, whom voters hated for the war, and wrecking the republic that made concern for voters necessary. Westarp failed to resolve the puzzle. He backed the Kapp Putsch (1920) but tried, without success, to stop the DNVP's further rightward lurch under Hugenberg. He formed a powerless small breakaway party and wrote a multivolume history of German conservatism.

Whigs and Jacksonians in the United States: American Whigs emerged in the 1820s and 1830s as opponents of Jacksonian Democrats, forming the second of five commonly identified party systems in the nineteenth and twentieth centuries: Federalists and Democrat-Republicans (1792–1824), Whigs and Democrats (1824–56), Republicans and Democrats from the Civil War to Gilded Age (1856–92), Business Republicanism and Progressive Democrats (1892–1932), and Republicans either resisting or copying New Deal Democrats (1932–80).

Leading Whigs were the New Englander Webster and the Kentuckian Clay. When the Whigs broke up in the 1850s, the Free Soil (Republican) Party was founded (1854) that under Lincoln became the cause, in sequence, of union, war, and abolition.

Edward Wood, Lord Irwin, Earl of Halifax (1881–1959): A controversial Tory might-have-been who passed up Britain's wartime premiership for Churchill (May 1940) and whose later reputation was overdarkened by his rival's disciples. Economist, 1914–18 veteran, and devout Christian, Halifax (as Irwin) sought compromise with Ghandi as viceroy in India (1926–31) but was obstructed by arch-imperialists, including Churchill. Historians still argue over his actions and opportunities as foreign secretary when faced with the German threat (1938–40). Halifax (as Wood) cowrote *The Great Opportunity* (1918), a manifesto-gospel for a social conservatism mixing social services, high employment, anti-unionism, and imperial free trade with "national unity" and the "spirit of sacrifice."

2. *Thinkers*

Henry Adams (1838–1918): American author and historian of the United States. Grandson and great grandson of presidents, Adams was born to wealth and standing in a society where the first was prized, the second discredited. The tension runs through his autobiographical masterwork, *The Education of Henry Adams* (1907) and through *Democracy* (1880), a satire of lobbying and corruption in Gilded Age Washington. Its venal antihero, a US senator, expresses Adams's dim view of mass suffrage and social reform: "No representative government can long be much better or much worse than the society it represents. Purify society and you purify the government."

Steve Bannon (1953–): A former US naval officer, banker, news executive, and Trump aide, Bannon speaks for an American hard right with aspirations for links in Europe. Siding with the little guys, he opposes free trade and immigration, without otherwise threatening the rich. Popular discontent comes from exporting jobs and banks' undue power. The US offers "socialism for rich and poor," "Darwinian capitalism" to everyone else. Left liberals, for Bannon, are both a domineering elite and a crowd of out-of-touch "pussies." Free-market liberals are the people's enemy. His self-described "right-wing populism" to put nation first and "maximize citizen value" is louder on diagnosis than cure.

Maurice Barrès (1862–1923): A French writer and hyperpatriot, Barrès was born near Nancy in part of Lorraine that escaped German annexation (1871). Belief in local roots, dislike of capitalism, a mythic vision of the nation as "la terre et les morts," and desire for revenge were blended by him into a politico-literary whole of strong appeal to the French right. Barrès despised the liberal center, which he took for corrupt and dogmatically secular, backed the feckless General Boulanger in his anti-parliamentarism, and sided with anti-Semites in the Dreyfus affair. Like Céline and Drieu, Barrès was a gifted writer who brought scorn and anger to the novel of ideas. *Les déracinés* (1897), a story of clever, disruptive young Lorrainers in Paris misled by their Kantian professor, was admired by opponents including Léon Blum and later by the Communist poet Louis Aragon. As with Maurras, eloquence and conviction gave Barrès weapons against liberal modernity that argument alone did not provide.

Alain de Benoist (1943–): A prominent figure in France's New Right, Benoist founded (1968) the Groupement de recherche et d'études pour la civilisation européenne (GRECE). Benoist proscribes condemnations in politics but permits contempt. He despises free-market globalization, democratic equality ("levelling down"), and human rights ("law contaminated by morality"). A self-described pagan and "ethnopluralist," he judges the great monotheisms to be "totalitarian" but defends "European civilization." Echoing Maurras and Drieu, Benoist takes societies to be distinct unities separated by incompatible moral traditions. His long, winding march against democratic liberalism began on the pro-French Algerian far right. Benoist says he is now "beyond left or right."

Mel Bradford (1934–93): Southern conservative writer and thinker who taught at University of Dallas. Bradford bridged the 1930s and 1950s traditionalism and 1980s paleoconservatism, an intellectual precursor of the present hard right. Paleoconservatism's vehicles included *The Southern Partisan* (from 1979) and the Rockford Institute's *Chronicles* (from 1977). Bradford derided Lincoln, opposed civil rights, and campaigned for George Wallace (1972). Liberals, he believed, travestied the American tradition. The nation was culturally Anglo-Saxon, its constitution conservative, not emancipatory, and the American people had never endorsed liberal progress. Reagan named Bradford to head the National Endowment of the Humanities but was thwarted by appalled mainstream conservatives.

F. H. Bradley (1846–1924): Philosopher at Oxford University from 1870 to his death. Britain's leading philosophical idealist, Bradley rejected a common associationist picture of mind, truth, and knowledge adopted from Locke by way of Mill in favor of treating them holistically. Error, for Bradley, lay in partiality, a multipurpose idea that influenced his ethical thought. Kantianism and Utilitarianism, he argued, each wrongly isolated one undisputed aspect of human personhood, hence morality. In "My Station and Its Duties" (1876), Bradley criticized the supposedly liberal picture of socially detachable people choosing aims and attachments at will. His political lesson was subtle, however. A person could fail society by self-isolation or refusal of duty. Society could fail people by not providing stations from which binding duties and a sense of themselves arose. Labeling Bradley a conservative is tentative, although he was more doubtful of social reform than an older British idealist whose work he followed, T. H. Green.

Jason Brennan (1979–): American political thinker versed in the study of elections and how little voters know. In *Against Democracy* (2016), Brennan revived earlier doubts raised, for example, by Schumpeter and Hayek about the compatibility of liberal capitalism with electoral democracy. Of right-wing libertarian outlook, Brennan was no longer confident that the rights to good and limited government enjoyed, on his view, by each citizen were still adequately protected from ignorant majorities. Brennan defended "epistocracy," that is, competent government by those who knew what they were doing as opposed to incompetent government confirmed by voters who didn't know what they were voting for or why.

Orestes Brownson (1803–76): Against Protestant prejudice, Brownson defended Catholics as loyal Americans. Born on a Vermont farm and self-taught, Brownson journeyed to Catholicism from strict Calvinism via Boston Unitarianism. An anti-Whig and paternalist social-Christian, Brownson defended workers' claims against bosses in "The Laboring Classes" (July 1840). *The American Republic* (1866) criticized liberalism for misrepresenting freedom and society. Being free, for government and citizen alike, amounted to obeying just laws. Society was not a compact but "an organism, and individuals live in its life as well as it in theirs." Brownson was conservative in seeking to temper democratic liberalism by beneficent moral guidance.

Patrick Buchanan (1938–): A Washington DC–born journalist, "Paleo-Republican," Catholic, and unilateralist, Buchanan was an aide, speechwriter, and campaign sidekick in Nixon's comeback (1966–68), who coined for him the phrase "silent majority." He urged Nixon to take a Jacksonian, "anti-elitist" line and raid the opposition's working-class preserves: "Daley-Rizzo Democrats" (Northern Catholic ethnics) and "Wallace Democrats" (Southern Protestant conservatives). After serving Reagan, Buchanan ran for president himself as an America Firster, winning a fifth of the vote in the Republican primaries (1992; 1996). He launched a unilateralist fortnightly, the *American Conservative* (2002), opposed the Iraq War (2003), and, dismayed by the Bush-Cheney White House, urged conservatives to vote for Democrats (2006).

William Buckley Jr. (1925–2008): Self-assured, quick-witted American Catholic controversialist, editor, and TV host who did much to restore conservatism to public argument in the US after 1945. His flagship was the magazine *National Review* (founded 1955). It united diverse streams of the American right: anticommunism, traditionalism, and the money interests. After sidelining the cranks, Buckley skillfully held together a fractious army of cold warriors, moral conservatives, and economic liberals. He was, he said of himself, "spiritually and philosophically" a conservative, but not "temperamentally." A balloon pricker and phrasemaker, Buckley could make prejudice sound urbane. On his talk show, *Firing Line*, bien-pensant liberals from ease and good schools like Buckley's often fell victim to his sly teasing and dialectical brio. More strategic than dogmatic, Buckley's contribution to the revival of intellectual self-confidence among American conservatives was political and managerial. By insisting it keep a common liberal adversary always in view, Buckley helped the right overlook its own differences.

Edmund Burke (1729–97): Anglo-Irish parliamentarian and political thinker. Politically, Burke was an aide and ideas man for the anti-centralist Rockingham Whigs, friend of American colonists, selective scourge of colonial corruption in India, and foe of all who put hope in the French Revolution. Celebrated and translated in life, largely ignored in the nineteenth century, Burke's speeches and writings served later conservatives as spiritual sources for a usable catechism. The French Revolution's faults, Burke judged, were selling church lands to creditors of the French state and unwarranted trust by men of letters in overbroad principles ("the science of constructing a commonwealth, or renovating it or restoring it, is . . . not to be taught à *priori*." Conservatives took from Burke negative lessons for use against social-minded, liberal reform. To shift resources, hence social power, from one class to another by government action was risky or futile. Requiring customary institutions to justify themselves was in general vain because those tests rested on custom. Since talents and inclinations were diverse, no all-purpose principles could show how people should be handled, directed, or listened to. Government was neither a moral teacher nor guarantor of human betterment. Positively, sound politics rested on shrewdness and prudence. Conservatism's surest guide, on a Burkean view, was well-judged expediency.

James Burnham (1905–87): American, ex-Catholic, ex-Marxist thinker, and Buckley's right hand at the *National Review*. In *The Managerial Revolution* (1941) Burnham opined that managers controlled Western society, and in *Suicide of the West* (1964) that liberalism controlled the managers. Born to railway money, Burnham was a college lecturer, Trotskyist militant, and intelligence operative. Buckley relied on Burnham's brains, his nose for spotting crackpots, and his feel for what the conservative mainstream would wear. In his "Third World War" column Burnham thundered as an anticommunist Ultra, although his actual proposals were less overwrought than the prose. A self-described moderating force on the *National Review*'s left wing," he grew obdurate with age.

John Calhoun (1782–1850): A lawyer from South Carolina, US senator, and vice-president (1825–32), Calhoun argued for the rights of minorities, notably the minority of Southern agrarian states hostile to manufacturing tariffs together with their landed slave owners. In *Disquisition on Government* and *Discourse on the Constitution* (both published posthumously), Calhoun looked to constitutional breakwaters against an intrusive, reforming liberal state. Constitutions were blocking devices against undue power. Democracy spoke for recognized interests, not people en masse. Particular regional interests required protection by, for example, concurrent majorities. People were equal morally but not equal in talent or energy. Liberty and equality were consequently at odds. "Liberty, when forced on a people unfit for it, would, instead of a blessing, be a curse." Later dubbed "the Marx of the master class," Calhoun looked beyond the North-South conflict to labor's battle with capital: "After we are exhausted, the contest will be between the capitalists and the operatives" (1828).

Thomas Carlyle (1795–1881): British author and historian (*French Revolution*, 1837; *Cromwell*, 1845), believer in the influence of great men (*On Heroes, Hero-Worship and the Heroic in History*, 1841), and critic of laissez-faire capitalism (*Past and Present*, 1843). Steeped in German thought and writing, Carlyle rejected worship of "that monster, Utilitaria." When cash payment became the "sole nexus between man and man," true worth was forgotten and social revolution threatened. Tolerant of slavery, he supported the South in America's Civil War. Medieval admirations, electoral hostilities, and weakness for strong leaders misaligned him with party-political conservatism. As an ethico-cultural critic of liberal capitalism, Carlyle's influence was enduring.

François-René de Chateaubriand (1768–1848): Breton Romantic for whom passionate attachment counted more in life and politics than prudential reasoning or partisan obedience; antirevolutionary army volunteer, exile, Napoleonic envoy and later scourge of Napoleon, and founder-editor of *Le Conservateur* (1818). As France's foreign minister (1822–24) Chateaubriand promoted intervention to suppress Spain's liberals only to turn, in opposition, against France's conservative Ultras. His post-Enlightenment *Génie du christianisme* (1802) stressed faith's aesthetic and emotional appeal ("I wept, so I believed") and helped make Catholicism fashionable. The autobiographical *Mémoires d'outre-tombe* (1849–50) ranks with Augustine's and Rousseau's *Confessions* as a masterpiece in the unconservative genre of self-invention. He called himself "Republican by nature, monarchist by reason, Bourbon from honour." Although Maurras begrudgingly took him for a pagan egoist and liberal anarchist in disguise, Chateaubriand passed down to conservatism a Romantic distaste for the "empty world" of liberal modernity and counterpart trust in the "full heart" of faith and loyalty.

Rufus Choate (1799–1859): Conservative Massachusetts Whig and lawyer, US congressman and senator (1841–45). Choate in court made florid, ingenious defenses (e.g., his "sleepwalking" acquittal for murder). As did Beecher's and Emerson's, Choate's civic oratory replaced the church sermon. Friend and eulogist of Webster, his predecessor in the Senate, Choate spoke for the lawful institutions of a settled East, was troubled by an expanding frontier, and was opposed to annexing Texas. His best-known addresses were on soft power and the stabilizing work of law, "The Power of a State Developed by Mental Culture" (1844) and "The Conservative Force of the American Bar" (1845).

William Cobbett (1763–1835): A people's Tory, who loved crown and country, while loathing upstart trade, as well as courtiers, moneymen, and "boroughmongers" (bought politicians) who fed off "the Wen" (London). Son of a Surrey innkeeper, Cobbett was a lawyer's clerk, soldier, publisher-editor of his weekly paper, *The Political Register* (1802–35), and MP (1832–35). Taxation for Cobbett was the conspiracy of upper-class idlers to despoil the common people from self-serving greed or in order to fight pointless wars. Unconvinced by government proposals to relieve agricultural distress, Cobbett set out to see the condition and needs of the countryside for himself, recording his observations in *Rural Rides* (1830).

Samuel Taylor Coleridge (1772–1834): English Romantic poet and anti-liberal social critic who called for a "clerisy" of intellectuals to resist undue freedom and cultural leveling in mass democracy. A clerisy would keep up the nation's ethico-cultural traditions and civilize politics. German idealism stamped Coleridge's prose but his core ideas, presented in *The Constitution of Church and State* (1830), were detachable from philosophical borrowings. Coleridge saw a "wretchedness of division" in society, which he contrasted with the supposed unity of premodern times. Although responsible government had to listen to property, in industrial capitalism Coleridge feared an "overbalance of commercial spirit." Its boisterous energies needed restraining by the landed interest, that is, oversight by the Lords or the Commons. As in the Hegelian system, the crown symbolized the higher unity of state and people. Coleridge's verbose redescriptions of then current English institutions mattered less to conservative tradition than his recognition and promotion of the need for conservative intellectuals.

R. G. Collingwood (1889–1943): Roman historian and archeologist, philosopher of history, and quiet exponent of conservative moderation. He was born in a town on the edge of Britain's Lake District, where his father was Ruskin's secretary. Collingwood was against turning history into empirical science or politics into Utilitarian calculation. In *The New Leviathan* (1942), he wrote that liberals "pictured themselves as dragging the vehicle of progress against the dead weight of human stupidity; and I think they believed Conservatives to be a part of that dead weight. Conservatives understood that there must be a party of progress. Liberals, I think, never understood that there must be a party of reaction."

Joseph Conrad (1857–1924): Polish-British sailor and novelist who combined storytelling craft with a sense of human imperfection and, in his political novels, the counter-Enlightenment belief that historical destiny was opaque. Conrad touched on the corruptions of colonialism (*Heart of Darkness*, 1899) and capitalism (*Nostromo*, 1904), as well as would-be revolutionary follies (*The Secret Agent*, 1907; *Under Western Eyes*, 1911). Not conservative in a partisan sense, Conrad lacked the right-wing commitments of Barrès or Jünger. Unlike Maurras, he had no worked-through outlook. Conrad deflected liberal hope for human progress less directly by focusing on people's moral vulnerabilities and how little they tended to foresee.

Patrick Deneen (1964–): An American politics professor at Notre Dame University, Deneen follows the ethico-cultural anti-liberalism of the late John Neuhaus. In *Why Liberalism Failed*

(2018), a display of prosecutorial oratory in classical periods, Deneen charged liberalism with espousing equal rights but creating material inequality, resting legitimacy on consent but discouraging civic commitment, and emptily defending personal autonomy while sustaining an overly intrusive state. The answer was local communities and free institutions where a conservative counterculture might flourish. With the anti-liberal Adrian Vermeule at Harvard Law School and Jason Brennan at Georgetown, Deneen belies the claim that liberals monopolize American law schools and politics departments.

Benjamin Disraeli (1804–81): As a statesman, political novelist, party leader, and prime minister (1868; 1874–80), Disraeli exemplified the British right's gradual accommodation to liberal modernity. A Romantic "Young England" Tory, he opposed suffrage extension and defended established institutions—landed estates, church, and crown—which embodied, in his vision, the conservative ideals of loyalty, deference, and faith. He ended as a pragmatic manager-tactician largely reconciled to mass democracy, social reform, and the upper classes' loss of cultural privileges. A *Vindication of the English Constitution* (1835) attacked Whigs as self-interested ins tied in Utilitarianism to a flawed philosophy. Disraeli was at once social reformer, imperialist, People's Democrat, and One-Nation Tory, which led critics to call him unprincipled. Charming, raffish, often in debt, and self-promoting, he was to his Liberal rival Gladstone "all display." In partisan loyalty, feel for maneuver, and nose for office, Disraeli showed an instinct for self-preservation that also underlay his party's own remarkable continuity.

Rod Dreher (1967–): A hopeful story told by American conservatives about their tainted, godless culture is that after 1945 an unrepresentative secular-liberal elite seized the churches, universities, media, and courts from a fundamentally God-fearing and virtuous people. Conservatives, leading a moral majority, had to win them back. A bleak story, shared by the American conservative thinker Rod Dreher, is that secular decadence was too seductive not to prevail. Americans were, and would remain, an immoral majority. The righteous response was not politics but spiritual and intellectual renewal in small countercultural communities, which Dreher, a spirited controversialist influenced by Alasdair MacIntyre, argued for in *The Benedict Option* (2017).

Pierre Drieu la Rochelle (1893–1945): A French novelist, journalist, and literary editor during the German occupation (1940–44), Drieu elegantly vilified liberals, parliamentarians, and Jews. With the chauvinist Barrès and the anti-Semitic Céline, Drieu fortified the claim that France's right in the 1930s had the worst authors but the best prose. In *Gilles* (1939), Drieu's bewitching antihero, wounded like him in the trenches, drifts through Paris despising himself, his rich Jewish mistress, his Marxist-Bohemian friends, and France's besieged republican liberals. More a patriotic nihilist than a fascist, Drieu offered no alternative. "The only way to love France today," he wrote, "is to hate it in its present form" (1937).

Maxime Du Camp (1822–94): French author, photographer, and friend of Flaubert, noted for a multivolume account of the 1871 Commune, *Convulsions de Paris* (1878–80), a masterpiece of conservative vituperation and scorn set in a deceptively factual frame of Communal documents and official reports. Du Camp created a polemical, fantastical picture of Paris's common people as weak-willed, malady-prone simpletons led astray by half-educated villains. Driving the Communards was envy, "that primal vice" of "base people with suspect minds." "Collectivists, French communards, German social democrats, Russian nihilists, different labels, similar tendencies . . . different labels, all poison." Du Camp vented conservative fears of mass democracy at their most overwrought.

T. S. Eliot (1888–1965): Eminent American-born literary modernist and conservative dissenter from liberal modernity, as poet, playwright, critic, publisher, and essayist. What stable institutions were for conservatism politically, aesthetic tradition was for Eliot culturally. Tradition answered modernity's spiritual emptiness, as explored poetically in *The Waste Land* (1922). Traditions were not inherited but had to be worked into and upheld. *The Sacred Wood* (1920) aimed to fix a poetic canon and establish, neither puritanically nor didactically, poetry's distinctive moral value as "truth seen in passion." The best course in pagan, materialistic England was "pessimistic renunciation" (*The Idea of a Christian Society*, 1939). More hopefully, high sensibility might yet "permeate" the broader culture (*Notes towards a Definition of Culture*, 1948). Eliot admired Coleridge and wrote a thesis on Bradley's ethical thought. Personal liberty, duties to others, and social order were not for Eliot disentangleable. His appeals for aesthetic retreat from democratic culture nourished conservatism intellectually but without political guidance.

Alain Finkielkraut (1949–): French thinker and cultural critic who has defended Western tradition, especially French tradition, against the confusions of multiculturalism and moral relativism. An essayist and radio-cum-Web controversialist, Finkielkraut was a Maoist in the 1960s, doubter of the sexual revolution in the 1970s, scourge of the postmodern, anti-Enlightenment left in the 1980s, and agonizer about France's loss of civic identity and betrayal of its republican values since the 1990s. As timid Europe abandoned democratic Spain (1936), so, he charged, it deserted Bosnia (1991–95). The French left, Finkielkraut has complained, ducks the sociocultural challenge of Muslim immigration and hides from growing anti-Semitism.

John Finnis (1940–): Australian-born philosopher of law at Oxford University with distinguished students including Neil Gorsuch, justice of the US Supreme Court. Finnis has led scholarly opposition to a common liberal view of law as bound to neutrality over personal morals. In *Natural Law and Natural Rights* (1980; 2011), Finnis defended a neo-Thomist picture of proper law as speaking with authority about the good in human life and what sustaining that good required. Though independent of choices and conventions, human good was neither simple nor unified. Finnis picked out seven separate, basic goods: life and health, noninstrumental knowledge, friendship, play, aesthetic experience, practical reasonableness, and religious faith. Within that framework, Finnis has defended a strict personal morality, notably on abortion, sex, and marriage. Though a steadfast Catholic, he argues in secular terms for the state's duty to police morals. In liberal democracies, moral policing, he allows, must respect established procedures and democratic consent.

Arnold Gehlen (1904–76): Leipzig-born social philosopher who, following an early flirt with "conservative revolution," sought after 1945 to deradicalize and modernize conservative thought in Germany by severing it from exclusionary hatreds, discredited philosophy, and fear of modern society. Conservatism's deep insight, Gehlen believed, was people's need for stable institutions. Humans were creatures of early helplessness and bewilderingly open biological aptitude. Family bonds and social guidance were essential. Technocratic modernity was stabilizing, hence legitimate. Technology was not to be bemoaned in Heideggerian manner but handled. Liberal modernity's demands, by contrast, were indeterminate or unachievable, hence Utopian. They uprooted established norms yet demanded too much ethically of people, who needed "unburdening" from impossible duties. The challenge was to embrace technocratic modernity without ditching embedded norms. Gehlen's answer, in "realist" spirit, was to severe political-institutional morality from small-group, personal morality. He worried, though, whether liberal society had the discipline to sustain the second sort, a link to American neoconservatism.

Friedrich von Gentz (1764–1832): Prussian publicist and diplomat who (from 1802) worked for Austrians, notably Metternich, and was secretary-drafter to the congresses of the post-Napoleonic settlement (1814–22). A pupil of Kant's, Gentz translated and clarified Burke's *Reflections*. The revolutionaries' mistake, Gentz insisted, was not in having ideas about politics at all but in having the wrong ones. Gentz updated *raison d'état* in service of social and international order. He was "realist" in making politics the exercise of power and power's task the keeping of established order. Among Europe's states that meant a balance of power; within them, locally chosen institutions, unless disturbing to continental peace; and for Germans, the promotion of faith (which fostered obedience), not democracy (opinion was to be formed, not followed). "We do not want the mass to become wealthy and independent of us. How could we govern them if we were?" Gentz asked. His legacy to "realist" conservatism was linking institutional order within states to durable order among states.

Otto von Gierke (1841–1921): German jurist and historian of law who stressed the historical and juridical independence of civil associations. Historically, citizens and state had not created political society without aid of intermediary bodies. Juridically, a healthy society needed self-regulating, voluntary institutions shielded from the state and mutable private interests. Gierke's chief work, in four parts, *The German Law of Associations* (1868–1913) viewed law not as legislated from above but grown from below by custom for society's sake without preestablished pattern. Corporate bodies gave members a sense of themselves. They stored customs, norms, and knowledge. Gierke saw a perilous slope from Locke and Grotius (who tied associations' rights to members' rights) to the French Revolution (putting associations under central legal control). A monarchist, Gierke was close to Germany's National Liberals but concerned for social welfare. His conservatism lay in stressing the harmony and intrinsic healthiness of society, which had little need for an omnicompetent, reforming liberal state.

Ian Gilmour (1926–2007): British Conservative MP (1962–92), minister, and exemplary Wet, who spoke up for middle-of-the-road social-minded Toryism as it was dying. *Inside Right* (1977) contained urbane mini-portraits of historical Conservatives and essays on right-wing thought. Conservatism was celebrated negatively: neither reaction, ideology, exclusion (a slap at Powell), nor blind anti-liberalism and antisocialism. Gilmour's canon, stretching back to the eighteenth century, included Bolingbroke and Disraeli (Tories as the national party); Hume (our intellectual fallibility and need for cheerfulness); Burke and Hailsham (social health required faith); and Oakeshott (against "rationalism" in politics). Notable was Gilmour's attack on Hayek-inspired economic liberalism then sweeping the Conservatives as new orthodoxy.

Karl Ludwig von Haller (1768–1854): Swiss-born government official and theorist of conservative reaction, as argued for in his six-volume *Restoration of Politics* (1816–34). Haller's insistence on the unchallenged authority of church and state, a view popular in legitimist courts, was challenged by liberal constitutionalists, notably Hegel, who treated Haller as a silent opponent in

The Philosophy of Right (1820). Haller claimed the natural superiority of the strong, propertied, and clever. The state, to Haller, was a giant household, a "patrimonial state." Haller's authority worship was a constant in an up-and-down life of isolation followed by celebrity and double exile, once from French Republicans and once from Bernese Protestants.

Nathaniel Hawthorne (1804–64): A Salem, Massachusetts–born American writer and moral pessimist. Hawthorne's novels and allegorical tales offered a powerful reimagination of the Puritan element in American thought, with its assurance of human depravity and scorn for ameliorative hope. A Democrat tax official done down by Boston Whigs, Hawthorne believed neither in liberal progress nor the abolitionist cause. A sense of sin and folly pervaded his writing. Every new society, a Hawthorne character said, soon found itself needing a prison and a graveyard. His popular allegory "The Earth's Holocaust" (1844) mocked evangelical hopes for this-worldly reform of imperfect humankind. *The Blithedale Romance* (1852) satirized the Fourierist commune at Brook Farm, which he helped pay for and where he briefly lived. *The Scarlet Letter* (1850) posed, without resolving, Puritanism's abiding conflict between personal conscience and social shame. Hawthorne was a conservative counterinstance to the callow picture of the American spirit as liberal and optimistic at birth.

Martin Heidegger (1889–1976): German philosopher of heroic depth to admirers and evasive obscurity to doubters. His chief work, *Being and Time* (1927), fed existentialist and other anti-naturalistic philosophies in France, Germany, and elsewhere. Heidegger aimed to retrieve (and aggrandize) the authoritative integrity of everyday experience from scientistic, objectifying views of human life. The project involved the pocketable claims that we were "thrown" into life and must find our own purposes; our attitudes to the world and to our fellows had in common a practical-minded "care," that is, outward-looking concern; our most reliable moral beacon in a post-religious world was authenticity, a mix of not hiding behind social roles and stoically facing mortality. After embracing Nazism (1933), Heidegger fell silent but never shook off the taint. He was not conservative in a party-political sense; his conservatism lay in the high-level rejection of naturalistic views of people and their concerns, on which liberal modernism was alleged to depend.

Charles Hodge (1797–1878): American theologian at Princeton Theological Seminary whose bleak Calvinism and literal readings of scripture stamped twentieth-century Fundamentalism and Evangelicalism. Hodge opposed religious revivalism and its political cousin, abolitionism. For revivalists, faith could silence anxieties about our ultimate end. Hodge's Calvinism denied us knowledge or control over the whether and when of redemption. A slaveholder, Hodge took slavery as biblically approved but decried Southern maltreatment and thought denying slaves schooling was abhorrent. An American nationalist, he backed the Union. Twentieth-century political evangelicals drew selectively on Hodge's theology. Liberal evangelicals recalled his disavowal of self-reliance; conservative evangelicals, his disbelief in human equality or progress.

Quintin Hogg, Lord Hailsham (1907–2001): British lawyer-politician, long-serving Lord Chancellor (justice minister), and Conservative party stalwart, who in *The Case for Conservatism* (1947) set out a middle-of-the-road Toryism. Like Disraeli and Baldwin, Hogg presented conservatism as the common sense of a solid, competent, and fair-minded nation, which liberals and socialists refused to heed. Society was an organism, not a machine. Though inevitable, change must be gradual and respect tradition. Reformers tended to "dictatorial methods" that provoked "self-defeating reaction." Progress was possible, but "to combat evil" mattered politically as much as "to create good." Politics was not all of life; family, neighbors, and faith mattered more.

Bertrand de Jouvenel (1903–87): Conservative French social thinker who, after an early flirt with the authoritarian right, turned to criticizing post-1945 democratic liberalism. *On Power* (1945) argued that liberalism's resistance to power had perversely empowered an "ubiquitous Minotaur," the modern state. The authority of "intermediary bodies" preceded the state's, but theirs was now eroded. To restore them, Jouvenel looked to republican-minded civic elites but doubted the modern rich would supply them. *Sovereignty* (1955) traced the historical emergence of domineering power justified by popular sovereignty. Without a party-political home, dogma preoccupied him less than practical tasks at which democratic liberalism seemed to fail: housing, schools, pollution, economic management, and city planning. At either end of life, Jouvenel drew attention outside the world of ideas. At seventeen, he had an affair with his stepmother, the novelist Collette. In his eighties, he won token damages in French court against a historian who labeled his early thinking fascist.

Ernst Jünger (1895–1998): A decorated German soldier, author, essayist, and insect collector, Jünger fought in the 1914–18 and 1939–45 wars. *Storm of Steel* (1920), drafted from his trench diaries, stressed war's moral opportunity: courage in facing its horrors could elevate humdrum lives. In the 1920s, Jünger joined the "conservative revolution," the loose search on the German right for a redemption of liberal society that, to its critics, aimed to blend conservatism with Bolshevism. Unwilling to be a Nazi literary star, Jünger went into retirement (1933). His fable *On the Marble Cliffs* (1939) was for some a veiled attack on Hitlerism, for others a neo-Nietzschean grumble about the democratic loss of excellence and daring. Admirers found Jünger's cool, modernist prose honest and observant. To doubters, it was mannered and amoral. His implicit politico-moral message was stoical service in war, aloof withdrawal in peace. Jünger's conservatism was aesthetic and largely negative, a turning of his back on democratic liberalism without suggesting a constructive alternative.

Wilhelm von Ketteler (1811–77): Bishop of Mainz, active locally and nationally in the cause of social Catholicism. In Hesse-Darmstadt, he was right-hand man to its reactionary, anti-Prussian premier. For the sake of social peace, Ketteler thought the working classes' economic, not political, demands should be met. He opposed Bismarck's anti-Catholic *Kulturkampf* and favored Catholic-Protestant reconciliation. In *The Labour Question and Christianity* (1864), Ketteler blamed liberals for promoting a ruinous picture of society that took people for "atoms of stuff" to be "pulverized" and "blown over the earth." Ketteler's writings and sermons stamped the conservative, top-down, social Catholicism promulgated in the papal encyclical *Rerum Novarum* (1891).

Willmoore Kendall (1909–67): Yale professor, CIA officer, *National Review* writer, and hard-right herald. Trotskyist, Democrat, and anti-liberal conservative (though never Republican), Kendall espoused a right-wing populism of his own devising. A majoritarian, he trusted "the people" against out-of-touch liberals who had seized society's heights. Kendall saw the people as a virtuous, neglected majority deliberating under God. American society was not open or diverse. Its schools and churches were correct to expel Communists. Immigration of "certain types that some . . . regard as undesirable" was undesirable. In "What Is Conservatism?" (1962), Kendall saw it negatively as a set of counter-ideas in an asymmetric war with democratic liberalism.

Russell Kirk (1918–94): Michigan-born American author of *The Conservative Mind* (1953), which aimed to answer Lionel Trilling's challenge (1950) that liberalism was the only tradition in American politics. A "traditionalist" conservative, Kirk proposed a Burke-led canon of eighteenth- to twentieth-century British and American thinkers. He also picked out six conservative precepts: belief in a transcendent order, acceptance of mystery, inevitability of class-based social order, interdependence of freedom and property, trust in custom, which innovation, though welcome, must respect, and recognition of prudence as a guiding political value. A Tridentine Catholic, who favored the Latin ritual, Kirk was noted for personal generosity and care for the needy.

Aurel Kolnai (1900–73): Austrian-born emigré philosopher who settled in England. A student of Husserl, Kolnai attended to the character of everyday experience and to neglected moral emotions such as hatred and disgust. His *Struggle against the West* (1938) took Utopian faith in social progress and human equality as the common flaw of communism, fascism, and liberalism. Democratic society needed stable leadership and guidance from a "head," a settled atmosphere of respect for excellence, and "social nobility"; otherwise, societies were on "lethal course to qualitative egalitarianism." Kolnai's conservatism lay in his defense of high standards against cultural majoritarianism and the sovereignty of personal opinion.

Irving Kristol (1920–2009): Eminent neoconservative New Yorker whose career tracked the long search for a political home among intellectuals on the American right. Brooklyn-born war veteran and anti-Stalinist, Kristol broke with the left (early 1950s) on declining to be "anti-anti-Communist." He cofounded the CIA-backed *Encounter* (1953) and, with Daniel Bell, the *Public Interest* (1965). Kristol's targets (1960s) were well-intentioned-but-counterproductive social reform and unchecked, antinomian dissent (anti-war protest, denial of tutorial authority, sexual liberty). Now a Republican, Kristol moved to Washington (1978). A hawk in the Second Cold War (1978–86), Kristol launched the *National Interest* (1985). The US had a "proprietary claim to the world's future" and should shape a world order against destabilizing threats, alone if necessary. Second-generation neoconservatives, inspired by such unilateralism, encouraged war in Iraq (2003). After the Tea Party and Trump, homeless neoconservatives resought a shrinking center-right. Polemical in philosophy, Kristol equated liberalism with a nihilist denial of morality.

Félicité de Lamennais (1782–1854): French Catholic priest who swung from Ultramontane (pro-papal) reaction to Christian socialism. His *Indifference in Religion* (1817) attacked Enlightenment skeptics, anticlericals, and anti-papalists for sapping the moral-intellectual order society needed to survive. As an Ultra, he wrote for Chateaubriand's *Conservateur*. Lamennais hoped first for a Europe of Christian theocracies but soon despaired of France's Bourbons. In 1830, he helped found a short-lived daily, *L'Avenir*, which was promptly condemned by the Vatican. His support for the Polish uprising (1831) drew further papal censure. By the hungry 1840s, Lamennais's open embrace of popular, social-minded Catholicism put him at war with the church hierarchy. Now more socialist than liberal, Lamennais treated liberalism as war of all against all unless grounded on social responsibility and common faith. He favored personal liberties but questioned how achievable liberties were amid unfettered economic markets. As a newspaper publisher, he remarked how much money was needed to enjoy free speech.

Gustave Le Bon (1841–1931): Omnicurious French doctor, social thinker, and scientific popularizer who put immemorial fear of the mob on a factual-sounding, nonclass basis. In *The Crowd: A Study of the Popular Mind* (1895), Le Bon suggested that crowds had a collective mind driven by hidden instincts that silenced even reasonable members. "Isolated, a man may be a cultivated individual; in a crowd, he is a barbarian." Crowds occurred at all social levels. They could be criminal (riots) or heroic (battle). Both "primitive" and "civilized" peoples, elites and masses might form crowds. So could parliaments. Crowds were dominable by strong leaders. Or they might dissolve spontaneously. When crowd-thinking seized a social caste (for example, priests, judges, military officers, industrial workers), it tended to crystallize and endure. The caste then claimed authority over the masses. Le Bon's conservatism lay in a suspicion of democratic leveling and rejection of political liberalism's picture of the self-reliant, reasonable citizen.

Alasdair MacIntyre (1929–): Scottish ex-Marxist, Catholic philosopher, and anti-liberal scourge. In *After Virtue* (1981) MacIntyre took incoherence about morality to be liberalism's primal stain, passed down from the Enlightenment, "a machine for demolishing outlooks." Enlightenment had abandoned the Aristotelian conviction that people found moral purpose only as social beings. Whereas a socially anchored morality gave guidance, liberal morality was argumentative, detached, impersonal, indecisive, and inconclusive. The only moral guides left were "the aesthete" and "the therapist"; the only political guide, "the manager," tasked with impartial, cost-effective balancing of people's wants. Empty, morality-like talk continued as claims to rights, as Nietzschean unmasking of hidden interests, or as protest, the only dissent short of civil conflict. MacIntyre's bleak account of liberalism's intellectual disorder paralleled postmodernist despair at theoretical incoherence generally. MacIntyre proposed an archipelago of nonliberal institutions to shelter countertraditions from an indifferent, secular society, an idea taken up on the American Catholic right.

James Madison (1751–1836): American lawyer, drafter of Virginia's constitution, campaigner for a national government (*The Federalist Papers*, 1788, with Hamilton and Jay), framer of the US Constitution, and president (1809–17). Madison's triple aim was to establish a single national authority, recognize popular sovereignty, and prevent the tyranny of majorities. He shared Jefferson's democratic belief that government should answer to popular control but believed peace and prosperity unattainable without overall central power and uniform national laws. Poor in health and small, Madison missed the Revolutionary War but became a leading force in the creation of a new republic. Having secured religious liberties in Virginia, he won inclusion of the Bill of Rights in the Constitution. As an opposition leader to Adams, he opposed the Alien and Sedition Acts (1798). He served Jefferson as secretary of state (Louisiana Purchase, 1803). His presidency was marked by renewed war with Britain over territory (Canada) and British interference with American shipping.

Joseph de Maistre (1753–1821): Exile Savoyard lawyer, ambassador to Russia (1803–17), and anti-revolutionary thinker, best known for the *Saint-Petersburg Dialogues* (1821). Maistre's conservatism rested on a grim vision of humanity as irrational, incurably wicked, and governable only by unbridled power. In the superheated prose of the *Dialogues* and other works, recurring themes stood out. The Terror in the French Revolution was God's punishment for the Enlightenment denial of faith. Once purged in blood, France merited salvation and was duly rescued from Napoleonic captivity by the European allies. The callow Enlightenment ignored human irrationality and violence, as well as humanity's need for sacrifice, obedience, and submission. There were no presocial humans nor any "man in general," only particular men of some national type. Maistre followed Burke in rejecting institutional ideals while insisting on theocracy as the best form of government. Social order required undivided, sovereign power, submitted to in awe. Institutions could not endure impious doubt: "If you wish to conserve all, consecrate all." Faith was required but not enough. Fear of punishment was prior. The emblem of good government was not the wise ruler but the executioner. Among forerunners, Maistre would never sit well in conservatism's front parlor, but he belonged in the household as much as Burke.

William Mallock (1849–1923): English novelist of ideas, political author, and spokesman for conservative causes. Mallock was an inegalitarian who disbelieved in human progress. Material betterment and sustainable prosperity depended on the wise guidance of talented elites. Politics should not reflect popular opinion; it was a contest for control among small groups. Taxing wealth to help manual workers penalized the mental work of entrepreneurs, on which prosperity depended. Mallock's novel *The New Republic* (1877) satirized liberal intellectuals who abandoned religious orthodoxy. The Conservative Central Office used his writings for campaigning. Mallock thought conservatives should resist any further extension of electoral democracy because it promised too much economic democracy.

Jacques Maritain (1882–1973): Together with Emmanuel Mounier (1905–50), Maritain espoused a French Catholic understanding of politics, drawn from Thomist tradition, known as personalism. Although anti-liberal, it sought a path between secular radicals and socialism on the one hand, and the anti-republican hard right (condemned by the Vatican in 1926) on the other. Maritain, a neo-Thomist scholar in the natural-law tradition, was France's ambassador to the Vatican (1945–48). In *Man and the State* (1951), Maritain set out a morality of politics organized around a distinction between the (spiritual) person, with unassailable, common rights and duties of a moral kind, and the (legal) individual, with positive rights and duties of a local, civic kind. His thinking influenced the drafting of the Universal Declaration of Human Rights in 1948. Mounier, a teacher and publicist, launched and ran the influential personalist journal *L'Esprit*.

Odo Marquard (1928–2015): German aphoristic defender of humanities and storytelling as necessary compensation in an ever more technocratic society. "The more modern the world, the more dispensable are the human sciences: sciences that tell a story." After philosophical and theological studies, Marquard assisted Joachim Ritter, theorist of culture as "compensation." Though versed in Freudianism and sympathetic to the Frankfurt School critics of liberalism, Marquard doubted the left's trust in grand ideas and stressed human imperfectability. As if to excuse conservatism's lack of an all-in theory, Marquard, in quietist spirit, saw the history of philosophy as a movement from early omnicompetence, through service as "handmaiden" (for Christianity, science, and politics), to its only remaining usefulness, which was to acknowledge its own limits.

Charles Maurras (1868–1952): Editor, writer, and thinker, founding member of Action Française (1898), and right-wing thorn of the Third Republic. Maurras loved the classical past; admired, without believing in, Catholicism; and claimed, like Comte, to found a political outlook on facts. Liberals, who were libertarians or anarchists, mistook the facts. Society did not consist of personal units cooperating for mutual advantage, and authority did not depend on choice. Society needed shared a belief, no matter which, and in France, Catholicism was near to hand. Personal rights masked commercial interests. Liberals, mistaking authority for state power, neglected the authoritative collectivities that composed society. Parliament, a sham, spoke for a "legal" France captured by Protestants, Jews, Freemasons, and immigrants. As corrupt "insider-outsiders," they self-servingly betrayed the "real" France of people, towns, parishes, and associations. A patriotic anti-German, Maurras nevertheless welcomed Pétainism as an authoritarianism that was second-best to monarchy. Maurras fashioned a rhetorical arsenal for hard-right populism in use to this day.

H. L. Mencken (1880–1956): Conservative Baltimore journalist and critic for the *Smart Set* and the *American Mercury* who delighted readers (1920s) by mocking political follies and cultural pretension. Mencken's prejudices—against blacks, Jews, women, and foreigners save Germans—were unconfined, proudly expressed, and now unprintable. He called democracy "the art of running the circus from the monkey cage." Without positive opinions, he declined into out-of-touch grumpiness and rated Roosevelt below Hitler. To admirers, Mencken deflated political correctness and was so outrageous as to mock bigotry itself. Nonadmirers found it progress that people (for a time) learned not to sound off in public in the same way as Mencken wrote.

Arthur Moeller van den Bruck (1876–1925): An advocate of Germany's "conservative revolution" and author of *The Third Reich* (1923), his clotted vision of a socialist conservatism grown "organically" from the German nation. Son of an architect who named him "Arthur" after the philosophical pessimist Schopenhauer, Moeller left school with no diploma and made his name by writing popular lives of eminent Germans, arranged to typify national characters. An admirer of Dostoevsky's anti-modernism, Moeller supervised a complete edition of his works in German before suffering a crack-up and killing himself. The visible thread in Moeller's tangled thought was abiding hostility to liberalism, which he called "the death of nations."

Gouverneur Morris (1752–1816): A rich, witty New Yorker, tireless speaker at the Constitutional Convention (1787), and crafter of the final draft, Morris did not share the rhetorical enthusiasm for France's revolution of Jefferson, his predecessor as American envoy in Paris. Morris in France (1792–94) so feared the crowd and favored the crown that the republic asked for his recall. Morris was strongly federalist, antislavery, and undemocratically exclusive in his understanding of "We the people," the opening phrase of the Constitution's preamble, the writing of which he supervised.

Adam Müller (1779–1829): Berlin-born conservative writer, Austrian official, and friend of Gentz. Müller fashioned a hostile picture of revolutionary thought for use against political liberalism. People for Müller were not "thinkable" outside the state, which blurred for him with society. In *Von der Idee des Staates* (The idea of the state, 1809), Müller argued that people could not leave a state at will. States were never conjured into life; they had no date of birth or death. They were not tools for people's purposes. In answer, Müller wrote that each person "stands in the middle of civic life, wrapped into the state on all sides"; nobody joined a new society, but "every citizen stands in the middle of lifetime of a state" with unbounded past behind and future ahead. States were not instruments for the satisfaction of citizen's needs and demands but "the whole of civic life itself, necessary and inevitable as soon as there are people."

Henry, Cardinal Newman (1801–90): British religious thinker and prominent clergyman who disbelieved in liberal progress and mass democracy. Newman, first an Anglican, joined the Roman Catholic Church in 1845. Politically, he moved from die-hard Toryism to social-minded, Catholic paternalism. Humanity, in his view was corrupt and society imperfect; not even a society of good Christians would be just. Society could nevertheless be stable and healthy with religion. A common faith would bind society, enabling authority to govern with police rule by consent. Of ways to govern—"subordination" (authoritarianism), "participation" (mass democracy), and "co-ordination," Newman preferred the last, a social union offering protections and liberties under a single, overarching belief.

Robert Nozick (1938–2002): American philosopher whose venture into political thought, *Anarchy, State and Utopia* (1974), invoked rights and liberties against social-minded liberal reform. Trying to redistribute wealth to reduce inequality was bound, Nozick believed, to infringe on personal rights. Equal rights expressed an ungainsayable natural liberty in people that no government could properly curtail save to protect their security and enforce freely struck contracts. Nozick included among the liberties held by right the freedoms from taxation, economic regulation, military conscription, and moral policing. Nozick's libertarianism is awkward for conservatives. They may welcome principled arguments against taxes and welfare but still worry that other social values of importance to conservatism—for example, patriotism, sense of communal duty, and neighborliness—vanish from the libertarian picture, save as contingent outcomes of self-regarding choices.

Michael Oakeshott (1901–90): British political philosopher, claimed by liberals and conservatives alike. Oakeshott forswore political rationalism (attempts to guide society on a chosen course) together with ideology (aims snatched from the context of thinking in which they sprang). Since forms of political life shaped political discourse, they could not be rejected wholesale without the risk of incoherence. "Rationalism in Politics" (1947) attacked the errors of thinking that any social arrangement was open to criticism and that social remedies, if uniform, well-grounded, and universally applied, could improve society overall. Politics was not an enterprise with a common aim but arose as a by-product of life together in a "civil association," akin to clubs or societies without single purposes but under accepted rules. In *On Human Conduct* (1975), Oakeshott invoked the enterprise-association distinction when contrasting two pictures of politics: purpose-governed, tradition-ignoring teleocracy (bad) and purposeless, rule-governed, tradition-respecting nomocracy (good). From one hero, Hobbes, Oakeshott took the moral authority of civil association as compatible with liberty, understood as the absence of external constraint. From another, Hegel, he took morality as pointless unless "suspended in a religious or social tradition." Oakeshott was liberal in his hostility to dogma, systems, and social interference with people, conservative in his refusal to believe in liberal progress.

Enoch Powell (1912–1998): A scholarly, polyglot, long-serving Conservative MP and minister (health, treasury), Powell was herald of Britain's present-day hard right. Although Powell was spurned in his day and sacked (1968) by Heath from the shadow cabinet for an inflammatory speech on immigration, a shrewd Tory editorialist wrote that containing Powellism would occupy his party for a decade. Half a century later, liberal Conservatives were still floundering and in the end failing at their efforts to contain Powellism. As a right-wing member of the One Nation group of young Tory MPs (early 1950s), Powell hardened the one-nation theme, dear to Disraeli and Baldwin, into three interlocking claims: postimperial Britain was alone in the world (the Commonwealth was a sham; the US, not a friend but a bully; Europe, a trap); the postwar liberal British state was at war with British society (aka "people of Britain"); and the British national character was precious and unique. Each idea came into its own on the British hard right after 2010.

Ayn Rand (1905–82): A self-possessed, dogmatic writer-thinker and founder of a movement she called Objectivism, Rand wrote two novels of ideas that won her a huge readership, *The Fountainhead* (1943) and *Atlas Shrugged* (1957). Both expressed her belief that the Judeo-Christian morality of duty and care should give way to bracing self-promotion, decisiveness, and bold projects, a plea repeated in *The Virtue of Selfishness* (1964). Rand left the exposition of Objectivism to her followers. Although her celebration of capitalism and diagnosis of socialism as politicized envy was welcome on the right, worldly wise American conservatives in the main took Randism for an ill-adapted and poorly reasoned eccentricity.

Wilhelm Riehl (1823–97): German conservative folklorist and pioneer of social geography, admired and translated by George Eliot. Riehl contrasted the healthiness of the countryside with the unhealthiness of cities. His "natural history of society" included *Land and People* (1854), which stressed how land shaped society (German woods against French and English fields; artificial cities dependent on transport for resources against "natural," self-sufficient cities); *Middle-Class Society* (1851), which lamented cities presided over by commercial bourgeoisie and rootless intellectuals; *The Family* (1855), which took the masculine-feminine distinction as natural and "individualist" equality as corrosive; and *Walking* (1869), which noted the growing fashion for country walks, anticipating nature conservation and Greenism.

Phyllis Schlafly (1924–2016): A pioneer of recent American "values" conservatism and antifeminist, Schlafly won notice as author of *A Choice Not an Echo* (1964), an attack on center-right Republicanism that sold, it was claimed, three million copies. Schlafly, a conservative Catholic, led the successful national campaign against ratification of the Equal Rights Amendment, which she derided as a charter for "Typhoid Marys carrying a germ called lost identity." She founded the Eagle Forum (1972), a Tea Party precursor, which opposed detente with the Soviet Union and in the name of American or "family values" attacked abortion, "activist judges," bilingual schooling, and government-sponsored health care.

Carl Schmitt (1888–1985): German constitutional scholar, right-wing Catholic conservative, Nazi apologist, and disgraced post-1945 refusenik. The connecting thread in Schmitt's political thought was a corrosive mistrust of democratic liberalism. His charged epigrams included: "Dictatorship is not antithetical to democracy," "When you talk of humanity, you are lying," and "The distinction specific to politics . . . is that between friend and enemy." His presidentialist *Constitutional Theory* (1928) defended extreme measures to protect the constitution and became a standard text. Unlike Heidegger's, Schmitt's engagement with Hitlerism was long and open. After 1945, he turned to geopolitics, writing that Britain and the US hypocritically pursued their global interests in humanity's name. Schmitt's political essays (1920s) pressed at democratic liberalism's weaknesses: slowness to defend its values; recurrent astonishment at passions of nation and faith; undue trust in argument; deafness to myth. Representative parliaments had had their day, but plebiscitary democracy was no better. By exclusion, Schmitt argued himself toward nationalist authoritarianism under a "temporary" dictator.

Joseph Schumpeter (1883–1950): Austrian-born US economist and conservative defender of liberal capitalism, which he treated in *Capitalism, Socialism and Democracy* (1942) as the best of bad ways to organize society, the good ways being unachievable. His picture of capitalism was dialectical: creative but destructive; reliant on entrepreneurial innovation but needing bureaucratic rationalization; unsustainable without popular acceptance but hindered by democratic interference. Could capitalism survive democracy? Yes, Schumpeter thought, given an open, authoritative upper class; an efficient, uncorrupt bureaucracy; social consensus; and institutional breakwaters against majority pressure, especially in economics. A disbeliever, like Italian elite theorists, in popular sovereignty, Schumpeter saw electoral democracy as a contest among small groups for office: "Democracy is the rule of politicians." Though wary of socialist intellectuals, Schumpeter welcomed a left that accepted capitalism. His contribution to conservatism was to map a space at the center-right where conservatives might compete for office with a center-left similarly reconciled to capitalism, liberalism, and democracy.

Roger Scruton (1944–2020): Eloquent British philosopher-polemicist of daunting range—from the aesthetics of art, architecture, and music to moral and political thought. In many books, beginning with *The Meaning of Conservatism* (1980), Scruton laid out, in defense of conservative values, a philosophical critique of political liberalism. His cardinal thought was that people needed established institutions and established institutions needed people's "allegiance." "Establishment," Scruton wrote, "is the great internal aim of politics." Liberals who mistook state and society for contractual arrangements among "rationally calculating" citizens treated politics as an endless lawsuit for noncompliance, thus exaggerating the cogency and relevance of social criticism. The typical liberal was a vexatious litigant; the typical conservative, a pious believer. Society could not cohere without a common faith and government was not possible "without the propagation of myths." Conservatism's *conservandum* was established order, which varied from country to country; conservatism had, accordingly, no one form. A polyglot exegete of the Western tradition, he annoyed the intellectual left by careful, but not always fair or respectful, readings of its post-1945 totems, both liberal and nonliberal. His own intellectualism taxed workaday conservatives. His output was prodigious, but he lacked right-wing equals to argue with. Scruton's prowess shows a weakness of present-day conservative thought, which has too few Scrutons.

Noel Skelton (1880–1935): Scottish Unionist, lawyer, war veteran, *Spectator* journalist, MP (1293; 1924–35), and author of *Constructive Conservatism* (1924), a pamphlet that popularized "property-owning democracy." Skelton hoped wider private ownership, as against collective ownership, would steady British democracy by matching electoral enfranchisement with higher economic status for wage earners, "bridge the economic gulf . . . between Labour and Capital," and serve as "vehicle for the moral and economic progress of the individual."

Skelton's ideas inspired young Conservatives such as Macmillan and others looking for an economic "middle way." By the 1950s, British Conservatives had transmuted Skelton's call for property-owning democracy into a campaign for private home ownership, and by the 1970s into the call for wide ownership of company shares.

Peter Sloterdijk (1947–): An idiosyncratic German social thinker and essayist, professor at the Karlsruhe University of Art and Design, host of television philosophy show (2002–12), and bête noir of liberal left, Sloterdijk occupies an intellectual space in Germany not unlike that of Scruton in Britain—disliked by the left but too detached from policy and party politics to be directly useful to the right. Sloterdijk made his name with the 950-page *Critique of Cynical Reason* (1983), followed by a three-volume illustrated rumination on the human condition, *Spheres* (1998–2004). We are, for Sloterdijk, inventive toolmakers in a cluttered space who must "immunize" and shelter ourselves from present-day chaos. His politics is hard to pigeonhole. He finds the center's discomfort salutary. He can sound libertarian (taxes are theft and voluntary contributions should replace income tax), hard right (toying with its slogan words), or simply turned off (liberal democracy is boring). Much as Scruton needs an interlocutor, Sloterdijk needs an editor. In the runaway prose lurk telling insights. Rage, Sloterdijk has written, is the characteristic social emotion of our day.

Georges Sorel (1847–1922): French social critic and civil engineer, who retired early on a small inheritance to write. His *Illusions of Progress* (1906) and *On Violence* (1908) derided Utopian trust in public reason. Sorel looked to working-class revolt to expose the shortfall between liberal pieties and the actual condition of liberal society. Liberal democracy stifled the sources of vitality—irrationality, myth, and force—with procedures, argument, and talk. Only aimless popular energy could expose the sham. Sorel, who admired Lenin, was not straightforwardly conservative. His contemptuous picture of liberal democracy as a mask for interests ran with electric charge into twentieth-century anti-liberalism on the right.

Friedrich Julius Stahl (1802–61): Prussian conservative, constitutional monarchist (against the Ultras), and legal rationalist (against the Romantics). A converted Jew, Stahl upheld the equal but separate authorities of church and state. Social order lay not in liberal progress or mass democracy but in property and faith. Strategically, Stahl aimed to persuade Germany's landed nobility to drop obstructive privileges in return for governmental primacy while giving bourgeois wealth a secondary share in the three-class Prussian franchise. Constitutionally, sovereign authority could not be shared and did not derive from the common people. Crown and church were each uncontested in their sphere. Both, however, were constrained by the rule of law, "an insurmountable limit to any reactionary programme." Revolution had to be understood, not simply abhorred. Law and reason, not tradition and custom were his guides. Conservatives had to look to the present. "The will of earlier people should be no limitation on the will of present people."

James Fitzjames Stephen (1829–94): English lawyer, political writer, and judge who used literary scorn and Utilitarian arguments in defense of moral policing and established religion. Stephen served as a high-court judge (1879–91) after service in colonial India, where he reformed the legal codes. In *Liberty, Equality, Fraternity* (1873) he held that social order depended on moral restraint. There would always be "an enormous mass of bad and indifferent people," whose "depth of moral failings" could be checked only by compulsion. People were not much improvable, so liberal hope for progress was delusory. Nor were people equal, making hopes for democratic sovereignty blind: "Wise and good men ought to rule over foolish and bad." Since people were not fraternal but partial, "the religion of humanity" was a fraud. More controversialist than thinker, Stephen marked a shift for conservatism in public argument's ground rules. The case made for moral policing and respect for religious authority now had to be secular.

William Graham Sumner (1840–1910): An American anti-Progressive, who agreed that people had natural rights and needed socializing but who disagreed on the existence of a common human nature or people's unlimited improvability. Progressivism, resting on those mistakes, included income taxes and imperialist wars to improve Spanish America. A professor of political economy at Yale (1873), Sumner wrote *What Social Classes Owe Each Other* (1883) and *The Science of Society* (1927). His "forgotten man" argument took aim at liberal social help for the needy, which fell on taxpayers unevenly. The "forgotten man" was the A who paid taxes to help B with programs chosen by C.

Heinrich von Treitschke (1834–96): Dresden-born conservative historian and journalist, who fostered an exclusionary self-understanding of the German nation popular among middle-class voters that stamped conservative politics before 1914. Treitschke had platforms as a university professor, editor of the *Prussian Yearbooks* (1866–89), and pro-Bismarck deputy for the National Liberals in the Reichstag. Poorly regarded by historians, Treitschke's dynastic worship of the Hohenzollerns and anti-Semitic prejudice ("The Jews are our misfortune") had a wide following. He turned Karl Rochau's coinage *Realpolitik* (1853) from a liberal warning to themselves to pay less attention to their dreams, into a conservative call for the uninhibited exercise of power: by Prussia over Germany, by Germany over Europe (especially hypocritical England), and by the German empire over inferior colonial peoples. "The state," Treitschke wrote, was not "a good little boy, to be brushed and washed and sent to school." For Treitschke, all elements of national life—identity, well-being, security—converged in the state.

Peter Viereck (1916–2006): Poet, writer, and quiet exponent of a moderate, historically minded conservatism who taught at Mount Holyoke (1948–97). Viereck was the New York–born son of a pro-German Hearst journalist and Nazi apologist. An anti-anticommunist who rejected McCarthyism, he irked fellow contributors to the *National Review* by engaging with liberal opponents. One colleague, Willmoore Kendall, said of Viereck that he told Americans how to be conservative but agreed on everything with the liberals. In "The New Conservatism: One of Its Founders Asks What Went Wrong" (1962), Viereck charged religious fundamentalists, deluded superpatriots, and rich conservatives with destroying the centrist pivot of American politics.

Eric Voegelin (1901–85): German-born American emigré who taught the history of ideas mostly at Louisiana State University (1942–58). Voegelin hoped to shake liberal modernity from its philosophical self-satisfaction by showing that it shared with early Jewish-Christian thinkers an error he called "gnosticism." By gnosticism Voegelin meant the pervasive mistake of confusing foundational ideas that bind together present society with ideal depictions of some future society. Late in *Order and History* (1956–87), modern gnosticism took the stage as liberalism, an impatient attempt to cash in Christianity's redemptive promises in this world. Political ideas included philosophy, myth, and religious revelation. Without sympathetic understanding of them, history could not be grasped as it was experienced. In the gnostic error—which led to judging society by how ideally it should be—Voegelin believed he had diagnosed the commonly identified ills of modernity: excessive individuality and social "massification," twin enablers of totalitarianism. By denying human limitations, on his view, liberals invited near-certain failure, aggrieved disappointment, and an ill-grounded search for culprits.

Richard Weaver (1910–63): North Carolina–born conservative thinker and scholar, author of *Ideas Have Consequences* (1948). Liberal modernity's mistake was to abandon a medieval-classical view of the world in which everything had a value whether humans liked it or not for a view on which humans gave things value for their own purposes. Freed from that error, modern people might yet return to respect for property, piety toward nature, and due care for their neighbors. Although Weaver's idiosyncratic book went unnoticed on publication, Weaver's themes—liberals had no fixed morals; society needed sacredness; Burkeanism was expedient, not principled—later became widely accepted on the American right. His *Ethics of Rhetoric* (1953), also neglected, gave proper due to the political speech as a primary vehicle of political ideas. In "Rhetorical Strategies of the Conservative Cause" (1959), Weaver proposed a Gramscian program of anti-liberal warfare for the American right: nourish cadres and sharpen arguments in well-financed institutions and lobbies.

For this historical essay on the parties and ideas of the political right, I have relied on writings of thinkers and politicians as well as on interpretations and commentaries of scholars and journalists. I am in their debt and thank them all. In the book, there are no item-by-item references to works mentioned or quoted. Below, however, is a selective list of works consulted for each of the book's six parts. It is not meant as a scholarly bibliography but as a guide to how my book grew and to where readers interested in conservatism can find a selection of original sources, histories, and lives, as well as later commentary. Works, accordingly, are limited to those by or about the political right. They are arranged, chapter by chapter, in date order of publication. Book titles and publication names are in italics; article, speech, and pamphlet titles are in quotation marks. For changeable online sources, the date of download or date of latest state at time of download is given.

General

Karl Mannheim, "Das konservative Denken," *Archiv für Sozialwissenschaft und Sozialpolitik* (1927); *Conservatism* (1936); Roberto Michels, "Conservatism," in *Encyclopaedia of the Social Sciences* (1930; 1937); Clinton Rossiter, "Conservatism," in *The International Encyclopedia of the Social Sciences* (1968), ed. Sills and Merton; Russell Kirk, *The Conservative Mind* (1953); Samuel P. Huntington, "Conservatism as an Ideology," *American Political Science Review* (*APSR*) (June 1957); Mathias Greiffenhagen, "Konservativ, Konservatismus," in *Historisches Wörterbuch der Philosophie* (1976), ed. Ritter and Gründer; Anthony Quinton, *The Politics of Imperfection* (1978); Russell Kirk, *The Portable Conservative Reader* (1982); David Kettler, Volker Meja, and Nico Stehr, "Karl Mannheim and Conservatism: The Ancestry of Historical Thinking," *American Sociological Review* (February 1984); Theo Schiller, "Konservatismus," in *Pipers Wörterbuch zur Politik* (1985), ed. Nohlen and

Schultze; Robert Nisbet, *Conservatism: Dream and Reality* (1986); Noel O'Sullivan, "Conservatism," in *The Blackwell Encyclopedia of Political Thought* (1987), ed. Miller; Alain Compagnon, *Les cinq paradoxes de la modernité* (1990); *Conservative Texts: An Anthology* (1990), ed. Scruton; Anthony Quinton, "Conservatism," in *A Companion to Contemporary Political Philosophy* (1993), ed. Goodin and Pettit; Stephen Holmes, *The Anatomy of Antiliberalism* (1993); Jeremy Rabkin, "Conservatism," in *The Oxford Companion to Politics of the World* (1993), ed. Krieger; Brian Girvin, *The Right in the Twentieth Century* (1994); *Lexikon des Konservatismus* (1996), ed. Schrenk-Notzing; Michael Freeden, "The Adaptability of Conservatism," Part III of *Ideologies and Political Theory: A Conceptual Approach* (1996); *Conservatism: An Anthology of Social and Political Thought from David Hume to the Present* (1997), ed. Muller; Noel O'Sullivan, "Conservatism"; Steven Lukes (on left and right), "The Grand Dichotomy of the Twentieth Century"; both in *The Cambridge History of Twentieth-Century Political Thought* (2003), ed. Ball and Bellamy; Arthur Aughey, "Conservatism," in *The New Dictionary of the History of Ideas* (2005), ed. Horowitz; John Morrow, "Conservatism, Authority and Tradition," in *Encyclopedia of Nineteenth-Century Thought* (2005), ed. Claeys; Alain Compagnon, *Les Antimodernes de Joseph Maistre à Roland Barthes* (2005); Alexander Moseley, "Political Philosophy: Methodology," *Internet Encyclopedia of Philosophy* (February 2017); Andy Hamilton, "Conservatism," *Stanford Encyclopedia of Philosophy* (*SEP*) *Online* (April 2017); *Le dictionnaire du conservatisme* (2017), ed. Rouvillois, Dard, and Boutin.

France

The French Right from Maistre to Maurras (1970), ed. McClelland; Eric Cahm, *Politics and Society in Contemporary France 1789–1971* (1972); Theodore Zeldin, *France 1848–1945* (1973); P. Mazgaj, "The Right," in *Historical Dictionary of The Third French Republic: 1870–1940* (1986), ed. Hutton; *Histoire de l'extrême droite en France* (1993), ed. Azéma et al.; René Rémond (with Jean-François Sirinelli), *Notre Siècle de 1918 à 1988*

(1988); *A Biographical Dictionary of French Political Leaders since 1870* (1990), ed. Bell, Johnson, and Morris; *Histoire des droites en France: I. Politique, II. Cultures, III. Sensibilités* (1992), ed. Sirinelli; Sudhir Hazareesingh, *Political Traditions of Modern France* (1994); *Dictionnaire historique de la vie politique française au XXe siècle* (1995), ed. Sirinelli; Robert Tombs, *France 1814–1914* (1996); Peter Davies, *The Extreme Right in France* (2002); François Huguenin, *Le conservatisme impossible: libéraux et réactionnaires en France depuis 1789* (2006); Kevin Passmore, *The Right in France from the Third Republic to Vichy* (2012); *Les grandes textes de la droite* (2017), ed. Franconie; *Dictionnaire de la droite* (2017), ed. Jardin.

Britain

Ian Gilmour, *Inside Right* (1977); Anthony Quinton, *The Politics of Imperfection* (1978); Frank O'Gorman, *British Conservatism: Conservative Thought from Burke to Thatcher* (1986); Anthony Seldon, "Conservative Century"; Brian Girvin, "The Comparative and International Context"; Vernon Bogdanor, "The Selection of the Party Leader"; John Barnes, "Ideology and Factions"; John Barnes and Richard Cockett, "The Making of Party Policy"; Kevin Theakston and Geoffrey Fry, "The Party and the Civil Service"; Ken Young, "The Party and Local Government"; Keith Middlemas, "The Party Industry and the City"; Andrew Taylor, "The Party and the Trade Unions"; Robert Waller, "Conservative Electoral Support and Social Class"; John Lovendoski, Pippa Norris, and Catriona Burness, "The Party and Women"; Peter Catterall, "The Party and Religion," all in *Conservative Century* (1994), ed. Seldon and Ball; *Conservative Realism* (1996), ed. Minogue; Bruce Coleman, "Conservatism," in *The Oxford Companion to British History* (1997); E.H.H. Green, *Ideologies of Conservatism* (2002); *The Oxford Companion to Twentieth-Century British Politics* (2002), ed. Ramsden; John Charmley, *A History of Conservative Politics since 1830* (2008); a general online source, though not free, is *The Oxford Dictionary of National Biography Online* (https://www.oxforddnb.com/)

Germany

Reinhold Aris, *History of Political Thought in Germany from 1789 to 1815* (1936); Klaus Epstein, *The Genesis of German Conservatism* (1966); Hans-Jürgen Puhle, "Conservatism in Modern German History," *Journal of Contemporary History* (special issue: "A Century of Conservatism," October 1978); Martin Greiffenhagen, "The Dilemma of Conservatism in Germany," *Journal of Contemporary History* (October 1979); Geoffrey Eley, *Reshaping the German Right* (1980); H. W. Koch, *A Constitutional History of Germany* (1984); H. A. Turner, *German Big Business and the Rise of Hitler* (1985); Jerry Z. Muller, *The Other God That Failed: Hans Freyer and the Deradicalization of German Conservatism* (1987); S. Davis, "German Conservatism," in *A Dictionary of Conservative and Libertarian Thought* (1991), ed. Ashford and Davies; Frederick Beiser, *Enlightenment, Revolution, and Romanticism: The Genesis of Modern German Political Thought* (1992); *Between Reform and Reaction: Studies in the History of German Conservatism from 1789 to 1945* (1993), ed. Jones and Retallack; David Blackbourn, *The Long Nineteenth Century* (1997); Axel Schildt, *Conservatismus in Deutschland* (1998); H. A. Winkler, *Der Lange Weg nach Westen, Vol. I: 1789–1933, Vol. II: 1933–1990* (2001), trans. Sager, *Germany: The Long Road West, Vols. I: 1789–1933, Vol. II: 1933–1990* (2006); Beiser, *The German Historicist Tradition* (2011); Oded Heilbronner, "Conservatism," in *Ashgate Research Companion to Imperial Germany* (2015), ed. Jefferies; Gerritt Dworok, *"Historikerstreit" und Nationswerdung* (2015); Daniel Ziblatt, *Conservative Parties and the Birth of Democracy* (2017); Matthias Heitmann, "Die Zwillingskrise," *Cicero Online* (February 18, 2018); two excellent free online sources: *German Historical Documents and Images (GHDI Online)* at http:// germanhistorydocs.ghi-dc.org/, German Historical Institute, Washington DC); *Deutsche Biographie Online* at http://www.deutsche -biographie.de, a joint project of the Historical Commission at the Bavarian Academy of Sciences and Humanities with the Bavarian State Library to update and e-publish the *Allgemeine Deutsche Biographie* and *Neue Deutsche Biographie*.

United States

Ralph Waldo Emerson, "The Conservative" (lecture, December 9, 1841); Russell Kirk, *The Conservative Mind* (1953); Clinton Rossiter, *Conservatism in America* (1955; 1962); Richard Hofstadter, *The Paranoid Style in American Politics* (1964); *The Radical Right* (1963), ed. Bell; Peter Steinfels, *The Neoconservatives: The Men Who Are Changing America's Politics* (1979; 2013); Jeffrey Crawford, *Thunder on the Right: The "New Right" and the Politics of Resentment* (1980); E. J. Dionne, *Why Americans Hate Politics* (1991); John Micklethwait and Adrian Wooldridge, *The Right Nation* (2004); *American Conservatism: An Encyclopedia* (2006), ed. Frohnen, Beer, and Nelson; Jacob Heilbrunn, *They Knew They Were Right* (2008); Patrick Allitt: *The Conservatives: Ideas and Personalities Throughout American History* (2009); Julian E. Zelizer, "Rethinking the History of American Conservatism," *Reviews in American History* (June 2010); Corey Robin, *The Reactionary Mind* (2011); Yuval Levin, *The Fractured Republic: Renewing America's Social Contract in the Age of Individualism* (2016); Lily Geismer, *Don't Blame Us: Suburban Liberals and the Transformation of the Democratic Party* (2014); E. J. Dionne *Why the Right Went Wrong* (2016); *American Conservatism: Reclaiming an Intellectual Tradition* (2020), ed. Bacevich; a general online source, though not free, is *American National Biography* (https://www.anb.org/)

Conservatism's Forerunners

Möser: "No Promotion According to Merit" (1770); "On the Diminished Disgrace of Whores and Their Children in Our Day" (1772); both in *Conservatism: An Anthology* (1997), ed. Muller; Jerry Z. Muller, *The Mind and the Market: Capitalism in Western Thought* (2002); Frederick Beiser, *The German Historicist Tradition* (2011).

Müller: "Von der Idee des Staates" (1809); "Adam Smith" (1808); both in *Ausgewählte Abhandlungen* (1921), ed. Spann; Hans Reiss, *Politisches Denken in der deutschen Romantik* (1966); James Retallack, *The German Right 1860–1920* (2006).

REHBERG: *Über den deutschen Adel* (1803); "Die französische Revolution der 1789," in *Sämmtliche Schriften* (1831); Hans-Kristoff Klaus, "Rehberg, August Wilhelm," *NDB* (2003), *Deutsche Biographie Online*; Frederick Beiser, "August Wilhelm Rehberg," *Stanford Encyclopedia of Philosophy Online* (Spring 2019).

MAISTRE: *Oeuvres Complètes, Vols. I–XIV* (1884); *Les Carnets du comte Joseph de Maistre, Livre Journal, 1790–1817* (1923); *The Works of Joseph de Maistre* (1965), ed. Lively; *Joseph de Maistre: Oeuvres* (2007), ed. Glaudes; Augustin Sainte-Beuve, "Joseph de Maistre" (1843), in *La Littérature française à 1870* (1927); Charles de Rémusat, "Traditionalisme: Louis de Bonald et Comte de Maistre," *Revue des deux mondes* 9 (1857); Albert Blanc, *Mémoires politiques et correspondance diplomatique de J. de Maistre* (1859); John Morley, "The Champion of Social Regress," in *Critical Miscellanies* (1871; 1886); Emile Faguet, "Joseph de Maistre," in *Politiques et moralistes du dix-neuvième siècle I* (1891); George Cogordan, *Joseph de Maistre* (1894); Peter Richard Rohden, *Joseph de Maistre als politischer Theoretiker* (1929); Elisha Greifer, "Joseph de Maistre and the Reaction against the Eighteenth Century," *APSR* (September 1961); Jack Lively, "Introduction," in *The Works of Joseph de Maistre*, ed. Lively (1965); E. D. Watt, " 'Locked In': De Maistre's Critique of French Lockeanism," *Journal of the History of Ideas* (January–March 1971); Stephen Holmes, *The Anatomy of Antiliberalism* (1983); Richard Lebrun, *Joseph de Maistre: Intellectual Militant* (1988); Massimo Boffa, "Maistre," in *Dictionnaire Critique de la Révolution Française* (1988); Isaiah Berlin, "Joseph de Maistre and the Origins of Fascism," *New York Review of Books* (*NYRB*) (September 27, October 11, October 25, 1990); Owen Bradley, *A Modern Maistre: The Social and Political Thought of Joseph de Maistre* (1999); Philippe Sollers, "Eloge d'un maudit," in *Discours parfait* (2010); Emile Perreau-Saussine, "Why Maistre Became Ultramontane," trans. Lebrun, in *Joseph Maistre and the Legacy of the Enlightenment* (2011), ed. Armenteros and Lebrun; Sollers, "Prodigieux Joseph de Maistre," interview at www. Philippesollers.net (August 2014).

BURKE: *Vindication of Natural Society* (1756); *Philosophical Enquiry into the Origin of Our Ideas of the Sublime and Beautiful* (1757); *Reflections on the Revolution in France* (1790); *Letter to a Noble Lord* (1796); *Letters on a Regicide Peace* (1796); William Hazlitt, "Edmund Burke" in *The Eloquence of the British Senate* (1807); S. T. Coleridge, "On the Grounds of Government," *The Friend: A Series of Essays* (October 1809); Thomas Moore, *Literary Chronicle* (November 12, 1825); T. E. Kebbell, *A History of Toryism* (1886); James Shelley, "British 18th-Century Aesthetics," *SEP Online* (December 2008); Iain Hampsher-Monk, "Edmund Burke," in *The Routledge Encyclopedia of Philosophy*, disc version, *REP 1.0* (2001); Michael A. Mosher, "The Skeptic's Burke: Reflections on the Revolution in France, 1790–1990," *Political Theory* (August 1991); Jerry Z. Muller, *The Mind and the Market* (2002); Francis Canavan, SJ, "Foreword," *Reflections on the Revolution in France* (Repr., E. J. Payne ed. [1874–78], 1999), *Online Library of Liberty*; Richard Bourke, *Empire and Revolution: The Political Life of Edmund Burke* (2015); Emily Jones, "Conservatism, Edmund Burke and the Invention of a Political Tradition, c. 1885–1914," *Historical Journal* (December 2015); Jones, *Edmund Burke and the Invention of a Political Tradition, 1830–1914* (2017).

CHATEAUBRIAND: *Génie du Christianisme* (1802); "De la nouvelle proposition rélative au banissement de Charles X" (1831); *Mémoires d'outre tombe* (1850); Victor-Louis Tapié, *Chateaubriand* (1965); Pierre Manent, *Intellectual History of Liberalism* (1987; trans. Balinski (1994); Jean d'Ormesson, *Album Chateaubriand* (1988); René Clément, *Chateaubriand* (1998); Robert Tombs, review of Clément, *Times Literary Supplement* (*TLS*) (November 27, 1998); Bertrand Aureau, *Chateaubriand* (1998); Jean-Pierre Chalin, *La Restauration* (1998); *Mémoires de Comtesse de Boigne*; Henri Astier, review of Marc Fumaroli, *Chateaubriand: Poésie et Terreur*, *TLS* (March 19, 2004).

GENTZ: *Briefe*, Vol. 3 (1913), ed. Wittichen and Salzer; *Ausgewählte Schriften V* (1838), ed. Weick; *Tagebücher I, 1800–1819* (1861); *Revolution und Gleichgewicht* (2010), ed. Hennecke; Robert Owen, *Life of Robert Owen by Himself* (1857); Abraham Hayward, "Friedrich v Gentz," *Edinburgh Review* (January 1863); Paul Reiff, *Friedrich Gentz: An Opponent of the French Revolution and Napoleon* (1912); André Robinet de Cléry, *Un diplomate d'il y a cent ans: Friedrich de Gentz* (1917); Paul Sweet,

Friedrich von Gentz: Defender of the Old Order (1941); Golo Mann, *Friedrich von Gentz* (1947; 1972); Hubert Rumpel, "Gentz, Friedrich" (1964), *Deutsche Biographie Online* (July 2016); *New Cambridge Modern History IX: War and Peace in an Age of Upheaval, 1793–1830* (1965), ed. Crawley; Harro Zimmermann, *Friedrich Gentz: Die Erfindung der Realpolitik* (2012); Charles Esdaile, *Napoleon's Wars: An International History 1803–1815* (2007); Mark Jarrett, *The Congress of Vienna and Its Legacy* (2013); Waltraud Heindl, *Gehorsame Rebellen: Bürokratie und Beamte in Österreich 1780–1848* (2014); Jonathan Allen Green, "Friedrich Gentz's Translation of Burke's *Reflections*," *Historical Journal* (August 2014).

MADISON: Letter to Jefferson, October 24, 1787, in *Debates on the Constitution*, 2 vols. (1993), ed. Bailyn; *The Federalist Papers* (1788; 1987), ed. Kramnick; *The Diaries and Letters of Gouverneur Morris* (1888), ed. Morris; Philipp Ziesche, "Exporting American Revolutions: Gouverneur Morris, Thomas Jefferson, and the National Struggle for Universal Rights in Revolutionary France," *Journal of the Early Republic* (Fall 2006); Avishai Margalit, *On Compromise and Rotten Compromises* (2010); Thomas Jefferson, *Diplomatic Correspondence 1784–89* (2016), ed. Woods; Max Mintz, "Gouverneur Morris," *American National Biography Online* (July 2018).

Resisting Liberalism (Parties and Politicians)

France

Eric Cahm, *Politics and Society in Contemporary France, 1789–1971* (1972); Sirinelli (1992); Sudhir Hazareesingh, *Political Traditions of Modern France* (1994); Robert Tombs, *France 1814–1914* (1996).

Britain

PEEL: Tamworth Manifesto (1834); Boyd Hilton, *A Mad, Bad and Dangerous People? England 1783–1846* (2006); John Prest, "Peel, Sir Robert (1788–1850)," in *Oxford Dictionary of National Biography* (*ODNB*)

Online (July 2016); James Sack, "Ultra Tories (1827–1834)," *ODNB Online* (July 2016).

STANLEY (LORD DERBY): Speech at Glasgow, the "Knowsley Creed" (1834); Angus Hawkins, "Stanley, Edward George Geoffrey Smith, Fourteenth earl of Derby," *ODNB Online* (May 2009); John Charmley, *A History of Conservative Politics since 1830* (2008).

DISRAELI: *Vindication of the English Constitution* (1835); *Coningsby* (1844); *Sybil* (1845); speech, "On the Conservative Programme" (April 1872); speech, "On Conservative and Liberal Principles" (June 1872); Anthony Quinton, *The Politics of Imperfection* (1978); Frank O'Gorman, *British Conservatism: Conservative Thought from Burke to Thatcher* (1986); Jonathan Parry, "Disraeli, Benjamin, Earl of Beaconsfield (1804–1881)," *ODNB Online* (June 2016).

Germany

H. W. Koch, *A Constitutional History of Germany* (1984), Axel Schildt, *Conservatismus in Deutschland* (1998); David Blackbourn, *The Long Nineteenth Century* (1997); H. von Petersdorff, "Wagener, Hermann" (1896); Hans-Joachim Schoeps, "Gerlach, Leo von" and "Gerlach, Ludwig von" (1964); Günter Richter, "Kleist-Retzow, Hans von" (1979); Helmut Neubach, "Oldenburg-Januschau, Elard von" (1999), all at *Deutsche Biographie Online*.

United States

John Quincy Adams, *The Diaries of John Quincy Adams 1779–1848* (2017), ed. Waldstreicher; Horace Greeley, "Why I am a Whig" (1840); "Yes, more, more, more . . . ," *Democratic Review* (July–August 1845); Rufus Choate, "The Power of a State Developed by Mental Culture" (1844); "The Position and Functions of the American Bar as an Element of Conservatism in the State" (1845); both in *Addresses and Orations of Rufus Choate* (1883); Daniel Walker Howe, *The Political Culture of the American Whigs* (1979); Mary W. M. Hargreaves, "Adams, John Quincy,"

American National Biography (ANB) Online (December 1999); The Conservative Press in Eighteenth- and Nineteenth-Century America (1999), ed. Lora and Langton; Walter Russell Mead, "The Jacksonian Tradition" (1999), National Interest (Fall–Winter 1999); Maurice G. Baxter, "Daniel Webster," ANB Online (December 1999); Robert V. Remini, "Henry Clay," ANB Online (February 2000).

Resisting Liberalism (Ideas and Thinkers)

CALHOUN: Disquisition on Government (posth.); Discourse on Government (posth.); Senate speeches, "On Anti-Slavery Petitions" (1837); "On Compromise Resolution" (1850); both in American Speeches (2006), ed. Wilmer; The Essential Calhoun (1992), ed. Wilson; Gunnar Hecksher, "Calhoun's Idea of 'Concurrent Majority' and the Constitutional Theory of Hegel," APSR (August 1939); Richard Hofstadter, "The Marx of the Master Class," in The American Political Tradition (1948); Russell Kirk, "Southern Conservatism: Randolph and Calhoun," in The Conservative Mind (1953); George Kateb, "The Majority Principle: Calhoun and His Antecedents," Political Science Quarterly (December 1969); Pauline Maier, "The Road Not Taken: John C. Calhoun and the Revolutionary Tradition in South Carolina," South Carolina Historical Magazine (January 1981); Lacy K. Ford, "Recovering the Republic: Calhoun, Southern Carolina, and the Concurrent Majority," South Carolina Historical Magazine (July 1988); Robert Herzberg, "The Relevance of John C. Calhoun's Theory for Institutional Design," Journal of Politics (September 1992); Warren Brown, John C. Calhoun (1993); Lacy K. Ford, "John Calhoun," in Companion to American Thought (1995), ed. Fox and Kloppenberg; Zoltan Vajda, "John C. Calhoun's Republicanism Revisited," Rhetoric and Public Affairs (Fall 2001); W. Kirk Wood, "Calhoun, John C.," in American Conservatism: An Encyclopedia (2006), ed. Frohen, Beer, and Nelson; Christian Esh, "The Rights of Unjust Minorities," review of James H. Read, Majority Rule versus Consensus, The Political Thought of John C. Calhoun (2009), Review of Politics (Spring 2010); Vajda, "Complicated Sympathies: John C. Calhoun's Sentimental Union and the South," South Carolina

Historical Magazine (July 2013); John Niven, "Calhoun, John C.," *ANB Online* (April 2015).

STAHL: Speech to Evangelical Association (1852); *Der Protestantismus als politische Prinzip* (1853); *Die gegenwärtigen Parteien in Staat und Kirche* (1863); Ernst Landsberg, "Stahl, Friedrich Julius," *Allgemeine Deutsche Biographie* (1893); Hans-Jürgen Puhle, "Conservatism in Modern German History," *Journal of Contemporary History* (October 1978); Rudolf Vierhaus, "Konservativ, konservatismus," in *Geschichtliche Grundbegriffe III* (1982), ed. Brunner et al.; Michael Stolleis, *Public Law in Germany 1800–1914* (2001); Johann Baptist Müller, "Der politische professor der Konservativen: Friedrich Julius Stahl (1802–61)," in *Konservativer Politiker in Deutschland* (1995), ed. Kraus; Axel Schildt, *Konservatismus in Deutschland* (1998); James Retallack, *The German Right 1860–1920: The Political Limits of the Authoritarian Imagination* (2006).

LAMENNAIS: Émile Faguet, "Lamennais," *Revue des Deux Mondes* (April 1897); Waldemar Gurian, "Lamennais," *Review of Politics* (April 1947); Robert Nisbet, "The Politics of Social Pluralism: Some Reflections on Lamennais," *Journal of Politics* (November 1948); C. B. Hastings, "Hugues-Félicité Robert de Lamennais: A Catholic Pioneer of Religious Liberty," *Journal of Church and State* (Spring 1988); David Nicholls, "Scepticism and Sovereignty: The Significance of Lamennais, I and II," *New Blackfriars* (April–May 1996).

KETTELER: *Die Arbeiterfrage und das Christentum* (1864), *The Labour Question and Christianity*, extracts on *GHDI Online*; J. E. Le Rossignol, review of Eduard Rosenbaum, *Ferdinand Lassalle* (1911), and Johannes Mundwiler, *Bischof von Ketteler als Vorkämpfer der christliche Sozialreform* (June 1912); Edward C. Bock, "Wilhelm Emmanuel von Ketteler: His Social and Political Philosophy" (Ph.D. diss., 1967); Erwin Iserloh, "Ketteler, Wilhelm Emmanuel Freiherr von," *Deutsche Biographie Online* (1977); Jonathan Sperber, "The Shaping of Political Catholicism in the Ruhr Basin, 1848–1881," *Central European History* (December 1983); Margaret Lavinia Anderson, "Piety and Politics: Recent Work on German Catholicism," *Journal of Modern History* (1991).

NEWMAN: *Development of Christian Doctrine* (1845); *Idea of a University* (1853); *Apologia pro vita sua* (1864); *The Grammar of Assent* (1870); "The Religion of the Day," in *Parochial and Plain Sermons* (1896); Lytton Strachey, *Eminent Victorians* (1918); Owen Chadwick, *Newman* (1983); Eamonn Duffy, "A Hero of the Church," *NYRB* (December 23, 2010); Anthony Kenny, "Cardinal of Conscience," *TLS* (July 30, 2010).

BROWNSON: "The Laboring Classes," *Boston Quarterly Review* (July 1840); *The Spirit-Rapper, An Autobiography* (1854); *The American Republic* (1865); *Literary, Scientific and Political Views of Orestes A. Brownson* (1893), ed. Brownson; *Watchwords* (1910); Arthur Schlesinger Jr., *Orestes A. Brownson: A Pilgrim's Progress* (1939); David Hoeveler, "Brownson, Orestes Augustus," *ANB Online* (February 2000).

HODGE: *The Way of Life* (1841), ed. Noll (1987); "A Discourse on the Re-Opening of the Chapel" (September 27, 1874); *Index to Systematic Theology* (1877); A. A. Hodge, *The Life of Charles Hodge* (1880).

COLERIDGE: *Coleridge* (1933; 1962), ed. Potter; *The Works of Coleridge* (1985), ed. Jackson; *Coleridge's Notebooks: A Selection 1798–1820* (2002), ed. Perry; J. H. Muirhead, *Coleridge as Philosopher* (1930); Paul Deschamps, *Formation de la pensée de Coleridge, 1772–1804* (1964); Michael Moran, "Coleridge," in *Encyclopedia of Philosophy* (1966), ed. Edwards; R. W. Harris, *Romanticism and the Social Order* (1969); Owen Barfield, *What Coleridge Thought* (1972); Anthony Quinton, "Against the Revolution: Burke, Coleridge, Newman," in *The Politics of Imperfection* (1978); Marilyn Butler, *Romantics, Rebels and Reactionaries: English Literature and its Background, 1760–1830* (1982); Richard Holmes, *Coleridge: Early Visions* (1989); John Morrow, *Coleridge's Political Thought* (1990); Julia Stapleton, "Political Thought, Elites and the State in Modern Britain," *Historical Journal* (March 1999); John Skorupski, "Between Hume and Mill: Reid, Bentham and Coleridge," in *English-Language Philosophy, 1750–1945* (1993); Mary Anne Perkins, "Coleridge, Samuel Taylor (1772–1834)," *REP 1.0* (2001); *Coleridge: Darker Reflections* (1998); Richard Holmes, "The Passionate Partnership," review of Adam Sisman, *The Friendship* (2006), *NYRB* (April 12,

2007); Pamela Clemit, "So Immethodical," review of Coleridge, *Biographia Literaria*, ed. Roberts, *TLS* (May 22, 2015); John Beer, "Coleridge, Samuel Taylor (1772–1834); Poet, Critic and Philosopher," *ODNB Online* (January 2017).

STEPHEN: *Liberty, Equality, Fraternity* (1873), ed. and intro. White (1967); Anthony Quinton, on Stephen, in *The Politics of Imperfection* (1978); K.J.M Smith, *James Fitzjames Stephen: Portrait of a Victorian Rationalist* (1988); Le Play, cited in Compagnon (2005); Smith, "James Fitzjames Stephen," *ODNB Online* (June 2012).

GIERKE: *Political Theories of the Middle Ages* (1900), trans. and intro. Maitland; "Der germanische Staatsgedanke" (1919), "L'idée germanique de l'état," trans. Argyriadis-Kervegan, in *Revue Française d'Histoire des Idées Politiques* 23 (2006); *Community in Historical Perspective: A Translation of Selections from "Das deutsche Genossenschaftsrecht"* (1990), trans. Fischer, intro. and ed. Black; Michael F. John, "The Politics of Legal Unity in Germany, 1870–1896," *Historical Journal* (June 1985); Michael Stolleis, *Public Law in Germany, 1800–1914* (1994).

BRADLEY: *Ethical Studies* (1876; 1927); *Appearance and Reality* (2nd ed., 1930); Richard Wollheim, *F. H. Bradley* (1959); Guy Stock, "Bradley, Francis Herbert," *ODNB Online* (September 2004); Terence Irwin, *The Development of Ethics, Vol. III: From Kant to Rawls* (2009); Stewart Candlish, "Francis Herbert Bradley," *SEP Online* (February 2015).

Adaptation and Compromise
(Parties and Politicians)

France

Historical Dictionary of The Third French Republic: 1870–1940 (1986), ed. Hutton; *Biographical Dictionary of French Political Leaders since 1870* (1990), ed. Bell, Johnson, and Morris; Julian Jackson, *France: The Dark Years, 1940–1944* (2001); Tardieu, in *Les grandes textes de la droite* (2017), ed. Franconie (2017).

Britain

SALISBURY: Michael Pinto-Duschinsky, *The Political Thought of Lord Salisbury, 1854–1868* (1967); Anthony Quinton, *The Politics of Imperfection* (1978); Frank O'Gorman, *British Conservatism: Conservative Thought from Burke to Thatcher* (1986); Paul Smith, "Cecil, Robert Arthur Talbot Gascoyne-, Third Marquess of Salisbury (1830–1903)," *ODNB Online* (June 2016); and John Greville, "Robert Arthur Talbot Gascoyne-Cecil, 3rd Marquess of Salisbury," *Encyclopedia Britannica Online*; Hugh Cecil, *Conservatism* (1912); Keith Feiling, *Toryism* (1913).

BALDWIN: *On England* (1925); Frank O'Gorman, *British Conservatism: Conservative Thought from Burke to Thatcher* (1986); John Charmley, *A History of Conservative Politics from 1830* (2008); Stuart Ball, "Baldwin, Stanley, First Earl Baldwin of Bawdley (1867–1947)," *ODNB Online* (July 2016); Anthony Ludovici, *A Defence of Conservatism* (1927); Robert Boothby et al., *Industry and the State: A Conservative View* (1927); Macmillan, *The Middle Way* (1938).

CHURCHILL: Paul Addison, "Churchill, Sir Winston Leonard Spencer (1874–1965)," *ODNB Online* (July 2016).

Germany

Theodor Barth, "On the need for left-liberal opposition to Bismarck" (June 26, 1886), on *GHDI Online*; Otto von Bismarck, *Gedanken und Errinerungen* (1898; 1919); James Joll, "Prussia and the German Problem, 1830–66," in *The New Cambridge Modern History, Vol. X: Zenith of European Power* (1960); Lothar Gall et al., *Bismarck: Preussen, Deutschland und Europa* (1990); Henry Kissinger, *Diplomacy* (1994); Edgar Feuchtwanger, *Bismarck* (2002); Jonathan Steinberg, *Bismarck* (2011); Friedrich Freiherr Hiller von Gaertringen, "Helldorff, Otto von" (1969); Klaus-Peter Hoepke, "Hugenberg, Alfred" (1974); Hans-Günther Richter, "Kardorff, Wilhelm von" (1977); Alf Christophersen, "Stoecker, Adolf" (2013), all at *Deutsche Biographie Online*; *Fascists and Conservatives: The*

Radical Right and the Establishment in Twentieth-Century Europe (1990), ed. Blinkhorn.

United States

Hugh Brogan, *The Penguin History of the United States* (1985; 1999); David Kennedy, *Freedom from Fear: The American People in Depression and War, 1929–45* (1999); relevant entries from *The Oxford Companion to United States History* (2001), ed. Boyer; Andrew Carnegie, "Wealth" (June 1889); Carnegie, *Autobiography* (posth., 1920); Richard Lowitt, "Cannon, Joseph"; Paul Kens, "Field, Stephen"; Donald A. Ritchie, "Hanna, Marcus Alonzo"; all at *ANB Online* (December 1999); Kim Phillips-Fein, *Invisible Hands: The Businessmen's Crusade against the New Deal* (2009).

Adaptation and Compromise
(Ideas and Thinkers)

MALLOCK, *The New Republic* (1877); *Is Life Worth Living?* (1879); *Labour and the Popular Welfare* (1893); *Aristocracy and Evolution: A Study of the Rights, the Origin, and the Social Functions of the Wealthier Classes* (1898); *Memoirs of Life and Literature* (1920); Robert Eccleshall, *English Conservatism since the Restoration: An Introduction and Anthology* (1990); *Conservatism: An Anthology*, ed. Muller (1997).

SUMNER, *What the Classes Owe Each Other* (1883); "Sociological Fallacies"; "An Examination of a Noble Sentiment" (1887), extracts; both in *Conservatism*, ed. Muller (1997); *Folkways* (1906); J. H. Abraham, *The Origin and Growth of Sociology* (1973); Bruce Curtis, *William Graham Sumner* (1981); *Conservatism*, ed. Muller (1997); Mike Hawkins, *Social Darwinism in European and American Thought, 1860–1945* (1997).

SCHUMPETER, "The Sociology of Imperialisms" (1918); *Capitalism, Socialism and Democracy* (1942); "Introduction," Thomas McCraw (1975); McCraw, "Schumpeter Ascending," *American Scholar* (Summer

1991); Jerry Z. Muller, "Joseph Schumpeter," in *Conservatism*, ed. Muller (1997); Mark Thornton, "Schumpeter, Joseph Alois Julius," *ANB Online* (2000).

TREITSCHKE, "Freedom" (1861), in *Heinrich von Treitschke: His Life and Works* (1914), ed. Hausrath; "Socialism and Its Patrons" (1874); "A Word about Our Jews" (1880); both in *GDHI Online*; Herman von Petersdorff, "Treitschke, Heinrich," *ADB* (1910); Hausrath, "The Life of Treitschke," in *Heinrich von Treitschke* (1914), ed. Hausrath; Pierre Nora, "Ernest Lavisse: Son rôle dans la formation du sentiment national," *Revue Historique* (1962); Andreas Dorpalen, "Heinrich von Treitschke"; P. M. Kennedy, "The Decline of Nationalistic History," both in *Historians in Politics* (1974), ed. Lacqueur and Mosse; Jens Nordalm, "Der gegängelte Held: 'Heroenkult' im 19. Jahrhundert am Beispiel Thomas Carlyles und Heinrich von Treitschkes," *Historische Zeitschrift* (June 2003); *Deutsche Erinnerungsorte, Vols. I, II, and III* (2001), ed. François and Schulze; George Y. Kohler, "German Spirit and Holy Ghost: Treitschke's Call for Conversion of German Jewry; The Debate Revisited," *Modern Judaism* (May 2010); John Bew, *Realpolitik: A History* (2016).

LE BON, *La Psychologie des foules* (1895), trans. Fisher, *The Crowd* (1896); Robert A. Nye, *The Origins of Crowd Psychology: Gustave Le Bon and the Crisis of Mass Democracy in the Third Republic* (1975); Susanna Barrows, *Distorting Mirrors: Visions of the Crowd in Late Nineteeth-Century France* (1981); Cathérine Rouvier, *Gustave Le Bon* (1986); J. S. McClelland, *The Crowd and the Mob: From Plato to Canetti* (1989); Raymond Queneau, *Gustave Le Bon* (Posth., 1990); Jaap van Ginneken, *Crowds, Psychology and Politics: 1871–99* (1992); Benoit Marpeau, *Gustave le Bon: Parcours d'un intellectuel, 1841–1931* (2000) James Surowiecki, *The Wisdom of Crowds* (2004); Detmar Klein, "Le Bon, Gustave (1841–1931)," in *Encyclopedia of Nineteenth Century Thought* (2005), ed. Claeys.

DU CAMP, *Convulsions de Paris* (1878–80).

ADAMS, *Democracy, An American Novel* (1880); *The Education of Henry Adams* (1918).

MENCKEN, *"What I Believe,"* Forum (September 1930); *The Vintage Mencken* (1990), ed. Cooke; *Prejudices* (2010).

SOREL, *Réflexions sur la violence* (1906; 1908), trans. Hulme, *Reflections on Violence*, ed. Jennings (1999); *Les Illusions du progrès* (1908).

SPENGLER, *Preussentum und Sozialismus* (1919); *Der Untergang des Abendlandes* (1918; 1922), trans. Atkinson, *Decline of the West* (1926; 1928); Detlev Felken, "Spengler, Oswald Arnold Gottfried," *Deutsche Biographie Online* (2010).

MOELLER, *Der Preußischer Stil* (1916); *Das dritte Reich* (1923); Fritz Stern, *The Politics of Cultural Despair* (1961); J. B. Müller, "Liberaler und autoritärer Konservatismus," *Archiv für Begriffsgeschichte* (1985); Klemens von Klemperer, "Moeller van den Bruck," *Deutsche Biographie Online* (1994).

JÜNGER, *Ernst Jünger In Stahlgewittern*, (1920), trans. Hofmann, *Storm of Steel* (2003); *In Stahlgewittern: Historische-kritische Ausgabe* (2013), ed. Kiesel; *Der Arbeiter* (1932); *Auf den Marmorklippen* (1939), trans. Hood, *On the Marble Cliffs* (1939), intro., George Steiner; *Strahlungen I and II* (1988); *A German Officer in Occupied Paris: War Journals 1941–45*, trans. Hansen and Hansen (2018); J. P. Stern, *Ernst Jünger: A Writer of Our Time* (1953); Paul Fussell, *The Great War and Modern Memory* (1975); Karlheinz Bohrer, *Die Aesthetik des Schreckens: Die pessimistische Romantik und Ernst Jüngers Frühwerk* (1978); Bruce Chatwin, "An Aesthete at War," *NYRB* (March 5, 1981); *Ernst Jünger: Leben und Werk in Bildern und Texten* (1988), ed. Schwik; George L. Mosse, *Fallen Soldiers: Reshaping the Memory of the World Wars* (1990); Ian Buruma, "The Anarch at Twilight," *NYRB* (June 24, 1993); Nicolaus Sombart, "Der Dandy in Forsthaus," *Tagesspiegel* (March 29, 1995); Thomas Nevin, *Ernst Jünger and Germany: Into the Abyss, 1914–45* (1997); Paul Noack, *Ernst Jünger: eine Biographie*

(1998); Helmuth Kiesel, *Ernst Jünger, Die Biographie* (2007); *No Man's Land: Writings from a World at War* (2014), ed. Ayrton; Elliot A. Neaman, "Ernst Jünger and *Storms of Steel*," in *Key Thinkers of the Radical Right: Behind the New Threat to Liberal Democracy* (2019), ed. Sedgwick.

DRIEU LA ROCHELLE, *Socialisme Fasciste* (1934); *Le feu follet* (1931); *Gilles* (1939).

SOUTHERN AGRARIANS, *I'll Take My Stand The South and the Agrarian Tradition* (1930); Paul Murphy, *The Rebuke of History: The Southern Agrarians and American Conservative Thought* (2001).

ELIOT, *The Sacred Wood* (1920); "The Humanism of Irving Babbitt" (1928), in *Selected Essays, (1917–32)*; *The Use of Poetry and Use of Criticism* (1933); *After Strange Gods* (1934); *The Idea of a Christian Society* (1939); *What Is a Classic?* (1954); *Notes towards the Definition of Culture* (1948); *Selected Essays* (1951); *On Poetry and Poets* (1957); *Knowledge and Experience in the Philosophy of F. H. Bradley* (1964); Roger Kojecky, *T. S. Eliot's Social Criticism* (1971); Craig Raine, *In Defence of T. S. Eliot* (2000).

SCHMITT, *Politische Romantik* (1919); *Die Diktatur* (1921); *Politische Theologie* (1922; 1934), trans. Schwab, *Political Theology*, (1985); *Parliamentarismus* (1923); *Der Begriff des Politischen* (1927; 1933; 1971); *Verfassungslehre* (1927); *Legalität und Legitimät* (1932), trans. Seitzer, *Legality and Legitimacy* (2004); "Der Führer schützt das Recht" (1934); "Das Judentum in der Rechtswissenschaft" (1937); Leo Strauss, "Anmerkungen zu Carl Schmitts *Der Begriff des Politischen*," *Archiv für Sozialwissenschaft und Sozialpolitik* (August–September 1932); Joseph Bendersky, *Carl Schmitt: Theorist for the Reich* (1983); Paul Noack, *Carl Schmitt: Eine Biographie* (1993); Heinrich Meier, *Carl Schmitt and Leo Strauss: The Hidden Dialogue* (1995); Mark Lilla, "The Enemy of Liberalism," *NYRB* (May 15, 1997); Jan-Werner Mueller, *A Dangerous Mind: Carl Schmitt in Post-War European Thought* (2003); Reinhard

Mehring, *Carl Schmitt: Aufstieg und Fall* (2009); Lars Vinx, "Carl Schmitt," *SEP Online* (July 2019).

MAURRAS, "La vision du moi de Maurice Barrès" (1891); *Trois idées politiques: Chateaubriand, Michelet, Sainte-Beuve* (1898; 1912); *Mes idées politiques* (1937), ed. Chardon; extracts, in McClelland (1970); Ernst Nolte, *Der Faschismus in seiner Epoche* (1963), trans. Vennewitz, *Three Faces of Fascism* (1966); Zeev Sternhell, *Ni droite, ni gauche: L'Idéologie fasciste en France* (1983), trans. Maisel, *Neither Right nor Left: Fascist Ideology in France* (1986); Robert Paxton, *The Anatomy of Fascism* (2004); John Rogister, review of Stéphane Giocantis, *Maurras: le chaos et l'ordre* (2007), *TLS* (September 21, 2007); Jeremy Jennings, *Revolution and the Republic: A History of Political Thought in France since the Eighteenth Century* (2011).

Political Command and the Search for Ideas
(Parties and Politicians)

France

Antoine Pinay, *Un Français comme les autres: Entretiens* (1984); Charles de Gaulle: *Le Fil de l'épée* (1932); *Vers l'armée de métier* (1934); *Mémoires de Guerre* (1954–59; 2000); *Lettres, notes et carnets: Juin 1951–Mai 1958* (1985), *Juin 1958–Décembre 1960* (1985), *Juillet 1966–Avril 1969* (1987); *Mémoires d'espoir* (1970); Charles Péguy, *Notre patrie* (1905); Jean-François Revel, *Le style du Général* (1959); Pierre Viansson-Ponté, *Histoire de la République Gaullienne: May 1958–April 1969* (1971); Eric Cahm, *Politics and Society in Contemporary France, 1789–1971* (1972); Jean Lacouture, *De Gaulle I: Le Rebelle* (1984), *II: Le Politique* (1985), *III: Le Souverain* (1986); Brian Bond and Martin Alexander, "Liddell Hart and de Gaulle: The Doctrines of Limited Liability and Mobile Defence," in *The Makers of Modern Strategy* (1986), ed. Paret; Vincent Wright, *The Government and Politics of Modern France* (1978; 1989); Régis Debray, *A demain, De Gaulle* (1990); Sudhir Hazareesingh, *Political Traditions in*

Modern France (1994); Robert A. Dougherty, "The Illusion of Security: France 1919–40," in *The Making of Modern Strategy* (1994), ed. Murray, Knox, and Bernstein; Eric Roussel, *Charles de Gaulle* (2002); Julian Jackson, *De Gaulle: Life and Times* (2003); John Lewis Gaddis, *The Cold War* (2005); *Dictionnaire de Gaulle* (2006), ed. Andrieu, Braud, and Piketty; Jonathan Fenby, *The General: Charles de Gaulle and the France He Saved* (2010); Hazareesingh, *In the Shadow of the General* (2012); William Nester, *De Gaulle's Legacy* (2014); Julian Jackson, *A Certain Idea of France: The Life of Charles De Gaulle* (2018).

Britain

Margaret Thatcher, *Margaret Thatcher: The Downing Street Years* (1993); Raphael Samuel, "Mrs Thatcher's Return to Victorian Values," British Academy lecture (1990); David Cannadine, "Thatcher, Margaret," *ODNB Online* (January 2017).

Germany

Axel Schildt, *Conservatismus in Deutschland* (1998); Horst Teltschik, *329 Tage* (1991); "Not as Grimm as It Looks: A Survey of Germany," *Economist* (May 23, 1992).

United States

James T. Patterson, *Grand Expectations: The United States 1945–74* (1996); Richard Reeves, *President Reagan: The Triumph of Imagination* (2005).

Political Command and the Search for Ideas (Ideas and Thinkers)

POWELL, *Still to Decide Speeches 1969–71* (1972); T. E. Utley, *Enoch Powell: The Man and His Thinking* (1968); Humphrey Berkeley, *The Odyssey of Enoch Powell* (1977); Ian Gilmour, *Inside Right* (1977); Maurice Cowling, *Religion and Public Doctrine in Modern England I* (1980); Patrick

Cosgrave, *The Lives of Enoch Powell* (1989); Simon Heffer, *Like the Roman: The Life of Enoch Powell* (1998); "Powell, (John) Enoch (1912–1998)," *ODNB Online*; *Enoch at 100* (2012), ed. Howard; Camilla Schofield, *Enoch Powell and the Making of Post-Colonial Britain* (2013).

GEHLEN, *Der Mensch; Seine Natur und seine Stellung in der Welt* (1940); *Man in the Age of Technology* (1983), trans. Lipscomb; *Man: His Nature and Place in the World* (1988), trans. McMillan and Pillemer, intro. Karl-Siegbert Rehberg; "On Culture, Nature and Naturalness" (1958); "Man and Institutions" (1960); both in *Conservatism*, ed. Muller (1997); *Moral und Hypermoral: Ein pluralistische Ethik* (1969); Jürgen Habermas, review of Gehlen, *Urmensch und Spätkultur* (1956), in *Philosophische-politische Profile* (1971); Manfred Stanley, review of Gehlen, *Man* (1983), *American Journal of Sociology* (January 1983); Jerry Z. Muller, *The Other God That Failed: Hans Freyer and the Deradicalization of German Conservatism* (1987); Karlheinz Weißmann, "Gehlen, Arnold," in *Lexikon des Konservatismus* (1996).

WEAVER, *Ideas Have Consequences* (1948); *Ethics of Rhetoric* (1953); "Rhetorical Strategies of the Conservative Cause" (1959), talk to the Intercollegiate Society of Individualists at Madison, Wisconsin (April 26, 1959), cited in Richard L. Johannesen, "A Reconsideration of Richard M. Weaver's Platonic Idealism," *Rhetoric Society Quarterly* (Spring 1991).

VOEGELIN, *Uber die Form des amerikanischen Geistes* (1928), trans. Hein, *On the Form of the American Mind* (1995); *Die Rassenidee in der Geistesgeschichte* (1933); *Der autoritäre Staat: Ein Versuch über das österreichische Staatsproblem* (1936), trans. Weiss, *The Authoritarian State: An Essay on the Problem of the Austrian State* (1999); *Die Politische Religionen* (1938), trans. Schildhauer, *The Political Religions* (2000); *The New Science of Politics* (1952); *History of Political Ideas, Vols. I–VIII* (1939–54; posth. publ.); *Anamnesis* (1966), trans. Niemeyer (1978); *Autobiographical Reflections* (transcription 1973; publ. 1989); H. M. Höpfl, "Voegelin, Eric," in *REP 1.0* (2001); Michael Federici, *Eric Voegelin* (2002); *Robert B. Heilman and Eric Voegelin: A Friendship in*

Letters 1944–84 (2004), ed. Embry; Mark Lilla, "Mr Casaubon in America," *NYRB* (June 28, 2007).

MACINTYRE, *A Short History of Ethics* (1966); *After Virtue* (1981); *Whose Justice, Which Rationality?* (1988); *Three Rival Versions of Moral Enquiry* (1990); "Politics, Philosophy and the Common Good"; "Interview with Giovanna Boradori"; both in *The MacIntyre Reader* (1998), ed. Knight; *After MacIntyre* (1994), ed. Mendus and Horton; Thomas Nagel, "MacIntyre versus the Enlightenment," review of MacIntyre, *Whose Justice, Which Rationality, TLS* (July 8, 1988); Alan Ryan, review of MacIntyre, *Three Rival Versions, New Statesman* (August 17, 1990).

BUCKLEY, *God and Man at Yale: The Superstitions of "Academic Freedom"* (1951); *Up from Liberalism* (1957); "Publisher's Statement" (November 1955); "Why the South Must Prevail" (August 1957); "The Question of Robert Welch" (February 1962); all in *National Review*; Niels Bjerre-Poulsen, *Right Face: Organizing the American Conservative Movement 1945–65* (2002); Jeffrey Hart, *The Making of the American Conservative Mind* (2005); George Will, interview with Buckley, ABC News, October 9, 2005; John Judis, *William F. Buckley Jr: Patron Saint of the Conservatives* (1988); Carl T. Bogus, *Buckley* (2011).

BURNHAM, "Science and Style: A Reply to Comrade Trotsky" (February 1940); *The Managerial Revolution* (1941); *The New Machiavellians: Defenders of Freedom* (1943); "Lenin's Heir," *Partisan Review* (Winter 1945); *The Struggle for the World* (1947); *The Coming Defeat of Communism* (1950); *Containment or Liberation?* (1953); *Web of Subversion* (1954); *Suicide of the West* (1964); John Diggins, "Four Theories in Search of a Reality: James Burnham, Soviet Communism and the Cold War," *APSR* (June 1976); Kevin Smant, "James Burnham," *ANB Online* (January 2017)

KENDALL, *John Locke and the Doctrine of Majority Rule* (1959); "The Open Society and Its Fallacies," *APSR* (December 1960); *The Conservative Affirmation in America* (1963); *Willmoore Kendall Contra Mundum* (posth., 1971), ed. Kendall; Saul Bellow, "Mosby's Memoirs" (1968); John P. East, "The Political Thought of Willmoore Kendall," *Political Science Reviewer* (Fall 1973); George H. Nash, "Willmoore Kendall: Iconoclast," *Modern Age* (Spring 1975); *Willmoore Kendall: Maverick of American Conservatives* (2002), ed. Alvis and Murley; George Carey, "Kendall, Willmoore (1909–67), in *American Conservatism: An Encyclopedia* (2006); William D. Pederson, "Willmoore Kendall," *ANB Online*.

ON AMERICAN NEOCONSERVATISM, Peter Steinfels, *The Neoconservatives: The Men Who Are Changing America's Politics* (1979; 2013); Jürgen Habermas, "Neoconservative Culture Criticism in the United States and West Germany: An Intellectual Movement in Two Political Cultures," *Telos* 56 (1983); Francis Fukuyama, "After Neoconservatism," *New York Times* (February 19, 2006); Jacob Heilbrunn, *They Knew They Were Right* (2008); Justin Vaïsse, *Histoire du néo-conservatisme aux Etats Unis: Le Triomphe de l'idéologie* (2008), trans. Goldhammer, *Neoconservatism: The Biography of a Movement* (2011)

AMERICAN NEOCONSERVATIVE AUTHORS, Irving Kristol: *Two Cheers for Capitalism* (1978); *Neo-conservatism: The Autobiography of an Idea* (1995); "American Conservatism," *Public Interest* (Fall 1995); Norman Podhoretz: "My Negro Problem and Ours" (1963); *Making It* (1967); *Breaking Ranks: A Political Memoir* (1979); *The Present Danger: Do We Have the Will to Reverse the Decline of American Power?* (1980); *Ex-Friends* (1999); "Why Are Jews Liberals?" (2009); Daniel Bell: *The End of Ideology* (1960); "The Dispossessed" (1962), in *The Radical Right* (2nd ed., 1963), ed. Bell; "Unstable America," *Encounter* (June 1970); *The Cultural Contradictions of Capitalism* (1976).

Hyper-liberalism and the Hard Right
(Parties and Politicians)

C. Vann Woodward, "Pennies from Heaven," review of Alan Brinkley, *Voices of Protest* (1982), *NYRB* (September 23, 1982); Keith Thomas, "Inventing the People," *NYRB* (November 24, 1988); *Histoire de l'extrême droite en France* (1993), ed. Winock; Walter Russell Mead, "The Jacksonian Tradition," *National Interest* (Winter 1999–2000); Peter Davies, *The Extreme Right in France, 1789 to the Present* (2002); Thilo Sarrazin, *Deutschland schafft sich ab* (Germany is destroying itself) (2010); Eric Zemmour, *Le Suicide français* (2014); Marc Jongen, "The Fairytale of the Ghost of the AfD," *Cicero Online* (January 22, 2014); Jan-Werner Mueller, *What Is Populism?* (2016); "Le Front National," *Pouvoirs* (2016); George H. Nash, "American Conservatism and the Problem of Populism," *New Criterion* (September 2016); Hajo Funke, *Von Wutbürgern und Brandstiften: AfD, Pegida, Gewaltnetze* (2016); "The Power of Populism" issue of *Foreign Affairs* (November–December 2016); Alan Brinkley, "Coughlin, Charles Edward," and "Long, Huey Pierce," *ANB Online* (March 2017); Martin Wolf, "The Economic Origins of the Populist Surge," *Financial Times* (June 28, 2017); George Hawley, "The European Roots of the Alt-Right," *Foreign Affairs* (October 27, 2017); Frédéric Brahami, "Quel peuple?," review of Gérard Bras, *Les voies du peuple: Éléments d'une histoire, Vie des idées* (October 2018); Cas Mudde, "How Populism Became the Concept That Defines Our Age," *Guardian* (November 22, 2018); Jascha Mounk and Jordan Kyle, "What Populists Do to Democracies," *Atlantic* (December 26, 2018); *The Oxford Handbook of the Radical Right* (2018), ed. Rydgren; Gérard Courtois, "La fracture démocratique"; Cathérine Tricot, "Les categories populaires se révèlent profondément fragmentées"; Charles Zarka, "Pour une consultation de mi-mandat"; all in *Le Monde* (January 3, 2019); Lucie Soullier, "Marion Maréchal, les mots de l'extrémisme"; Tal Bruttman, "Chez Eric Zemmour, la 'lutte des races' tient lieu de programme politique," both in *Le Monde* (October 2, 2019); *Key Thinkers of the Radical Right: Behind the New Threat to Liberal Democracy* (2019), ed. Sedgwick.

Hyper-liberalism and the Hard Right
(Ideas and Thinkers)

Taguieff, *Résister au bougisme: Démocratie forte contre mondialisation-marchande* (2000).

BUCHANAN, *Right from the Beginning* (1988); *Death of the West: How Dying Populations and Immigrant Invasions Imperil Our Culture and Civilization* (2001); *Where the Right Went Wrong: How Neoconservatives Subverted the Reagan Presidency and Hijacked the Bush Administration* (2004); Tim Alberta, "The Ideas Made It, But I Didn't," *Politico* (May–June 2017); Paul Gottfried, *Conservatism in America* (2007); E. Christian Kopff: Buchanan, *American Conservatism: An Encyclopedia*.

BANNON, "Remarks to Vatican Conference on Poverty" (Summer 2014), *Buzzfeed News Online*; "How 2008 Planted the Seed for the Trump Presidency," Bannon interview with Noah Kulwin, *New York Magazine Online* (August 6, 2018); Joshua Green, *Devil's Bargain* (2017); Josh Kraushaar, "Bannon's Bark Is Worse Than His Bite," *National Journal* (October 17, 2017); Jason Horowitz, "Steve Bannon Is Done Wrecking the American Establishment. Now He Wants to Destroy Europe's," *New York Times* (March 9, 2018).

DREHER, *The Benedict Option* (2017).

FINKIELKRAUT, *Le nouveau désordre amoureux* (The new love disorder) (1977), with Pascal Bruckner; *Défaite de la pensée* (1987); trans. Friedlander, *The Defeat of the Mind* (1995); *L'identité malheureuse* (2015); Daniel Lindenberg, *Le Rappel à l'ordre* (2002).

BENOIST, *Vu de droite: Anthologie critique des idées contemporaines* (1977), trans. Lindgren, *The View from the Right, Vols. I–III* (2017–2019); *Le moment populiste: Droite-gauche, c'est fini!* (2017); *Contre le libéralisme: La société n'est pas un marché* (2019).

FINNIS, *Natural Law and Natural Rights* (1980); "Persons and Their Associations," reply to Scruton, *Proceedings of the Aristotelian Society*, suppl. vol. 63 (1989); "Political Neutrality and Religious Arguments" (1993), in *Religion and Public Reasons: Collected Essays, Vol. V* (2011); Neil MacCormick "Natural Law Reconsidered," on Finnis, *Natural Law and Natural Rights* (1980), *Oxford Journal of Legal Studies* (Spring 1981);

Kent Greenawalt, on Finnis, *Natural Law and Natural Rights* (1980), *Political Theory* (February 1982); William H. Willcox, review of Finnis, *Natural Law and Natural Rights* (1980), *Philosophical Review* (October 1983); Charles Covell, *The Defence of Natural Law* (1992); Mark Murphy, "Natural-Law Theories in Ethics," *SEP Online* (May 2018); Patrick Deneen, "Unsustainable Liberalism," *First Things* (May 2012); Cécile Laborde, *Liberalism's Religion* (2017); Deneen, *Why Liberalism Failed* (2018).

SCRUTON, *Art and Imagination* (1974); *The Aesthetics of Architecture* (1979); "The Significance of Common Culture," *Philosophy* (January 1979); *The Meaning of Conservatism* (1980; 1984); *A Dictionary of Political Thought* (1982); *Sexual Desire* (1986); "Modern Philosophy and the Neglect of Aesthetics" (inaugural lecture, Birkbeck College), *TLS* (June 5, 1987); *Untimely Tracts* (1987); "How to Be a Non-Liberal, Anti-Socialist Conservative," *Intercollegiate Review* (Spring 1993); *The Aesthetics of Music* (1997); "The Philosophy of Love," in *Death-Devoted Heart* (2004); *Gentle Regrets* (2005); *A Political Philosophy* (2006); *Beauty* (2009); "Classicism Now," in *The Roger Scruton Reader* (2011), ed. Dooley; "Nonsense on Stilts," Lincoln's Inn Conference on Human Rights (2011); *How to Be a Conservative* (2014); "Parfit the Perfectionist," *Philosophy* (July 2014); "The Good of Government," *First Things* (June–July 2014); *Fools, Frauds and Firebrands* (2015); *On Human Nature* (2017); *Conservatism* (2017); John Hallowell, review of Scruton, *The Meaning of Conservatism, Journal of Politics* (May 1982); Jeremy Rayner, "Philosophy into Dogma: The Revival of Cultural Conservatism," *British Journal of Political Science* (October 1986); Martha Nussbaum, "Sex in the Head," *NYRB* (December 18, 1986); T. E. Utley, "A Thinker for the Tories," *Times* (October 26, 1987); Stefan Collini, "Hegel in Green Wellies," *London Review of Books* (March 8, 2001); Mark Dooley, *Roger Scruton: The Philosopher on Dover Beach* (2009); *The Roger Scruton Reader* (2011), ed. Dooley; Daniel Cullen, "The Personal and the Political in Roger Scruton's Conservatism"; Peter Augustine Lawler, "Roger Scruton's Conservatism: between Xenophobia and Oikophobia"; Daniel J. Mahoney, "Defending the West in All Its Amplitude: The Liberal

Conservative Vision of Roger Scruton"; Stephen Wirls, "Roger Scruton's Conservativism and the Liberal Regime"; Scruton, "Reply to Critics"; all in *Perspectives on Political Science* (October 2016); Samuel Freeman, "The Enemies of Roger Scruton," *NYRB* (April 21, 2016); Roger Scruton and Mark Dooley, *Conversations with Roger Scruton* (2016); Andy Hamilton, "Conservatism," *SEP Online* (August 2018).

SLOTERDIJK, *Kritik der zynischen Vernunft* (1983), trans. Eldred, *Critique of Cynical Reason* (1988); *Sphären I: Blasen (Mikrosphärologie)* (1988); *Sphären II: Globen (Makrosphärologie)* (1999), trans. Hoban, *Bubbles* (2011), *Globes* (2014); "Regeln für den Menschenpark" (1999), trans. "Rules for the Human Zoo," in *Society and Space* (special issue: "The Worlds of Peter Sloterdijk," February 2009); *Sphären III: Schäume (Plurale Sphärologie)* (2004), trans. Hoban, *Foams* (2016); *Zorn und Zeit* (2006), trans. Wenning, *Rage and Time* (2010); *Du mußt dein Leben ändern* (2009), trans. Hoban, *You Must Change Your Life* (2013); *Ausgewählte Übertreibungen: Gespräche und Interviews, 1993–2102*, trans. Margolis, *Selected Exaggerations: Conversations and Interviews, 1993–2012* (2016)

Liberal-Conservative Status Quo

Anthony Quinton, *The Politics of Imperfection* (1978); David Willetts, *Modern Conservatism* (1992); Willetts, *Is Conservatism Dead?* (1997); Willetts, *The Pinch* (2010); Noel Malcolm, "Conservative Realism and Christian Democracy," in *Conservatism Realism: New Essays in Conservatism* (1996), ed. Minogue; John Kekes, "What Is Conservatism?," *Philosophy* (July 1997); Kekes, *A Case for Conservatism* (1998); Pierre Rosanvallon : "Il faut refaire le bagage d'idées de la démocratie française," *Le Monde* (November 21, 2002); Nicholas Rescher, "The Case for Cautious Conservatism," *Independent Review* (Winter 2015); Yuval Levin, *The Fractured Republic: Renewing America's Social Contract in the Age of Individualism* (2016); Jason Brennan, *Against Democracy* (2016); Julius Krein, review of Alvin S. Felzenberg, *A Man and His Presidents: The Political Odyssey of William F. Buckley Jr.* (2017), *Washington Post* (July 6, 2017); David Brooks, "The Rise of the Refuseniks and the Populist War on

Excellence," *New York Times* (November 15, 2018); George Will, *The Conservative Sensibility* (2019); "The Global Crisis in Conservatism" issue of the *Economist* (July 6, 2019); Nick Timothy, *Remaking One Nation: Conservatism in an Age of Crisis* (2020); Ferdinand Mount, "Après Brexit: On the New Orthodoxy," *London Review of Books* (February 20, 2020).

NAME INDEX

Abraham, J. H., 214

Abrams, Elliott, 322

Acton, Lord, 212–13; on Stahl, 118

Adams, Henry, 206, 447; background of, 98; *Democracy*, 159, 235–36; disillusioned view of the people of, 224, 235–36; works of, 483

Adams, John, 31, 446

Adams, John Quincy, 31, 96–98, 112, 428

Adelson, Sheldon, 343

Adenauer, Konrad, 286–88, 334, 338, 428

Adorno, Theodor, 52, 53

Agnew, Spiro, 370

Allitt, Patrick, 251

Ames, Fisher, 317

Apollinaire, 159

Aquinas, Thomas, 383

Aristotle, 423, 424

Arnold, Matthew, 140, 210

Aron, Robert, 249

Attlee, Clement, 298

Austin, John, 120

Babbitt, Irving, 252, 254

Bachelard, Gaston, 401

Bacon, Francis, 8

Bagehot, Walter, 3, 55

Baldwin, Stanley, 18, 201, 428–29; background and career of, 180–82; bibliography for, 480; postwar reputation of, 183–84; social-unity Toryism of, 298

Balfour, Arthur, 178

Bancroft, George, 228

Bannon, Steve, 371–72, 447; bibliography for, 492

Barnes, Thomas, 83

Barrès, Maurice, 447

Barthes, Roland, 327

Bartley, Robert, 320

Baudelaire, Charles, 52, 352

Beard, Charles, 102

Bell, Daniel, 320, 359–60

Belloc, Hilaire, 252

Bellow, Saul, 314

Benedict of Nursia, 372

Benoist, Alain de, 367, 376, 379–82, 448; bibliography for, 493

Bentham, Jeremy, 141, 146

Berlioz, Hector, 71

Bethmann-Hollweg, Theo von, 429

Bibesco, Marthe, 229

Bidault, Georges, 429

Bismarck, Otto von, 79–80, 168, 334; antisocialist laws of, 64, 190; conservatives' division over, 90–91, 93; fall and resignation of, 187; as Iron Chancellor, 187–88; pursuit of German unification by, 188; successes and failures of, 95–96; supporting free trade, 189–90

Blum, Léon, 262

Bock-Côté, Mathieu, 378–79

Bodin, Jean, 425

Bohrer, Karl-Heinz, 248

Bolingbroke, Viscount (Henry St. John), 13, 81–82

Bonald, Louis de, 21, 51

Borges, Jorge Luis, 247

Bourdieu, Pierre, 377

Boutin, Christine, 379

Boutwood, Arthur, 182

Bradford, Mel, 448

Bradley, F. H., 448; anti-individualism of, 110, 144–45; bibliography for, 479; ethical and social thoughts of, 151–56, 254; *Ethical Studies*, 152–53; on morality's claims, 144–45

SUBJECT INDEX

Where the sense of a term as used in this book is explained in "Conservative Keywords" (Appendix A), the entry here is in italics. Where listed without comment or attribution, ideas indexed here are to be taken de dicto as they occur in conservative thoughts and arguments dealt with in the book.

collectivists in, 233–35; colonialism of, 275; conservative label originated in, 60; constitutional *Charte* of, 75–76; corrupt *classe politique* in, 350; disappointment of liberal monarchy in, 76; end of monarchism in, 74–76; Fourth Republic of, 272; growing prosperity in, 272–73; hard right in, 277, 343, 346–50, 434–35, 442, 438; hard-right roots in, 353; hard-right themes in, 350; improvisations of right in, 74–80; interwar hard right in, 249–50; liberal conservatism in, 56; liberal democracy in, 74; mainstream right of, 61; moral conservatism in, 379; National Front (Front National) in, 340, 343, 344, 346–47, 350, 377, 438; National Revolution of, 445–46; nationalism in, 228; New Right in, 379–80, 448; new voices of right in, 376–82; opposition to immigrants in, 377–78; overthrow of Restoration monarchy in, 71; Popular Front in, 170, 172, 262–63, 437–38; post-1945, 271–77, 442; post–WW I decline in, 249–50; post–WW II right in, 270; Quatorze Juillet made a holiday in, 166; Republics of, 43; Restoration era in, 75–76; Second Republic of, 77, 78, 233–34; singularity of, 379; Socialist Party in, 336–37; "trentes glorieuses" in, 272; UDF-RPR center-right in, 380; Vichy regime of, 173–74. *See also* French Revolution; The Terror; Vichy France

franchise, extended, 73–74; universal, 93, 101, 226, 230–31

Franco-German ties, 174, 192, 274, 333, 433

fraternity, false hope of, 148

Free Conservatives. *See* Frei Konservative Partei (FKP)

free love, 376–77

free-market conservatism, 384, 414

free-market radicalism, suspicion of, 397

free markets: damage of to society, 389–90; political promotion of, 413–14

Free Soil Republicans, 98, 447

free trade, 78, 84, 93, 169, 178, 186, 189, 330, 332, 369–70, 437

freedom: British *vs.* American concepts of, 397–98; just laws and, 134–35, 448–49. *See also* liberties

Frei Konservative Partei (FKP, Germany), 92–93, 189, 190, 437

French Africa, independence for, 275

French Communist Party, strength of, 272

French pride, 23–24

French Revolution, 459; American's responses to, 31–32; Burke on, 3, 5, 10–11, 13; conservative arguments against, 36–37; contrasted with American Revolution, 30–31; Declaration of the Rights of Man and, 27; German philosophers' views on, 28–30; Maistre on, 5, 7–9; queen's fate in, 18; roots of, 75; Third Republic linked to, 166; writers against, 119–20

friend-enemy distinction, for Schmitt, 255–56, 258–59

frontier society, 99–102

frustration: mutual, 36; conservative, 62; and rage, 271

fundamentalists: Christian, in 20th-century U.S., 135, 335; conservatives as, for Sloterdijk, 403

Gaullism, 272, 274–75; difficulty categorizing, 276

geopolitics, 17–18, 26, 256, 328; oracular, 347, 438

German Confederation, unstable, 90

German conservatism: cross-tensions in, 89–90; distinctive factors in, 187–88; purged of chauvinism and pagan irrationalism, 304

German unification, 92, 95, 188–89, 333–34; army as national bond in, for Treitschke, 227

Germanness (German national feeling), 149–50, 227; disappointments of with unification, 334; before Napoleonic age, 225–26

Monroe Doctrine, 97, 428

moral conservatives, 59, 148, 317, 336, 385, 449

moral majority, 452

moral permissiveness, 292; neoconservatives and, 322

moral policing, 214, 464–65

moral regeneration, need for, 409–10

moral resistance ethic, 313

morality: changing public views of, 386–87; contradictoriness of, 153–55; disorder of, 306–0; of duty, 22; good and bad in, 385; of interest, 22; liberal flawed picture of, 312; liberal misunderstandings of for Scruton, 393; in local custom, 396–97; for MacIntyre, 312–15; medieval traditional approach to, 383–84; Nietzschean, 239; as protection of weak against strong, 146; psychology of, 152; rooted in extra-human order, 405; universal standards of, 385

Mugwumps, 196

multiculturalism, 376–78

multilateralism, 271; abandonment of, 351

Munich Agreement, 432

mutual frustration, U.S. Constitution as harmonious system of, 36

myths: nostalgic, 299; rational and irrational, for Schmitt, 257

nation: as community, for Calhoun, 113; decline of, 349–50; devotion to, 257–58; as ethnos, 351; formation of, 222–23; fostering of feeling for, 228–29; friend-enemy distinction binding, 258–59; inner and outer enemies of, 350–51; as keyword, 422; mindedness of, 225, 333–34, 360, 411; national people, idea of, 45, 222, 360; need for diversity and disagreement in, 391; order in and among, 25–31; patriotism and pride in, 23–24; recovery of pride in, in post-1945 France, 272; renewal of values of, 206; as unifying ideas and myths of, 224–25; unity of in diverse society, 294–95; unwritten laws constituting, 9. *See also* state

nation-state, creation of, 121–22

National Centre of Independents and Farmers (CNIP, France), 272–74, 437, 441

National Front (France): decline and capture themes of, 350; finances of, 343; herald for, 377; rise of, 346–47; supporters of, 344

National Liberals (NL, Germany), 92, 93, 150, 189–91, 193, 454, 465

national power, uninhibited use of, 226–27

National Rally (France), 346–47

National Review, 317, 318, 319–20, 369, 449, 465

nationalists/nationalism, 57, 119, 167, 191, 330; competitive, 57; exclusionary, 57, 227; *vs.* globalism, 330; among historians, 225–27, 332, 443; 19th-century and present-day sense of contrasted, 35; Powell's "indexical," 299; supercharged by hard right, 345. *See also* nativist/nativism

nativist/nativism, conservative, 342–43; exclusionary, 340

Navigation Acts, 28

Nazism, 194, 217, 255, 256, 258, 355; unselfconsciousness about, 305

neoconservatives, 320–21, 457; achievements of, 323–24; belief of in power of ideas, 323; Christian conservatives and, 323; in Germany, 218, 232, 410; in government, 322–23; Iraq occupation as nemesis of, 323; paleoconservatives and, 368–69; targets of, 321–22; three generations of, 408–9, 457; in U.S., 101, 141, 218, 297, 305, 317, 320–24, 338, 408–9, 457

Neues Abendland, 304

New Deal, 199–200, 363; conservative opposition to, 291, 315; dime-store, 292, 434; opposition to, 443

normality, in post-1945 France, 271–73

norms: authority for, 19; natural resistance of, 213–14; universal need for, 301–2

North-South compromise (U.S.), 35–36

nostalgia, reason replacing, 117–24

A NOTE ON THE TYPE

This book has been composed in Arno, an Old-style serif typeface in the classic Venetian tradition, designed by Robert Slimbach at Adobe.